LASERJET

COMPANION

The Cobb Group supports many business software programs with books, workbooks, and journals:

IBM PC and Compatibles

BORLAND PARADOX
Douglas Cobb's Paradox 3.0 Handbook
Hands-On Paradox
Paradox User's Journal *

BORLAND QUATTRO
Quattro Companion
For Quattro *

HEWLETT-PACKARD LASERJET
LaserJet Companion
LaserJet Companion TechNotes

LOTUS SYMPHONY
Mastering Symphony
The Hidden Power of Symphony
The Symphony User's Journal *

LOTUS 1-2-3
Douglas Cobb's 1-2-3 Handbook
123 User's Journal *

MICROSOFT EXCEL
Running Microsoft Excel
The Expert *

MICROSOFT WORKS
Works Companion
The Workshop *

MICROSOFT WORD
Word for Word *

Apple Macintosh

PROVUE OVERVUE
Understanding OverVUE

MICROSOFT WORD
Word Companion
Inside Word *

MICROSOFT EXCEL
Excel in Business
Doug Cobb's Tips for Microsoft Excel
Hands-On Microsoft Excel
Microsoft Excel Functions Library
Excellence *

* *A monthly technical journal devoted exclusively to this program.*

LASERJET
COMPANION

Mark W. Crane
Joseph R. Pierce

With:
Jeff Yocom

Louisville, Kentucky

LASERJET COMPANION

Published by
The Cobb Group, Inc.
9420 Bunsen Parkway, Suite 300
Louisville, Kentucky 40220

Library of Congress Catalog Card Number: 88-072331
ISBN 0-936767-08-1

Editing	Production	Design
Toni Frank	Maureen Pawley	Julie Baer Tirpak
Jody Gilbert	Elayne Noltemeyer	
Linda Baughman	Tara Billinger	
Linda Watkins	Beth Riggle	
Clyde Zellers		

Throughout this book, the trade names and trademarks of many companies and products have been used, and no such uses are intended to convey endorsement of or other affiliations with this book.

Apple® is a registered trademark of Apple Computer, Inc. BitStream® and Fontware® are registered trademarks of BitStream, Inc. CompuServe® is a registered service trademark of CompuServe, Inc. dBASE III Plus™ and dBASE IV™ are trademarks of Ashton-Tate. Glyphix™ is a trademark of SWFTE International, Ltd. IBM® is a registered trademark of International Business Machines, Inc. IBM PC™, IBM PC XT™, IBM PC AT™, IBM PS/2™, and DisplayWrite™ are trademarks of International Business Machines, Inc. ITC™ is a trademark of International Typeface Corporation. JetScript™ and PS Jet Plus™ are trademarks of QMS, Inc. LaserJet™, LaserJet Plus™, LaserJet 500 Plus™, LaserJet Series II™, LaserJet IID™, LaserJet 2000™, PCL™, FontLoad™ and PCLPak™ are trademarks of Hewlett-Packard Company. LaserWriter®, LaserWriter Plus®, and LaserWriter II® are registered trademarks of Apple Computer, Inc. Lotus® and 1-2-3® are registered trademarks of Lotus Development Corporation. Macintosh™ is a trademark licensed to Apple Computer, Inc. Microsoft® is a registered trademark of Microsoft Corporation. MS-DOS™, Microsoft Word™, Microsoft Chart™, Microsoft GW-BASIC™, Microsoft Windows™, Microsoft Excel™, and Microsoft Write™ are trademarks of Microsoft Corporation. PageMaker® is a registered trademark of Aldus Corporation. PostScript® is a registered trademark of Adobe Systems, Inc. Publisher's Typefoundry™ is a trademark of Z-Soft Corporation. Quattro™ and Paradox™ are trademarks of Borland International. Tandy® is a registered trademark of Tandy Corporation. Times Roman® and Helvetica® are registered trademarks of Linotype Corporation. Ventura Publisher™ is a trademark of Ventura Software, Inc. WordPerfect® is a registered trademark of WordPerfect Corporation. WordStar Professional® is a registered trademark of MicroPro International Corporation. WYSIfonts!®, Font Effects®, SoftCraft Font Editor®, and Laser Fonts® are registered trademarks of SoftCraft, Inc. Xerox® is a registered trademark of Xerox Corporation. XyWrite III Plus™ is a trademark of XyQuest, Inc.

Printed in the United States of America

RRD-H 0 9 8 7 6 5 4 3 2

TABLE OF CONTENTS

SECTION TWO: USING THE LASERJET WITH DOS APPLICATIONS

SECTION THREE: USING THE LASERJET WITH MICROSOFT WINDOWS

SECTION FOUR: ENHANCING THE LASERJET

SECTION FIVE: PROGRAMMING THE LASERJET

Dedication

To my sister, Amanda, and my brother, Jeff
MWC

To Mom—I think this one's above 90
JRP

To Brady, my new addition
JPY

Acknowledgments

No project of this magnitude can be carried out successfully without the help and encouragement of dozens of people. Therefore, we'd like to take this opportunity to say thanks.

Douglas Cobb—boss man and basketball player, for the opportunity, encouragement, and advice.

Tom Cottingham—marketing guru and musician, for setting up the deal and travelling the country on an expense account.

Toni Frank, Jody Gilbert, Linda Baughman, Linda Watkins, Clyde Zellers, Allan McGuffey, and Rose Fairfax—editors extraordinaire, for yet another marathon editing session.

Maureen Pawley, Elayne Noltemeyer, Beth Riggle, and Tara Billinger—the tireless group of PageMaker magicians, for putting it all together.

Julie Baer Tirpak—dynamite designer, for the insanely great cover.

Jeri Peterson, Judy Ross, and Scott Lokken at Hewlett-Packard, for assistance above and beyond the call of duty.

The friendly folks on HP's LaserJet Customer Assist Line, for hundreds of tips, techniques, and shortcuts.

Dave Parks and all the folks at Printer's Type Service, for accommodating our hectic schedule.

Tim Landgrave and Judy Harvey at Citizens Fidelity Bank, for the tips and advice, and other special favors.

Bud and Wanda, for the opportunities and for caring day in and day out.

Nita, for inspiring, humoring, caring, and keeping it in perspective.

The crew of STS-26 and everyone involved in the Discovery launch, for doing it right.

Finally, to the rest of The Cobb Group—Doug Been, Julia Bennett, Sandy Bozarth, Grand Britt, Gena Cobb, Steve Cobb, Teresa Codey, Bob Evans, Donald Fields, Luanne Flynn, Patty Flynn, Laura Heuser, Lori Houston, Lori Junkins, Kathleen Lane, Becky Ledford, Jo McGill, Tracy Milliner, Judy Mynhier, Keith Nicholson, Doug Roach, Raven Sexton, Margaret Walz, Jeff Warner, Barbara Wells, and Kellie Woods—thanks for sharing the experience.

PREFACE

Before Hewlett-Packard introduced the original LaserJet printer in 1984, personal computer users were forced to choose between two types of printers: impact (or letter-quality) printers and dot-matrix printers. While impact printers are capable of printing great-looking business letters, monthly reports, and so forth, they are not capable of printing graphics. As with a standard typewriter, you can use an impact printer only to print a finite set of fixed-space characters. Dot-matrix printers, on the other hand, are capable of printing both text and bit-mapped graphics. In fact, most dot-matrix printers allow you to print characters in a variety of font types and sizes. However, the printed text generated by most dot-matrix printers does not have the professional look required by most businesses.

Needless to say, people had to give up something when they wanted to buy a new PC printer. They could either buy an impact printer and sacrifice graphics capability, or buy a dot-matrix printer and sacrifice letter-quality text capability. In addition, no matter which printer they chose, they had to put up with some rather disturbing noises, along with incredibly slow print speeds. (A few dot-matrix printers were relatively fast, but impact printers worked at the dreadful rate of 40 characters per second.)

In the spring of 1984, Hewlett-Packard introduced one of the most significant computer peripheral devices of all time—the HP LaserJet printer. Since that time, HP has added five additional members to the LaserJet family: the LaserJet Plus, LaserJet 500 Plus, LaserJet Series II, LaserJet IID, and LaserJet 2000. Today's base of installed LaserJet printers exceeds one million units, making the HP LaserJet the world's most popular laser printer.

ABOUT THIS BOOK

We began using LaserJet printers at The Cobb Group when they were introduced in 1984. While we were always pleased with the LaserJet's speed and the quality of documents it produced, we often had to spend several hours tinkering to produce the desired output. This was a problem for two reasons.

First, while the manuals included with each member of the LaserJet printer family and other HP documents contain a large amount of useful information, they are not particularly easy to digest. Second, it was virtually impossible to obtain documentation that explained how to configure word processors and other applications for the specific set of LaserJet fonts and/or features we wanted to use.

Since there are more than one million LaserJet printers in the world, we realized that we couldn't be the only ones who were frequently aggravated by the LaserJet's idiosyncrasies. Consequently, the idea for *LaserJet Companion* was born.

We focused on three goals when writing *LaserJet Companion*. First, we wanted to provide you with the essential information you need about each member of the LaserJet printer family. Second, we wanted to show you how to use your particular LaserJet's fonts and features with software applications. Finally, we wanted to provide a comprehensive guide to Hewlett-Packard's Printer Command Language (PCL).

Philosophy

As we mentioned earlier, most of the documentation available for the LaserJet printer family is informative but extremely difficult to digest. Therefore, our primary concern in writing *LaserJet Campanion* was to present, in a comprehensible manner, the information you need to use your LaserJet easily and efficiently.

We tried to strike a balance in *LaserJet Companion*—providing the technical information you need to use your LaserJet effectively and teaching by example. *LaserJet Companion* explains each concept in detail, then takes you through the procedures step by step.

Organization

LaserJet Companion is divided into five sections. Section One introduces the LaserJet printer family, as well as a number of concepts and procedures. Here, you'll learn about the LaserJet's control panel, the various features and fonts you can use with a LaserJet, and relevant terminology.

Section Two shows you how to use a LaserJet with major DOS applications, such as WordPerfect, Lotus 1-2-3, and Ventura Publisher. Section Three shows you how to use a LaserJet with Microsoft Windows and Windows-based applications, such as Aldus PageMaker. In each of these sections, we'll begin by showing you how to add LaserJet support to the products we discuss. Once we've done this, we'll explain how to overcome any LaserJet support limitations a product may have, and we'll provide several practical examples showing you how to print various types of documents using different LaserJet fonts and features.

In Section Four, we'll look at products you can use to enhance the performance of your LaserJet. For example, we'll show you how to create fonts with the BitStream Fontware Installation Kit, and we'll show you how to add Adobe's PostScript page description language to a LaserJet Series II. Finally, in Section Five, we'll document Hewlett-Packard's Printer Command Language (PCL).

Index

At The Cobb Group, we take pride in the comprehensive indexes we create for our books. *LaserJet Companion*'s index contains hundreds of entries covering all the concepts, topics, and applications we discuss. In addition, many entries are cross-referenced to facilitate your search for a particular subject. If you have a question about your LaserJet or any of the applications discussed in *LaserJet Companion*, the index will help you locate the answer in a matter of seconds.

CONVENTIONS

This book uses a few conventions that make it easier to read and understand. For example, when we show you how to use the LaserJet, we will tell you to push keys on the control panel. The names of these keys will always be uppercase, as in, "Press the MENU key on the control panel."

The names of keys on your PC, PS/2, or compatible keyboard, like [F1], [Esc], [Pg Up], and [Home], are enclosed in brackets. The Return/Enter key is represented by the symbol ↵, and the cursor-movement keys are represented by the symbols →, ←, ↑, and ↓.

When we show you how to use the LaserJet with applications, any characters or entries you must type or keys you must press will be in boldface, as in "type **c:\fonts**" and "press **[Esc]**." Additionally, when two keys must be pressed at the same time, those key names will be shown side by side, as in "press **[Alt]P**."

Throughout *LaserJet Companion*, we will discuss PCL commands. PCL commands always contain an escape character (ASCII 27 decimal, 1B hexadecimal), which we will represent with the symbol $^E s_c$. In addition, whenever it is necessary to represent a lowercase *l* (ASCII 108 decimal, 6C hexadecimal) in a PCL command, we will use the symbol ℓ, while we will use the symbol Ø to represent zero. For example, the PCL command $^E s_c$&ℓØL contains each of these symbols.

ABOUT THE COBB GROUP

Based in Louisville, Kentucky, The Cobb Group was founded in 1984 by Douglas Cobb—co-author of the best-selling computer book of all time: *Using 1-2-3*. Since then, The Cobb Group has become a leading publisher of books and journals for users of personal computer software and related products. Best-selling books written and/or published by The Cobb Group include *Quattro Companion*, *Douglas Cobb's 1-2-3 Handbook*, *Running Microsoft Excel*, *Mastering Symphony*, *Word Companion*, *Paradox Companion*, and *Works Companion*.

In addition to its best-selling books, The Cobb Group publishes *The Expert*, a monthly journal written for users of Microsoft Excel on the PC. Other Cobb Group journals include *Word for Word*, for users of Microsoft Word on the PC; *The*

Workshop, for users of Microsoft Works on the PC; *For Quattro*; *1-2-3 User's Journal*; *The Symphony User's Journal*; and *Paradox User's Journal*. For more information on any Cobb Group book or journal, call 800-223-8720 (502-491-1900 in Kentucky).

ABOUT THE AUTHORS

Mark W. Crane is editor-in-chief of two monthly Cobb Group publications, *The Expert* and *Excellence*, and co-author of The Cobb Group's book *Quattro Companion*. Mark holds a B.S. in electrical engineering from Purdue University. He has served as a PC specialist with IBM and with the Citizens Fidelity Corporation in Louisville, Kentucky.

Joseph R. Pierce co-authored The Cobb Group's book *Quattro Companion* and is the editor-in-chief of The Cobb Group's *LaserJet Companion TechNotes*. Joe was formerly the technical editor of a monthly magazine for users of Tandy personal computers and is currently working on degrees in computer science and business administration at Bellarmine College.

Jeff Yocom is editor-in-chief of the *Paradox User's Journal* and holds a B.A. in psychology from the University of Louisville. Jeff was a writer and software specialist at the University of Louisville Office of News and Public Information before joining The Cobb Group.

THERE'S MORE!

When we began to write *LaserJet Companion*, we quickly realized it would be impossible to include every application that can be used with the LaserJet. Therefore, we limited our discussion of applications to those our market research found to be most popular among LaserJet users.

To supplement the selected DOS applications we have included in *LaserJet Companion*, The Cobb Group publishes *LaserJet Companion TechNotes*. Each edition of *LaserJet Companion TechNotes* is comparable to a chapter in *LaserJet Companion*. For example, Chapter 5 of *LaserJet Companion* explains how to use your LaserJet with WordPerfect 5.0. Likewise, we have published *LaserJet Companion TechNotes* that discuss the procedures, applications, and utilities for using your LaserJet with Paradox, Quattro, and XyWrite III Plus.

In addition to discussing applications not covered in *LaserJet Companion*, *LaserJet Companion TechNotes* provide current information on upgrades of products that are included in *LaserJet Companion*. For example, when Lotus 1-2-3 Release 3 becomes available, we will publish an edition of *LaserJet Companion TechNotes* that shows you how to use the upgrade with the LaserJet. Likewise, we will publish *LaserJet Companion TechNotes* for dBASE IV and other products discussed in *LaserJet Companion* as they are updated.

Chapters 12 and 17 explain our procedures for publishing *LaserJet Companion TechNotes* and tell you how you can obtain them. For more information on specific applications, call The Cobb Group at 800-223-8720 (502-491-1900 in Kentucky).

THE COBB GROUP

The
Best

· GUARANTEED ·

Section One

Using the LaserJet

LaserJet printers are incredibly powerful and relatively easy to use. However, before you can get the most out of your LaserJet, there are a number of concepts and procedures with which you should become familiar. Section One introduces these concepts and procedures.

We'll begin in Chapter 1 by introducing you to each member of the LaserJet printer family. Once we've done this, we'll look at the process LaserJets use to print text and graphics on a page, and we'll discuss several LaserJet accessories.

In Chapter 2, we'll show you how to operate and control the LaserJet. For example, we'll document each function of the LaserJet control panel, and we'll show you how to insert font cartridges and paper trays.

Chapter 3 is dedicated to maintenance and the prevention and resolution of problems that you may experience when using a LaserJet. For instance, we'll show you how to change toner cartridges, and we'll document each of the error messages that may appear on the control panel.

Finally, in Chapter 4, we'll take an in-depth look at the heart and soul of the LaserJet's ability to produce high-quality text output—fonts. We'll explain how to obtain and use fonts, and we'll discuss the concepts and terms used throughout *LaserJet Companion* when referring to fonts.

LASERJET BASICS 1

In this chapter, we'll cover the fundamentals of printing with a Hewlett-Packard LaserJet printer. First, we'll take a close look at each member of the HP LaserJet family, pointing out the features and capabilities of each. Next, we'll discuss how the LaserJet prints, and we'll point out a few of the common quirks associated with LaserJet printing, such as the LaserJet's inability to print to the edges of a page. We will also tell you about the LaserJet's standard page description language (PCL) and how you can add PostScript capabilities to any of HP's LaserJet printers. Finally, we'll discuss the most important accessories that are available for the LaserJet printers—memory options, font cartridges, and downloadable soft fonts.

There are six members of Hewlett-Packard's LaserJet printer family: the LaserJet, LaserJet Plus, LaserJet 500 Plus, LaserJet Series II, LaserJet IID, and LaserJet 2000. Although Hewlett-Packard has discontinued production of the LaserJet, LaserJet Plus, and LaserJet 500 Plus, these three printers still account for a large percentage of installed LaserJet printers. Hewlett-Packard has promised to provide supplies and support services for these printers until at least 1992.

Hewlett-Packard's current line of laser printers consists of the LaserJet Series II, LaserJet IID, and LaserJet 2000. Of course, in the process of manufacturing and selling its first three laser printers, Hewlett-Packard learned a few things that helped make its new generation of laser printers better than the previous generation. As we take a quick look at the history of the LaserJet printer family, we'll highlight the similarities and differences between family members. Regardless of which

THE LASERJET FAMILY

LaserJet printer you own, you'll probably find the information in this section helpful, since we'll specifically refer to each of these printers in our discussions throughout the book.

The Original HP LaserJet

After Hewlett-Packard introduced the original HP LaserJet printer in 1984, personal computer users could purchase a single printer that was capable of printing both letter-quality text and bit-mapped graphics. The HP LaserJet could print much faster and much more quietly than either impact or dot-matrix printers, and an abundance of LaserJet printer options (like font cartridges and paper trays) gave the LaserJet tremendous flexibility. The only thing that kept the LaserJet out of many offices was its high retail price—a whopping $3,495.

Although the LaserJet's high price limited its appeal to most small businesses, Hewlett-Packard sold enough LaserJet printers to realize it had found an attractive niche in the fast-moving personal computer industry. Other manufacturing companies realized this too, and soon there were dozens of HP LaserJet compatibles available in stores and in mail-order catalogs. Although third-party manufacturers helped lower the prices of laser printers to some extent, small businesses still had a difficult time justifying the purchase of this expensive printer—especially since most companies already had both an impact printer (or a typewriter) for printing business correspondence, and a dot-matrix printer for printing graphics.

As we have said, the original HP LaserJet printer offered almost everything you would ever want in a personal printer: letter-quality text, fine graphics resolution, a slot for optional font cartridges, and rapid output speed (eight pages per minute). In addition, the LaserJet's nearly silent method of printing was a welcome relief to office workers who thought they'd never escape those dreadful days of *clackity-clackity-clack*.

Figures 1-1, 1-2, and 1-3 identify the features of the original LaserJet printer. As you read through the remainder of this book, you should refer to these figures whenever we discuss a location that is unfamiliar to you.

Since the LaserJet uses a unique method to print the data it receives from the computer (which we'll discuss later in this chapter), most software companies had to provide special printer drivers so their programs could work correctly with the LaserJet printer. Fortunately, these drivers became available rather quickly.

As more and more users became familiar with the LaserJet and its capabilities, they began to want more printing features. For instance, many users wanted to use a parallel interface (instead of a serial interface) to connect their computer to their printer. Others wanted a more convenient method for printing groups of envelopes. Still others wanted to overcome the LaserJet's memory limitations, which handicapped the LaserJet's graphics capabilities. Hewlett-Packard listened to the users' concerns, and in 1985, they introduced two new members of the LaserJet family: the LaserJet Plus and the LaserJet 500 Plus.

FIGURE 1-1

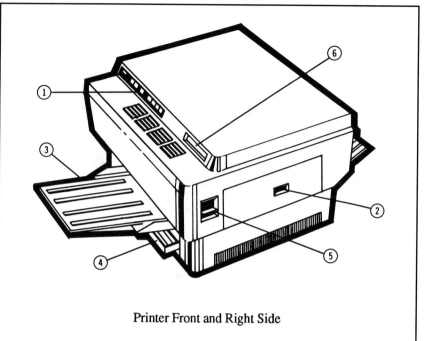

Printer Front and Right Side

1. **Operator Control Panel--**
   controls printer
   operations
2. **Right Door--**open to access
   EP cartridge
3. **Print Tray--**collects
   printed paper
4. **Paper Input Cassette--**
   load paper in here
5. **Upper Unit Release Lever--**
   pull up to open upper
   main body of printer
6. **Font Cartridge Slot--**
   insert font cartridges
   in here

This diagram shows the front and right side of the LaserJet.

FIGURE 1-2

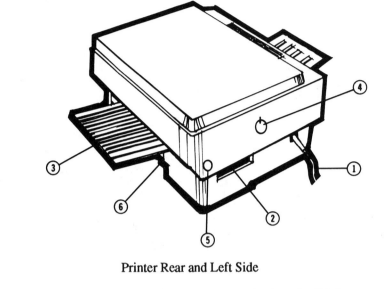

Printer Rear and Left Side

1. **AC Power Cord**
2. **Interface Connector--**
   plug interface cable
   in here
3. **Manual Feed Tray--**
   manually feed paper
   and envelopes from here

4. **Print Density Dial--**
   adjusts lightness and
   darkness of print
5. **Test Print Button--**press
   for printer self-test
6. **Rear Door--**open to clear
   paper jams in the cassette
   feed area

This diagram shows the locations on the rear and left side of the LaserJet.

FIGURE 1-3

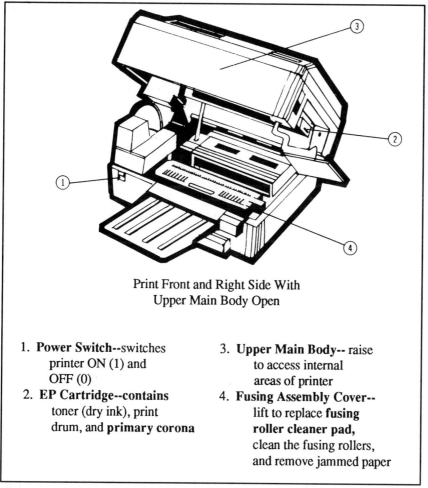

Print Front and Right Side With
Upper Main Body Open

1. **Power Switch--**switches
   printer ON (1) and
   OFF (0)
2. **EP Cartridge--contains**
   toner (dry ink), print
   drum, and **primary corona**

3. **Upper Main Body--** raise
   to access internal
   areas of printer
4. **Fusing Assembly Cover--**
   lift to replace **fusing
   roller cleaner pad,**
   clean the fusing rollers,
   and remove jammed paper

This diagram shows the inside of the LaserJet.

**The LaserJet
Plus**

The HP LaserJet Plus printer is a significantly enhanced version of the original LaserJet printer. Along with the standard features offered on the LaserJet printer, the LaserJet Plus printer offers both a serial and a parallel interface port, seven additional resident fonts, and 512K of built-in random access memory (RAM). As we'll explain, these additional features make the LaserJet Plus much more powerful than the original LaserJet printer.

The LaserJet Plus' parallel interface makes it much easier to configure the LaserJet with the computer. In addition to eliminating the need for messy DOS MODE commands and a special serial cable, the LaserJet Plus' parallel interface allows for very rapid data transfer. Needless to say, the LaserJet Plus' parallel interface alone constitutes a really big "plus."

In addition to providing a parallel interface on its LaserJet Plus printer, HP included seven additional resident fonts on the LaserJet Plus: an additional Portrait 16.66-pitch Line Printer font, as well as Roman-8, ASCII, and Roman Extended symbol sets available for all internal fonts.

The LaserJet Plus' third "plus" is its 512K of built-in memory (RAM). This memory lets you download soft fonts, store print macros, draw patterns and shading, and print larger graphics images with higher resolution. Table 1-1 on pages 14 and 15 illustrates the graphics sizes and resolutions possible for all of the LaserJet printers. As you can see, the LaserJet Plus' standard 512K of RAM lets you print a full page of 150 dpi (dots per inch) graphics, and a half page of 300 dpi graphics. You can provide your LaserJet Plus printer with the ability to print full-page 300 dpi graphics images by purchasing HP's 2MB upgrade kit. This kit must be installed by a Hewlett-Packard service technician.

Along with the features we've mentioned so far, HP added a few others to the LaserJet Plus printer. Of course, HP figured that if you really needed all of these nice features, you'd be willing to pay for them, so they set the price of the LaserJet Plus at $3,995, while they dropped the price of the original LaserJet to $2,995.

The LaserJet 500 Plus

At the same time HP introduced the LaserJet Plus printer, they introduced a third member of the LaserJet family—the LaserJet 500 Plus. The HP LaserJet 500 Plus has the same features as the LaserJet Plus with the addition of dual input paper trays and a larger output stacker. The LaserJet 500 Plus also has manually selectable correct-order/reverse-order stacking, and program-controlled job offsetting and paper bin selection. Originally, the HP LaserJet 500 Plus printer sold for a retail price of $4,995—$1,000 more than the LaserJet Plus.

The LaserJet Series II

In the spring of 1987, Hewlett-Packard replaced the LaserJet and LaserJet Plus printers with a brand new LaserJet printer: the LaserJet Series II. Like the LaserJet Plus, the LaserJet Series II is equipped with both a serial and a parallel interface, and with 512K of built-in RAM. In addition, the LaserJet Series II's front control panel allows users to access various printer options, such as interface selection, number of copies, and number of lines per page, without using any complicated software commands. The LaserJet Series II also comes with six resident fonts (in 23 symbol sets) and two font cartridge slots, and it is capable of handling more sheets of paper than the older LaserJet models. The LaserJet Series II takes up less space than the older machines, and it weighs 20 pounds less. Perhaps the LaserJet Series II's neatest feature of all, however, was its list price of $2,495—$1,000 less than you would have paid for the original LaserJet just three years earlier.

As we have said, to increase the graphics capability of an HP LaserJet Plus, you must increase the amount of RAM (random access memory) by purchasing HP's 2MB upgrade kit and have an HP technical specialist perform the installation. Fortunately, HP has made it much easier to upgrade the RAM inside a LaserJet Series II printer. To do this, you simply buy a 1MB, 2MB, or 4MB memory expansion board and plug it into the printer's RAM expansion slot. These expansion boards are much less expensive than the 2MB upgrade kit for the older LaserJet printers, and you can install them as easily as you can install an adapter board in your PC.

Figures 1-4, 1-5, and 1-6 on the following pages identify the features of the LaserJet Series II printer. As you read through the remainder of this book, you should refer to these figures whenever we discuss a location that is unfamiliar to you.

The HP LaserJet 2000

The HP LaserJet 2000 printer is the Cadillac of LaserJet printers. Hewlett-Packard designed this printer for use with personal computer networks, departmental systems, and minicomputers. The standard HP LaserJet 2000 printer (Model 2684A) prints up to 20 pages per minute and is equipped with 34 internal fonts, three font cartridge slots, 1.5MB of RAM (expandable to 5.5MB), two 250-sheet input bins, and a 1,500-page correct-order output stacker. Of course, this printer isn't cheap—it currently sells for a little under $20,000.

HP also offers two enhanced versions of the HP LaserJet 2000. Model 2684P includes a 2,000-sheet input bin, and Model 2684D includes both the 2,000-sheet input bin and a duplex feature, which allows for printing on both sides of the paper.

The HP LaserJet IID

The newest member of the HP LaserJet family is the HP LaserJet IID. Perhaps a more suitable name for this printer would be the "HP LaserJet Series II Plus," since it offers everything you'll find on the LaserJet Series II printer, plus the following three features: two-sided (duplex) printing; two paper trays; and font rotation capability, which allows all of your fonts to appear in both Portrait and Landscape orientation.

FIGURE 1-4

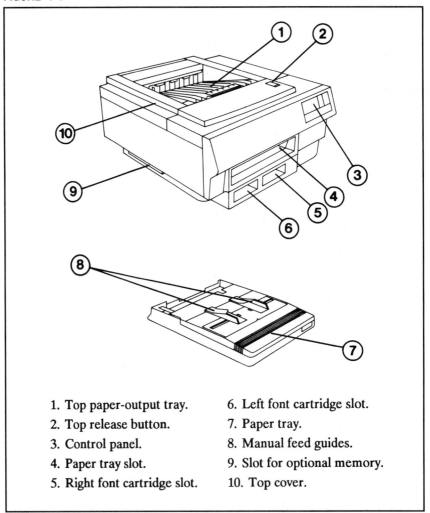

1. Top paper-output tray.
2. Top release button.
3. Control panel.
4. Paper tray slot.
5. Right font cartridge slot.
6. Left font cartridge slot.
7. Paper tray.
8. Manual feed guides.
9. Slot for optional memory.
10. Top cover.

This diagram shows the front and left side of the LaserJet Series II.

FIGURE 1-5

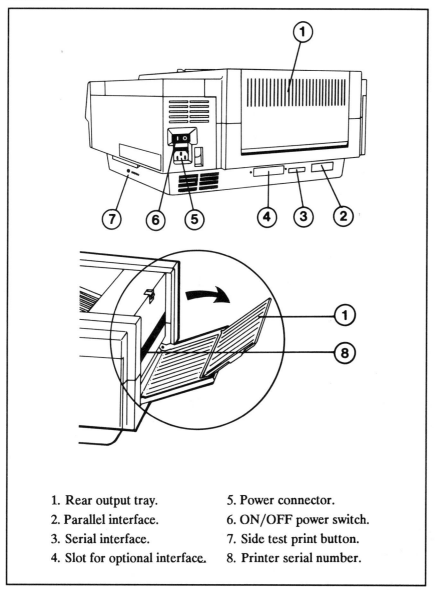

1. Rear output tray.
2. Parallel interface.
3. Serial interface.
4. Slot for optional interface.
5. Power connector.
6. ON/OFF power switch.
7. Side test print button.
8. Printer serial number.

This diagram shows the rear and right side of the LaserJet Series II.

FIGURE 1-6

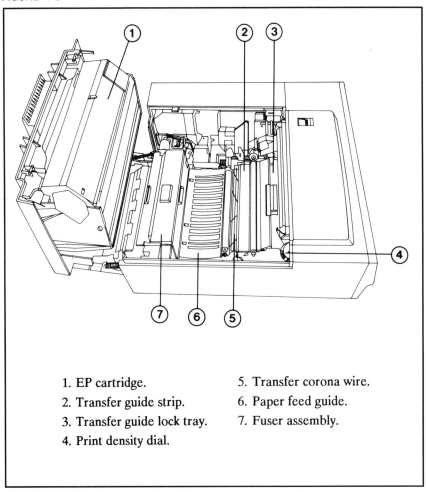

1. EP cartridge.
2. Transfer guide strip.
3. Transfer guide lock tray.
4. Print density dial.

5. Transfer corona wire.
6. Paper feed guide.
7. Fuser assembly.

This diagram shows the inside of the LaserJet Series II.

Summary of the LaserJet Family

Table 1-1 on pages 14 and 15 lists all of the printers we've discussed so far and summarizes each printer's capabilities. Most of our explanations of LaserJet printing will be general enough to cover the various models. However, we will occasionally discuss matters that concern only a specific member of the family. In those instances, just select the section that pertains to your printer.

Perhaps you've wondered how your LaserJet can produce extremely sharp documents in just a few seconds when it takes other printers much longer to produce documents that are far less attractive. In this section, we'll first explain how the LaserJet stores incoming print data and how it uses that data to create a printed page. In addition, we'll discuss some quirks associated with laser printing, including the unprintable region of the page.

HOW THE LASERJET PRINTS

Although it's not essential for you to understand how the LaserJet stores print data in memory and how it uses that data to print a page, you might wonder why it takes only a few seconds for the LaserJet to print a full page of text, while it takes several minutes to print graphics images.

Creating the Page

Before we explain what takes place when you send data to the LaserJet, first consider what happens when you send data to a conventional PC printer. For example, let's suppose you have a dot-matrix printer, and that you use a word processor to send the words *Dear John* to your printer. When you issue the print command, your computer will send ASCII representations for each of the letters in the words *Dear John*. When your dot-matrix printer receives the ASCII representation for the letter *D*, the printer translates that ASCII code and tells the printhead to create a matrix of dots forming the letter *D*. Next, the printer translates the ASCII representation for the letter *e*, and tells the printhead to create the matrix forming the letter *e*. This process continues until the printer receives an end-of-line command, which will cause the printhead to return to the left edge of the page.

Now, let's consider what happens when you send the words *Dear John* to the LaserJet. When the LaserJet receives the ASCII code for the letter *D*, it first looks up the bit-mapped representation for that letter. (This representation exists either in the printer's internal ROM, in an installed font cartridge, or in a soft font that is stored in the printer's RAM). After the LaserJet obtains a bit-mapped image of the letter *D*, it stores that image in memory at the current position of the LaserJet's cursor. (The LaserJet's cursor marks the position where the next printed character will appear—much like your screen's cursor marks the place where the next typed character will appear.) When the LaserJet receives the letter *e*, it looks up the bit-mapped representation for that letter and stores that bit-mapped image at the cursor's new position. This process continues until all the letters in *Dear John* have been translated into bit-mapped images and have been stored in memory. We'll discuss how fonts are managed in more detail in Chapter 23.

If you send a raster graphics image to the printer, the image is transferred in groups of bytes that contain a dot-per-bit representation of the row. If a bit in a row is set to one, the LaserJet will print the corresponding dot on the page. Figure 1-7 on page 16 shows an example of a raster image that forms an arrow. As you might guess, raster images require considerably more transfer time and printer memory than that required by characters. We'll discuss raster graphics in more detail in Chapter 24.

TABLE 1-1

	LaserJet	LaserJet Plus (&500 Plus)
Hardware interface	Serial	Serial or parallel
Internal fonts	Courier (10 cpi, portrait & landscape)	Courier (10 cpi, port & land) Compressed Lineprinter (16.66 cpi, portrait)
Internal symbol sets	Roman-8	Roman-8, ASCII, Roman Extended
Font cartridge slots	1	1
Downloadable font support	No	Yes
Character height	Up to 18 point	Up to 30 point
Font rotation	No	No
Pages per minute	Up to 8	Up to 8
Paper input trays	1	1
Sheets per input tray	100	100 (250 for 500 Plus)
Sheets per output tray	20	20 (250 for 500 Plus)
Correct order output	No	No (Yes for 500 Plus)
Job offsetting	No	No (Yes for 500 Plus)
Duplex printing	No	No
Standard memory **Expandable to**	128K 2 M	512K 2 M
Graphics resolution (letter size page): **75 dpi** **100 dpi** **150 dpi** **300 dpi**	Full page 1/2 page 1/4 page 1/16 page	Full page Full page Full page 1/2 page

LaserJet Series II	LaserJet IID	LaserJet 2000
Serial, parallel, or I/O	Serial, parallel, or I/O	Serial, parallel, or I/O
Courier reg and bold (10 cpi, port & land) Compressed Lineprinter (16.66 cpi, port & land)	Courier reg, bold, italic (10 & 12 cpi, port & land), Compressed Lineprinter (16.66 cpi, port & land) Tms Rmn reg, bold, italic (12 point, port & land), Helv bold (14 pt, port & land)	34 internal fonts, including many variations of Courier, Prestige Elite, Line Draw, Lineprinter, Tms Rmn, and Helv
Roman-8, ASCII, IBM-US (PC-8), IBM-DN (PC-8 DN), ECMA-94, 17 ISO sets, and 2 HP 7-bit sets	Roman-8, ASCII, IBM-US (PC-8), IBM-DN (PC-8 DN), ECMA-94, Legal, IBM-850 (PC-850), 17 ISO sets, and 2 HP 7-bit sets	34 symbol sets, including those found in the LJet IID, plus a few more ISO and HP 7- and 8-bit sets
2	2	3
Yes	Yes	Yes
Up to 655 point (9 inches)	Up to 655 point (9inches)	Unlimited
No	Yes	Yes
Up to 8	Up to 8	Up to 20
1	2	2, plus 2000 sheet input deck
200	200	250
100	100	1500
Yes	Yes	Yes
No	No	Yes
No	Yes	Yes
512K 4.5 M	512K 4.5 M	1.5M 5.5 M
Full page Full page Full page 1/2 page	Full page Full page Full page 1/2 page	Full page Full page Full page Full page

This table summarizes the capabilities of each member of the HP LaserJet family.

FIGURE 1-7

Dot Row	Binary Representation			
	Byte 1	Byte 2	Byte 3	Byte 4
1	00000000	00000000	10000000	00000000
2	00000000	00000000	11000000	00000000
3	00000000	00000000	11100000	00000000
4	00000000	00000000	11110000	00000000
5	00000000	00000000	11111000	00000000
6	00000000	00000000	11111100	00000000
7	00000000	00000000	11111110	00000000
8	00000000	00000000	11111111	00000000
9	00000000	00000000	11111111	10000000
10	11111111	11111111	11111111	11000000
11	11111111	11111111	11111111	11100000
12	11111111	11111111	11111111	11110000
13	11111111	11111111	11111111	11111000
14	11111111	11111111	11111111	11111100
15	11111111	11111111	11111111	11111110
16	11111111	11111111	11111111	11111111
17	11111111	11111111	11111111	11111111
18	11111111	11111111	11111111	11111110
19	11111111	11111111	11111111	11111100
20	11111111	11111111	11111111	11111000
21	11111111	11111111	11111111	11110000
22	11111111	11111111	11111111	11100000
23	11111111	11111111	11111111	11000000
24	00000000	00000000	11111111	10000000
25	00000000	00000000	11111111	00000000
26	00000000	00000000	11111110	00000000
27	00000000	00000000	11111100	00000000
28	00000000	00000000	11111000	00000000
29	00000000	00000000	11110000	00000000
30	00000000	00000000	11100000	00000000
31	00000000	00000000	11000000	00000000
32	00000000	00000000	10000000	00000000

Raster graphics are transferred to the LaserJet as a string of bytes containing a dot-per-bit representation of the row.

Printing the Page

In most cases, the LaserJet will keep storing the incoming print data in memory (in the print buffer) until it has enough data to print an entire page. At this point, the LaserJet will accept a sheet of paper and begin printing. Figure 1-8 shows the six printing stages through which the paper passes.

Conditioning and writing

The heart of your LaserJet printer is its photosensitive drum. In the conditioning stage of printing, the LaserJet prepares the drum to receive an image by applying a uniform electrostatic charge to the drum's photosensitive material. After the entire drum has been uniformly charged, the writing process begins.

FIGURE 1-8

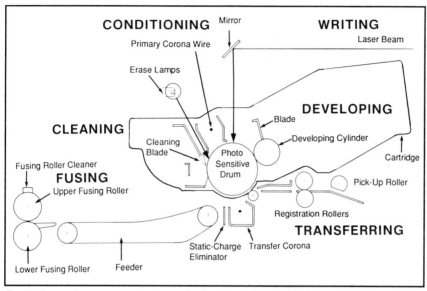

Each sheet of paper passes through six stages inside the LaserJet.

As you can see in Figure 1-8, the LaserJet uses a laser beam to write information on its photosensitive drum. As the laser beam scans across the drum's surface, it removes "dots" of static charge. After the beam has scanned a single row, the drum rotates a very small distance, and the beam scans across the next row, again removing "dots" of static charge where an image should appear. As the laser beam continues scanning the surface of the drum, the area of the drum containing the electrostatic image waits for the developing stage.

Developing

After the photosensitive drum has been properly charged, the LaserJet exposes a cloud of toner to the freshly charged photosensitive drum. As you might guess, the toner particles are attracted to the areas of the drum that were struck by the laser beam and are repelled by all the other areas. After the drum passes through this developing stage, it is ready to transfer the toner particles to a sheet of paper.

Transferring to the paper

Before a sheet of paper enters the LaserJet's transfer station, it receives an electrostatic charge that is opposite the charge of the toner particles on the photosensitive drum. After the paper receives this charge, it is fed into the transfer station where it comes into contact with the drum. Since the toner particles and the sheet of paper contain opposing charges, the toner particles are transferred from the drum onto the surface of the paper when the paper separates from the drum. As the drum rotates around to the cleaning station to prepare for the next page, the sheet of paper moves on to the printer's fusing station.

Fusing the image

When the paper leaves the transfer station, the toner particles are held in place by only a small static charge. The fusing station's high-intensity lamps permanently melt the toner particles onto the paper. After the entire image has been fused onto the page, the paper proceeds to the LaserJet's output tray, where you can retrieve and inspect the printed page.

Cleaning

After the photosensitive drum transfers the developed image to the paper, it rotates to the cleaning station, where residual toner particles are scraped from the drum's surface. The cleaning station's erase lamps also neutralize all the electrostatic charges left over from the previous image. After physical and electrostatic cleaning have taken place, the drum rotates to the conditioning stage and prepares to begin the process all over again.

What's that noise?

If you own a LaserJet Series II or LaserJet IID printer, you've probably noticed that the printer makes a strange noise every 30 seconds or so when it is turned on and standing idle. The noise is natural—the LaserJet is simply rotating the photosensitive drum a half turn. By keeping the drum active during long periods of printer inactivity, the LaserJet is able to extend the life of your EP toner cartridge and to maintain a more consistent print quality.

Printing and Ejecting Pages

As we mentioned in the previous section, your LaserJet stores print data from the computer in an area of memory called the print buffer. The LaserJet usually waits until you send it a whole page of data before it prints a page. Unfortunately, if you send less than a full page of data to your LaserJet, you won't immediately see the printed output—instead, you'll see your LaserJet's FORM FEED indicator turn on, telling you that there is page data currently stored in the print buffer.

In most cases, you'll want your LaserJet to eject partial pages from the printer after they've been sent. For example, if you use a word processor to send a $3^1/_2$-page document to your LaserJet, the LaserJet will print the document's first three pages but will not print page 4, since it contains less than a full page of data. Chances are, you'll want to tell the LaserJet to go ahead and eject the last page as well. To do this, you'll either have to issue a form feed command from your word processor or use the FORM FEED key on the LaserJet's control panel.

As we'll explain in Chapter 2, the LaserJet's FORM FEED key is operational only when the printer is off-line and in a ready state. To take the printer off-line, simply press the LaserJet's ON LINE key to make the LaserJet's ON LINE indicator turn off. Once the printer is off-line, you can press the FORM FEED key to eject the current page. After you've ejected the current page, the FORM FEED indicator will turn off, and you should then press the ON LINE key again to put the printer back on-line. We'll discuss the LaserJet's ON LINE and FORM FEED keys in more detail in the next chapter.

Pressing the LaserJet's FORM FEED key is not the only way to make the LaserJet print the contents of the print buffer. The LaserJet will print the current page whenever any of the following conditions exist:

• The printer receives enough data from the computer to fill an entire page.
• The printer receives a form feed command from the computer.
• The printer receives a reset command from the computer.
• The printer receives a command that changes the page orientation.
• The printer receives a command that specifies the paper source (either manual feed or cassette feed).

If none of the above conditions exist, then the LaserJet will add any incoming print data to the current page. Because the LaserJet ejects printed pages in this fashion, it is called a page printer.

The Unprintable Region

Unfortunately, the HP LaserJet printer is incapable of printing to a small region along the outside edges of a page. Figure 1-9 on the next page shows the location and size of the unprintable region for an $8^1/_2$- by 11-inch sheet of paper. As you can see, this region occupies approximately $^1/_4$ inch of space at the top and bottom edges of the page, as well as $^1/_4$ inch of space at the left and right edges. By default, the LaserJet reserves $^1/_2$ inch at the top and bottom of each page as a default top and bottom margin. When you consider the unprintable areas along with the default top and bottom margins, a sheet of letter-size paper has an effective print area of only 8 inches by 10 inches. You should think of these unprintable areas as default margins—you will print only to the area of the page that lies inside these boundaries.

If you print your documents in Landscape orientation, the LaserJet's default margins will be a $^1/_2$-inch top and bottom margin and a $^1/_4$-inch left and right margin, reducing the effective print area from 11 by $8^1/_2$ inches to $10^1/_2$ by $7^1/_2$ inches.

Table 1-2 on the next page summarizes the LaserJet's printable areas. Remember, although it is possible to print 62 lines of six lines per inch text on a letter-size sheet of paper, the default top and bottom margins leave room for only 60 lines of text. Also, remember that when you're printing with the LaserJet's default font (Courier, 10 characters per inch), the LaserJet has a page width of 80 characters.

You'll soon realize that the LaserJet's default margins cause many problems for some of your PC applications. Most applications add default top and bottom margins to the LaserJet's default margins when you print, leaving huge areas of white space around the edges of your page. Furthermore, since your documents will contain only 60 lines of text instead of the standard 66, your application's default settings may produce erratic page breaks in your printed documents. Consequently, if you want to use your PC applications to print documents on your LaserJet, you'll have to adjust the print settings within that application. We'll show you how to do this for 11 applications in Sections Two and Three of this book.

FIGURE 1-9

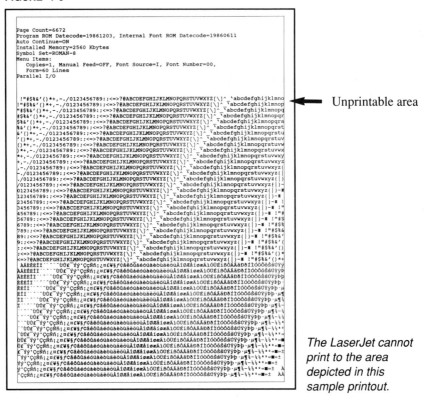

Unprintable area

The LaserJet cannot print to the area depicted in this sample printout.

TABLE 1-2

		Printable Areas				
		Lines		Columns		
Paper size	**Orient.**	**6 lpi**	**8 lpi**	**10 cpi**	**12 cpi**	**16.66 cpi**
Letter	Port.	62	84	80	96	132
	Land.	48	63	106	127	176
Legal	Port.	80	108	80	96	132
	Land.	48	63	136	163	226

This table summarizes the LaserJet's printable areas.

All of HP's LaserJet printers use Hewlett-Packard's Printer Command Language (PCL). In short, PCL is the language spoken by your LaserJet. If you want the LaserJet to carry out specific operations, such as changing the margin settings or changing the number of copies, you'll need to issue a PCL command to do so. PCL commands are often referred to as escape commands or escape sequences.

In most cases, you will not need to interact directly with PCL. Instead, your applications will automatically handle the task of sending PCL commands to the LaserJet. In the first four sections of this book, we'll discuss the specific capabilities of PCL commands as they relate to PC applications. In Section Five of this book, we'll discuss in more detail the structure of PCL commands and the concepts related to PCL programming.

Although Hewlett-Packard's PCL language is standard on all HP LaserJet printers, many of today's laser printers use an alternative page description language called PostScript, popularized by Apple Computer, Inc.'s LaserWriter family of printers. PostScript's main advantage over PCL is that it lets you dynamically scale, rotate, shade, shadow, half-tone, and crop fonts and bit-mapped graphics.

Hewlett-Packard has announced several hardware products that allow you to add the PostScript page description language to your LaserJet. If you own an HP LaserJet Series II, you can give your printer PostScript capabilities with HP's JetScript Accessory Kit. If you own a LaserJet, LaserJet Plus, or LaserJet 500 Plus, you can contact HP and have a service representative install a PostScript upgrade on your printer. For more information on PostScript accessories for the LaserJet printer, contact HP's Direct Marketing Division at 800-538-8787, or call 408-708-4133 in California.

For most of our discussions in this book, we'll assume that your LaserJet is not equipped with PostScript capabilities. However, we'll mention PostScript again when we discuss using the LaserJet with your computer's Windows applications in Section Three.

If you are like most LaserJet users, you'll find that your standard LaserJet printer is powerful enough to handle most of your printing needs. Sooner or later, however, you'll want to enhance the capabilities of your LaserJet with some of the LaserJet's many options and accessories. In this section, we'll give you a brief overview of the options and accessories available for the LaserJet printers. (Appendix 2 lists all of the HP's current accessory offerings for the HP LaserJet family.)

LASERJET OPTIONS AND ACCESSORIES

As we mentioned earlier in this chapter, your LaserJet stores data sent from the computer into its memory. Although text data requires a relatively small amount of printer memory, graphics data consumes an enormous amount of memory. For instance, to give your printer the capability to print a 300 dpi graphics image occupying an entire $8^1/_2$- by 11-inch sheet of paper, your printer must be equipped with over 1MB of memory.

Memory Options

In addition to storing print data, your printer also uses memory to store downloadable soft fonts and print macros. Soft fonts occupy anywhere from a few kilobytes to over 150K of printer memory. If you download a few soft fonts to your printer before you send a graphics image to be printed, the LaserJet will not have as much memory left to store the graphics image. As we'll explain in a moment, if you plan to use soft fonts and to print graphics images on your LaserJet printer, you should purchase a memory upgrade.

LaserJet

The original LaserJet printer comes equipped with only 128K—enough memory to print a full-page graphics image at 75 dpi, or a half-page image at 100 dpi. Unfortunately, the only way you can expand the original LaserJet's memory is by purchasing HP's 2MB upgrade kit, which must be installed by an HP technician. If you own an original LaserJet printer and you've outgrown its memory limitations, you're probably better off buying a new HP LaserJet Series II printer instead of ordering HP's memory upgrade.

LaserJet Plus and LaserJet 500 Plus

As we mentioned earlier, the LaserJet Plus and LaserJet 500 Plus printers are equipped with 512K of memory—395K of which is available for graphics, downloadable soft fonts, and downloadable macros. This amount of memory is enough to print a full-page graphics image with a resolution of 150 dpi, or to print a half-page image at 300 dpi.

Unfortunately, to expand the memory capabilities of these printers, you must order the same 2MB upgrade kit that you would for the original LaserJet.

LaserJet Series II and IID

Like the LaserJet Plus and LaserJet 500 Plus, a standard LaserJet Series II and LaserJet IID printer is equipped with 512K of memory. However, these newer printers have a RAM expansion slot that will accept cards containing an additional 1, 2, or 4MB of memory. If you own a LaserJet Series II or LaserJet IID printer and are not sure how much memory you need, you might use the following general guidelines. To order these memory options, contact your local computer vendor or call HP Direct Marketing at 800-538-8787.

Adding 1MB

When you install HP's 1MB memory expansion card in your printer, your printer will have a total of 1.5MB. Since a full-page graphics image requires about 1.2MB of memory, you can download a couple of soft fonts to your LaserJet and still have enough memory left over to print a full-page graphics image at 300 dpi. If you plan to use several downloaded fonts at once, however, or if you frequently download large headline fonts, an additional 1MB of memory probably won't be enough.

HP's 2MB memory expansion card is designed for people who use their LaserJet for desktop publishing. This card boosts the printer's total memory capacity to 2.5MB, and allows you to download several soft fonts at once and still print full-page 300 dpi graphics images.

Adding 2MB

You may not be sure whether you'll need an additional 1MB or 2MB of memory for your LaserJet; however, there are two reasons you should buy the 2MB card. First, as you continue to use more complicated applications on your computer, your printing needs will increase. So, if you're running up against a 1.5MB memory limitation now, you'll outgrow your printer when your computing needs change in the future.

The second reason you should opt for the 2MB memory card over the 1MB card is that you cannot increase the memory capacity of the 1MB memory card. If you buy the 1MB card and then need additional memory later, you'll have to purchase a new 2MB card to replace the first one. If you're like most LaserJet users, it will be worth the additional expense to upgrade to 2.5MB instead of to 1.5MB.

Only a few LaserJet users need HP's 4MB memory expansion card, which boosts the LaserJet's total memory to 4.5MB. If you need to download more than just a few soft fonts and forms, then still produce 300 dpi graphics images, you probably need the 4MB memory expansion card for your LaserJet.

Adding 4MB

When the LaserJet prints characters in a document, it prints them in one of the LaserJet's available fonts. Before we tell you the different ways you can supply your LaserJet with fonts, it's important for you to understand how the LaserJet uses font sources to print a document.

Fonts

Suppose you are in charge of updating the marquee for a large convention center. Each day, your part-time employee takes letters out of a big box and spells out words that announce the week's upcoming events. Let's also suppose that the box of letters is so big that he never runs out of letters, and that all of the letters in the box are the same size and have the same style.

An analogy

Now, suppose that one day you decide you are tired of seeing the same letters on the marquee every day, so you buy a new box of letters that are a little larger and fancier than the letters in the first box. You can now vary the marquee's appearance; you can tell the marquee builder to use the letters in the old box to give the marquee a "traditional" look, or you can tell him to use the letters in the new box to produce a more contemporary look. If you want, you can even tell him to use the old box of letters to create some words and to use the new box to create the rest. All he has to do is find out which box of letters to use for each word, then place those letters on the marquee.

Your LaserJet printer is very much like the person building the marquee in our analogy. When you want the LaserJet to print your documents with characters of a particular size or style, you must make sure that your LaserJet has access to the appropriate font source (as you had to provide the marquee builder with the appropriate box of letters). Of course, instead of giving your LaserJet a new box of letters, you install a font cartridge or a downloadable soft font to get some variety.

If you want your marquee builder to add boldface or italics to some of the words on the marquee, then you'll need to provide him with a box of bold or italic letters—he can't transform the regular letters into bold or italic letters with his bare hands. Similarly, your LaserJet can't modify your fonts in any way. If you want to use both upright and italic fonts in your document, then you must make sure that your LaserJet has access to both upright *and* italic fonts. The LaserJet can't turn upright characters into italic characters, just as the marquee builder can't slant his letters to make them look italic.

Unfortunately, only the LaserJet IID and LaserJet 2000 printers have the ability to rotate fonts. If you have any of the other LaserJet printers, and you need to print documents in both Portrait and Landscape orientation, you must make sure you've equipped your LaserJet with both Portrait and Landscape fonts.

Once you've equipped your LaserJet with the appropriate fonts, it's up to your software to tell the LaserJet which font to use in your printed document. For instance, you could tell the LaserJet to print an entire page in the first font, an entire page in the second font, or part of the page in one font and part of it in another.

Each LaserJet comes equipped with a few internal fonts. If you want to add additional fonts to your printer, you can do so with either font cartridges or downloadable soft fonts. Let's look briefly at each of these font sources.

Internal fonts

The internal (built-in) fonts for each LaserJet printer are listed in Table 1-3. (Some of the fonts in Table 1-3 come in more than one symbol set.) As you can see, the newer LaserJet printers are equipped with more fonts than the older LaserJet models. The original LaserJet is equipped with only the Courier, 10-pitch, medium, upright font. The LaserJet Plus and LaserJet 500 Plus are also equipped with a Line Printer font, which is a 16.66-pitch, medium, upright typeface. The other three LaserJet printers (Series II, IID, and 2000) have many other fonts. If you use one of these printers, you can easily print all of the fonts installed on your printer. We'll show you how to do this in Chapter 3.

TABLE 1-3

Printer	Internal fonts
LaserJet	Courier
LaserJet Plus	Courier, Line Printer
LaserJet 500 Plus	Courier, Line Printer
LaserJet Series II	Courier, Courier Bold, Line Printer
LaserJet IID	Courier, Courier Bold, Courier Italic, Courier 12, Courier 12 Bold, Courier 12 Italic, Line Printer
LaserJet 2000	Courier 10, Courier 10 Bold, Courier 10 Italic, Prestige Elite, Prestige Elite Bold, Prestige Elite Italic, Tms Rmn, Tms Rmn Bold, Tms Rmn Italic, Helv Bold, Line Draw, Line Printer

This table shows the internal fonts available for each of the LaserJet printers.

The easiest way to add additional fonts to your LaserJet printer is to install a font cartridge. HP offers a large number of font cartridges for all LaserJet printers, and many third-party manufacturers have developed LaserJet font cartridges as well. The catalog in Appendix 2 lists all of HP's current font cartridge offerings. We'll show you how to install font cartridges in Chapter 3, and we'll show you how to tell the LaserJet to use your optional fonts in Chapter 4.

Font cartridges

Another way you can provide additional fonts for your LaserJet printer is with downloadable soft fonts. Unlike font cartridges, which are pieces of hardware you can just plug in and use, soft fonts are little software files that you must transfer from a disk in your computer to the printer's memory. (The process of transferring soft fonts from disk to the printer's memory is called downloading.) All of HP's LaserJet printers can use downloaded soft fonts except the original LaserJet printer. If you have an original LaserJet printer, you can only use font cartridges to add fonts to your printer.

Downloadable soft fonts

Once you've downloaded a soft font to your LaserJet, it behaves pretty much the same as a cartridge font. Because the font exists in memory, however, your soft fonts will get erased when you turn off the power to the printer. In addition to HP's soft font offerings, which are listed in Appendix 2, a large number of soft fonts are available from third-party manufacturers. We'll talk about soft fonts in more detail in Chapter 4.

**Other
Accessories**

In addition to memory and fonts, HP offers many other options and accessories for your LaserJet printer. For example, if you use legal-size paper to print most of your documents, you'll probably want to purchase the LaserJet's legal paper cassette tray. Appendix 2 lists some of the accessories that are currently available from HP's Direct Marketing Division. As we have said, many third-party manufacturers sell LaserJet accessories, so consult your local computer vendor to find out which accessories are available for your HP LaserJet printer.

CONCLUSION

In this chapter, we've discussed the fundamental features of all HP LaserJet printers. After we introduced you to each member of the LaserJet family, we told you how the LaserJet prints images on the page. Next, we explained the page printing nature of the LaserJet, and we pointed out that each page has an unprintable region around its edges. Finally, we told you how you can enhance your printer's capabilities with memory options and font options. Now that you're familiar with these LaserJet basics, you can better grasp the concepts we'll introduce throughout the remainder of this book.

OPERATING THE LASERJET 2

Now that you're familiar with the basics of LaserJet printing, you need to become acquainted with some standard LaserJet operating procedures. In this chapter, we'll show you how to configure your LaserJet for either serial or parallel printing. We'll discuss the purpose of the keys and indicators on the LaserJet's control panel, and show you how to use the control panel to issue a few printer commands. After we briefly explain how to set the print density and how to use font cartridges and soft fonts, we'll give you some valuable paper-handling tips, and show you how to feed paper and envelopes into the printer manually. Finally, we'll explain a few ways you can share a LaserJet printer with your co-workers.

Before you install and configure your Hewlett-Packard LaserJet printer, you must decide whether you will run it as a parallel printer or as a serial printer. (Of course, if you own an original LaserJet printer, you have no choice—you can run it only as a serial printer.) You should be able to obtain parallel and serial printer cables from any dealer that sells the HP LaserJet printer.

Your LaserJet user's manual will tell you how to unpack and set up your printer. After you follow the setup procedures in your printer manual, you simply connect the printer cable to your printer and to your computer, and then configure your printer and computer so that they can communicate with each other. In this section, we'll show you how to configure your computer and your LaserJet for both serial printing and parallel printing.

CONFIGURING YOUR LASERJET

**Serial vs.
Parallel Printing**

Except for the original LaserJet printer, every printer in the LaserJet family lets you use either its serial or parallel interface to talk to your computer. (The original LaserJet is equipped only with a serial interface.) As you can see in Figure 2-1, the printer's parallel and serial interface ports look different.

FIGURE 2-1

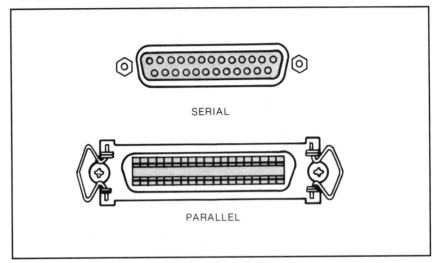

The printer's serial and parallel interface ports have distinct pin configurations.

If you own any member of the LaserJet family except the original LaserJet, you'll probably want to connect your computer to the printer's parallel interface since parallel data transfer occurs much faster than serial data transfer. In addition, unlike your computer's parallel ports, which require no special configuring procedure, your computer's serial ports require a couple of DOS MODE commands that define the baud rate, data bits, stop bits, and parity settings for your printer.

The only reasons you would want to use your LaserJet's serial interface instead of its parallel interface are if your computer does not have an extra parallel port or if your computer is located over 15 feet away from your LaserJet. If you need more than 15 feet of cable to connect your LaserJet to your computer, you cannot use a standard parallel printer cable; instead, you must use either a serial cable (which can be as long as 150 feet) or a special parallel cable that is allowed to exceed 15 feet. (One example of such a cable is Long Link, from the Intellicom Corporation.) For more information on parallel and serial cables, contact your local computer vendor or simply call Hewlett-Packard's Direct Marketing Division at 800-538-8787 (in California, call 408-708-4133).

The original HP LaserJet printer is equipped with only a serial interface—you cannot run the original LaserJet as a parallel printer. You will connect the LaserJet to your computer's Asynchronous Communications Adapter (which we usually call a serial port). Make sure you note whether the LaserJet is connected to the Primary Asynchronous Adapter (COM1:) or the Secondary Asynchronous Adapter (COM2:). If your PC is equipped with only one serial port, that port is probably configured as the Primary Asynchronous Adapter. If you have two serial ports, you'll have to determine which one is configured as the Primary Asynchronous Adapter and which is configured as the Secondary Asynchronous Adapter. To determine which is which, consult your adapter's technical reference manual or ask your local PC guru.

LaserJet

Once you've used a serial printer cable to connect your LaserJet to your computer, you'll need to configure the appropriate serial port so that it can talk to your LaserJet. The way you'll configure your computer's serial port is by entering a couple of DOS MODE commands in an AUTOEXEC.BAT file.

To install the appropriate MODE commands on your computer's boot disk, first move into your boot disk's root directory, then type the command **DIR** at the DOS prompt. When DOS presents a listing of the files in that directory, look for MODE.COM and AUTOEXEC.BAT. If you don't see the file MODE.COM, copy the MODE.COM file from your DOS disk into the root directory of your boot disk.

If an AUTOEXEC.BAT file already exists, use EDLIN or any other text processor to add the lines

```
MODE COM1:=9600,n,8,1,p
MODE LPT1:=COM1:
```

to the existing AUTOEXEC.BAT file. If you don't have an AUTOEXEC.BAT file on your disk, use EDLIN or any other text processor to create one that contains the two lines shown above. If your LaserJet printer is connected to your computer's Secondary Asynchronous Adapter, you'll need to change the device name in the two MODE commands listed above from COM1: to COM2:, like this:

```
MODE COM2:=9600,n,8,1,p
MODE LPT1:=COM2:
```

After you've added the appropriate commands to your AUTOEXEC.BAT file, reboot your computer. Assuming you've set up the AUTOEXEC.BAT file correctly and that you've copied the file MODE.COM into the disk's root directory, your computer will automatically configure itself to print to your LaserJet printer each time you boot with this disk.

If more than one printer is connected to your computer, you may need to assign the device name LPT2: or LPT3: to your LaserJet printer. (Parallel printers that are connected to your computer's primary parallel port automatically take on the device name LPT1:.) To assign the name LPT2: or LPT3: to your LaserJet, just change the device name in the second MODE command from LPT1: to either LPT2: or LPT3:.

LaserJet Plus and LaserJet 500 Plus

Unlike the original LaserJet printer, which is equipped with only a serial interface, the LaserJet Plus and LaserJet 500 Plus printers are equipped with a parallel interface, allowing you to connect these printers to either your computer's serial port or to its parallel port. Since a parallel LaserJet runs up to three times faster than a serial LaserJet, you'll probably want to run your LaserJet Plus or LaserJet 500 Plus as a parallel printer. If you want, however, you can still run either the LaserJet Plus or LaserJet 500 Plus as a serial printer.

Configuring for serial printing

By default, the LaserJet Plus and LaserJet 500 Plus printers are configured for serial printing. Consequently, if you want to connect your LaserJet Plus or LaserJet 500 Plus printer to one of your computer's serial ports, just follow the procedures above for configuring the original LaserJet printer.

Configuring for parallel printing

Since HP configures the LaserJet Plus and LaserJet 500 Plus printers for serial printing by default, you'll have to reconfigure your printer if you want to use it as a parallel printer. Although it involves some minor printer disassembly and switch throwing, you need not possess superior mechanical know-how to perform this simple procedure.

To select your LaserJet Plus' parallel interface, first unplug the printer's power cord from both the wall and the printer. Next, remove the four screws that secure the LaserJet's rear panel, as shown in Figure 2-2.

FIGURE 2-2

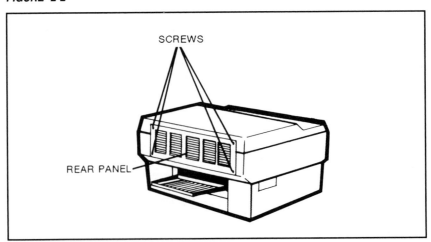

You must remove the four screws on the LaserJet's rear panel to uncover the printer's vertical support bracket.

Then, remove the screw that secures the printer's vertical support bracket at the center of the cabinet, as shown in Figure 2-3. When you remove this bracket, you will expose a set of eight DIP switches labeled SW1. When you see these switches, set switch number 1 of SW1 to the ON position, as shown in Figure 2-4 on the following page.

FIGURE 2-3

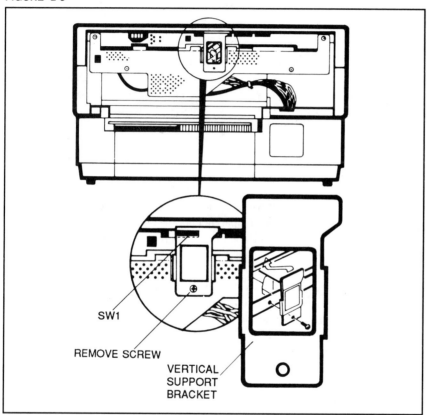

SW1

REMOVE SCREW

VERTICAL
SUPPORT
BRACKET

You must remove the screw holding the vertical support bracket to uncover the printer's SW1 switch bank.

After you've changed switch 1 from the OFF position to the ON position, replace the printer's vertical support bracket and rear panel. Finally, plug in the power cord and turn on the printer. Your LaserJet Plus printer should now accept data through its parallel interface, and not through its serial interface. (For more information on the LaserJet Plus' parallel interface, refer to the *LaserJet Printer Family Technical Reference Manual.*)

FIGURE 2-4

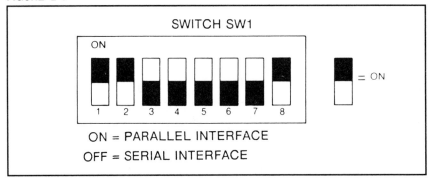

Set switch number 1 of SW1 to the ON position to select the parallel interface port. (Switches 2 through 8 need not match those in this figure.)

LaserJet Series II and LaserJet IID

Like the LaserJet Plus and LaserJet 500 Plus printers, the LaserJet Series II and LaserJet IID printers are equipped with both a serial and a parallel interface. Unlike the previous laser printers, however, these printers can be reconfigured with the control panel on the front—no screwdrivers or DIP switches come into play when you want to change the default configuration. As we said earlier, since a LaserJet that is connected to your computer's parallel port runs much faster than one that is connected to your computer's serial port, you'll probably want to configure your LaserJet as a parallel printer.

Configuring for serial printing

By default, the LaserJet Series II and LaserJet IID printers are configured for serial printing. Consequently, if you want to connect your printer to one of your computer's serial ports, just follow the procedures described at the beginning of this chapter for configuring the original LaserJet printer. We'll show you how to change the baud rate, robust XON, or DTR polarity in the section entitled "Configuration Menu" later in this chapter.

Configuring for parallel printing

Since HP configures the LaserJet Plus, LaserJet Series II, and LaserJet IID printers for serial printing by default, you'll have to reconfigure your printer if you want to connect it to your computer's parallel port. Fortunately, these printers allow you to reconfigure the interface (along with many other configuration settings) directly from the LaserJet's control panel.

To configure your printer for parallel printing, first make sure that the printer is turned on and is off-line. Once this is done, press and hold the MENU key on the LaserJet's control panel until the message *SYMBOL SET=ROMAN-8* appears in the display window (this normally takes about five seconds). At this point, press the LaserJet's MENU key twice to display the message *I/O=SERIAL**. Now, press the LaserJet's + key to display the message *I/O=PARALLEL*, then press the ENTER/ RESET MENU key to save your selection. (As soon as you press that key, an asterisk (*) will appear on the right side of the display window to indicate that the ENTER/RESET MENU key has saved your selection.) Finally, press the LaserJet's ON LINE key to exit the Configuration menu and to put the printer back on-line. (We'll discuss the Configuration menu in more detail later in this chapter.)

After you've reconfigured the LaserJet for parallel printing, you can simply hook up your LaserJet to your computer's parallel port as you would any other parallel printer. If your computer has more than one parallel port, you'll need to determine which parallel port is configured as LPT1: and which is configured as LPT2:. You need not make any modifications to your AUTOEXEC.BAT file when you run the LaserJet as a parallel printer—DOS automatically knows how to talk to the LaserJet's parallel interface.

USING THE CONTROL PANEL

The LaserJet's control panel is the place where you will communicate with your printer. You can use the keys and indicators on the control panel to issue printer commands (such as turning on manual feed or running a self-test), and the LaserJet can use the display area of the control panel to display status information and error codes that keep you informed of its current condition. If you own a LaserJet Series II or LaserJet IID printer, you can use the control panel to configure your printer and to change many of LaserJet's default print settings, such as form length and number of copies. While reading the section on the control panel, remember that many of the commands you can issue from the control panel are normally handled directly by your software applications. (We'll discuss how specific software applications communicate with the LaserJet in Sections Two and Three.)

LaserJet, LaserJet Plus, and LaserJet 500 Plus

Figures 2-5 and 2-6 show the control panels that appear on the front of the LaserJet and LaserJet Plus printers. As you can see, these two control panels are very similar. After we consider the purpose of the keys and indicators on these control panels, we'll show you how to use the control panels to reset the printer and perform a self-test.

FIGURE 2-5

This control panel appears on the original LaserJet printer.

FIGURE 2-6

This control panel appears on the LaserJet Plus printer.

Keys and indicators

The keys and indicators on the LaserJet's control panel allow you to issue many important printer commands and monitor the printer's current status. Although most of the keys and indicators that appear on the control panel of the first-generation LaserJets are the same, there are a few features that apply only to the LaserJet Plus or to the LaserJet 500 Plus. We'll point out those special features along the way.

The READY indicator

The green READY indicator in the upper-left corner of the control panel can appear in any of three states: on, off, and flashing. When the READY indicator is on, the printer is turned on and ready for printing, but is not necessarily on-line. The READY indicator will also appear when the printer performs a self-test.

When the READY indicator is off, the printer is either turned off or is experiencing a problem. If the printer is not ready for printing, the LaserJet will indicate the cause of the problem with a number in the status display.

A flashing READY indicator on an original LaserJet printer indicates that the printer is warming up. During a warm-up, the LaserJet will display the number *02* in the status display. When the READY indicator flashes on a LaserJet Plus or LaserJet 500 Plus printer, however, it indicates that the printer is receiving data from the computer.

The status display

The two-digit LED display on the left side of the control panel is called the status display. The LaserJet uses the status display to indicate the status of the printer and to inform you of printer errors.

When the number in the status display is not flashing, the LaserJet is displaying a status code. When the number is flashing, the LaserJet is making a request or displaying an error condition. There are quite a few status codes and error numbers that the LaserJet can display. Table 2-1 lists these numbers and gives a brief description of their meanings.

When an error code appears, you should look up the cause of that error in Table 2-1 and try to correct the problem. You can correct most of these problems by pressing the CONTINUE key. (If the problem persists, however, refer to Chapter 3. This section of the book explains the error and status codes in detail, and outlines the steps you should take to correct them.)

TABLE 2-1

	Printer Status
Number	**Meaning**
00	Printer ready
02	Wait
05	Self-test (non-printing)
06	Self-test (printing, staggered characters)
07	Reset
15	Test print (striped pattern)

Operator Service Conditions	
Number	**Meaning**
11*	Paper tray empty (add paper)
LC 11	No paper in lower cassette (LaserJet 500 Plus only)
UC 11	No paper in upper cassette (LaserJet 500 Plus only)
12*	Printer engine power off—upper main body of printer open
13*	Paper jam
14*	No EP toner cartridge installed
PC*	Request for different size paper tray
PF*	Manual paper feed request—printer ready for manual feed
PE*	Envelope feed request—printer ready for envelope feed
FC*	Check font cartridge
FE	Font cartridge removed
Error Conditions	
Number	**Meaning**
20*	Memory overflow
21*	Print overrun error
22	Receiving buffer overflow
40*	Line error
41*	Print check error
50*	Fusing assembly malfunction
51*	Beam detect malfunction
52*	Scanner malfunction
53*	Laser temperature control circuit malfunction
54*	Main motor malfunction
55*	Printer command error
60	Bus error
61	Program ROM checksum error
62	Internal font ROM checksum error
63	D-RAM error
64	Scan buffer error
65	D-RAM controller error
67	Illegal I/F microprocessor number
* These conditions/errors can be cleared by pressing the CONTINUE key.	

You can use this table to determine the status or the error condition of your LaserJet printer.

The ON LINE key

Pressing the LaserJet's ON LINE key switches the printer between on-line and off-line status. The orange indicator light on this key is on when the printer is on-line and off when the printer is off-line.

When the LaserJet printer is on-line, it is ready to accept print data from your computer. (The data can be in the form of text, graphics, or escape sequences.) When the printer is on-line, it will not respond to any of the commands you issue from the control panel (except the ON LINE key, of course). When your LaserJet is off-line, it will not respond to your computer, but instead will wait for you to issue a command from the control panel. By default, the LaserJet will be on-line after you turn it on.

The CONTINUE key

The CONTINUE key on the LaserJet and LaserJet Plus allows you to resume printing after the printer has been taken off-line due to an error condition. In most cases, pressing the CONTINUE key clears the error and places the printer back on-line. Table 2-1 on pages 34 and 35 uses an asterisk (*) to denote the error conditions that can be cleared with the CONTINUE key.

In the case of a paper jam, pressing the CONTINUE key after you've removed the jammed page will cause the LaserJet to reprint the page on which the jam occurred. After the LaserJet successfully reprints the problem page, it will continue printing the rest of the document. We will discuss paper jams in more detail in Chapter 3.

The HOLD TO RESET/CONTINUE key

The HOLD TO RESET/CONTINUE key on the LaserJet Plus and LaserJet 500 Plus serves double duty. When you momentarily press this key, it performs the same function as the LaserJet's CONTINUE key. When you hold down this key for about three seconds, however, the LaserJet will display *07* in the status display, then will reset itself. Resetting the printer returns all print settings (page length, symbol set, number of copies, etc.) to their defaults. The reset function also clears temporary soft fonts, temporary macros, and any data that is stored in the print buffer. We'll talk about resetting the printer in more detail in the section of this chapter called "Resetting the Printer."

The SELF TEST key

Pressing the SELF TEST key causes the printer to perform an internal test of the controller and to print a test printout. Holding this key down for more than three seconds causes the printer to continue the self-test until you press the SELF TEST key again or the ON LINE key. Like all of the keys on the control panel, the SELF TEST key is operational only when the printer is off-line.

You'll want to perform the self-test procedure only when you suspect there may be a problem with your LaserJet. During the LaserJet's self-test procedure, the printer will display the number *05* in the status display, and all of the indicator lights on the control panel will turn on. When the printing portion of the self-test begins, the LaserJet will display the number *06*. Finally, when the self-test has been completed, the LaserJet will display the number *00*, which indicates that the printer is ready. If any errors occur during the self-test, the printer will display an error number that pinpoints the problem.

As we explained in Chapter 1, when the computer sends print data to the LaserJet, that data gets stored in the LaserJet's memory, and the orange indicator on the FORM FEED key lights up. If the computer sends less than a full page of data, then that data will reside in the printer's memory until the computer sends enough additional data to fill the page, or until you press the LaserJet's FORM FEED key. Pressing the FORM FEED key tells the LaserJet to print all of the stored page data and to empty the contents of the printer's memory. After the current page has been printed, the indicator on the FORM FEED key will turn off, telling you that there is no longer any page data stored in memory. The section entitled "How the LaserJet Prints" in Chapter 1 explains in detail what causes a partial page to eject.

The FORM FEED key

As we have said, you'll want to press the FORM FEED key whenever you've sent the LaserJet less than a page of data and are ready to eject the current page. Of course, the FORM FEED key is functional only when the printer is off-line and in a ready state. If a paper jam or other error occurs during the form feed procedure, the form feed is cancelled. Finally, if you have placed the LaserJet in the manual feed mode and you press the FORM FEED key, the printer will begin printing when you manually feed paper into the printer.

Pressing the MANUAL FEED key on the LaserJet or LaserJet Plus' control panel switches the printer between manual feed mode and cassette feed. (The LaserJet 500 Plus has a PAPER SELECT key instead of a MANUAL FEED key, as we'll discuss in a moment.) Of course, the MANUAL FEED key is operational only when you've taken the printer off-line. After you've placed the LaserJet in manual feed mode and have placed the printer back on-line, the indicator on the MANUAL FEED key will be lit.

The MANUAL FEED key

If there is no data waiting to be sent to the printer when you press the MANUAL FEED key, the number *00* will appear in the status display. As soon as the printer is ready to draw a sheet of paper, the status display will prompt you by alternately flashing *PF* and the selected letter size (*L* for letter, *LL* for legal, *A4* for A4, and *b5* for B5). If envelope feed has been requested, then the status display will flash *PE*. For a detailed discussion on manually feeding paper into the LaserJet, see the section "Using Manual Feed" on page 60.

Because the LaserJet 500 Plus accepts two paper trays, its control panel features a PAPER SELECT key instead of a MANUAL FEED key. You can use its PAPER SELECT key, along with the four indicator lights on the right edge of the control panel, to activate any of the LaserJet 500 Plus' paper sources. By default, the LaserJet 500 Plus uses the paper in its upper cassette tray. As you might guess,

LaserJet 500 Plus' PAPER SELECT key and paper indicators

pressing the PAPER SELECT key while the printer is off-line causes the indicator light to move among the AUTO, U CASSETTE, L CASSETTE, and MANUAL settings. Let's consider how the LaserJet 500 Plus reacts when you've selected each of these settings.

AUTO

When the AUTO indicator is lit, the printer is in auto-select mode, which tells the LaserJet 500 Plus to switch automatically from one paper cassette to the other when one runs out of paper. In order for the auto-select mode to work, of course, you must insert the same size cassette trays in both the upper and lower cassette slots. The orange indicator light will illuminate either the U CASSETTE or L CASSETTE setting to indicate from which cassette the printer is now drawing.

When either the upper or lower cassette tray runs out of paper, the LaserJet 500 Plus will flash either *UC 11* or *LC 11* to let you know that you need to add paper. If both trays run out of paper, the number *11* will appear in the status display. Printing is not interrupted unless both cassettes are empty or are removed. As you might expect, attempting to run your printer in auto-select mode with two different size cassette trays will result in a paper out message (error message 11) when the first tray runs out of paper.

U CASSETTE & L CASSETTE

When the U CASSETTE indicator is lit, the LaserJet 500 Plus will draw paper only from the upper cassette tray. If the upper cassette tray runs out of paper while the printer is in upper cassette mode, the printer will alternately flash *UC* and *11* in the status display, indicating that you must remove the upper cassette and add paper.

Similarly, when the L CASSETTE indicator is lit, the LaserJet 500 Plus will draw paper only from the lower cassette tray. If the lower cassette tray runs out of paper while the printer is in lower cassette mode, the printer will alternately flash *LC* and *11* in the status display, indicating that the LaserJet will not resume printing until you add paper to the lower cassette.

MANUAL

When the MANUAL indicator is lit, the printer will draw paper from the printer's manual feed slot instead of from either of the paper cassette trays. When the printer is ready to draw a sheet of paper, the status display will prompt you by alternately flashing *PF* and the selected letter size (*L* for letter, *LL* for legal, *A4* for A4, and *b5* for B5). If envelope feed has been requested, then the status display will flash *PE*. For a detailed discussion on manually feeding paper into the LaserJet, see the section "Using Manual Feed" on page 60.

Resetting the printer

As we said earlier, resetting the LaserJet returns all print settings (page length, symbol set, number of copies, etc.) to their defaults. Table 2-2 shows a few of the LaserJet's default settings. In addition to restoring the default print settings, resetting your printer also clears temporary soft fonts, temporary macros, and any data that is stored in the print buffer.

TABLE 2-2

Orientation	Portrait
Characters per inch	10
Lines per inch	6
Lines per page	60
Top margin	0.5
Bottom margin	0.5
Left margin	0.25
Right margin	0.25

Whenever you reset the LaserJet, the default settings shown here become active.

The only way you can reset the original LaserJet printer is to turn it off and back on again. You can reset the LaserJet Plus and LaserJet 500 Plus printers either by turning them off and back on again, or by holding down the HOLD TO RESET/ CONTINUE key on the printer's control panel.

If you share a LaserJet with other people in your office, it's a good idea to reset the printer before you print your document, just in case the person before you has changed any print settings. For instance, if someone in your office uses the LaserJet to print a document with compressed print, and then you send a document to the printer without first resetting the printer, your document will appear in compressed print too. By resetting the printer before you send your document, however, you ensure that your document will not be adversely affected by the person who prints just before you.

If you think there is a hardware problem with your LaserJet printer, you should instruct your printer to perform a self-test. There are two kinds of self-tests you can execute: (1) a print quality test, which you invoke with the TEST PRINT button on the left side of the printer, and (2) an interface test, which you invoke with the SELF TEST key on the control panel. If an error occurs during the testing phase, the printer will display an error message in the status display that notifies you of the problem.

To invoke the print quality test, take the printer off-line and press the TEST PRINT button located on the left side of the printer (shown in Figure 2-7). After a brief pause, the LaserJet will eject a page with a pattern of striped lines. You should check the test printout to make sure the lines are smooth and clear and that they do not contain smudges, missing areas, or any other irregularities. If any signs of poor print quality appear, refer to the section entitled "Optimizing Print Quality" in Chapter 3.

Performing a self-test

FIGURE 2-7

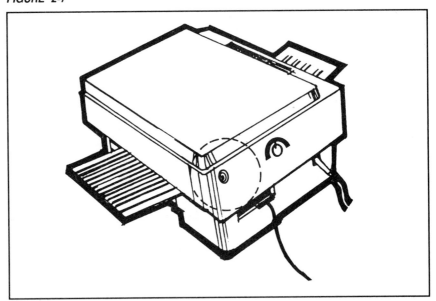

The TEST PRINT button is located on the left side of the LaserJet.

To invoke the interface test, simply press the SELF TEST key on the LaserJet's control panel. Holding this key down for more than three seconds causes the printer to continue the self-test until you press the SELF TEST key again or until you press the ON LINE key. Like all of the keys on the control panel, the SELF TEST key is operational only when the printer is off-line.

During the LaserJet's interface test procedure, the printer will display the number *05* in the status display, and all of the indicator lights on the control panel will turn on. When the printing portion of the test begins, the LaserJet will display the number *06*. Finally, when the test has been completed, the LaserJet will display the number *00*, which indicates that the printer is ready. If any errors occur during the test, the printer will display an error number that pinpoints the problem.

**LaserJet
Series II and
LaserJet IID**

Figures 2-8 and 2-9 show the control panels that appear on the front of the LaserJet Series II and LaserJet IID printers. As you can see, these control panels are considerably different from the control panels on the older LaserJet printers. In this section, we'll explain the purpose of each key and indicator on the Series II and IID control panels. After that, we'll show you how to use the LaserJet's control panel to configure the printer, reset the printer, perform a self-test, print a font sample, and change the default print settings.

FIGURE 2-8

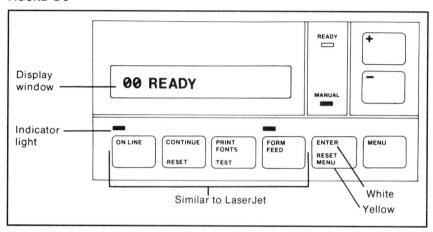

This control panel appears on the LaserJet Series II printer.

FIGURE 2-9

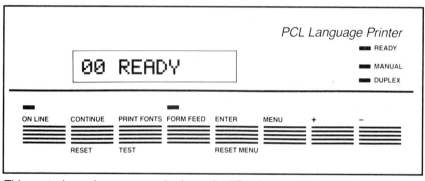

This control panel appears on the LaserJet IID printer.

You might notice that the first four keys along the bottom of the control panel on the LaserJet Series II and LaserJet IID are very similar to the four keys on the older LaserJet printers. The additional keys on this control panel, however, allow you to change many of the LaserJet's printing parameters (such as lines per page and number of copies), as well as all of the printer's configuration settings (baud rate, interface port, and so forth).

Some of the printer functions are listed on the upper half of the keys (in white letters); these functions are invoked by pressing the key momentarily. Other functions are listed on the lower half of the keys (in yellow letters) and are invoked by holding down the key for about three seconds.

Keys and indicators

The display window

The display window is the LaserJet's bulletin board. The LaserJet uses the display window to show you status messages, which tell you about the printer's current condition; attendance messages, which tell you to perform the necessary task at hand; error or service messages, which tell you when the printer has encountered a problem; and menu items along with their associated values or choices.

The LaserJet can display quite a few status and error messages. When a message appears, you can try to correct the problem by pressing the CONTINUE key and re-sending the print job. Most printing problems can be resolved this way. If the problem persists, however, you should look up the cause of the error message in Chapter 3 and follow the instructions given there to correct the error condition.

The ON LINE indicator

The orange light above the ON LINE key comes on when the computer is on-line and stays off when the printer is off-line. When the LaserJet printer is on-line, it is prepared to receive data from your computer, and it will not respond to any of the commands you issue from the control panel (except when you press the ON LINE key). When your LaserJet is off-line, it will not respond to your computer—it waits for you to issue a command from the control panel. By default, the LaserJet powers up on-line.

The ON LINE key

Pressing the LaserJet's ON LINE key switches the printer between on-line and off-line status. The printer must be on-line to receive data from your computer, and it must be off-line to respond to the other keys on the control panel.

If the printer is on-line and you want to issue a command from the control panel, you'll have to press the ON LINE key to take the printer off-line before you can issue the command. Similarly, if the printer is off-line and you want to send some data to the printer from your computer, you'll have to press the ON LINE key to put the printer back on-line before the printer will be able to receive the print data.

The CONTINUE/ RESET key

The CONTINUE/RESET key performs two distinct functions. If you momentarily press the CONTINUE/RESET key, the printer performs the continue function, which clears most printer errors and places the printer back on-line. For a list of printer errors that can be cleared with the CONTINUE key, see Table 2-1.

In the case of a paper jam, pressing the CONTINUE key after you've removed the jammed page will cause the LaserJet to reprint the page on which the jam occurred. After the LaserJet successfully reprints the problem page, it will continue printing the rest of the document.

If you hold down the CONTINUE/RESET key for about three seconds, the LaserJet will display the message *07 RESET* on the display window of the control panel. When this message appears, the LaserJet returns all print settings (page length, symbol set, number of copies, etc.) to the control panel's current defaults. The reset function also clears temporary soft fonts, temporary macros, and any data that is stored in the print buffer.

The PRINT FONTS/ TEST key

The PRINT FONTS/TEST key performs two distinct functions. If you momentarily press the PRINT FONTS/TEST key, the printer performs the print fonts function, which tells the LaserJet to print sample characters from each font that is currently available. While the LaserJet is producing the print sample, it will display the message *06 FONT PRINTOUT* in the display window of the control panel. Figure 2-10 shows a sample font printout.

FIGURE 2-10

```
                 -------- PORTRAIT FONTS --------

FONT                                   POINT SYMBOL
 ID            NAME              PITCH SIZE   SET        PRINT SAMPLE
---- -------------------------- ----- ----- ------ ------------------------

"PERMANENT" SOFT FONTS

LEFT FONT CARTRIDGE

RIGHT FONT CARTRIDGE

INTERNAL FONTS

I00  COURIER                     10    12      8U ABCDEfghij#$@[\]^`{|}~123
                                                  ÀÂ˚ÇÑ¡¿£§êéàèëöÅØåæÄÜßÁÐÒ
I01  COURIER                     10    12     10U ABCDEfghij#$@[\]ˆ˙{|}˜123
                                                  ió│┤╢╖╣╗╜┴┼╚╔╩╦╠═╬╧╤╙╘╒╓╫┘█▐απΦ
I02  COURIER                     10    12     11U ABCDEfghij#$@[\]ˆ˙{|}˜123
                                                  ió│┤╢╖╣╗╜┴┼╚╔╩╦╠═╬╧╤╙╘╒╓╫┘█▐απΦ
I03  COURIER                     10    12      0N ABCDEfghij#$@[\]ˆ˙{|}˜123
                                                  ¡¢³´¶¸¹»½ÁÂÈÉÍÎÐÒÔ×ØÛÞàãè
I04  COURIER BOLD                10    12      8U ABCDEfghij#$@[\]^`{|}~123
                                                  ÀÂ˚ÇÑ¡¿£§êéàèëöÅØåæÄÜßÁÐÒ
I05  COURIER BOLD                10    12     10U ABCDEfghij#$@[\]ˆ˙{|}˜123
                                                  ió│┤╢╖╣╗╜┴┼╚╔╩╦╠═╬╧╤╙╘╒╓╫┘█▐απΦ
I06  COURIER BOLD                10    12     11U ABCDEfghij#$@[\]ˆ˙{|}˜123
                                                  ió│┤╢╖╣╗╜┴┼╚╔╩╦╠═╬╧╤╙╘╒╓╫┘█▐απΦ
I07  COURIER BOLD                10    12      0N ABCDEfghij#$@[\]ˆ˙{|}˜123
                                                  ¡¢³´¶¸¹»½ÁÂÈÉÍÎÐÒÔ×ØÛÞàãè
I08  LINE_PRINTER               16.6   8.5     8U ABCDEfghij#$@[\]^`{|}~123
                                                  ÀÂ˚ÇÑ¡¿£§êéàèëöÅØåæÄÜßÁÐÒ
I09  LINE_PRINTER               16.6   8.5    10U ABCDEfghij#$@[\]ˆ˙{|}˜123
                                                  ió│┤╢╖╣╗╜┴┼╚╔╩╦╠═╬╧╤╙╘╒╓╫┘█▐απΦ
I10  LINE_PRINTER               16.6   8.5    11U ABCDEfghij#$@[\]ˆ˙{|}˜123
                                                  ió│┤╢╖╣╗╜┴┼╚╔╩╦╠═╬╧╤╙╘╒╓╫┘█▐απΦ
I11  LINE_PRINTER               16.6   8.5     0N ABCDEfghij#$@[\]ˆ˙{|}˜123
                                                  ¡¢³´¶¸¹»½ÁÂÈÉÍÎÐÒÔ×ØÛÞàãè
```

Momentarily pressing the PRINT FONTS/ TEST key causes the LaserJet to print sample characters from each available font.

If you hold down the PRINT FONTS/TEST key for about three seconds to invoke the test function, the LaserJet will test its built-in controller and produce a test printout. The LaserJet will then display the message *05 SELF TEST* in the display window. When the printing portion of the test begins, this message will change to *06 PRINTING TEST*. Figure 2-11 shows a sample test printout.

If the test is completed successfully, the LaserJet will display the message *00 READY* to let you know that the self-test is over. If an error occurs during the test, however, the LaserJet will display the appropriate error message in the display window. You'll only want to use the TEST key when you suspect there may be a problem with your LaserJet. For a listing of printer error messages, refer to the section entitled "Error and Status Messages" in Chapter 3.

FIGURE 2-11

```
Page Count=6692
Program ROM Datecode=19861203, Internal Font ROM Datecode=19860611
Auto Continue=ON
Installed Memory=2560 Kbytes
Symbol Set=ROMAN-8
Menu Items:
   Copies=1, Manual Feed=OFF, Font Source=I, Font Number=00,
   Form=60 Lines
Parallel I/O


 !"#$%&'()*+,-./0123456789:;<=>?@ABCDEFGHIJKLMNOPQRSTUVWXYZ[\]^_`abcdefghijklmno
!"#$%&'()*+,-./0123456789:;<=>?@ABCDEFGHIJKLMNOPQRSTUVWXYZ[\]^_`abcdefghijklmnop
"#$%&'()*+,-./0123456789:;<=>?@ABCDEFGHIJKLMNOPQRSTUVWXYZ[\]^_`abcdefghijklmnopq
#$%&'()*+,-./0123456789:;<=>?@ABCDEFGHIJKLMNOPQRSTUVWXYZ[\]^_`abcdefghijklmnopqr
$%&'()*+,-./0123456789:;<=>?@ABCDEFGHIJKLMNOPQRSTUVWXYZ[\]^_`abcdefghijklmnopqrs
%&'()*+,-./0123456789:;<=>?@ABCDEFGHIJKLMNOPQRSTUVWXYZ[\]^_`abcdefghijklmnopqrst
&'()*+,-./0123456789:;<=>?@ABCDEFGHIJKLMNOPQRSTUVWXYZ[\]^_`abcdefghijklmnopqrstu
'()*+,-./0123456789:;<=>?@ABCDEFGHIJKLMNOPQRSTUVWXYZ[\]^_`abcdefghijklmnopqrstuv
()*+,-./0123456789:;<=>?@ABCDEFGHIJKLMNOPQRSTUVWXYZ[\]^_`abcdefghijklmnopqrstuvw
)*+,-./0123456789:;<=>?@ABCDEFGHIJKLMNOPQRSTUVWXYZ[\]^_`abcdefghijklmnopqrstuvwx
*+,-./0123456789:;<=>?@ABCDEFGHIJKLMNOPQRSTUVWXYZ[\]^_`abcdefghijklmnopqrstuvwxy
+,-./0123456789:;<=>?@ABCDEFGHIJKLMNOPQRSTUVWXYZ[\]^_`abcdefghijklmnopqrstuvwxyz
,-./0123456789:;<=>?@ABCDEFGHIJKLMNOPQRSTUVWXYZ[\]^_`abcdefghijklmnopqrstuvwxyz{
-./0123456789:;<=>?@ABCDEFGHIJKLMNOPQRSTUVWXYZ[\]^_`abcdefghijklmnopqrstuvwxyz{|
./0123456789:;<=>?@ABCDEFGHIJKLMNOPQRSTUVWXYZ[\]^_`abcdefghijklmnopqrstuvwxyz{|}
/0123456789:;<=>?@ABCDEFGHIJKLMNOPQRSTUVWXYZ[\]^_`abcdefghijklmnopqrstuvwxyz{|}~
0123456789:;<=>?@ABCDEFGHIJKLMNOPQRSTUVWXYZ[\]^_`abcdefghijklmnopqrstuvwxyz{|}~■
123456789:;<=>?@ABCDEFGHIJKLMNOPQRSTUVWXYZ[\]^_`abcdefghijklmnopqrstuvwxyz{|}~■ 
23456789:;<=>?@ABCDEFGHIJKLMNOPQRSTUVWXYZ[\]^_`abcdefghijklmnopqrstuvwxyz{|}~■ !
3456789:;<=>?@ABCDEFGHIJKLMNOPQRSTUVWXYZ[\]^_`abcdefghijklmnopqrstuvwxyz{|}~■ !"
456789:;<=>?@ABCDEFGHIJKLMNOPQRSTUVWXYZ[\]^_`abcdefghijklmnopqrstuvwxyz{|}~■ !"#
56789:;<=>?@ABCDEFGHIJKLMNOPQRSTUVWXYZ[\]^_`abcdefghijklmnopqrstuvwxyz{|}~■ !"#$
6789:;<=>?@ABCDEFGHIJKLMNOPQRSTUVWXYZ[\]^_`abcdefghijklmnopqrstuvwxyz{|}~■ !"#$%
789:;<=>?@ABCDEFGHIJKLMNOPQRSTUVWXYZ[\]^_`abcdefghijklmnopqrstuvwxyz{|}~■ !"#$%&
89:;<=>?@ABCDEFGHIJKLMNOPQRSTUVWXYZ[\]^_`abcdefghijklmnopqrstuvwxyz{|}~■ !"#$%&'
9:;<=>?@ABCDEFGHIJKLMNOPQRSTUVWXYZ[\]^_`abcdefghijklmnopqrstuvwxyz{|}~■ !"#$%&'(
:;<=>?@ABCDEFGHIJKLMNOPQRSTUVWXYZ[\]^_`abcdefghijklmnopqrstuvwxyz{|}~■ !"#$%&'()
;<=>?@ABCDEFGHIJKLMNOPQRSTUVWXYZ[\]^_`abcdefghijklmnopqrstuvwxyz{|}~■ !"#$%&'()*
<=>?@ABCDEFGHIJKLMNOPQRSTUVWXYZ[\]^_`abcdefghijklmnopqrstuvwxyz{|}~■ !"#$%&'()*+
 ÀÂÈÊËÎÏ´`ˆ¨˜ÙÛ₤¯Ýý°ÇçÑñ¡¿¤£¥§ƒ¢âêôûáéóúàèòùäëöüÅîØÆåíøæÄìÖÜÉïßÔÁÃãÐðÍÌÓÒÕõŠšÚŸÿ
ÀÂÈÊËÎÏ´`ˆ¨˜ÙÛ₤¯Ýý°ÇçÑñ¡¿¤£¥§ƒ¢âêôûáéóúàèòùäëöüÅîØÆåíøæÄìÖÜÉïßÔÁÃãÐðÍÌÓÒÕõŠšÚŸÿÞ
ÂÈÊËÎÏ´`ˆ¨˜ÙÛ₤¯Ýý°ÇçÑñ¡¿¤£¥§ƒ¢âêôûáéóúàèòùäëöüÅîØÆåíøæÄìÖÜÉïßÔÁÃãÐðÍÌÓÒÕõŠšÚŸÿÞþ
ÈÊËÎÏ´`ˆ¨˜ÙÛ₤¯Ýý°ÇçÑñ¡¿¤£¥§ƒ¢âêôûáéóúàèòùäëöüÅîØÆåíøæÄìÖÜÉïßÔÁÃãÐðÍÌÓÒÕõŠšÚŸÿÞþ·
ÊËÎÏ´`ˆ¨˜ÙÛ₤¯Ýý°ÇçÑñ¡¿¤£¥§ƒ¢âêôûáéóúàèòùäëöüÅîØÆåíøæÄìÖÜÉïßÔÁÃãÐðÍÌÓÒÕõŠšÚŸÿÞþ·µ
ËÎÏ´`ˆ¨˜ÙÛ₤¯Ýý°ÇçÑñ¡¿¤£¥§ƒ¢âêôûáéóúàèòùäëöüÅîØÆåíøæÄìÖÜÉïßÔÁÃãÐðÍÌÓÒÕõŠšÚŸÿÞþ·µ¶
ÎÏ´`ˆ¨˜ÙÛ₤¯Ýý°ÇçÑñ¡¿¤£¥§ƒ¢âêôûáéóúàèòùäëöüÅîØÆåíøæÄìÖÜÉïßÔÁÃãÐðÍÌÓÒÕõŠšÚŸÿÞþ·µ¶¾
Ï´`ˆ¨˜ÙÛ₤¯Ýý°ÇçÑñ¡¿¤£¥§ƒ¢âêôûáéóúàèòùäëöüÅîØÆåíøæÄìÖÜÉïßÔÁÃãÐðÍÌÓÒÕõŠšÚŸÿÞþ·µ¶¾—
´`ˆ¨˜ÙÛ₤¯Ýý°ÇçÑñ¡¿¤£¥§ƒ¢âêôûáéóúàèòùäëöüÅîØÆåíøæÄìÖÜÉïßÔÁÃãÐðÍÌÓÒÕõŠšÚŸÿÞþ·µ¶¾—¼
`ˆ¨˜ÙÛ₤¯Ýý°ÇçÑñ¡¿¤£¥§ƒ¢âêôûáéóúàèòùäëöüÅîØÆåíøæÄìÖÜÉïßÔÁÃãÐðÍÌÓÒÕõŠšÚŸÿÞþ·µ¶¾—¼½
ˆ¨˜ÙÛ₤¯Ýý°ÇçÑñ¡¿¤£¥§ƒ¢âêôûáéóúàèòùäëöüÅîØÆåíøæÄìÖÜÉïßÔÁÃãÐðÍÌÓÒÕõŠšÚŸÿÞþ·µ¶¾—¼½ª
¨˜ÙÛ₤¯Ýý°ÇçÑñ¡¿¤£¥§ƒ¢âêôûáéóúàèòùäëöüÅîØÆåíøæÄìÖÜÉïßÔÁÃãÐðÍÌÓÒÕõŠšÚŸÿÞþ·µ¶¾—¼½ªº
˜ÙÛ₤¯Ýý°ÇçÑñ¡¿¤£¥§ƒ¢âêôûáéóúàèòùäëöüÅîØÆåíøæÄìÖÜÉïßÔÁÃãÐðÍÌÓÒÕõŠšÚŸÿÞþ·µ¶¾—¼½ªº«
ÙÛ₤¯Ýý°ÇçÑñ¡¿¤£¥§ƒ¢âêôûáéóúàèòùäëöüÅîØÆåíøæÄìÖÜÉïßÔÁÃãÐðÍÌÓÒÕõŠšÚŸÿÞþ·µ¶¾—¼½ªº«■
Û₤¯Ýý°ÇçÑñ¡¿¤£¥§ƒ¢âêôûáéóúàèòùäëöüÅîØÆåíøæÄìÖÜÉïßÔÁÃãÐðÍÌÓÒÕõŠšÚŸÿÞþ·µ¶¾—¼½ªº«■»
₤¯Ýý°ÇçÑñ¡¿¤£¥§ƒ¢âêôûáéóúàèòùäëöüÅîØÆåíøæÄìÖÜÉïßÔÁÃãÐðÍÌÓÒÕõŠšÚŸÿÞþ·µ¶¾—¼½ªº«■»±
¯Ýý°ÇçÑñ¡¿¤£¥§ƒ¢âêôûáéóúàèòùäëöüÅîØÆåíøæÄìÖÜÉïßÔÁÃãÐðÍÌÓÒÕõŠšÚŸÿÞþ·µ¶¾—¼½ªº«■»± 
Ýý°ÇçÑñ¡¿¤£¥§ƒ¢âêôûáéóúàèòùäëöüÅîØÆåíøæÄìÖÜÉïßÔÁÃãÐðÍÌÓÒÕõŠšÚŸÿÞþ·µ¶¾—¼½ªº«■»±  
ý°ÇçÑñ¡¿¤£¥§ƒ¢âêôûáéóúàèòùäëöüÅîØÆåíøæÄìÖÜÉïßÔÁÃãÐðÍÌÓÒÕõŠšÚŸÿÞþ·µ¶¾—¼½ªº«■»±  À
°ÇçÑñ¡¿¤£¥§ƒ¢âêôûáéóúàèòùäëöüÅîØÆåíøæÄìÖÜÉïßÔÁÃãÐðÍÌÓÒÕõŠšÚŸÿÞþ·µ¶¾—¼½ªº«■»±  ÀÂ
```

Holding down the PRINT FONTS/TEST key for three seconds causes the LaserJet to produce a test printout showing your menu selections and printer configuration.

As you can see, the test printout lists all of your current menu settings, as well as your printer configuration settings. We'll talk about these settings in more detail later when we discuss the LaserJet's MENU key.

If you hold down the PRINT FONTS/TEST key too long (about six seconds), the LaserJet will display the message *04 SELF TEST* and will continuously produce test printouts. To stop the continuous test printouts, press the ON LINE key. After you press the ON LINE key, the *04* portion of the message will flash and the printer will return on-line. (Unfortunately, the printer may print up to four additional pages before it returns on-line.)

The FORM FEED indicator

As we explained in Chapter 1, when the computer sends print data to the LaserJet, the printer stores that data in an area of its memory. (We usually call this memory the print buffer.) If less than a full page of data is sent, the LaserJet's FORM FEED indicator will turn on to indicate that some unprinted data currently resides in the print buffer. For this reason, you should not turn off the printer when the FORM FEED indicator is turned on, or you'll lose the data stored in the print buffer. To empty the contents of the print buffer onto a new page, simply take the printer off-line and press the FORM FEED key.

Pressing the FORM FEED key tells the LaserJet to print all of the data that is currently stored in the LaserJet's print buffer. After the current page has been printed, the indicator on the FORM FEED key will turn off, telling you that there is no longer any page data stored in memory. For a more detailed discussion on how the LaserJet receives data and ejects pages, see the section entitled "How the LaserJet Prints" in Chapter 1.

The FORM FEED key

You'll want to press the FORM FEED key whenever you have sent the LaserJet less than a full page of data and are ready to eject the current page. (Of course, the FORM FEED key is only functional when the printer is off-line and in a ready state.) If a paper jam or other error occurs during the form feed procedure, the form feed is cancelled. Finally, if you have placed the LaserJet in the manual feed mode and you press the FORM FEED key, the printer will begin printing when you manually feed paper into the printer.

The MENU key allows you to access the LaserJet's Printing menu and Configuration menu. The settings on the Printing menu affect the final appearance of the printed page, while the settings on the Configuration menu determine how the computer communicates with the printer.

The MENU key

When you want to change a setting on the LaserJet's Printing menu, press the MENU key momentarily. As soon as you do this, the LaserJet will enter the Printing menu and will display *COPIES=01* in the display window. From that point, you can continue pressing the MENU key to step through the Printing menu items. After you've stepped through the entire list, the LaserJet will display the message *00 READY* in the display window. We'll show you how to change the settings on the Printing menu in the section entitled "The Printing Menu" later in this chapter.

If you hold down the MENU key for about five seconds, the LaserJet will enter the Configuration menu and display *SYM SET=ROMAN-8** in the display window. Once the LaserJet has entered the Configuration menu, you can step through the items on the menu by repeatedly pressing (and quickly releasing) the MENU key. After you've moved through all of the items on the menu, the LaserJet will present the message *00 READY* in the display window. For a detailed discussion of how to configure your LaserJet with the control panel, see the section entitled "Configuring Your LaserJet" at the beginning of this chapter.

The ENTER/RESET MENU key performs two distinct functions. Pressing this key while you are in the LaserJet's Printing menu or Configuration menu saves the current menu choice. When you save a menu value or a menu choice, the LaserJet places an * in the display window. We'll discuss the use of menus later in this chapter.

The ENTER/RESET MENU key

If you hold down the ENTER/RESET MENU key for about three seconds to invoke the reset menu function, the LaserJet will display *09 MENU RESET* in the display window and will return the Printing menu items to the factory default settings. The reset menu function also clears temporary soft fonts, temporary macros, and stored page data. You'll want to reset the menus only when someone has changed the default menu settings and those settings are not producing satisfactory documents.

The Plus (+) and Minus (-) keys

You will use the LaserJet's Plus (+) and Minus (-) keys to step through the choices of a particular menu item. For instance, if the message *COPIES=03* appears in the display window, pressing the + key will change the message to *COPIES=04*. Pressing the - key at this point will change the message back to *COPIES=03* again. If you hold down either of these keys, the LaserJet will scroll through the values or choices for the current menu item. We'll show you how to change the settings on the Configuration menu in the section of this chapter entitled "Configuration Menu."

The READY indicator

The READY indicator in the upper-right corner of the control panel can appear in any of three states: on, off, and flashing. When the READY indicator is on, the printer is turned on and ready for printing but is not necessarily on-line. The READY indicator will also come on when the printer performs a self-test.

When the READY indicator is off, the printer is either turned off or is experiencing a problem. If the printer is not ready for printing, the LaserJet will indicate the cause of the problem in the display window.

A flashing READY indicator means that the printer is receiving data from the computer. You should not interfere with the LaserJet while it is receiving data from the computer, or you'll lose data.

The MANUAL indicator

The orange MANUAL indicator lights up when you select manual paper feed. We'll tell you how to select manual feed from the control panel in the section of this chapter entitled "Manual Feed."

The DUPLEX indicator (LaserJet IID only)

The DUPLEX indicator lights up when you select duplex (two-sided) printing. We'll tell you how to select duplex printing from the control panel in the section "Two-sided Printing" on page 63.

The Printing menu

The LaserJet's Printing menu allows you to redefine the default settings that control the appearance of the printed page. Table 2-3 shows the items on the Printing menu, the default settings for each item, and the range of choices for each item. In most cases, the printer's factory default settings will suit your printing needs. In most other cases, you'll want to use your software's print commands to change these settings. You'll seldom (if ever) use the LaserJet's Printing menu to change your printer's default settings. When you want to change the factory default settings, however, you can just use the keys on the LaserJet's control panel to change them.

TABLE 2-3

Printing menu item	Default setting	Possible settings
Number of copies	COPIES=01	01 through 99
Manual feed	MANUAL FEED=OFF	ON or OFF
Font source	FONT SOURCE=I	I (internal fonts) L (left cartridge) R (right cartridge) S (soft fonts)
Font	FONT NUMBER=00	00 through 99
Form length	FORM=060 LINES	005 through 128

This table shows the choices available for each item on the LaserJet Series II's Printing menu.

To enter the Printing menu, just press the LaserJet's MENU key momentarily, which will bring the message *COPIES=01* into the display window. Once you've entered the Printing menu, you can scroll through the available items by pressing the MENU key. To change the setting for a particular item, press the LaserJet's + or - keys to scroll through the menu values or choices. Once the desired value or choice appears in the display window, you can save it as the default by pressing the LaserJet's ENTER key. As soon as you press ENTER to save a value or choice, an * will appear in the window to indicate that your new value or choice has been saved as the new default.

Now that we've explained how to make choices from the Printing menu, let's consider how each menu item affects the appearance of the printed page.

Copies

The Copies setting tells the LaserJet how many copies to print. The default setting, of course, is 1. To change the default setting, first make sure that the printer is turned on and is off-line. Next, press the MENU key to bring the message *COPIES=01* into the display window, then press the LaserJet's + or - keys to select the desired number of copies—the + key increases the setting (up to 99), while the - key decreases it. After you've defined the appropriate number of copies, press the LaserJet's ENTER key to save the setting, then press the MENU key five times so that the display window contains the message *00 READY*. Finally, activate your new settings by holding down the CONTINUE/RESET key until the message *07 RESET* appears in the display window. (You must reset the printer to activate the new settings.) In a few seconds, the LaserJet will be on-line. The next time you print, the LaserJet will print the number of copies you've specified.

When the LaserJet prints more than one copy of a multiple-page document, it will not collate the copies as they print. For example, if you've used the Printing menu to select two copies, and you send a three-page document to the printer, the LaserJet will print two copies of the first page, then two copies of the second page, and, finally, two copies of the third page.

Manual Feed

The Manual Feed setting tells the LaserJet whether it should accept paper from the printer's paper tray or from hand-fed sheets inserted above the paper tray. If you leave the Manual Feed setting on OFF (the default), the LaserJet will take paper from the paper tray. If you change the Manual Feed setting to ON, however, the LaserJet will wait for you to insert paper in the manual feed slot on top of the paper tray. You'll want to turn the Manual Feed setting on whenever you're printing on odd-size sheets of paper or on envelopes.

To turn Manual Feed on, first make sure that the printer is turned on and that it is off-line. Next, press the MENU key twice so that the message *MANUAL FEED=OFF* appears in the display window, then press the + key to change the display to *MANUAL FEED=ON*. Now, press the LaserJet's ENTER key to save your new setting (which will cause an * to appear in the display window), then press the MENU key four times to display the message *00 READY*. Finally, hold down the CONTINUE/RESET key until the message *07 RESET* appears in the display window (you must perform this step to activate your new print settings). In a few seconds, the LaserJet will return on-line and will expect you to feed sheets of paper manually each time it prints a document.

Font Source and Font Number

The Font Source and Font Number settings specify the default font used when the LaserJet prints a document. Before you adjust these settings, you will probably want to see a sample printout of all the fonts installed on your printer. To generate a sample printout, take the printer off-line and press the PRINT FONTS/TEST key. Figure 2-10 on page 43 shows one page of a sample font printout.

As you can see, the first column in the font printout lists the two-part font ID number for each font that is installed in the LaserJet. The first part of the font ID is a letter indicating the font source (*I* for internal, *L* for left cartridge, *R* for right cartridge, and/or *S* for soft font). The second part of the font ID is the font number assigned to that particular font. For example, the font ID I11 represents the LaserJet's internal font, number 11.

The font ID for the LaserJet's factory default font is I00. As you can see on your font printout, this font is a 10-pitch Courier font in the Roman-8 symbol set. If you want to change the default font from I00 to another font, you must specify the appropriate Font Source and Font Number settings on the LaserJet's Printing menu.

Changing the Printing menu default

To change the LaserJet's default Font Source, first take the printer off-line and press the MENU key three times to display the message *FONT SOURCE=I* in the display window. Now, press the + or - key to select the desired font source (the

LaserJet will display only the sources that are currently available). Once you've chosen the desired font source, press the LaserJet's ENTER key to save your selection (as soon as you press ENTER, an * will appear next to the font source you've chosen).

After you've identified the appropriate font source, press the MENU key once more to display the message *FONT NUMBER=00* in the display window. As you might guess, you should now use the + and - keys to select the number that matches the numeric portion of the font ID in your sample font printout. Once you've selected the appropriate number, press the LaserJet's ENTER key to bring the * into view, indicating that your selection has been saved. Finally, press the MENU key two times to display the message *00 READY*, then hold down the CONTINUE/ RESET key until the message *07 RESET* appears in the display window (you must perform this step to activate your new print settings). In a few seconds, the LaserJet will return on-line and will use the new default font each time it prints a document.

Notes about default fonts

Many of the LaserJet's font cartridges contain a font that is designated as a default font. On HP font cartridges, an * appears next to the name of the cartridge's default font. If you install one of these cartridges into your LaserJet Series II printer and have not used the Printing menu to change the LaserJet's default font, then the default font on that cartridge will become the new default font. However, if you've used the Printing menu to change the LaserJet's default font, then the font cartridge's default font will not replace the LaserJet default you've defined.

Regardless of which method you've used to specify a default font, if the LaserJet receives a software escape sequence that selects a different font, that escape sequence has priority over all printer defaults. Table 2-4 summarizes the font priority system used by the LaserJet when it prints a document.

TABLE 2-4

First:	A font selected by an escape sequence sent by the computer.
Second:	A default font selected on the control panel's Printing menu.
Third:	A default font contained on an installed font cartridge. (The left slot has priority over the right slot.)
Fourth:	The printer's factory default font (which is stored inside the printer).

The LaserJet uses this priority system to determine which font it should use in the printed document.

Form Length

The Form Length setting tells the LaserJet how many lines to print on each page of a document. You can change the default Form Length setting from 60 lines per page to any length between five and 128 lines per page. To accommodate a form length that is either larger or smaller than 60 lines per page, the LaserJet simply adjusts the amount of space between each line of print. Consequently, when you try to squeeze 128 lines of Courier 12 print on an $8\frac{1}{2}$- by 11-inch piece of paper, the printed lines will overlap and make a confusing mess of the printout.

Most software applications automatically send escape codes that specify a form length before printing actually begins. When this happens, that new form length overrides the default form length you've specified with the LaserJet's Printing menu. We recommend that you leave the LaserJet's default Form Length setting at 60, then use your software applications to change the form length when necessary. (Sections Two and Three of this book deal with specific software applications; if we've covered your application in this book, read the appropriate chapter; if we haven't covered your application in this book, read Chapters 12 and 17.

If you want to change the LaserJet's default form length with the Printing menu, first make sure that the LaserJet is off-line, then press the MENU key five times so that the message *FORM=060 LINES* appears in the display window. Now, you can use the LaserJet's + and - keys to change the form length to any value between five and 128. After you've specified the desired form length, press the ENTER key to save your new Form Length setting (which will cause an * to appear in the display window), and press the MENU key once to display the message *00 READY*. Finally, hold down the CONTINUE/RESET key until the message *07 RESET* appears in the display window (you must perform this step to activate your new print settings). In a few seconds, the LaserJet will return on-line and will use the new form length you've defined as the default length.

Configuration menu

Unlike the Printing menu, which controls the appearance of the LaserJet's printed pages, the LaserJet's Configuration menu controls how the LaserJet will communicate with your computer. Table 2-5 shows the items on the Configuration menu and the choices that are available for each item. If you plan to run your LaserJet as a serial printer, you probably won't need to change any of the settings on the Configuration menu—you can just follow the procedures outlined in the first section of this chapter to configure your printer. If you plan to use the LaserJet as a parallel printer, however, or if you need to change any of the default serial settings shown in Table 2-5, you can do so by using the keys on the LaserJet's control panel.

To enter the Configuration menu, just press and hold the LaserJet's MENU key until the message *SYM SET=ROMAN-8* appears in the display window (this usually takes about five seconds). Once you've entered the Configuration menu, you can scroll through the items on the menu by pressing the MENU key. To change the setting for a particular item, just press the LaserJet's + or - keys to scroll quickly through the menu values or choices. Once the desired value or choice appears in the display window, you can save it as the default by pressing the LaserJet's ENTER key. As soon as you press ENTER to save a value or choice, an * will appear in the window to indicate that your new value or choice has been saved as the new default.

TABLE 2-5

Configuration menu item	Default setting	Possible settings
Symbol set	SYM SET = ROMAN-8	All available symbol sets
Auto continue	AUTO CONT = OFF	ON or OFF
Interface	I/O = SERIAL	SERIAL or PARALLEL
Baud rate	BAUD RATE = 9600	300, 600, 1200, 2400, 4800, 9600, or 19200
Robust XON	ROBUST XON = ON	ON or OFF
DTR polarity	DTR POLARITY = HI	HI or LO

This table shows the choices available for each item on the LaserJet Series II's Configuration menu.

Now that we've explained how to enter the Configuration menu and how to make choices from it, let's consider each menu item in more detail.

Symbol set

A symbol set is a subgrouping of all the characters available in a particular font. Most symbol sets are designed for a specific type of application. For example, the IBM-US (PC-8) symbol set was designed to support IBM PC applications.

In most cases, the LaserJet's default symbol set (Roman-8) will work fine with your PC applications. If you need to use a different subgrouping of characters with your application, however, you can use the Configuration menu to select one of the LaserJet Series II's other symbol sets. Table 2-6 lists all of the LaserJet Series II's built-in symbol sets.

To select a new symbol set, make sure that the printer is turned on and is off-line. Then, hold down the MENU key until the message *SYM SET=ROMAN-8* appears in the display window. Now, press the LaserJet's + or - key until the desired symbol set appears in the display window. Finally, press the LaserJet's ENTER key to save your choice (an * will appear in the display window at this point), then press the ON LINE key to put the printer back on-line.

TABLE 2-6

Font printout symbol set #	Control panel display	Symbol set	Font printout symbol set #	Control panel display	Symbol set
8U	ROMAN-8		10U	IBM-US	
11U	IBM-DN	Denmark/Norway	0N	ECMA-94	ISO 100 Latin 1
2U	ISO 2	ISO IRV	0F	ISO 25	ISO French
1E	ISO 4	ISO United Kingdom	2K	ISO 57	ISO Chinese
0U	ISO 6	ANSI ASCII	0D	ISO 60	ISO Norwegian v1
3S	ISO 10	ISO Swedish	1D	ISO 61	ISO Norwegian v2
0S	ISO 11	ISO Swedish: names	1F	ISO 69	ISO French
0K	ISO 14	JIS ASCII	5S	ISO 84	ISO Portuguese: IBM
01	ISO 15	ISO Italian	6S	ISO 85	ISO Spanish: IBM
4S	ISO 16	JIS ASCII	0G	German	HP German
2S	ISO 17	ISO Italian	1S	Spanish	HP Spanish
1G	ISO 21	ISO Portuguese			

These symbol sets are built into the LaserJet Series II printer.

Auto Continue

The Auto Continue setting determines how your LaserJet responds to error conditions. When Auto Continue is off (the default), the LaserJet will continue to display error messages or status messages until you correct the current error condition. The printer will not resume printing until you press the CONTINUE key to put the printer back on-line.

When Auto Continue is on, the LaserJet will display most error messages for about ten seconds, then automatically go back on-line and resume printing. We recommend that you leave the Auto Continue setting off so that you can tend to each error condition as it appears.

If you want to change the Auto Continue setting from OFF to ON, first make sure that the printer is turned on and is off-line. Then, press and hold the MENU key until the message *SYM SET=ROMAN-8* appears in the display window. Now, press the MENU key again to display *AUTO CONT=OFF**. Next, press the LaserJet's + key to display *AUTO CONT=ON*, and press the LaserJet's ENTER key to save your choice (an * will appear in the display window to indicate that your choice has been saved). Finally, press the ON LINE key to put your printer back on-line.

Interfaces

In an earlier section of this chapter, we showed you how to use the Configuration menu to configure the LaserJet Series II for parallel printing. As you'll recall, to configure the LaserJet for parallel printing, you must connect your LaserJet to your computer with a standard parallel printer cable and then use the Configuration menu to change the I/O setting from SERIAL (the default) to PARALLEL.

If you want to change the LaserJet's configuration from PARALLEL to SERIAL, you'll first need to purchase a serial printer cable for your LaserJet printer, and then use that cable to connect the LaserJet to your computer. After you've installed the serial cable, make sure that the printer is turned on and is off-line, then hold down the MENU key until the message *SYM SET=ROMAN-8* appears in the display window. Now, press the MENU key twice to display the message *I/O= PARALLEL*, press the LaserJet's - key to change the I/O setting to SERIAL, and press the LaserJet's ENTER key to save your selection.

Now, press the MENU key again to display the message *BAUD RATE=9600* (this message will not appear if you've configured the LaserJet for parallel printing). If you need to change the computer's baud rate, just press the + or - keys until the desired baud rate appears in the display, then press the ENTER key to save your selection.

When you press the MENU key again, the message *ROBUST XON=ON* will appear. Unless your computer requires robust XON to be turned off (a rare occurrence), you should press the MENU key again to display the message *DTR POLARITY=HI*. As you might guess, most computers require the DTR polarity setting to be HI. However, if you need to change either the robust XON or DTR polarity settings, use the LaserJet's + or - key to change the setting, then use the ENTER key to save your selection. After you've made all the necessary changes, press the ON LINE key to put the LaserJet back on-line.

ADJUSTING THE PRINT DENSITY

Your LaserJet printer allows you to adjust the density of your printed images. The print density setting, which can range from 1 to 9, is controlled by your LaserJet's print density dial. When you print an image with the density set on a lower number (like 1 or 2), the LaserJet uses toner at a rapid rate and produces images that look blacker than images produced with the density set on a higher number (like 8 or 9). On older LaserJet printers, the print density dial is located on the left side of the printer. On the LaserJet Series II and LaserJet IID printers, this dial is located just underneath the toner cartridge rack. Figures 2-12 and 2-13 show the locations of these dials.

If you experiment with the print density dial, you'll notice only a slight difference between images printed on position 1 and images printed on position 9. Since increasing the density causes the LaserJet to use more toner, your EP toner cartridge won't last as long if you print with the density setting on 1 instead of on 9. If you are like most LaserJet users, you'll want to leave the print density dial in the center position on 5.

FIGURE 2-12

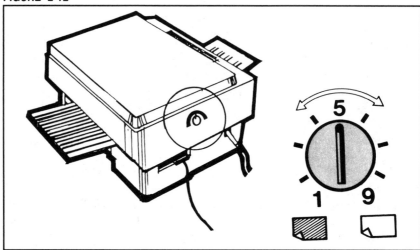

The print density dial is located on the left side of the LaserJet and LaserJet Plus printers.

FIGURE 2-13

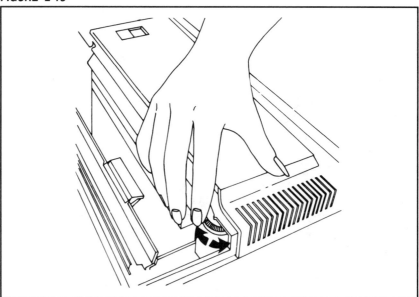

The print density dial is located just underneath the toner cartridge rack on the LaserJet Series II and LaserJet IID printers.

As you probably know, you can expand the font capabilities of your LaserJet printer by purchasing and installing optional font cartridges. (Appendix 2 lists all of the optional font cartridges currently offered by Hewlett-Packard.) Although we will talk in detail about using fonts in Chapter 4, we now would like to introduce a few operating procedures that apply to your LaserJet's font accessories.

FONTS

Before you insert a font cartridge, check the LaserJet's ON LINE indicator to see if the printer is on-line. If it is, press the ON LINE key to take the printer off-line. Once the LaserJet is off-line, slide the cartridge into the font cartridge slot, as shown in Figure 2-14. Make certain that you push the cartridge in as far as it will go before you continue (you should feel the cartridge "snap" into place). After you've securely seated the cartridge in the slot, press the ON LINE key again to put the printer back on-line. At this point, you're ready to print using your new fonts. (We'll talk about printing with fonts in Chapter 4.)

Inserting and Removing Font Cartridges

FIGURE 2-14

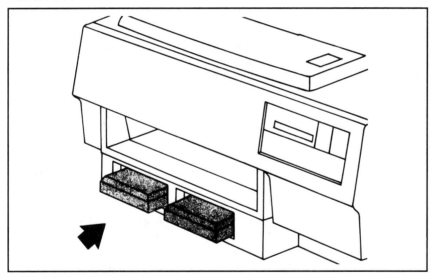

To insert a font cartridge, simply push it in the LaserJet's cartridge slot until it "snaps" into place.

To remove a font cartridge, first press the ON LINE key to take the printer off-line. (This step is very important, as you'll see in a moment.) After you've taken the printer off-line, grasp the edges of the font cartridge and slowly pull it out of the slot (don't yank it out). Finally, press the ON LINE key again to put the printer back on-line.

If you remove a font cartridge while the printer is on-line, the LaserJet will display the message *FE* (on the LaserJet and LaserJet Plus) or *FE CARTRIDGE* (on the LaserJet Series II and LaserJet IID) in the display window and will not respond to any of the keys on the control panel. The only way to recover from this situation is to turn the printer off and back on again.

Font Cartridge Life

Your HP LaserJet font cartridges have an estimated life of 500 insertions. For this reason, you should try to minimize the number of times you insert and remove them. If both you and another user in your office frequently use the same font cartridge in two different LaserJet printers, you're much better off buying two cartridges (one for each printer) instead of taking turns using the same one.

If one of your older font cartridges begins acting strangely, you may have inserted and removed it enough times to wear out its electrical contacts. When this happens, you'll need to purchase a new font cartridge. Remember, you can make your cartridges last longer by cutting down on the number of times you insert and remove them.

Using Soft Fonts

If you use an original LaserJet printer, the only way you can expand its font capabilities is by installing a font cartridge. If you use any other LaserJet printer, however, you can add fonts using either of two methods: by installing a font cartridge or by downloading soft fonts to the printer's memory.

A soft font is essentially a file on your computer's disk that contains a bit-mapped representation of every character in that font. After you transfer a soft font from your computer's disk to the printer's memory, the printer can use that font just as it uses cartridge fonts. (The process of transferring a soft font from the disk to the printer is called downloading.) As you might guess, dozens of companies produce soft fonts for the LaserJet, including Hewlett-Packard. Contact your local computer vendor for information on soft font offerings.

When you download a soft font to the printer, you can specify the soft font as either a temporary soft font or as a permanent soft font. If you download a temporary soft font, the LaserJet will clear that font from memory the next time it encounters a printer reset command, or when you turn off the power to the printer. If you download a permanent soft font, that font will not be cleared by a printer reset. Instead, it will be erased from memory only when the printer gets turned off, or when you send a specific PCL command to remove that font from memory. We'll discuss soft fonts in more detail in Chapter 4, and we'll cover PCL commands in Chapter 23.

PAPER HANDLING

Many LaserJet users do not take time to learn proper paper-handling procedures—they simply fill their paper trays with paper and begin printing. In this section, we'll explain how to load paper into the paper tray, and how to feed standard-size and odd-size sheets of paper manually into the LaserJet. After we explain these paper-handling procedures, we'll tell you what kinds of paper, envelopes, labels, and transparencies work best in a LaserJet printer.

Using Paper Trays

If you typically print to letter- or legal-size paper, you'll almost always use a paper tray to feed paper into your LaserJet printer. When you load the paper tray with paper and insert it into the printer, the LaserJet automatically knows what size paper is in the tray, and will use that paper for printing until you place the printer in manual feed mode or until the tray becomes empty.

When your paper tray runs out of paper, refill it with more than just a few sheets. If possible, add at least a half-tray of paper each time you reload. By refilling the tray with a whole stack of paper instead of only a few sheets, you can reduce the time spent on maintaining paper supplies and reduce the frequency of paper jams. Because the paper trays for the older-generation LaserJets are different from the newer generation's, you'll need to follow the paper replacement procedures that apply to the type of LaserJet printer you own.

LaserJet and LaserJet Plus

If you use a LaserJet or LaserJet Plus printer, follow these steps to refill your paper tray with paper:

1) Hold a stack of paper by the edges and tap the stack against the desktop to line up the sheets in the stack (much like you line up a stack of playing cards after shuffling).

2) Hold the stack along either of the short ends and slide the opposite end of the stack into the paper tray, as shown in Figure 2-15.

FIGURE 2-15

Slide one short edge of the paper stack into the deep end of the paper tray.

3) After you've placed the paper in the tray, use your fingers to line up the edges of the stack, as shown in Figure 2-16 on the next page, then push the edges of the stack underneath the paper tray's retaining clips, as shown in Figure 2-17.

FIGURE 2-16

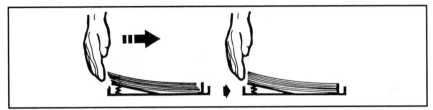

Use your fingers to line up the edges of the sheets in the paper tray.

FIGURE 2-17

After you've lined up the sheets in the stack, push the end of the stack under the tray's retaining clips.

4) Re-insert the paper tray into the printer until it's firmly seated, as shown in Figure 2-18. The arrow on the right side of the tray reminds you that the end with the retaining clips goes in first.

LaserJet Series II and LaserJet IID

If you use a LaserJet Series II or LaserJet IID printer, follow these steps to refill your paper tray with paper:

1) Hold a stack of paper by the edges and tap the stack against the desktop to line up the sheets in the stack (much like you line up a stack of playing cards after shuffling).

2) Hold the stack along either of the long ends and slide the opposite end of the stack into the paper tray, as shown in Figure 2-19. Make sure that your stack does not exceed the height indicated by the silver tabs on the edge of the tray.

FIGURE 2-18

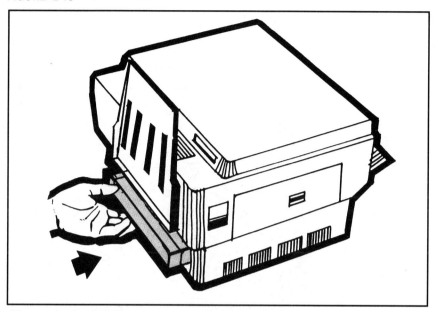

After you've loaded the paper tray, push the tray firmly into its slot .

FIGURE 2-19

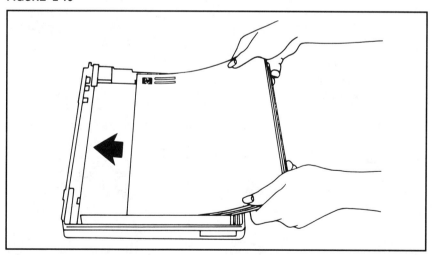

When you refill the LaserJet Series II's or LaserJet IID's paper tray, make sure your paper does not exceed the height of the silver tabs on the edge of the tray, then slide one of the long ends of the stack into the paper tray.

3) After you've placed the paper in the tray, replace the paper tray cover, as shown in Figure 2-20.

FIGURE 2-20

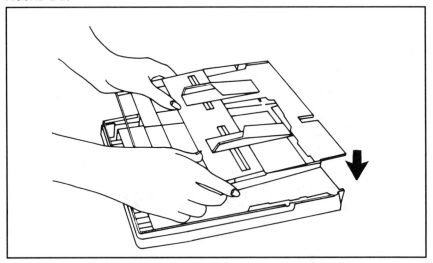

Replace the paper tray cover before inserting the tray into the printer.

4) Re-insert the paper tray into the printer until it's firmly seated, as shown in Figure 2-21. At this point, the LaserJet's READY indicator should come on, and the message in the display window should change from *11 PAPER OUT* to *00 READY*. If the printer does not return to the ready mode after you've refilled and re-inserted the paper tray, remove the tray and check it for misaligned sheets, paper fragments, and so forth. Also make sure that you push the tray all the way into the printer so that it is seated firmly into place.

A note

One thing you need to remember about paper trays is that when you remove a tray and replace it with a different size tray, the LaserJet will not expect the new paper size until you reset the printer. As we have said, you'll almost always want to use paper trays when you are printing on standard-size sheets of paper. If you need to print on envelopes, labels, or odd-size sheets of paper, you'll have to feed these items into the LaserJet by hand.

Using Manual Feed

By default, every LaserJet printer draws paper from its paper tray when it prints a page. If you want, however, you can tell your LaserJet to use the paper in its manual feed slot instead of the paper in its tray. You'll find the LaserJet's manual feed option especially helpful when you want to print on odd-size sheets of paper or on envelopes. Since the procedure you use to select manual feed differs considerably between the two generations of LaserJet printers, we'll discuss each generation separately.

FIGURE 2-21

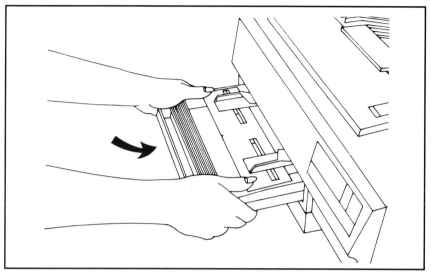

After you've loaded the paper tray, push the tray into its slot until it's firmly seated.

To invoke the manual feed feature on the LaserJet or LaserJet Plus, just take the printer off-line and press the LaserJet's MANUAL FEED key. When you do this, the indicator on the MANUAL FEED key will turn on to indicate that the LaserJet is now in manual feed mode. After the MANUAL FEED indicator comes on, press the ON LINE key to put the printer back on-line.

LaserJet, LaserJet Plus, and LaserJet 500 Plus

If you have a LaserJet 500 Plus and you want to invoke the manual feed feature, first take the printer off-line, then press the PAPER SELECT key on the control panel until the MANUAL FEED indicator is illuminated. After you've selected MANUAL, just press the ON LINE key to put the printer back on-line.

When the LaserJet is ready to draw a page in manual feed mode, it will alternately flash the letters *PF* and the paper size in the printer's display window (*L* for letter, *LL* for legal, *A4* for A4, and *b5* for B5). When this happens, you should insert a sheet of paper into the manual feed slot, as shown in Figure 2-22. As you insert your sheet of paper, make sure that you place the paper face up and that you keep it against the paper feed guide on the right side of the manual feed slot. When you've slid the paper in far enough, the LaserJet will grab the sheet of paper and pull it out of your hands.

FIGURE 2-22

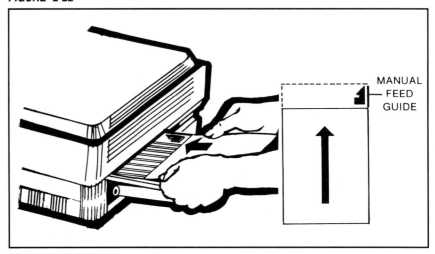

When you insert a sheet of paper into the manual feed slot, make sure you keep the right edge of the paper against the paper feed guide.

When the LaserJet is ready for another sheet of paper, it will again flash the letters *PF* and the paper size in the display window. Of course, when you see this message, you should insert an additional sheet of paper into the manual feed slot (with the right edge against the paper feed guide).

To exit the manual feed mode, take the printer off-line and press the MANUAL FEED key. When you do this, the indicator on the MANUAL FEED key will turn off, indicating that the printer is no longer in manual feed mode. When you put the printer back on-line, it will once again draw paper from its paper tray.

Printing to odd-size paper and envelopes

Printing to odd-size paper and envelopes with your LaserJet is no different from printing to standard-size paper. However, you must remember that the LaserJet formats the page as if it were standard size. For example, suppose you want to print an address on a business envelope and you've loaded letter-size paper in your LaserJet's paper tray. To print the address correctly, you must format the page so that it prints to the area indicated by a dotted line, as shown in Figure 2-23. As you can see, you must tell the LaserJet to print in Landscape orientation with a top margin of about $1^1/_2$ inches and a left margin of about 5 inches. We'll talk more about formatting the page with escape sequences in Chapter 22. We'll also discuss printing envelopes with specific applications in the chapters of this book that explain each application.

FIGURE 2-23

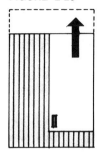

When you manually feed an envelope into the LaserJet, you must format the page so that it prints to the specific area.

Two-sided printing

If you want to print to both sides of a sheet of paper, you can do so by first pressing the MANUAL FEED key on your LaserJet's control panel to activate manual feed mode. (When you do this, the MANUAL FEED indicator will come on.) After you press the ON LINE key to put the printer back on-line, send your document to the printer. When the printer asks for a sheet of paper, manually feed the piece of paper into the printer as usual. After the page has been printed, take the page from the output tray, flip it over so that the printed side is facing down, and manually feed the page back into the printer, as shown in Figure 2-24. If the paper becomes curled during its first pass through the printer, make sure it is straight before sending it through a second time.

FIGURE 2-24

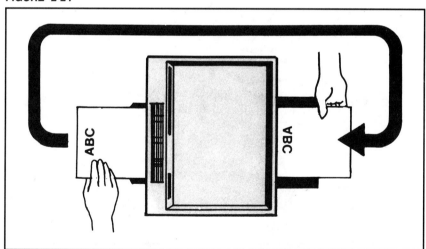

To print to both sides of the page, manually feed the page back through the printer.

LaserJet Series II and LaserJet IID

Like the first-generation LaserJets, the LaserJet Series II and LaserJet IID printers allow you to feed sheets of paper and envelopes manually. To invoke the manual feed feature, first take the printer off-line and press the LaserJet's MENU key twice to display the message *MANUAL FEED=OFF* in the display window. Next, press the LaserJet's + key to change the setting from OFF to ON, and press the ENTER/RESET MENU key to save your selection (an * will appear next to your selection to indicate that it has been saved). Now, press the MENU key repeatedly until the message *00 READY* appears in the display window, then hold down the CONTINUE/RESET key until the message *07 RESET* appears in the display window. In a moment, the LaserJet will come back on-line, and the MANUAL indicator will turn on, indicating that the printer is now in manual feed mode.

When the LaserJet is ready to draw a page in manual feed mode, it will display the message *PF FEED* along with the expected page size (*LETTER*, *LEGAL*, *EXEC*, or *A4*). When this happens, you should adjust the manual feed guides to the appropriate width, as shown in Figure 2-25. After you've adjusted the width of the manual feed guides, insert a sheet of paper into the manual feed slot. When you've slid the paper in far enough, the LaserJet will grab the sheet of paper and pull it out of your hands.

FIGURE 2-25

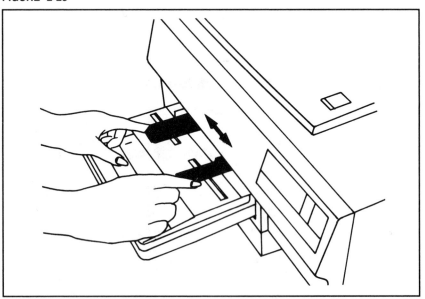

Adjust the manual feed guides to the appropriate width before you insert paper.

When the LaserJet is ready for another sheet of paper, it will again display the *PF FEED* message in the display window. Of course, when this message appears, you should insert an additional sheet of paper into the manual feed slot.

To exit the manual feed mode, take the printer off-line and press the MENU key twice to display the message *MANUAL FEED=ON*. Next, press the LaserJet's - key to change the setting from ON to OFF, and press ENTER/RESET MENU key to save your selection. Now, press the MENU key repeatedly until the message *00 READY* appears in the display window, then hold down the CONTINUE/RESET key until the message *07 RESET* appears in the display window. In a moment, the LaserJet will come back on-line, and the MANUAL indicator will turn off, indicating that the printer will once again draw paper from its paper tray.

Printing to odd-size paper and envelopes

Printing to odd-size paper and envelopes with your LaserJet is like printing to standard-size paper. However, you must remember that the LaserJet formats the page as if it were standard size. For example, to print the address on a business envelope correctly, you must tell the LaserJet to print in Landscape orientation with a top margin of about 25 lines and a left margin of about 50 characters. We'll discuss printing envelopes with specific applications later in this book.

Two-sided printing

Although the LaserJet IID printer has duplex printing capabilities, the LaserJet Series II printer does not. Consequently, if you want to print on both sides of a sheet of paper, you'll need to follow the procedures that apply to the type of LaserJet printer you use.

LaserJet Series II

To print on both sides of a sheet of paper with the LaserJet Series II, first use the Printing menu to activate manual feed. After you put the printer back on-line, send your document to the printer. When it asks for a sheet of paper, manually feed a piece of paper into the printer as usual. After the page has been printed, take the page from the output tray, flip it over so that the printed side is facing down, and manually feed the page back into the printer.

LaserJet IID

If you use a LaserJet IID printer, you can tell your printer to print on both sides of the paper automatically. To do this, first take the printer off-line, then press the MENU key four times to bring the message *DUPLEX=OFF* into the display window. Now, press either the + or - key to change the setting to *DUPLEX=ON*, and press the ENTER key to save your selection (an * will appear in the display window to indicate that you've saved your selection).

When you press the MENU key again, the message *BIND=LONG-EDGE* will appear in the display window. The Bind setting tells the LaserJet which edge of the page you plan to punch and bind. Figure 2-26 illustrates long-edge and short-edge binding for both Portrait- and Landscape-oriented documents. You should use the LaserJet's + or - key to define the desired Bind setting, then press the ENTER key to save your selection. Finally, press the ON LINE key to exit the menus and place the printer back on-line.

FIGURE 2-26

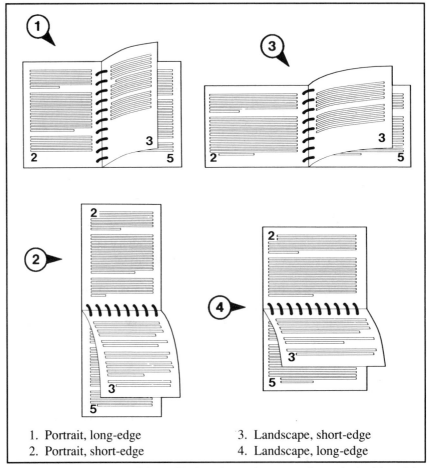

1. Portrait, long-edge
2. Portrait, short-edge
3. Landscape, short-edge
4. Landscape, long-edge

You need to select one of these Bind settings when you print on both sides of the page with the LaserJet IID printer.

Notes on manual feed

As we have said, when you invoke manual feed on the LaserJet printer, it expects you to feed the same size paper as what is in its paper tray. If you want to feed a different size sheet of paper, you must send an escape sequence that changes the paper size. We'll discuss escape sequences in Chapter 22.

If you manually feed a sheet of paper that is not the same size as that indicated in the display window, you may lose some of your data, or the LaserJet may report a false paper jam. Chapter 3 explains how to recover from these situations.

Many software applications automatically send a reset command to the printer before they send the data to be printed. If your application does this, your printer will not stay in manual feed mode when you send a document to the printer. If you want to use the manual feed feature with such an application, you'll have to send the LaserJet the escape sequence that turns on manual feed—$E_s{}_c\&\ell 2H$. We'll tell you how specific applications handle manual feeding later in this book.

In order to obtain the best print quality possible from your LaserJet printer, you must provide the printer with good paper. Although almost any kind of paper will work with the LaserJet, some materials in the paper can significantly affect both the quality of your printed documents and the frequency of paper jams. Make the effort not only to find good paper for your LaserJet, but also to store the paper properly.

Choosing Paper and Envelopes

To obtain the clearest, sharpest image possible from your printer, use paper that is specifically manufactured for photocopying. In general, this kind of paper has a smooth surface that allows for excellent print quality, as well as reliable handling.

Choosing paper

For applications where photocopying paper is too unprofessional in appearance, you should use cotton bond paper. Although most kinds of cotton bond paper work fine in your LaserJet, always test paper before you invest in large quantities of a particular brand. Remember to test for both the quality of the print on the paper and the frequency of paper handling problems. Some kinds of cotton bond paper (especially those that are textured) tend to jam rather frequently—make sure the paper you buy feeds easily.

The kinds of paper you want to avoid are:

- Extremely smooth or shiny paper, or paper that is highly textured
- Coated paper
- Letterheads using low temperature dyes or thermography (these materials may melt onto the fusing roller and cause serious damage; use preprinted paper whose inks can handle 200 degrees Celsius for 0.1 second)
- Damaged or wrinkled paper, or paper with irregularities such as tabs, staples, and so forth
- Multipart forms or carbonless paper

The most important rule concerning paper is this: Do not purchase large quantities of any kind of paper before you test that paper in your LaserJet. Your computer vendor will usually let you test samples from different manufacturers before you purchase any paper. If you cannot obtain a small quantity of the paper before you make your purchasing decision, make sure your vendor will allow you to return the paper if it does not perform satisfactorily.

Envelopes

If you plan to print envelopes on your LaserJet printer, you can probably feed your normal envelopes without any problems. However, if you find that your envelopes are jamming or wrinkling on a regular basis, you should consider purchasing envelopes that are specially designed for laser printing. Figure 2-27 shows one type of envelope that works well with LaserJet printers.

FIGURE 2-27

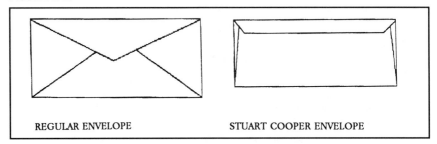

REGULAR ENVELOPE   STUART COOPER ENVELOPE

Envelopes that are specifically designed for use with laser printers (like the Stuart Cooper envelope) are less likely to jam inside the LaserJet.

As you can see, the laser envelopes are folded and glued only at the edges, rather than across the entire back in a "V" pattern. In addition, the laser envelopes contain uniform fiber patterns that run in the optimum direction for laser printing. As you might guess, these two features allow laser envelopes to pass through the printer with fewer problems than regular envelopes.

Check with your local computer vendor or office supplier for more information on laser envelopes. If they seem difficult to find, contact Stuart F. Cooper Company, 1565 E. 23rd St., Los Angeles, CA 90011, 800-821-2920. If you want to test the Cooper Company's laser envelopes, ask them to send you some free samples.

Labels

If you need to print labels with your LaserJet printer, the labels must completely cover the backing material, as shown in Figure 2-28. If you attempt to feed labels that have portions of the carrier sheet exposed, the edge of the labels can easily get caught inside the LaserJet and cause extensive damage to the printer's internal parts. Of course, if your local computer vendor does not carry the right kind of labels, you can order them from HP's Direct Marketing Division.

Transparencies

Many kinds of special paper can be used in the LaserJet, including overhead transparencies. Once again, the best rule to follow is to test whatever samples you have available, then choose the kind that does the best job. For a detailed discussion on paper and on the kinds of paper that perform well in the LaserJet, order the *LaserJet Series II Printer Paper Specification Guide* (Part No. 5954-7339) from HP's Direct Marketing Division.

FIGURE 2-28

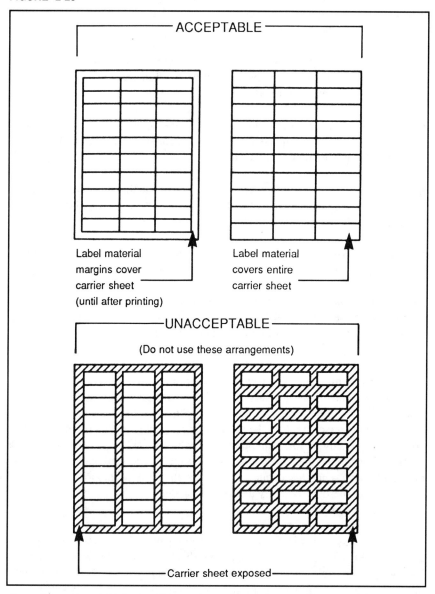

If you intend to print labels with your LaserJet, make sure that your labels completely cover the carrier sheet.

Storing paper

It is very important for you to store your paper properly in order to maintain a high level of print quality and reliability. In order to keep your paper in top condition, follow these simple tips:

- Store and use the paper in an area that is protected from temperature extremes. If possible, store it at a temperature of 63 to 73 degrees Fahrenheit and at a relative humidity of 40 to 50%.

- Allow time for the paper to adjust to the temperature of its new environment. If the paper has been shipped in extremely cold or hot weather, the natural fibers in the paper need time to adjust to your office environment.

- Load only the amount of paper that you plan to use that day in the LaserJet's paper tray. Leaving sheets of paper in the paper tray overnight dries out the paper and builds up static electricity.

- Stack reams of paper flat, one on top of the other. If you stack paper on its edges, the paper can easily curl or warp, increasing the possibility of a paper jam.

SHARING YOUR LASERJET

If you are like most LaserJet users, you share your LaserJet printer with at least one other person in your office. Let's consider three of the most common ways users share a LaserJet printer in a small office: cable swapping, switchboxes, and networks.

Cable Swapping

Perhaps the most common way for office workers to share a LaserJet printer is to give each user a printer interface cable, and then to plug in the appropriate cable when it's time to print. For example, if one person in the office needs to print a document, that person unplugs the cable currently seated in the printer's interface port, plugs in his own cable, and prints the document. When someone else needs to print a few minutes later, that person unplugs the first person's cable, plugs in his own cable, and sends his document. Although this type of printer sharing is somewhat troublesome, it's very inexpensive and is probably the most commonly used method of sharing.

Switchboxes

Another way to share a single LaserJet among multiple users is to use a printer switchbox. In offices that use a switchbox to share a LaserJet, each employee plugs his own printer cable into the switchbox, which is connected to the LaserJet's interface port. Unfortunately, printer switchboxes have been responsible for damaging many LaserJet interface/formatter components. If you know what to look for in a printer switchbox, however, you'll probably find that a good switchbox will save you time and trouble in your office. Let's consider the two types of printer switchboxes: electronic and mechanical.

Electronic switchboxes

Electronic switchboxes are the safest kind of switchboxes to use with your LaserJet printer. Since these kinds of switchboxes don't require a physical flip of a switch, there is no danger of sending a voltage spike into the LaserJet's interface port. Not only are electronic switchboxes safer than mechanical switchboxes, they are also easier to use (when they are working properly). For instance, if three office workers are connected to an electronic switchbox, and one worker sends something to the printer, then the switchbox should automatically route his data into the LaserJet just as if he were connected by himself. Later, if a different worker sends something to the printer, the switchbox should automatically detect the incoming print data and route it to the LaserJet.

Several manufacturers sell electronic printer switchboxes that vary widely in features and in price. If you go shopping for an electronic switchbox, make sure you buy one with enough input ports to accommodate all of the users who will need access to the LaserJet. Also, make sure that the input ports on the switchbox are configured correctly for your environment (either parallel or serial). Some other features that are nice to have include a print buffer, which will free up your computer while the LaserJet is printing, and a spooling device, which will process print requests on a first-come, first-served basis and will let you change the order in which print jobs are processed. Contact your local computer vendor for more information on electronic switchboxes.

Mechanical switchboxes

Mechanical switchboxes are an inexpensive way to avoid cable-swapping hassles. As an example of how a switchbox system should operate, suppose an office has installed a mechanical switchbox, and one worker wants to send something to the printer. To do this, he would first need to move the switch to the location that patches his cable through to the printer. Next, he prints his document. Later, if another person wants to send something to the printer, he simply changes the switchbox setting before he prints. Although this process still involves some inconvenience for users, it's much easier to throw a little switch than it is to swap printer cables.

As we mentioned, some mechanical switchboxes send voltage spikes into the printer's interface port that may damage some of the printer's expensive internal components. Before you purchase a mechanical switchbox for your printer, make sure that it offers surge suppression, which prevents the box from sending voltage spikes into the printer.

As with electronic switchboxes, mechanical switchboxes are manufactured by dozens of companies. Make sure that the switchbox you buy has enough interface ports for the users in your office, and that its ports are appropriately configured for your printer interface cables (parallel or serial).

Networks   A third method you can use to share your LaserJet printer is to place the LaserJet on a personal computer network. In offices using a PC network to share a LaserJet printer, each user can print to the LaserJet as if he were directly connected to his own printer. Of course, installing a personal computer network in your office is not an easy or inexpensive task. However, in many cases, a PC network is the most efficient way to share a LaserJet printer. For more information on PC networks, contact your local computer vendor.

CONCLUSION   In this chapter, we've familiarized you with the LaserJet's control panel, and we've discussed the various ways you can configure your LaserJet to communicate with your computer. We've also discussed how to handle the LaserJet's font cartridges properly, how to handle paper, and how to share a single LaserJet with several co-workers. Regardless of which LaserJet printer you own or which software applications you use, you'll want to make sure you're familiar with the operational aspects we've discussed in this chapter.

MAINTENANCE AND TROUBLESHOOTING 3

Like any sophisticated piece of hardware, your HP LaserJet printer requires a small amount of maintenance in order to continue working smoothly, and it will probably have a few mechanical problems at some point down the road. In this chapter, we'll give you a few maintenance tips that will keep your LaserJet in top shape, and we'll show you how to recover from unexpected problems.

EP CARTRIDGES

The EP (electrophotographic) cartridge is the lifeblood of your LaserJet. It supplies your LaserJet with all the "consumable" items needed in the printing process, including the photosensitive print drum and a supply of toner. If you fail to keep a good EP cartridge in your LaserJet, your pages will look faded, blotted, or smeared.

Cartridge Life

The EP cartridges for the LaserJet, LaserJet Plus, and LaserJet 500 Plus printers need to be replaced after printing approximately 3,000 pages of text. The EP cartridges for the LaserJet Series II and LaserJet IID will print approximately 4,000 pages. Of course, if your average page coverage is relatively light, then your EP cartridge will last a little longer. On the other hand, if your printed pages typically contain graphics or other relatively "dense" images, then your EP cartridge won't last quite as long.

One way to extend the life of your EP cartridge is to change the setting of the print density dial. If you set your print density dial on a higher setting (like 8 or 9), then the LaserJet will use toner at a slower rate than it will when the dial is set on a lower setting (like 1 or 2). For more information on the print density dial, see Chapter 2.

**Replacing the
EP Cartridge**

Sooner or later, your LaserJet's EP cartridge will run out of toner and will need to be replaced. Whenever you replace your EP cartridge, you should also clean your LaserJet by following the procedures outlined in this chapter.

Although the process of replacing an EP cartridge is similar for all types of LaserJet printers, we've broken down our discussion into two sections: one for first-generation LaserJet users (LaserJet, LaserJet Plus, and LaserJet 500 Plus), and one for second-generation LaserJet users (LaserJet Series II and LaserJet IID).

*LaserJet,
LaserJet Plus,
and LaserJet
500 Plus*

If you use a LaserJet, LaserJet Plus, or LaserJet 500 Plus printer, you'll want to keep an eye on the indicator window on the side of the printer. As you can see in Figure 3-1 on the facing page, the color in the indicator window gives you a general idea of how much "life" the toner cartridge has left. When it turns red, you'll know that your EP cartridge will soon need replacing. When the toner level falls far enough, you'll begin to see defects in your printed documents.

You can slightly extend the life of your EP cartridge by removing it and rocking it from side to side, as shown in Figure 3-2. Although the indicator window will still be red, the fading will clear up for about 60 to 100 more pages. If the fading persists, however, you'll need to replace the old cartridge with a new one.

FIGURE 3-2

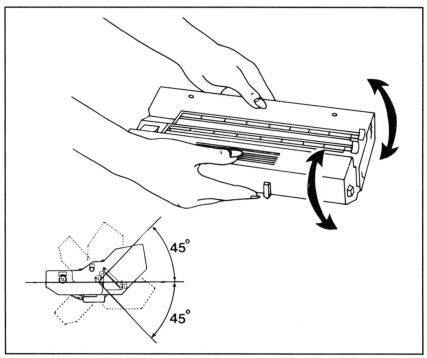

You can slightly extend the life of your EP cartridge by rocking it from side to side to distribute the remaining toner evenly.

FIGURE 3-1

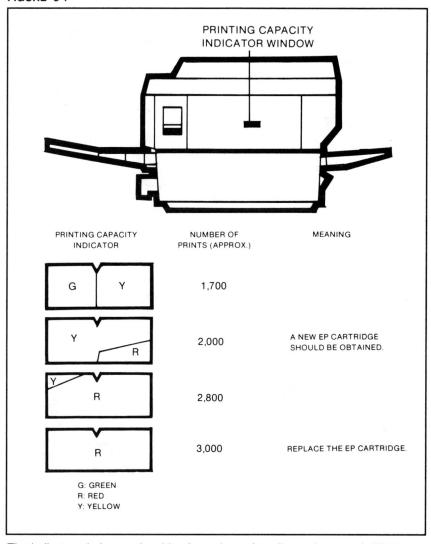

The indicator window on the side of your LaserJet tells you how much "life" remains in your EP cartridge.

To replace your LaserJet's EP cartridge, follow these steps:

1) First, open the main body of the printer, then open the door on the right side of the printer, as shown in Figure 3-3. Pull out the old EP cartridge, as shown in Figure 3-4, and discard it.

FIGURE 3-3

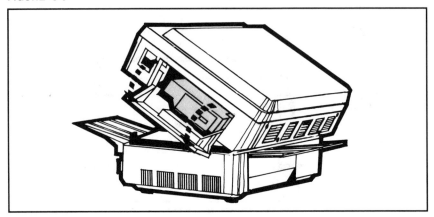

Open the door on the right side of the printer to expose the EP cartridge.

FIGURE 3-4

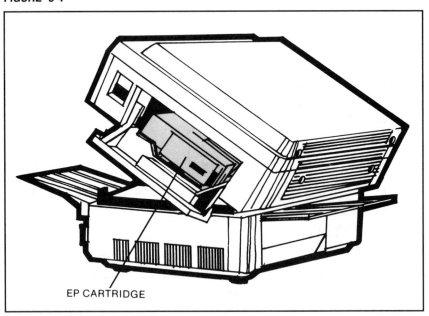

EP CARTRIDGE

After you've opened the printer's right door, remove the old EP cartridge.

2) Hold your new EP cartridge as shown in Figure 3-2, and rock it from side to side about five times. This procedure helps distribute the toner evenly throughout the cartridge.

3) Insert the new EP cartridge into the printer, as shown in Figure 3-5. Make sure you insert the cartridge all the way into the printer.

4) Firmly hold the cartridge in place and bend the cartridge's tab back and forth, as shown in Figure 3-6 on the next page, until it breaks free from the cartridge. Next, pull the tab all the way out of the cartridge to remove the attached sealing tape, as shown in Figure 3-6. If the tab breaks loose from the sealing tape, grab the end of the sealing tape with your finger or with some pliers, and pull it completely out of the cartridge. If the sealing tape breaks off inside the cartridge, return the defective cartridge to your vendor.

5) Once you've removed the sealing tape from the new EP cartridge, close the printer's right door.

FIGURE 3-5

Make sure you slide the new EP cartridge all the way into the cartridge slot on the right side of the printer.

FIGURE 3-6

Bend the black tab on the EP cartridge back and forth until it breaks free from the sealing tape, then pull the tab to completely remove the sealing tape.

6)   Raise the fusing assembly cover and slide the green-handled fusing roller cleaner pad to the right, as shown in Figure 3-7. Insert the new cleaner pad included with your EP cartridge into the slot, and lower the fusing assembly cover. Be careful! The fusing assembly gets very hot.

7)   It's a good idea to clean your LaserJet every time you install a new EP cartridge. Follow the procedures on pages 87-99 for cleaning your LaserJet printer.

LaserJet Series II and LaserJet IID

If you use a LaserJet Series II or LaserJet IID printer, the message *16 TONER LOW* will appear in the display window when the toner level gets low. When the toner level falls far enough, you'll begin to see defects in your printed documents.

You can slightly extend the life of your EP cartridge by removing the cartridge and rocking it from side to side, as shown in Figure 3-2 on page 74. Although the message *16 TONER LOW* will still appear in the display window, the fading will clear up for about 60 to 100 more pages. If the fading persists, however, you'll need to discard the old cartridge and replace it with a new one.

FIGURE 3-7

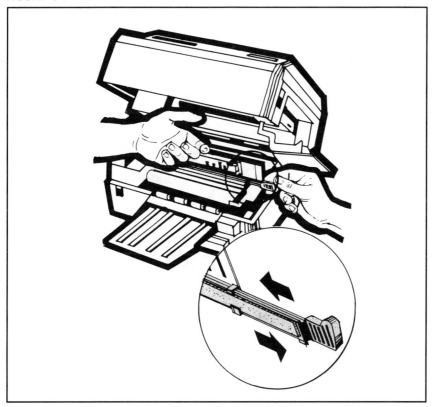

Remember to replace the fusing roller cleaning pad each time you replace the printer's EP cartridge.

To replace your LaserJet's EP cartridge, follow these steps:

1) Open the cover of the printer by pulling the release button on the top of the printer toward you, as shown in Figure 3-8. Remove the old EP cartridge from the cartridge holder inside the printer's main body cover, as shown in Figure 3-9 on page 81.

FIGURE 3-8

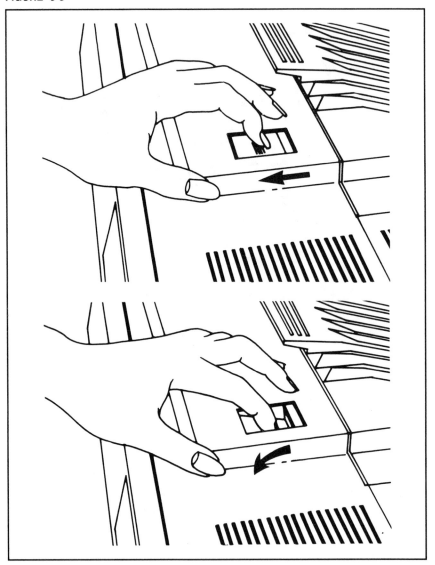

Pull the release button on top of the printer to open the main body cover.

FIGURE 3-9

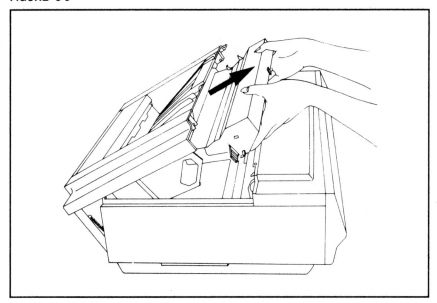

Slide the old EP cartridge out of the cartridge rack.

2) Hold your new EP cartridge as shown in Figure 3-2 on page 74, and rock it from side to side a few times. This procedure helps distribute the toner evenly throughout the cartridge.

3) Insert the new EP cartridge into the cartridge holder on the top of the printer, as shown in Figure 3-10 on the following page. Make sure you insert the cartridge all the way into the printer.

4) Once the new EP cartridge is in place, bend the white tab on the cartridge until it breaks free, as shown in Figure 3-11 on page 83. Next, pull the tab out to remove the sealing tape. If the tab breaks off the sealing tape, grab the end of the tape with your fingers or with a pair of pliers, and pull it completely out of the cartridge. If the sealing tape breaks off inside the cartridge, return the defective cartridge to your vendor.

FIGURE 3-10

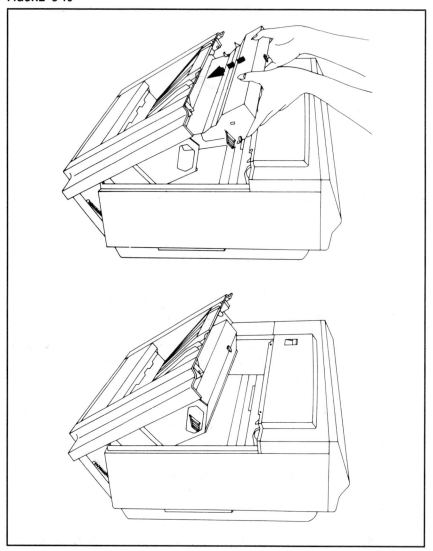

Insert the new EP cartridge into the cartridge holder on the top of the printer.

FIGURE 3-11

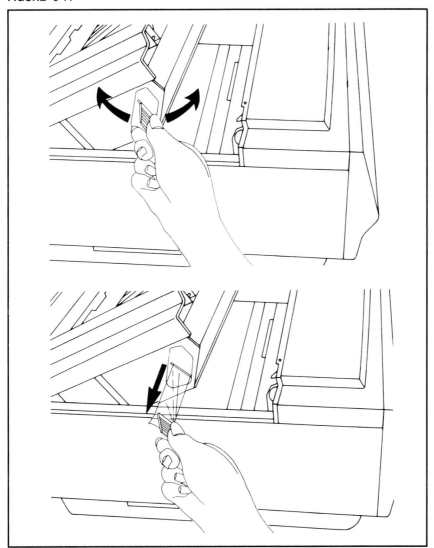

Flex the white tab on the EP cartridge until it breaks free, then pull it out to remove the sealing tape.

5) Open the LaserJet's green fusing assembly cover, as shown in Figure 3-12 on the following page, and remove the old fusing roller cleaning pad, as shown in Figure 3-13 on page 85.

FIGURE 3-12

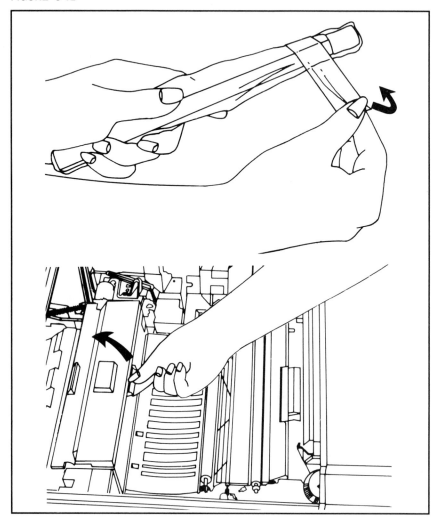

Lift the green fusing assembly cover to expose the fusing roller cleaning pad.

FIGURE 3-13

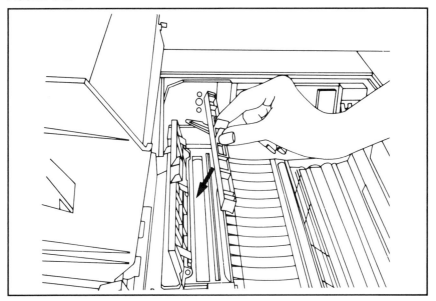

Carefully remove the old fusing roller cleaning pad.

6) Use the cloth end of the new fusing roller cleaning pad to wipe off the toner residue that has collected on the fusing roller. (A new cleaning pad should be included with your new EP cartridge.) You should carefully wipe the pad back and forth across the roller, as shown in Figure 3-14 on the next page. Be careful! The area around the fusing assembly gets very hot.

7) After you've cleaned off the fusing roller, remove and discard the cloth end of the cleaning pad, and insert the new cleaning pad into the groove in the top part of the fusing assembly.

8) Once the new cleaning pad is in place, lower the fusing assembly cover. Don't press hard on the fusing assembly cover—it should not close tightly. Remember, the area around the fusing assembly gets very hot.

9) As we mentioned earlier, it's a good idea to clean your LaserJet every time you install a new EP cartridge. Follow the procedures on pages 87-99 for cleaning your LaserJet printer.

FIGURE 3-14

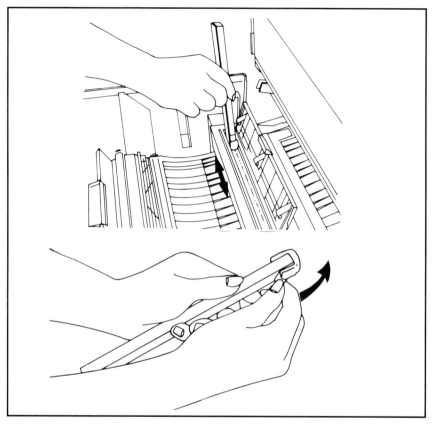

Use the cloth end of the new fusing roller cleaning pad to wipe off the fusing roller.

Notes on EP cartridges

Although many companies now allow you to trade in your old EP cartridges for inexpensive recycled cartridges, we highly recommend that you always buy new EP cartridges for your LaserJet printer. In addition to toner, the EP cartridge contains many consumable parts (like the corona wires, imaging drum, and developer units) that the recycling manufacturers don't replace. As these parts wear out over time, the quality of your printouts will deteriorate. In addition, when these parts become worn, they can permanently damage some of the parts inside the LaserJet. You've made a large investment in your LaserJet printer—don't cut corners with accessories that will diminish your print quality and shorten your printer's life. Always purchase new EP cartridges for the HP LaserJet printer.

From time to time, you'll need to clean the toner debris that builds up inside the printer. In addition to wiping away any visible toner with a damp cloth, you need to occasionally follow the cleaning procedure described in this section. The areas that you need to keep clean depend on whether you own a first-generation LaserJet printer (LaserJet, LaserJet Plus, or LaserJet 500 Plus), or a second-generation LaserJet printer (LaserJet Series II or LaserJet IID).

If you own a LaserJet, LaserJet Plus, or LaserJet 500 Plus printer, you need to clean the following four areas: primary corona wire, transfer corona wire, transfer guide, and separation belt. *Make sure that you turn the printer off before you perform any of these cleaning procedures.*

To clean the primary corona wire (which is housed inside the EP cartridge), first open the printer's main body cover and pull out the EP cartridge. Next, insert the green-handled wire cleaner (which is stored next to the fusing assembly) into the long slot of the EP cartridge (behind the shutter) and move it back and forth several times in the slot, as shown in Figure 3-15. After cleaning the primary corona wire, re-insert the EP cartridge into the printer.

CLEANING THE PRINTER

LaserJet, LaserJet Plus, and LaserJet 500 Plus

Primary corona wire

FIGURE 3-15

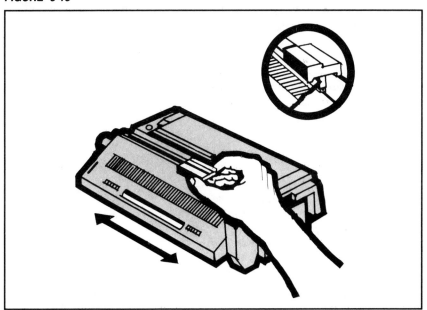

Use the green-handled wire cleaner that came with your LaserJet to clean the primary corona wire inside the EP cartridge.

Transfer corona wire

To clean the LaserJet's transfer corona wire, dip a cotton swab into some rubbing alcohol and gently rub the swab back and forth across the transfer corona wire, as shown in Figure 3-16. Continue rubbing the transfer corona wire until you've removed all the toner residue.

FIGURE 3-16

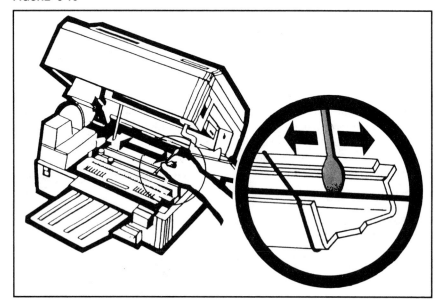

Use a cotton swab dipped in alcohol to clean the transfer corona wire.

Transfer guide

To clean the transfer guide, take a damp cloth (moist, but not wet) and wipe across the transfer guide, as shown in Figure 3-17.

Separation belt replacement and cleaning

Your LaserJet's separation belt, which guides paper through the inside of the printer, has an average life of 50,000 pages. If the separation belt breaks, your paper will not feed correctly and will jam inside the printer. For this reason, you'll need to replace the separation belt when the old one breaks. You'll also want to keep your separation belt free from toner debris.

Replacing the belt

You should follow the steps on the next page to replace your printer's separation belt. Fortunately, HP provides a spare separation belt near the wire cleaner, as shown in Figure 3-18 on page 90. You can order a new separation belt from either Hewlett-Packard's Direct Marketing Division (Part No. RF1-0224-000CN) or from your local computer vendor.

FIGURE 3-17

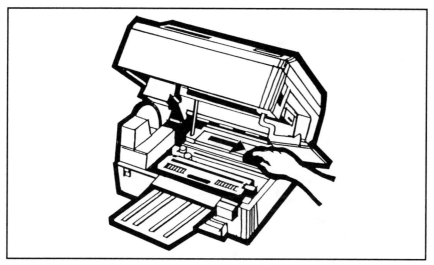

Use a damp cloth to wipe off the transfer guide.

1) Open the upper main body of the printer and locate the separation belt on the left side of the printer, as shown in Figure 3-18 on the next page. You will notice that the belt is attached to the printer by loop A and loop B, as depicted in Figure 3-19 on the next page. You should remove the broken belt by sliding loop A from its hanger and loop B from the spring suspender.

2) Open loop A of the new separation belt so that you can fit the loop around the upper transfer guide.

3) Attach loop A to the hanger located on the right side of the upper transfer guide, as shown in Figure 3-20 on page 91. Make sure you keep the separation belt's indentation on the right-hand side.

4) Pass the separation belt over the transfer roller and under the upper separation roller, and hook loop B on the spring suspender, as shown in Figure 3-20.

5) After you've installed the separation belt, make sure there are no twists or cuts in the belt. Also make sure the indentation is on the right-hand side, and the belt is securely fastened on both ends. Once the belt is properly in place, close the main body of the printer.

FIGURE 3-18

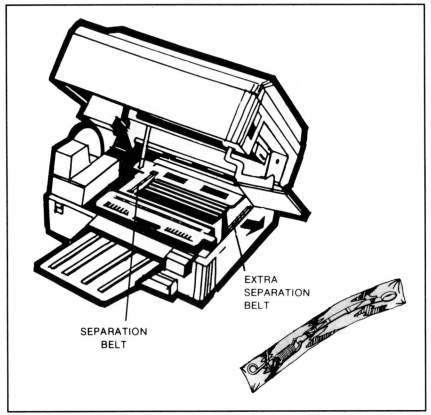

The separation belt is located on the left side of the printer, while the extra separation belt is located on the right side.

FIGURE 3-19

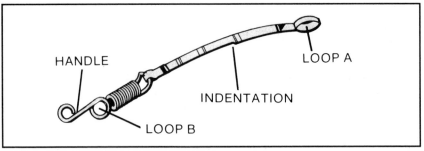

Don't confuse loop A with loop B when installing a new separation belt.

FIGURE 3-20

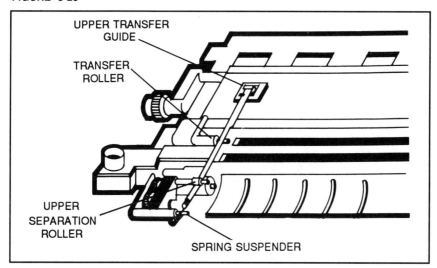

UPPER TRANSFER
GUIDE

TRANSFER
ROLLER

UPPER
SEPARATION
ROLLER

SPRING SUSPENDER

After you attach loop A of the separation belt to the upper transfer guide, pass the belt over the transfer roller and under the upper separation roller, and hook loop B on the spring suspender.

Cleaning the belt

If a black line appears along the right edges of your printed sheets, your separation belt has probably become soiled with toner residue. If you see any soil on your separation belt, clean it with a cotton swab and a little alcohol. If the separation belt is permanently stained, replace it with a new one.

LaserJet Series II

If you own a LaserJet Series II printer, you need to clean four areas: the transfer corona wire, the transfer guide, the transfer guide lock tray, and the paper feed guide. *Make sure that you turn the printer off before performing any of these cleaning procedures.*

Transfer corona wire

To clean the transfer corona wire, first locate the small green brush inside the printer to the left of the paper feed guide (see Figure 3-21 on the next page). Then, use the brush to wipe off the transfer corona wire, as shown in Figure 3-22. Be sure to wipe the top, bottom, and sides of the wire until you've removed all of the toner residue. Also, use the brush to clean the monofilament lines that cross above the transfer corona wire.

FIGURE 3-21

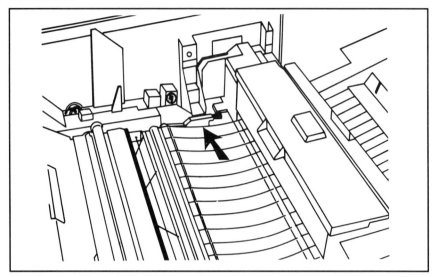

A cleaning brush is located inside the LaserJet just to the left of the paper feed guide.

FIGURE 3-22

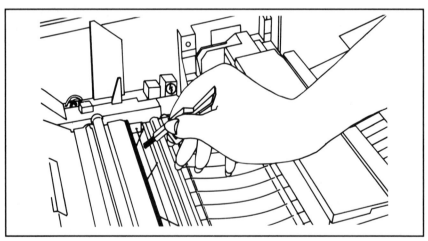

Use the cleaning brush to clean the printer's transfer corona wire.

If you cannot find your LaserJet's green brush, use a cotton swab dampened with alcohol or water to clean the transfer corona wire. Be careful not to break either the monofilament lines that cross above the transfer corona wire or the transfer corona wire itself. Also be careful not to get any excess alcohol on any parts inside the printer. Finally, use the green brush or the cotton swab to clean the orange pads around the wire area (area a), the area under the plastic lip, along the length, (area b), and the area along the back of the casing (area c), as shown in Figure 3-23.

FIGURE 3-23

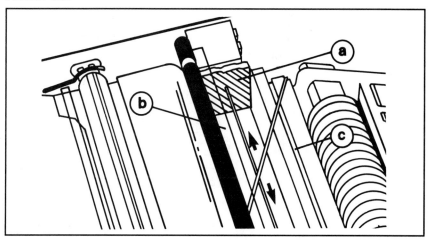

In addition to cleaning the transfer corona wire itself, you need to clean these three areas around the transfer corona wire.

Transfer guide

To clean the transfer guide, dampen a cloth with water and wipe the silver strip, as shown in Figure 3-24 on the following page. Use water only—don't use alcohol. Make sure that the cloth is only damp—if water drips into the printer, it can damage the printer's internal parts.

Transfer guide lock tray

To clean the transfer guide lock tray, lift the cover of the transfer guide lock and wipe the area underneath, as shown in Figure 3-25 on the next page.

Paper feed guide

To clean the paper feed guide, simply dampen a cloth with water and wipe it, as shown in Figure 3-26 on page 95. Be careful—the fusing area gets very hot. Also be careful not to get any toner on your clothing since toner can permanently stain it.

FIGURE 3-24

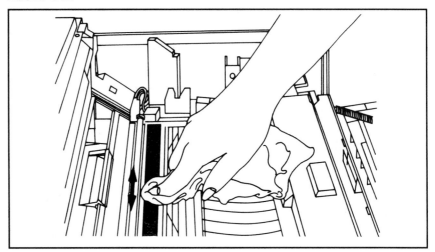

Use a damp cloth to wipe the silver strip of the transfer guide.

FIGURE 3-25

Use a damp cloth to wipe the transfer guide lock tray.

FIGURE 3-26

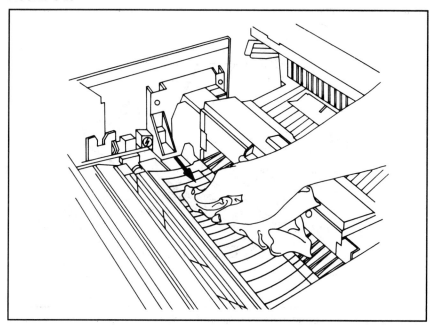

Don't forget to wipe the LaserJet's paper feed guide.

LaserJet IID

If you use a LaserJet IID printer, you need to clean the following five areas: the transfer corona wire, the transfer guide, the transfer guide lock tray, the paper feed guide, and the primary corona wire. In addition, you need to replace the LaserJet IID's ozone filter approximately every 50,000 pages. *Make sure that you turn the printer off before performing any of these cleaning procedures.*

Transfer corona wire

To clean the transfer corona wire, use a cotton swab dipped in rubbing alcohol or water. Make sure the swab is not dripping. Clean the top, bottom, and sides of the wire, as shown in Figure 3-27 on the next page , until you remove all of the toner residue. Be careful not to break either the monofilament lines that cross above the transfer corona wire or the transfer corona wire itself. Also be careful not to get any alcohol on the rollers or on any of the plastic parts in the printer.

After you've cleaned the transfer corona wire, use the swab to clean the orange pads around the wire area, the area under the plastic lip (along the length), and the area along the back of the casing.

FIGURE 3-27

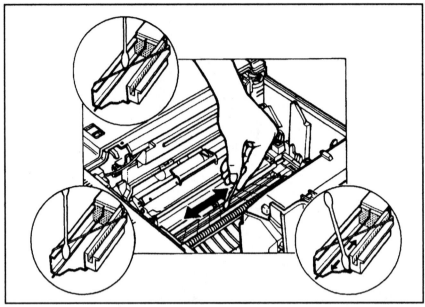

Use a cotton swab dipped in rubbing alcohol to clean the transfer corona wire.

Transfer guide   To clean the transfer guide, dampen a cloth with water (use water only) and wipe the silver strip, as shown in Figure 3-28. Make sure that the cloth is only damp—if water drips into the printer, it can damage your machine.

Transfer guide   To clean the transfer guide lock tray, lift the cover and wipe the area underneath,
lock tray   as shown in Figure 3-29.

Paper feed guide   To clean the paper feed guide, dampen a cloth with water and wipe it, as shown in Figure 3-30 on page 98. Be careful—the fusing area gets very hot. Also be careful not to get any toner on your clothing.

FIGURE 3-28

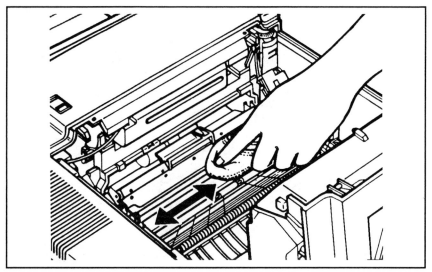

Use a damp cloth to clean the silver strip of the transfer guide.

FIGURE 3-29

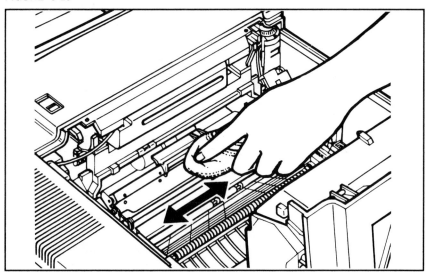

Use a damp cloth to wipe the transfer guide lock tray.

FIGURE 3-30

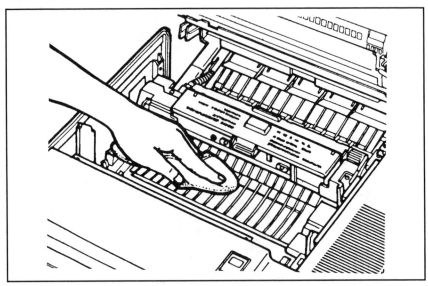

Use a damp cloth to wipe the paper feed guide.

Primary corona wire

The LaserJet IID's primary corona wire is located inside the EP cartridge. You do not need to clean this wire as often as the transfer corona wire. In fact, the primary corona wire is delicate, so you should clean it only when absolutely necessary.

To clean the primary corona wire, first remove the EP cartridge from the printer, and locate the cleaning brush shown in Figure 3-21 on page 92. Now, carefully insert the felt-tipped end of the brush in the EP cartridge slot, as shown in Figure 3-31. Clean the wire by carefully moving the brush back and forth a few times along the wire's surface. (Be very careful—if you break the primary corona wire, you'll have to replace the entire EP cartridge.) After you've removed all the toner residue, return the brush and the EP cartridge to their appropriate locations in the printer.

Replacing the ozone filter

The LaserJet IID's ozone filter needs to be replaced approximately every 50,000 pages. To replace the ozone filter, open the printer's main body cover and locate the filter on the inner-right side of the printer, as shown in Figure 3-32. Flip the filter cover down, and pull on the filter's clear plastic tab until the filter slides out of the printer. After you've removed the old filter, insert a new filter (HP Part No. RF1-2130-000CN) in place of the old one.

FIGURE 3-31

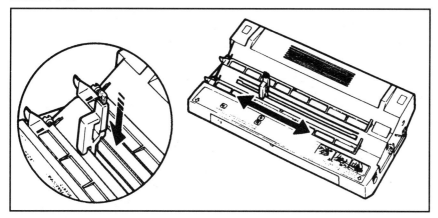

Use the cleaning brush to clean the primary corona wire on the EP cartridge.

FIGURE 3-32

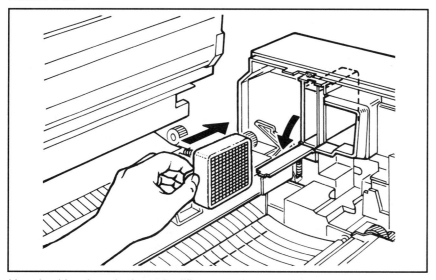

You should replace the LaserJet IID's ozone filter every 50,000 pages.

TROUBLE-SHOOTING

Because the LaserJet is a complex machine used to perform a very complex task, you'll inevitably run into problems from time to time. Some of the problems you'll face will be simple, like running out of paper, while other problems will be serious, like an incorrect computer-to-printer configuration.

In this section, we'll show you how to solve the sundry problems that can surface with your LaserJet. We've organized this section into four parts: "Optimizing Print Quality," "Error and Status Messages," "Clearing Paper Jams," and "Troubleshooting Communication Problems."

If you are unable to solve your problem using the information in this section, don't fret—you can turn elsewhere for assistance. One source of help is the HP dealership where you purchased your printer. Alternatively, you can get help by calling HP's LaserJet Customer Assist Line during business hours (208-323-2551).

Optimizing Print Quality

If you notice a decline in the quality of your printed documents, you should use the following checklist to identify and resolve your problem. This list of problems and solutions covers the most common causes of poor print quality.

Vertical fade

If your page contains white streaks or faded areas that run top to bottom on the page as shown in Figure 3-33, the cause of your problem could be:

- The EP cartridge toner supply is low. Try rocking the cartridge from side to side as shown in Figure 3-2 on page 74. If that does not fix the problem, replace the current EP cartridge with a new one.

- The print density setting is too high. Try turning the print density dial to a lower number. (Refer to Chapter 2 for a more detailed discussion of the print density setting.)

Dropouts

Figure 3-34 shows a page that contains faded areas, generally round in shape, that occur in random locations. The cause of this problem could be:

- The paper has moist spots on its surface, or it has an uneven moisture content. Try using a different supply of paper.

- The paper lot is bad. A careless manufacturing process may have produced paper that cannot accept toner in some areas. Try using a different supply of paper.

- The transfer corona wire needs cleaning. Follow the instructions in the preceding section of this chapter for cleaning the inside of the printer.

FIGURE 3-33

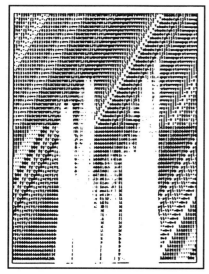

This page has vertical fade problems.

FIGURE 3-34

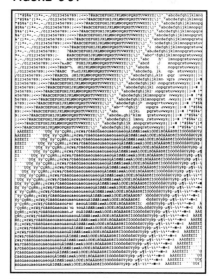

This page has dropout problems.

If your paper contains black streaks or smeared ink spots that run the length of the page like the one in Figure 3-35 on the next page, the cause of your problem could be:

Vertical lines

• The photosensitive drum inside the EP cartridge has been scratched, causing thin lines to appear on the page. Replace the EP cartridge with a new one.

• The fusing roller cleaning pad has become dirty or worn, causing smeared vertical lines to appear on the page. Follow the instructions on page 78 or 83 to replace the pad. If you don't have an extra pad on hand, you can temporarily alleviate the problem by wiping excess toner off the surface of the pad and cleaning the inside of the printer, as shown in the section entitled "Cleaning the Printer," earlier in this chapter.

If dark horizontal stains appear repeatedly down the back side of the page like the one in Figure 3-36 on the next page, your problem could be:

Staining

• The transport rollers need cleaning. Follow the instructions in the section entitled "Cleaning the Printer" for cleaning the inside of the printer.

• The fusing roller cleaning pad has become dirty or worn. Follow the instructions on page 78 or 83 for replacing the pad. If you don't have an extra pad, you can temporarily remedy the problem by wiping excess toner from the surface of the pad and cleaning the inside of the printer, as shown earlier in this chapter.

FIGURE 3-35

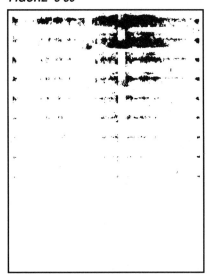

This page has vertical line problems.

FIGURE 3-36

This page has staining problems.

Repetitive defects

If marks like the ones in Figure 3-37 appear repeatedly on the printed side of the page, the cause of the problem could be:

- A defective EP cartridge. Since the circumference of the EP cartridge drum is 3.75 inches, a defect on the drum will result in print defects exactly 3.75 inches apart on the page. If your print defects are 3.75 inches apart, simply replace the old EP cartridge with a new one.

- The transport roller needs cleaning. Follow the instructions given earlier in this chapter for cleaning the inside of the printer.

Black stripe

If a black stripe appears on the right side of the printed page, as shown in Figure 3-38, your LaserJet's primary corona wire has probably become dirty. To resolve this problem, follow the instructions on page 87, 91, or 98 for cleaning your printer's primary corona wire.

FIGURE 3-37

FIGURE 3-38

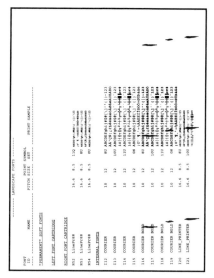

This page has repetitive defects.

This black stripe results from a dirty corona wire.

The messages that appear on your LaserJet's status display or display window fall into one of the following three categories: status messages (that inform you of the printer's current operating condition), attendance messages (that request a specific task before printing continues), and error messages (that tell you when the printer has experienced some difficulty).

After we discuss the messages that can appear on the LaserJet, LaserJet Plus, and LaserJet 500 Plus printers, we'll discuss the messages you might see on the LaserJet Series II and LaserJet IID printers.

When a two-digit message appears on your LaserJet's status display, you should look up the message in this section, learn the cause of the problem, and take the recommended action. We've divided the messages that appear in the status display into three sections: "Status Messages," "Attendance Messages," and "Error Messages."

**Error and
Status Messages**

*LaserJet,
LaserJet Plus,
and LaserJet
500 Plus*

Status messages

First, we'll discuss the status messages. These messages do not indicate an error condition—they merely inform you of the printer's current status. As you'll see, status messages are represented by relatively low numbers.

00

If *00* appears in your status display, the printer is in ready mode. In other words, the printer is turned on and is ready to print. You do not need to take any action when this status code appears.

02

Status message *02* tells you that the printer is warming up and will be ready to print shortly. This message always appears for a few seconds when you first turn on the LaserJet. After a few seconds, the message *02* will be replaced by the message *00* to tell you that the printer is warmed up and ready to print.

05

Status message *05* appears while the printer is performing the nonprinting portion of its interface self-test. After the nonprinting portion of the self-test is completed, the message *05* will be replaced with the status message *06* to indicate that the printing portion of the self-test is taking place.

06

Status message *06* indicates that the printer is performing the printing portion of its interface self-test. After the test is completed, the message *06* will be replaced by the status message *00* to indicate that the printer is ready to resume printing. Of course, you'll need to press the ON LINE key to put the printer back on-line before you can continue printing.

07

Status message *07* indicates that you have reset the LaserJet Plus or LaserJet 500 Plus with the HOLD TO RESET/CONTINUE key on the control panel. After the printer resets itself, the message *07* will be replaced by the message *00*.

15

Status message *15* indicates that you have invoked the print engine self-test by pressing the TEST PRINT key on the control panel. (This message does not appear on the original LaserJet printer.) After the printer completes the test print, the message *15* will be replaced by the message *00*. Of course, you'll need to press the ON LINE key to put the printer back on-line before you can continue printing.

Attendance messages

Next, we'll discuss the LaserJet's attendance messages. These messages require you to perform some sort of basic printer operation, such as closing the printer's main body cover or refilling the printer's paper tray.

11

Message *11* appears when the printer's paper tray becomes empty or when the paper tray is not installed in its slot. When you see this message, reload the paper tray with a fresh stack of paper, re-insert the tray into the printer, and press the CONTINUE key on the LaserJet's control panel to put the printer back on-line (you need not press the CONTINUE key on the LaserJet Plus or LaserJet 500 Plus—the printer will automatically return on-line when you re-insert the paper tray).

If you insert the wrong size paper tray into the printer, the message *PC* will appear on the status display when you try to print again. If you need to change from one size paper tray to another, make sure you reset the printer immediately after you insert the new tray into the printer. For more information on paper trays, see the section entitled "Paper Trays" in Chapter 2.

Message *12* appears when the printer's main body cover is open. When you see this message, close the cover and make sure that it is seated firmly in place. Once you've closed the cover securely, press the CONTINUE key to put the printer back on-line, and resume printing.

12

Message *13* appears when a paper jam occurs inside the printer. When you see this message, open the printer's main body cover, and follow the procedures outlined in the section "Clearing Paper Jams" on page 117. After you've removed the jammed page, close the body cover, and put the printer back on-line. The LaserJet will reprint the jammed page and continue printing your document.

13

Message *14* appears when the EP cartridge is either not installed or is installed improperly. To correct this problem, insert an EP cartridge or reseat the existing cartridge. If you cannot make your existing cartridge work properly, discard it and install a new EP cartridge. For more information on this subject, read the section entitled "EP Cartridges" at the beginning of this chapter.

14

When the status display alternately flashes the message *PC* and a paper size number (*L* for letter, *LL* for legal, *A4* for A4, or *b5* for B5), the printer expects you to insert the appropriate paper tray. For example, if the messages *PC* and *LL* are alternately flashing, the LaserJet expects you to insert a legal-size paper tray.

PC

When you see this message, you should insert the requested paper tray and press the CONTINUE key to resume printing. If you do not have the requested size paper tray, you can insert another size tray and press the CONTINUE key to force the LaserJet to print on the paper in that tray. If you do this, however, the LaserJet will format the printed pages for the requested paper size—not for the size you've installed. Consequently, the LaserJet might "clip" the images on your printed pages, or it might print some images completely off the edge of the page. For information on how to request paper tray sizes using escape sequences, see Chapter 22.

When the status display alternately flashes the message *PF* and a paper size number (*L* for letter, *LL* for legal, *A4* for A4, or *b5* for B5), it expects you to insert a sheet of the requested size paper into the printer's manual feed slot. For example,

PF

if the messages *PF* and *LL* are alternately flashing, the LaserJet expects you to insert a sheet of legal-size paper into the manual feed slot. For instructions on manually feeding paper into the LaserJet, see the section entitled "Using Manual Feed" in Chapter 2.

If you do not have a sheet of the requested size paper, you can insert another size sheet into the manual feed slot and print on that sheet of paper. If you do this, however, the LaserJet will format the printed page for the requested paper size—not for the size you've manually fed. Consequently, the LaserJet might clip the images on your printed pages, or it might print some images completely off the edge of the page. If the paper you use is longer than the requested paper size, it will probably get stuck inside the printer and result in a paper jam error.

PE

When the message *PE* appears in the status display, the LaserJet expects you to manually feed an envelope into the printer. As soon as the printer receives the envelope, the LaserJet will remove the *PE* message from the status display and begin printing the envelope. For more information on feeding envelopes into the printer, see the section entitled "Printing Envelopes" in Chapter 2.

FC

The message *FC* appears whenever you remove a font cartridge while the LaserJet is formatting a page. To resolve this situation, re-insert the font cartridge and press the CONTINUE key. At this point, the LaserJet should reformat the page and continue printing as usual.

FE

The message *FE* appears whenever you remove a font cartridge while the printer is on-line. The only way to recover from this situation is to re-insert the font cartridge, turn off the power to the printer, then turn the power back on again.

FF

The message *FF* appears whenever the LaserJet experiences a printer malfunction. The only way to recover from this situation is to turn off the power to the printer, then turn the power back on again. If this problem persists, call your HP service representative for assistance.

Error messages

The last group of messages consists of error messages. Error messages usually require you to reset the printer by turning off the power, then turning it back on again. If the action we recommend below does not correct the error, or if the error condition persists, contact your HP service representative for assistance.

20

Error message *20* indicates a memory overflow error. This error message appears whenever the data sent by the computer exceeds the LaserJet's memory capacity. As you may know, the kinds of data that require large amounts of memory are soft fonts, graphics, and macros.

When you see this message, press the CONTINUE key to clear the error and to resume printing. Since a memory overflow error has occurred, however, the LaserJet will print only the data that fit in the printer's memory. To reprint your image without running into error *20* again, reformat your page so that it requires less printer memory to print. Some ways to reduce the amount of required memory include decreasing print resolution and decreasing the point size of your larger fonts. If error *20* persists, you should consider adding more memory to your LaserJet. HP offers a 2MB upgrade kit for the LaserJet, LaserJet Plus, and LaserJet 500 Plus (HP Part No. 26054A). For more information on memory options for the LaserJet printer, see the section entitled "Memory Options" in Chapter 1.

Error message *21* indicates a print overrun error. During the printing process, the LaserJet's formatter starts formatting the page before the laser begins writing to the photosensitive drum. Under normal circumstances, the formatter works about 20 scan lines ahead of the laser. If the page being formatted is very complex, however, the laser catches up to the formatter, and a print overrun error occurs.

21

The problem usually results from complex printer commands that cause the LaserJet's formatter to "jump around" the page instead of letting it work from left to right, top to bottom. For example, if your printer's software tells the LaserJet to print all text first, then all shading, then all graphics, the formatter will be moving back up to portions of the page it has already formatted. All of this up-and-down, back-and-forth movement will allow the laser to catch up to the formatter and will cause a print overrun error.

When you see this message, you can clear the error condition by pressing the LaserJet's CONTINUE key. After you've cleared the error, decrease the complexity of the page you are sending. For example, take shading off text, remove an image that overlaps another image, and so forth. After you've decreased the complexity as much as possible, re-send your document. If the problem persists, contact your software vendor or call the HP LaserJet Customer Assist Line.

Error message *22* indicates a receiving buffer overflow error. This message appears when the computer sends print data so quickly that it fills and overflows the LaserJet's receiving buffer.

22

When you see this message, press the CONTINUE key to resume printing, and check to see what data was lost in the overflow. If this error condition occurs on a regular basis, reread the section entitled "Configuring Your LaserJet" in Chapter 2 to ensure that you've configured the printer correctly. Also make sure you are not using a defective printer cable.

40   Error message *40* indicates that a data error (parity, framing, or line overrun) occurred while the printer was receiving data from the computer. This message will appear if the LaserJet's configuration settings do not match the configuration settings on your computer. In addition, this message can appear when you reboot your computer while the LaserJet is on-line.

When you see this message, simply press the CONTINUE key to clear the error condition and to resume printing. If error message *40* occurs repeatedly, check to make sure that your printer cable is not defective and that it is securely fastened to both the printer and to the computer. Also make sure your computer is correctly configured for your LaserJet printer. If the error still occurs, contact your HP dealer or HP service representative for assistance.

41   Error message *41* indicates that a temporary error occurred while the LaserJet was printing the current page. When you see this message, remove the paper from the output paper tray, then press the CONTINUE key to clear the error condition and to resume printing. After you press the CONTINUE key, the LaserJet will reprint the page on which the error occurred.

50   Error message *50* indicates a fusing assembly malfunction. Unfortunately, the printer cannot immediately recover from this type of error. When you see this message, turn off the power to the printer for at least ten minutes. After you turn it back on, re-send the document the LaserJet was printing when the error occurred.

51   Error message *51* indicates a beam detect malfunction. When you see this message, just press the CONTINUE key to clear the error and to resume printing. If this error occurs repeatedly, contact your HP service representative.

52   Error message *52* indicates a scanner malfunction. When you see this message, just press the CONTINUE key to clear the error and to resume printing. If this error occurs repeatedly, contact your HP service representative.

53   Error message *53* indicates a laser temperature control circuit malfunction. Unfortunately, the LaserJet cannot immediately recover from this type of error. When you see this message, turn off the power to the printer for at least ten minutes. After you turn it back on, re-send the document you were printing when the error occurred. If this error occurs repeatedly, contact your HP service representative.

Error message *54* indicates a main motor malfunction. When you see this message, first make sure that the paper tray does not contain more than 100 sheets of paper. After you've checked the paper tray (and removed any excess paper), press the CONTINUE key to clear the error and to resume printing. If this error occurs repeatedly, contact your HP service representative.

54

Error message *55* indicates a printer command error, which means that the print engine and its controller are not communicating clearly. When you see this message, just press the CONTINUE key to clear the error and to resume printing. If this error occurs repeatedly, contact your HP service representative.

55

Error message *60* indicates a bus error, which can be caused by a circuit malfunction. This message can also appear when you've improperly inserted a font cartridge into the printer's cartridge slot. When you see this message, make sure your font cartridges are firmly seated in the cartridge slot. After you've checked your font cartridges, turn off power to the printer, then turn it back on again. If this error occurs repeatedly, contact your HP service representative.

60

Error message *61* indicates a program ROM checksum error. When you see this message, turn off power to the printer, then turn it back on again. If this error occurs repeatedly, contact your HP service representative.

61

Error message *62* indicates an internal font ROM checksum error. When you see this message, turn off power to the printer, then turn it back on again. If this error occurs repeatedly, contact your HP service representative.

62

Error message *63* indicates a dynamic RAM error. When you see this message, turn off power to the printer, then turn it back on again. If this error occurs repeatedly, contact your HP service representative.

63

Error message *64* indicates a scan buffer error. When you see this message, turn off power to the printer, then turn it back on again. If this error occurs repeatedly, contact your HP service representative.

64

Error message *65* indicates a dynamic RAM controller error. When you see this message, turn off power to the printer, then turn it back on again. If this error occurs repeatedly, contact your HP service representative.

65

Error message *67* indicates a miscellaneous interface hardware error. When you see this message, turn off power to the printer, then turn it back on again. If this error occurs repeatedly, contact your HP service representative.

67

**LaserJet Series II
and LaserJet IID**

When a message appears in your LaserJet's display window, you should look up that message in the following section and take the recommended action. We've divided the messages that appear in the display window into three sections: "Status Messages," "Attendance Messages," and "Error Messages."

Status messages

First, we'll discuss status messages. These messages do not indicate an error condition—they merely inform you of the printer's current status.

00 READY

If *00 READY* appears in your display window, the printer is in ready mode. In other words, the printer is turned on and ready to print. You do not need to take any action when this status code appears.

02 WARMING UP

Status message *02 WARMING UP* tells you that the printer is warming up and will be ready to print shortly. This message always appears for a few seconds when you first turn on the LaserJet. After a few seconds, the message *02 WARMING UP* will be replaced by the message *00 READY* to tell you the printer is warmed up and ready to print.

04 SELF TEST

Status message *04 SELF TEST* tells you that the printer is continuously generating test printouts. To stop the continuous test printouts and return the printer on-line, just press the ON LINE key. After printing a few more pages, the printer will go back on-line.

05 SELF TEST

Status message *05 SELF TEST* appears while the printer is performing the nonprinting portion of its interface self-test. After the nonprinting portion of the self-test is completed, the message *05 SELF TEST* will be replaced with the status message *06 PRINTING TEST* to indicate that the printing portion of the self-test is taking place.

06 PRINTING TEST

Status message *06 PRINTING TEST* indicates that the printer is performing the printing portion of its interface self-test. After the test is completed, the message *06 PRINTING TEST* should be replaced by the status message *00 READY* to indicate that the printer is ready to resume printing. Of course, you'll need to press the ON LINE key to put the printer back on-line before you can continue printing.

06 FONT PRINTOUT

Status message *06 FONT PRINTOUT* appears while the printer is printing sample characters from each of its available fonts.

07 RESET

Status message *07 RESET* indicates that you have reset the printer with the RESET key on the LaserJet's control panel. Resetting the printer returns all printing menu items to user-selected settings and clears buffer pages, temporary soft fonts, and temporary macros. After the printer resets itself, the message *07 RESET* will be replaced by the message *00 READY*.

Status message *08 COLD RESET* indicates that the printer is returning all configuration and printing menu selections to their factory default settings.

08 COLD RESET

Status message *09 MENU RESET* indicates that you have reset the LaserJet's printing menu items with the control panel's RESET MENU key. Resetting the printing menu returns all printing menu items to the factory settings and clears buffer pages, temporary soft fonts, and temporary macros.

09 MENU RESET

Status message *15 ENGINE TEST* indicates that the printer is performing a print engine self-test. After the printer completes the test, press the LaserJet's ON LINE key to put the printer back on-line and continue printing.

15 ENGINE TEST

Next, we'll discuss the LaserJet's attendance messages. These messages require you to perform a basic printer operation, such as closing the printer's main body cover or refilling the printer's paper tray.

Attendance messages

Message *10 RESET TO SAVE* (which appears only on the LaserJet IID) appears whenever you have made changes to the printing menu while data, temporary soft fonts, or temporary macros are present in printer memory. When you see this message, you can press the LaserJet's RESET key, which will activate your new menu selections but delete your data, fonts, and macros. You can also press the CONTINUE or ON LINE key to postpone saving your new menu selections until you're willing to delete the data, fonts, or macros in your printer's memory.

10 RESET TO SAVE

Message *11 PAPER OUT* appears when the printer's paper tray becomes empty, or when the paper tray is not installed in its slot. When you see this message, reload the paper tray with a fresh stack of paper, and re-insert the tray into the printer.

11 PAPER OUT

If you re-insert the wrong size paper tray into the printer, the message *PC* will appear on the status display when you try to print again. If you need to change from one size paper tray to another, make sure you reset the printer immediately after you insert the new tray into the printer. For more information on paper trays, see the section entitled "Paper Trays" in Chapter 2.

Message *12 PRINTER OPEN* appears when the upper main body of the printer is open or is not closed properly. When you see this message, close the cover and make sure that it is seated firmly in place. Once you've closed the cover securely, the message *12 PRINTER OPEN* will be replaced by the message *02 WARMING UP*, and then by the message *00 READY*. At this point, you can press the ON LINE key to put the printer back on-line and resume printing.

12 PRINTER OPEN

13 PAPER JAM

Message *13 PAPER JAM* appears when a paper jam occurs inside the printer. When you see this message, open the main body cover of the printer, and follow the procedures outlined in the section "Clearing Paper Jams" on page 117. After you've removed the jammed page, close the body cover and put the printer back on-line. LaserJet will reprint the page and continue printing your document.

14 NO EP CART

Message *14 NO EP CART* appears when the EP cartridge is either not installed or is installed improperly. To correct this problem, insert an EP cartridge or reseat the existing cartridge. If you cannot make your existing cartridge work properly, discard it and install a new one. For more information on EP cartridges, read the section entitled "EP Cartridges" at the beginning of this chapter.

16 TONER LOW

Message *16 TONER LOW* appears when the EP cartridge is almost out of toner. When the message first appears, there is enough toner to print 30 to 100 more "quality" pages. You can slightly extend the life of the toner cartridge by taking it out and rocking it from side to side, as shown in Figure 3-2 on page 74. However, you should replace the EP cartridge as soon as possible after you see this message.

PC LOAD [paper size]

Message *PC LOAD* and a paper size (*A4*, *EXEC*, *LETTER*, or *LEGAL*) appear when the printer expects you to insert the appropriate paper tray. For example, if the message *PC LOAD LEGAL* appears, the LaserJet expects you to insert a legal-size paper tray.

When you see this message, you should insert the requested paper tray and press the CONTINUE key to resume printing. If you do not have the requested size paper tray, you can insert another size tray and press the CONTINUE key to force the LaserJet to print on the paper in that tray. If you do this, however, the LaserJet will format the printed pages for the requested paper size—not for the size you've installed. Consequently, the LaserJet might "clip" the images on your printed pages, or it might print some images completely off the edge of the page. For information on how to request paper tray sizes using escape sequences, see Chapter 22.

PE FEED
[envelope size]

Message *PE FEED* and an envelope size (*COM-10*, *MONARCH*, *DL*, *C5*, or *ENVELOPE*) appear when the LaserJet expects you to manually feed the requested size envelope into the printer. As soon as the printer receives the envelope, the LaserJet will remove the *PE FEED* message from the display window and begin printing the envelope. For more information on feeding envelopes into the printer, see the section entitled "Printing Envelopes" in Chapter 2.

Message *PF FEED* and a paper size (*A4*, *EXEC*, *LETTER*, or *LEGAL*) appear when the printer expects you to insert a sheet of the requested size paper into the printer's manual feed slot. For example, if the message *PF FEED LEGAL* appears, the LaserJet expects you to insert a sheet of legal-size paper into the manual feed slot. For instructions on manually feeding paper into the LaserJet, see the section entitled "Using Manual Feed" in Chapter 2.

PF FEED [paper size]

If you do not have a sheet of the requested size paper, you can insert another size sheet into the manual feed slot and print on that sheet of paper. If you do this, however, the LaserJet will format the printed page for the requested paper size—not for the size you've manually fed. Consequently, the LaserJet might clip the images on your printed pages, or it might print some images completely off the edge of the page. If the paper you use is longer than the requested paper size, the paper will probably get stuck inside the printer and result in a paper jam error.

Message *EC LOAD* and an envelope size (*COM-10*, *MONARCH*, *DL*, *C5*, or *ENVELOPE*) appear when the printer expects you to load the correct size envelopes in the envelope tray, then insert the envelope tray into the printer.

EC LOAD [envelope size]

The message *FC LEFT*, *FC RIGHT*, or *FC BOTH* appears whenever you remove a font cartridge while the LaserJet is off-line and contains buffered data. To resolve this situation, re-insert the appropriate font cartridge and press the CONTINUE key.

FC [LEFT, RIGHT, BOTH]

Message *FE CARTRIDGE* appears whenever you remove a font cartridge while the printer is on-line. The only way to recover from this situation is to re-insert the font cartridge, turn the printer off, and turn it back on again.

FE CARTRIDGE

Message *UC LOAD* and a paper size (*A4*, *EXEC*, *LETTER*, or *LEGAL*) appear when the LaserJet IID printer expects you to load the appropriate size paper into the appropriate paper tray, then insert that paper tray into the LaserJet IID's upper printer slot.

UC LOAD [paper size]

Message *LC LOAD* and a paper size (*A4*, *EXEC*, *LETTER*, or *LEGAL*) appear when the LaserJet IID printer expects you to load the appropriate size paper into the appropriate paper tray, then insert that paper tray into the LaserJet IID's lower printer slot.

LC LOAD [paper size]

Message *UE LOAD* and an envelope size (*COM-10*, *MONARCH*, *DL*, *C5*, or *ENVELOPE*) appear when the LaserJet IID printer expects you to load the appropriate size envelope into the envelope tray, then insert that envelope tray into the LaserJet IID's upper printer slot.

UE LOAD [envelope size]

LE LOAD
[envelope size]

Message *LE LOAD* and an envelope size (*COM-10*, *MONARCH*, *DL*, *C5*, or *ENVELOPE*) appear when the LaserJet IID printer expects you to load the appropriate size envelope into the envelope tray, then insert that tray into the LaserJet IID's lower printer slot.

UC or LC EMPTY

The message *UC EMPTY* or *LC EMPTY* appears whenever the upper or lower paper tray runs out of paper. When you see this message, you should remove the paper tray, refill it, and re-insert it into the printer.

UE, LE, or EE TRAY
[envelope size]

When the message *UE TRAY*, *LE TRAY*, or *EE TRAY* appears in the display window along with an envelope size (*COM-10*, *MONARCH*, *DL*, *C5*, or *ENVE-LOPE*), the printer has detected a new stack of envelopes in the upper, lower, or optional envelope feeder. When you see this message, make sure the envelopes you've inserted match the size shown in the display window. If they don't match, use the control panel's printing menu to select and save the envelope size.

Error messages

The last group of messages consists of printer error service messages. These messages usually indicate that a hardware problem has been detected inside the printer. If the action we recommend below does not correct the error, or if the error condition persists, contact your HP service representative for assistance.

20 ERROR

Error message *20 ERROR* indicates a memory overflow error. This error message appears whenever the data sent by the computer exceed the LaserJet's memory capacity. As you may know, the kinds of data that require large amounts of memory are soft fonts, graphics, and macros.

When you see the message *20 ERROR*, press the CONTINUE key to clear the error and to resume printing. Since a memory overflow error has occurred, however, the LaserJet will print only the data that fit in the printer's memory. To reprint your image without running into *20 ERROR* again, reformat your page so that it requires less printer memory. Some ways to reduce the amount of required memory include decreasing print resolution and decreasing the point size of your larger fonts. If the message *20 ERROR* persists, you should consider adding more memory to your LaserJet. HP offers 1, 2, and 4MB memory cards that you can buy and install for the LaserJet Series II printer. For more information on memory options for the LaserJet printer, see the section entitled "Memory Options" in Chapter 1.

21 ERROR

Error message *21 ERROR* indicates a print overrun error. During the printing process, the LaserJet's formatter starts formatting the page before the laser begins writing to the photosensitive drum. Under normal circumstances, the formatter works about 20 scan lines ahead of the laser. If the page being formatted is complex, however, the laser catches up to the formatter, and a print overrun error occurs.

The problem usually results from complex printer commands that cause the LaserJet's formatter to "jump around" the page instead of letting it work from left to right, top to bottom. For example, if your printer's software tells the LaserJet to print all text first, then all shading, then all graphics, the formatter will be moving back up to portions of the page it has already formatted. All of this up-and-down, back-and-forth movement will allow the laser to catch up to the formatter and will cause a print overrun error.

When you see this message, you can clear the error condition by pressing the LaserJet's CONTINUE key. After you've cleared the error, decrease the complexity of the page you are sending. For example, take shading off text, remove an image that overlaps another image, and so forth. After you've decreased the complexity as much as possible, re-send your document. If the problem persists, contact your software vendor or your HP service representative.

Error message *22 ERROR* appears when your printer and computer are not communicating properly, and improper signal protocols are being used. When you see this message, press the CONTINUE key to resume printing, and refer to the section entitled "Configuring Your LaserJet" in Chapter 2 to make sure you've configured the printer correctly. (Note: The LaserJet Series II uses XON/XOFF and DTR signal protocols, and does not use Enquire/Acknowledge.) Also make sure you are not using a defective printer cable. If the problem persists, contact your HP service representative.

22 ERROR

Error message *40 ERROR* indicates that a data error (parity, framing, or line overrun) occurred while the printer was receiving data from the computer. This message will appear if the LaserJet's configuration settings do not match the configuration settings on your computer. In addition, this message can appear when you reboot your computer while the LaserJet is on-line.

When you see this message, simply press the CONTINUE key to clear the error condition and to resume printing. If message *40 ERROR* occurs repeatedly, make sure your printer cable is not defective and is securely fastened to both the printer and to the computer. Also make sure your computer is correctly configured for your LaserJet printer. If the error still occurs, contact your HP dealer or service representative for assistance.

40 ERROR

Error messages *42 ERROR* and *43 ERROR* indicate that a problem has occurred on the card installed in the optional interface slot. When you see either of these messages, press the CONTINUE key to clear the error, and make sure the card in the optional I/O slot is configured properly. If the problem persists, contact your HP service representative.

42 or 43 ERROR

41, 51, 52, or 55 ERROR

If error message 41, 51, 52, or 55 appears in the display window, simply press the CONTINUE key to clear the error and resume printing. (You may experience some data loss in the process of clearing the error.) If the problem persists, contact your HP service representative.

53 ERROR

Error message *53 ERROR* indicates that a problem has occurred with the optional memory card in your printer. When you see this message, make sure you've obtained the appropriate card for your printer and the card has been installed correctly. Reset the printer by turning it off and back on again, then resume printing. If the problem persists, contact your HP service representative.

54 SERVICE

Error message *54 SERVICE* indicates that a problem has occurred while the printer was duplexing (printing to both sides of the paper). When you see this message, make sure your paper is the correct size, and then reset the printer by turning it off and back on again. If the problem persists, contact your HP service representative.

56 ERROR

Error message *56 ERROR* indicates an output selector error. When you see this message, reset the printer by turning it off and back on again. If the problem persists, contact your HP service representative.

50 SERVICE

Error message *50 SERVICE* indicates a fusing assembly malfunction. Unfortunately, the printer cannot immediately recover from this type of error. When you see this message, turn off the power to the printer, and leave it turned off for at least ten minutes. After you turn the printer back on, re-send the document that the LaserJet was printing when the error occurred.

63 SERVICE

Error message *63 SERVICE* indicates an internal memory check error, which means the LaserJet encountered a problem while checking its internal memory. If you have not installed any optional memory boards in your LaserJet, simply turn the printer off and then back on. If this does not clear the error condition, contact your HP service representative.

If you've installed a memory expansion board in your LaserJet, and you receive the error message *63 SERVICE*, turn off your printer and make sure you've installed the memory board correctly. Next, turn the printer back on. If the message still appears, turn off the printer, remove the memory board from your LaserJet, and turn the printer back on again. If no error message appears this time, your memory board is defective and needs to be replaced. If the message still appears, however, contact your HP service representative.

These error messages indicate various internal service errors. If any of these error messages appear on your printer, turn off the power to the printer, then turn it back on again. If the error message persists, contact your HP service representative.

61, 62, 64, 65, 67, or 68 SERVICE

Error message *69 SERVICE* indicates an optional interface error, which means a problem has occurred on the card installed in the optional interface slot. When you see this message, turn the printer off, and make sure the card in the optional I/O slot is configured properly and is seated firmly. If the message still appears when you turn the printer back on, contact your HP service representative.

69 SERVICE

Error message *70 ERROR* indicates that you've installed a font cartridge that is not designed for the LaserJet printer. When you see this message, turn the printer off, remove the font cartridge, then turn the printer back on again.

70 ERROR

Error message *71 ERROR* indicates a miscellaneous font cartridge error. When you see this message, turn the printer off, remove the font cartridge, and turn the printer back on again. If you are unable to re-insert the font cartridge without generating a *71 ERROR* message, return the defective font cartridge to your HP dealer.

71 ERROR

Error message *72 SERVICE* indicates that a font cartridge was removed too quickly after it was inserted. When you see this message, turn the printer off, then turn it back on again.

72 SERVICE

Error message *79 SERVICE* indicates that the LaserJet has detected a firmware error. When you see this message, turn the printer off, then turn it back on again. If the error condition persists, contact your HP service representative.

79 SERVICE

Sooner or later, a sheet of paper will get jammed as it passes through the LaserJet. When this happens, the LaserJet's control panel will display a message that notifies you of the problem. If you use a LaserJet, LaserJet Plus, or LaserJet 500 Plus, the number *13* will appear in the status display; if you use a LaserJet Series II or LaserJet IID, the message *13 PAPER JAM* will appear in the display window.

Clearing Paper Jams

The procedure you should use to clear a paper jam depends on which LaserJet model you use. We'll outline the steps necessary to clear paper jams in the LaserJet, LaserJet Plus, LaserJet Series II, and LaserJet IID.

LaserJet and
LaserJet Plus

Figure 3-39 shows the path of the paper as it flows through the LaserJet and LaserJet Plus. Paper jams usually occur in one of four areas: (1) the manual feed area, (2) the cassette feed area, (3) the separation/feeder area, or (4) the fusing/delivery area. When a paper jam occurs, take the following steps to correct the problem:

FIGURE 3-39

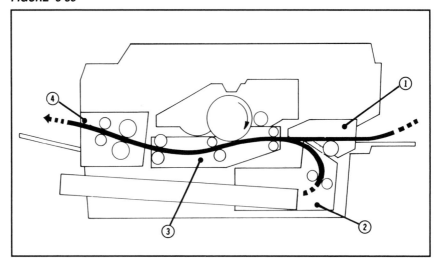

Paper that passes through the LaserJet and LaserJet Plus usually jams in one of these four areas.

1) Press the release lever and open the main body cover of the printer, as shown in Figure 3-40. (Since some parts of the printer are light-sensitive, make sure you close the cover as soon as you've cleared the paper jam.)

2) Look for the jammed paper in the separation/feeder area, as shown in Figure 3-41 on page 120. If the paper is stuck in this area, firmly grasp the edges of the paper and carefully pull it out of the printer.

3) If the jammed paper is not in the separation/feeder area, open the green fusing assembly cover and look for the jammed sheet. If you see it there, firmly grasp the edges of the paper and gently pull it out of the printer, as shown in Figure 3-42 on page 121. If you can't remove the jammed paper, proceed to step 4.

FIGURE 3-40

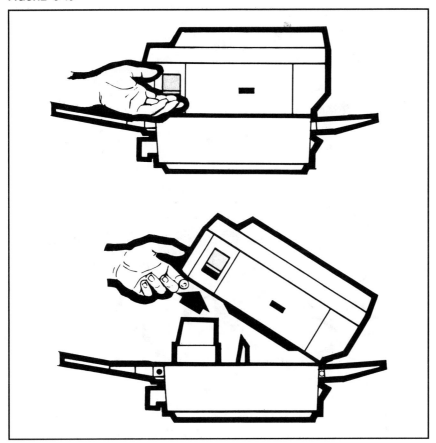

Press the release lever to open the printer's main body cover.

FIGURE 3-41

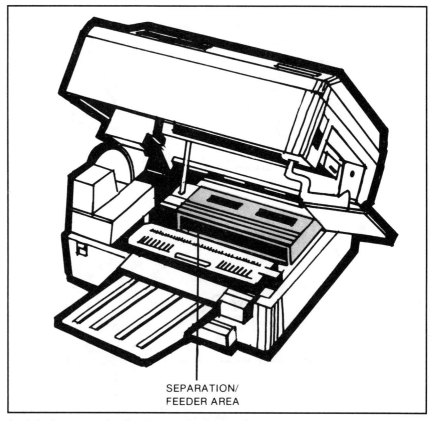

SEPARATION/
FEEDER AREA

Look in the separation/feeder area for jammed paper.

4)   If you could not remove the jammed paper in step 3, open the rear door and look
     for the jammed sheet. If you see it there, gently pull the paper out of the printer,
     as shown in Figure 3-43, and close the rear door.

5)   After you've removed the jammed paper, close the main body cover and press
     the CONTINUE key on the control panel to resume printing. The LaserJet will
     automatically reprint the page that was being printed when the jam occurred.

FIGURE 3-42

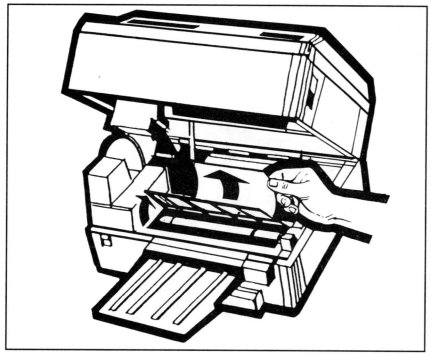

Look under the fusing assembly cover for the jammed page.

FIGURE 3-43

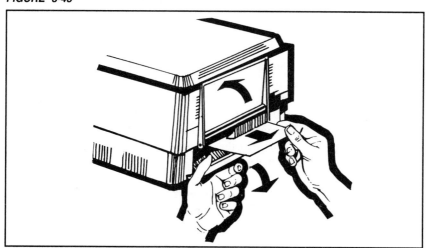

If the jammed page is behind the printer's rear door, remove it and close the door.

LaserJet Series II

Figure 3-44 shows the path of the paper as it flows through the LaserJet Series II. Paper jams usually occur in (a) the fusing assembly area, (b) the transfer guide, or (c) the paper pick-up area.

FIGURE 3-44

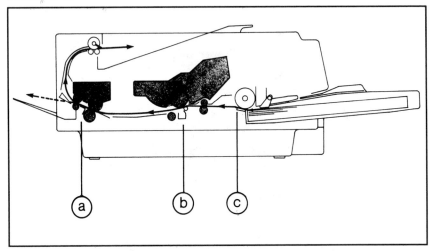

Paper that passes through the LaserJet Series II usually jams in one of these three areas.

When a paper jam occurs, take the following steps to correct the problem:

1) Open the printer's main body cover and look for the jammed paper. (Since some parts of the printer are light-sensitive, make sure you close the cover as soon as you've cleared the paper jam.)

2) If the paper is jammed in the paper pick-up area (area c in Figure 3-44), open the transfer guide lock tray and pull the paper out of the printer, as shown in Figure 3-45. If you cannot remove the jammed sheet of paper, remove the paper tray and pull the jammed paper out of the paper tray slot. (Note: Don't bend the transfer guide lock tray past the upright position. The tray will stand upright when fully opened. If you force the tray beyond the upright position, you can obstruct your LaserJet's paper path.)

3) If the paper is jammed in the transfer guide area (area b), open the transfer guide lock tray, and pull the paper out of the printer, as shown in Figure 3-46.

FIGURE 3-45

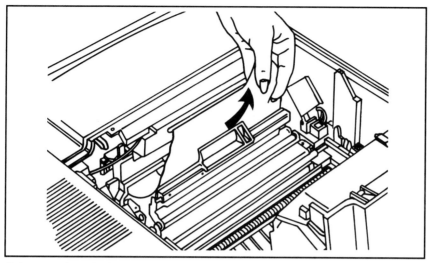

If the page jams in the paper pick-up area, simply pull the jammed page out of the printer.

FIGURE 3-46

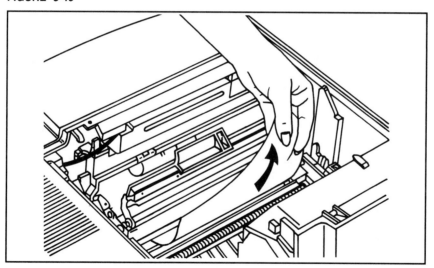

If the page jams in the transfer guide area, pull the jammed page out of the printer.

4) If the paper is jammed in the fusing assembly/final delivery area (area a in Figure 3-44), open the fusing assembly and remove the jammed paper, as shown in Figure 3-47. (Note: The fusing assembly area gets very hot, so be careful whenever you're working with the interior of the printer. Also be careful not to get any toner on your clothing—if you do, the toner will permanently stain it.)

FIGURE 3-47

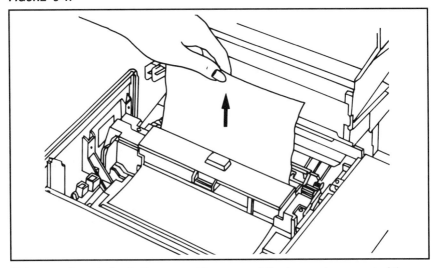

If the page jams in the fusing assembly area, pull the jammed page out of the printer.

5) After you've removed the jammed paper, close the main body cover of the printer. When the message *00 READY* appears in the display window, press the LaserJet's CONTINUE key or the ON LINE key to resume printing. The LaserJet will automatically reprint the page that was being printed when the jam occurred.

LaserJet IID

Figure 3-48 shows the path of the paper as it flows through the LaserJet IID. Paper jams usually occur in (1) the paper pick-up area, (2) the transfer guide area, (3) the fusing assembly area, (4) the duplex area, or (5) the switchback area.

Before we outline the procedures for clearing paper jams, take a moment to familiarize yourself with the LaserJet IID's paper paths. Figure 3-49 shows the rear exit paper path; Figure 3-50 shows the top exit paper path; and Figure 3-51 on page 126 shows the duplex paper path.

FIGURE 3-48

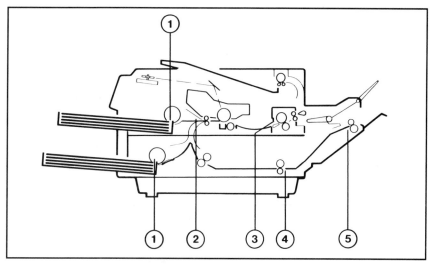

Paper that passes through the LaserJet IID can jam in any of these five areas.

FIGURE 3-49

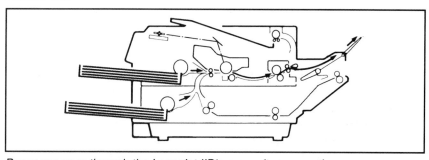

Paper can pass through the LaserJet IID's rear exit paper path.

FIGURE 3-50

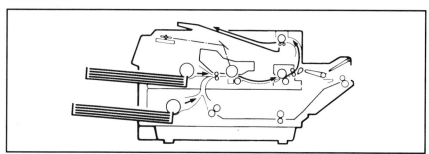

Paper can pass through the LaserJet's top exit paper path.

FIGURE 3-51

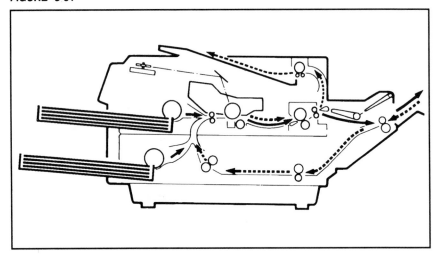

Paper can pass through the LaserJet's duplex paper path.

When a paper jam occurs, take the following steps to correct the problem:

1) Open the printer's main body cover and look for the jammed paper. (Since some parts of the printer are light-sensitive, make sure you close the cover as soon as you've cleared the paper jam.)

2) If the paper is jammed in the paper pick-up area, open the transfer guide lock tray and pull the paper out of the printer, as shown in Figure 3-52. If you cannot remove the jammed sheet of paper, remove the paper tray and pull the jammed paper out of the paper tray slot. (Note: Don't bend the transfer guide lock tray past the upright position. The tray will stand upright when fully opened. If you force the tray beyond the upright position, you can obstruct your LaserJet's paper path.)

3) If the paper is jammed in the transfer guide area, open the transfer guide lock tray and pull the paper out of the printer, as shown in Figure 3-53.

FIGURE 3-52

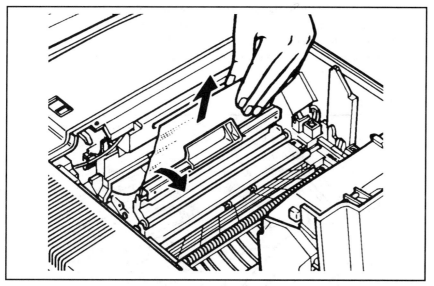

If the page is jammed in the paper pick-up area, simply open the transfer guide lock tray and pull the page out.

FIGURE 3-53

If the page is jammed in the transfer guide area, open the transfer guide lock tray and pull out the jammed page.

4) If the paper is jammed in the fusing assembly/final delivery area, open the transfer guide lock tray, then open the fusing assembly and remove the jammed paper, as shown in Figure 3-54. (Note: The fusing assembly area gets very hot—be careful whenever you're working with the interior of the printer. Also be careful not to get any toner on your clothing—if you do, the toner will permanently stain it.)

FIGURE 3-54

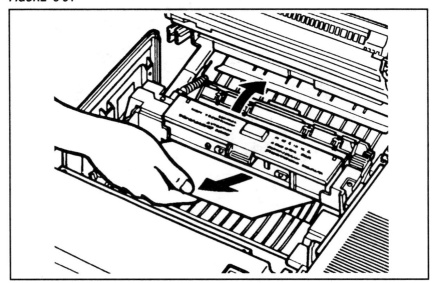

If the page jams in the fusing assembly area, grasp either end of the paper and pull it out of the printer.

5) If the jam occurs in the duplexing area, open the transfer guide lock tray and look for the jammed paper. Next, lift the handle on the printer's right side door, and remove the jammed paper. If necessary, open the rear output tray cover and remove the jammed paper, as shown in Figure 3-55.

6) If the jam occurs in the switchback area, open the left side door and remove the paper, as shown in Figure 3-56.

FIGURE 3-55

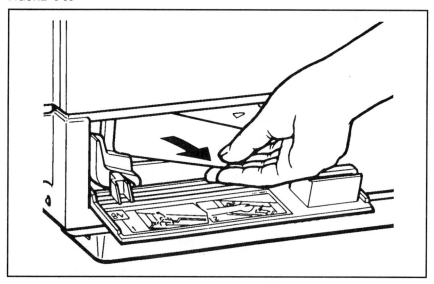

If the page is jammed in the duplexing area, open the rear output tray cover and remove the page.

FIGURE 3-56

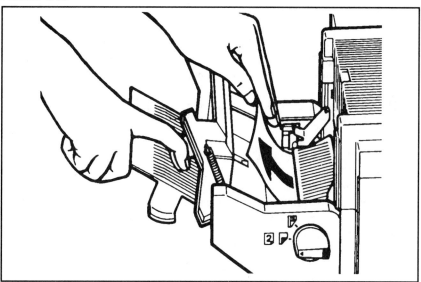

If the page is jammed in the switchback area, open the left side door and remove the page.

7) After you've removed the jammed paper, close the printer's main body cover. When the message *00 READY* appears in the display window, press the LaserJet's CONTINUE key or the ON LINE key to resume printing. The LaserJet will automatically reprint the page that was being printed when the jam occurred.

Trouble-shooting Communication Problems

If you cannot get your computer and your printer to communicate with each other, read the items on this troubleshooting checklist to see if you can identify the problem. If you follow the instructions in this section and you still cannot print, call HP's LaserJet Assist line for help.

1) Is the AC power cord attached properly and plugged into a 115 V power outlet?

2) Is the power switch in the ON (|) position?

3) Have you followed the instructions in Chapter 2 for configuring your LaserJet and your computer?

4) Are the interface cable connectors seated properly on both the printer end and on the computer end?

5) Does the printer come on-line when your turn on the power? (Is the ON LINE indicator lit after you flip on the power switch?)

6) Do any messages other than *00* (or *00 READY*) appear in the status display (or the display window)? If so, refer to the previous section, "Error and Status Messages," and take the steps recommended to solve your problem.

7) Have you performed a self-test? If not, follow the instructions on page 39 or 43 to test your printer.

If you've worked through the checklist and are still having trouble, your problem is probably either a paper jam, a faulty EP cartridge, or, if you use a LaserJet or LaserJet Plus, a broken separation belt.

Refer to the appropriate sections of this chapter for instructions to remedy these kinds of problems. As we have said, the operators on HP's LaserJet Assist line (208-323-2551) may be able to help you when all else fails.

CONCLUSION

Because the HP LaserJet printer is a very sophisticated piece of equipment, it requires regular maintenance in order to run smoothly. In this chapter, we've given you several maintenance tips and shown you how to resolve most of the problems you may encounter with your printer.

EQUIPPING YOUR LASERJET WITH FONTS 4

The first time you used an HP LaserJet printer, you probably thought it would have an immediate and dramatic effect on the appearance of your documents. However, if your experience was similar to ours, you were probably disappointed the first time the LaserJet issued a document printed with its internal 10-pitch Courier font. Although it may have appeared professionally printed, it probably lacked the flair you expect from a LaserJet.

In this chapter, we will show you how to add flair to your LaserJet documents. We'll explain how to take advantage of the LaserJet's ability to use several different sizes and types of fonts. We'll begin by looking at the different types of fonts that you can use with your LaserJet. After we've done this, we'll familiarize you with the terminology that we will use throughout *LaserJet Companion* when we discuss fonts. Finally, we'll end the chapter by showing you how to add fonts to your LaserJet.

FONT TYPES

A font is a collection of characters whose design is based on a specific set of physical or conceptual design characteristics. Each font has a unique name and is identified by its height, pitch, spacing, style, stroke weight, symbol set, and orientation. For example, the name of the font used to produce this text is Times. Its height is 10 points, its style is upright, and its stroke weight is medium. We'll define the terms height, spacing, style, stroke weight, symbol set, and orientation later in this chapter. In this section, we'll take a look at the types of fonts that we will encounter in *LaserJet Companion*.

PCL Fonts

All LaserJets support a specific set of internal fonts that can be used by any application. In addition, you can add fonts to your LaserJet by plugging in font cartridges, or by downloading them from your computer to RAM on the LaserJet. The fonts that you can use with a LaserJet are called PCL (Printer Control Language) fonts because they are designed to be used with the LaserJet's internal command language. In this section, we'll take a brief look at the types of fonts that are supported by or can be added to PCL- and PostScript-equipped LaserJets.

Internal fonts

All members of the LaserJet printer family support a specific set of internal fonts. For example, every LaserJet sports an Internal Medium Courier font. The bit maps—patterns of dots—that define the characters in these fonts are stored in ROM (Read Only Memory) within the LaserJet.

Cartridge fonts

You can add fonts to any LaserJet by plugging in a font cartridge. A font cartridge contains ROM on which the bit maps of characters supplied on that cartridge are stored. Font cartridges are available from HP as well as several third-party suppliers.

Soft fonts

Soft fonts are fonts whose bit maps are stored as software in a disk-based data file. Soft fonts can be used with any member of the LaserJet family except the original LaserJet. To use a soft font, you must download it from your PC to your LaserJet's RAM (Random Access Memory). We'll discuss the process of downloading soft fonts later.

HP SuperFonts

Most soft fonts you will encounter are designed for Portrait or Landscape orientation and support a specific symbol set. The orientation for which a font has been designed determines if a font can be used to print text along the width or along the length of a page. The symbol set refers to the actual set of characters supported by a font.

The bit-mapped image of an HP SuperFont is stored in a data file just as the bit map of any other soft font is stored in a data file. However, you cannot download SuperFonts directly to the LaserJet. Instead, you must use HP's MakeFont utility to specify which orientation and symbol set you want to use. Once you have done this, MakeFont will build the appropriate soft font file, which can be downloaded to the LaserJet with a utility such as FontLoad. We'll discuss SuperFonts later.

BitStream Fontware

Throughout *LaserJet Companion*, we'll encounter BitStream's Fontware and various forms of the Fontware Installation Kit. These products allow you to create bit-mapped PCL soft fonts from an outline.

An outline is a mathematical formula that describes the shape of a character. The main advantage of outlines is that they can be used to create characters of various sizes dynamically.

As we pointed out earlier, PCL soft fonts are based on bit maps. Therefore, outline-based fonts, such as those sold by BitStream under the trademark Fontware, cannot be sent directly to the LaserJet. Instead, you must use a utility program to convert outlines into bit maps. For example, you may use BitStream's Fontware Installation Kits to convert outline-based Fontware fonts into PCL bit-mapped fonts. We'll take a detailed look at the Fontware Installation Kit in Chapter 18.

Bit maps

All characters in PCL fonts are stored in the form of bit maps. A bit map is just what it sounds like: a map, or pattern, of bits that describes a shape—in this case, a letter or a number. The bit map for a PCL character is made up of hundreds of dots, each of which is $\frac{1}{300}$ inch tall and $\frac{1}{300}$ inch wide. These dots are arranged in a rectangle, called a cell, whose height is determined by the height (point size) of the character and whose width is determined by the width of the character. For example, the bit map for a character in a font that is 72 points (1 inch) high will be 300 dots high.

The bit map for any particular character tells the LaserJet which dots in the cell to print and which not to print to form that character. The status of each dot is controlled by a particular bit in the character's bit map. If the bit for a particular dot has the value 1, then the dot is printed. If the bit has the value 0, then the dot is left blank. The pattern of printed and nonprinted dots in the cell results in a character of the appropriate size and width.

The maximum height of a bit map varies according to the capabilities of your printer. For example, the LaserJet Series II can handle fonts that are 1,008 points (14 inches) tall, while the LaserJet Plus and LaserJet 500 Plus can handle only fonts that are 30 points (less than half an inch) tall. The height of characters used with the original LaserJet is limited to 18 points.

If you want to know more about bit maps, you can refer to Chapter 26. In that chapter, we'll show you how to create an actual bit-mapped character using the PCL.

PostScript Fonts

If your LaserJet is equipped with PostScript, you have access to a specific set of fonts that are supported by the version of PostScript you are using. For example, if you have a LaserJet Series II equipped with JetScript, you have access to 35 different fonts.

While PCL fonts exist as bit maps, all PostScript fonts exist in the form of outlines. A font outline is a mathematical formula that describes the shape of a font. The outline formula that describes the shape of a character can be manipulated to produce various sizes of that character.

The size of PostScript fonts can be automatically scaled from 4 points to infinity. In addition, PostScript fonts can be printed at any position on a page's x-y plane.

While you can't add PostScript fonts to your LaserJet by plugging in a font cartridge, you can add soft fonts. These are fonts whose outlines are stored in a disk-based data file that must be downloaded from your PC to the PostScript controller's RAM before they can be used.

Screen Fonts

Later in *LaserJet Companion*, we'll show you how the LaserJet can be used with several major PC software applications. Many of these applications have the ability to represent facsimiles of LaserJet fonts on your screen. In order to differentiate these fonts from LaserJet fonts, we'll refer to them as screen fonts.

With very few exceptions, screen fonts are application specific and cannot be printed by the LaserJet. Their sole purpose is to provide you with an on-screen WYSIWYG (What You See Is What You Get) representation of a document. In Chapter 16, we'll take a look at products that can be used to generate screen fonts that match LaserJet fonts.

FONT FEATURES

As we mentioned earlier, each font is based on a distinct set of design characteristics. In this section, we'll examine each of the characteristics that a font may possess and define the terms we will use to refer to these characteristics throughout *LaserJet Companion*.

Font Names

Each of the fonts we will encounter in *LaserJet Companion* has a unique name. A name is usually given to a font by the person or corporation that designed it. For example, the font used to produce this text, Times, was named by its designer, Linotype Corporation.

In most cases, the name of a font won't tell you much about the physical characteristics of the font, just as a person's name usually doesn't tell you much about the physical characteristics of a person. For instance, it's probable that upon hearing that BitStream produces a font called Broadway, you won't be able to form a mental picture of the font based on the name Broadway.

Typefaces

The set of physical and conceptual characteristics on which a font's design is based is called a typeface. All typefaces are identified by a unique name. Often the name of a typeface on which a font is based is the same as the name that has been given to the font. For example, the typeface on which the Courier font is based is known as the Courier typeface.

All typefaces are members of specific typeface families. These families are identified by specific sets of design characteristics on which they are based. Table 4-1 lists each of the typeface families you will encounter as you read *LaserJet Companion*. This table will help you make assumptions about the physical characteristics of fonts before you have actually seen them. For example, if someone tells you that the design of a font is based on a Modern typeface, you will be able to use the information in Table 4-1 to determine that it will be a fixed-space font with serifs and a constant stroke weight.

TABLE 4-1

Typeface	Characteristics			
	Stroke Weight	*Spacing*	*Serifs*	*Example*
Modern	Constant	Fixed	Yes	Courier
Swiss	Variable	Proportional	No	Helvetica
Roman	Variable	Proportional	Yes	Times
Script	Based on handwriting			*Chancery*
Decorative	Ornamental/Symbols			◀▶ ↵ ➡ ⬅ ↓ ↑

The design characteristics common to five typeface families are listed in this table.

Character Style

The style of a font refers to the angle at which characters appear in relation to the vertical axis of a page. For example, upright characters are those that stand straight on the vertical axis, while italic characters are slanted slightly to the right. Examples of upright and italic characters are shown in Figure 4-1.

FIGURE 4-1

Upright: ABCDEFGHIJKLMNOPQRSTUVWXYZ
Italic: ABCDEFGHIJKLMNOPQRSTUVWXYZ

The style of a character is determined by the position in which it appears in relation to the vertical axis of a page.

In some cases, you may find that characters slanted to the right on the vertical axis are referred to as oblique rather than as italic. When hand-tooled fonts (those that were originally created by hand) are slanted to the right, they have historically been referred to as italic. On the other hand, geometric fonts (those originally created with the assistance of drafting instruments) have historically been referred to as oblique. With the passage of time, the original intent of these terms, which was to differentiate two different classes of fonts, has been widely forgotten. As a result, you will find that characters slanted to the right on the vertical axis are usually referred to as italic.

Italic or oblique characters are usually used to draw the reader's attention to, or place emphasis on, a particular word within a sentence. For example, as you can see in this sentence, it's very *easy* to see that the word *easy* is the one we want you to notice.

Stroke Weight

Stroke weight is a term used to describe the thickness, or width, of the lines used to construct a particular character. A font's stroke weight can be varied or fixed, depending on the typeface on which its design is based. There are three general measures of stroke weight—light, medium, and bold. Examples of each are shown in Figure 4-2.

FIGURE 4-2

Light
Medium
Bold

The thickness of lines used to produce a character determines its stroke weight.

Characters that are classified as light are formed by a series of extremely thin lines, while those classified as medium, such as the one used to produce this text, are formed by a series of double lines. You should use light and medium characters to produce the body of a document.

Bold characters are formed by a series of extremely thick lines. Like italic characters, bold characters are usually used to bring the reader's attention to a particular word within a paragraph. For example, in this sentence, it's very **easy** to determine that the word **easy** is the one we want you to notice.

Character Spacing

Since the LaserJet can print text using fixed-space and proportionally spaced fonts, it's important to understand the concepts behind fixed and proportional character spacing. Likewise, it's equally important to understand the effect character spacing can have on your documents. In this section, we'll define the concepts and terminology related to character spacing.

Proportional spacing

The amount of space that a character occupies on a line has a dramatic effect on the appearance of your documents. The Times font used to produce this paragraph is a proportionally spaced font. In other words, each character in this font occupies space on a line in accordance with its size. For example, a character such as *i* occupies less space on a line in this paragraph than does a character such as *G*. As a result, the number of *G*s you can print on a line when using a proportional font will be smaller than the number of *i*'s you can print on a line.

Fixed spacing

On the other hand, the Courier font is a fixed-space font. In other words, each character in this font occupies a fixed amount of space on a line, regardless of the fact that some characters are smaller or bigger than others.

For example, while characters such as *i* are smaller than characters such as *G*, they each occupy the same amount of space on a line.

The unit used to measure the width of characters in a fixed font is called pitch. Technically, a font's pitch is equivalent to the number of characters that can appear in a single inch. For example, a 10-pitch font is one in which each character will occupy $^1/_{10}$ inch on a line. Therefore, when using a 10-pitch font, you can expect ten characters to appear in each inch. Figure 4-3 shows a sample of the LaserJet's Internal 10-pitch Medium Courier font.

FIGURE 4-3

```
1234567890
```

The number of characters that can be printed in one inch determines the pitch of those characters.

Symbol Set

All of the fonts we will encounter in *LaserJet Companion* are based on sets of 256 symbols. Each of these symbols is associated with a unique value from Ø to 255. The specific set of symbols a font supports, as well as the values that represent them, is referred to as the font's symbol set.

Standard symbols

The American Standard Code for Information Interchange (ASCII), which is recognized by Hewlett-Packard, specifies values that must be assigned to particular symbols within a symbol set. For example, in any symbol set based on the ASCII standard, the character *A* should be identified by the decimal value 65.

Unfortunately, the ASCII standard only defines the symbols that must be assigned to codes Ø through 127. Therefore, as you might suspect, the symbols assigned to the values 128 through 255 can, and usually do, vary.

Symbol conflicts

In *LaserJet Companion*, we will deal primarily with two symbol sets: the HP Roman-8 symbol set and the PC symbol set. PCs and PS/2s use the IBM PC symbol set to display text on the video screen, while the Roman-8 symbol set is used by most HP and third-party LaserJet fonts. As a result, you can expect to run into conflicts between the symbols displayed by your PC and the symbol that will be printed when the decimal value that represents the PC symbol on your video screen is sent to the LaserJet. A table that shows the IBM PC and Roman-8 symbol set appears in Appendix 1.

The primary conflict between the Roman-8 and IBM PC symbol sets is the difference in the values used to represent characters beyond those defined by the ASCII standard. Consequently, when you send a document created with a PC or PS/2 to the LaserJet, the text the LaserJet prints will not match the text that appears on your screen if the font you are using does not support the PC symbol set, or if the application you are using does not adjust for the difference between the PC symbol set and the one supported by the font you are using.

For example, if you create a document with your PC or PS/2 that contains a pound sign (£), and try to print it using a LaserJet font that supports the Roman-8 symbol set, the result will not be satisfactory. The symbol for British pounds sterling (£) is associated with the decimal value 156 in the IBM PC symbol set, while it is associated with the decimal value 187 in the Roman-8 symbol set. Therefore, when the PC sends the value 156 to the LaserJet, the pound sign will not be printed. Instead, the character associated with the value 156 within the Roman-8 character set will be printed.

Unfortunately, there is no magic solution to the problem of conflicts between the PC and Roman-8 symbol sets. However, as we look at several popular PC applications, we will point out solutions when they exist.

Character Height

The height of a character is measured in units called points. One point is equivalent to $1/_{72}$ inch. However, if you measure a particular character, you will usually find that it is smaller than its point size suggests.

The reason for this is quite simple. A character's point size does not define the height of the character itself. Instead, it defines the height of a conceptual rectangle in which a character exists. All LaserJet characters exist in such a rectangle, which is known as a character cell.

For example, the character shown in Figure 4-4 is 72 points tall. If you measure this character, you will find that it is not 1 inch tall. However, if you measure the cell in which the character exists, you will find that it is 72 points, or 1 inch, tall.

FIGURE 4-4

1"

While the cell occupied by this character is 72 points tall, the character itself is less than $3/_4$ inch tall.

The reason characters do not occupy all of the space in the cell in which they exist is simple. Different characters naturally occupy different amounts of space. For example, the character *i* is much smaller than the character *M*. Therefore, while the height of the cell in which each character font can exist is constant, the amount of space each character occupies within its particular cell will vary according to its size.

As we mentioned earlier in this chapter, LaserJet fonts are often designed for a specific orientation. In other words, you can use them to print text in Portrait or Landscape mode. As you can see in Figure 4-5, when you use Portrait orientation, the LaserJet will print text along what you would normally consider to be the width of a page. On the other hand, when you use Landscape orientation, the LaserJet will print text along the length of a page.

FIGURE 4-5

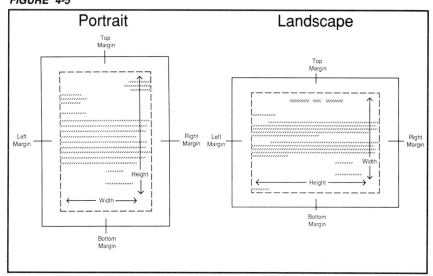

LaserJet fonts are often designed for use with a specific orientation.

The LaserJet IID and LaserJet 2000 can print any font in any orientation because all fonts are designed in relation to the PCL coordinate system. This system defines a grid on which fonts can be designed independent of orientation. We'll discuss the PCL coordinate system in detail in Chapter 20.

Serifs

Serifs are short lines that appear at the ends of, and at angles to, the main strokes of some characters. The Times font that was used to produce this text is a serif font.

Generally, you'll find that either serif or sans serif type works just fine for display type such as headings. However, studies have shown that serif type is more readable in the body of your document because the serifs help the reader to distinguish characters and words easily. They also add "horizontal stability," establishing a flow from left to right across a line of text.

As an example, a Helvetica *E* and a Times Roman *E* are shown in Figure 4-6. The Times Roman *E* has serifs, while the Helvetica *E* does not.

FIGURE 4-6

The tiny lines that terminate the ends of characters are known as serifs; characters that do not have these tiny lines are referred to as sans serif.

Ascenders and Descenders

An ascender is a portion of a character that appears above the main body of the character, while a descender is the portion of a character that appears below the main body of a character. Figure 4-7 shows some examples of ascenders and descenders. Most LaserJet fonts contain characters that feature ascenders and/or descenders.

FIGURE 4-7

Ascenders and descenders are design features common to most LaserJet fonts.

FONT MANAGEMENT

Throughout this chapter, we have familiarized you with several terms and concepts that we will use throughout *LaserJet Companion* when discussing fonts. In this section, we'll show you how these concepts and terms apply in practical situations.

Internal Fonts

As we showed you in Chapter 1, each member of the LaserJet family supports a certain number of internal fonts. For example, the LaserJet Series II supports internal versions of the Courier 10, Courier 10 Bold, and Line Printer fonts. Table 4-2 summarizes the fonts supported by each member of the LaserJet family.

As you can see, the only internal font common to all members of the LaserJet family is the Courier 10 font, which is the default internal font. In other words, if you (or the application you're using) do not specifically tell the LaserJet to use another font, it will automatically print all text using Courier 10.

If you want to use an internal font other than Courier 10, PC applications such as Microsoft Word will allow you to select the internal font you want to use to print a document. If the application you are using does not allow you to select another font, you can select fonts manually by sending PCL commands to the LaserJet. We'll show you how to select fonts with PCL in Chapter 23.

Finally, if you have a LaserJet Series II, LaserJet IID, or LaserJet 2000, you can use the control panel located on the front of your printer to change the default font. We showed you how to do this in Chapter 2.

TABLE 4-2

Printer	Internal fonts
LaserJet	Courier 10
LaserJet Plus	Courier 10, Line Printer
LaserJet 500 Plus	Courier 10, Line Printer
LaserJet Series II	Courier 10, Courier 10 Bold, Line Printer
LaserJet IID	Courier 10, Courier 10 Bold, Courier 10 Italic, Courier 12, Courier 12 Bold, Courier 12 Italic, Line Printer
LaserJet 2000	Courier 10, Courier 10 Bold, Courier 10 Italic, Prestige Elite, Prestige Elite Bold, Prestige Elite Italic, Tms Rmn, Tms Rmn Bold, Tms Rmn Italic, Helv Bold, Line Draw, Line Printer

Each member of the LaserJet family offers internal fonts.

Cartridge Fonts

If you need or want to use fonts other than those stored in ROM within your LaserJet, the easiest way to do so is to add a font cartridge. As we showed you in Chapter 2, you can plug at least one font cartridge into any member of the LaserJet printer family. If you have a LaserJet Series II or LaserJet IID, you can use two font cartridges at once, while the LaserJet 2000 allows you to use three.

Availability

At the time *LaserJet Companion* went to press, a total of 25 font cartridges were available from HP, while several others were available from third-party manufacturers. A list of font cartridges available for the LaserJet appears in Appendix 2.

Pros and cons

One of the most attractive aspects of cartridge fonts is the fact that they are easy to install. Also, since they are stored on ROM, cartridge fonts do not have to be downloaded to RAM. They are available as soon as you plug them into the LaserJet, or turn the LaserJet on while they are plugged in.

The main drawback of a cartridge font is that they are usually quite expensive. For example, a typical font cartridge will cost $100 to $300, while soft fonts can be purchased for as little as $15. Also, each font cartridge contains a specific set of fonts. Therefore, you may have to swap cartridges in and out of your LaserJet continually in order to gain access to the specific font you want to use.

Using cartridge fonts

If you want to use a cartridge font, begin by making sure your LaserJet is not on-line. As we showed you in Chapter 2, you can immediately determine if a LaserJet is on-line by checking the ON LINE LED on the control panel. If the LED is on, the LaserJet is on-line. If it is off, the LaserJet is not on-line. You can turn the ON LINE LED on and off by pressing the ON LINE button on your LaserJet.

Once you are sure that your LaserJet is not on-line, simply plug into one of your LaserJet's font cartridge slots the cartridge that contains the font you want to use. After you have done this, press the ON LINE button on the control panel to turn the LaserJet on. A more detailed explanation of how to plug a font cartridge into your LaserJet appears in Chapter 2.

Most PC applications can use the fonts stored in ROM within a cartridge to print a document. If the application you are using does not allow you to select and use a cartridge font, you can select it manually by sending PCL commands to the LaserJet. We'll show you how to select fonts with PCL in Chapter 23.

Many font cartridges, such as HP's Legal Courier H cartridge, contain a default font. When you plug a cartridge that contains a default font into your LaserJet , that font will immediately become the font the LaserJet will use to print all the text if you (or the application you are running) do not specifically select another font. The names of default fonts on HP-produced font cartridges are always marked with an *.

Finally, if you have a LaserJet Series II, LaserJet IID, or LaserJet 2000, you can use the control panel located on the front of your printer to select and use cartridge fonts. We explained how to do this in Chapter 2.

Soft Fonts

Soft fonts reside in data files that are stored on disk. To use these fonts, you must download them from disk to the LaserJet. We'll show you how to download soft fonts to your LaserJet in this section after we have discussed their availability, advantages, and drawbacks.

Availability

At the time *LaserJet Companion* went to press, 11 soft font packages were available from HP, while several others were available from third-party manufacturers. A list of soft fonts available for the LaserJet appears in Appendix 2.

Pros and cons

One of the most attractive aspects of soft fonts is their comparatively low price. For example, soft fonts can be purchased for as little as $15, while font cartridges may cost as much as $300. Another advantage soft fonts have over cartridge fonts is flexibility. For example, while it's possible you may pay $300 for a font cartridge and use only one of the fonts on the cartridge, you can buy soft fonts individually.

Soft fonts have four drawbacks. First, the files in which they are stored can occupy a large amount of disk space. Therefore, to use soft fonts, you'll need a hard disk. Second, the number of soft fonts you can use at one time is limited by the amount of RAM installed in your LaserJet. As a result, if you plan to use a large number of soft fonts, you may have to purchase more memory for your LaserJet.

Third, before you can use a soft font, you must download it to the LaserJet's RAM. This may take only a few seconds, or it can take several minutes, depending on the size and number of fonts you are downloading and the speed of the physical connection between your LaserJet and computer. Finally, since soft fonts are RAM based, they are volatile. In other words, whenever you turn off your LaserJet, any fonts that have been downloaded to RAM are lost. Therefore, you must download fonts each time you turn on your LaserJet.

The process of transferring soft font data from your PC to your LaserJet is called downloading. There are three ways to download fonts to the LaserJet. First, you can manually send a specific sequence of PCL commands to the LaserJet, followed by the bit mapped data that forms the font. We'll discuss the PCL commands that you must send to the LaserJet to download a soft font in Chapter 23.

Downloading

Second, you can use a download utility to automate the process of downloading soft fonts. Most soft fonts that you purchase are shipped with a download utility. We'll show you how to use the utilities that are included with HP soft fonts later in this section, and again in Chapter 18.

Finally, many PC applications have the ability to download soft fonts automatically. For example, we'll show you how Microsoft Windows and Microsoft Word can automatically download soft fonts when we discuss each product in Chapters 13 and 8, respectively.

If you have a LaserJet Plus or LaserJet 500 Plus, you can download as many as 32 soft fonts from your computer to your printer. On the other hand, if you have a LaserJet Series II, LaserJet IID or LaserJet 2000, you can download as many fonts to your printer as the amount of memory you have installed will allow. Unfortunately, the original LaserJet does not support soft fonts.

Hardware issues

HP now includes a utility called FontLoad with all HP-produced soft fonts. FontLoad can be used to automate completely the process of downloading soft fonts to your LaserJet. In this section, we'll explain the process of downloading a soft font to the LaserJet with FontLoad.

Downloading HP soft fonts with FontLoad

FontLoad requires MS-DOS 2.0 or later and 256K of memory. It also supports a Microsoft or Microsoft-compatible mouse. It is shipped with HP SuperFont packages, such as the HP Helv Headlines AG Soft Font, on a diskette titled SUPER FONT UTILITIES. FontLoad is shipped under separate cover with other HP soft fonts, where it is stored on a disk entitled FONT LOAD.

To run FontLoad, place the SUPER FONT UTILITIES or FONT LOAD disk in drive A, type **FLOAD** at the DOS prompt, and press ↵. After you have run FontLoad from the DOS prompt, the screen shown in Figure 4-8 will appear.

FIGURE 4-8

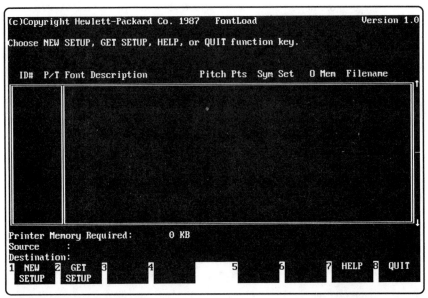

After you have run FontLoad from the DOS prompt, issue a NEW SETUP
command and enter the name of the directory in which the fonts you want to
download are stored.

*Issuing FontLoad
commands*

FontLoad can be operated with a mouse, or by pressing function keys. For
example, you can issue a NEW SETUP command by pressing [F1] or by clicking
on the box in the bottom-left corner of the screen with the mouse. Throughout our
discussion of FontLoad, we will refer to commands by mentioning the name that
identifies them at the bottom of FontLoad's display. Therefore, whenever we tell
you to execute one of these commands, remember that you can do so by pressing
the function key with which it is associated, or by clicking on the boxes at the bottom
of the screen with the left mouse button.

*Creating a new
SETUP file*

After you have run FontLoad, it will ask you to specify the name of the directory
in which PCL soft font data files are stored. At this prompt, you should type the
name of the directory and press ↵. For example, if the fonts you want to download
are stored in C:\FONTS, type **c:\fonts** at the prompt, and press ↵.

Once you have specified the directory in which your PCL soft font data files are
stored, FontLoad will prompt you to enter the name of the device to which your
LaserJet is connected. If your LaserJet is connected to LPT1:, you can press ↵ at
this prompt. Otherwise, at the prompt, type the name of the port to which your
LaserJet is connected and press ↵.

When you've provided FontLoad with the name of the directory in which your PCL soft font data files are stored and the port to which your LaserJet is connected, it will list on your screen all of the fonts found in the directory. For example, in Figure 4-9, FontLoad lists the soft fonts found in the directory C:\FONTS.

FIGURE 4-9

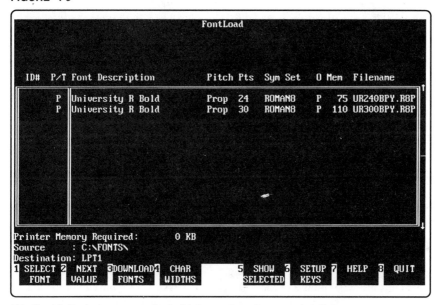

FontLoad displays a great deal of information about each soft font.

As you can see in Figure 4-9, FontLoad displays the ID number assigned to a font, along with its status (temporary or permanent). FontLoad also displays a description of each font, as well as its pitch, point size, symbol set, and orientation. Finally, FontLoad provides you with the name of the data file itself, as well as the amount of LaserJet memory that the font will occupy.

Before you select a font for downloading, you must tell FontLoad if it should be downloaded as a permanent or temporary soft font. If you download a soft font to your LaserJet as a permanent soft font, you must turn off the LaserJet's power to remove it from RAM. On the other hand, if you download a font to the LaserJet as a temporary soft font, you can remove it from RAM by issuing a printer reset from the control panel, or by sending a PCL command to the LaserJet. We'll discuss the PCL command that can be used to delete temporary soft fonts in Chapter 23; we explained how to issue a reset command with the control panel in Chapter 2.

To select a font's status, use your mouse, or the ↑,↓,→,←, or [Tab] keys to move the cursor to the line that contains the font's status setting. This setting is

Font status

located immediately below the heading P/T. Once you have placed the cursor on a font's status setting, click the mouse button once, or issue the NEXT VALUE command to toggle the setting from permanent to temporary or vice versa.

Font ID#

After you have specified whether a soft font should be downloaded as a temporary or permanent soft font, you may want to give it a specific ID number. If you do not want to assign a specific ID number to a soft font, FontLoad will automatically assign one to it when you select it for downloading. Soft font ID numbers must be unique and in the range of Ø to 32767. As we will show you in Chapter 23, they may be used in conjunction with a PCL command to select a font.

You may choose soft font ID numbers arbitrarily, or choose them to match ID numbers required by specific applications. If you plan to use soft fonts with products such as Microsoft Windows, the soft font ID you assign to the font when you download it with FontLoad must match the number Windows uses to select it. We'll show you how to use soft fonts with Microsoft Windows in Chapter 13.

To assign an ID number to a font, use your mouse or the ↑,↓,→,←, or [Tab] keys to move the cursor to the line that contains the font's ID number. This number is located immediately below the heading ID#. Once you have placed the cursor on a font's ID number, issue the NEXT VALUE command to increase the value, or use the keyboard to enter the value directly. For example, to assign the ID number 23 to a soft font, move the cursor above its ID # setting, and type **23**.

Selecting a font

The final step you must take to select a font for downloading is to highlight it. To do this, use your mouse or the ↑,↓,→, or ← keys to move the cursor to the line that contains the ID number, status setting, description, etc. When you have done this, issue the SELECT FONT command to select the font.

*Downloading more
than one soft font*

If you plan to download more than one font, repeat the process we've just described as many times as necessary. Regardless of the number of fonts you actually select, once you've finished making selections, you may issue the DOWN-LOAD command to download the fonts to the LaserJet. Once you have downloaded fonts to your LaserJet, you can quit FontLoad by issuing the QUIT command.

*Saving your
SETUP file*

After FontLoad has downloaded to the LaserJet the fonts you have selected, you may wish to save the present configuration to a disk file by issuing the SETUP KEYS command. As we will show you, you can use a saved configuration file to download the set of fonts automatically.

As you can see in Figure 4-10, when you issue the SETUP KEYS command, FontLoad will display a new set of commands in the command boxes that appear at the bottom of your screen. Once these commands have appeared, issue the SAVE SETUP command. At this time, FontLoad will prompt you to enter the name of the

file in which you want to save the present configuration. At this prompt, type the
file name, and press ↵. For example, if you want to save the present configuration
in a file called FAST, type **FAST** at the prompt, and press ↵.

FIGURE 4-10

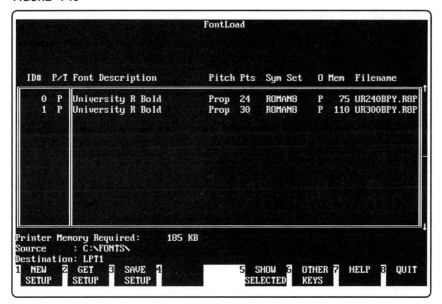

*When you issue the SETUP KEYS command, FontLoad will display a new set of
commands in the command boxes at the bottom of your screen.*

Once you have saved a SETUP file to disk, you can use it to simplify further
the task of downloading fonts with FontLoad. For example, after running Font-
Load, you can use the GET SETUP command to load a SETUP file from disk. By
loading a SETUP file from disk, you avoid the process of specifying the directory
in which PCL soft font data files are stored, selecting font ID numbers, etc.

You can completely avoid having to interact with FontLoad by specifying the
name of a SETUP file on the command line when you run it from the DOS prompt.
For example, if you have a SETUP file called AUTO that contains all of the settings
necessary to download a particular set of fonts to your LaserJet, you can invoke
FontLoad from the command **FLOAD AUTO /R**. The switch /R in this command
tells FontLoad to load the SETUP file AUTO and to download the fonts that are
selected within that SETUP file. If you want to load a SETUP file without
automatically downloading the fonts selected in that file, do not include the /R
switch on the command line.

*Using a saved
SETUP file*

Character widths

One feature of FontLoad that is not directly related to the process of downloading soft fonts is the CHAR WIDTHS command. This command produces a report listing the width of each character in a soft font. If you plan to use proportional soft fonts with products such as Microsoft Word, the report generated by the CHAR WIDTHS command can be very helpful. We'll discuss this command again in Chapter 18.

**Downloading
HP soft fonts
with PCLPak**

PCLPak is a utility that allows you to communicate with, and control the operation of, your LaserJet or LaserJet Plus. The only PCLPak feature we are concerned with at this point is soft font downloading. Therefore, in this section, we'll explain the process of downloading a soft font with PCLPak. We'll discuss PCLPak again in Chapter 18.

Before we move on, it is important to point out that PCLPak is not a state-of-the-art download utility. Therefore, if you have access to another soft font download utility, such as FontLoad, you'll probably find it to be superior to PCLPak. However, if PCLPak is what you have, it will get the job done.

PCLPak requires MS-DOS 2.0 or later and 256K of memory. In the past, it has been shipped as an independent product and has been included with HP packages. In both cases, it was provided on a disk labeled HP PCLPak. To run PCLPak, place the HP PCLPak disk in drive A, type **PCLPAK** at the DOS prompt, and press ↵.

Once you have run PCLPak from the DOS prompt, the screen shown in Figure 4-11 will appear. At this time, press **2** to select the LaserJet Plus as your printer. This will allow you to access PCLPak's soft font downloading features.

FIGURE 4-11

```
┌─────────────────────────────────────────────────────────┐
│ PCLPak  (A.00.02)            PRINTER SELECTION            │
│                                                          │
│ 1.LaserJet  2.LaserJet+  Help  Quitprogram               │
│                                                          │
│                                                          │
│ Type the number corresponding to your printer.           │
│                                                          │
│ >                                                        │
└─────────────────────────────────────────────────────────┘
```

When run from the DOS prompt, PCLPak will ask you to identify the printer you are using.

After you've told PCLPak that you are using a LaserJet Plus, the screen shown in Figure 4-12 will appear. At this time, issue the Fonts command by pressing **F**. As a result, PCLPak will display another series of commands. Now, issue the Download command by pressing **D**. Next, issue the File name command by pressing **F**, then type the name of the soft font file you want to download. For example, to download the file SYMBOL.USP, type **SYMBOL.USP** at this prompt, and press ↵.

FIGURE 4-12

```
┌──────────────────────────────────────────────────────────────────┐
│ PCLPak  (A.00.02)              MAIN                                 │
│                                                                    │
│ Pagesetup  Fonts  Managefiles  Others  Setdefaults  Help  Quitprogram │
│                                                                    │
│ Make sure your printer is on-line.  For help, type "H".            │
│                                                                    │
│ >                                                                  │
│                                                                    │
│ CURRENT FONT STATUS:                    CURRENT SETTINGS:           │
│                                                                    │
│ unknown                                 orientation:    portrait assumed │
│                                         paper source:   unknown    │
│                                         lines per page: not set    │
│                                         lines per inch: unknown    │
│                                         left margin:    unknown    │
│                                         right margin:   not set    │
│                                         copies:         unknown    │
│                                                                    │
│                                                                    │
│ DESTINATION:  LPT1:                                                │
└──────────────────────────────────────────────────────────────────┘
```

The Fonts command on PCLPak's main menu allows you to access the commands that may be used to download soft fonts.

Next, issue the Temp/perm command by pressing **T**. This command will allow you to tell PCLPak if the font you are about to download should be treated as a temporary or permanent soft font. If you want to download the font as a permanent font, press **P**. If you want to download it as a temporary font, press **T**. As we mentioned during the discussion of HP's FontLoad utility, permanent soft fonts will survive a printer reset, while temporary soft fonts will not. Also, temporary soft fonts can be removed from LaserJet RAM using PCL commands that we will discuss in Chapter 23.

The next step is to assign to the soft font a unique ID number in the range Ø to 32767. As we will show in Chapter 23, you may use ID numbers with PCL commands to select and use a font.

You may choose soft font ID numbers arbitrarily or choose them to match ID numbers required by a specific application. If you plan to use soft fonts with products such as Microsoft Windows, the soft font ID you assign to the font when you download it with FontLoad must match the number Windows uses to select it. We'll show you how to use soft fonts with Microsoft Windows in Chapter 13.

To assign an ID number to a soft font with PCLPak, issue the Id command by pressing **I**, then type the ID number at the prompt, and press ↵. For example, to assign the ID number 32 to a soft font, press **I**, type **32** at the prompt, then press ↵.

Once you have defined the name of the soft font you want to download, and have given it a temporary or permanent status in addition to an ID number, you can download it by pressing **G** to issue the Go command. Once the font has been downloaded, you may repeat the process to download any number of additional fonts. Finally, to quit PCLPak, press **Q** to issue the Quitmenu command to return to the main menu, then issue the Quitprogram command by pressing **Q** again.

Downloading HP soft fonts with DOWNLOAD.BAT

DOWNLOAD.BAT is a batch file that HP supplies with many of its soft fonts. For example, all of the BitStream soft fonts marketed by HP are shipped with a copy of DOWNLOAD.BAT. In this section, we'll explain the process of downloading a soft font with DOWNLOAD.BAT.

Before we move on, we need to point out that DOWNLOAD.BAT is a rather Spartan product. In other words, it has no superfluous features. Therefore, if you have access to a download utility such as FontLoad, you may want to use it instead. If you have only DOWNLOAD.BAT, don't worry; it will get the job done.

To use DOWNLOAD.BAT, place the soft font diskette that contains the files DOWNLOAD.BAT, PERMTEMP.EXE and IDFONT.EXE in drive A and type **DOWNLOAD** followed by the name of the soft font you wish to download. If the soft font data file UR240BPY.R8P is stored in a directory on your hard disk called C:\FONTS, you can use DOWNLOAD.BAT to download it to the LaserJet by typing **DOWNLOAD C:\FONTS\UR240BPY.R8P** at the DOS prompt.

When you invoke DOWNLOAD.BAT, it will run IDFONT.EXE, which will display the text shown in Figure 4-13. As you can see in this figure, IDFONT.EXE prompts you to assign a unique ID number to the font. As we will show you in Chapter 23, a font's ID number can be used in conjunction with a PCL command to select and use the font. Font ID numbers must be unique for each font and must be in the range Ø to 32767.

You may choose soft font ID numbers arbitrarily or choose them to match ID numbers required by specific applications. If you plan to use soft fonts with products such as Microsoft Windows, the soft font ID you assign to the font when you download it with FontLoad must match the number Windows uses to select it. We'll show you how to use soft fonts with Microsoft Windows in Chapter 13.

FIGURE 4-13

```
C:\FONTS
.download c:\fonts\ur240bpy.r8p

C:\FONTS
.echo off
First, ensure the printer is powered ON


What font ID number would you like to assign
to the downloaded font?
(Enter a number between 0 and 32767, then press RETURN)

Font ID # =
```

IDFONT.EXE will ask you to assign ID numbers to each soft font before it is downloaded.

To assign an ID number to a font with DOWNLOAD.BAT, type the number at the prompt shown in Figure 4-13, and press ↵. For example, to assign the font ID number 69 to a soft font, type **69** at the prompt, and press ↵.

After you have assigned an ID number to a soft font, DOWNLOAD.BAT will execute PERMTEMP.EXE. As you can see in Figure 4-14, PERMTEMP.EXE prompts you to specify whether the font you are about to download should be downloaded as a permanent or temporary soft font. Permanent soft fonts will survive a printer reset, while temporary soft fonts will not. Also, as we will show you in Chapter 23, temporary soft fonts can be deleted from LaserJet RAM with a PCL command. When DOWNLOAD.BAT prompts you to specify whether a soft font should be permanent or temporary, reply by choosing **P** or **T**, then press ↵.

FIGURE 4-14

```
.echo off
First, ensure the printer is powered ON


What font ID number would you like to assign
to the downloaded font?
(Enter a number between 0 and 32767, then press RETURN)

Font ID # =  69

        1 File(s) copied


Would you like the downloaded font to be
permanent or temporary?
Please enter a P (permanent) or T (temporary) & press RETURN

Permanent or Temporary?
```

PERMTEMP.EXE will ask you if the font it is about to download should be downloaded as a permanent or temporary font.

After you have specified whether the font should be treated as permanent or temporary, PERMTEMP.EXE will ask if you would like to see a sample of text printed with the font. If you do not want to print a sample, press **N** and you will be returned to the DOS prompt. On the other hand, if you do want to print a sample, press **Y**. As a result, PERMTEMP will ask you if the font you have just downloaded is designed for Portrait or Landscape printing. If the font is a Portrait font, type **P**, then press ↵. If it is a Landscape font, type **L**, then press ↵. Once you have done this, PERMTEMP will produce a print sample similar to the one shown in Figure 4-15 and will return you to the DOS prompt.

FIGURE 4-15

```
!"#$%&'()*+,-./0123456789:;<=>?
@ABCDEFGHIJKLMNOPQRSTUVWXYZ[\]^_
'abcdefghijklmnopqrstuvwxyz{|}~▓

ÀÁÊÈÈÏÍ´`^¨˜ÙÛ£¯Ý°ÇçÑñì¿¤£¥§ƒ¢
âêôûáéóúàèòùäëöüÅîØÆåíøæÄíÖÜÉñßÔ
ÁÅãÐðÍÓÒÕõšÚŸÿÞþµ¶¾–¼½ªº«■»±
```

The font ID for this font is 69 .

*PERMTEMP.EXE
will generate a
sample printout
using the font you
have just downloaded.*

If you want, you can download as many soft fonts as the amount of memory in your LaserJet will allow by repeating the process we have just described. However, one of the limitations of DOWNLOAD.BAT is that it will allow you to download only one font at a time.

HP SuperFonts

As we discussed earlier in this chapter, HP SuperFonts are essentially data files that contain the bit-mapped images of fonts. However, before you can download these images to the LaserJet with a utility such as FontLoad, you must specify the symbol set and orientation of the fonts. To do this, you must run a utility program included with SuperFonts called MakeFont.

MakeFont requires MS-DOS 2.0 or later, 256K of memory, and supports a Microsoft or Microsoft-compatible mouse. MakeFont is shipped with HP Super-Font packages, such as the HP Helv Headlines AG Soft Font, on a disk titled SUPERFONT UTILITIES. To run MakeFont, place this disk in drive A, type **MFONT** at the DOS prompt, and press ↵.

*Specifying the
SuperFont directory*

After you have run MakeFont from the DOS prompt, the screen shown in Figure 4-16 will appear. When this screen appears, MakeFont asks you to enter the name of the directory that contains the SuperFont data files from which you want to create PCL bit-mapped data files that can be downloaded to the LaserJet.

FIGURE 4-16

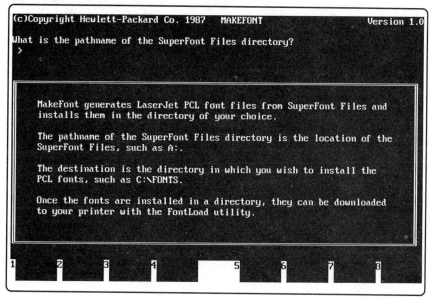

After you run MakeFont from the DOS prompt, it will ask you to provide the name of the directory in which SuperFont data files are stored.

When MakeFont prompts you to specify the name of the directory in which SuperFont data files are stored, type the name of the directory at the prompt, and press ↵. For example, if you plan to use SuperFont data files stored on a disk in drive B, type **b:** at the prompt, and press ↵.

After you have provided MakeFont with the location of the SuperFont files from which you want to create PCL bit-mapped data files, it will display a screen similar to the one shown in Figure 4-17. As you can see in this figure, MakeFont lists the names of the SuperFont data files found in the directory you specified and prompts you to enter the name of the directory in which the data files should be written. For example, if you want data files to be stored in a directory named C:\FONTS, type **c:\FONTS** at this prompt, and press ↵.

Specifying a soft font directory

FIGURE 4-17

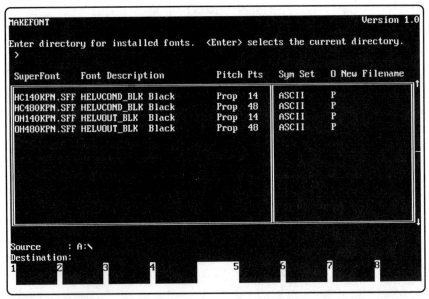

After you have specified the directory in which SuperFont data files are stored, MakeFont will display a list of those files and ask you where the PCL bit-mapped data files should be written.

After you have supplied MakeFont with the name of the directory in which you want it to install PCL bit-mapped data files, it will prompt you to enter the name of the directory containing the symbol list file. MakeFont uses the symbol list file to build fonts based on one of the symbol sets listed in Table 4-3. This file is stored on the same disk with MakeFont. Therefore, place the SUPERFONT UTILITIES disk in a floppy disk drive, and enter the name of the drive at the prompt. For example, if the SUPERFONT UTILITIES disk is in drive A, type **a:** at the prompt, and press ↵.

TABLE 4-3

ASCII	ISO UK
Roman-8	ISO GER
EC-94 L1	ISO IT
Legal	ISO SWED
PC-8	ISO SP17
PC-8 D/N	ISO DN
PC-850	ISO FR69

MakeFont can create SuperFonts using any of these symbol sets.

Once you have provided MakeFont with the location of the symbol list file, you can begin the process of creating PCL bit-mapped data files. As you can see in Figure 4-18, MakeFont lists the name of each SuperFont data file, a description, and the pitch, point size, symbol set, and orientation of each font.

FIGURE 4-18

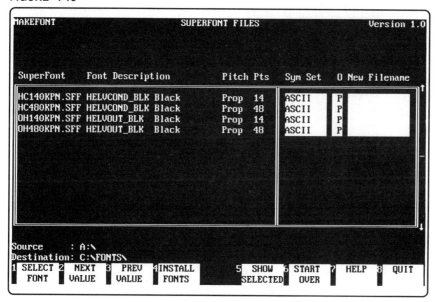

```
MAKEFONT                 SUPERFONT FILES                    Version 1.0



   SuperFont     Font Description        Pitch Pts   Sym Set   O New Filename
  HC140KPN.SFF  HELVCOND_BLK  Black      Prop  14   ASCII    P
  HC480KPN.SFF  HELVCOND_BLK  Black      Prop  48   ASCII    P
  OH140KPN.SFF  HELVOUT_BLK   Black      Prop  14   ASCII    P
  OH480KPN.SFF  HELVOUT_BLK   Black      Prop  48   ASCII    P








Source      : A:\
Destination: C:\FONTS\
 1 SELECT  2  NEXT   3  PREV  4 INSTALL      5  SHOW   6 START  7  HELP  8  QUIT
   FONT       VALUE     VALUE   FONTS         SELECTED  OVER
```

FontLoad displays a great deal of information about each HP SuperFont.

MakeFont can be operated with a mouse or by pressing function keys. For example, as you can see in Figure 4-18, you can issue the SELECT FONT command by pressing [F1] or by clicking on the box in the bottom-left corner of the screen with the mouse. Throughout our discussion of MakeFont, we will refer to commands by providing the name that identifies them at the bottom of MakeFont's display. Therefore, whenever we tell you to execute one of these commands, remember that you can do so by pressing the function key with which it is associated, or by clicking on the boxes at the bottom of the screen with the left mouse button.

Issuing MakeFont commands

To create a PCL bit-mapped data file, use the ↑ and ↓ keys or your mouse to move the cursor to the line that contains the name and description of the font, and issue the SELECT FONT command. If you are using a mouse, you can click on the arrow keys to the right of the window that displays the names of the SuperFonts to scroll through the list of SuperFonts.

Creating a soft font

Once you have selected all of the fonts you want to install, you can use the cursor-movement keys, [Tab] key, or mouse to position the cursor above each font's symbol set, orientation, or new file name setting. You can toggle the symbol set and orientation setting by issuing either the NEXT VALUE or PREV VALUE command, and you can use the keyboard to enter the file name in which the bit-mapped data for that font will be stored.

After you have chosen the symbol set, orientation, and new file name for each font you want to install, issue an INSTALL FONTS command to create the PCL bit-mapped data files. When the files have been created, you may quit MakeFont by issuing the QUIT command.

Using soft fonts

After you have downloaded a soft font, PC applications such as Microsoft Word will allow you to use the font to print a document. If the application you are using will not allow you to select and use a particular soft font, you can select it manually by sending PCL commands to the LaserJet. We'll show you how to select fonts with PCL in Chapter 23.

CONCLUSION

In this chapter, we've defined several terms and concepts that you'll encounter as you use *LaserJet Companion*. If you understand all of the definitions we've presented, you're ready to proceed to the next section of *LaserJet Companion*.

Also, in this chapter, we've taken a look at three utilities that you can use to download soft fonts to the LaserJet. If you plan to use soft fonts with your LaserJet, it is essential that you understand the process of downloading. Therefore, if you do not feel confident that you understand the process at this time, take a few moments to reread the section on downloading, and experiment with your own soft fonts.

THE COBB GROUP

The
Best

· GUARANTEED ·

DOS Applications

Section Two

Using the LaserJet
with DOS Applications

While the vast majority of DOS applications now support the LaserJet family of printers, adding this support to an application can be tricky. Furthermore, once you have added LaserJet support to an application, the procedures and/or commands that allow you to take advantage of that support are usually poorly documented. With these facts in mind, our goal in Section Two is to explain in detail the process of adding support for the LaserJet to several major DOS applications. Once we've done this, we'll look at the procedures and/or commands that allow you to use that support.

In Chapters 5 through 11, we'll show you how to add LaserJet support to WordPerfect, Lotus 1-2-3, WordStar, Microsoft Word, DisplayWrite, dBASE III Plus, and Ventura Publisher. When necessary, we'll show you how to build printer drivers that support the fonts and features you want to use with these applications. Additionally, we'll discuss issues you should consider when using these features.

Finally, in Chapter 12, we'll introduce you to *LaserJet Companion TechNotes* for other DOS applications. Essentially the equivalent of a chapter in *LaserJet Companion*, *LaserJet Companion TechNotes* provide you with all the information you need to use applications not discussed in *LaserJet Companion*.

WORDPERFECT 5 **5**

WordPerfect 5 is the latest version of WordPerfect Corporation's popular word processing product. While previous versions of WordPerfect have featured a great amount of support for the LaserJet, WordPerfect 5's LaserJet support is truly exceptional. For example, WordPerfect 5 provides full support for all members of the LaserJet printer family, all HP cartridge and soft fonts, and all types of paper and envelopes that you might use.

In this chapter, we'll show you how to take advantage of the LaserJet features that WordPerfect supports directly. More importantly, we'll show you how to add support to WordPerfect for third-party soft fonts—a task that is not explained in documentation shipped with WordPerfect.

INSTALLING LASERJET SUPPORT

Support for the LaserJet is not a built-in feature of WordPerfect 5—you must add it after you have installed WordPerfect on your system. The command that allows you to add LaserJet support to WordPerfect is located on the Print menu. To access this menu, which is shown in Figure 5-1 on the next page, press **[Shift][F7]**.

The only command on this menu that we will be concerned with at this time is the Select Printer command. You must use this command to add LaserJet support to WordPerfect. To execute the Print menu's Select Printer command, type **S**. When you do this, the Print: Select Printer screen shown in Figure 5-2 will appear on your monitor. The commands located at the bottom of this screen allow you to add, edit, or delete printer support.

FIGURE 5-1

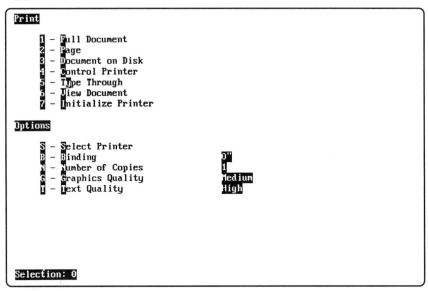

The Select Printer command on WordPerfect 5's Print menu allows you to add or modify LaserJet support.

FIGURE 5-2

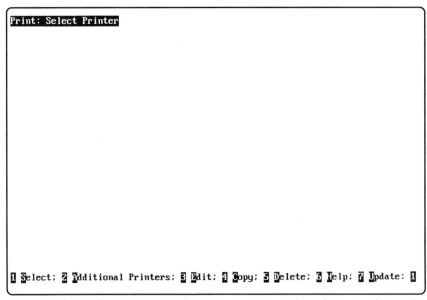

The Print: Select Printer screen will appear on your monitor when you choose the Print menu's Select Printer command.

To add support for a LaserJet to WordPerfect, choose the Print: Select Printer screen's Additional Printers command by typing **2** or **A**. WordPerfect will respond by informing you that it was not able to find any printer files. When this occurs, place the Printer 1 disk in drive A, then choose the Other Disk command by pressing **2** or **O**. This command will display the prompt *Directory for printer files:* in the bottom-left corner of the screen. Type **A:** at this prompt, press ↵, and the Select Printer: Additional Printers menu shown in Figure 5-3 will appear on your monitor.

FIGURE 5-3

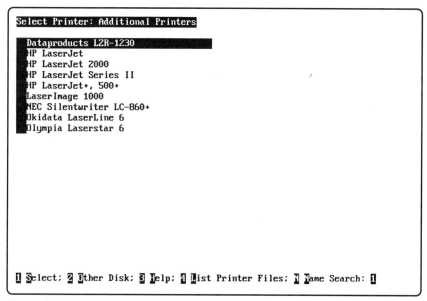

The Select Printer: Additional Printers menu allows you to choose the specific LaserJet you are using.

Selecting a LaserJet

When the Select Printer: Additional Printers menu appears on your screen, use the ↑, ↓, →, or ← key to highlight the name of the printer you plan to use with WordPerfect, then press 1 or ↵. For example, if you plan to use a LaserJet Series II, highlight **HP LaserJet Series II**, then press **1** or ↵.

While the Printer 1 disk did not contain support for the LaserJet IID when *LaserJet Companion* went to press, WordPerfect Corporation has assured us that LaserJet IID support will be provided in future releases. Until that support is provided, you should choose the **HP LaserJet 2000** option if you plan to use a LaserJet IID with WordPerfect. Later in this chapter, we'll discuss the changes you must make to the HPLAS200.PRS printer resource file to ensure complete compatibility with the LaserJet IID.

After you have selected the printer you plan to use, WordPerfect will display a prompt asking you to confirm the name to be assigned to the printer resource file containing the information needed to use that printer. For instance, if you select HP LaserJet Series II, WordPerfect will display the prompt *Printer Filename: HPLASEII.PRS*. Table 5-1 lists the file names WordPerfect will suggest for the printer resource files that let you use each member of the LaserJet printer family.

TABLE 5-1

Printer	Filename
LaserJet	HPLASERJ.PRS
LaserJet Plus	HPLAS500.PRS
LaserJet 500 Plus	HPLAS500.PRS
LaserJet Series II	HPLASEII.PRS
LaserJet 2000	HPLAS200.PRS

WordPerfect 5 will suggest that you use these file names when creating a printer resource file.

If you want to use a file name other than the one displayed at the *Printer Filename:* prompt, simply enter at the prompt the file name you want, then press ↵. If, however, you find that the file name WordPerfect displays at the prompt is satisfactory, press ↵ to continue.

Once you have supplied or accepted a file name that WordPerfect will use to store the information needed to use your LaserJet, WordPerfect will display a screen of helps and hints specific to the printer you have chosen. For example, it will display the screen shown in Figure 5-4 if you choose LaserJet Series II.

While the screen shown in Figure 5-4 is displayed on your monitor, Word-Perfect will use information stored on the Printer 1 disk to build a printer file that will allow you to take advantage of your LaserJet's internal fonts capabilities. When WordPerfect has finished the process of creating this file, press **[F7]** to continue adding support for your LaserJet to WordPerfect.

**Customizing
Your Printer
Resource File**

After you have read the helps and hints screen that pertains to your printer and have pressed [F7] to continue the printer installation process, WordPerfect 5 will display the Select Printer: Edit menu shown in Figure 5-5. The commands on this menu allow you to customize your LaserJet printer file. Once you have used the commands on the Select Printer: Edit menu to make changes to your printer, press Ø, ↵, or [F7] to return to the Select Printer menu.

FIGURE 5-4

```
┌──────────────────────────────────────────────────────────────────────┐
│ Printer Helps and Hints:  HP LaserJet Series II                        │
│                                                                        │
│  ▪  If you choose the option to initialize the printer, all soft fonts │
│     in its memory will be erased and those fonts marked with an        │
│     asterisk (*) will be downloaded.                                   │
│                                                                        │
│  ▪  The graphics feature is not supported in landscape mode.           │
│                                                                        │
│  ▪  Do not set any margins less than 1/4 of an inch.                   │
│                                                                        │
│  ▪  Line draw does not work correctly with proportionally spaced fonts.│
│                                                                        │
│                                                                        │
│                                                                        │
│                                                                        │
│                                                                        │
│                                                                        │
│                                                                        │
│ Press Exit to quit, Cursor Keys for More Text, Switch for Sheet Feeder │
│ Help                                                                   │
└──────────────────────────────────────────────────────────────────────┘
```

While building a printer resource file for the LaserJet Series II, WordPerfect 5 will display this screen of helps and hints.

FIGURE 5-5

```
┌──────────────────────────────────────────────────────────────────────┐
│ Select Printer: Edit                                                   │
│                                                                        │
│         Filename                       HPLASEII.PRS                    │
│                                                                        │
│     1 - Name                           HP LaserJet Series II           │
│                                                                        │
│     2 - Port                           LPT1:                           │
│                                                                        │
│     3 - Sheet Feeder                   None                            │
│                                                                        │
│     4 - Forms                                                          │
│                                                                        │
│     5 - Cartridges and Fonts                                           │
│                                                                        │
│     6 - Initial Font                   Courier 10 pitch (PC-8)         │
│                                                                        │
│     7 - Path for Downloadable                                          │
│           Fonts and Printer                                            │
│           Command Files                                                │
│                                                                        │
│                                                                        │
│ Selection: 0                                                           │
└──────────────────────────────────────────────────────────────────────┘
```

The Select Printer: Edit menu contains options that you can use to customize a printer resource file.

Printer name

The Name command allows you to change the name assigned to a printer. For example, if you have installed support for a LaserJet Plus or LaserJet 500 Plus, WordPerfect 5 will identify the printer as the HP LaserJet + or 500+, respectively. You might want to use the Name command to change the name of the printer to LaserJet Plus or LaserJet 500 Plus. To change the name assigned to your printer, press **1** or **N**, type the new name at the prompt, then press ↵.

Port

The Port command allows you to choose the port to which your LaserJet is connected. By default, WordPerfect 5 assumes that your LaserJet is connected to LPT1:. To choose another port, press **2** or **P**. When you do this, WordPerfect will display a list of ports across the bottom of your screen, as shown in Figure 5-6.

FIGURE 5-6

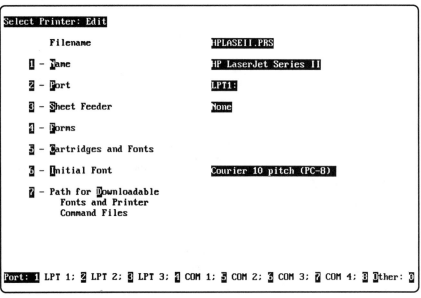

When you choose the Select Print: Edit menu's Port command, WordPerfect 5 will display a list of ports across the bottom of your screen.

To choose one of the ports shown in Figure 5-6, press the number that corresponds to it. For example, to choose LPT 2:, you would press **2**. If the port to which your LaserJet is connected is not listed, or if you want to send all printer output to a disk file, you should choose the Other option by pressing **8** or **O**. When you do this, WordPerfect will display the prompt *Device or Filename:*. At this prompt, you should enter the name of the device or disk file to which you want WordPerfect to send all printer output. For example, if you want to send printer output to LPT4:, type **LPT4:** then press ↵.

The Sheet Feeder command allows you to associate a specific paper source with a WordPerfect 5 paper bin value. You can do this with the Select Printer: Edit menu's Forms command. We'll show you how to do this later.

When you issue a Sheet Feeder command by pressing 3 or S, WordPerfect will display the Select Printer: Sheet Feeder menu shown in Figure 5-7. This menu contains a list of possible paper sources. To choose a paper source, use the ↓ or ↑ key to highlight its name, then press ↵. For instance, if you are adding support to WordPerfect for a LaserJet 2000, highlight **HP LaserJet 2000**, then press ↵.

Sheet Feeder

FIGURE 5-7

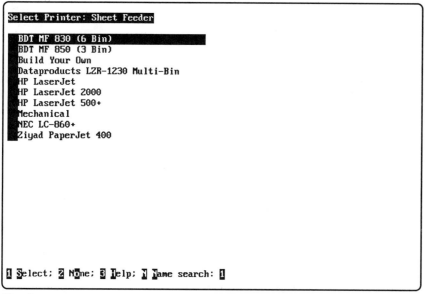

The Select Printer: Sheet Feeder menu lists each of the paper sources that can be used with the LaserJet and WordPerfect 5.

When you select a paper source from the Select Printer: Sheet Feeder menu, WordPerfect 5 will display a screen that shows which bin provided by that source is assigned to which WordPerfect bin value. As you may expect, if you plan to use one of the commercial sheet feeders listed in Figure 5-7, you should choose that feeder. Likewise, if you have a LaserJet 500 Plus, you should choose the HP LaserJet 500+ option. However, if you have an original LaserJet, LaserJet Plus, LaserJet Series II, or LaserJet IID, you should choose the HP LaserJet option. When you choose the HP LaserJet option, the screen shown in Figure 5-8 will appear on your screen.

FIGURE 5-8

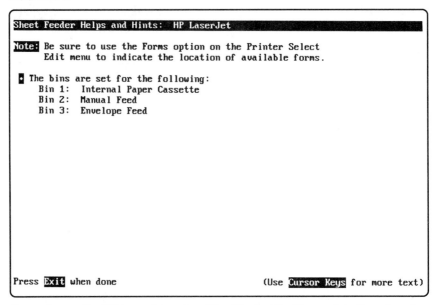

```
Sheet Feeder Helps and Hints:  HP LaserJet

Note: Be sure to use the Forms option on the Printer Select
      Edit menu to indicate the location of available forms.

■ The bins are set for the following:
    Bin 1:  Internal Paper Cassette
    Bin 2:  Manual Feed
    Bin 3:  Envelope Feed
```

```
Press Exit when done                   (Use Cursor Keys for more text)
```

If you choose the HP LaserJet option, WordPerfect 5 will associate the internal, manual, and envelope feed with Bins 1, 2, and 3, respectively.

Forms

The Select Printer: Edit menu's Forms command allows you to define the types of forms you may use with the LaserJet. To issue this command, press **4** or **F**. When you do this, a Select Printer: Forms screen similar to the one shown in Figure 5-9 will appear on your monitor.

Editing a form

As you can see in Figure 5-9, the Select Printer: Forms screen lists each type of form that can be used with a LaserJet. In addition, it also lists each form's size, orientation, initial presentation status, location, and offset settings. If you find it necessary to make changes to a form's settings, use the ↓ or ↑ key to highlight the form, then press **E**, **3**, or ↵. When you do this, a Select Printer: Forms menu similar to the one shown in Figure 5-10 will appear on your screen.

FIGURE 5-9

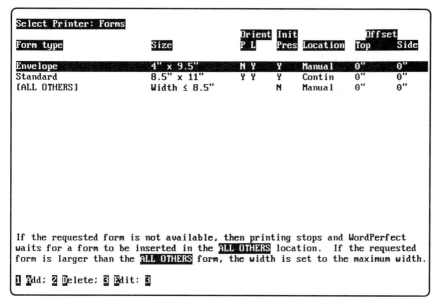

WordPerfect 5 allows you to describe the types of forms that you want to use when printing with a LaserJet.

FIGURE 5-10

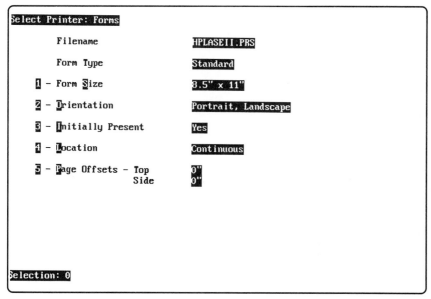

This menu allows you to describe the form you want to use with the LaserJet.

The commands on the menu shown in Figure 5-10 allow you to change the settings that define a form's size, orientation, initially present status, location, and page offset values. To change a specific setting, press the highlighted number or character of the command associated with each setting. For example, to select the Orientation command, press **2** or **O**.

Form Size

When you select the Form Size command by pressing **1** or **S**, WordPerfect 5 will display the menu shown in Figure 5-11. You can use the commands on this menu to select or define a form's dimensions.

FIGURE 5-11

```
┌─────────────────────────────────────────────────────────────────┐
│ Select Printer: Form Size                                        │
│                                   Inserted                       │
│                                   Edge                           │
│                                                                  │
│        1 - Standard              8.5"   x    11"                 │
│                                                                  │
│        2 - Standard Wide         11"    x    8.5"                │
│                                                                  │
│        3 - Legal                 8.5"   x    14"                 │
│                                                                  │
│        4 - Legal Wide            14"    x    8.5"                │
│                                                                  │
│        5 - Envelope              9.5"   x    4"                  │
│                                                                  │
│        6 - Half Sheet            5.5"   x    8.5"                │
│                                                                  │
│        7 - US Government         8"     x    11"                 │
│                                                                  │
│        8 - A4                    210mm  x    297mm               │
│                                                                  │
│        9 - A4 Wide               297mm  x    210mm               │
│                                                                  │
│        0 - Other                                                 │
│ Selection: 1                                                     │
└─────────────────────────────────────────────────────────────────┘
```

You can specify a form's dimensions by choosing one of the options on the Select Printer: Form Size menu.

Of the nine paper sizes you can choose from the menu shown in Figure 5-11, all but Half Sheet and A4 Wide may be used with the LaserJet printer family. However, if you select the US Government size, the LaserJet will treat it as a standard $8^1/_2$- by 11-inch letter-size page. Therefore, you must adjust the top and bottom margins to allow for the $^1/_2$ inch difference in page length.

Finally, while it is not directly supported by WordPerfect, you can use B5 (182mm x 257mm) stationery with the LaserJet 500 Plus by entering its width and length manually via the Other option.

You can use the Orientation command to specify whether a particular form can be used in Portrait and/or Landscape mode. To select the Orientation command, press **2** or **O**. When you do this, WordPerfect 5 will ask you if Portrait, Landscape, or both Portrait and Landscape modes can be used with the form in question. If you want to use a form in Portrait mode only, press **1** or **P** at this prompt. If you want to use a form in Landscape mode only, press **2** or **L**. Finally, if you want to use a form in both Portrait and Landscape modes, press **3** or **B**.

Orientation

The Initially Present command on the Select Printer: Forms menu allows you to specify whether the form whose profile you are editing will always be loaded when you attempt to print a document. To select this command, you should press **3** or **I**. When you do this, you should press **Y** if the form in question will always be available, while you should press **N** if the form will not always be available.

Initially Present

The effect of the Initially Present setting is very important. If you instruct WordPerfect to print text using a particular form, it will use the Initially Present setting to determine if it should prompt you to feed that form into the LaserJet before it actually prints the text. For example, if you instruct WordPerfect 5 to print a document on standard letter-size paper while the Initially Present setting has been set to No, it will prompt you to feed standard letter-size paper before it attempts to send the document to the LaserJet. On the other hand, if you instruct WordPerfect to print a document on standard letter-size paper while the Initially Present setting is set to Yes, it will assume that letter-size paper is available and will not request intervention.

You can use the Location command on the Select Printer: Forms menu shown in Figure 5-10 to specify the location of the form whose profile you are editing. To select the Location command, press **4** or **L**. When you select the Location command, WordPerfect 5 will prompt you to choose one of three paper locations—Continuous, Bin Number, or Manual.

Location

If you want to feed paper from the LaserJet's internal paper tray, you should choose the Continuous option by pressing **1** or **C**. On the other hand, if you want to feed paper via the LaserJet's manual feed slot, you should choose the Manual option by pressing **3** or **M**.

Finally, if you have used the Select Printer: Edit menu's Sheet Feeder command to inform WordPerfect that you have a LaserJet IID, LaserJet 2000, or an external sheet feeder, you should select the Bin Number option by pressing **2** or **B**. When you select this option, WordPerfect will display the prompt *Bin Number:*. At this prompt, type the bin value that corresponds to the specific bin from which you want to feed paper. For example, to feed the form in question from the LaserJet 2000's paper deck, you should type **3** at the *Bin Number:* prompt.

When you use the Select Printer: Edit menu's Sheet Feeder command to select a paper source, WordPerfect will display a screen that shows bin number assignments for that paper source. If you did not make a note of these assignments when they appeared on your monitor, use the Sheet Feeder command to reselect the paper source and display the list of bin value assignments.

Page Offsets

The last command on the Select Printer: Forms menu shown in Figure 5-10—Page Offsets—allows you to set an offset from the left or top margin of a form. For example, if you want the LaserJet to reserve an extra inch of white space along the left margin for binding, you may use the Page Offsets command to do so. To select the Page Offsets command, press **5** or **P**.

When you select the Page Offsets command, WordPerfect 5 will allow you to enter the amount of space that it should reserve along the top margin. Once you have entered this value and have pressed ↵ to save it, you can then enter the amount of space for WordPerfect to reserve along the left margin. After you have entered this value, press ↵ to save it.

Adding forms

In addition to the ability to edit a form's profile, the Select Printer: Forms screen shown in Figure 5-9 allows you to add a new form profile. Therefore, if you want to use a form other than the ones supported by default, you should select the Add command by pressing **1** or **A**. This command will produce the Select Printer: Form Type menu shown in Figure 5-12, which allows you to describe the physical characteristics of the form you want to add.

If the form you want to use appears on the Select Printer: Form Type menu, you should choose it. However, if the form you want to use does not appear on the menu, you may choose the [ALL OTHERS] option, or you may assign a name to the form type by choosing the Other option.

Once you have informed WordPerfect 5 of the type of form you are defining, it will display the Select Printer: Forms menu shown in Figure 5-10 on your monitor. As we indicated, you can use the commands on this menu to define the size, orientation, and location of the form along with the size of an offset. In addition, if a form will not always be loaded into the paper bin you define, you can use the Initially Present option to instruct WordPerfect to specifically request the form before sending a document to the LaserJet.

FIGURE 5-12

```
Select Printer: Form Type
     1 - Standard

     2 - Bond

     3 - Letterhead

     4 - Labels

     5 - Envelope

     6 - Transparency

     7 - Cardstock

     8 - [ALL OTHERS]

     9 - Other




Selection: 1
```

The Select Printer: Form Type menu allows you to describe the physical characteristics of a form.

Cartridge and soft fonts

The most important command on the Select Printer: Edit menu shown in Figure 5-6 is the Cartridges and Fonts command. This command lets you specify which fonts you want to use with WordPerfect 5. To select this command, press **5** or **C**.

When you select the Cartridges and Fonts command, the Printer 1 disk must be in drive A because WordPerfect will use data on this disk to determine which fonts can be used with your LaserJet. Once it has made this determination, WordPerfect will display a Select Printer: Cartridges and Fonts menu similar to the one shown in Figure 5-13 on the next page.

The Select Printer: Cartridges and Fonts menu provides you with a list of fonts you can use with your LaserJet, as well as the number of font cartridge slots and the amount of soft font memory that is available. You can use commands available from the Select Printer: Cartridges and Fonts menu to select the fonts you want to use with your LaserJet, or you can update the values expressing the number of cartridge slots or the amount of soft font memory that is available.

FIGURE 5-13

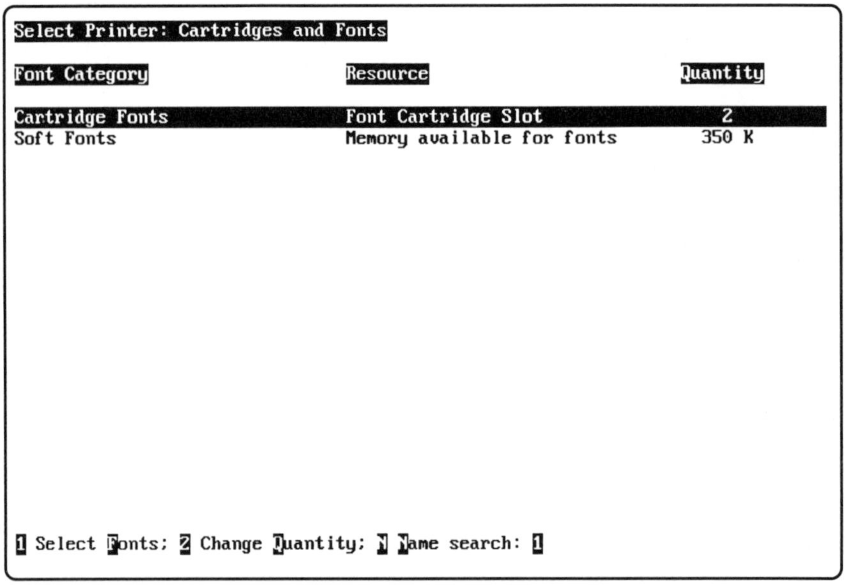

```
┌──────────────────────────────────────────────────────────────────┐
│ Select Printer: Cartridges and Fonts                               │
│                                                                    │
│ Font Category              Resource                    Quantity    │
│                                                                    │
│ Cartridge Fonts            Font Cartridge Slot             2       │
│ Soft Fonts                 Memory available for fonts    350 K     │
│                                                                    │
│                                                                    │
│                                                                    │
│                                                                    │
│                                                                    │
│                                                                    │
│                                                                    │
│                                                                    │
│                                                                    │
│                                                                    │
│                                                                    │
│                                                                    │
│ 1 Select Fonts; 2 Change Quantity; N Name search: 1               │
└──────────────────────────────────────────────────────────────────┘
```

You can use the Select Printer: Cartridges and Fonts menu to choose the specific fonts you want to use with WordPerfect 5.

Printer memory

The Select Printer: Cartridges and Fonts menu's Soft Fonts command allows you to specify the amount of memory installed in your LaserJet that is available for use by soft fonts. For example, the Select Printer: Cartridges and Fonts menu shown in Figure 5-13 indicates that 350K of memory is available for soft fonts. If you want to increase or decrease this amount, use the ↓ or ↑ key to highlight the **Soft Fonts** entry, then press **2** or **Q** to issue the Change Quantity command.

WordPerfect 5 will display the prompt *Quantity:* when you issue the Change Quantity command. At this prompt, type a value equal to the amount of available soft font memory, then press ↵. For example, if you have a LaserJet Series II equipped with a 2MB memory upgrade, a total of 2350K of memory is available for use by soft fonts. Therefore, you should type **2350** at the *Quantity:* prompt.

Cartridge slots

While you can use the Change Quantity command to change the number of cartridge slots that are available, it shouldn't be necessary. When you choose the specific type of LaserJet you are using, WordPerfect 5 will automatically determine the appropriate number of cartridge slots that are supported by that printer.

If you plan to use cartridge fonts with WordPerfect, select the Cartridge Fonts entry on the Select Printer: Cartridges and Fonts menu, then issue the Select Fonts command. To do this, use the ↓ or ↑ key to highlight the **Cartridge Fonts** entry, then press **1**, **F**, or **↵**.

Adding support for cartridge fonts

When you select the Cartridge Fonts entry and issue the Select Fonts command, WordPerfect 5 will display a screen that lists each HP-produced font cartridge. This screen should be similar to the one shown in Figure 5-14. To select the cartridge(s) you want to use from this list, use the ↓ or ↑ key to highlight the name(s), then press *. Finally, once you have selected the cartridge(s) that you want to use, press **[F7]** to return to the Select Printer: Cartridges and Fonts menu.

HP cartridge fonts

FIGURE 5-14

```
┌─────────────────────────────────────────────────────────────────────┐
│ Select Printer: Cartridges and Fonts                                │
│                                                                      │
│                                      Total Quantity:    2            │
│                                  Available Quantity:    2            │
│                                                                      │
│ Cartridge Fonts                              Quantity Used           │
│   A Cartridge                                      1                 │
│   B Cartridge                                      1                 │
│   C Cartridge                                      1                 │
│   D Cartridge                                      1                 │
│   E Cartridge                                      1                 │
│   F Cartridge                                      1                 │
│   G Cartridge                                      1                 │
│   H Cartridge                                      1                 │
│   J Cartridge                                      1                 │
│   K Cartridge                                      1                 │
│   L Cartridge                                      1                 │
│   M Cartridge                                      1                 │
│   N Cartridge                                      1                 │
│   P Cartridge                                      1                 │
│   Q Cartridge                                      1                 │
│                                                                      │
│ Mark Fonts:  ▪ Present when print job begins    Press Exit to save   │
│                                            Press Cancel to cancel     │
└─────────────────────────────────────────────────────────────────────┘
```

When this screen appears on your monitor, you can select the font cartridge(s) you want to use with WordPerfect 5.

If you want to use a non-HP cartridge font with WordPerfect 5, you must use the WordPerfect PTR program to manually add support for the font to your printer file. We'll show you how to do that later in this chapter.

Non-HP cartridge fonts

If you have selected the HP LaserJet 2000 as your printer, WordPerfect 5 will display a Duplex option on the Select Printer: Cartridges and Fonts menu. If you want to print text on both sides of a page, use the ↓ or ↑ key to highlight **Duplex**,

Adding support for duplex printing

then press **1**, **F**, or ↵. When you do this, WordPerfect will display the screen shown in Figure 5-15. At this time, press * to select the Duplex option, then press **[F7]** to return to the Select Printer: Cartridges and Fonts menu.

FIGURE 5-15

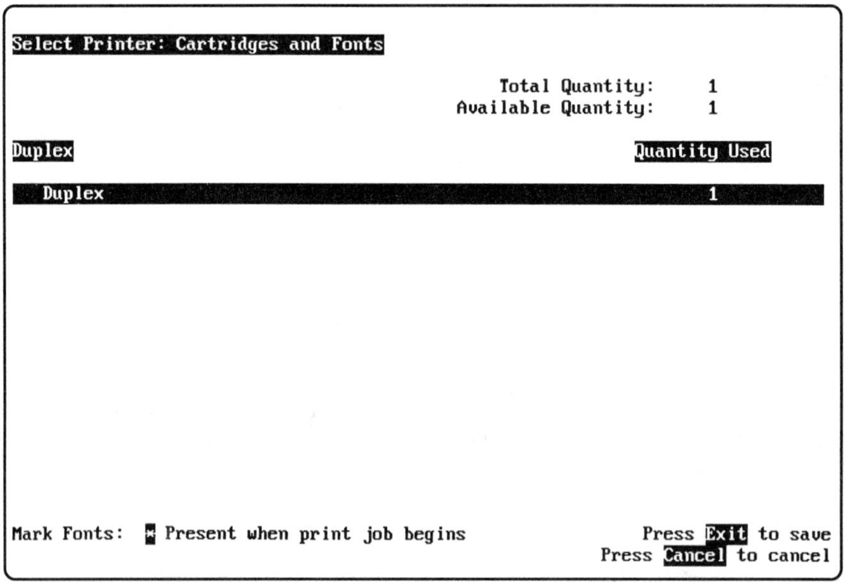

```
┌─────────────────────────────────────────────────────────────────────────┐
│ Select Printer: Cartridges and Fonts                                      │
│                                                                           │
│                                          Total Quantity:      1           │
│                                      Available Quantity:      1           │
│                                                                           │
│ Duplex                                                    Quantity Used   │
│                                                                           │
│    Duplex                                                          1      │
│                                                                           │
│                                                                           │
│                                                                           │
│                                                                           │
│                                                                           │
│                                                                           │
│                                                                           │
│                                                                           │
│                                                                           │
│ Mark Fonts:  * Present when print job begins          Press Exit to save  │
│                                                     Press Cancel to cancel │
└─────────────────────────────────────────────────────────────────────────┘
```

If you have a LaserJet 2000, select the Duplex entry if you want to print on both sides of a page.

Finally, as we mentioned earlier, when *LaserJet Companion* went to press, WordPerfect was not shipped with a printer resource file specifically designed for the LaserJet IID. As a result, we suggested that you should choose the HP LaserJet 2000 from the Select Printer: Additional Printers menu.

If you have a LaserJet IID and selected the HP LaserJet 2000 option, you can use the method we have just described to install support for duplex printing. Likewise, if the version of WordPerfect that you are using does include a LaserJet IID printer resource file, the procedure you must use to install duplex support will be very similar to the one we have just outlined.

Adding support for soft fonts

If you plan to use a soft font with WordPerfect, select the Cartridge Fonts entry on the Select Printer: Cartridges and Fonts menu, then issue a Select Fonts command. To do this, use the ↓ or ↑ key to highlight the **Soft Fonts** entry, then press **1**, **F**, or ↵.

When you select the Soft Fonts entry and issue the Select Fonts command, *HP soft fonts*
WordPerfect 5 will display a list of several HP-produced soft fonts. This screen will
be similar to the one shown in Figure 5-16. To select a soft font from this list, use
the ↓ or ↑ key to highlight its name, then press + if you want WordPerfect to
automatically download it whenever you use it in a document. On the other hand,
you should press * if you plan to use a utility program such as HP's FontLoad to
download the font to the LaserJet before running WordPerfect, or if you plan to use
the Initialize Printer command on WordPerfect's Print menu to accomplish the
same task. We'll elaborate on the Initialize Printer command later.

FIGURE 5-16

```
┌─────────────────────────────────────────────────────────────────────────┐
│ Select Printer: Cartridges and Fonts                                      │
│                                                                           │
│                                            Total Quantity:    350 K       │
│                                        Available Quantity:    350 K       │
│                                                                           │
│ Soft Fonts                                                Quantity Used   │
│                                                                           │
│    (AC) Helu 06pt                                             8 K          │
│    (AC) Helu 06pt (Land)                                     8 K          │
│    (AC) Helu 06pt Bold                                       8 K          │
│    (AC) Helu 06pt Bold (Land)                               8 K          │
│    (AC) Helu 06pt Italic                                    8 K          │
│    (AC) Helu 06pt Italic (Land)                            8 K          │
│    (AC) Helu 08pt                                            9 K          │
│    (AC) Helu 08pt (Land)                                    9 K          │
│    (AC) Helu 08pt Bold                                      11 K          │
│    (AC) Helu 08pt Bold (Land)                              11 K          │
│    (AC) Helu 08pt Italic                                   10 K          │
│    (AC) Helu 08pt Italic (Land)                           10 K          │
│    (AC) Helu 10pt                                           13 K          │
│    (AC) Helu 10pt (Land)                                   13 K          │
│    (AC) Helu 10pt Bold                                     13 K          │
│                                                                           │
│ Mark Fonts:  * Present when print job begins      Press Exit to save      │
│              + Can be loaded during print job     Press Cancel to cancel  │
└─────────────────────────────────────────────────────────────────────────┘
```

*When this screen appears on your monitor, you can select the soft fonts you
want to use with WordPerfect 5.*

If you want to use a non-HP soft font with WordPerfect 5, you must use the *Non-HP soft fonts*
WordPerfect PTR program to build support manually into your printer file for the
font. However, as we will show you later in this chapter, you can use the support
provided by WordPerfect Corporation for an HP soft font as a template when you
use PTR to build support for a non-HP soft font.

If you plan to use a non-HP font with WordPerfect, you may use the Select
Printer: Edit menu's Cartridges and Fonts command at this point to select an HP soft
font that is similar to the non-HP soft font you want to use. For example, if you want
to use a 14-point non-HP soft font with WordPerfect, go ahead and add support for
a 14-point HP soft font. Later in this chapter, we'll show you how to modify support
for an HP soft font so that it provides support for a non-HP soft font.

Finally, once you have selected each soft font that you want to use with WordPerfect, press **[F7]** to return to the Select Printer: Cartridges and Fonts menu.

Initial Font

After you have added support to your printer file for the fonts you want to use, you can use the Select Printer: Edit menu's Initial Font command to specify which of those fonts should be treated as the default font. In other words, you can use this command to choose the font that WordPerfect 5 will use to print text when no other font is specified. To issue the Initial Font command, press **6** or **I**.

When you issue the Initial Font command, WordPerfect will display a list of the fonts that are supported by your printer file. This list will include each of the internal fonts supported by your particular LaserJet, as well as any cartridge or soft fonts you have added to the file. For example, the screen shown in Figure 5-17 lists the LaserJet Series II's internal fonts. To choose the font WordPerfect will treat as the default font, use the ↓ or ↑ key to highlight the name of the font, then press *****.

FIGURE 5-17

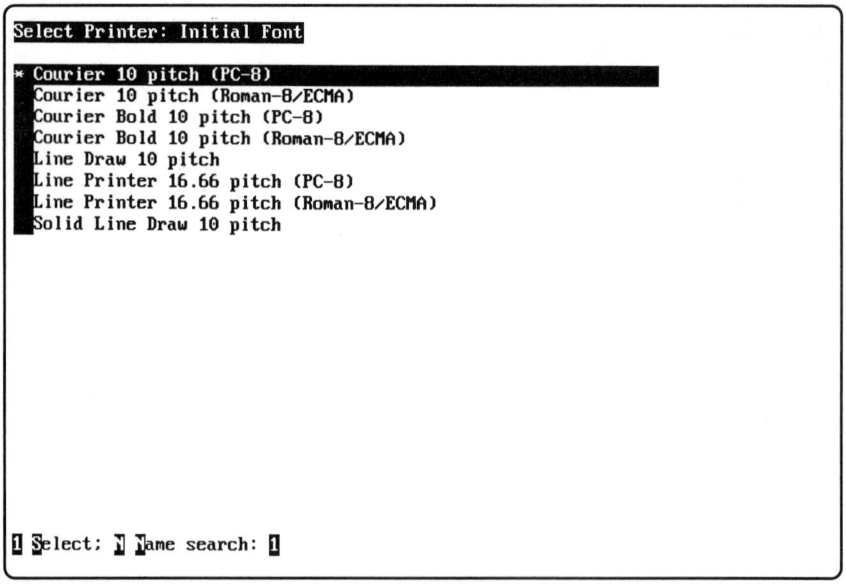

```
┌──────────────────────────────────────────────────────────────────────┐
│ Select Printer: Initial Font                                           │
│ ┌────────────────────────────────────────────────────────────────┐   │
│ │* Courier 10 pitch (PC-8)                                         │   │
│ │ Courier 10 pitch (Roman-8/ECMA)                                  │   │
│ │ Courier Bold 10 pitch (PC-8)                                     │   │
│ │ Courier Bold 10 pitch (Roman-8/ECMA)                             │   │
│ │ Line Draw 10 pitch                                               │   │
│ │ Line Printer 16.66 pitch (PC-8)                                  │   │
│ │ Line Printer 16.66 pitch (Roman-8/ECMA)                          │   │
│ │ Solid Line Draw 10 pitch                                         │   │
│ │                                                                  │   │
│ │                                                                  │   │
│ │                                                                  │   │
│ │                                                                  │   │
│ │                                                                  │   │
│ │                                                                  │   │
│ │                                                                  │   │
│ │ 1 Select; N Name search: 1                                       │   │
│ └────────────────────────────────────────────────────────────────┘   │
└──────────────────────────────────────────────────────────────────────┘
```

This screen lists the LaserJet Series II's internal fonts.

Choosing a soft font directory

The last command on the Select Printer: Edit menu is critical because it allows you to define the name of the directory in which soft font data files are stored. To issue the Path for Downloadable Fonts and Printer Command Files command, press **7** or **D**. When you do, WordPerfect will prompt you to enter the name of the directory in which soft font data files are stored. For example, if your soft font data files are stored in C:\PCLFONTS, type **c:\pclfonts** at the prompt and press ↵.

After you have used the commands on the Select Printer: Edit menu to make changes and/or additions to your printer file and have pressed 0, ↵, or [F7] to return to the Select Printer menu, it's time to save those changes and additions to disk. You can do this by pressing **7** or **U** to issue the Update command.

When you issue the Update command, WordPerfect 5 will display a helps and hints screen similar to the one we looked at in Figure 5-4. While this screen is displayed, any changes and/or additions you have made to your printer resource file will be written to disk. Finally, when WordPerfect completes the task of updating your printer resource file, press **[F7]** twice to return to the Select Printer menu shown in Figure 5-2.

Updating a Modified Printer File

Once you have saved a modified printer file to disk, you must select that printer file before WordPerfect 5 will recognize those changes. To do this, use the ↓, ↑, →, or ← key to highlight the font's name, then press **1** or ↵ to select it. When you do this, WordPerfect will return you to the Print menu.

Using a Modified Printer File

Now that we've shown you how to add LaserJet support to WordPerfect 5, we will show you how to print a document. Therefore, in this section, we'll take a look at the commands, concepts, and procedures that you must use to send text and/or graphics to the LaserJet.

PRINTING

Once you have created a document, you can send it to the LaserJet by pressing [Shift][F7] to issue the Print command. As you can see in Figure 5-18 on the next page, the menu WordPerfect 5 will display on your screen when you issue the Print command contains a number of options. Each of these options allows you to specifically control the performance of the LaserJet.

The Print Command

If you want to send the entire document in the current document window to the LaserJet, you should choose the Print menu's Full Document command by pressing **1** or **F**. When you choose this command, WordPerfect 5 will display the message *Please Wait* in the bottom-left corner of your screen as it sends the document in the currently active document window to the print spooler. Once the document has been sent to the print spooler, you may continue using WordPerfect to edit documents. We'll discuss the print spooler in more detail later in this section.

Printing an entire document

If you want to send a single page to the LaserJet, you must place the cursor on that page within the document. Once you have done this, issue the Print command by pressing **[Shift][F7]**, then select the Page command by pressing **2** or **P**. Then, WordPerfect 5 will print the page on which the cursor was located.

When you send a single page to the LaserJet, WordPerfect will display the message *Please Wait* in the bottom-left corner of your screen as it sends the page to the print spooler. Once the page has been sent to the print spooler, you may continue using WordPerfect to edit documents.

Printing a single page

FIGURE 5-18

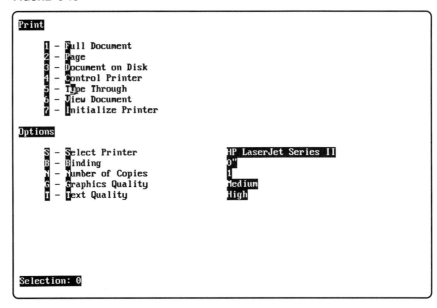

```
Print

    1 - Full Document
    2 - Page
    3 - Document on Disk
    4 - Control Printer
    5 - Type Through
    6 - View Document
    7 - Initialize Printer

Options

    S - Select Printer          HP LaserJet Series II
    B - Binding                 0"
    N - Number of Copies        1
    G - Graphics Quality        Medium
    T - Text Quality            High




Selection: 0
```

When you issue the Print command, this menu will appear on your screen.

Printing from a disk file

If you want to print a document that is stored on disk, press **[Shift][F7]** to activate the Print menu, then select the Document on Disk command by pressing **3** or **D**. When you do this, WordPerfect 5 will display the prompt *Document Name:*. At this prompt, you should type the name of the WordPerfect document that you want to send to the LaserJet. For example, if you want to print the document stored in the file C:\TEXT\SAMPLE.DOC, type **c:\text\sample.doc** at the *Document Name:* prompt, then press ↵.

When you print a document that is stored on disk, WordPerfect will display the message **Please Wait** in the bottom-left corner of your screen as it sends the document to the print spooler. Once the document has been sent to the print spooler, you may continue using WordPerfect to edit documents.

Controlling the print spooler

When we looked at the commands you must issue to print a document, we mentioned that WordPerfect 5 sends documents to a print spooler, which sends them to the LaserJet. This procedure allows you to continue editing as the print spooler prints documents in the background. You can monitor and alter the operation of the print spooler with the Print menu's Control Printer command. To issue this command, press **[Shift][F7]** to activate the Print menu, then press **4** or **C**. When you do this, a Print: Control Printer screen similar to the one shown in Figure 5-19 will appear.

FIGURE 5-19

```
┌─────────────────────────────────────────────────────────────────────┐
│ Print: Control Printer                                                │
│                                                                       │
│ Current Job                                                           │
│                                                                       │
│ Job Number: None                     Page Number:  None               │
│ Status:     No print jobs            Current Copy: None               │
│ Message:    None                                                      │
│ Paper:      None                                                      │
│ Location:   None                                                      │
│ Action:     None                                                      │
│                                                                       │
│                                                                       │
│ Job List                                                              │
│                                                                       │
│ Job  Document            Destination       Print Options              │
│                                                                       │
│                                                                       │
│                                                                       │
│ Additional Jobs Not Shown: 0                                          │
│                                                                       │
│                                                                       │
│                                                                       │
│ 1 Cancel Job(s); 2 Rush Job; 3 Display Jobs; 4 Go (start printer); 5 Stop: 0 │
└─────────────────────────────────────────────────────────────────────┘
```

The Print: Control Printer screen will appear when you issue the Print menu's Control Printer command.

The Print: Control Printer screen displays the status of the current job (the document that is currently being spooled to the LaserJet), as well as a list of jobs that are waiting in a queue to be spooled to the LaserJet. In addition, the Print: Control Printer screen allows you to cancel a job, rush a job, display a complete list of jobs in the queue, stop a job, and restart a job.

If you want to cancel a job, press **1** or **C** to issue the Cancel Job(s) command. **Cancelling a job** When you do this, WordPerfect 5 will display the prompt *Cancel which job? (*=All Jobs)*. At this prompt, you should type the number of the job that you want to cancel. For example, if you want to cancel job 7, type **7** at the *Cancel which job? (*=All Jobs)* prompt, then press ↵.

When you attempt to cancel the job that is currently being spooled to the LaserJet, WordPerfect will finish printing the page that is being printed. As it is printing this page, WordPerfect will display the message *Trying to cancel job* in the Status field of the Current Job section of the Print Control: Printer screen, and the message *Press "C" to cancel job immediately* in the Action field.

While these messages will disappear when the current page has been printed and the remainder of the job has been cancelled, you should press C if you do not want to continue printing the current page. However, when you do this, Word-

Perfect will display a message informing you that you may have to re-initialize the LaserJet before you can send other documents to it. We'll show you how to initialize the LaserJet in a few moments.

Rushing a job

Since each document you send to the print spooler must wait in a queue before it is printed, you may run into an occasion where you may want to rush a job. For example, if you have sent ten documents to the spooler but need to print one document right away, you can do so by using the Rush Job command to move your most important document to the front of the queue. To issue the Rush Job command, press **2** or **J**.

When you issue the Rush Job command, WordPerfect 5 will display the prompt *Rush which job?* At this prompt, you should type the number of the job you want to move to the front of the queue. For example, if you want to move job 10 to the front of the queue, type **10** at the *Rush which job?* prompt, then press ↵.

Once you have entered the number of the job you want to move to the front of the queue, WordPerfect will display the prompt *Interrupt current job? (Y/N)*. If you type Y at this prompt, the current job will be cancelled, and the rush job will be sent to the LaserJet. If you type N, the rush job will not be processed until the current job has been sent to the LaserJet.

Displaying a complete list of jobs

The maximum number of jobs that may appear on the Print: Control Printer screen's job list is four. Therefore, if you send more than four jobs to the print spooler, you must use the Display Jobs command to display the entire job list. To issue the Display Jobs command, press **3** or **D**.

Restarting the spooler after a printer error

From time to time, it's possible that an error may occur as a document is being spooled to the LaserJet. For example, if you run out of paper as a document is being spooled, the print spooler will automatically stop until you correct the situation. After you correct an error, you can instruct the spooler to continue processing a document by pressing **4** or **G** to issue the Go (start printer) command.

Stopping a job

If you must stop the job that is currently being processed, you can do so by pressing **5** or **S** to issue the Stop command. When you issue this command, WordPerfect 5 will display a message informing you that you may have to re-initialize the LaserJet before you can send other documents to it.

Page preview

One of the most attractive and useful features of WordPerfect 5 is its ability to display an on-screen WYSIWYG representation of a page before you send it to your printer. If you want to view a page on the screen before you send it to the LaserJet, you must place the cursor on that page. Once you have done this, issue the Print command by pressing **[Shift][F7]**, then select the View Document command by pressing **6** or **V**. When you do this, WordPerfect displays a graphic representation of the page on your monitor. Figure 5-20 shows a typical screen view of a page.

FIGURE 5-20

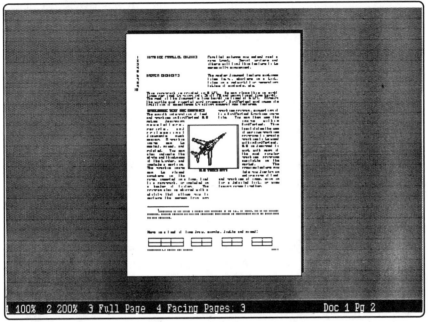

WordPerfect 5 can provide on-screen representations of any document.

While viewing a document on the screen, you can use the ↓, ↑, →, ←, [Pg Up], [Pg Dn], [Expand], and [Contract] keys to scroll the display. As you can see in Figure 5-20, you may also choose any of four viewing options while viewing a document on the screen. If you want to view a document at 100% of its actual size, you should press **1**, while you should press **2** if you want to view a document at 200% of its actual size. To view an entire page at once, press **3** to select Full Page. Finally, if you want to view two facing pages at once, press **4**.

The next command on the Print menu allows you to initialize your printer. This command is particularly important if you plan to use soft fonts in a document, or if you are using a LaserJet IID or 2000 and want to take advantage of its ability to print on both sides of a page. To issue the Initialize Printer command, press **7** or **I**.

Initializing the LaserJet

If you added support for soft fonts to your printer resource file by marking them with an *, they must be downloaded to the LaserJet before you try to print a document. You can use a utility such as HP's FontLoad to manage this task, or you can issue the Initialize Printer command. When you issue the Initialize Printer command while using a printer driver that contains support for soft fonts, WordPerfect 5 will delete any of these present in your LaserJet's memory and will then download all the soft fonts supported by your printer file that are marked with an *.

Downloading soft fonts

Duplex printing

If you are using an HP LaserJet 2000 or LaserJet IID, WordPerfect 5 will let you add duplex support to your printer file. Consequently, if you have added duplex support to your printer file, you must issue the Initialize Printer command to activate that support. Likewise, to deactivate duplex printing, you must use the Print menu's Select Printer command to select a printer file that does not contain duplex support, then you must re-initialize the printer with the Initialize Printer command.

Binding

The Print menu's Binding option is extremely important if you have a LaserJet IID or LaserJet 2000 and want to print a document on both sides of a page. When you select the Binding option by pressing B, WordPerfect 5 will allow you to specify the distance to the right that text will be shifted on odd-numbered pages and the distance to the left that text will be shifted on even-numbered pages to allow for binding. For example, if you select the Binding option and type 1", WordPerfect will automatically shift all output one inch to the right on odd-numbered pages, and one inch to the left on even-numbered pages.

Number of Copies

The Number of Copies option allows you to specify how many copies WordPerfect 5 should generate when you print a document. To specify the number of copies WordPerfect should print, press **N** to choose the Number of Copies option. When you do this, WordPerfect will allow you to enter a value between 1 and 9999.

Graphics Quality

The Graphics Quality option allows you to specify the resolution at which WordPerfect 5 should print graphics. It also allows you to inform WordPerfect that it should not print graphics. To choose the Graphics Quality option, press **G**.

When you select the Graphics Quality option, you will be given four choices: Do Not Print, Draft, Medium, and High. If you choose the Do Not Print option by pressing **N**, WordPerfect will not send graphics to the LaserJet when you print a document. On the other hand, if you choose the Draft option by pressing **D**, all graphics will be printed at 75 dpi; if you choose the Medium option by pressing **M**, all graphics will be printed at 150 dpi; and if you choose the High option by pressing **H**, all graphics will be printed at 300 dpi. As an example, Figure 5-21 shows a document printed without graphics, with draft quality graphics, medium quality graphics, and high quality graphics.

The option you choose should depend on the quality of the output you require, as well as the amount of time it takes to print a document loaded with graphics. For example, if your goal is to print a draft copy of a document for review purposes, you should choose the Draft option. On the other hand, if speed is your only goal and you do not need to review the appearance of the graphics, you should choose the Do Not Print option. Finally, if your goal is to produce the most attractive document possible, you should choose the High option.

FIGURE 5-21

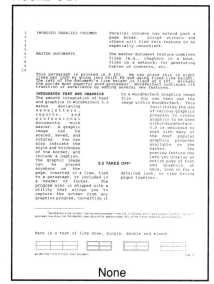

None

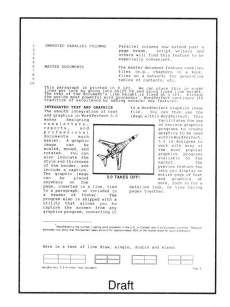

Draft

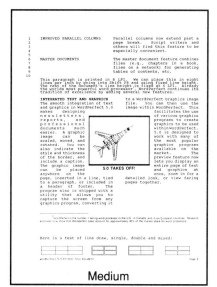

Medium

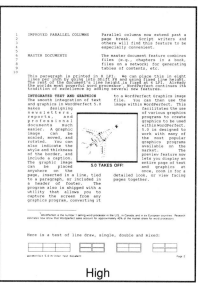

High

This figure shows an example of a document printed without graphics, and with draft quality graphics, medium quality graphics, and high quality graphics.

Text Quality

The Print menu's Text Quality option allows you to specify the quality at which WordPerfect 5 should print text. However, since LaserJets always print high quality text, the only purpose the Text Quality option serves is to allow you to remove text from a document. To choose the Text Quality option, press **T**.

When you select the Graphics Quality option, you will be given four choices: Do Not Print, Draft, Medium, and High. If you choose the Draft, Medium, or High option, nothing will happen because these options are not supported. However, if you choose the Do Not Print option by pressing N, WordPerfect will remove text from any document you send to the LaserJet. This is a useful feature if want to preview graphics that you have embedded in a document. As an example, Figure 5-22 shows a document printed without text.

FIGURE 5-22

This figure shows the document used in Figure 5-21 printed without text.

Setting Margins

LaserJets cannot print text in an area just inside each border of a page. This area is known as the unprintable region. While WordPerfect 5 is aware that the unprintable region exists when you set margins, you must be careful not to set a margin less than $\frac{1}{4}$ inch. If you set a margin less than $\frac{1}{4}$ inch, WordPerfect will attempt to print text and/or graphics in the unprintable region. While this will not cause WordPerfect or the LaserJet to generate an error message, it will result in a loss of printed data since the LaserJet will simply ignore anything WordPerfect attempts to print in the unprintable region.

Using Fonts

Now that we've shown you how to add support for fonts to your LaserJet printer file, it's time to consider the procedures and commands you must issue to include fonts in a document. The Fonts command is the heart of WordPerfect's ability to place fonts in a document. When you issue the Fonts command by pressing [Ctrl][F8], WordPerfect 5 will allow you to select one of five options: Size, Appearance, Normal, Base Font, and Print Color.

Of the five options you can choose when you issue the Fonts command, all but the Print Color command can be used with the LaserJet. However, before you issue the Fonts command, you should place the cursor at the point in your document at which you want to change the font, or you should define the block of text whose font you want to change.

Finally, while WordPerfect allows you to include fonts in a document, the method it will use to represent fonts on your screen will differ according to the type of video system you are using. For example, if you have a monochrome, CGA, EGA, or VGA video system, WordPerfect will display various fonts by underlining, inversing, or boldfacing text. On the other hand, if you have a Hercules RAMfont video system, WordPerfect can display fonts on the screen as you edit a document.

Font size

If you want to specify the size of the font you want to use, or if you want to print text in the superscript or subscript position, you should press **1** or **S** to select the Size option after issuing the Fonts command. When you select the Size option, WordPerfect 5 will display seven size options — Suprscpt, Subscpt, Fine, Small, Large, Vry Large, and Ext Large.

When you want to print text in the superscript position, you should press **1** or **p** to select the Suprscpt option. If you want to print text in the subscript position, you should press **2** or **b** to select the Subscpt option. If you want to print text with the smallest version of the base font, you should press **3** or **F** to choose the Fine option. Likewise, you should press **4** or **S** to select the Small option, **5** or **L** to select the Large option, **6** or **V** to select the Vry Large option, and **7** or **E** to select the Ext Large option.

Appearance

To define the appearance or style of a font, press **[Ctrl][F8]** to issue the Fonts command, then press **2** or **A** to select the Appearance option. When you select the Appearance option, WordPerfect 5 will display nine options, each of which corresponds to a particular form of the currently selected font.

If you want to select the bold version of the base font, you should press **1** or **B** to select the Bold option, while, if you want to underline a block of text, you should press **2** or **U** to select the Undrln option. If you want to double-underline a block of text, you should press **3** or **D** to select the Dbl Und option, while you should press **4** or **I** to select the Italc option if you want the italic version of the base font.

If an outline version of the base font is available, you can press **5** or **O** to select the Outln option, while you can press **6** or **a** to select the Shadw option if a shadow version of the font is available. Likewise, by pressing **7** or **C**, you can select the Sm Cap option, while you can press **8** or **R** to select the Redln (Red Line) option. Finally, to select the Stkout option, you should press **9** or **S**.

Normal

After you have selected a new font, you may want to reselect the default font. Press **[Ctrl][F8]** to issue the Print command, then press **3** or **N** to select the Normal option. You can use the Select Printer: Edit menu's Initial Font command to specify the default font when you add font support to your printer file.

Base Font

To select a font other than the default font, press **[Ctrl][F8]** to issue the Fonts command, then select the Base Font option by pressing **4** or **F**. When you select the Base Font option, WordPerfect 5 will display a list of the fonts supported by your printer. For example, if your printer file supports a LaserJet Series II equipped with an HP Microsoft Z1A font cartridge, the list shown in Figure 5-23 will appear on your screen when you select the Base Font option.

FIGURE 5-23

```
┌─────────────────────────────────────────────────────────────┐
│ Base Font                                                     │
│                                                               │
│ * Courier 10 pitch (PC-8)                                     │
│   Courier 10 pitch (Roman-8/ECMA)                             │
│   Courier Bold 10 pitch (PC-8)                                │
│   Courier Bold 10 pitch (Roman-8/ECMA)                        │
│   Helv 08pt (Z1A)                                             │
│   Helv 10pt (Z1A)                                             │
│   Helv 10pt Bold (Z1A)                                        │
│   Helv 10pt Italic (Z1A)                                      │
│   Helv 12pt (Z1A)                                             │
│   Helv 12pt Bold (Z1A)                                        │
│   Helv 12pt Italic (Z1A)                                      │
│   Helv 14pt Bold (Z1A)                                        │
│   Line Draw 10 pitch                                          │
│   Line Printer 16.66 pitch (PC-8)                             │
│   Line Printer 16.66 pitch (Roman-8/ECMA)                     │
│   Solid Line Draw 10 pitch                                    │
│   Tms Rmn 08pt (Z1A)                                          │
│   Tms Rmn 10pt (Z1A)                                          │
│   Tms Rmn 10pt Bold (Z1A)                                     │
│   Tms Rmn 10pt Italic (Z1A)                                   │
│   Tms Rmn 12pt (Z1A)                                          │
│                                                               │
│ 1 Select; N Name search: 1                                    │
└─────────────────────────────────────────────────────────────┘
```

WordPerfect 5 allows you to use any font for which support is provided within your printer file.

To choose a font from the font list WordPerfect will display on your screen when you choose the Base Font option, use the ↑ or ↓ key to highlight the name of the font you want to use, then press **1**, ↵, or *****. Once you have chosen a font, WordPerfect will allow you to continue editing your document.

One of the most interesting features of WordPerfect 5 is its ability to draw lines and boxes using a line draw font. This is a feature that is fully supported by the LaserJet printer family. However, you must be careful not to use WordPerfect's line draw features in conjunction with a proportionally spaced font. If you do, the results will be unsatisfactory.

Using Line Draw

While each member of the LaserJet printer family can take advantage of WordPerfect 5's ability to embed graphics in text, there are two limitations that you must consider when printing graphics. First, due to the limited amount of RAM available, the original LaserJet cannot print full-page graphics. Table 5-2 lists the maximum size of graphics that the original LaserJet can print using WordPerfect's draft, medium, and high resolution graphics modes.

Graphics

TABLE 5-2

Graphics Mode	Maximum Graphic Size
Draft (75 dpi)	85.9"
Medium (150 dpi)	48.3"
High (300 dpi)	21.5"

The size of a graphics image that can be printed by the original LaserJet is limited by the amount of memory available.

Secondly, WordPerfect does not allow you to include graphics in a document when printing in Landscape mode.

PTR is a program included with WordPerfect 5 that allows you to edit WordPerfect printer files. The only time you should have to use PTR is when you want to use an unsupported font with WordPerfect. For example, while most HP-produced soft fonts are supported by the printer file shipped with WordPerfect, third-party soft fonts are not. Therefore, to use these fonts with WordPerfect, you must use PTR.

USING PTR

At the time *LaserJet Companion* went to press, WordPerfect Corporation did not include documentation with WordPerfect illustrating the use of PTR. In this section, we'll explain how to use PTR to add support for a font to a printer file. We'll also show you how to use PTR to modify the LaserJet 2000 printer resource file so that it may be used with a LaserJet IID.

Getting Started

Once you have used WordPerfect 5's Select Printer command to build a printer resource file that supports a specific set of fonts, you can use PTR to make changes and/or additions to that file. To begin, place the PTR program disk in drive A:, or copy the files PTR.EXE and PTR.HLP into the \WP50 directory on your hard disk. Once you have done this, type **A:** and press ↵ at the DOS prompt if you want to run PTR from drive A:, or type **CD \WP50** and press ↵ if you want to run PTR from your hard disk. Finally, to run PTR, type **PTR** and the name of the printer file you want to edit at the DOS prompt, then press ↵. For example, if you want to edit the printer file HPLASEII.PRS, type **PTR HPLASEII.PRS** at the DOS prompt, then press ↵. When you do this, PTR will display the Printers screen shown in Figure 5-24.

FIGURE 5-24

```
File: C:\WP50\HPLASEII.PRS

                              Printers
┌──────────────────────────────────────────────────────────────────┐
│ HP LaserJet Series II                                              │
│                                                                    │
│                                                                    │
│                                                                    │
│                                                                    │
│                                                                    │
│                                                                    │
│                                                                    │
│                                                                    │
│                                                                    │
│                                                                    │
│                                                                    │
│                                                                    │
│                                                                    │
└──────────────────────────────────────────────────────────────────┘
1 Add; 2 Delete; 3 Rename; 4 Copy;
Press Enter to Look or Edit; A - Z Name Search;
```

PTR's Printers screen will appear when you run PTR from the DOS prompt.

The Printers screen shown in Figure 5-24 lists each printer supported by a specific printer resource file. For example, in Figure 5-24, the Printers screen indicates that the printer resource file HPLASEII.PRS supports the HP LaserJet Series II. When the Printers screen displays a list of printers on your monitor, use the ↓, ↑, →, or ← key to highlight the name of the printer to which you want to add support for a font, then press ↵.

After you have selected a printer, PTR will display a Printer: screen similar to the one shown in Figure 5-25. This screen lists categories that provide access to the technical information WordPerfect uses to format a document for output to a

LaserJet. For example, the Initialize and Reset category defines all the commands WordPerfect uses to initialize and/or reset the LaserJet, while the Fonts category defines all the information needed to select and use a LaserJet font.

FIGURE 5-25

```
File: C:\WP50\HPLASEII.PRS

                    Printer: HP LaserJet Series II

  Initialize and Reset
  Horizontal Motion
  Vertical Motion
  Margins and # Fonts/Page
  Type Through
  Miscellaneous Printer Commands
  Miscellaneous Information
  Fonts
  Groups
  Resources
  Forms
  Graphics Resolutions
  Bitmap Graphics
  Rules and Shaded Boxes
  Bold
  Underline
  Double Underline
▼ Italics

Press Enter to Look or Edit; A - Z Name Search;
Do all that apply
```

To modify the information WordPerfect 5 uses to format a document for output to the LaserJet, you must select the appropriate category from the Printer: screen.

To add support for a font to a printer resource file and to modify the LaserJet 2000 printer resource file for use with the LaserJet IID, use the Fonts category. This category defines all the commands and technical information WordPerfect needs to select and print text with internal, cartridge, and soft fonts. To select the Fonts category, use the ↓, ↑, →, or ← key to highlight **Fonts**, then press ↵.

Adding Font Support

As we mentioned earlier, the Fonts category keeps track of all fonts that can be used with your LaserJet. You must modify this category whenever you want to add to a printer file or remove from a printer file support for a particular font.

When you select the Fonts category on the Printer: screen, PTR will display a list containing the names of each of the fonts supported by the currently loaded printer file. For example, if you used the procedures we described earlier to select a printer and specified that you were using a LaserJet Series II equipped with an HP 92286Z Microsoft 1A font cartridge and (SB) Century Schoolbook soft fonts, the list of fonts shown in Figure 5-26 would appear on your screen.

FIGURE 5-26

```
File: C:\WP50\HPLASEII.PRS

                    Printer: HP LaserJet Series II
                              Fonts

  Courier 10 pitch (PC-8)
  Courier 10 pitch (PC-8) (Land)
  Courier 10 pitch (Roman-8/ECMA)
  Courier 10 pitch (Roman-8/ECMA) (Land)
  Courier Bold 10 pitch (PC-8)
  Courier Bold 10 pitch (PC-8) (Land)
  Courier Bold 10 pitch (Roman-8/ECMA)
  Courier Bold 10 pitch (Roman-8/ECMA) (Land)
  Line Draw 10 pitch
  Line Draw 10 pitch (Land)
  Line Printer 16.66 pitch (PC-8)
  Line Printer 16.66 pitch (PC-8) (Land)
  Line Printer 16.66 pitch (Roman-8/ECMA)
  Line Printer 16.66 pitch (Roman-8/ECMA) (Land)
  Solid Line Draw 10 pitch
  Solid Line Draw 10 pitch (Land)
▼ (SB) Century Schoolbook 14pt

1 Add; 2 Delete; 3 Rename;
Press Enter to Look or Edit; A - Z Name Search;
```

When you select the Fonts category, PTR will display a list of the fonts currently supported by your printer file.

Once PTR displays a list of fonts similar to the list shown in Figure 5-26, you can begin the process of adding support for a new cartridge and/or soft font to your printer file. To do this, issue the Add command by pressing **1**. When you issue this command, PTR will prompt you to choose a font to use as a template around which you can build support for the new font. To do this, use the ↓, ↑, →, or ← key to highlight the name of a font and press ↵. If you want to choose the currently selected default font as a template, press **[Ctrl]**↵.

If you are adding support for a cartridge font, you should choose a cartridge font as a template. You should choose a soft font as template if you are adding support for a soft font. For example, if you are adding support to your printer file for BitStream's 14-point Broadway font, the best choice from the list of fonts shown in Figure 5-26 is (SB) Century Schoolbook 14pt.

When you select the font that you want to use as a template, PTR will prompt you to enter the name of the font for which you are adding support. At this prompt, simply type the name of the font, then press ↵. For example, if you are adding support for BitStream's 14-point Broadway font, you should type **Broadway 14pt** at this prompt.

After you have supplied PTR with the name of the font for which you are adding support, it will place that name in the list of font names shown in Figure 5-26. At this time, use the ↓, ↑, →, or ← key to highlight the name of that font and press ↵. As a result, PTR will display the list of categories shown in Figure 5-27.

FIGURE 5-27

```
File: C:\WP50\HPLASEII.PRS

                        Printer: HP LaserJet Series II
                          Font: Broadway 14pt

  Typeface
  Orientations
  Character Map
  Size and Spacing Information
  Load and Select Strings
  Groups
  Resources
  Automatic Font Changes
  Substitute Fonts
  Quality
  Miscellaneous Font Features




Press Enter to Look or Edit; A - Z Name Search;
Do all that apply
```

*Once you have selected the name of the font you want to edit, PTR will display
this list of categories.*

The information associated with each category listed in Figure 5-27 allows
WordPerfect 5 to use a specific font. Therefore, at this time, you must provide the
appropriate information within each category. We'll begin by discussing the
Typeface category.

*Choosing a
typeface*

The Typeface category allows you to provide PTR with a summary of the
physical characteristics on which a font's design is based. To select this category,
highlight **Typeface**, then press ↵. As a result, PTR will list each typeface supported
by the current selection of fonts. For example, Figure 5-28 on the next page shows
the typeface names that will appear on your screen if your printer file contains
support for LaserJet Series II internal fonts, the HP 92286Z Microsoft 1A font
cartridge, and the 14-point (SB) Century Schoolbook soft font.

If the typeface of the font for which you are adding support appears on your
screen, use the ↓, ↑, →, or ← key to highlight its name, then press * to select it. If you
are installing a font whose design is based on a typeface that does not appear in the
list, you must build a description of the typeface.

FIGURE 5-28

```
File: C:\WP50\HPLASEII.PRS

                        Printer: HP LaserJet Series II
                           Font: Broadway 14pt
                                Typeface
  ┌────────────────────────────────────────────────────────────────┐
  │*Century                        Century (Bold)                   │
  │ Century (Italic)               Courier                          │
  │ Courier (Bold)                 Helvetica                        │
  │ Helvetica (Bold)               Helvetica (Oblique)              │
  │ LtrGothic                      Roman                            │
  │ Roman (Bold)                   Roman (Italic)                   │
  │                                                                 │
  │                                                                 │
  │                                                                 │
  │                                                                 │
  │                                                                 │
  │                                                                 │
  │                                                                 │
  └─────────────────────────────────────────────────────────────────┘
1 Add; 2 Delete; 3 Rename; 4 Copy;
Press * to Select, Enter to Look or Edit; A - Z Name Search;
```

This screen allows you to create, select, or modify a typeface on which a font's design is based.

For example, none of the typefaces that appear in the list shown in Figure 5-28 are appropriate for BitStream's Broadway font. Therefore, if you are adding support for the Broadway font, you must build a description of the typeface on which its design is based. To do this, press **1** to issue the Add command.

When you issue the Add command, PTR will prompt you to select a typeface that will be used as a pattern or template around which you can build a new typeface description. When this prompt appears, you should use the ↓, ↑, →, or ← key to highlight the name of a typeface that is similar to the one you are going to describe, then press ↵. If you want to choose the currently selected default font as a template, press **[Ctrl]**↵. For instance, if you are going to describe the Broadway font's typeface, you should select **Helvetica (Bold)** as a template.

Once you have selected the typeface you want to use as a template, PTR will prompt you to enter the name of the typeface you are adding. At this prompt, simply type the name of the typeface, then press ↵. You should include the style of the typeface in its name where appropriate. For example, if you are describing the typeface on which the Broadway font is based, you should type **Broadway** at this prompt; if you are describing an italic version of the Broadway font, you should type **Broadway (Italic)** at the prompt.

After you have supplied PTR with the name of the typeface you are adding, it will place that name in the list of typeface names shown in Figure 5-28. At this time, use the ↓, ↑, →, or ← key to highlight the name of that typeface, press * to select it, then press ↵. As a result, PTR will display a Typeface: screen similar to the one shown in Figure 5-29.

FIGURE 5-29

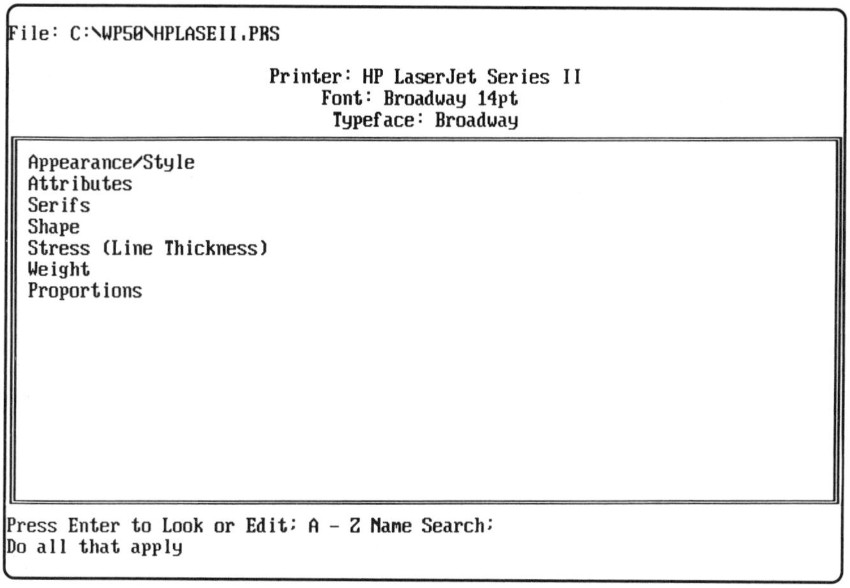

```
File: C:\WP50\HPLASEII.PRS

                    Printer: HP LaserJet Series II
                        Font: Broadway 14pt
                     Typeface: Broadway
┌──────────────────────────────────────────────────────────────┐
│ Appearance/Style                                               │
│ Attributes                                                     │
│ Serifs                                                         │
│ Shape                                                          │
│ Stress (Line Thickness)                                        │
│ Weight                                                         │
│ Proportions                                                    │
│                                                                │
│                                                                │
│                                                                │
│                                                                │
│                                                                │
│                                                                │
│                                                                │
│                                                                │
└──────────────────────────────────────────────────────────────┘
Press Enter to Look or Edit; A - Z Name Search;
Do all that apply
```

Once you have selected the name of the typeface that you want to edit, PTR will display this list of options.

As you can see in Figure 5-29, the Typeface: screen contains several options that you can use to describe the physical characteristics upon which a font's design is based. For example, the Appearance/Style option allows you to describe a font's appearance, while the Serifs option allows you to describe the shape of serifs.

Appearance/Style

The first typeface characteristic you must define is the appearance or style. To do this, use the ↓ or ↑ key to highlight Appearance/Style on the list of options that appear on the Typeface: screen shown in Figure 5-29, then press ↵. As a result, PTR will display the list of Appearance/Style options shown in Figure 5-30 on the following page.

Choosing the options that describe the appearance/style of a typeface is quite simple. Select the Casual option if the typeface you are describing can be used in less formal text, the Connected Letters option if the font is cursive, or the Decorative option if symbols, dingbats, and other special characters are present.

FIGURE 5-30

```
File: C:\WP50\HPLASEII.PRS

                    Printer: HP LaserJet Series II
                       Font: Broadway 14pt
                       Typeface: Broadway
                       Appearance/Style
┌─────────────────────────────────────────────────────────────┐
│ Casual                                                        │
│ Connected Letters                                             │
│ Decorative                                                    │
│ Formal                                                        │
│ Futuristic                                                    │
│ Old Style                                                     │
│ Script or Calligraphic                                        │
│                                                               │
│                                                               │
│                                                               │
│                                                               │
│                                                               │
│                                                               │
└─────────────────────────────────────────────────────────────┘
Press * to Mark or Select, Backspace to Unmark
Mark all that apply
```

When you select the Appearance/Style option, you may choose any of the options on this screen to describe a typeface's appearance or style.

If a font's typeface is appropriate for use in a formal document, you should select the Formal option, while fonts based on a futuristic theme should be classified as Futuristic. Finally, Old Style should be chosen for fonts such as Old English, while Script or Calligraphic is the proper choice for fonts that resemble calligraphy.

Once you have determined which appearance/style options are appropriate for a font, use the ↓ or ↑ key to highlight them, then press * to select them. For example, if you feel that it is appropriate to use the Broadway font in casual situations, highlight **Casual** and type *. Finally, once you have selected each option that is proper for a font, press **[F7]** to return to the Typeface: screen shown in Figure 5-29.

Attributes

Once you have described a typeface's appearance or style, you must specify which attributes are featured by the font whose typeface you are defining. To do this, use the ↓ or ↑ key to highlight Attributes on the list of options that appear on the Typeface: screen shown in Figure 5-29, then press ↵. As a result, PTR will display the list of attributes shown in Figure 5-31.

If a font is italic or oblique, you should choose the Italic or Oblique attribute, while you should choose Outline if the characters in a font are white with a black outline. Finally, if a font has a shadow, you should choose the Shadow attribute, while you should choose Small Caps if the lowercase characters in a font are essentially smaller versions of capital characters.

FIGURE 5-31

```
File: C:\WP50\HPLASEII.PRS

                    Printer: HP LaserJet Series II
                       Font: Broadway 14pt
                   Typeface: Broadway
                      Attributes
   ┌─────────────────────────────────────────────────────────┐
   │  Italic or Oblique                                        │
   │  Outline                                                  │
   │  Shadow                                                   │
   │  Small Caps                                               │
   │                                                           │
   │                                                           │
   │                                                           │
   │                                                           │
   │                                                           │
   │                                                           │
   │                                                           │
   └─────────────────────────────────────────────────────────┘

Press * to Mark or Select, Backspace to Unmark
Mark all that apply
```

When you select the Attributes category, this list will appear on your screen.

Once you have determined which attributes are appropriate for a font, use the ↓ or ↑ key to highlight them, then press * to select them. For example, if a font is italic or oblique, highlight Italic or Oblique and press *.

If you are dealing with a font that carries none of these attributes, you shouldn't select any of them. The Broadway font is a prime example of this type of font. Once you have selected each attribute that is carried by a particular font, press [F7] to return to the Typeface: screen shown in Figure 5-29.

Serifs

Fonts may have serifs—tiny crosslines that extend from the main lines that form a character. If a font whose typeface you are describing has serifs, use the ↓ or ↑ key to highlight Serifs on the list of options that appears on the Typeface: screen shown in Figure 5-29, then press ↵. When you do this, PTR will display the list of serif types shown in Figure 5-32 on the following page.

If a font features serifs that are curved or cupped, you should select Cupped, while you should choose Exaggerated if the serifs are extremely long. When serifs are very thin, you should choose Hairline. Conversely, if serifs are quite thick, you should choose Slab.

If serifs are slanted in relation to the main strokes of a character, you should choose Slanted. If the angle formed between the main stroke of a character and a serif is curved, you should choose Transitional, while you should choose Triangular if the angles are straight. Finally, if a font features serifs that are round, you should select Ball.

FIGURE 5-32

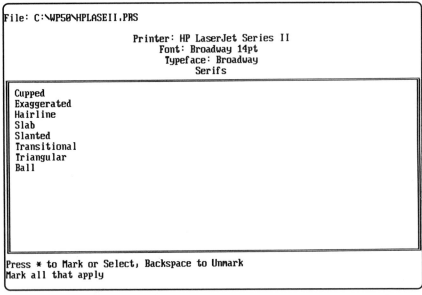

```
File: C:\WP50\HPLASEII.PRS

                        Printer: HP LaserJet Series II
                          Font: Broadway 14pt
                          Typeface: Broadway
                              Serifs

    Cupped
    Exaggerated
    Hairline
    Slab
    Slanted
    Transitional
    Triangular
    Ball




Press * to Mark or Select, Backspace to Unmark
Mark all that apply
```

If a font has serifs, you must specify which type of serif by choosing one of the options from this list.

Once you have determined which type of serifs a font features, use the ↓ or ↑ key to highlight those features, then press * to select them. For example, if a font has serifs that are extremely thick and rounded on the edges, highlight **Slab**, press *, then highlight **Ball** and press *. Once you have selected the type of serifs featured by a font, press **[F7]** to return to the Typeface: screen shown in Figure 5-29 .

Shape

The next category on the Typeface: screen allows you to describe the general shape of the lines or strokes that form the characters in a font. To select this category, use the ↓ or ↑ keys to highlight **Shape** on the list of options that appear on the Typeface: screen, then press ↵. When you do this, PTR will display on your screen the list of shapes shown in Figure 5-33.

If the diagonal lines that form characters in a font are slightly curved or bowed, you should select **Curved or Bowed Lines**, while you should choose **Non-connecting Enclosures** if the lines that form enclosures in characters such as *B* and *D* do not connect. Finally, if characters such as *O* and *C* are generally square, you should select **Square**, while you should choose **Round** if they are generally round. Once you've determined the shape of the characters in a font, use the ↓ or ↑ key to highlight the appropriate choices, then press * to select them. After you've selected the appropriate choice(s) for a font, press **[F7]** to return to the Typeface: screen.

FIGURE 5-33

```
File: C:\WP50\HPLASEII.PRS

                    Printer: HP LaserJet Series II
                       Font: Broadway 14pt
                    Typeface: Broadway
                       Shape
 ┌─────────────────────────────────────────────────────────┐
 │ Curved or Bowed Lines                                     │
 │ Nonconnecting Enclosures                                  │
 │ Round                                                     │
 │ Square                                                    │
 │                                                           │
 │                                                           │
 │                                                           │
 │                                                           │
 │                                                           │
 │                                                           │
 │                                                           │
 │                                                           │
 └─────────────────────────────────────────────────────────┘
Press * to Mark or Select, Backspace to Unmark
Mark all that apply
```

PTR allows you to describe the general shape of the characters in a font.

Stress (Line Thickness)

After you have described the general shape of the characters in a font, it's time to describe the thickness of the lines that form the characters. To do this, use the ↓ or ↑ key to highlight **Stress (Line Thickness)** on the list of options that appear on the Typeface: screen shown in Figure 5-29, then press ↵. As a result, PTR will display the list of attributes shown in Figure 5-34.

If the slanted lines that form characters are thicker than the horizontal and vertical lines that form characters, you should choose **Angular**, while you should select **Exaggerated** if characters feature thick horizontal and vertical lines and thin slanted lines. Finally, you should select **Uniform** if all lines that form characters are equally thick.

After you have examined the thickness of the lines that form characters in a font, use the ↓ or ↑ key to highlight the appropriate choices, then press * to select them. For example, the only choice that pertains to the Broadway font is Exaggerated. Therefore, if you are adding support for this font, highlight **Exaggerated**, then press *. Finally, once you have selected the appropriate choice(s) for a font, press **[F7]** to return to the Typeface: screen shown in Figure 5-29.

FIGURE 5-34

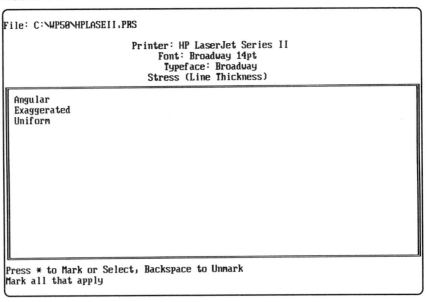

```
File: C:\WP50\HPLASEII.PRS
                    Printer: HP LaserJet Series II
                       Font: Broadway 14pt
                    Typeface: Broadway
                      Stress (Line Thickness)
 ┌────────────────────────────────────────────────────────────────┐
 │ Angular                                                          │
 │ Exaggerated                                                      │
 │ Uniform                                                          │
 │                                                                  │
 │                                                                  │
 │                                                                  │
 │                                                                  │
 │                                                                  │
 │                                                                  │
 │                                                                  │
 │                                                                  │
 └────────────────────────────────────────────────────────────────┘
 Press * to Mark or Select, Backspace to Unmark
 Mark all that apply
```

Each of these attributes describes the thickness of the lines that form characters.

Weight

      The Weight option on the Typeface: screen lets you spec-ify the stroke weight of a font. To select this option, use the ↓ or ↑ key to highlight **Weight** on the list of options that appear on the Typeface: screen, then press ↵. When you do this, PTR will display the list of choices shown in Figure 5-35.

      If a font's stroke weight is normal, you should choose that option, while you should choose Extra Light, Light, Bold, or Extra Bold when appropriate. After you have determined which stroke weight is appropriate, use the ↓ or ↑ key to highlight it, then press * to select it. For example, since the Broadway font is considered a boldface font, highlight **Bold** and press *. Finally, once you have selected the appropriate choice(s) for a font, press **[F7]** to return to the typeface category screen.

Proportions

      The Proportions option allows you to describe the height of characters in relation to the height of the conceptual cell in which they exist. To select this category, use the ↓ or ↑ key to highlight **Proportions** on the list of options that appear on the Typeface: screen shown in Figure 5-29, then press ↵. When you do this, PTR will display the Proportions screen shown in Figure 5-36.

FIGURE 5-35

```
File: C:\WP50\HPLASEII.PRS

                    Printer: HP LaserJet Series II
                       Font: Broadway 14pt
                    Typeface: Broadway
                        Weight

 ┌─────────────────────────────────────────────────────────┐
 │  Extra Light                                              │
 │  Light                                                    │
 │  Normal                                                   │
 │ *Bold                                                     │
 │  Extra Bold                                               │
 │                                                           │
 │                                                           │
 │                                                           │
 │                                                           │
 │                                                           │
 │                                                           │
 │                                                           │
 └─────────────────────────────────────────────────────────┘

A - Z Name Search;
Mark one
```

PTR allows you to specify a font's stroke weight.

FIGURE 5-36

```
File: C:\WP50\HPLASEII.PRS

                    Printer: HP LaserJet Series II
                       Font: Broadway 14pt
                    Typeface: Broadway
                       Proportions

 ┌─────────────────────────────────────────────────────────┐
 │ Capital Height (% of Font Cell Height)        79          │
 │ Descender Height (% of Font Cell Height)      21          │
 │ Lowercase x Height (% of Font Cell Height)    57          │
 │ Lowercase t Height (% of Font Cell Height)    75          │
 │ Maximum Ascender Height (% of Font Cell Height) 79        │
 │ Slant Adjust (± % of Font Cell Height)         0          │
 │                                                           │
 │                                                           │
 │                                                           │
 │                                                           │
 │                                                           │
 │                                                           │
 └─────────────────────────────────────────────────────────┘

Enter Values
```

A great deal of technical information is needed to define the proportions of a font.

As you can see in Figure 5-36, the Proportions screen contains six entries that allow you to describe the proportions of a character. To assign a value to an entry, use the ↓ or ↑ key to highlight it, type the value in the field that appears to the right of the entry, then press ↵.

Capital Height

The first entry on the Proportions screen shown in Figure 5-36 allows you to define the height of a font's capital characters as a percentage of the height of the cells in which the characters exist. For example, the entry shown in Figure 5-36 indicates that capital characters occupy 79% of a 14-point cell.

Descender Height

The second entry on the Proportions screen allows you to define the distance from the bottom of descenders to the conceptual line on which each character sits (baseline). For example, the entry shown in Figure 5-36 indicates that descenders occupy 21% of the total height of a 14-point cell.

Lowercase x Height

The third entry on the Proportions screen allows you to define the height of all lowercase characters excluding ascenders and descenders. This is called x height because the height of a lowercase x is usually equal to the height of all lowercase characters excluding ascenders and descenders. As an example, the Lowercase x Height entry that appears in Figure 5-36 indicates that x occupies 57% of the total height of a 14-point cell.

Lowercase t Height

The fourth entry on the Proportions screen is used to define the height of the character t. This value should include the height of ascenders, but should exclude the height of descenders. For example, the Lowercase t Height entry that appears in Figure 5-36 indicates that the character t occupies 75% of the total height of a 14-point cell.

Maximum Ascender Height

The fifth entry on the Proportions screen allows you to define the height of the tallest ascender. In other words, it allows you to define the height of characters such as $b, d, l,$ and h. For example, the Maximum Ascender Height entry shown in Figure 5-36 indicates that characters such as $b, d, l,$ and h occupy 79% of a cell's total height.

Slant Adjust

Finally, the sixth entry on the Proportions screen allows you to define as a percentage of total cell height the amount by which italic characters are shifted from an upright position. If characters are shifted to the right, this value should be positive, while it should be negative if characters are shifted to the left. Also, if characters stand upright, this value should be zero. For example, the Slant Adjust entry that appears in Figure 5-36 indicates that characters are shifted 0%.

Obtaining proportions

At the time *LaserJet Companion* went to press, there was no quick and easy way to obtain the values you must supply for each of the six entries on the Proportions screen. For example, if you are describing a cartridge font's typeface, the only way to obtain the information concerning a font's proportions is to contact the company that produced the font.

On the other hand, if you are describing a soft font's typeface, it is possible to write a program that extracts this information from a soft font data file. If you're an accomplished programmer and wish to tackle the task of writing such a program, the technical characteristics of a soft font data file are presented in Chapter 26.

If you're not an accomplished programmer, however, and it is impossible to obtain a font's proportions from the company that produced it, your best bet is to use the proportional values defined for the font you are using as a template. If you notice peculiarities when using the font, then adjust the values until the results are satisfactory.

After looking at the proportional values assigned to all of the HP fonts supported by WordPerfect 5, we have constructed Table 5-3. This table lists the range of values that you can use when trying to determine the appropriate proportional values for a font.

TABLE 5-3

Proportion	Range
Capital Height (% of Font Cell Height)	70-85
Descender Height (% of Font Cell Height)	20-30
Lowercase x Height (% of Font cell Height)	50-60
Lowercase t Height (% of Font Cell Height)	65-80
Maximum Ascender Height (% of Font Cell Height)	70-85
Slant Adjust (+/- % of Font Cell Height)	0, +/- 10-20

This table shows a common range of values for each proportional value required by WordPerfect 5.

Orientation

Once you have described a font's typeface, you can specify the orientation of the font. To do this, press **[F7]** twice to return to the Font: screen shown in Figure 5-27, use the ↓ or ↑ key to highlight the **Orientations** category, then press ↵. When you do this, the Orientations screen shown in Figure 5-37 will appear.

To specify the orientation of a font, use the arrow keys to highlight the appropriate entry on the Orientations screen, then press *. For example, the Broadway font can be used only in Portrait mode. Therefore, if you are installing support for this font, highlight the entry **Portrait**, then press *. Finally, after you have specified a font's orientation, press **[F7]** to return to the Font: screen shown in Figure 5-27.

FIGURE 5-37

```
File: C:\WP50\HPLASEII.PRS

                         Printer: HP LaserJet Series II
                             Font: Broadway 14pt
                               Orientations
 ┌─────────────────────────────────────────────────────────────────┐
 │*Portrait                                                          │
 │ Landscape                                                         │
 │ Reverse Portrait                                                  │
 │ Reverse Landscape                                                 │
 │ Portrait & Landscape                                              │
 │ Portrait, Landscape, Reverse Portrait, & Reverse Landscape        │
 │                                                                   │
 │                                                                   │
 │                                                                   │
 │                                                                   │
 │                                                                   │
 │                                                                   │
 │                                                                   │
 │                                                                   │
 │                                                                   │
 │                                                                   │
 └─────────────────────────────────────────────────────────────────┘
A - Z Name Search;
Mark one
```

The Orientations screen lets you choose the orientation(s) for which a font was designed.

Character maps

The actual collection of symbols supported by a font, as well as the decimal values that represent each symbol, is known as a symbol set. The Character Map category on the Font: screen shown in Figure 5-27 allows you to choose, modify, or create a symbol set. To choose, modify, or create a symbol set, use the ↓ or ↑ key to highlight the **Character Map** category, then press ↵. As a result, the Character Maps screen shown in Figure 5-38 will appear.

Choosing a character map

Fortunately, Word Perfect 5 creates a printer file that supports the majority of LaserJet fonts. If your font is based on the HP PC-8 (IBM PC), HP Roman-8, or HP+ Line Draw symbol set, you should use the ↓ or ↑ key to highlight the appropriate entry on the Character Maps screen, then press ↵. For example, BitStream's Broadway font is based on the Roman-8 symbol set. Therefore, when installing support for this font, you should choose the HP Roman 8 (Extended)/ ECMA entry.

FIGURE 5-38

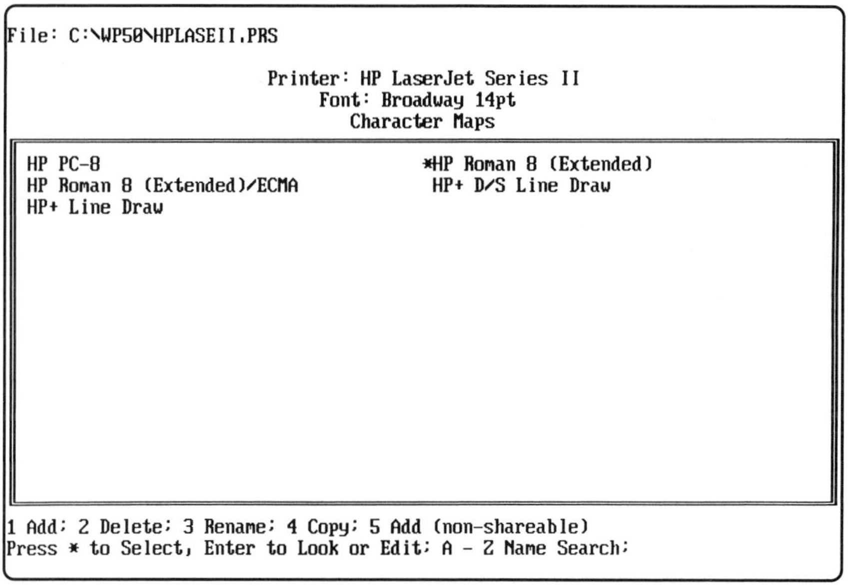

```
┌─────────────────────────────────────────────────────────────────┐
│File: C:\WP50\HPLASEII.PRS                                         │
│                                                                   │
│                      Printer: HP LaserJet Series II               │
│                         Font: Broadway 14pt                       │
│                        Character Maps                             │
│  ┌─────────────────────────────────────────────────────────────┐ │
│  │HP PC-8                          *HP Roman 8 (Extended)       │ │
│  │HP Roman 8 (Extended)/ECMA        HP+ D/S Line Draw           │ │
│  │HP+ Line Draw                                                 │ │
│  │                                                             │ │
│  │                                                             │ │
│  │                                                             │ │
│  │                                                             │ │
│  │                                                             │ │
│  │                                                             │ │
│  │                                                             │ │
│  │                                                             │ │
│  │                                                             │ │
│  │                                                             │ │
│  │                                                             │ │
│  └─────────────────────────────────────────────────────────────┘ │
│                                                                   │
│1 Add; 2 Delete; 3 Rename; 4 Copy; 5 Add (non-shareable)          │
│Press * to Select, Enter to Look or Edit; A - Z Name Search;      │
└─────────────────────────────────────────────────────────────────┘
```

The Character Maps screen lists each symbol set supported by your printer file.

Creating a character map

If you run into a situation where your printer file does not contain support for a particular font's symbol set, it is possible to create a new character map. To do this, issue the Add command by pressing **1**, use the ↓ or ↑ key to highlight the character map that you want to use as a template, then press ↵. When you do this, PTR will prompt you to enter the name of the new character map. For example, if you are creating a character map for a font called Zingduds, type **Zingduds** when PTR prompts you to enter the name of the new character map, then press ↵.

After you have provided PTR with the name of the new character map, you may begin to associate the symbols supported by WordPerfect 5 with the symbols supported by the font for which you are adding support to your printer file. To do this, use the ↓ or ↑ key to highlight the name of the character map you are creating, then press ↵. When you do this, the screen shown in Figure 5-39 will appear.

The Character Map: screen shown in Figure 5-39 is divided into two sections. The left section lists the numeric character ID and a description of each symbol supported by WordPerfect, while the right section lists the character or command that must be sent to the LaserJet to produce that character. For example, to print the WordPerfect symbol 0,33 ! (Exclamation Point) using the Zingduds symbol set, you must send the decimal value 33 to the LaserJet. Similarly, to print the symbol 0,34" (Neutral Double Quote), you must send the decimal value 34 to the LaserJet.

FIGURE 5-39

```
File: C:\WP50\HPLASEII.PRS

                       Printer: HP LaserJet Series II
                           Font: Broadway 14pt
                       Character Map: Zingduds

   Number Description                            Printer Command String

    0,32    (Space)                                " "
    0,33  ! (Exclamation Point)                    "!"
    0,34  " (Neutral Double Quote)                 [34]
    0,35  # (Number/Pound)                         "#"
    0,36  $ (Dollars)                              "$"
    0,37  % (Percent)                              "%"
  ▼ 0,38  & (Ampersand)                            "&"




Ctrl Home Go To; F2 Search Char; Cursor Key Edit; Non Cursor Key New String;
Ctrl Enter Edit in Window
```

You can use this screen to associate the symbols supported by a LaserJet font with those supported by WordPerfect 5.

If you need to send a character that cannot be generated by a standard keystroke, you can enter the character by holding down the [Alt] key and entering its decimal ASCII value on the numeric keypad. For example, to generate the character associated with the symbol that represents British pounds sterling, press the **[Alt]** key, type **156** on the numeric keypad, then release the **[Alt]** key.

Finally, once you have associated a WordPerfect character with the symbol set supported by the LaserJet font for which you are adding support to your printer file, press **[F7]** twice to return to the Font: screen shown in Figure 5-27.

Size and Spacing Information

The Size and Spacing Information category on the Font: screen shown in Figure 5-27 allows you to provide WordPerfect with information it needs to use the font. To select this category, use the ↓ or ↑ key to highlight Size and Spacing Information, then press ↵. When you do this, the screen shown in Figure 5-40 will appear.

FIGURE 5-40

```
File: C:\WP50\HPLASEII.PRS

                    Printer: HP LaserJet Series II
                      Font: Broadway 14pt
                    Size and Spacing Information

 Point Size (1 Point = 1/72 Inch)              14
 Font Cell Height (Points)                     14
 Default Leading (Points)                      1.4
 PS Table Width Scaling Factor                 1
 Optimal Character Width (% of Font Width)     100
 Optimal Space Width (% of Font Width)         75
 Character Cell Adjust (± 1200ths)             0
 Baseline Bias Factor (Points)                 0
 Horizontal Spacing Units                      1/300
 Vertical Spacing Units                        1/300
 Proportional Spacing Table: Century SB 14R

            PS Table Information (change in PS Table)
 Average PS Table Width (PS Table Units):      33/300
 Average Scaled Width (PS Table Units):        33/300
 Point Size PS Table Was Created for:    14

Enter Values
Press Enter to Edit
```

The Size and Spacing Information screen allows you to provide WordPerfect with the information it needs to use a font.

As you can see in Figure 5-40, there are a number of options on the Size and Spacing Information screen that can be adjusted. However, if you followed our instructions and chose as a template a font that is similar to the one you are adding to your printer file, the only option on this screen to be concerned with is the Proportional Spacing Table.

Entering character width information

If you are adding to your printer file support for a proportionally spaced font, you must use the Proportional Spacing Table option to define the width of each character in the font. WordPerfect 5 will use the information in this table to calculate line endings when you are printing justified text. To define the width of each character in a proportionally spaced font, use the ↓ or ↑ key to highlight the Proportional Spacing Table option on the Size and Spacing Information screen shown in Figure 5-40, then press ↵. When you do this, a screen similar to the one shown in Figure 5-41 will appear.

The Proportional Spacing Tables screen shown in Figure 5-41 allows you to select a proportional spacing table that you can use as a template when creating a new proportional spacing table. To create a new table, issue an Add command by pressing 1, use the ↓ or ↑ key to highlight the name of the table you want to use as a template, then press ↵. When you do this, PTR will display the prompt *Name:*.

At this prompt, you should enter a name for the proportional spacing table you are about to create, then press ←. For example, if you are creating a proportional spacing table for the 14-point Broadway font, type **Broadway 14** at the *Name:* prompt, then press ←.

FIGURE 5-41

```
File: C:\WP50\HPLASEII.PRS

                        Printer: HP LaserJet Series II
                           Font: Broadway 14pt
                        Size and Spacing Information
                        Proportional Spacing Tables
 ┌─────────────────────────────────────────────────────────────────────┐
 │  Century SB 14B                    Century SB 14I                     │
 │ *Century SB 14R                    HP AD Helv10B                      │
 │  HP AD Helv10I                     HP AD Helv10R                      │
 │  HP AD Helv12B                     HP AD Helv12I                      │
 │  HP AD Helv12R                     HP AD Helv14B                      │
 │  HP AD Helv8R                      HP AD TmsRmn10B                     │
 │  HP AD TmsRmn10I                   HP AD TmsRmn10R                     │
 │  HP AD TmsRmn12B                    HP AD TmsRmn12I                    │
 │  HP AD TmsRmn12R                   HP AD TmsRmn14B                     │
 │  HP AD TmsRmn8R                                                       │
 │                                                                       │
 │                                                                       │
 │                                                                       │
 │                                                                       │
 └─────────────────────────────────────────────────────────────────────┘
 1 Add; 2 Delete; 3 Rename; 4 Copy;
 * Select; Backspace Unmark; Enter Look or Edit; A - Z Name Search;
```

The Proportional Spacing Tables screen allows you to select an existing proportional spacing table as a template.

Once you have assigned a name to a new table, use the arrow keys to highlight its name, then press ←. When you do this, a screen similar to the one shown in Figure 5-42 will appear on your monitor.

When this screen appears, use the ↓ or ↑ key to scroll through the list of symbols and characters supported by WordPerfect. When you reach the specific character that is supported by the LaserJet font in question, simply enter its width in dots (one dot = $1/_{300}$ inch). For example, if a font's exclamation point character is 17 dots wide, use the ↓ or ↑ key to scroll through the list of characters shown in Figure 5-42, highlight the exclamation point character's width field, and type **17**.

FIGURE 5-42

```
File: C:\WP50\HPLASEII.PRS

                    Printer: HP LaserJet Series II
                         Font: Broadway 14pt
                     Size and Spacing Information
                 Proportional Spacing Table: Broadway 14

  Number Description                        Width   Adjust   Kern?

    0,32    (Space)                           16              ----
    0,33  ! (Exclamation Point)               16              ----
    0,34  " (Neutral Double Quote)            19              ----
    0,35  # (Number/Pound)                    45              ----
    0,36  $ (Dollars)                         32              ----
    0,37  % (Percent)                         48              ----
    0,38  & (Ampersand)                       47              ----
    0,39  ' (Neutral Single Quote)            16              ----
    0,40  ( (Left Parenthesis)                21              ----
    0,41  ) (Right Parenthesis)               21              ----
  ▼ 0,42  * (Asterisk)                        29              ----

  Units: 300ths                       Point Size: 14

Number Width:
Press Tab to edit Units or Font Cell Height
```

This screen allows you to define the width of each character in a proportionally spaced font.

Obtaining character width information

There are several ways to obtain character width information depending on the form of the font in question. If it is a cartridge font, you must obtain character width information from the font's manufacturer. For example, the widths of all characters in cartridge fonts produced by HP are available from HP. Similarly, you can obtain the widths of proportionally spaced soft fonts from most manufacturers.

If you have HP's FontLoad utility, you can use it to generate a report listing the widths of all characters in a proportional soft font. If you're an accomplished programmer, you can extract character width information from a soft font data file. The technical information necessary to write such a program is presented in Chapter 26.

Kern values

In addition to allowing you to enter character width information, the Proportional Spacing Table: screen shown in Figure 5-42 allows you to enter kern values for each character. In other words, if you want to increase the amount of white space that will appear between two specific characters, you can do so by supplying the appropriate kern value. To specify kern values for a specific character, use the ↑ or ↓ key to highlight the character's description, press the → key twice to select the Kern option, then press ↵. When you do this, a screen similar to the one shown in Figure 5-43 will appear.

FIGURE 5-43

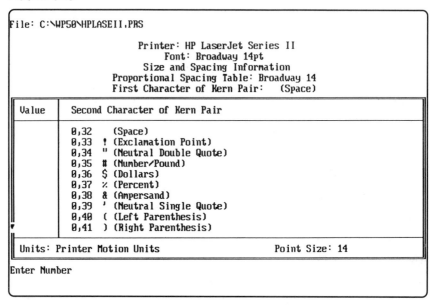

```
File: C:\WP50\HPLASEII.PRS

                      Printer: HP LaserJet Series II
                          Font: Broadway 14pt
                      Size and Spacing Information
                 Proportional Spacing Table: Broadway 14
                 First Character of Kern Pair:    (Space)

 ┌────────┬──────────────────────────────────────────────────┐
 │ Value  │ Second Character of Kern Pair                     │
 ├────────┼──────────────────────────────────────────────────┤
 │        │   0,32    (Space)                                 │
 │        │   0,33  ! (Exclamation Point)                     │
 │        │   0,34  " (Neutral Double Quote)                  │
 │        │   0,35  # (Number/Pound)                          │
 │        │   0,36  $ (Dollars)                               │
 │        │   0,37  % (Percent)                               │
 │        │   0,38  & (Ampersand)                             │
 │        │   0,39  ' (Neutral Single Quote)                  │
 │        │   0,40  ( (Left Parenthesis)                      │
 │▼       │   0,41  ) (Right Parenthesis)                     │
 ├────────┴──────────────────────────────────────────────────┤
 │ Units: Printer Motion Units              Point Size: 14    │
 └────────────────────────────────────────────────────────────┘
Enter Number
```

This screen allows you to enter kern values for a specific pair of characters.

Once the screen shown in Figure 5-43 appears, use the ↑ or ↓ key to select the second character of a kern pair. For example, if you want to reserve two dots of white space between the space character and the exclamation point, use the ↑ or ↓ key to select the exclamation point value field, type **2** and press ↵. After you have assigned kern values to all appropriate characters, press **[F7]** to return to the Proportional Spacing Table: screen shown in Figure 5-42.

Scaling a spacing table

It's quite likely that you may eventually add support to your printer file for several sizes of the same font. For example, you might want to add support for 12- and 24-point versions of the same font. When you do this, it is not always necessary to build a proportional spacing table for each size of the font. Instead, you can create a single table and use the Size and Spacing Information screen's PS Table Width Scaling Factor option to scale the table.

As an example, let's assume that you have created a spacing table for the 12-point version of a font, and want to use it with the 24-point version of the font. To do this, use the ↑ or ↓ key to select the PS Table Width Scaling Factor option, type **2**, and press ↵. Consequently, whenever WordPerfect uses the 24-point version of the font, it will use the 12-point spacing table by multiplying all values in that table by a factor of 2.

Perhaps the most important category on the Font: screen is the Load and Select Strings category. This category allows you to define the name of the file in which a soft font exists, as well as the PCL command that WordPerfect 5 must send to the LaserJet to select the font. To select this category, use the ↑ or ↓ key to highlight Load and Select Strings, then press ↵. When you do this, you will see a Load and Select Strings screen similar to the one that appears in Figure 5-44.

FIGURE 5-44

```
File: C:\WP50\HPLASEII.PRS

                    Printer: HP LaserJet Series II
                         Font: Broadway 14pt
                      Load and Select Strings

 ┌────────────────────┬─────────────────────────────────────────────┐
 │ Function           │ Expression                                  │
 ├────────────────────┼─────────────────────────────────────────────┤
 │ Load Font          │ font DOWNLOAD("CN140RPN.R8P")perm REPOSITION │
 │ Unload Font        │ ulfont                                      │
 │ Select Font        │ r8 prop"14vsb23T"                           │
 │ Deselect Font      │                                             │
 │                    │                                             │
 ├────────────────────┴─────────────────────────────────────────────┤
 │                                                                   │
 │                                                                   │
 │                                                                   │
 │                                                                   │
 └───────────────────────────────────────────────────────────────────┘
A - Z Name Search;
Press Enter to Edit
```

The Load and Select Strings screen allows you to specify the name of the data file in which a soft font is stored and to specify the PCL command that WordPerfect 5 must use to select the font.

As you can see in Figure 5-44, the Load and Select Strings screen is divided into two sections. The left section defines the name of a function, while the right section defines the expression that WordPerfect will use to execute that function.

The first function that appears in Figure 5-44 is the Load Font function. This function must be defined only if the font you want to load is a soft font. To edit the expression that executes the Load Font function, use the ↑ or ↓ key to highlight the function, then press ↵. When you do this, PTR will allow you to edit the expression. The format of the expression that allows WordPerfect 5 to download a font automatically is:

Downloading soft fonts

font DOWNLOAD("*FILENAME.EXT*")*status* REPOSITION

If you want WordPerfect to download a soft font automatically, place the name of the data file in which the font is stored in the expression to the right of the Load Font function. You must also indicate the status of the font once it has been downloaded by replacing the status field shown above with the word *perm* or *temp*. Fonts with *perm* status will be downloaded as permanent soft fonts, while fonts with *temp* status will be downloaded as temporary soft fonts.

For example, let's assume that you want WordPerfect to automatically download the soft font BC140BPY.USP as a permanent font. To do this, edit the expression associated with the Load Font function so that it reads

font DOWNLOAD (*"BC140BPY.USP"*)*perm* REPOSITION.

Selecting a font

The next function you must define before WordPerfect 5 can successfully use a font in a document is the Select Font function. This expression is nothing more than a PCL command. For example, to select the 14-point version of the Broadway font, you should edit the expression associated with the Select Font function so that it reads **"(8Us1p14vs3b21T"**. Finally, you must define an expression for the Select Font function for all forms of LaserJet fonts.

Resources

If you are installing support for a cartridge font, you must select the Resources option on the Font: screen shown in Figure 5-27 on page 193 to assign a cartridge slot to the cartridge. To select this category, use the ↑ or ↓ key to highlight **Resources**, then press ↵. When you do this, the screen shown in Figure 5-45 will appear on your monitor.

As an example, let's assume you are adding support for a Broadway font cartridge to your printer file. Let's also assume that you have previously installed support for two other font cartridges. Whenever you use the Broadway font in a document, it will be necessary for WordPerfect 5 to request that the Broadway font be inserted into the appropriate cartridge slot. To inform WordPerfect that it should make this request, you must change the intervention status of the font to Yes.

To change the intervention status of a font, use the ↑ or ↓ key to highlight the Font Cartridge Slot entry on the Resources screen, press the → key six times, type **Y**, then press ↵. Finally, to save this change, press **[F7]**.

Automatic font changes

As we showed you earlier in this chapter, WordPerfect 5 associates styles of fonts with keywords or features such as Bold, Italic, Small, etc. Consequently, if you have added to your printer file support for a font and want to associate it with one of these features, you may do so by selecting the Automatic Font Changes option on the Font: screen shown in Figure 5-27. To select this option, use the ↑ or ↓ key to highlight Automatic Font Changes, then press ↵. When you do this, a screen similar to the one shown in Figure 5-46 will appear on your monitor.

FIGURE 5-45

```
File: C:\WP50\HPLASEII.PRS

              Printer: HP LaserJet Series II
                   Font: Broadway 14pt
                      Resources
```

Resource Name	Font or Group Type	Quan-tity	Units	ID	Type/ Order	I
Font Cartridge Slot	Cartridge Fonts	2		1	Fixed	N
*Memory available for	Soft Fonts	350	K	2	Load/Any	N

```
I=Intervention Required?

1 Add; 2 Delete; 3 Rename;
* Select; Backspace Unmark; Enter Look or Edit; A - Z Name Search;
```

The Resources screen allows you to assign printer resources such as cartridge slots and memory.

FIGURE 5-46

```
File: C:\WP50\HPLASEII.PRS

              Printer: HP LaserJet Series II
                   Font: Broadway 14pt
              Automatic Font Changes For
                   Broadway 14pt
```

Feature	Font Name
Extra Large Print	(SB) Century Schoolbook 14pt Bold
Very Large Print	(SB) Century Schoolbook 14pt Bold
Large Print	(SB) Century Schoolbook 14pt Bold
Small Print	(Z1A) Tms Rmn 10pt
Fine Print	(Z1A) Helv 08pt
Superscript	(Z1A) Helv 08pt
Subscript	(Z1A) Helv 08pt
Outline	
Italics	(SB) Century Schoolbook 14pt Italic
Shadow	
Redline	
Double Underline	
Bold	(SB) Century Schoolbook 14pt Bold

```
Enter Select Automatic Font Change;
Switch Cross Reference List;
```

The Automatic Font Changes screen allows you to associate a feature with a specific font.

The Automatic Font Changes screen, shown in Figure 5-46, is divided into two sections. The left (Feature) section lists the feature that may be associated with a font, while the right (Font Name) section lists the name of the font associated with that feature/keyword.

If you want to associate a feature with a font, use the ↑ or ↓ key to highlight the feature, then press ↵. When you do this, PTR will list each font supported by your printer file. At this time, use the ↑ or ↓ key to highlight the name of the font that you want to associate with the feature, press * to select it, then press [F7] to return to the Automatic Font Changes screen. Finally, when you have finished the task of associating features with fonts, press [F7] to return to the Font: screen.

Building a LaserJet IID Printer Resource File

Earlier in this chapter, we mentioned that a LaserJet IID printer resource file had not been shipped with WordPerfect 5 at the time *LaserJet Companion* went to press. Therefore, when we showed you how to add LaserJet support to Word-Perfect, we recommended you choose the HP LaserJet 2000 option if you have a LaserJet IID.

The only critical difference between the LaserJet IID and LaserJet 2000 is the number of internal fonts. Therefore, if you are using the LaserJet 2000 printer resource file, you must use PTR to remove support for the LaserJet 2000 internal fonts not supported by the LaserJet IID. To do this, type **PTR HPLAS200.PRS** at the DOS prompt, then press ↵ to run PTR. When you do this, PTR will display on your monitor the Printers screen shown in Figure 5-47.

FIGURE 5-47

```
File: C:\WP50\HPLAS200.PRS

                            Printers

    HP LaserJet 2000













 1 Add; 2 Delete; 3 Rename; 4 Copy;
 Press Enter to Look or Edit; A - Z Name Search;
```

PTR's Printers screen will appear when you run PTR from the DOS prompt.

When the Printers screen appears on your monitor, use the ↓, ↑, →, or ← key to highlight **HP LaserJet 2000**, then press ↵. After you've done this, PTR will display the Printer: screen shown in Figure 5-25 on page 191. When this screen appears on your monitor, use the ↑ or ↓ key to select the **Fonts** category, then press ↵.

Once you've selected the Fonts category from the screen shown in Figure 5-25, PTR will display a list of each of the fonts supported by the HP LaserJet 2000 printer resource file. You can then remove the internal fonts not supported by the LaserJet IID. To remove support for a font from the HP LaserJet 2000 printer resource file, use the ↑ or ↓ key to highlight its name, then press **2** or **D**.

Table 5-4 shows the internal fonts supported by the LaserJet 2000 appearing on the list of fonts that will be displayed by PTR. The fonts you must remove to ensure compatibility with the LaserJet IID are marked with an *.

TABLE 5-4

Courier 12pt Bold (PC-8D/N)	* Prestige 07pt (PC-8D/N)
Courier 12pt Bold (R8)	* Prestige 07pt (R8)
Courier 12pt Italic	* Prestige 10pt
Courier 12pt Italic (ISO-100)	* Prestige 10pt (ISO-100)
Courier 12pt Italic (Legal)	* Prestige 10pt (Legal)
Courier 12pt Italic (OEM-1)	* Prestige 10pt (Math)
Courier 12pt Italic (PC-8D/N)	* Prestige 10pt (Math 8)
Courier 12pt Italic (R8)	* Prestige 10pt (OEM-1)
* Helv 14pt Bold	* Prestige 10pt (PC-8D/N)
* Line Draw 12pt 10 pitch	* Prestige 10pt (R8)
* Line Draw 12pt 12 pitch	* Prestige 10pt Bold
* Line Printer 8.5pt 15 pitch	* Prestige 10pt Bold (ISO-100)
* Line Printer 8.5pt 15 pitch (ISO-100)	* Prestige 10pt Bold (Legal)
* Line Printer 8.5pt 15 pitch (OEM-1)	* Prestige 10pt Bold (OEM-1)
* Line Printer 8.5pt 15 pitch (PC-8D/N)	* Prestige 10pt Bold (PC-8DN)
* Line Printer 8.5pt 15 pitch (R8)	* Prestige 10pt Bold (R8)
Line Printer 8.5pt 16.66	* Prestige 10pt Italic
Line Printer 8.5pt 16.66 pitch (ISO-100)	* Prestige 10pt Italic (ISO-100)
Line Printer 8.5pt 16.66 pitch (OEM-1)	* Prestige 10pt Italic (Legal)
Line Printer 8.5pt 16.66 pitch (PC-8D/N)	* Prestige 10pt Italic (OEM-1)
Line Printer 8.5pt 16.66 pitch (R8)	* Prestige 10pt Italic (PC-8D/N)
* LineDraw 08.5pt	* Prestige 10pt Italic (R8)
* LineDraw 12pt	* Tms Rmn 08pt
* Prestige 07pt	* Tms Rmn 10pt
* Prestige 07pt (ISO-100)	* Tms Rmn 10pt Bold
* Prestige 07pt (OEM-1)	* Tms Rmn 10pt Italic

These internal fonts are supported by the HP LaserJet 2000 printer resource file. To ensure compatibility with the LaserJet IID, delete each of the fonts marked with an *.

Saving a Printer Resource File

After you have added support for a font to a printer file, you should save the printer file. To do this, press **[F7]**, then press **Y** when PTR displays the message *Save File (Y/N)* in the bottom-left corner of your screen.

Before PTR actually writes a printer file to disk, it will prompt you to supply a name for the file. At this prompt, type a new file name if you do not want to overwrite the previous version of the file you have been editing, then press ↵. If you want to overwrite the previous version of the file, simply press ↵ at this prompt, and type **Y** when PTR asks if you want to replace the file.

Using a Modified Printer Resource File

If you save a modified printer resource file to disk using a file name other than that of the printer resource file you have previously created and selected with WordPerfect 5, you must use the procedures and commands we outlined at the beginning of this chapter to select that printer resource file. For example, if you have saved a modified printer file as NEW.PRS, run WordPerfect from the DOS prompt, then issue a Print command by pressing **[Shift][F7]**. When the Print menu appears, press **1** or **S** to issue a Select Printer command, then press **2** or **A** to issue the Additional Printers command followed by **4** or **L** to issue the List Printer Files command.

At this time, WordPerfect will display a list of all printer files stored in the WordPerfect directory on your screen. To select NEW.PRS, use the ↑ or ↓ key to highlight its name, then press ↵. When you do this, WordPerfect will display a helps and hints screen, which you may exit by pressing **[F7]**.

After you have chosen NEW.PRS, WordPerfect will display the Select Printer: Edit screen. You should make any changes to the settings on this screen before exiting to the Print: Select Printer screen by pressing **[F7]**. Finally, once you have returned to the Print: Select Printer screen, use the ↑ or ↓ key to select the printer that has been added to the list of printers by NEW.PRS, then press **1** or **S** to select it. You can return to the Print menu where you print a document, or you can return to edit the document in the currently active document window by pressing **[F7]**.

BITSTREAM FONTWARE

At the time *LaserJet Companion* went to press, registered users of WordPerfect 5 could obtain a free copy of the BitStream Fontware Installation Kit for Word Perfect and Fontware typefaces—Charter, Dutch (Times Roman) and Swiss (Helvetica). The BitStream Fontware Installation Kit is a software package that lets you generate soft fonts of any size from 2 to 144 points. The Fontware Installation Kit for WordPerfect also adds to your printer file the information necessary to use each font. We'll discuss the Fontware Installation Kit in Chapter 18.

CONCLUSION

In this chapter, we showed you how to add support for the LaserJet to WordPerfect 5 and how to use each of the LaserJet capabilities that can be accessed with WordPerfect. Finally, we showed you how to use WordPerfect's PTR program to add font support to a LaserJet printer file.

LOTUS 1-2-3 6

Although many new spreadsheet application programs have appeared on the market in the last few years, Lotus 1-2-3 is still the most widely used spreadsheet program of all time. In fact, without Lotus 1-2-3, the personal computer industry would not have grown into the force that it is today. People in almost every industry can put 1-2-3 to work, and 1-2-3 will one day take its place in the Smithsonian Institution right next to the original IBM PC.

Anyone can use Lotus 1-2-3 and an HP LaserJet printer to create attractive reports and graphs. However, 1-2-3 can use only fixed-space fonts in its printed reports—it cannot print worksheets correctly with HP's proportionally spaced fonts. In this chapter, we'll show you how to use 1-2-3 to generate both professional reports and attractive graphs on your HP LaserJet printer.

Before you can print either a 1-2-3 worksheet or a 1-2-3 graph on an HP LaserJet printer, you need to use 1-2-3's Install Program to tell 1-2-3 a few things about the printer. You'll probably need to run through this installation procedure only once—from that point on, you'll be able to print your worksheets without any hardware setup.

HARDWARE SETUP

Lotus 1-2-3's Install Program lets you tell 1-2-3 about your computer equipment. When you run the Install Program, 1-2-3 will present the main menu shown in Figure 6-1. Since the Install Program can be used either to tell 1-2-3 about your equipment for the first time or to modify some specific information you've already supplied 1-2-3, you'll use one of two approaches to set up your HP LaserJet printer with the Install Program.

Running the Install Program

FIGURE 6-1

```
┌─────────────────────────────────────────────────────────────┐
│                    M A I N   M E N U                          │
│───────────────────────────────────────────────────────────────│
│                                                               │
│                                    ┌──────────────────────────┐│
│                                    │Select First-Time Installation│
│  Use  ↓  or  ↑  to move menu pointer.│for a guided path through the │
│                                    │installation procedure.  This │
│  ┌─────────────────────┐           │path lets you select drivers  │
│  │First-Time Installation│          │for screen display and for    │
│  └─────────────────────┘           │printers.                 │
│    Change Selected Equipment       │                          │
│    Advanced Options                │                          │
│    Exit Install Program            │                          │
│                                    └──────────────────────────┘│
│                                                               │
│                                                               │
│───────────────────────────────────────────────────────────────│
│  ↓  and  ↑  move menu pointer.      [F1] displays a Help screen.│
│  [RETURN] selects highlighted choice.  [F9] takes you to main menu.│
│  [ESCAPE] takes you to previous screen.  [F10] shows current selections.│
└─────────────────────────────────────────────────────────────┘
```

You must use the Install Program to install the LaserJet's printer drivers before you can print either worksheets or graphs.

Running Install for the first time

     If you're using the Install Program for the first time to tell 1-2-3 about your computer equipment, you'll want to choose the First-Time Installation option from the main menu shown in Figure 6-1. When you do this, Install will ask you some questions about your computer, including whether you have a hard disk and what type of monitor you have. After you've answered these questions, Install will present the question *Do you have a text printer?* When this question appears, you should choose the **Yes** option to bring up the list of printer manufacturers shown in Figure 6-2. When you see this list, press **[Pg Dn]** to display the printers at the bottom of the list, as we've done in Figure 6-3, and choose the **Unlisted** option (NOT the HP Option). When you choose the Unlisted option, Install will bring up the menu shown in Figure 6-4 on page 220, from which you should choose the **No Backspace** option.

FIGURE 6-2

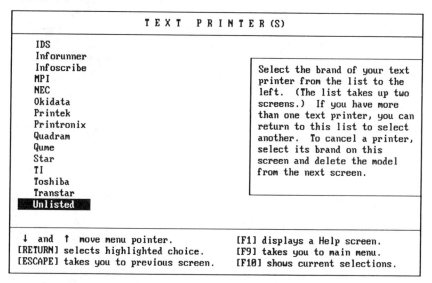

```
                    T E X T   P R I N T E R (S)

   Anadex
   C. Itoh
   Canon                        Select the brand of your text
   DEC                          printer from the list to the
   Diablo                       left. (The list takes up two
   Epson                        screens.) If you have more
   GE/Genicom                   than one text printer, you can
   HP                           return to this list to select
   IBM                          another. To cancel a printer,
   IDS                          select its brand on this
   Inforunner                   screen and delete the model
   Infoscribe                   from the next screen.
   MPI
   NEC
   Okidata
Use ↓ to see more selections below.

  ↓  and  ↑  move menu pointer.        [F1] displays a Help screen.
 [RETURN] selects highlighted choice.  [F9] takes you to main menu.
 [ESCAPE] takes you to previous screen. [F10] shows current selections.
```

The Install Program presents this list of printer manufacturers when you are installing a text printer.

FIGURE 6-3

```
                    T E X T   P R I N T E R (S)

   IDS
   Inforunner
   Infoscribe                   Select the brand of your text
   MPI                          printer from the list to the
   NEC                          left. (The list takes up two
   Okidata                      screens.) If you have more
   Printek                      than one text printer, you can
   Printronix                   return to this list to select
   Quadram                      another. To cancel a printer,
   Qume                         select its brand on this
   Star                         screen and delete the model
   TI                           from the next screen.
   Toshiba
   Transtar
   Unlisted

  ↓  and  ↑  move menu pointer.        [F1] displays a Help screen.
 [RETURN] selects highlighted choice.  [F9] takes you to main menu.
 [ESCAPE] takes you to previous screen. [F10] shows current selections.
```

The Unlisted option appears at the end of the list of printers.

FIGURE 6-4

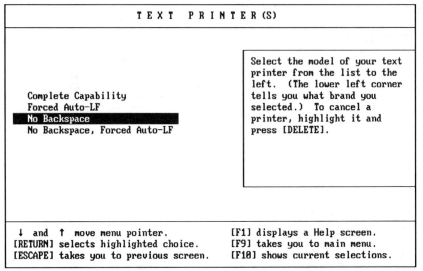

The Install Program will present this menu when you choose the Unlisted option.

After you answer another question or two, the Install program will present the prompt *Do you want to print graphs?* You should answer **Yes** to this prompt to bring up the list of graphics printer manufacturers shown in Figure 6-5. When you see this list, choose the **HP** option from the list of printer manufacturers to bring up the list of HP printers shown in Figure 6-6. If you have an original HP LaserJet printer, choose that option. If you have a LaserJet Plus, a LaserJet 500 Plus, a LaserJet Series II, or a LaserJet IID printer, choose the **LaserJet +** option from this list.

After the Install Program finishes prompting you for the necessary information, it will save your driver set under the name 123.SET, which contains all the information you provided during the installation procedure. Once Install has saved your driver set, you can exit the Install Program and load the 1-2-3 spreadsheet program. (For more information on the Install Program, see your 1-2-3 manuals.)

FIGURE 6-5

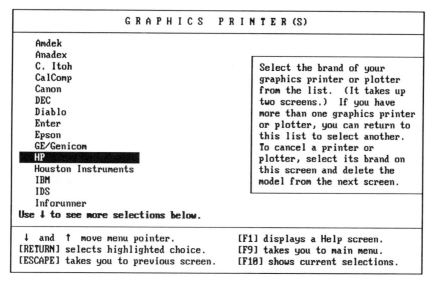

The Install Program presents this list of graphics printer manufacturers.

FIGURE 6-6

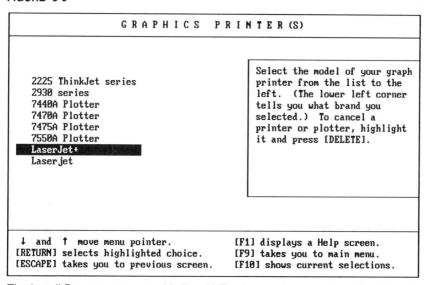

The Install Program presents this list of HP printers after you select the HP option from the list in Figure 6-5.

*Modifying the
existing driver set*

If you've previously saved a driver set with the Install Program and you want to add the HP LaserJet printer's driver to your existing driver set, you should run the Install Program and choose the **Change Selected Equipment** option from the main menu in Figure 6-1. When you choose this option, the Install Program presents the menu shown in Figure 6-7.

FIGURE 6-7

```
┌─────────────────────────────────────────────────────────────┐
│              S E L E C T E D    E Q U I P M E N T             │
├─────────────────────────────────────────────────────────────┤
│                                                               │
│                              ┌──────────────────────────────┐ │
│                              │ Select Return to Main Menu if │ │
│                              │ you have finished using this  │ │
│  ┌─────────────────────┐     │ menu. If you want to follow a │ │
│  │ Return to Main Menu │     │ guided path through the       │ │
│   Screen Display             │ installation procedure, choose│ │
│   Text Printer(s)            │ First-Time Installation from  │ │
│   Graphics Printer(s)        │ the main menu.                │ │
│   Save Changes               │                               │ │
│   Exit Install Program       │                               │ │
│                              │                               │ │
│                              └──────────────────────────────┘ │
│                                                               │
├─────────────────────────────────┬─────────────────────────────┤
│ ↓ and ↑ move menu pointer.      │ [F1] displays a Help screen.│
│ [RETURN] selects highlighted choice. │ [F9] takes you to main menu. │
│ [ESCAPE] takes you to previous screen. │ [F10] shows current selections. │
└─────────────────────────────────┴─────────────────────────────┘
```

*The Install Program presents this menu when you want to change your existing
driver set.*

You should now choose the **Text Printer(s)** option from this menu, choose the **HP** option from the list of printer manufacturers, and choose the **Unlisted** option (not the HP option) from the list of HP printers. Next, choose the **No Backspace** option to the menu shown in Figure 6-7.

If you intend to print graphs on your HP LaserJet printer, choose the **Graphics Printer(s)** option from the menu in Figure 6-7, choose the **HP** option from the list of printer manufacturers, and choose the **LaserJet** or **LaserJet +** option from the list of HP printers. (Lotus 1-2-3 Release 2.01 does not have a driver for the LaserJet 500 Plus, LaserJet Series II, or LaserJet IID printer; if you have any of these printers, just choose the **LaserJet +** option.)

After you've completed the procedures for installing the HP LaserJet as both a text printer and a graphics printer, you must save your changes in 1-2-3's driver set. To do this, choose the **Save Changes** option from the menu in Figure 6-7, and press ↵ to save the changes to the current file containing the driver set. After you've saved your changes, you can exit the Install Program and load 1-2-3's spreadsheet program. (For more information on the Install Program, see your 1-2-3 manuals.)

You'll probably need to use the Install Program to tell 1-2-3 about your LaserJet printer only once—just before you use 1-2-3 with your LaserJet for the first time. From that point on, you'll be able to print using the settings you've defined.

After you've used the Install Program to tell 1-2-3 that you're using an HP LaserJet printer, you need to load 1-2-3 and configure your printer with 1-2-3's / **W**orksheet **G**lobal **D**efault **P**rinter command. When you issue this command, 1-2-3 will present the menu shown in Figure 6-8. Before you try to print a 1-2-3 worksheet on the LaserJet, you need to adjust the following settings on this menu: Interface, Name, Pg-Length, Left, Right, Top, and Bottom.

Configuring the Printer

FIGURE 6-8

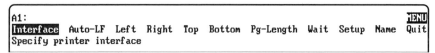

You'll use the / Worksheet Global Default Printer command to configure 1-2-3 for your LaserJet.

As we said in Chapter 1, you can run the LaserJet Series II and the LaserJet Plus printers as either parallel or serial printers. Since most PC printers are parallel printers, 1-2-3's default Interface setting is Parallel 1. If your LaserJet is connected to your computer's primary parallel interface, you probably won't need to adjust the Interface setting. However, if your LaserJet is connected to a second or third parallel interface, or if you are running your LaserJet as a serial printer, you must specify the appropriate Interface setting before you can print.

The Interface setting

To select a printer interface, choose the **Interface** option from the menu in Figure 6-8. When you do this, 1-2-3 will present a menu with eight options, as shown in Figure 6-9.

FIGURE 6-9

You'll use the Interface option on the / Worksheet Global Default Printer menu to specify the appropriate printer interface.

As we said, if your LaserJet is using your computer's primary parallel interface, you should leave the Interface setting at Parallel 1 (the default). If you are using anything other than the primary parallel interface, you should choose the option that corresponds to the interface used by your LaserJet. To choose the appropriate interface, just point to that option (or type the number of that option) and press ↵.

Although the HP LaserJet Series II and the HP LaserJet Plus are equipped with both a parallel and a serial interface, the original HP LaserJet is equipped with only a serial interface. If you have an original LaserJet printer, or if you want to run your LaserJet Plus or LaserJet Series II as a serial printer, you need to choose the appropriate serial interface setting from the Interface menu (options 2 or 4). You must also ensure that you've used DOS's MODE command to define the baud rate, number of stop bits, and parity for your printer. (Parallel printers don't require you to specify the baud rate, stop bits, and parity.) For instance, suppose you have connected your LaserJet to your computer's primary serial interface (COM1:). To define the baud rate, parity, data bits, and stop bits for COM1:, you must issue the DOS command

MODE COM1:9600,n,8,1,p

before you load 1-2-3. Once you have issued this MODE command and have started your 1-2-3 session, just choose the appropriate Interface setting for the serial port you defined in your MODE command (Serial 1 in this case).

The Name setting

The Name setting in Figure 6-8 on page 223 specifies which printer driver you want 1-2-3 to use when it prints your 1-2-3 worksheet. If you've installed more than one printer driver, you should choose the option that corresponds to the Unlisted, No Backspace printer driver. (If you don't see the Unlisted, No Backspace option on the Name menu, you need to run 1-2-3's Install Program.)

The Pg-Length setting

The Pg-Length setting specifies the default page length for your 1-2-3 reports. Since most PC printers automatically print 66 lines on a standard-size page, 1-2-3's default page length is 66. Because LaserJet printers automatically print only 60 lines per page, however, you'll need to change 1-2-3's default Pg-Length setting from 66 to 60. If you print a worksheet on the LaserJet printer with a Pg-Length setting of 66, 1-2-3 will not break the pages of the report in the proper locations.

To specify a page length setting of 60, simply choose the **P**g-Length option from the Printer menu shown in Figure 6-8, type **60**, and press ↵.

Margin settings

The Left, Right, Top, and Bottom margin settings specify the default margins for your 1-2-3 reports. You should set the Left, Top, and Bottom margin settings to 0 and the Right margin setting to 80.

To set the Left margin setting to 0, choose the **L**eft option from the Printer menu, type **0**, and press ↵. Similarly, to set the Top or Bottom margin settings to 0, choose **T**op (or **B**ottom), type **0**, and press ↵. Finally, to set the Right margin setting to 80, choose **R**ight, type **80**, and press ↵.

You should not change 1-2-3's default Auto-LF, Wait, and Setup settings. The Auto-LF and Wait settings should remain No, and the Setup setting should remain blank. If you inadvertently change these default settings, use the / Worksheet Global Default Printer command to restore them.

Other settings

After you've defined all the appropriate settings on the Printer menu, press [**Esc**] to return to the Default menu and choose the **U**pdate option. Once you've updated the default settings, 1-2-3 will use those defaults every time it prints a worksheet.

Updating and Viewing Your Print Settings

You can view your current printer defaults at any time by issuing the / **W**orksheet **G**lobal **D**efault **S**tatus command. When you issue this command, 1-2-3 will present a screen like the one in Figure 6-10. Notice that all the settings you just defined are shown in the upper-left portion of the screen.

FIGURE 6-10

```
A1:                                                          STAT

    Printer:                          International:
       Interface..... Parallel 1         Punctuation..... A
       Auto-linefeed. No                     Point Dot
                                          Argument Comma
       Margins                           Thousands Comma
          Left 0      Top 0
          Right 80  Bottom 0           Currency........ $ (Prefix)
                                       Date format D4.. A (MM/DD/YY)
       Page length... 60               Time format D8.. A (HH:MM:SS)
       Wait.......... No
       Setup string..
       Name.......... Unlisted No Backspace

    Directory at startup: B:\

    Help access method: Removable

    Clock on screen: None
```

You can view your current printer defaults at any time by issuing the / Worksheet Global Default Status command.

1-2-3 offers several tools that allow you to create attractive worksheet reports with your HP LaserJet printer. In this section, we'll show you how to use these tools to create worksheet reports that suit your specific needs.

PRINTING WORKSHEETS

The / **P**rint **P**rinter command is the tool you will use to print reports in 1-2-3. When you issue this command, 1-2-3 will present the menu shown in Figure 6-11. The options on this menu allow you to define the area of the worksheet you want to print, set up various formatting options, advance the paper in the printer, and print.

Printing Basics

FIGURE 6-11

```
A1:                                                          MENU
Range Line Page Options Clear Align Go Quit
Specify a range to print
```

You will use the / Print Printer command to print your 1-2-3 worksheets.

To print a worksheet, you need to choose the Range option from the Printer menu, select the range of cells you want to include in the report, align the paper in the printer, choose the Align command from the Printer menu, and then choose Go. The Options command on the Printer menu lets you customize your reports in a number of ways. We'll show you how to use these options to produce different kinds of reports on the LaserJet in a few pages.

Aligning paper

As with other types of printers, you must align the paper in the HP LaserJet printer before you send the data to be printed. To align paper in the LaserJet, press the ON LINE key on the LaserJet's control panel to take the printer off-line, and then press the FORM FEED key to eject the current page. After you press the ON LINE key again to put the printer back on-line, issue 1-2-3's / **P**rint **P**rinter Align command. This command tells 1-2-3 that the LaserJet is ready to begin printing on a new sheet of paper. If you do not follow this aligning procedure, 1-2-3 may insert page breaks in the wrong places in your report.

An example

Figure 6-12 shows part of a worksheet that contains a sales forecast for a fictitious company. The worksheet shows the expected level of sales for several cities beginning in January 1990 and extends from cell A1 to cell L69.

To print this worksheet, first issue the / **P**rint **P**rinter command and choose the **R**ange option. When 1-2-3 prompts you to specify the range of the worksheet you want to print, select the range **A1..L69** (either by typing or by pointing), and press ↵. Next, check the LaserJet's printer tray to make sure that it contains paper and that the ON LINE light is on. When the printer is ready, choose **A**lign from the Printer menu to tell 1-2-3 that you're ready to begin printing at the top of a new sheet of paper. Finally, print the report by choosing **G**o. As soon as you choose the Go option, 1-2-3's Mode indicator will change from MENU to WAIT, and 1-2-3 will begin sending the worksheet data to the printer. When 1-2-3 returns to the MENU mode, you'll need to choose the **P**age option from the Printer menu to eject the last page. Figure 6-13 on page 228 shows the resulting report as it will appear when printed on any HP LaserJet printer.

FIGURE 6-12

```
A1: [W22] 'Sales Forecast by Region                                      READY

           A           B        C        D        E        F
1   Sales Forecast by Region
2   ================================================================
3                     Jan-90   Feb-90   Mar-90   Apr-90   May-90
4                     ------   ------   ------   ------   ------
5   East
6     Raleigh, NC     $1,145   $1,264   $1,383   $1,502   $1,621
7     Providence, RI    $873     $882     $891     $900     $909
8     Baltimore, MD   $1,179   $1,298   $1,417   $1,536   $1,655
9     Washington, DC  $1,196   $1,315   $1,434   $1,553   $1,672
10    Virginia Beach, VA  $736   $848     $960   $1,072   $1,184
11    Carson City, NJ   $792     $904   $1,016   $1,128   $1,240
12    Syracuse, NY    $1,213   $1,332   $1,451   $1,570   $1,689
13    Boston, MA      $1,230   $1,349   $1,468   $1,587   $1,706
14    Atlantic City, NJ $1,247 $1,366   $1,485   $1,604   $1,723
15    Hartford, CT      $945     $956     $967     $978     $989
16                    ------   ------   ------   ------   ------
17      East Total    $9,611  $10,558  $11,505  $12,452  $13,399
18                    ======  =======  =======  =======  =======
19
20  South
```

We'll use this worksheet to demonstrate 1-2-3's printing capabilities.

Printing partial pages

Because the HP LaserJet does not eject a printed page until it receives a full page of information, you'll need to issue 1-2-3's / Print Printer Page command to eject the last page of your worksheet almost every time you print a report. Issuing this command has the same effect as pressing the FORM FEED key on the LaserJet's control panel—it tells the printer that the current page is finished and should be ejected from the printer. Of course, you can always tell when a partial page has been sent to the LaserJet by observing the FORM FEED light on the LaserJet's control panel. When this light is on, you can use either the LaserJet's FORM FEED key or 1-2-3's / Print Printer Page command to eject the current page.

Formatting Reports

1-2-3 offers several formatting options that you can use to improve the appearance and clarity of the reports you print on the HP LaserJet. In addition to modifying the report's margins, you can change the page length, define a header and footer, define a setup string, and designate certain rows and columns in your report as headings. In this section, we'll demonstrate how to make these kinds of changes to your reports.

FIGURE 6-13

Sales Forecast by Region

Page 1 (upper left)

	Jan-90	Feb-90	Mar-90	Apr-90	May-90
East					
Raleigh, NC	$1,145	$1,264	$1,383	$1,502	$1,621
Providence, RI	$873	$882	$891	$900	$909
Baltimore, MD	$1,179	$1,298	$1,417	$1,536	$1,655
Washington, DC	$1,196	$1,315	$1,434	$1,553	$1,672
Virginia Beach, VA	$736	$848	$960	$1,072	$1,184
Carson City, NJ	$792	$904	$1,016	$1,128	$1,240
Syracuse, NY	$1,213	$1,332	$1,451	$1,570	$1,689
Boston, MA	$1,230	$1,349	$1,468	$1,587	$1,706
Atlantic City, NJ	$1,247	$1,366	$1,485	$1,604	$1,723
Hartford, CT	$945	$956	$967	$978	$989
East Total	$9,611	$10,558	$11,505	$12,452	$13,399
South					
Miami, FL	$879	$1,023	$1,167	$1,311	$1,455
Atlanta, GA	$903	$1,047	$1,191	$1,335	$1,479
Jackson, MS	$927	$1,071	$1,215	$1,359	$1,503
Nashville, TN	$1,001	$1,047	$1,093	$1,139	$1,185
Hilton Head, SC	$1,024	$1,070	$1,116	$1,162	$1,208
Louisville, KY	$951	$1,095	$1,239	$1,383	$1,527
Knoxville, TN	$975	$1,119	$1,263	$1,407	$1,551
Tallahassee, FL	$1,325	$1,367	$1,409	$1,451	$1,493
Boca Raton, FL	$1,346	$1,388	$1,430	$1,472	$1,514
Myrtle Beach, SC	$1,162	$1,281	$1,400	$1,519	$1,638
Birmingham, AL	$999	$1,143	$1,287	$1,431	$1,575
South Total	$11,492	$12,651	$13,810	$14,969	$16,128
Midwest					
Indianapolis, IN	$2,179	$2,270	$2,361	$2,452	$2,543
Chicago, IL	$2,192	$2,283	$2,374	$2,465	$2,556
Dayton, OH	$2,205	$2,296	$2,387	$2,478	$2,569
Springfield, IL	$2,218	$2,309	$2,400	$2,491	$2,582
St. Louis, MO	$2,231	$2,322	$2,413	$2,504	$2,595
Fort Wayne, IN	$2,244	$2,335	$2,426	$2,517	$2,608
Milwaukee, WI	$3,210	$3,223	$3,236	$3,249	$3,262
Kansas City, MO	$2,257	$2,348	$2,439	$2,530	$2,621
Midwest Total	$18,736	$19,386	$20,036	$20,686	$21,336
West					
Denver, CO	$3,921	$4,411	$4,901	$5,391	$5,881

Page 2 (upper right)

	Jun-90	Jul-90	Aug-90	Sep-90	TOTALS
$1,740	$1,859	$1,978	$2,097	
$918	$927	$936	$945	
$1,774	$1,893	$2,012	$2,131	
$1,791	$1,910	$2,029	$2,148	
$1,296	$1,408	$1,520	$1,632	
$1,352	$1,464	$1,576	$1,688	
$1,808	$1,927	$2,046	$2,165	
$1,825	$1,944	$2,063	$2,182	
$1,842	$1,961	$2,080	$2,199	
$1,000	$1,011	$1,022	$1,033	
$14,346	$15,293	$16,240	$17,187	$120,591
$1,599	$1,743	$1,887	$2,031	
$1,623	$1,767	$1,911	$2,055	
$1,647	$1,791	$1,935	$2,079	
$1,231	$1,277	$1,323	$1,369	
$1,254	$1,300	$1,346	$1,392	
$1,671	$1,815	$1,959	$2,103	
$1,695	$1,839	$1,983	$2,127	
$1,535	$1,577	$1,619	$1,661	
$1,556	$1,598	$1,640	$1,682	
$1,757	$1,876	$1,995	$2,114	
$1,719	$1,863	$2,007	$2,151	
$17,287	$18,446	$19,605	$20,764	$145,152
$2,634	$2,725	$2,816	$2,907	
$2,647	$2,738	$2,829	$2,920	
$2,660	$2,751	$2,842	$2,933	
$2,673	$2,764	$2,855	$2,946	
$2,686	$2,777	$2,868	$2,959	
$2,699	$2,790	$2,881	$2,972	
$3,275	$3,288	$3,301	$3,314	
$2,712	$2,803	$2,894	$2,985	
$21,986	$22,636	$23,286	$23,936	$192,024
$6,371	$6,861	$7,351	$7,841	

Page 3 (lower left)

Reno, NV	$3,970	$4,460	$4,950	$5,440	$5,930
Salem, OR	$4,019	$4,509	$4,999	$5,489	$5,979
Albuquerque, NM	$4,068	$4,558	$5,048	$5,538	$6,028
Columbia, WA	$2,621	$2,714	$2,807	$2,900	$2,993
Boise, ID	$2,652	$2,745	$2,838	$2,931	$3,024
Flagstaff, AZ	$2,683	$2,776	$2,869	$2,962	$3,055
Phoenix, AZ	$4,117	$4,607	$5,097	$5,587	$6,077
San Diego, CA	$4,166	$4,656	$5,146	$5,636	$6,126
San Francisco, CA	$4,215	$4,705	$5,195	$5,685	$6,175
Santa Monica, CA	$4,264	$4,754	$5,244	$5,734	$6,224
Pasadena, CA	$4,313	$4,803	$5,293	$5,783	$6,273
Dallas, TX	$4,362	$4,852	$5,342	$5,832	$6,322
Houston, TX	$5,217	$5,230	$5,243	$5,256	$5,269
West Total	$49,371	$54,550	$59,729	$64,908	$70,087
GRAND TOTAL	$89,210	$97,145	$105,080	$113,015	$120,950

Page 4 (lower right)

$6,420	$6,910	$7,400	$7,890	
$6,469	$6,959	$7,449	$7,939	
$6,518	$7,008	$7,498	$7,988	
$3,086	$3,179	$3,272	$3,365	
$3,117	$3,210	$3,303	$3,396	
$3,148	$3,241	$3,334	$3,427	
$6,567	$7,057	$7,547	$8,037	
$6,616	$7,106	$7,596	$8,086	
$6,665	$7,155	$7,645	$8,135	
$6,714	$7,204	$7,694	$8,184	
$6,763	$7,253	$7,743	$8,233	
$6,812	$7,302	$7,792	$8,282	
$5,282	$5,295	$5,308	$5,321	
$75,266	$80,445	$85,624	$90,803	$630,783
$128,885	$136,820	$144,755	$152,690	$1,088,550

This is a printout of the complete worksheet represented in Figure 6-12.

Margin settings

Figure 6-14 shows a larger view of page 1 from the report in Figure 6-13. We will use this page to illustrate how 1-2-3's margin settings affect the format of the printed report.

As you probably know by now, the LaserJet printer does not print at the very top, bottom, left, and right edges of the page. This "unprintable" area occupies the first three and last three lines of the page, and the first $2^1/_2$ and last $2^1/_2$ character spaces of each row. In other words, the unprintable area on a standard $8^1/_2$- by 11-inch page is $^1/_2$ inch at the top and bottom and $^1/_4$ inch at the left and right edges of each page.

The unprintable area

We have recommended that you use a default Top and Bottom margin setting of 0 for your reports so that you can fit as much information as possible onto each page. As you probably know, 1-2-3 reserves three rows at the top of each page for a header. When you consider the three unprintable lines along with a three-line header, you'll see that a Top margin setting of 0 creates an effective top margin of six lines for each page in the report. Similarly, since there are three unprintable lines at the bottom of the page, along with a three-line footer, a Bottom margin setting of 0 produces an effective bottom margin of six lines, as well.

Top and bottom margins

FIGURE 6-14

```
Sales Forecast by Region
================================================================
                      Jan-90    Feb-90    Mar-90    Apr-90    May-90
                      ------    ------    ------    ------    ------
East
  Raleigh, NC         $1,145    $1,264    $1,383    $1,502    $1,621
  Providence, RI        $873      $882      $891      $900      $909
  Baltimore, MD       $1,179    $1,298    $1,417    $1,536    $1,655
  Washington, DC      $1,196    $1,315    $1,434    $1,553    $1,672
  Virginia Beach, VA    $736      $848      $960    $1,072    $1,184
  Carson City, NJ       $792      $904    $1,016    $1,128    $1,240
  Syracuse, NY        $1,213    $1,332    $1,451    $1,570    $1,689
  Boston, MA          $1,230    $1,349    $1,468    $1,587    $1,706
  Atlantic City, NJ   $1,247    $1,366    $1,485    $1,604    $1,723
  Hartford, CT          $945      $956      $967      $978      $989
                      ------    ------    ------    ------    ------
      East Total      $9,611   $10,558   $11,505   $12,452   $13,399
                      ======    ======    ======    ======    ======

South
  Miami, FL             $879    $1,023    $1,167    $1,311    $1,455
  Atlanta, GA           $903    $1,047    $1,191    $1,335    $1,479
  Jackson, MS           $927    $1,071    $1,215    $1,359    $1,503
  Nashville, TN       $1,001    $1,047    $1,093    $1,139    $1,185
  Hilton Head, SC     $1,024    $1,070    $1,116    $1,162    $1,208
  Louisville, KY        $951    $1,095    $1,239    $1,383    $1,527
  Knoxville, TN         $975    $1,119    $1,263    $1,407    $1,551
  Tallahassee, FL     $1,325    $1,367    $1,409    $1,451    $1,493
  Boca Raton, FL      $1,346    $1,388    $1,430    $1,472    $1,514
  Myrtle Beach, SC    $1,162    $1,281    $1,400    $1,519    $1,638
  Birmingham, AL        $999    $1,143    $1,287    $1,431    $1,575
                      ------    ------    ------    ------    ------
      South Total    $11,492   $12,651   $13,810   $14,969   $16,128
                      ======    ======    ======    ======    ======

Midwest
  Indianapolis, IN    $2,179    $2,270    $2,361    $2,452    $2,543
  Chicago, IL         $2,192    $2,283    $2,374    $2,465    $2,556
  Dayton, OH          $2,205    $2,296    $2,387    $2,478    $2,569
  Springfield, IL     $2,218    $2,309    $2,400    $2,491    $2,582
  St. Louis, MO       $2,231    $2,322    $2,413    $2,504    $2,595
  Fort Wayne, IN      $2,244    $2,335    $2,426    $2,517    $2,608
  Milwaukee, WI       $3,210    $3,223    $3,236    $3,249    $3,262
  Kansas City, MO     $2,257    $2,348    $2,439    $2,530    $2,621
                      ------    ------    ------    ------    ------
      Midwest Total  $18,736   $19,386   $20,036   $20,686   $21,336
                      ======    ======    ======    ======    ======

West
  Denver, CO          $3,921    $4,411    $4,901    $5,391    $5,881
```

This sample page from the report shown in Figure 6-13 has a left, top, and bottom margin of 0 and a right margin of 80.

If you want to change the Top margin setting for any of your 1-2-3 worksheets, first retrieve the worksheet, then issue the **/ Print Printer Options Margins Top** command. Issuing this command causes 1-2-3 to display the prompt *Enter Top Margin (0..32):*, followed by the current Top margin setting. When you see this prompt, type the new Top margin setting, and press ↵. You change the Bottom margin setting in much the same way: Issue the **/ Print Printer Options Margins Bottom** command, type the new bottom margin, and press ↵.

Although you may specify Top and Bottom margin settings ranging from 0 lines to 32 lines, you will rarely use a setting greater than 2 or 3 lines when printing to a LaserJet printer. As we have said, you'll almost always want to use Top and Bottom margin settings of 0 so that you can fit as much information as possible onto each page. Remember that even when you specify a top margin of 0, the LaserJet will still have an effective six-line top and bottom margin—three lines that are unprintable, and three lines that are reserved for a header or a footer.

If you want 1-2-3 to remove the lines that are reserved for the header and footer, you can issue the **/ Print Printer Options Other Unformatted** command. Unfortunately, this command affects more than just the header and footer—it also causes 1-2-3 to ignore the top and bottom margin, manual page breaks, and the page length. We'll discuss this command in more detail in the section "Printing Unformatted Reports" on page 242. As you might expect, 1-2-3 reserves either a full three lines for the header or footer, or no lines at all. Consequently, when you set your Top margin setting to 0, your effective top margin will be either three lines (the LaserJet's three unprintable lines) or six lines (the three unprintable lines plus the three lines reserved for the header or footer). There is no way you can print a report with an effective top margin of zero lines.

Left and right margins

We've recommended that you set your default Left margin setting to 0, which tells 1-2-3 to insert no blank characters at the beginning of each line in the report. However, since the LaserJet cannot print in the first $1/_4$-inch area at the left edge of each page, a Left margin setting of 0 produces an effective left margin of $2^1/_2$ characters.

If you want to insert additional spaces at the beginning of each line in the report, you can use the **/ Print Printer Options Margins Left** command to change the Left margin setting. When you issue this command, 1-2-3 will present the prompt *Enter Left Margin (0..240):*, followed by the current Left margin setting. When you see this prompt, just type the Left margin setting you want to use, and press ↵.

As the prompt indicates, you can enter a Left margin setting ranging from 0 to 240 characters. However, the Left margin setting must always be less than the Right margin setting. You will seldom use a Left margin setting of more than eight characters. We almost always use a Left margin setting of 0 in our reports so that we can fit as much information as possible onto each page.

1-2-3's Right margin setting is a little different from the other margin settings. While the Top, Bottom, and Left margin settings tell 1-2-3 how many blank rows or characters to reserve at the edge of a page, the Right margin setting tells 1-2-3 how many characters to print on each line of the page. A default Right margin setting of 80 means that each line of the report may contain a maximum of 80 characters. If you've specified a non-zero Left margin setting, however, then those characters count as part of the 80. For instance, a Left margin setting of 4 along with a Right margin setting of 80 allows 1-2-3 to print a maximum of 76 characters on each line of the report.

As you can see in Figure 6-14, Left and Right margin settings of 0 and 80, respectively, keep the report centered on the page. When you print a report with compressed characters, however, or in Landscape orientation, you'll need to change the Right margin setting in order to print more characters per line and to keep the lines centered on the page.

To change the Right margin setting, issue the / **Print Printer Options Margins & Length R**ight command. This command causes 1-2-3 to display the prompt *Enter Right Margin (0..240):*, followed by the current Right margin setting. When you see this prompt, type the new Right margin setting and press ↵.

The Right margin setting can range from 0 to 240 and must be larger than the Left margin setting. In fact, the difference between the Right margin setting and the Left margin setting must be equal to or greater than the widest column in your Print range. If the Right margin setting is less than the Left margin setting, 1-2-3 will not be able to print any data.

Always remember to use a Right margin setting that is consistent with the paper size you are using and with the setup string you have specified (if any). If you specify a Right margin setting that is greater than the maximum number of characters your printer can print on one line, each line of the report will wrap around to the next page. Not only does this make a confusing mess of the printout, it also disrupts 1-2-3's page breaks.

The maximum line length you use for 10 cpi type on a standard $8^1/_2$- by 11-inch sheet of paper is 80 characters. If you use a setup string to print in compressed type, the maximum length increases to about 132 characters. If you print a report with normal type in Landscape orientation, then the maximum line length can be as much as 106 characters. However, if you use compressed print and Landscape orientation, the maximum length increases to about 176 characters. We've included a summary of some popular report formats and their associated Right margin and Setup String settings in Table 6-1 on pages 236 and 237.

Page length

The number of lines that 1-2-3 prints on each page of a report is determined by the Pg-Length setting. Since the LaserJet cannot print on the first or last three lines of a page, 60 lines is the maximum the LaserJet can print on a standard-size sheet of paper. Consequently, you must make certain that 1-2-3's default page length is 60 before printing on a standard-size sheet of paper with the LaserJet.

Since the Pg-Length setting determines where 1-2-3 will place page breaks in a report, it is very important that you specify the appropriate page length. As we have said, a Pg-Length setting of 60 assumes that you are using the LaserJet to print text that occupies six vertical lines per inch on $8^{1}/_{2}$- by 11-inch paper in Portrait orientation. If you use a setup string that changes the character size or the paper orientation, or if you use paper that is longer or shorter than 11 inches (including legal-size paper, mailing labels, and special forms), you will need to adjust the Pg-Length setting accordingly.

To change the Pg-Length setting, issue the / **Print Printer Options Pg**-Length command. This command causes 1-2-3 to display the prompt *Enter Lines per Page (1..100):*, followed by the current Pg-Length setting. When you see this prompt, just type the new Pg-Length setting and press ↵.

You can specify any Pg-Length setting from one line to 100 lines. However, you must make sure that the page length you specify is at least as long as the sum of the top and bottom margins, the header and footer spaces, the lines that fall in the page's unprintable area, and one line of data. For example, if the Top and Bottom margin settings are both 0, then the minimum Pg-Length setting will be 13. We obtained this result by adding the two margin settings (0+0), the header and footer spaces (3+3), the lines that fall in the unprintable area at the top and bottom of the page (3+3), plus one line of data. If you enter a Pg-Length setting that is too small, 1-2-3 will alert you when you select Go to print your report by displaying the error message *Margins, header and footer equal or exceed page length.*

If you issue the / Print Printer Options Other command and choose the Unformatted option, 1-2-3 will completely ignore the Pg-Length setting. We'll discuss the Unformatted command in more detail on page 242.

Headers and footers

As you probably know, 1-2-3 lets you define a header, a footer, or both for your printed reports. A header is a line of text that is printed once at the top of every page in a report, while a footer is a line of text that is printed at the bottom of every page. You will probably use headers and footers to title your reports or to date and number the pages in your reports.

As we've explained, the LaserJet will not print on the first three or last three lines of a page. 1-2-3 reserves three additional lines just below the unprintable area at the top of the page for the header and three lines just above the unprintable area at the bottom of each page for the footer, even if you haven't defined a header or a footer. If you have defined a header, it will be printed on the first of the three header lines, with two blank lines between it and the first line of the report. Similarly, if you've defined a footer, it will appear on the third footer line at the bottom of the page, with two blank lines between it and the last line of the report.

The position of the first character in the header or footer is determined by the Left margin setting. (Of course, the "built-in" $^{1}/_{4}$-inch margin at the left edge of the page affects the header line—just as it affects the printed lines in the worksheet.)

Although headers and footers may contain up to 240 characters, the Left and Right margin settings determine the number of characters that can actually fit on the page. If your header or footer is too long to fit within your left and right margins, 1-2-3 will truncate the header or footer. The default left margin (4) and right margin (76) allow 1-2-3 to print a header or footer that is up to 72 characters long.

Since 1-2-3 is a character-based product, it can display only fixed-space characters on your screen, and it expects your printer to use only fixed-space characters in printed reports. For this reason, you'll find that it is impractical to print worksheet reports with proportionally spaced fonts on the HP LaserJet. If you want to use proportionally spaced fonts in your printed worksheets, you'll have to use a graphics-based spreadsheet application like Microsoft Excel.

Font options

Each LaserJet printer is equipped with a few internal fonts. Table 4-2 on page 141 lists the internal fonts that come with each member of the LaserJet family. As you can see in that table, almost every LaserJet printer is equipped with both Courier and Line Printer fonts. If your LaserJet is not equipped with the font you want to use, you'll have to purchase an optional font cartridge for your LaserJet.

The catalog in Appendix 2 lists HP's current font cartridge offerings. You should decide which fonts you'll most want to use in your printed worksheets, then identify the font cartridges that best suit your needs. You need to consider more than just the size of the fonts when purchasing a font cartridge. You should also consider the style of the fonts on each cartridge (Medium, Bold, Italics) and the orientations in which the fonts are available (Portrait, Landscape). One of the most popular font cartridges for 1-2-3 users with older LaserJet models is the "L" cartridge (HP Part No. 92286L), which contains Courier 12 Bold and Italic fonts, along with the Line Printer Compressed font (both fonts are offered in Portrait and in Landscape orientation). If you use a LaserJet Series II printer, you'll find that the "S1" cartridge (HP Part No. 92290S1) supplements the Series II's internal fonts quite nicely.

Although 1-2-3 is capable of using the LaserJet's soft fonts, we recommend that you not use soft fonts with 1-2-3 for two reasons. First of all, almost all soft fonts are proportionally spaced, which usually fouls up the spacing of your rows and columns in the printed worksheet. Second, soft fonts occupy a portion of your printer's RAM, which reduces the amount of printer RAM available for printing graphs. (We'll talk about printing graphs on the LaserJet in the next section of this chapter.) You'll save yourself plenty of time and trouble by using font cartridges instead of soft fonts when printing your 1-2-3 reports.

Setup strings

By default, the LaserJet uses the Courier 12 font to print 1-2-3 reports. This font occupies six lines per inch vertically and ten characters per inch horizontally. As you know, however, the LaserJet also has the ability to print more lines per inch, to print in boldface and in italics, to print in Portrait or in Landscape orientation, or even to print in completely different fonts. You can take advantage of the LaserJet's special print features by sending special strings of characters called setup strings.

The / Print Printer Options Setup command allows you to specify a setup string for your printed reports. When you issue this command, 1-2-3 will present the prompt *Enter Setup String:*. When you see this prompt, simply type the setup string that activates the print feature you want to use, and press ↵. If you use a setup string that changes the size of the type or the orientation of the page, you'll also need to change either the Pg-Length setting, the Right margin setting, or both.

The particular print options that are available depend on the LaserJet model you own and on the font options you've installed. Setup strings don't import any special features—they merely ask the LaserJet to use the features that are already there. For example, since none of the LaserJet printers contain a built-in italic font, you cannot use a setup string to create italic type on your LaserJet printer unless you've installed a font cartridge or a soft font that provides italic type. Table 6-1 on pages 236 and 237 lists the built-in fonts for each LaserJet model, while Appendix 2 lists the font options that are available for each printer. Make sure your printer has access to the font you want to use before you attempt to activate that font with a setup string.

Table 6-1 shows the common setup strings that are used for all LaserJet printers. As you can see, all of these setup strings have a similar form: They begin with \Ø27, are followed by various strings of characters, and end with a capital letter. For example, the character sequence that activates 12 cpi printing is \Ø27(sØp12H, while the sequence that activates 16.66 cpi printing is \Ø27(s16.66H. When you use the / Print Printer Options Setup command to define a setup string, you should type the appropriate string exactly as it appears in Table 6-1. Make sure you distinguish the number Ø from the capital letter O, and the number 1 from the lowercase letter *ℓ*. If you transpose these characters, your setup strings will not produce the results you expect.

After you have defined a setup string, 1-2-3 will automatically send that string to the printer each time you print a worksheet. Once a setup string has told the printer to use a particular print feature, the printer will continue using that feature until you use another setup string to turn off the feature or power off the printer. Any setup string you define with the / Print Printer Options Setup command will affect your entire worksheet, including headers and footers.

Using setup strings with soft fonts

If you download a soft font to your LaserJet printer before you load 1-2-3, you can tell 1-2-3 to use that font when you print your worksheet by sending the appropriate setup string. There are two ways to activate a downloaded soft font with a 1-2-3 setup string. First, you can specify the string that describes the soft font's orientation, pitch, and so forth, just as you would to activate a cartridge font. Alternatively, you can send a setup string that activates the font ID number of the font you've downloaded. (You must assign a font ID number between Ø and 32767 to each font you download.) For more information on how to activate soft fonts with setup strings, refer to the documentation included with your soft fonts.

If you can't make a setup string correctly alter the format of your printed report, use these tips to help debug the problem:

- First reset your LaserJet. If you have a Series II model, take the printer off-line, then press and hold the ENTER/RESET MENU key on the printer's control panel until the message *09 MENU RESET* appears. If you have a LaserJet Plus or LaserJet 500 Plus, press and hold the HOLD TO RESET key until *07* appears. If you have an original LaserJet printer, you must power the printer off and back on again.

- Check to see if your setup string has been typed correctly. The most common causes of setup string problems are the accidental use of the number one (1) in place of the lowercase letter *ℓ* and the use of the number zero (Ø) in place of the capital letter O. Also make sure you've used a backslash (\) instead of a forward slash (/). All the letters in the setup string should be lowercase letters, except the last letter, which must be uppercase.

- Make sure your printer is equipped with the print feature you are trying to activate. If you are attempting to use a particular font, make sure either that that font is one of your LaserJet's built-in fonts or that you've installed a font cartridge or a soft font that contains the font you're trying to use. If you're using a font cartridge, take the printer off-line, remove the cartridge, re-insert it firmly in the printer, and then put the printer back on-line before you test the setup string again.

After you've entered a setup string, you may want to remove that string so you can print a report in the LaserJet's standard typeface (Courier 12). To delete a setup string, issue the / **P**rint **P**rinter **O**ptions **S**etup command, press **[Esc]** to delete the existing string, then press ↵ to lock in the change.

You will find that deleting a setup string has no immediate effect on your printer. Although you've deleted the string, you'll still see the current special print features the next time you print. As we have said, once you turn on a special print attribute, that attribute remains in effect until you either turn off the printer or send another setup string that turns off the special attribute. Consequently, just deleting a setup string is usually not enough to reverse that string's effect. To restore normal printing, you must delete the setup string and reset the printer by turning it off and on again.

TABLE 6-1

	Setup	Pg-Length	Right
Portrait			
Letter-size paper			
60 lines per page			
10 cpi	\Ø27E	60	80
12 cpi	\Ø27(sØp12H	60	96
16.66 cpi	\Ø27(s16.66H	60	132
66 lines per page			
10 cpi	\Ø27&ℓ7.27C	66	80
12 cpi	\Ø27&ℓ7.27C\Ø27(sØp12H	66	96
16.66 cpi	\Ø27&ℓ7.27C\Ø27(s16.66H	66	132
89 lines per page			
10 cpi	\Ø27&ℓ5.39C	89	80
12 cpi	\Ø27&ℓ5.39C\Ø27(sØp12H	89	96
16.66 cpi	\Ø27&ℓ5.39C\Ø27(s16.66H	89	132
Legal-size paper (legal tray)			
78 lines per page			
10 cpi	\Ø27E	78	80
12 cpi	\Ø27(sØp12H	78	96
16.66 cpi	\Ø27(s16.66H	78	132
104 lines per page			
10 cpi	\Ø27&ℓ8D	100	80
12 cpi	\Ø27&ℓ8D\Ø27(sØp12H	100	96
16.66 cpi	\Ø27&ℓ8D\Ø27(s16.66H	100	132
150 lines per page			
16.66 cpi	\Ø27&ℓ4.16C\Ø27(s16.66H	100	132
Legal-size paper (manual feed)			
78 lines per page			
10 cpi	\Ø27&ℓ84p2H	78	80
12 cpi	\Ø27&ℓ84p2H\Ø27(sØp12H	78	96
16.66 cpi	\Ø27&ℓ84p2H\Ø27(s16.66H	78	132
104 lines per page			
10 cpi	\Ø27&ℓ84p2hØo8D	100	80
12 cpi	\Ø27&ℓ84p2hØo8D\Ø27(sØp12H	100	96
16.66 cpi	\Ø27&ℓ84p2hØo8D\Ø27(s16.66H	100	132
150 lines per page			
16.66 cpi	\Ø27&ℓ84p2hØo4.16C\Ø27(s16.66H	100	132

Landscape	Setup	Pg-Length	Right
Letter-size paper			
45 lines per page			
10 cpi	\Ø27&ℓ1O	45	106
12 cpi	\Ø27&ℓ1O\Ø27(sØp12H	45	127
16.66 cpi	\Ø27&ℓ1O\Ø27(s16.66H	45	176
66 lines per page			
10 cpi	\Ø27&ℓ1o5.45C	66	106
12 cpi	\Ø27&ℓ1o5.45C\Ø27(sØp12H	66	127
16.66 cpi	\Ø27&ℓ1o5.45C\Ø27(s16.66H	66	176
Legal-size paper (legal tray)			
45 lines per page			
10 cpi	\Ø27&ℓ1O	45	136
12 cpi	\Ø27&ℓ1O\Ø27(sØp12H	45	163
16.66 cpi	\Ø27&ℓ1O\Ø27(s16.66H	45	226
66 lines per page			
10 cpi	\Ø27&ℓ1o5.45C	66	136
12 cpi	\Ø27&ℓ1o5.45C\Ø27(sØp12H	66	163
16.66 cpi	\Ø27&ℓ1o5.45C\Ø27(s16.66H	66	226
Legal-size paper (manual feed)			
45 lines per page			
10 cpi	\Ø27&ℓ84p2h1O	45	136
12 cpi	\Ø27&ℓ84p2h1O\Ø27(sØp12H	45	163
16.66 cpi	\Ø27&ℓ84p2h1O\Ø27(s16.66H	45	226
66 lines per page			
10 cpi	\Ø27&ℓ84p2h1o5.45C	66	136
12 cpi	\Ø27&ℓ84p2h1o5.45C\Ø27(sØp12H	66	163
16.66 cpi	\Ø27&ℓ84p2h1o5.45C\Ø27(s16.66H	66	226

You can use these common setup strings to activate your printer's special print features.

Instead of simply deleting a setup string, you can replace the existing setup string with a new string that resets the printer to its default condition. For all LaserJet printers, this setup string is \Ø27E. When 1-2-3 sends this string to the printer, it will reset all formatting options.

Embedded setup strings

If you want to assign some special attributes to just a portion of your worksheet, you can embed setup strings that control those attributes directly in the worksheet. To embed a setup string in your worksheet, you must first insert a blank row directly above the first row that you want to print with the special attribute. Then, you must move the cell pointer to the leftmost column in the Print range in that row (this is usually column A). When the cell pointer is in place, type two vertical bars (‖), followed by the setup string that signals the beginning of the print attribute.

You'll usually want to include a second embedded setup string that turns off the special print attribute activated by the first string. You repeat the procedure to insert a second embedded setup string, except that you move the cell pointer to the row below the last row that you want to print with the special attribute. Table 6-2 shows a few popular setup strings you can embed in your 1-2-3 worksheets.

TABLE 6-2

Feature	Setup String
Underline On	\Ø27&dD
Underline Off	\Ø27&d@
Boldface On	\Ø27(s3B
Boldface Off	\Ø27(sØB
Italic On	\Ø27(s1S
Italic Off	\Ø27(sØS
Printer Reset	\Ø27E

You might want to embed these setup strings in your 1-2-3 worksheets.

An example

As an example of how you might use these strings, consider the worksheet shown in Figure 6-15. As you can see, we've embedded the setup string that turns on underlining (\Ø27&dD) in row 2 of this worksheet, and we've embedded the string that turns off underlining (\Ø27&d@) in row 4 of the worksheet. (Notice that the first vertical bar characters of the embedded setup strings are not displayed in the cells of the worksheet.) When we print this worksheet on an HP LaserJet printer, we will generate the report shown in Figure 6-16. As you can see, the entry in cell A3, *Sales Forecast for 1989*, is underlined, while the rest of the page is printed without underlines.

FIGURE 6-15

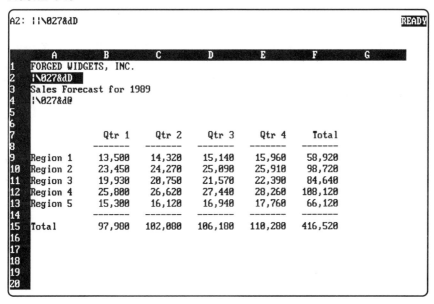

We've used embedded setup strings in this worksheet to underline the title.

FIGURE 6-16

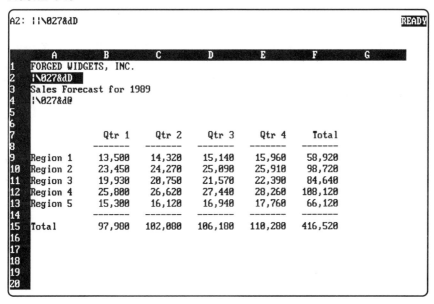

This is how the worksheet in Figure 6-15 looks when we print it on a LaserJet printer.

Troubleshooting

If your embedded setup string does not generate the results you expect, first check to see whether you have typed the embedded setup string correctly. Make sure you have not confused any number Øs with capital Os, or any number 1s with lowercase letter ℓs. Also, make sure you've preceded the setup string with two vertical bar characters (∥).

If you're certain that you've entered the setup string correctly, make sure you've defined the correct Print range. If you've inserted a blank row above the first row in your worksheet to hold an embedded setup string, you'll probably need to redefine the Print range to include the new row 1. Also, remember that your embedded setup string must appear in the leftmost column of the Print range (usually column A) in order to work properly.

Finally, make sure that your LaserJet is capable of printing with the special attribute you are attempting to invoke. If you're attempting to turn on bold printing, for example, make sure your printer has access to a bold font in the appropriate typeface. Remember that the setup string does not create any special print features, it merely activates the print features that already exist inside your LaserJet.

Sample reports

The sample reports and accompanying page layout settings in this section should help you decide which style to use for your 1-2-3 reports. You'll notice that most of these reports require either a LaserJet Series II printer or a font cartridge. In all of these examples, we've set the top, bottom, and left margins to 0.

If you need to fit more than 80 characters on a single line of a report, then you'll want to use the settings in Figure 6-17 to generate compressed characters in Portrait orientation.

FIGURE 6-17

Requires: LaserJet Series
  II or font cartridge
Right: 132
Page Length: 60
Setup String:
  \Ø27E\Ø27(s16.66H

This report is printed in Portrait orientation at 16.66 cpi and 60 lines per page.

If your worksheet report is relatively small (fewer than 45 lines) and is wider than it is tall, you may prefer to print the report in uncompressed print in Landscape orientation. To do this, you should use the layout settings in Figure 6-18.

FIGURE 6-18

```
Sales Forecast by Region
=================================================================================
                    Jan-90   Feb-90   Mar-90   Apr-90   May-90   Jun-90   Jul-90
                    ------   ------   ------   ------   ------   ------   ------
East
  Raleigh, NC       $1,145   $1,264   $1,383   $1,502   $1,621   $1,740   $1,859
  Providence, RI      $873     $882     $891     $900     $909     $918     $927
  Baltimore, MD     $1,179   $1,298   $1,417   $1,536   $1,655   $1,774   $1,893
  Washington, DC    $1,196   $1,315   $1,434   $1,553   $1,672   $1,791   $1,910
  Virginia Beach, VA  $736     $848     $960   $1,072   $1,184   $1,296   $1,408
  Carson City, NJ     $792     $904   $1,016   $1,128   $1,240   $1,352   $1,464
  Syracuse, NY      $1,213   $1,332   $1,451   $1,570   $1,689   $1,808   $1,927
  Boston, MA        $1,230   $1,349   $1,468   $1,587   $1,706   $1,825   $1,944
  Atlantic City, NJ $1,247   $1,366   $1,485   $1,604   $1,723   $1,842   $1,961
  Hartford, CT        $945     $956     $967     $978     $989   $1,000   $1,011
                    ------   ------   ------   ------   ------   ------   ------
    East Total      $9,611  $10,558  $11,505  $12,452  $13,399  $14,346  $15,293
                    ======   ======   ======   ======   ======   ======   ======

South
  Miami, FL           $879   $1,023   $1,167   $1,311   $1,455   $1,599   $1,743
  Atlanta, GA         $903   $1,047   $1,191   $1,335   $1,479   $1,623   $1,767
  Jackson, MS         $927   $1,071   $1,215   $1,359   $1,503   $1,647   $1,791
  Nashville, TN     $1,001   $1,047   $1,093   $1,139   $1,185   $1,231   $1,277
  Hilton Head, SC   $1,024   $1,070   $1,116   $1,162   $1,208   $1,254   $1,300
  Louisville, KY      $951   $1,095   $1,239   $1,383   $1,527   $1,671   $1,815
  Knoxville, TN       $975   $1,119   $1,263   $1,407   $1,551   $1,695   $1,839
  Tallahassee, FL   $1,325   $1,367   $1,409   $1,451   $1,493   $1,535   $1,577
  Boca Raton, FL    $1,346   $1,388   $1,430   $1,472   $1,514   $1,556   $1,598
  Myrtle Beach, SC  $1,162   $1,281   $1,400   $1,519   $1,638   $1,757   $1,876
  Birmingham, AL      $999   $1,143   $1,287   $1,431   $1,575   $1,719   $1,863
                    ------   ------   ------   ------   ------   ------   ------
    South Total    $11,492  $12,651  $13,810  $14,969  $16,128  $17,287  $18,446
                    ======   ======   ======   ======   ======   ======   ======

Midwest
  Indianapolis, IN  $2,179   $2,270   $2,361   $2,452   $2,543   $2,634   $2,725
  Chicago, IL       $2,192   $2,283   $2,374   $2,465   $2,556   $2,647   $2,738
  Dayton, OH        $2,205   $2,296   $2,387   $2,478   $2,569   $2,660   $2,751
```

Requires: LaserJet Series II or font cartridge   Right: 105
Page Length: 45   Setup String: \Ø27EØ27&ℓ1O
This report is printed in Landscape orientation at 10 cpi and 45 lines per page.

If you need to squeeze a few more characters on each line of a Landscape-oriented report, use the layout settings in Figure 6-19 on the following page to set up your LaserJet for compressed print in Landscape orientation.

If your worksheet is extremely wide in comparison to its length (as will be the case with a five-year sales forecast), you may prefer to use the layout settings in Figure 6-20 on page 243, which produce a compressed report in Landscape orientation on legal-size paper.

FIGURE 6-19

Sales Forecast by Region

	Jan-90	Feb-90	Mar-90	Apr-90	May-90	Jun-90	Jul-90	Aug-90	Sep-90	Oct-90	Nov-90	Dec-90	TOTALS
East													
Raleigh, NC	$1,145	$1,264	$1,383	$1,502	$1,621	$1,740	$1,859	$1,978	$2,097	$1,383	$1,502	$1,621	
Providence, RI	$873	$882	$891	$900	$909	$918	$927	$936	$945	$891	$900	$909	
Baltimore, MD	$1,179	$1,298	$1,417	$1,536	$1,655	$1,774	$1,893	$2,012	$2,131	$1,417	$1,536	$1,655	
Washington, DC	$1,196	$1,315	$1,434	$1,553	$1,672	$1,791	$1,910	$2,029	$2,148	$1,434	$1,553	$1,672	
Virginia Beach, VA	$736	$848	$960	$1,072	$1,184	$1,296	$1,408	$1,520	$1,632	$960	$1,072	$1,184	
Carson City, NJ	$792	$904	$1,016	$1,128	$1,240	$1,352	$1,464	$1,576	$1,688	$1,016	$1,128	$1,240	
Syracuse, NY	$1,213	$1,332	$1,451	$1,570	$1,689	$1,808	$1,927	$2,046	$2,165	$1,451	$1,570	$1,689	
Boston, MA	$1,230	$1,349	$1,468	$1,587	$1,706	$1,825	$1,944	$2,063	$2,182	$1,468	$1,587	$1,706	
Atlantic City, NJ	$1,247	$1,366	$1,485	$1,604	$1,723	$1,842	$1,961	$2,080	$2,199	$1,485	$1,604	$1,723	
Hartford, CT	$945	$956	$967	$978	$989	$1,000	$1,011	$1,022	$1,033	$967	$978	$989	
East Total	$9,611	$10,558	$11,505	$12,452	$13,399	$14,346	$15,293	$16,240	$17,187	$11,505	$12,452	$13,399	$157,947
South													
Miami, FL	$879	$1,023	$1,167	$1,311	$1,455	$1,599	$1,743	$1,887	$2,031	$1,167	$1,311	$1,455	
Atlanta, GA	$903	$1,047	$1,191	$1,335	$1,479	$1,623	$1,767	$1,911	$2,055	$1,191	$1,335	$1,479	
Jackson, MS	$927	$1,071	$1,215	$1,359	$1,503	$1,647	$1,791	$1,935	$2,079	$1,215	$1,359	$1,503	
Nashville, TN	$1,001	$1,047	$1,093	$1,139	$1,185	$1,231	$1,277	$1,323	$1,369	$1,093	$1,139	$1,185	
Hilton Head, SC	$1,024	$1,070	$1,116	$1,162	$1,208	$1,254	$1,300	$1,346	$1,392	$1,116	$1,162	$1,208	
Louisville, KY	$951	$1,095	$1,239	$1,383	$1,527	$1,671	$1,815	$1,959	$2,103	$1,239	$1,383	$1,527	
Knoxville, TN	$975	$1,119	$1,263	$1,407	$1,551	$1,695	$1,839	$1,983	$2,127	$1,263	$1,407	$1,551	
Tallahassee, FL	$1,325	$1,367	$1,409	$1,451	$1,493	$1,535	$1,577	$1,619	$1,661	$1,409	$1,451	$1,493	
Boca Raton, FL	$1,346	$1,388	$1,430	$1,472	$1,514	$1,556	$1,598	$1,640	$1,682	$1,430	$1,472	$1,514	
Myrtle Beach, SC	$1,162	$1,281	$1,400	$1,519	$1,638	$1,757	$1,876	$1,995	$2,114	$1,400	$1,519	$1,638	
Birmingham, AL	$999	$1,143	$1,287	$1,431	$1,575	$1,719	$1,863	$2,007	$2,151	$1,287	$1,431	$1,575	
South Total	$11,492	$12,651	$13,810	$14,969	$16,128	$17,287	$18,446	$19,605	$20,764	$13,810	$14,969	$16,128	$190,059
Midwest													
Indianapolis, IN	$2,179	$2,270	$2,361	$2,452	$2,543	$2,634	$2,725	$2,816	$2,907	$2,361	$2,452	$2,543	
Chicago, IL	$2,192	$2,283	$2,374	$2,465	$2,556	$2,647	$2,738	$2,829	$2,920	$2,374	$2,465	$2,556	
Dayton, OH	$2,205	$2,296	$2,387	$2,478	$2,569	$2,660	$2,751	$2,842	$2,933	$2,387	$2,478	$2,569	

Requires: LaserJet Series II or font cartridge   Right: 175

Page Length: 45   Setup String: \Ø27E\Ø27&ℓ1O\Ø27(s16.66H

This report is printed in Landscape orientation at 16.66 cpi and 45 lines per page.

Printing unformatted reports

1-2-3 offers you the option of printing "unformatted" reports—that is, reports that ignore the Top and Bottom margin settings, the Pg-Length setting, and any header or footer you have defined. Instead of reserving lines for the header, footer, top margin, and bottom margin areas at the top and bottom of each page, 1-2-3 will begin printing on the first printable line of the page and will continue printing to the last printable line of the page. Of course, the first and last printable lines of the page are $^1/_2$ inch from the top and bottom edges of the page.

To create an unformatted report, issue the / **Print Printer Options Other Unformatted** command. To turn formatting back on, issue the / **Print Printer Options Other Formatted** command.

Although the Unformatted option causes 1-2-3 to ignore the headers, footers, and manual page breaks, it will not affect your left and right margins or your setup string. The Left and Right margin settings still determine where the vertical page breaks in the report should occur. In addition, the printer will use whatever setup string you have defined.

If you have defined column headings before printing an unformatted report, those headings will appear on each vertical section of the report. However, because an unformatted report has no horizontal page breaks, the row headings will appear only once at the top of the report.

FIGURE 6-20

Sales Forecast by Region

Requires: LaserJet Series II or font cartridge   Right: 225
Page Length: 66   Setup String: \Ø27EØ27&ℓ84p2h1o5.45CØ27(s16.66H

This report is printed on legal-size paper in Landscape orientation at 16.66 cpi and 66 lines per page.

Resetting print defaults

After you change the default print settings for a worksheet, you might decide to return some or all of the print settings to their default values. The quickest way to do this is to issue the / Print Printer Clear command.

If you want to reset all the print settings to their defaults, issue the / **P**rint **P**rinter **C**lear **A**ll command. This command will delete your header and footer, remove any headings you have defined, and return the settings for the setup string, margins, and page length to their defaults. It also will remove the range you have defined as your Print range. The only settings that are not affected by this command are the manual page breaks you have defined, embedded setup strings, and the printer settings defined by the / Worksheet Global Default Printer command.

If you want to retain the current settings for the Print range, left heading, and top heading but reset the header, footer, margins, page length, and setup string, issue the / **P**rint **P**rinter **C**lear **F**ormat command. If you just want to clear the headings settings, issue the / **P**rint **P**rinter **C**lear **B**orders command. Finally, if you want to reset the Print range, issue the / **P**rint **P**rinter **C**lear **R**ange command.

PRINTING
GRAPHS

The process of printing a 1-2-3 graph on an HP LaserJet printer is entirely different from the process of printing a 1-2-3 worksheet. In this section, we'll tell you how to take advantage of the LaserJet's graphics capabilities, and we'll walk you through the process of printing some sample 1-2-3 graphs.

As you probably know, in order to print a graph you have created with 1-2-3, you must save that graph into a .PIC file, exit from 1-2-3, and then load 1-2-3's graph-printing utility program, PrintGraph. Once you've loaded PrintGraph, you must retrieve the appropriate .PIC file and adjust a few of the print settings. After you've done all of this, you can print the graph on your LaserJet.

You will not be able to use PrintGraph to print a graph on your LaserJet unless you have used the Install Program to install the LaserJet's graphics output driver. For an explanation of how to use the Install Program to install graphics output drivers, see the section entitled "Hardware Setup" at the beginning of this chapter, or refer to your 1-2-3 manuals.

Configuring
PrintGraph

Before you can use PrintGraph to print a 1-2-3 graph on your LaserJet printer, you need to tell 1-2-3 a few things about your printer. Specifically, you must indicate what kind of printer you have and how your printer is connected to your computer. The command you will use to define these settings is the Settings Hardware command. When you issue the Settings Hardware command, PrintGraph will present the menu shown in Figure 6-21.

FIGURE 6-21

```
Copyright 1986 Lotus Development Corp.  All Rights Reserved. Release 2.01  MENU

Set directory containing graphs
Graphs-Directory  Fonts-Directory  Interface  Printer  Size-Paper  Quit

    GRAPH     IMAGE OPTIONS                      HARDWARE SETUP
    IMAGES      Size                             Graphs Directory:
   SELECTED      Top        .395  X Black          B:\
                 Left      1.102  A Black         Fonts Directory:
                 Width     5.805  B Black           C:\APPS\123
                 Height    4.191  C Black         Interface:
                 Rotate     .000  D Black           Parallel 1
                                  E Black         Printer Type:
                 Font             F Black           HP LaserJet+/hi
                 1  BLOCK1                        Paper Size
                 2  BLOCK1                          Width     8.500
                                                   Length   11.000

                                                 ACTION OPTIONS
                                                 Pause: No    Eject: No
```

The Settings Hardware command lets you tell PrintGraph about your printer.

Just as you told 1-2-3 where to send your printed worksheets, you must tell PrintGraph which printer interface your LaserJet is using. To select a printer interface, choose the **Interface** option from the menu in Figure 6-21. When you do, 1-2-3 will present a menu with eight options, as shown in Figure 6-22. You'll notice that these are the same eight options 1-2-3 presents when you are defining a printer interface with 1-2-3's / Worksheet Global Default Printer Interface command.

Choosing an interface

FIGURE 6-22

```
Copyright 1986 Lotus Development Corp.  All Rights Reserved. Release 2.01  MENU

Parallel 1
1 2 3 4 5 6 7 8

   GRAPH      IMAGE OPTIONS                   HARDWARE SETUP
   IMAGES     Size          Range Colors     Graphs Directory:
   SELECTED   Top      .395  X Black            B:\
              Left    1.102  A Black          Fonts Directory:
              Width   5.805  B Black            C:\APPS\123
              Height  4.191  C Black          Interface:
              Rotate   .000  D Black            Parallel 1
                             E Black          Printer Type:
              Font           F Black            HP LaserJet+/hi
              1  BLOCK1                       Paper Size
              2  BLOCK1                         Width    8.500
                                                Length  11.000

                                             ACTION OPTIONS
                                             Pause: No   Eject: No
```

You'll use the Interface option on the Settings Hardware menu to specify the appropriate printer interface.

If your LaserJet is using your computer's primary parallel interface, you should leave the Interface setting at Parallel 1 (the default). If you are using anything other than the primary parallel interface, you should choose the option that corresponds to the interface used by your LaserJet. To choose the appropriate interface, just point to that option (or type the number of that option) and press ↵.

Although the HP LaserJet Series II and the HP LaserJet Plus are equipped with both a parallel and a serial interface, the original HP LaserJet is equipped with only a serial interface. If you have an original LaserJet printer, or if you want to run your LaserJet Plus or LaserJet Series II as a serial printer, you need to choose the appropriate serial Interface setting from the Interface menu (options 2 or 4). You must also make sure that you've used DOS's MODE command to define the baud rate, number of stop bits, and parity for your printer. (Parallel printers don't require you to specify baud rate, stop bits, and parity.) For instance, suppose you have connected your LaserJet to your computer's primary serial interface (COM1:). To define the baud rate, parity, data bits, and stop bits for COM1:, you must issue the DOS command

MODE COM1:9600,n,8,1

before you load PrintGraph. Once you have issued this MODE command and have started your PrintGraph session, choose the appropriate Interface setting for the serial port you defined in your MODE command (Serial 1 in this case).

Choosing
a printer

The Printer setting specifies which printer driver you want PrintGraph to use when it prints your 1-2-3 graphs. When you choose the Printer option, PrintGraph brings up a list of the printers you've installed with the Install Program. If you've installed the drivers for both the LaserJet and LaserJet Plus, PrintGraph will present the screen shown in Figure 6-23 when you choose the Printer option.

FIGURE 6-23

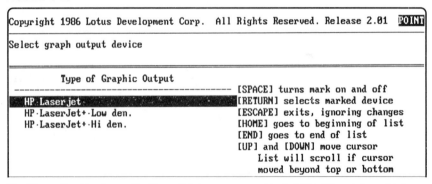

You'll use the Hardware Settings Printer command to tell PrintGraph for which LaserJet printer you have installed support, and in what mode you want to print.

If you have an original LaserJet printer, you need to choose the **HP Laserjet** option, which prints graphs at a resolution of 75 dpi. As you can see, PrintGraph automatically offers two density options for the LaserJet Plus—low density (100 dpi) and high density (300 dpi). If you have a LaserJet Plus, LaserJet 500 Plus, or LaserJet Series II printer, you'll have to choose one of the LaserJet Plus printer drivers. A full page of 300 dpi graphics requires about 1.5MB of printer memory. If you want to print full-page 300 dpi graphs, and your printer has less than 2MB of memory, you'll need to upgrade the memory on your printer.

After you use the ↓ and ↑ keys to highlight the appropriate LaserJet printer option, press the **[Spacebar]** to mark that choice. PrintGraph will place a # next to the device you select. When you've made your selection, press ↵ to lock in that choice and return to the Hardware Settings menu. If you change your mind, just repeat this procedure and select a new printer driver from the list.

Specifying paper size

The Settings Hardware Size-Paper command lets you specify the size of the paper you'll be using in your printer. PrintGraph's default paper size is $8^1/_2$ inches wide by 11 inches long. While this setting will probably be appropriate for most applications, you may need to change the Size-Paper setting in certain situations.

To specify a different paper size, just issue the Settings Hardware Size-Paper command to reveal the options Length and Width. To change the Page Length setting, choose the Length option and specify the new length in inches. To change the Page Width setting, choose the Width option and specify the new page width.

One common situation where you will need to change the Page Length setting is when you are using legal-size paper ($8^1/_2$-by 14-inches) to hold your printed graphs. To set up PrintGraph for legal-size paper, simply issue the Settings Hardware Size-Paper Length command, type **14**, and press ↵.

Defining the Graphs-Directory and Fonts-Directory

As you probably know, you must use the Graphs-Directory option to tell PrintGraph where you have stored the .PIC files you intend to print. Similarly, you must use the Fonts-Directory option to tell PrintGraph where you've installed PrintGraph's font files. If you do not define these two settings correctly, PrintGraph will be unable to print your graphs.

The Pause and Eject settings

The Pause and Eject settings are used to control the action of your printer when you are printing multiple graphs with one command. The Pause setting tells PrintGraph whether it should pause after it prints each graph in a series. If Pause is set to No (the default), PrintGraph will print all of the graphs in sequence without pausing. If Pause is set to Yes, however, PrintGraph will pause after it prints each graph and will make a beeping noise.

You'll probably want PrintGraph to pause between graphs whenever you are manually feeding sheets of paper to the LaserJet. To change the Pause setting from No (the default) to Yes, issue the Settings Action Pause command, and choose the **Yes** option.

When you issue the Settings Action Eject command, PrintGraph will offer you two choices: Yes and No. If you want to print each of your graphs on a separate page, then you should set Eject to **Yes**, which forces the LaserJet to eject the current page before printing a new graph. If you set Eject to **No**, PrintGraph will not advance your printer to the next page between graphs, enabling you to print more than one graph on a page. You must remember, however, that if there is not enough room to print an additional graph on the current page, PrintGraph will automatically eject the current page from the LaserJet.

Graph Print Basics

After you've configured PrintGraph for your LaserJet printer, you're ready to print your graphs. The Image-Select command on the main PrintGraph menu is the tool you use to retrieve .PIC files into PrintGraph. When you issue the Image-Select command, a list of all the .PIC files stored in the current graphs directory will appear on the screen, as shown in Figure 6-24.

FIGURE 6-24

```
┌─────────────────────────────────────────────────────────────────────────┐
│ Copyright 1986 Lotus Development Corp.   All Rights Reserved. Release 2.01 POINT │
│                                                                           │
│ Select graphs for output                                                  │
│ ───────────────────────────────────────────────────────────────────────  │
│                                                                           │
│     PICTURE     DATE      TIME     SIZE                                    │
│     ──────────────────────────────────────    [SPACE] turns mark on and off │
│     BUDGET    05-31-88  11:47     3528        [RETURN] selects marked pictures │
│     FORECAST  05-30-88  21:56     5673        [ESCAPE] exits, ignoring changes │
│     PROFITS   05-31-88  11:49     3816        [HOME] goes to beginning of list │
│     REVENUES  05-31-88  11:50     5540        [END] goes to end of list    │
│     SALES     05-31-88  11:50     4354        [UP] and [DOWN] move cursor  │
│                                                    List will scroll if cursor │
│                                                    moved beyond top or bottom │
│                                               [GRAPH] displays selected picture │
└─────────────────────────────────────────────────────────────────────────┘
```

The Image-Select command lets you choose the graphs you want to print.

To select a graph, use the ↓ and ↑ keys to position the cursor over the name of the graph you want to print, then press the **[Spacebar]** to select that graph. A # will appear next to the file name to indicate that it has been selected. If you want to deselect a selected graph, highlight it and press the [Spacebar] again.

If you want, you can select multiple graphs for printing. All you have to do is highlight the name of the first .PIC file that you want to print, press the **[Spacebar]**, then highlight the name of the second graph, press the **[Spacebar]** again, and so forth. After you've marked all the graphs you want to print, press ↵ to lock in your selections and return to the main PrintGraph menu.

Printing

Once you've selected a graph and returned to the main PrintGraph menu, issue the Align command to tell PrintGraph that the LaserJet is ready to print a new page, then issue the Go command to print the graph. As soon as you issue the Go command, PrintGraph will take a few seconds to load the appropriate font files and to form the print image. While this is taking place, 1-2-3 will display a message that informs you of the situation. When all of these preliminary tasks are out of the way, PrintGraph will begin sending data to the printer.

You'll find that the process of printing graphs on the LaserJet is relatively slow compared to printing worksheets. If your patience runs out and you want to stop printing before the graph is complete, press [Ctrl][Break], then [Esc].

As an example, suppose you have created the graph shown in Figure 6-25, and you want to print this graph using PrintGraph's default print settings. To do this, simply select the graph with the Image-Select command, make sure that the LaserJet printer is on-line and has no information in the print buffer, issue the Align command, then issue the Go command to print the graph. As soon as you choose the Go command, PrintGraph's Mode indicator will change to WAIT while PrintGraph loads the graph's fonts and generates the picture. When PrintGraph has finished printing the graph, the Mode indicator will change from WAIT to MENU to let you know that the graph is finished. Since the Eject option is set to No by default, you'll need to issue the Page command to eject the graph from the LaserJet. Figure 6-26 shows the printed graph as it appears when printed with PrintGraph's default settings.

An example

FIGURE 6-25

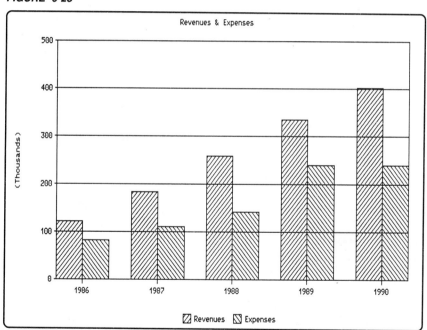

We'll use this 1-2-3 graph to demonstrate PrintGraph's printing capabilities.

FIGURE 6-26

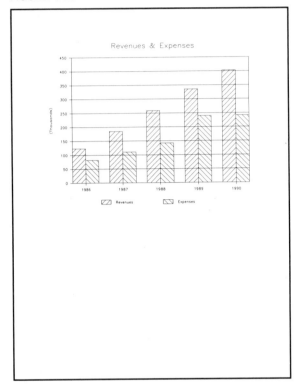

This graph was printed with PrintGraph's default format settings.

Notes

As you will recall, the LaserJet will not eject the current page until the page becomes full or until it receives a form feed command. If you have set the Eject setting to Yes, PrintGraph will automatically eject the current page after it prints each graph in the series. If, instead, you have set the Eject setting to No, you will need to issue the Page command on PrintGraph's main menu to eject the last page.

If you are using manual feed and you have set the Pause setting to Yes, PrintGraph will stop and beep after it prints each graph. During this time, you can insert a new sheet of paper and make any necessary adjustments to the printer. When you are ready to resume printing, press the [Spacebar].

Formatting the Graph

As you can see in Figure 6-26, PrintGraph's default settings cause graphs to be printed on half of the page in Portrait orientation. Although this format may be appropriate in most situations, you'll sometimes find that PrintGraph's default graph print settings do not suit your needs. Fortunately, the Settings Image command gives you control over the dimensions of the printed graph, its position on the page, and the fonts used in your printed graphs.

The Size options in PrintGraph let you change the size of a graph and its orientation on the page. The command for controlling graph size is Settings Image Size. There are three main choices for graph size: Full, Half, and Manual.

You can use the Full size option to make PrintGraph automatically adjust the width, height, margins, and orientation of your graph for a full-page graph. To do this, just issue the **Settings Image Size Full** command. When you issue this command, the Top, Left, Width, Height, and Rotate settings on the PrintGraph screen will change to reflect the new setting. Figure 6-27 shows the graph in Figure 6-26 printed full size. Notice that the full-size graph is rotated 90 degrees and completely fills the 8 $\frac{1}{2}$- by 11-inch page.

Full size

FIGURE 6-27

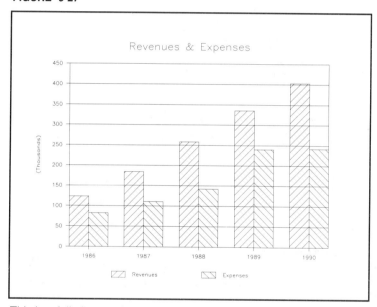

This is a full-size version of the graph in Figure 6-26.

With most printers, PrintGraph's Half option automatically adjusts the width, height, margins, and orientation settings for a half-page graph. When printing to a LaserJet printer, however, PrintGraph's Half settings do not allow you to print two half-size graphs on the same page because PrintGraph does not take into account the LaserJet's "built-in" $\frac{1}{2}$-inch margins at the top and bottom of each page. If you attempt to print two graphs on the same page with PrintGraph's Half settings, the second graph will spill over to the next page.

Half size

If you want to print a single graph that occupies only half of the page, you can issue the Settings Image Size Half command and print with PrintGraph's built-in Half page settings. If you need to print two graphs on a single page, however, or if you want to print a graph that occupies a true half page on the LaserJet printer, you'll have to manually change the sizing of the graph. Specifically, you need to define a left margin of 1.102, a width of 5.805, and a height of 4.191 (you can leave the top margin at the default setting of .395). We'll show you how to define these settings in the next section.

Manual sizing

If you want to specify a size other than PrintGraph's full or half sizes, you'll need to select the Manual option. When you select the Manual option, PrintGraph presents the menu shown in Figure 6-28. As you can see, this option allows you to define manually the top and left margins, the width and height, and the rotation of a graph.

FIGURE 6-28

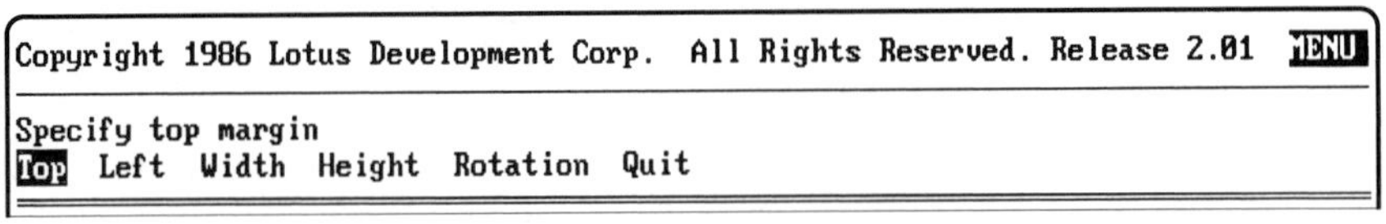

```
Copyright 1986 Lotus Development Corp.  All Rights Reserved. Release 2.01  MENU

Specify top margin
Top  Left  Width  Height  Rotation  Quit
```

1-2-3 presents this menu when you issue the Settings Image Size Manual command.

Redefining the
Half settings

When using manual sizing, you don't have to change all of the settings. If you want, you can use all of PrintGraph's default settings except the one or two you want to change manually. Manual sizing can come in handy when you need to make minor adjustments to the size and position of a printed graph.

As we mentioned a moment ago, you'll need to manually change PrintGraph's Half settings if you want to print two graphs on the same page. To print two graphs on the same page, first issue the Settings Image Size Half command to display PrintGraph's default Half settings on the screen. Next, choose Manual to bring up the menu in Figure 6-28, select Left, type **1.102**, and press ↵. Once you've changed the Left setting, choose Width, type **5.805**, and press ↵. Finally, choose Height, type **4.191**, and press ↵. After you've redefined these settings, use the Image-Select command to select the two graphs you want to print, and then issue the Align and Go commands. When you do this, both graphs will fit nicely on a single page, as shown in Figure 6-29.

FIGURE 6-29

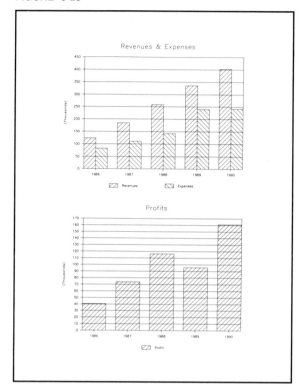

*You can print two
graphs on a single page
by manually redefining
PrintGraph's Half
settings.*

If you will often want to use the LaserJet to print two graphs on the same page, you'll probably want to make the adjusted Half page settings your defaults. To do this, first follow the instructions to define the new Half page settings, then issue the **S**ettings **S**ave command to save your changes.

Keep in mind that the margin settings you define with the Manual command do not take into account the LaserJet's "unprintable" area at the edges of the page. As you will recall, the LaserJet has a built-in margin of $\frac{1}{2}$ inch at the top and bottom of the page (regardless of orientation), and $\frac{1}{4}$ inch at the left and right of the page. For this reason, if you define a Top margin setting of 1 inch, the effective top margin will be $1\frac{1}{2}$ inches. Similarly, a Left margin setting of 1 inch results in an effective $1\frac{1}{4}$-inch left margin.

*Accounting for
unprintable areas*

The golden ratio

In order to keep your graphs from looking disproportionate, you should maintain a width-to-height ratio of 1.385 to 1. Although you can use manual sizing to produce any ratio you want, you'll want to maintain this ratio for almost all your printed graphs.

Choosing a text font

PrintGraph lets you specify the font in which your graph's text (titles, legends, and so forth) will be printed. Choosing text fonts for your LaserJet printer is no different than for other types of printers. The fonts that PrintGraph uses in its graphs are simply graphic fonts that are sent along with the graph—PrintGraph cannot take advantage of the LaserJet's font cartridges or soft fonts.

Resetting and saving print settings

After you've defined some new PrintGraph settings, you can save your changes to disk. To do this, just issue the Settings Save command. This command saves all of the current PrintGraph settings into a configuration file on the default directory. Once you've used this command to save your PrintGraph settings, those settings become the new defaults.

The Settings Reset command lets you call up your saved PrintGraph settings at any time. When you issue this command, 1-2-3 reads the settings from the configuration file into PrintGraph. The Settings Reset command lets you experimentally modify your permanent PrintGraph settings without losing your saved settings. Just remember to avoid the Settings Save command when you are experimenting with new PrintGraph settings that you don't want to save.

CONCLUSION

The HP LaserJet printer is the ideal printer for serious 1-2-3 users. The LaserJet's sundry font offerings let 1-2-3 print worksheet reports in many styles and sizes, and the LaserJet's graphics capabilities let 1-2-3's PrintGraph program generate handsome graphs from the data in your worksheets. In this chapter, we've shown you how to get the most out of 1-2-3 and an HP LaserJet printer.

WORDSTAR PROFESSIONAL RELEASE 5 7

In this chapter, we'll show you how to use your HP LaserJet printer with Word-Star Professional Release 5. We'll begin by showing you how to use the installation programs included with WordStar to build a printer description file (PDF) that supports the LaserJet, fonts, and features you want to use. Once we've done this, we'll show you how to format and print a WordStar document.

WordStar Professional Release 5 is shipped with several utility programs that you can use to add support for your LaserJet and the fonts and features you plan to use with WordStar. Determining which of these programs you will have to use, as well as the order in which you will have to run them, is quite simple.

INSTALLING LASERJET SUPPORT

If you plan to use a LaserJet Plus, 500 Plus, Series II, IID, or 2000 with third-party soft fonts, you should begin by running the utility program called LSRFONTS. This program produces a database with information that will allow you to add support for third-party soft fonts to WordStar. On the other hand, if you have an original LaserJet, or do not plan to use third-party soft fonts with WordStar, it is not necessary to run LSRFONTS.

Once you have determined if it is necessary to run LSRFONTS, you can begin the process of adding LaserJet support to WordStar. There are three utility programs included with WordStar that you can use to do this. The first of these utilities is called WINSTALL. As we will explain in a few moments, you can use WINSTALL to build a PDF that will provide WordStar with support for your LaserJet and the fonts and features you plan to use.

The second utility program you can use to add support for a LaserJet to WordStar is called WSCHANGE. Like WINSTALL, WSCHANGE allows you to build a PDF file. However, as we will show you later, WSCHANGE also provides you with the ability to change several printer-related settings such as default font and margin settings.

Finally, the third utility program you can use to add support for a LaserJet to WordStar is called PRCHANGE. PRCHANGE is different from WINSTALL and WSCHANGE in that it allows you to make changes to an existing PDF file in addition to allowing you to create a new one. Also, you can use PRCHANGE to create Advanced Page Preview screen fonts that match LaserJet soft fonts, as well as a batch file that automates the process of downloading soft fonts. We'll address each of these issues when we discuss PRCHANGE later in this chapter.

Using
LSRFONTS

LSRFONTS is a utility program that is included with every copy of WordStar Professional Release 5. As we mentioned earlier, if you want to use third-party soft fonts with WordStar, you should begin the installation process by using LSRFONTS. LSRFONTS creates a database, which we will refer to as the user printer database, that contains information that can be used by WINSTALL, WSCHANGE, and PRCHANGE whenever you add support for a third-party soft font to a PDF.

Preparing to
run LSRFONTS

If you want to use LSRFONTS to build a user printer database, you should begin by copying any third-party soft fonts you want to use with WordStar into a directory on your hard disk. For example, we store all our soft fonts in a directory called C:\PCLFONTS.

Once you have copied the third-party soft fonts you want to use with WordStar into a directory on your hard disk, the next step is to use the DOS CD command to move into that directory. For example, if you copy all the soft fonts you want to use into the directory C:\PCLFONTS, you should issue the command **cd \pclfonts** at the DOS prompt to move into that directory. When you have done this, you are ready to run LSRFONTS.

Running
LSRFONTS

The command you issue at the DOS prompt to run LSRFONTS should always include the name of the directory in which the LSRFONTS program file (LSRFONTS.EXE) is stored. For example, if you followed the installation procedure outlined in the *WordStar Reference Manual* and copied LSRFONTS.EXE from the WordStar PostScript Files Font Utility disk into the directory C:\WS5, you should type the command **\ws5\lsrfonts** at the DOS prompt to run LSRFONTS.

When you run LSRFONTS from the DOS prompt, a title screen will appear. Once you have read the information that appears on this screen, press any key to continue. When you do this, LSRFONTS will search the current directory specification for soft fonts and will display a list of font names on your screen. For example, if you run LSRFONTS from the directory C:\PCLFONTS, LSRFONTS will automatically search C:\PCLFONTS for soft font data files and will list their names on a screen similar to the one shown in Figure 7-1.

FIGURE 7-1

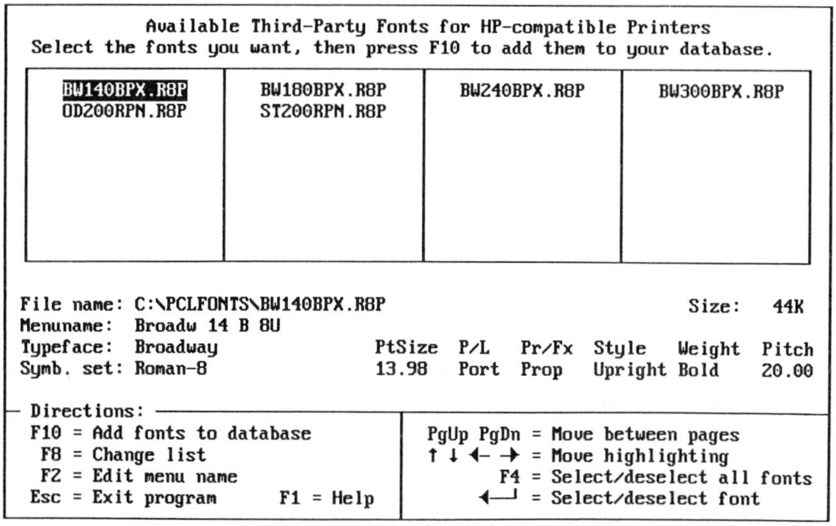

```
        Available Third-Party Fonts for HP-compatible Printers
    Select the fonts you want, then press F10 to add them to your database.

  ┌──────────────────┬──────────────────┬──────────────────┬──────────────────┐
  │ BW140BPX.R8P     │ BW180BPX.R8P     │ BW240BPX.R8P     │ BW300BPX.R8P     │
  │ OD200RPN.R8P     │ ST200RPN.R8P     │                  │                  │
  │                  │                  │                  │                  │
  │                  │                  │                  │                  │
  │                  │                  │                  │                  │
  └──────────────────┴──────────────────┴──────────────────┴──────────────────┘

  File name: C:\PCLFONTS\BW140BPX.R8P                        Size:   44K
  Menuname:  Broadw 14 B 8U
  Typeface:  Broadway              PtSize  P/L   Pr/Fx  Style    Weight  Pitch
  Symb. set: Roman-8               13.98   Port  Prop   Upright  Bold    20.00

  ┌─ Directions: ─────────────────────────────────────────────────────────────
  │ F10 = Add fonts to database    PgUp PgDn = Move between pages
  │ F8  = Change list              ↑ ↓ ← → = Move highlighting
  │ F2  = Edit menu name                F4 = Select/deselect all fonts
  │ Esc = Exit program   F1 = Help  ←──┘ = Select/deselect font
```

LSRFONTS will list the name of each soft font it finds in the current directory specification.

This screen allows you to select the fonts for which you want to add support to WordStar. One option on this screen allows you to change the name of a font as it will appear on WordStar's font menu. To select a font for which you want to add support to WordStar, use the →, ←, ↑, and ↓ keys to highlight its name, then press ↵. When you do this, LSRFONTS will display a small square to the left of the font's name to indicate that it has been selected. To change the name of a font on WordStar's font menu, use the cursor to highlight the name of the font, then press **[F2]**. When you do this, LSRFONTS will prompt you to enter the new font name. Once you have entered the name at this prompt, press ↵ to continue.

Finally, once you have selected all the fonts for which you want to add support to WordStar, press **[F10]**. When you do this, LSRFONTS will look in the current directory for the user printer database. If LSRFONTS does not find the user printer database, it will display the message shown in Figure 7-2 on the following page.

If the message shown in Figure 7-2 appears on your screen and you want LSRFONTS to automatically create the user printer database in the current directory, you should press ↵. On the other hand, if you want LSRFONTS to search for the user printer database in another directory, type the name of that directory at the prompt, and press ↵.

FIGURE 7-2

```
┌─────────────────────────────────────────────────────────────┐
│                                                             │
│   The user printer data base is not in the current directory: │
│                                                             │
│   ▐C:\PCLFONTS\          ·        ▌                         │
│                                                             │
│                                                             │
│   You may:                                                  │
│     Press ◄──┘ to create a new data base in this directory. │
│     Enter a new directory name and press ◄──┘ .             │
│     Press Esc to exit program.                              │
│                                                             │
└─────────────────────────────────────────────────────────────┘
```

If the user printer database does not exist in the current directory, LSRFONTS will display this message.

If the name of a font's typeface appears on the menu shown in Figure 7-1 as *Unknwn*, LSRFONTS will ask you to identify the typeface. When it does , the list of typefaces shown in Figure 7-3 will appear on your screen. To choose a typeface from this list, use the ➔, ◄, ↑, and ↓ keys to highlight its name, then press ↵.

FIGURE 7-3

```
┌─────────────────────────────────────────────────────────────┐
│  Select a new type style name:                              │
│                                                             │
│  ┌────────────────────────────────────────────────────────┐ │
│  │ Type style name              Type       Normal/Alt  Qual/Draft│
│  │ APL                          Sans Serif Alt        Draft │ │
│  │ Aachen                       Serif      Normal     Quality│ │
│  │ Adobe Collectors Edition1    Sans Serif Normal     Quality│ │
│  │ American Classic             Serif      Normal     Quality│ │
│  │ American Typewriter          Serif      Normal     Quality│ │
│  │ Amelia                       Serif      Normal     Quality│ │
│  │ Apollo                       Sans Serif Normal     Quality│ │
│  │ Artisan                      Sans Serif Normal     Quality│ │
│  └────────────────────────────────────────────────────────┘ │
│                                                             │
│  File name: C:\PCLFONTS\OD200RPN.R8P              Size:  34K │
│  Menuname:  Unknwn 20 8U                                    │
│  Typeface:  Unrecognized Typ   PtSize P/L  Pr/Fx Style  Weight Pitch│
│  Symb. set: Roman-8            19.98  Port Prop  Upright Medium 23.00│
│                                                             │
│  ┌ Directions: ──────────────────┬──────────────────────── │
│  │                               │ PgUp PgDn View more type styles│
│  │  ◄──┘  Select type style name │   ↑ ↓  Move highlighting │
│  │                               │   Esc  Previous screen   │
│  │                               │   F1   Help              │
│  └───────────────────────────────┴──────────────────────── │
└─────────────────────────────────────────────────────────────┘
```

LSRFONTS may ask you to identify the typeface on which a particular font's design is based.

Next, LSRFONTS will display a message on your screen that asks you to assign a name to the group of fonts you have just selected. This message is shown in Figure

7-4. As we will explain later in this chapter, the name you assign to a group of third-party fonts will appear on your screen when you use WINSTALL, WSCHANGE, and PRCHANGE to add support for those fonts to WordStar.

FIGURE 7-4

```
┌─────────────────────────────────────────────────────────────────────┐
│                                                                       │
│    Enter the font group name that PRCHANGE will use for these fonts   │
│    press ◄──┘                                                         │
│                    15:00:07 09/01/88                                  │
│                                                                       │
│                                                                       │
│    or press Esc to have PRCHANGE refer to this font group by date     │
│    and time of creation.                                              │
│                                                                       │
└─────────────────────────────────────────────────────────────────────┘
```

LSRFONTS allows you to assign a name to the information WINSTALL, WSCHANGE, and PRCHANGE will use to add support for a group of third-party soft fonts to WordStar.

As you can see in Figure 7-4, LSRFONTS uses the current time and date as the default name of a group of fonts. Therefore, if you want to accept the default name, you should press **[Esc]**. On the other hand, if you want to assign a unique name to the group of fonts, type the name, then press ◄──┘.

Finally, LSRFONTS will display a message informing you that it has updated the user printer database. When this message appears, press **Y** to exit LSRFONTS or **N** if you want to continue.

Using WINSTALL

WINSTALL is a utility program that allows you to customize WordStar for your system. You can use it to specify which monitor and printer you want to use, or to specify the location of dictionary files. In addition, you can use WINSTALL to choose the "classic" WordStar user interface or the new pull-down menu system. In this section, we'll show you how to add LaserJet support to WordStar.

Running WINSTALL

Once you have copied each of the disks included with the WordStar package into a directory on your hard disk called \WS5 (or have created a working disk for a floppy-based system), you should run WINSTALL to customize WordStar for your system. To do this, type **WINSTALL** at the DOS prompt and press ◄──┘.

When you run WINSTALL, the screen shown in Figure 7-5 will appear. This screen prompts you to enter the name of the WordStar program file you want to customize. Since the name of the standard WordStar program file is WS.EXE, when this screen and prompt appear on your monitor, type **WS** and press ◄──┘.

Once you have provided WINSTALL with the name of the WordStar program file, WINSTALL will ask you to enter the name that should be assigned to the customized version of the WordStar program file that WINSTALL will generate.

If you want to retain the file name WS.EXE, simply type **WS** and press ↵ when this prompt appears. On the other hand, if you want WINSTALL to write the customized version of the WordStar file to another file name, enter that file name at the prompt and press ↵.

FIGURE 7-5

```
WINSTALL  11 Aug 88
Copyright (C) 1983, 1988 MicroPro International Corporation.
All rights reserved

IBM PC Compatible PC-DOS/MS-DOS Version


To install WordStar, type ws and press ←┘ .




Note:  The uninstalled WordStar is called WS.  If you've renamed
the file, type the new name and press ←┘ .
```

WINSTALL will ask you to enter the name of the WordStar program file.

*Adding
LaserJet support*

Next, the Main Installation Menu shown in Figure 7-6 will appear on your screen. Options on this menu allow you to choose the type of user interface, monitor, and printer you want to use. To add LaserJet support to WordStar, you should press **B** to select the Printer option.

*Choosing a
printer type*

After you select the Printer option, the Printer Type Menu shown in Figure 7-7 will appear on your screen. As you can see, this menu allows you to choose the type of printer for which you want to add support to WordStar. Use the ↑ and ↓ keys to highlight the Laser printers option, then press ↵.

*Choosing a
LaserJet*

After you select the Laser printers option, the Printer Selection Menu shown in Figure 7-8 on page 262 will appear. As you can see, this menu lists a number of laser printers, including three LaserJets. To choose the printer you want to use with WordStar, use the →, ←, ↑, and ↓ keys to highlight its name, then press ↵. For example, if you want to use an original LaserJet with WordStar, you should choose the **Hewlett-Packard LaserJet** option. Likewise, if you want to use a LaserJet Plus or LaserJet Series II, you should choose the **Hewlett-Packard LaserJet Plus** or **Hewlett-Packard LaserJet Series II** option, respectively.

As you may have noticed, the Printer Selection Menu does not contain an option for the LaserJet 500 Plus, LaserJet IID, or LaserJet 2000. However, this does not mean that you cannot use these printers with WordStar. If you want to use a LaserJet 500 Plus, you should choose the Hewlett-Packard LaserJet Plus option, while you should choose the Hewlett-Packard LaserJet Series II option if you want to use a

LaserJet Series IID or LaserJet 2000. We'll show you later in this section how to add support to WordStar for the special features offered by these printers.

FIGURE 7-6

```
                          Main Installation Menu

  A   Console..........................Choose your monitor.

  B   Printer...........................Choose your printer.

  C   Default printer...................Choose a default printer.

  D   Computer..........................Choose operating system and disk
                                        drives on your computer.  Check the
                                        CONFIG.SYS and AUTOEXEC.BAT files.

  E   Dictionaries......................Specify location of the dictionaries.

  F   Help level........................Specify pull-down or classic menus.

  X   Finished with installation.


  Enter your menu selection...          ? = Help
                                        For detailed changes, run WSCHANGE.
```

WINSTALL's Main Installation Menu allows you to add LaserJet support to WordStar.

FIGURE 7-7

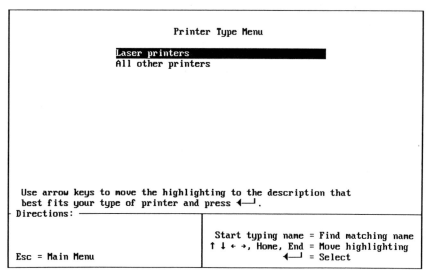

The Printer Type Menu allows you to choose the type of printer you want to use with WordStar.

FIGURE 7-8

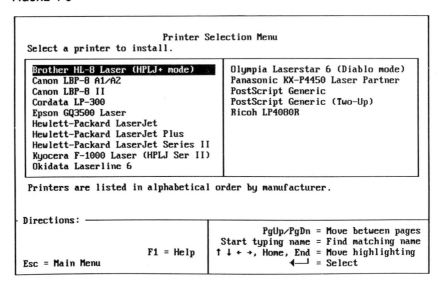

```
                      Printer Selection Menu
      Select a printer to install.

      ┌──────────────────────────────────┬──────────────────────────────────┐
      │Brother HL-8 Laser (HPLJ+ mode)   │ Olympia Laserstar 6 (Diablo mode)│
      │Canon LBP-8 A1/A2                 │ Panasonic KX-P4450 Laser Partner │
      │Canon LBP-8 II                    │ PostScript Generic               │
      │Cordata LP-300                    │ PostScript Generic (Two-Up)      │
      │Epson GQ3500 Laser                │ Ricoh LP4080R                    │
      │Hewlett-Packard LaserJet          │                                  │
      │Hewlett-Packard LaserJet Plus     │                                  │
      │Hewlett-Packard LaserJet Series II│                                  │
      │Kyocera F-1000 Laser (HPLJ Ser II)│                                  │
      │Okidata Laserline 6               │                                  │
      └──────────────────────────────────┴──────────────────────────────────┘

      Printers are listed in alphabetical order by manufacturer.


   ┌ Directions: ──────────────────────┬──────────────────────────────────┐
   │                                   │      PgUp/PgDn = Move between pages│
   │                                   │ Start typing name = Find matching name│
   │                         F1 = Help │ ↑ ↓ ← →, Home, End = Move highlighting│
   │ Esc = Main Menu                   │          ◄──┘ = Select            │
   └───────────────────────────────────┴──────────────────────────────────┘
```

When the Printer Selection Menu appears, you can choose the specific LaserJet model you want to use with WordStar.

Specifying the name of your PDF

After you specify which LaserJet you want to use with WordStar, the Installed Printer Menu shown in Figure 7-9 will appear. This menu allows you to specify the name of the PDF in which WINSTALL will store the information that provides WordStar with support for your LaserJet. When this menu appears, enter a file name whose length does not exceed eight characters, then press ↵. For example, if you want WINSTALL to store the information that provides WordStar with support for a LaserJet Series II in a file called SERIESII, type **SERIESII**, then press ↵.

Once you have entered the name of the file in which WINSTALL will store information about your LaserJet, the Additional Installation Menu shown in Figure 7-10 will appear. You can use the options on this menu to choose the port to which your LaserJet is connected, to specify the source from which your LaserJet will feed paper, or to add or remove support for fonts. The Additional Installation Menu also contains an option that will provide you with some tips related to the operation of your LaserJet.

Choosing a printer port

To specify the port to which your LaserJet is connected, you should choose the **Select printer adapter port** option. When you select this option, the menu shown in Figure 7-11 on page 264 will appear.

FIGURE 7-9

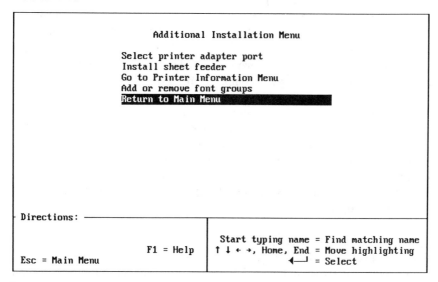

```
                        Installed Printer Menu
        The printer you selected is: Hewlett-Packard LaserJet Series II

        Type a new PDF name or select an old PDF to replace.
        PDF name: ASCII

        ┌─────────────────┬─────────────┬─────────────┬─────────────┐
        │ ASCII           │             │             │             │
        │ DRAFT           │             │             │             │
        │ WS4             │             │             │             │
        │                 │             │             │             │
        │                 │             │             │             │
        │                 │             │             │             │
        └─────────────────┴─────────────┴─────────────┴─────────────┘

        PDFs for installed printers are listed on this menu.

     ┌ Directions: ─────────────────┬─────────────────────────────────
     │                              │     PgUp/PgDn = Move between pages
     │                              │ Start typing name = Find matching name
     │                 F1 = Help    │ ↑ ↓ ← →, Home, End = Move highlighting
     │ Esc = Printer Selection Menu │       ◄──┘ = Select
```

The Installed Printer Menu allows you to specify the name of the file in which WINSTALL will store the information that provides WordStar with support for your LaserJet.

FIGURE 7-10

```
                        Additional Installation Menu

                Select printer adapter port
                Install sheet feeder
                Go to Printer Information Menu
                Add or remove font groups
                Return to Main Menu




     ┌ Directions: ─────────────────┬─────────────────────────────────
     │                              │ Start typing name = Find matching name
     │                 F1 = Help    │ ↑ ↓ ← →, Home, End = Move highlighting
     │ Esc = Main Menu              │       ◄──┘ = Select
```

The Additional Installation Menu allows you to choose a printer adapter port and sheet feeder and to add and delete support for fonts.

FIGURE 7-11

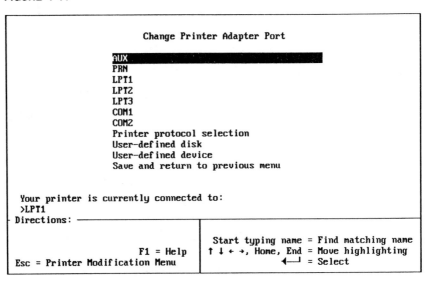

Change Printer Adapter Port

```
                                   AUX
                                   PRN
                                   LPT1
                                   LPT2
                                   LPT3
                                   COM1
                                   COM2
                                   Printer protocol selection
                                   User-defined disk
                                   User-defined device
                                   Save and return to previous menu


      Your printer is currently connected to:
      >LPT1
    Directions:
                                                Start typing name = Find matching name
                                  F1 = Help    ↑ ↓ ← →, Home, End = Move highlighting
      Esc = Printer Modification Menu                        ↵   = Select
```

This menu allows you to choose the port to which your LaserJet is connected.

As you can see, this menu lists the names of seven standard MS-DOS devices. You should press ↑ and ↓ to highlight the name of the device to which your printer is connected, then press ↵. If the name of the device to which your LaserJet is connected does not appear on the menu shown in Figure 7-11, you should choose the User-defined device option. When you do this, WINSTALL will prompt you to enter the device name associated with the port. For example, if your LaserJet is connected to LPT4:, choose the **User-defined device** option, type **LPT4:** at the *Enter User-defined device name:* prompt, and press ↵.

Sending output to a disk file

If you want WordStar to send all printer output to a disk file so you can send it to the LaserJet with the DOS COPY command, you should choose the User-defined disk option when the menu shown in Figure 7-11 appears. When you choose this option, WINSTALL will prompt you to enter a file name. For example, if you want to send all LaserJet output to a disk file named OUTPUT.PRN, choose the **User-defined disk** option, type **OUTPUT.PRN** at the *Enter User-defined disk file name:* prompt, then press ↵.

Choosing a paper source

The Install sheet feeder option allows you to choose the source (paper tray) from which your LaserJet will feed paper. When you choose this option, a menu similar to the one shown in Figure 7-12 will appear. The Sheet Feeder Selection Menu lists the name of each paper source that your printer supports.

FIGURE 7-12

```
                    Sheet Feeder Selection Menu
  Select a sheet feeder for your printer.
  ┌─────────────────────────────────┬─────────────────────────────────┐
  │ HPLJ II Internal & Manual Feed   │                                 │
  │                                  │                                 │
  │                                  │                                 │
  │                                  │                                 │
  │                                  │                                 │
  │                                  │                                 │
  │                                  │                                 │
  └─────────────────────────────────┴─────────────────────────────────┘
    Sheet feeders are listed in alphabetical order.


─ Directions: ──────────────────────┬────────────────────────────────────
                                     │ PgUp/PgDn = Move between pages
                                     │ Start typing name = Find matching name
                     F1 = Help       │ ↑ ↓ ← →, Home, End = Move highlighting
  Esc = Additional Install Menu      │      ◄─┘ = Select
```

*The Sheet Feeder Selection Menu allows you to select the source from which
your LaserJet will feed paper.*

As you can see in Figure 7-12, if you are adding support for a LaserJet to
WordStar, a single option will appear on the Sheet Feeder Selection Menu. This
option will provide WordStar with the ability to feed paper from each of the
LaserJet's standard paper sources. To select this option, use the →, ←, ↑, and ↓
keys to highlight its name, then press ↵. For example, to choose the option
that appears on the menu shown in Figure 7-12, highlight **HPLJ II Internal &
Manual Feed**, then press ↵.

As we mentioned earlier, the Additional Installation Menu contains an
option that provides you with a help screen relating to the use of your LaserJet
with WordStar. To display the help screen that relates to the LaserJet you have
selected, use the ↑ and ↓ keys to highlight **Go to Printer Information Menu**, then
press ↵. When you do this, the Printer Information Menu shown in Figure 7-13 will
appear on your screen.

When this menu appears on your screen, choose the **View printer information**
option. When you do this, WINSTALL will display a screen similar to the one
shown in Figure 7-14. At this time, you can read the information on this screen, or
you can press [Pg Dn] to read information on the next screen. When you're finished,
press **[F10]** to return to the Additional Installation Menu. You can send this
information directly to the LaserJet or to a disk file by choosing the Print printer
information or Save printer information to a disk file option.

*Printer
information*

FIGURE 7-13

```
                        Printer Information Menu

                 ┌────────────────────────────────────────┐
                 │View printer information                 │
                  Print printer information
                  Save printer information to a disk file
                  Return to Additional Installation Menu




            This information is for the printer you selected.
┌ Directions: ───────────────────────────────┐
│                                              Start typing name = Find matching name
│                               F1 = Help     ↑ ↓ ← →, Home, End = Move highlighting
│ Esc = Additional Install Menu                      ◄──┘ = Select
```

The Printer Information Menu allows you to read, print, or save information
concerning the operation of your printer with WordStar.

FIGURE 7-14

```
┌─────────────────── Printer Information ──────────────────────┐
│      Printer Information for your Hewlett-Packard LaserJet Series II

  To see another page, press PgUp or PgDn.
  Press F10 to end.

   You can use this installation with many LaserJet-compatible printers.
   However, it is unlikely that you will be able to match the internal fonts
   in compatible printers with the HP cartridge and internal font choices.

   Extended character set:  The printer compose tables for USASCII, Roman-8,
   Linedraw, ECMA-94, Latin 1, PC Set 1, OCR-B, and PC Line symbol sets remap
   characters so that they match the IBM character set more closely.
   Characters in other symbol sets maintain their original values.

   Fonts:  The default fonts are Courier 10 PC (portrait and landscape),
   Courier 10B PC8 (portrait and landscape), and Line Printer 17 PC8
   (portrait and landscape).




                                                          Pg 1 of 3
```

The Additional Installation Menu's Go to Printer Information Menu option displays
hints and helps related to the particular LaserJet you are using.

The next option on the Additional Installation Menu—Add or remove font groups—allows you to add support for LaserJet fonts to your PDF. If you plan to use any cartridge or soft fonts with WordStar, use the ↑ and ↓ keys to highlight the Add or remove font groups option, then press ↵. When you do this, WINSTALL will display a screen similar to the one shown in Figure 7-15.

Adding
font support
to WordStar

FIGURE 7-15

```
                        Current Fonts in PDF

      These fonts are in your printer description file (PDF).
      ┌──────────────┬──────────────┬──────────────┬──────────────┐
      │ Courier 12/10│              │              │              │
      │ LinePri 8.5/16.7            │              │              │
      │              │              │              │              │
      │              │              │              │              │
      │              │              │              │              │
      │              │              │              │              │
      │              │              │              │              │
      └──────────────┴──────────────┴──────────────┴──────────────┘
      Do you want to change the fonts in your PDF? (Y/N)

      If a font name appears twice, it represents two symbol sets.


  ┌ Directions: ──────────────┬─────────────────────────────────────┐
  │                           │         PgUp/PgDn = Move between pages│
  │                           │ Start typing name = Find matching name│
  │                F1 = Help   │ ↑ ↓ ← →, Home, End = Move highlighting│
  │ Esc = Printer Selection Menu                                      │
  └───────────────────────────┴─────────────────────────────────────┘
```

This screen lists each font supported by your PDF.

As you can see, this screen lists the fonts currently supported by your PDF. This screen also contains a prompt that allows you to specify whether you want to change the fonts supported by your PDF. To add additional font support to your PDF, press **Y**. When you do this, WINSTALL will display the screen shown in Figure 7-16 on the following page. From this screen, you can select the type of font for which you want to add support to your PDF.

All members of the LaserJet printer family support a specific set of internal fonts that can be used with WordStar. The Add internal fonts option on the screen shown in Figure 7-16 allows you to choose the specific internal fonts you want to use.

Adding support
for internal fonts

When you choose the Add internal fonts option, the name of each internal font supported by the type of LaserJet for which you are adding support to WordStar will appear. For example, if you are adding support to WordStar for a LaserJet or LaserJet Plus, WINSTALL will display the list of fonts shown in Figure 7-17.

LaserJet and LaserJet
Plus internal fonts

FIGURE 7-16

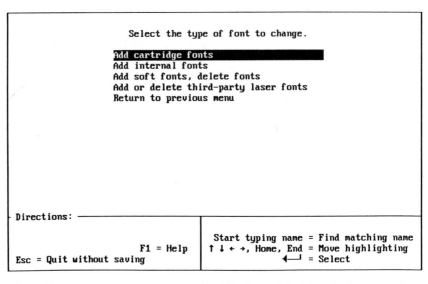

When this screen appears, you can select the type of font for which you want to add support to your PDF.

FIGURE 7-17

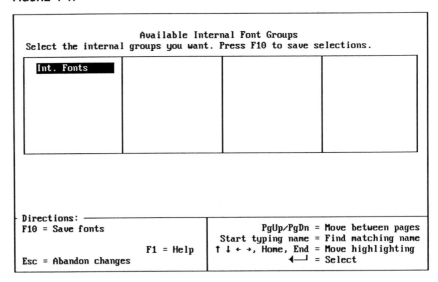

The Available Internal Font Groups menu will contain a single entry if you are adding support for LaserJet or LaserJet Plus internal fonts.

On the other hand, if you are adding support for a LaserJet Series II to WordStar, the list of fonts shown in Figure 7-18 will appear when you select the Add internal fonts option. As you can see, the Available Internal Font Groups menu contains four entries, each of which corresponds to a font and symbol set supported by the LaserJet Series II.

LaserJet Series II internal fonts

FIGURE 7-18

```
┌───────────────────────────────────────────────────────────────────────┐
│                    Available Internal Font Groups                       │
│          Select the internal groups you want. Press F10 to save selections. │
│  ┌─────────────────┬─────────────────┬─────────────────┬─────────────┐ │
│  │ PC-8 (Default)  │                 │                 │             │ │
│  │ ECMA-94         │                 │                 │             │ │
│  │ PC-8 D/N        │                 │                 │             │ │
│  │ Roman-8         │                 │                 │             │ │
│  │                 │                 │                 │             │ │
│  │                 │                 │                 │             │ │
│  │                 │                 │                 │             │ │
│  │                 │                 │                 │             │ │
│  └─────────────────┴─────────────────┴─────────────────┴─────────────┘ │
│                                                                         │
│                                                                         │
│  ┌ Directions: ──────────────────┬──────────────────────────────────┐  │
│  │ F10 = Save fonts              │        PgUp/PgDn = Move between pages │
│  │                               │  Start typing name = Find matching name │
│  │              F1 = Help        │ ↑ ↓ ← →, Home, End = Move highlighting │
│  │ Esc = Abandon changes         │           ◄─┘ = Select            │  │
│  └───────────────────────────────┴──────────────────────────────────┘  │
└───────────────────────────────────────────────────────────────────────┘
```

The Available Internal Font Groups menu will contain four entries if you are adding support for LaserJet Series II internal fonts.

If you want to add support to WordStar for all the fonts whose names appear on the Available Internal Font Groups menu, press **[F4]** to select them, then press **[F10]**. If you want to add support to WordStar for a specific font or group of fonts, use the →, ←, ↑, and ↓ keys to highlight the name or names, press ↵ to select them, then press **[F10]**. In either case, WINSTALL will return you to the menu shown in Figure 7-16 when you press [F10].

As we mentioned earlier, the version of WordStar Professional Release 5 that was available at the time *LaserJet Companion* went to press did not contain direct support for a LaserJet IID or LaserJet 2000. We told you to choose the Hewlett-Packard LaserJet Series II option from the Printer Selection Menu in the event a LaserJet IID or LaserJet 2000 option is not supported by your copy of WordStar.

LaserJet IID and LaserJet 2000 internal fonts

If you choose the Hewlett-Packard LaserJet Series II option from the Printer Selection Menu, WINSTALL will automatically add support for the LaserJet Series II's three internal fonts—Courier 10/12, Courier Bold 10/12, and Line Printer

8.5/16.66—to your PDF. However, if you want to use the additional internal fonts supported by the LaserJet IID or LaserJet 2000, it is necessary to add support for the additional internal fonts to your PDF manually.

Most of the LaserJet IID and LaserJet 2000 internal fonts that are not supported directly by WordStar are identical to cartridge and/or soft fonts produced by HP. Therefore, it is possible to use most of the LaserJet IID and 2000 internal fonts with WordStar by adding support for their cartridge and/or soft font twins. Table 7-1 lists the LaserJet 2000 and LaserJet IID internal fonts that are not supported by the LaserJet Series II, along with the font cartridge(s) or soft font package that contains each font's twin. Therefore, if you want to use these fonts with WordStar, you should use the procedures we will outline in the next two sections of this chapter to add support for them to your PDF.

TABLE 7-1

Internal Font	Font Cartridge	Soft Font
LaserJet 2000		
Line Printer 8.5/15	No match	No match
Line Draw 8.5/16.66	No match	No match
Line Draw 12/10	H, U, W, X	No match
Prestige Elite 7/16.66	G,H,J	EA
Prestige Elite 10/12	D,G,J,M	EA
Prestige Elite Bold 10/12	D,G,J,M	EA
Prestige Elite Italic 10/12	D,G,J,M	EA
Courier Italic 10/12	No match	No match
Courier 12/10	C,H,Y	No match
Courier Bold 12/10	A,C,H,L,Q,Y	No match
Courier Italic 12/10	A,C,H,L,Q,Y	No match
Tms Rmn 8	No match	AD
Tms Rmn 10	No match	AD
Tms Rmn Bold 10	No match	AD
Tms Rmn Italic 10	No match	AD
Helv Bold 14	No match	AD
LaserJet IID		
Courier Italic 10/12	No match	No match
Courier 12/10	C,H,Y	No match
Courier Bold 12/10	A,C,H,L,Q,Y	No match
Courier Italic 12/10	A,C,H,L,Q,Y	No match

To use the LaserJet IID's and LaserJet 2000's internal fonts with WordStar, you must add support for their cartridge or soft font twins to your printer file.

To add support for an HP cartridge font to your PDF, choose the **Add cartridge fonts** option from the menu shown in Figure 7-16 on page 268. When you do this, WINSTALL will display the Available Cartridges list shown in Figure 7-19. This list contains all the font cartridges produced by HP at the time *LaserJet Companion* went to press. In addition, it also contains separate entries for each symbol set supported by the fonts on specific cartridges.

Adding support for HP cartridge fonts

FIGURE 7-19

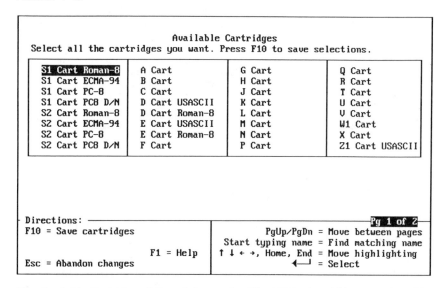

The Available Cartridges list contains each of the HP font cartridges produced by HP at the time LaserJet Companion went to press.

To add support to WordStar for a font cartridge that appears on the Available Cartridges list, use the →, ←, ↑, or ↓ key to highlight the font's name, then press ↵. When you do this, WINSTALL will display a square to the left of the selected font cartridge's name. Once you have used this procedure to select the font cartridges you want to use, press **[F10]** to add to your PDF the information WordStar needs to use the fonts stored on the cartridges. When you do this, WINSTALL will return you to the menu shown in Figure 7-16.

To use an HP-produced or marketed soft font with WordStar, choose the Add soft fonts, delete fonts option from the menu shown in Figure 7-16. When you choose this option, WINSTALL will display a Current Fonts in PDF screen similar to the one shown in Figure 7-20. As you can see, this screen lists each font supported by the PDF you are building.

Adding support for HP soft fonts

FIGURE 7-20

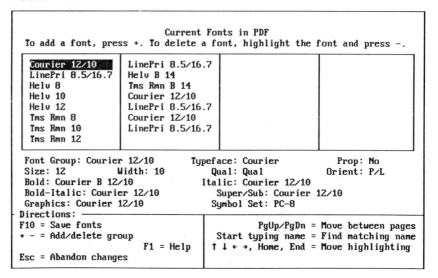

When the Current Fonts in PDF screen appears, you can add or delete support for HP soft fonts to WordStar by pressing + or -, respectively.

When the Current Fonts in PDF screen appears, you can remove support for any of the fonts that are listed, or you can add support for an HP soft font. If you want to remove support for a font, highlight its name, then press -. When you do this, the font's name will disappear. If you want to add support for an HP soft font to your PDF, press the + key. When you do this, WINSTALL will display the Purchased Soft Fonts list shown in Figure 7-21. This list includes entries for most HP soft fonts.

When the Purchased Soft Fonts list appears on your screen, highlight the name of the soft font package(s) for which you want to add support to WordStar, then press ↵. When you do this, WINSTALL will display a square to the left of the soft font package's name. Once you've selected the soft font package(s) for which you want to add support, press **[F10]** to save the selection(s). When you do this, WINSTALL will display an Available Typefaces list similar to the one shown in Figure 7-22.

The Available Typefaces list includes the name of each font supported by the soft font package(s) you have selected. For example, the Available Typefaces list shown in Figure 7-22 lists the names of the fonts included in the Headlines 1 soft font package.

If you want to add support to WordStar for all the fonts whose names appear on the Available Typefaces list, press **[F4]** to select them, then press **[F10]**. On the other hand, if you want to add support to WordStar for a specific font (or group of fonts) that appears on the list, use the ➡, ⬅, ⬆, and ⬇ keys to highlight the font (or group of fonts), press ↵ to select it, then press **[F10]**.

FIGURE 7-21

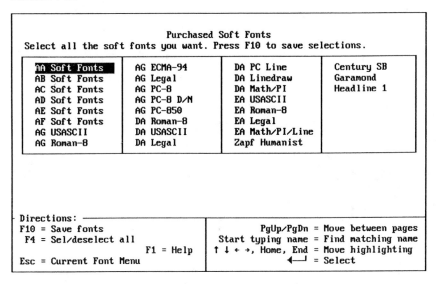

The Purchased Soft Fonts list contains entries for most HP soft fonts.

FIGURE 7-22

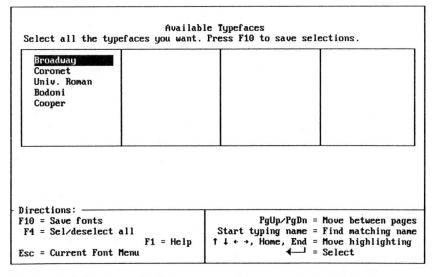

The Available Typefaces list lets you select the specific fonts included in a particular soft font package.

Once you have selected the specific fonts you want to use with WordStar from the Available Typefaces list, WINSTALL will display an Available Type Sizes list similar to the one shown in Figure 7-23. This list will provide the name and point size of each font contained within the specific font or group of fonts you have selected. For example, the Available Type Sizes list shown in Figure 7-23 will appear if you select the Broadway option from the Available Typefaces list.

FIGURE 7-23

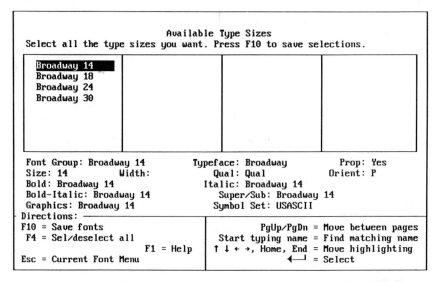

The Available Type Sizes list allows you to choose the specific fonts for which you want to add support to WordStar.

You can choose from the Available Type Sizes list the specific sizes of fonts you want to support. To add support to WordStar for every size that appears on this list, press **[F4]** to select the sizes, then press **[F10]**. If you want to add support to WordStar for a specific size (or group of sizes), highlight the size (or group of sizes), press ↵ to select it, then press **[F10]**. Regardless of the font or group of fonts you select, WINSTALL will return you to the menu shown in Figure 7-16 when you press [F10].

Adding support for third-party soft fonts

If you want to use a third-party soft font or an HP soft font that does not appear on the Purchased Soft Fonts menu with WordStar, you can do so by selecting the Add or delete third-party laser fonts option. When you select this option, WordStar will search the current directory specification for the user printer database. As we pointed out earlier in this chapter in the discussion of the LSRFONTS utility, the user printer database contains data WINSTALL uses to add support for third-party soft fonts to WordStar.

If WINSTALL doesn't find the user printer database in the current directory, it will display the message and prompt shown in Figure 7-24. When this message appears, enter the name of the directory in which the user printer database is stored, then press [**F10**].

FIGURE 7-24

```
Type the drive letter, a colon, a backslash, and the
directory name where Printer Data 0 is located. If you have
a two floppy computer, type a:, put the Printer Data disk
in drive A, and press F10.



Press Esc to cancel.              Press F10 when finished.
```

WINSTALL will ask you to enter the name of the directory in which the user printer database is stored.

Once it has located the user printer database, WINSTALL will display a Current Fonts in PDF screen similar to the one shown in Figure 7-20. When this screen appears, you can remove support for any of the fonts that are listed on the screen, or you can add support for a third-party soft font.

To remove support for a font, highlight its name, then press -. When you do this, the font's name will disappear. If you want to add support for a third-party soft font to your PDF, press the + key. WINSTALL will display the Purchased Soft Fonts list shown in Figure 7-25 on the next page. This list will include an entry for all groups of third-party soft fonts that exist within your user printer database. If you want to learn how to add support for a group of fonts to your user printer database, refer to the discussion of LSRFONTS that appeared earlier in this chapter.

When the list shown in Figure 7-25 appears on your screen, highlight the name of the group of fonts for which you want to add support to WordStar, then press ↵. Once you've selected the group(s) of fonts for which you want to add support, press [**F10**] to save the selection(s). WINSTALL will display an Available Typefaces list similar to the one shown in Figure 7-26 on the following page.

The Available Typefaces list includes the name of each font supported by the font group(s) you have selected. For example, the Available Typefaces list shown in Figure 7-26 allows you to choose the fonts that exist within the 15:00:07 09/01/ font group. Therefore, if you want to add support for all the fonts that appear on the Available Typefaces list to WordStar, press [**F4**] to select them, then press [**F10**]. On the other hand, if you want to add support to WordStar for a specific font (or group of fonts), use the →, ←, ↑, and ↓ keys to highlight your selection, press ↵, then press [**F10**].

FIGURE 7-25

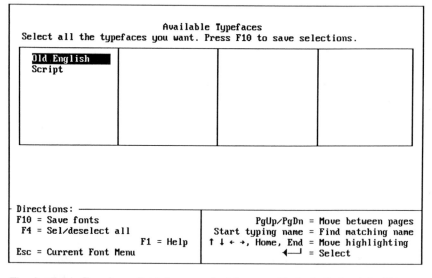

WINSTALL will display a list of the font groups that exist within your user printer database.

FIGURE 7-26

```
                        Available Typefaces
         Select all the typefaces you want. Press F10 to save selections.
      ┌─────────────────────┬─────────────┬──────────────┬─────────────┐
      │ Old English         │             │              │             │
      │ Script              │             │              │             │
      │                     │             │              │             │
      │                     │             │              │             │
      │                     │             │              │             │
      │                     │             │              │             │
      └─────────────────────┴─────────────┴──────────────┴─────────────┘



     Directions: ─────────
      F10 = Save fonts                    PgUp/PgDn = Move between pages
       F4 = Sel/deselect all        Start typing name = Find matching name
                            F1 = Help  ↑ ↓ ← →, Home, End = Move highlighting
     Esc = Current Font Menu                    ◄──┘ = Select
```

The Available Typefaces list lets you select the specific fonts that exist within a group of third-party soft fonts.

Once you have selected the specific fonts you want to use with WordStar from the Available Typefaces list, WINSTALL will display an Available Type Sizes list similar to the one shown in Figure 7-27. This list displays the name and point size of each font contained within the specific font or group of fonts you have selected. For example, the Available Type Sizes list shown in Figure 7-27 will appear if you select the Old English and Script options.

FIGURE 7-27

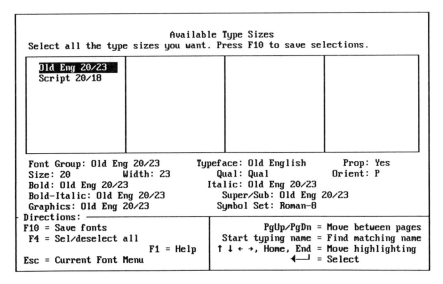

The Available Type Sizes list allows you to choose the specific fonts for which you want to add support to WordStar.

When the Available Type Sizes list appears, you can choose the specific sizes of fonts you want to use with WordStar. If you want to add support to WordStar for fonts that appear on this list, press [**F4**] to select them, then press [**F10**]. On the other hand, if you want to add support to WordStar for a specific size (or group of sizes), highlight your selection, press ↵, then press [**F10**]. Regardless of the font or group of fonts you select, WINSTALL will return you to the menu shown in Figure 7-16 when you press [F10].

Once you have added support for your LaserJet to WordStar, you're ready to select the LaserJet as your default printer. To do this, select the Choose a default printer option from the Main Installation Menu shown in Figure 7-6 on page 261 by pressing **C**. When you do this, WSCHANGE will display a list of printers similar to the list that appears on the Default Printer Selection Menu shown in Figure 7-28.

*Choosing a
default printer*

To choose a printer from this list, simply type the letter that appears to the left of its name. For example, to choose Hewlett-Packard LaserJet Series II from the list that appears in Figure 7-28, you should press **C**.

FIGURE 7-28

```
                           Default Printer Selection Menu

        Choose the printer (and printer description file) to use if no other printer
        is specified at print time.  Current PDF:  DRAFT

        Menu 1  of 1

        Printer Name                                          PDF Name
        A  ASCII                                              ASCII.PDF
        B  Draft                                              DRAFT.PDF
        C  Hewlett-Packard LaserJet Series II                 LJ.PDF
        D  WS4                                                WS4.PDF




        X  Finished with this menu

        Enter your menu selection...        | PgUp/PgDn = Move between menus
```

To choose a default printer, type the letter that appears to the left of a printer's name on the Default Printer Selection Menu.

Exiting
WINSTALL

Finally, when you have completed the task of using WINSTALL to add support for your LaserJet to your copy of WordStar and have chosen the LaserJet as your default printer, you should press **X** to select the Main Installation Menu's Finished with installation option. When you do this, WINSTALL will display a prompt that asks you if you are finished making changes. When this prompt appears, type **Y** to return to the DOS prompt. At this time, the PDF that provides your copy of WordStar with access to your LaserJet will be generated, and your copy of WordStar will automatically recognize the PDF the next time it is run.

Using
WSCHANGE

WSCHANGE is a utility program that is included with each copy of WordStar Professional Release 5. If you have already installed WordStar, you can use WSCHANGE to build a PDF that supports the specific LaserJet, fonts, and features that you want to use. You can also use WSCHANGE to make changes to several printer-related settings. We'll address both topics in this section.

Running
WSCHANGE

If you have a hard disk, WSCHANGE should be stored in the directory in which you have installed WordStar. If you are using a floppy-based system,

WSCHANGE is stored on the WordStar Professional Installation Customization disk. In either case, to run WSCHANGE, type **WSCHANGE** at the DOS prompt, then press ↵.

When you run WSCHANGE, the screen shown in Figure 7-29 will appear. This screen prompts you to enter the name of the WordStar program file you want to customize. Since the name of the standard WordStar program file is WS.EXE, when this prompt appears on your monitor, type **WS** and press ↵.

Once you have provided WSCHANGE with the name of the WordStar program file you want to customize, WSCHANGE will ask you to enter the name that should be assigned to the customized version of the WordStar program file that WSCHANGE will generate. If you want to retain the file name WS.EXE, simply type **WS**, and press ↵ when this prompt appears. On the other hand, if you want WSCHANGE to save the customized version of the WordStar file to another file name, enter that file name at the prompt, and press ↵.

FIGURE 7-29

```
WSCHANGE  11 Aug 88
Copyright (C) 1983, 1988 MicroPro International Corporation.
All rights reserved

IBM PC Compatible PC-DOS/MS-DOS Version


To install WordStar, type ws and press ◀┘.




Note:  The uninstalled WordStar is called WS.  If you've renamed
the file, type the new name and press ◀┘.
```

WSCHANGE will begin by asking you to enter the name of the WordStar program file.

Next, the Main Installation Menu shown in Figure 7-30 on the following page will appear on your screen. You can press the letter that appears to the left of each selection to change the settings related to that selection. For example, to make changes to Printer settings, you should press **B**.

As we mentioned earlier in this chapter, WSCHANGE allows you make changes to several settings that affect printing. If you want to change these settings, you should press **B** to select the Printer option from WSCHANGE's Main Installation Menu. When you do this, the Printer Menu shown in Figure 7-31 on the next page will appear on your screen.

Changing printer settings

If you want to add support for a LaserJet to WordStar, you should press **A** to choose the Printer menu's Install a printer option. When you choose this option,

Adding LaserJet support

FIGURE 7-30

```
                    Main Installation Menu

A  Console......Monitor              Function keys        Video attributes
                Monitor patches      Keyboard patches

B  Printer......Install a printer    Choose a default printer
                Change printer name  Printer defaults     Printer interface

C  Computer.....Disk Drives          Operating system     Memory usage
                WordStar files       Directory display    Patches

D  WordStar.....Page layout          Editing settings     Help level
                Spelling checks      Nondocument mode     Indexing
                Shorthand            Merge print          Miscellaneous

E  Patching.....General patches      Reset all settings   Auto-patcher

X  Finished with installation

────────────────────────────────────────────────────────────────────────

Enter your menu selection...      ? = Help
                                  ^C = Quit and cancel changes
```

WSCHANGE's Main Installation Menu allows you to add LaserJet support to WordStar.

FIGURE 7-31

```
                       Printer Menu

A  Install a printer

B  Choose a default printer

C  Change printer name on sign-on screen

D  Printing defaults...Print command answers    Character and line sizing

E  Printer interface...Printer busy handshaking  Printer subroutines
                       Background printing

X  Finished with this menu




────────────────────────────────────────────────────────────────────────

Enter your menu selection...      ? = Help
```

The Printer Menu allows you to make changes to WordStar printer settings.

WSCHANGE will display the Printer Type Menu shown in Figure 7-7 on page 261. As you may recall, this menu will also appear when you choose the Printer option from WINSTALL's Main Installation Menu.

At this point, the processes of using WSCHANGE and WINSTALL to install LaserJet support become identical. For a step-by-step look at this procedure, refer to the discussion in the section entitled "Adding LaserJet Support," which appears on page 260.

Choosing a default printer

Once you have added support for your LaserJet to WordStar, you're ready to select the LaserJet as your default printer. To do this, select the Choose a default printer option from the Printer Menu shown in Figure 7-31 by pressing **B**. When you do this, WSCHANGE will display a list of printers similar to the one shown in Figure 7-28. To choose a printer from this list, simply type the letter that appears to the left of its name. For example, to choose the Hewlett-Packard LaserJet Series II from the list that appears in Figure 7-28, you should press **C**.

Changing the printer name

The next option on WSCHANGE's Printer Menu—Change printer name on sign-on screen—lets you change the printer name that will appear on your screen when you run WordStar. If you want to personalize this name, simply press **C** to choose the Change printer name on sign-on screen option, type the new name at the prompt, then press ↵.

Changing printer defaults

You can use the fourth option on the Printer Menu shown in Figure 7-31—Printing defaults—to change several printer-related default settings. When you select this option by pressing **D**, the Printing Defaults Menu shown in Figure 7-32 will appear on your screen.

The Printing Defaults Menu lets you make changes to several default settings. To change a particular setting, simply press the letter that appears to the left of its name. For example, if you do not want WordStar to automatically print page numbers at the bottom of each page, press **L** to select the Print page numbers option, then type **N** at the prompt that will appear at the bottom of your screen.

Two default settings you should change are the Normal character font and Alternate character font settings. You can use these settings to associate any font supported by your PDF with WordStar's Normal and Alternate font commands. As we will show you later in this chapter, these commands are extremely handy when you want to switch between two fonts quickly.

To change the Normal and Alternate character font settings, press **G** and **H,** respectively. When you choose either of these options, WSCHANGE will display a list that contains the name of each font supported by your PDF. When this list appears, highlight the name of the font you want to select as Normal or Alternate, then press ↵. When you have done this, press **X** to return to the Printing Defaults Menu.

FIGURE 7-32

```
                    Printing Defaults Menu

    A  Print nondocument as default................OFF      PNODOC
    B  Bidirectional printing......................ON       .bp
    C  Letter quality printing (NLQ)...............DIS      .lq
    D  Microjustification..........................DIS      .uj
    E  Underline blanks............................OFF      .ul
    F  Proportional spacing........................DIS      .ps
    G  Normal character font.......................No font name
    H  Alternate character font....................No font name
    I  Strikeout character.........................."-"      STKCHR
    J  Line height (1440ths/inch)..................240      INIEDT+40
    K  Sub/superscript roll (1440ths/inch).........80       .sr
    L  Print page numbers..........................ON       .op

    X  Finished with this menu


    ┌─────────────────────────────────┬──────────────────────┐
    │  Enter your menu selection...   │   ? = Help           │
    └─────────────────────────────────┴──────────────────────┘
```

The Printing Defaults Menu lets you make changes to several default settings.

Changing printer interface settings

The last option on the Printer Menu, Printer interface, lets you change the method serial LaserJets will use to handshake with your computer. It also allows you to specify the location of the subroutines WordStar will use to communicate with your printer and allows you to speed up or slow down background printing. We have found it is not necessary to make changes to any of these settings when using a LaserJet with WordStar.

Changing default margin settings

As we first noted in Chapter 2, LaserJets cannot print in an area along each edge of a page. This area, known as the unprintable region, is approximately $1/4$ inch wide and must be considered whenever you print a document with WordStar.

You can use WSCHANGE to change the default margin settings so that WordStar will not attempt to print text in the unprintable region. To do this, press **D** to select the WordStar option from WSCHANGE's Main Installation Menu. When you do this, the WordStar Menu shown in Figure 7-33 will appear on your screen. At this time, press **A** to select the Page layout option.

When you select the Page layout option from the WordStar Menu shown in Figure 7-33, the Page Layout Menu will appear. You should press **A** to select the Page size and margins option. When you do this, the Page Sizing and Margins Menu shown in Figure 7-34 will appear.

The Page Sizing and Margins Menu lets you change WordStar's default margin settings. To do this, press the letter that appears to the left of the margin setting you want to change. For example, to change the default Page length setting, press **A** to select the Page length option, enter the new page length value, then press ↵.

FIGURE 7-33

```
                        WordStar Menu

A  Page layout........Page size and margins    Headers and footers
                      Tabs                      Footnotes and endnotes
                      Stored ruler lines        Paragraph numbering

B  Editing settings....Edit screen, help level  Typing
                      Paragraph alignment        Blocks
                      Erase and unerase          Lines and characters
                      Find and replace           WordStar compatibility
                      Printing defaults          Line numbering

C  Other features......Spelling checks          Nondocument mode
                      Indexing                   Shorthand (key macros)
                      Merge printing             Miscellaneous
                      Char conversion patches

X  Finished with this menu


Enter your menu selection...        ? = Help
```

From this menu, you can choose the Page layout option.

FIGURE 7-34

```
                  Page Sizing and Margins Menu

A  Page length.......................11.00"      INIEDT+18  .pl
B  Top margin........................00.50"      INIEDT+14  .mt
C  Bottom margin.....................01.33"      INIEDT+16  .mb
D  Header margin.....................00.33"      INIEDT+1F  .hm
E  Footer margin.....................00.33"      INIEDT+21  .fm
F  Page offset on even page..........00.80"      INIEDT+24  .poe
G  Page offset on odd page...........00.80"      INIEDT+26  .poo
H  Left margin.......................00.00"      RLRINI     .lm
I  Right margin......................06.50"      RLRINI+2   .rm
J  Paragraph margin (-1 for none).....(none)     RLRINI+4   .pm

X  Finished with this menu




Enter your menu selection...        ? = Help
```

The Page Sizing and Margins Menu lets you change WordStar's default margin settings.

To prevent the LaserJet from attempting to print text in its unprintable region, use the procedure we have just outlined to set the Top margin to **1.6** inches, the Bottom margin to **1.3** inches, the Header margin to **.3** inches and Page length to **11** inches. If you are printing in Landscape mode, set Page length to **8.5** inches. Then, press **X** three times to return to WSCHANGE's Main Menu.

Exiting
WSCHANGE

When you have finished using WSCHANGE to add support for your LaserJet to your copy of WordStar and have used it to select the LaserJet as your default printer, you should select from the Printer Menu the Finished with this menu option by pressing **X**. When you do this, WSCHANGE will return you to the Main Installation Menu, where you should choose the Finished with installation option by pressing **X**. As a result, WSCHANGE will display a prompt that asks you if you are finished making changes. When this prompt appears, type **Y** to return to the DOS prompt. At this time, the PDF that provides your copy of WordStar with access to your LaserJet will be generated, and your copy of WordStar will automatically recognize the PDF the next time it is run.

Using
PRCHANGE

Like WSINSTALL, PRCHANGE can be used to add LaserJet support to WordStar. It can also be used to make changes to existing levels of LaserJet support or to create screen fonts for WordStar's Advanced Page Preview feature. In addition, PRCHANGE will create a batch file that will automatically download to the LaserJet any soft fonts you want to use with WordStar. In this section, we'll look at the capabilities of PRCHANGE and show you how to use them.

Running
PRCHANGE

If you have a hard disk, PRCHANGE should be stored in the directory in which you have installed WordStar. On the other hand, if you are using a floppy-based system, PRCHANGE is stored on the WordStar Professional Installation Customization disk. In either case, to run PRCHANGE, type **PRCHANGE** at the DOS prompt, then press ↵.

When you run PRCHANGE, the Main Menu shown in Figure 7-35 will appear. From this menu, you can build a new PDF, or you can modify an existing PDF.

Adding LaserJet
support

To add support for a LaserJet to WordStar, you should choose the Main Menu's Install a printer option. When you choose this option, PRCHANGE will display the Printer Type Menu shown in Figure 7-7 on page 261. This menu will also appear when you choose the Printer option from WINSTALL's Main Installation Menu.

At this point, the processes of using PRCHANGE and WINSTALL to install LaserJet support become identical. For a step-by-step look at this procedure, please refer to the section entitled "Adding LaserJet Support," which appears on page 260.

Modifying a PDF

If you want to use PRCHANGE to make changes to an existing PDF, you should choose the Main Menu's Modify PDF settings option. When you do this, an

Installed Printer Menu similar to the one shown in Figure 7-9 on page 263 will appear. This menu will contain a list of each of the PDFs that are stored in the directory in which WordStar is installed. To make changes to one of these files, highlight its name, then press ↵.

FIGURE 7-35

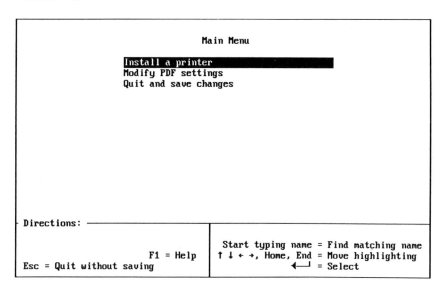

When PRCHANGE's Main Menu appears, you can create or modify a PDF.

Once you have selected the name of the PDF you want to modify, PRCHANGE will display the PDF Modification Menu shown in Figure 7-36. When this menu appears, highlight the name of the option you want to change, then press ↵. For example, to add or remove font support, highlight the **Add or remove fonts** option, then press ↵.

To add or delete support for fonts, you should choose the PDF Modification menu's Add or remove fonts option. When you choose this option, PRCHANGE displays a Current Fonts in PDF screen similar to the one shown in Figure 7-15 on page 267. As you may recall, this screen will also appear when you choose the Add or remove font groups option from WINSTALL's Additional Installation Menu.

At this point, the processes of using PRCHANGE and WINSTALL to add or remove font support become identical. For a step-by-step look at the procedure, please refer to the discussion that begins on page 267 in the section "Adding Font Support to WordStar."

Adding and deleting font support

FIGURE 7-36

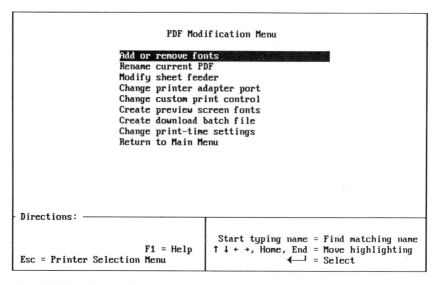

The PDF Modification Menu supports options that allow you to make changes to an existing PDF.

Changing the name of a PDF

The second option on the PDF Modification Menu—Rename current PDF—allows you to change the name of the PDF you are editing. When you select the Rename Current PDF option, PRCHANGE will display the Installed Printer Menu once again. At this time, you can select the name of an existing file, or you can enter a new name at the prompt.

Choosing a paper source

The third option that appears on the PDF Modification Menu—Modify sheet feeder—allows you to select the source from which your LaserJet will feed paper. When you select this option, the menu shown in Figure 7-12 on page 265 will appear on your screen. This menu will list each of the paper sources (sheet feeders) your printer supports.

As you can see in Figure 7-12, if you are adding support for a LaserJet to WordStar, a single option will appear on the Sheet Feeder Selection Menu. This option will provide WordStar with the ability to feed paper from each of the LaserJet's standard paper sources. To select this option, highlight its name, then press ↵. For example, to choose the option that appears on the menu shown in Figure 7-12, highlight **HPLJ II Internal & Manual Feed**, then press ↵.

Choosing a printer port

To choose the port to which your LaserJet is connected, you should choose the PDF Modification Menu's Change printer adapter port option. When you select this option, the menu shown in Figure 7-11 on page 264 will appear. This menu lists the names of seven standard MS-DOS devices. You should press ↑ and ↓ to highlight the name of the device to which your printer is connected, and press ↵. If the device name of the port to which your LaserJet is connected does not appear on the menu shown in Figure 7-11, choose the User-defined device option. When you do this, WINSTALL will prompt you to enter the device name associated with the port. For example, if your LaserJet is connected to LPT4:, choose the **User-defined device** option, type **LPT4:** at the *Enter User-defined device name:* prompt, and press ↵.

If you want WordStar to send all printer output to a disk file so you can send it to the LaserJet with the DOS COPY command, choose the User-defined disk option when the menu shown in Figure 7-11 appears. When you choose this option, WINSTALL will prompt you to enter a file name. For example, if you want to send all LaserJet output to a disk file named OUTPUT.PRN, choose the **User-defined disk** option, type **OUTPUT.PRN** at the *Enter User-defined disk file name:* prompt, then press ↵.

Sending output to a disk file

The fifth option on the PDF Modification Menu—Change custom print control—allows you to add custom printer commands to WordStar. For example, you can add custom printer commands to WordStar that allow you to activate the LaserJet IID and LaserJet 2000 to print text on both sides of a page. We'll show you how to use custom print control commands later in this chapter.

Adding custom print commands

When you select the Change custom print control option, PRCHANGE will display the Custom Print Control menu shown in Figure 7-37 on the following page. At this time, you can delete an existing print control command. To do this, highlight the name of the command, then press -.

On the other hand, if you want to add a custom print control command to your PDF, you should press +. When you do this, PRCHANGE will display a screen similar to the one shown in Figure 7-38 on the next page.

When this screen appears, begin by entering a name you want to associate with the command, then press ↵. For example, if you want to define a command that will activate the LaserJet IID and LaserJet 2000 to print text on both sides of a page, you might want to type **DUPLEX ON**.

After you have associated a name with a print control command, enter the actual PCL command that WordStar will send to the LaserJet to achieve the results you desire. For example, to activate the duplex mode of the LaserJet IID and LaserJet 2000, WordStar must send the PCL command ^{E}s$_c$&11S to the printer. To enter this command, begin by entering the escape character (ASCII 27 decimal, 1B hexadecimal). To do this, hold down the **[Alt]** key, type **27** on the numeric keypad, then release the [Alt] key. Once you've done this, type **&11S** to enter the remainder of the command, then press **[F10]** to return to the Custom Print Control Menu.

FIGURE 7-37

```
                    Custom Print Control Menu
     Add a custom print control or select one to modify or delete.
   ┌──────────────┬──────────────┬──────────────┬──────────────┐
   │ DUPLEX ON    │              │              │              │
   │              │              │              │              │
   │              │              │              │              │
   │              │              │              │              │
   │              │              │              │              │
   │              │              │              │              │
   └──────────────┴──────────────┴──────────────┴──────────────┘


 Directions: ──────────
 F10 = Finished
 + - = Add/delete item                Start typing name = Find matching name
                        F1 = Help     ↑ ↓ ← →, Home, End = Move highlighting
 Esc = Abandon changes                        ◄──┘ = Select
```

When this screen appears, you can add or remove custom print control commands by pressing + or -, respectively.

FIGURE 7-38

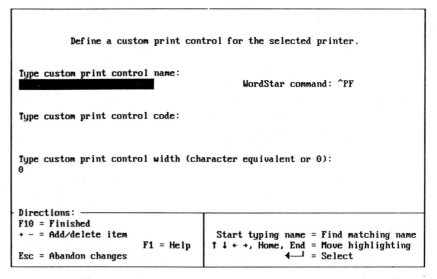

```
          Define a custom print control for the selected printer.

 Type custom print control name:
 ██████████████████████████████          WordStar command: ^PF


 Type custom print control code:


 Type custom print control width (character equivalent or 0):
 0



 Directions: ──────────
 F10 = Finished
 + - = Add/delete item                Start typing name = Find matching name
                        F1 = Help     ↑ ↓ ← →, Home, End = Move highlighting
 Esc = Abandon changes                        ◄──┘ = Select
```

This screen allows you to define a custom print control command.

One of the most interesting features of WordStar 5 is its ability to display an on-screen WYSIWYG representation of a document. However, if you want to take full advantage of this capability when using soft fonts, you must create screen fonts that match the soft fonts. To do this, you should choose the PDF Modification Menu's **Create preview screen fonts** option.

When you select this option, PRCHANGE will display the message and prompts shown in Figure 7-39. As you can see, when these prompts appear, it is necessary to specify the name of the directory in which you have installed WordStar, as well as the name of the directory in which the soft fonts for which you have added support to your PDF are stored. Once you have specified the location of these directories, PRCHANGE will automatically generate screen font files that match each soft font.

Creating screen fonts for Advanced Page Preview

FIGURE 7-39

```
In order for Advanced Page Preview to work properly, screen
font files must be created. These files must be kept in the
directory with your program files.

Type the drive and directory where your WordStar program files
are located.

C:\WS5\

Type the drive and directory where your font files are located.

C:\WS5\

Press Esc to cancel.                    Press F10 when done.
```

PRCHANGE will ask you to specify the names of the directories in which WordStar and soft font data files are stored.

The file name extension of a soft font data file may create a problem when you are using PRCHANGE'S Create preview screen font option. Sometimes, PRCHANGE expects the extension carried by HP soft fonts to be different from the actual file name extension. For example, PRCHANGE expects each of the Broadway fonts that are part of HP's Headlines 1 soft font package to carry the extension .USP, when they actually carry the extension .R8P.

When a soft font's file name extension does not match PRCHANGE's expectations, a message will appear on your screen informing you that PRCHANGE could not find the soft font. This message will include the file name of the soft font in question, as well as the extension PRCHANGE expects it to carry. If such a message should appear when you attempt to create screen fonts, rename the soft fonts so that their extensions agree with PRCHANGE's expectations.

Matching soft font file names with PRCHANGE's expectations

Avoiding problems
when using various
sizes of the same font

If PRCHANGE finds that various sizes of a particular soft font have been installed, it will create a screen font that matches each soft font. Because Advanced Page Preview has the ability to scale screen fonts, this step isn't necessary. In other words, if a 14-point screen font is available, Advanced Page Preview can automatically generate a larger version of that font.

If you are using several sizes of a soft font with WordStar and use PRCHANGE to generate matching screen fonts, you should delete all the screen fonts except the smallest. For example, if PRCHANGE creates 12-, 14-, and 18-point versions of a screen font, you should delete the 14- and 18-point versions.

Deleting a screen font is a two-step process. First, you must edit a text file called FONTID.CTL. This file contains entries that Advanced Page Preview uses to associate soft fonts with a screen font. You can edit this file using WordStar's nondocument mode.

The entries in FONTID.CTL that associate soft fonts with LaserJet fonts are always located at the end of the file and are preceded by a version entry. For example, Figure 7-40 shows the version entry and a group of entries that associate soft fonts with screen fonts, as they appeared after we used PRCHANGE to generate screen fonts that match the Broadway font in HP's Headlines 1 soft font package.

FIGURE 7-40

```
VER=V5.ØØ Ø157 154
Ø1=NPSHLV1   NPSHLV1 ,1ØØ Ø5Ø 4ØØ6
Ø2=NPSHLV2   NPSHLV2 ,1ØØ Ø5Ø 42Ø6
Ø3=NPSHLV3   NPSHLV3 ,1ØØ Ø5Ø 41Ø6
Ø4=NPSHLV4   NPSHLV1 ,1ØØ Ø5Ø 43Ø6
Ø5=NPSTMS1   NPSTMS1 ,1ØØ Ø6Ø 44Ø3
Ø6=NPSTMS2   NPSTMS2 ,1ØØ Ø6Ø 46Ø3
Ø7=NPSTMS3   NPSTMS3 ,1ØØ Ø6Ø 45Ø3
Ø8=NPSTMS4   NPSTMS4 ,1ØØ Ø6Ø 47Ø3
Ø9=BW14ØBPX
1Ø=BW18ØBPX
11=BW24ØBPX
12=BW3ØØBPX
```

These entries associate soft fonts with screen fonts.

The first entry that appears in Figure 7-40 is the version entry. This entry marks the point in a FONTID.CTL file at which entries that associate screen fonts with LaserJet fonts begin. The version entry also acts as a revision flag. In other words, whenever you make a change to the entries that associate screen fonts with LaserJet fonts, you should remove the version entry from your FONTID.CTL file. Consequently, the next time you run WordStar, it will detect the absence of the version entry and will recognize any changes you have made to the file.

When you use PRCHANGE to build a screen font that matches a soft font, an entry for each font will be placed in your FONTID.CTL. This entry will consist of a line number, an equal sign, and the file name of the soft font. For example, as you can see in Figure 7-40, PRCHANGE placed four entries in FONTID.CTL to indicate that screen fonts matching the 14-, 18-, 24- and 30-point Broadway fonts have been created. Since all of these fonts are identical, and Advanced Page Preview has the ability to automatically scale screen fonts, you should remove the 18-, 24-, and 30-point entries.

After you have removed entries from FONTID.CTL, you can remove the screen font data files that were associated with those entries. These files will always have the same file name as the soft font they match, followed by the extension .WSF. For example, the screen font data file that matches the 18-point Broadway font (whose file name is BW180BPX) will be named BW180BPX.WSF. Once you have removed these entries, you will be ready to use screen fonts with Advanced Page Preview.

The next option on the PDF Modification Menu—Create download batch file—can be used to create a standard MS-DOS batch file, which, when executed from the DOS prompt, will download to the LaserJet all the soft fonts your PDF supports. When you select this option, the Batch File Menu shown in Figure 7-41 will appear.

Creating a download batch file

FIGURE 7-41

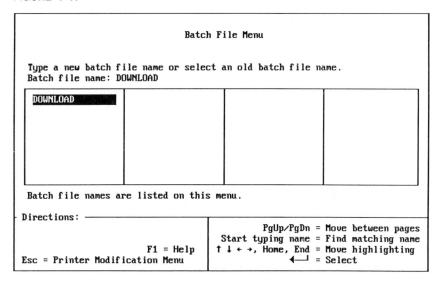

The Batch File Menu allows you to specify the name of a download batch file.

When the Batch File Menu appears on your screen, you can specify the name of the batch file PRCHANGE will create. For example, if you want PRCHANGE to create a batch file named DOWNLOAD.BAT, you should type **DOWNLOAD** at the prompt that appears at the top of the Batch File Menu, then press ↵.

Once you have specified the name of the batch file PRCHANGE should create, the message and prompts shown in Figure 7-42 will appear. At this time, you should enter the name of the directory in which WordStar is installed, as well as the name of the directory in which your font files are located. When you have done this, press [**F10**] to continue.

FIGURE 7-42

```
The batch file should be kept with your WordStar program files.


Type the drive and directory where your WordStar program files
are located.

C:\WS5\

Type the drive and directory where your font files are located.

C:\PCLFONTS\

Press Esc to cancel.                        Press F10 when done.
```

PRCHANGE will prompt you to specify the name of the directory in which WordStar is installed and soft fonts are stored.

After it has completed the process of creating a download batch file, PRCHANGE will inform you by displaying a message on the screen. When this message appears, press any key to return to the PDF Modification Menu.

Saving a PDF and exiting PRCHANGE

Once you have used the options on the PDF Modification Menu to make changes to your PDF, you should choose the **Return to Main Menu** option to return to PRCHANGE's Main Menu. After you have done this, choose the Main Menu's **Quit and save changes** option to save any changes you have made and to return to the DOS prompt.

USING WORDSTAR WITH A LASERJET

Now that we've shown you how to add LaserJet support to WordStar, we'll show you how to use the LaserJet with WordStar. In this section, we'll begin by showing you how to format a document for the LaserJet, then we'll show you how to use fonts. Finally, we'll show you how to print a document, and we'll look at WordStar's Advanced Page Preview feature.

To adjust WordStar's margins so that your LaserJet will not attempt to print text in the unprintable region, pull down the **Layout** menu and select the **Margins and tabs** command, or press **[Ctrl]OL**. When you do this, the MARGINS & TABS menu shown in Figure 7-43 will appear.

Setting Margins

FIGURE 7-43

```
════════════ M A R G I N S   &   T A B S ════════════
Margins
Left      .lm    .00"   ···.00"     Page length      .pl 11.00" 11.00"
Right     .rm   6.50"  ·6.50"
Paragraph .pm  (none)                Even page offset .poe   .80" ···.80"
Top       .mt    .50"  ···.50"       Odd page offset  .poo   .80" ···.80"
Bottom    .mb   1.33"  ·1.33"
Header    .hm    .33"  ···.33"       Line spacing     .ls     1 1
Footer    .fm    .33"  ···.33"

Tabs      .tb
.50" 1.00" 1.50" 2.00" 2.50" 3.00" 3.50" 4.00" 4.50" 5.00" 5.50"
·.50"·1.00"·1.50"·2.00"·2.50"·3.00"·3.50"·4.00"·4.50"·5.00"·5.50"
(none)

(none)

Press F1 for help.
```

The MARGINS & TABS menu allows you to adjust margins so that WordStar will not attempt to print text in the unprintable region.

When the MARGINS & TABS menu appears on your screen, set the Top margin to **1.6** inches, the Bottom margin to **1.3** inches, the Header margin to **.3** inches and Page length to **11** inches. If you 're printing in Landscape mode, set Page length to **8.5** inches. Once you've made these settings, press **[F10]** to return to edit mode.

When you change WordStar margin settings using the procedure outlined above, dot commands will be embedded in your document. For example, if you change the Top margin to 1.6 inches, the command .mt 1.6Ø″ will be embedded in your document. You can bypass the MARGINS & TABS menu and use dot commands to set margins. The dot commands you should embed in a document to set each margin are shown in Table 7-2.

Margin settings and dot commands

TABLE 7-2

Dot Command	Purpose
.mt 1.6Ø″	Set Top margin
.mb 1.3Ø″	Set Bottom margin
.hm .3Ø″	Set Header margin
.pl 11.ØØ″	Set Page length

These dot commands can be used to set the Top, Bottom, and Header margin and Page length settings.

Changing default margin settings

Finally, you can use WSCHANGE to change the default margin settings so they agree with the ones we have just recommended. To do this, use the procedure we outlined earlier in this chapter when we showed you how to use WSCHANGE.

Custom Print Control Commands

Custom print control commands are essentially WordStar [Ctrl] commands with which you can associate a LaserJet PCL command. For example, if you have a LaserJet IID or LaserJet 2000, you might want to use this capability to associate a custom print control command with the PCL commands necessary to activate the duplex printing feature.

In this section, we'll begin by showing you how to issue a custom print control command. Then, we'll show you how to use a dot command to associate custom print control commands with PCL commands.

Issuing a custom print control command

You can define up to six custom print control commands: [Ctrl]PQ, [Ctrl]PW, [Ctrl]PE, [Ctrl]PR, [Ctrl]PF, and [Ctrl]PG. You can issue these commands by pressing the [Ctrl] key and the two-key sequence that identifies the command.

When you issue a custom print control command, WordStar will embed the actual PCL command associated with the command in your document. For example, if you issue a custom print control command that is associated with the PCL command that activates the LaserJet IID and LaserJet 2000 to print text on both sides of a page, WordStar will place the following sequence of characters in your document: `<^[&l1S>`.

Defining custom print control commands

To define a custom print control command, you must place a dot command in your document. This dot command will associate the custom print control command with the hexadecimal values that make up a PCL command. Each custom print control command and the dot command you should use to associate a PCL command with it is shown in Table 7-3.

TABLE 7-3

Custom print control	Dot command
[Ctrl]PQ	.xq
[Ctrl]PW	.xw
[Ctrl]PE	.xe
[Ctrl]PR	.xr
[Ctrl]PF	.xf
[Ctrl]PG	.xg

You can use a dot command to associate each custom print control command with a PCL command.

As an example, let's assume that you want to associate the custom print control command [Ctrl]PQ with the PCL command needed to activate the duplex printing mode (^{E}s$_c$&l1S). To do this, you should embed the dot command `.xq 1B 26 6C 31 53` in your document.

In addition to the six custom print control commands we have just discussed, WordStar supports the User print control command. You can use this command to embed PCL commands not associated with a specific custom print control command in a document. To issue this command, press **[Ctrl]P!**.

When you issue a User print control command, the USER PRINT CONTROL menu shown in Figure 7-44 will appear. This menu allows you to enter any PCL command that you want to embed in a document, as well as a line of text that WordStar will use to represent the command on the screen.

Embedding other PCL commands in a document

FIGURE 7-44

```
═══════════════ U S E R   P R I N T   C O N T R O L ═══════
Characters to send to printer
       (none)


Characters to display on screen
       (none)


Number of inches to account for on printer    .00"
                                         ···.00"
Press F1 for help.
```

The USER PRINT CONTROL menu allows you to embed PCL commands in a document.

For example, let's assume you want to use the User print control command to embed the PCL command that activates the LaserJet IID or LaserJet 2000's duplex printing mode in your document. Let's also assume you want WordStar to use the phrase DUPLEX ON to represent this command on screen. To do this, press **[Ctrl]P!**, type ^{E}s$_c$&l1S, and press ↵. (To enter the escape character, hold down the **[Alt]** key, type **27** on the numeric keypad, then release the [Alt] key). Next, type **DUPLEX ON**, then press **[F10]** to embed the PCL command in your document.

Each member of the LaserJet printer family can feed paper from a number of sources. For example, the LaserJet Series II can feed paper from its internal paper tray or from the manual feed slot. On the other hand, the LaserJet IID can feed paper from either of its internal paper trays or from the manual feed slot.

To select the source from which your LaserJet will feed paper when you are using WordStar, you must embed a dot command in your document. Table 7-4 shows all these commands and the paper sources they select.

Choosing a Paper Source

TABLE 7-4

Dot command	Paper Source
.bn 1	Standard letter paper tray
.bn 2	Manual feed
.bn 3	Envelopes
.bn 4	Legal paper tray

You can choose the source from which your LaserJet will feed paper by embedding a .bn *command in your document.*

As we showed you earlier in this chapter, you can use custom print control commands to access LaserJet features that are not directly supported by WordStar. If you want to use any of the various paper sources supported by the LaserJet 500 Plus, LaserJet IID, and LaserJet 2000 that are not supported by the LaserJet Plus and LaserJet Series II PDFs, you should associate the PCL commands necessary to select these paper sources with a custom print control command. All the PCL commands you must send to the LaserJet 500 Plus, LaserJet IID, and LaserJet 2000 to select a paper source are discussed in Chapter 21.

Using Fonts in a Document

Choosing the font you want WordStar to use is extremely simple. To begin, pull down the **Style** menu and select the **Choose font** command, or type **[Ctrl]P=**. When you do this, WordStar will display the FONT menu shown in Figure 7-45.

FIGURE 7-45

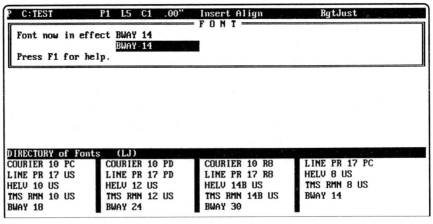

The FONT menu allows you to select the font you want to use in a Wordstar document.

As you can see in Figure 7-45, WordStar's FONT menu shows the name of the font that is currently being used and displays a list of available fonts at the bottom of the screen. To select a font from this list, simply type or highlight its name, then press ↵.

When you select a font, WordStar will embed its name and size in your document at the point where the cursor was located when you issued the Choose font command. For example, as you can see in Figure 7-46, WordStar has embedded the name and point size of each font used in the document within less than and greater than signs.

FIGURE 7-46

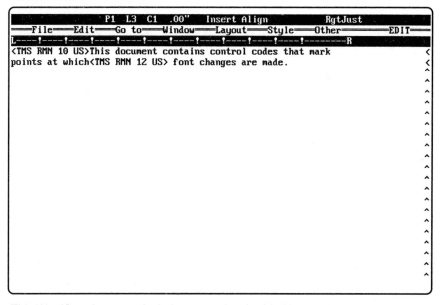

This WordStar document includes several embedded font codes.

Earlier in this chapter, we showed you how to use WSCHANGE to associate WordStar commands [Ctrl]PN and [Ctrl]PA with a normal and alternate font. Whenever you want to use the font you have defined as normal in a document, simply type **[Ctrl]PN**. Likewise, whenever you want to use the font defined as the alternate, you should type **[Ctrl]PA**. When you issue these commands, WordStar will embed the control codes <NORMAL> or <ALTERNATE> at the point at which the cursor is located.

Switching between popular fonts

When you use fonts larger than 14 points in a document, you may experience problems with line spacing. Specifically, WordStar may not leave enough white space between two lines of text, causing portions of one line to be printed on top of another. An example is shown in Figure 7-47.

Adjusting line spacing for large fonts

FIGURE 7-47

When you use fonts larger than 14 points, WordStar may not leave enough white space between two lines of text.

While this is annoying, it can be overcome easily with the help of the Line Height dot command. This command, which should be placed on a line by itself, will force WordStar to leave the appropriate amount of white space between two lines of text.

The format of the Line Height dot command is .lh followed by a value that specifies the height of each line in 48ths of an inch. For example, the Line Height dot command .lh 8 indicates that each line is $^8/_{48}$ inch tall and that six lines can appear in one inch.

After experimenting with several large fonts, we have found that you should embed a Line Height dot command on the line that precedes any line in which you plan to use a font larger than 14 points. We have also found that using a value in the Line Height command equal to half the height of a font in points works well. For example, if you want to use a 30-point font, you should place the Line Height dot command .lh 15 on the line that precedes the line in which you begin to use the 30-point font. Figure 7-48 shows a WordStar document as it will appear on your screen in which Line Height dot commands are used to adjust line spacing whenever a large font is used.

FIGURE 7-48

```
┌──────────────────────────────────────────────────────────────────┐
│  C:TEST          P1  L5  C1   .00"   Insert Align        RgtJust   │
│ ══File════Edit════Go to════Window════Layout════Style════Other════ ═EDIT══│
│L────!────!────!────!────!────!────!────!────!────!────!─────────R  │
│.lh 15                                                             1 │
│<BWAY 30>This is a 30 point test.                                 < │
│.lh 12                                                             1 │
│<BWAY 24>This is a 24 point test.                                 < │
│.lh 9                                                             1 │
│<BWAY 18>This is a 18 point test.                                 < │
│.lh 7                                                             1 │
│<BWAY 14>This is a 14 point test.                                 < │
│                                                                  ^ │
│                                                                  ^ │
│                                                                  ^ │
│                                                                  ^ │
│                                                                  ^ │
│                                                                  ^ │
│                                                                  ^ │
│                                                                  ^ │
│                                                                  ^ │
│                                                                  ^ │
│                                                                  ^ │
│                                                                  ^ │
│                                                                  ^ │
│                                                                  ^ │
└──────────────────────────────────────────────────────────────────┘
```

You should use the Line Height dot command to adjust line spacing whenever you use a large font with WordStar.

Finally, whenever you use the Line Height dot command in a document, you should issue the Reformat command by pressing **[Ctrl]QU** before saving and printing a document. This command will allow WordStar to recognize any Line Height dot command that may exist in the document.

Choosing an attribute

Although the LaserJet considers the bold and italic versions of a font to be separate and independent from the normal version of a font, you can't select a bold or italic font directly from the FONT menu. Instead, to select a bold or italic font, it is necessary to begin by selecting the normal version of the font. Once you have done this, you can select the bold or italic version of the font by selecting the **Bold** or **Italics** attribute from the **Style** menu, or by pressing **[Ctrl]PB** or **[Ctrl]PY**, respectively.

Likewise, whenever you want to underline a block of text or print it in superscript or subscript position, you can do so by choosing the appropriate attribute from the Style menu or by pressing the appropriate WordStar [Ctrl] key sequence. The Style menu, which shows each attribute command and its WordStar [Ctrl] key-sequence equivalent is shown in Figure 7-49.

FIGURE 7-49

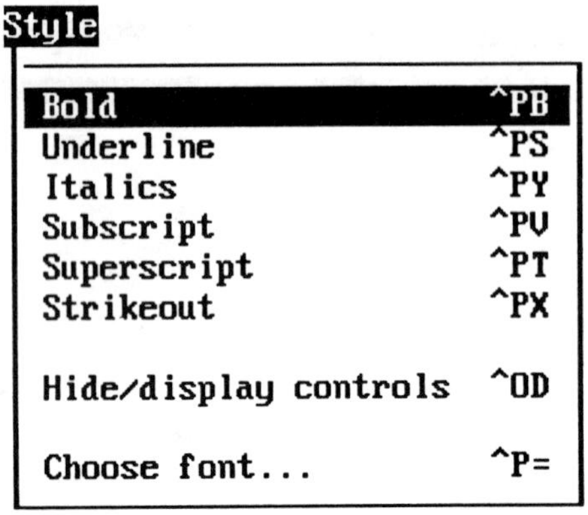

```
 Style 

┌─────────────────────────────────────────┐
│ ▐ Bold                          ^PB      │
│   Underline                     ^PS      │
│   Italics                       ^PY      │
│   Subscript                     ^PV      │
│   Superscript                   ^PT      │
│   Strikeout                     ^PX      │
│                                          │
│   Hide/display controls         ^OD      │
│                                          │
│   Choose font...                ^P=      │
└─────────────────────────────────────────┘
```

Each attribute command has a unique WordStar [Ctrl] key-sequence equivalent.

Assigning an attribute such as underlining to a block of text, or choosing the bold version of a font is a two-step process. First, move the cursor to the point in a document at which you want to begin using the attribute or font. Once you have done this, issue the command that activates the attribute. Next, enter the block of text or move the cursor to a point immediately beyond the block. Then, issue the attribute command again to deactivate the attribute or font.

As an example, let's assume that you want to underline a specific block of text. To do this, move the cursor to a point that precedes the block, then pull down the **Style** menu and choose **Underline,** or type **[Ctrl]PS**. Next, enter the block of text, or move the cursor to the point immediately following the block, then pull down the **Style** menu and choose **Underline** or type **[Ctrl]PS** to deactivate underlining.

When you issue an attribute command, WordStar will embed a control code in your document. For example, when you issue the Underline command, WordStar will embed the code ^S in a document. Figure 7-50 shows a document in which each attribute and the control codes that indicate the presence of the attributes have been used.

Avoiding spacing problems

When you switch from a larger to a smaller font, you may find that the amount of space WordStar will leave between the larger and smaller fonts will be too large. Likewise, when you switch from a smaller font to a larger font, you may find that the space WordStar will leave between the fonts will be too small. The document shown in Figure 7-51 on page 302 illustrates this problem.

To avoid this problem, follow two simple rules. First, whenever you want to switch from a large font to a smaller font, do not type a space following the last character that you want to print using the large font. Instead, use the Choose font command to select the smaller font, then type a space before entering the text that you want to print using that font.

FIGURE 7-50

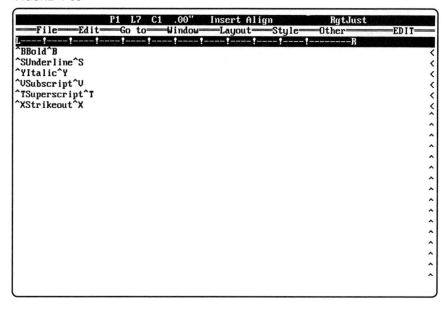

This is a document in which each attribute is marked by a unique control code.

Second, whenever you want to switch from a small font to a larger font, type a space following the last character that you want to print with the small font. Once you have done this, use the Choose font command to select the larger font and enter the text you want to print using that font.

Downloading soft fonts

WordStar cannot automatically download soft fonts to the LaserJet. Therefore, before running WordStar, you should download any soft fonts you want to use. As we showed you in Chapter 4, you can do this with a soft font download utility such as FontLoad. Also, as we mentioned earlier in this chapter, you can use PRCHANGE to generate a batch file that will download each of the soft fonts supported by your PDF to the LaserJet.

The only rule you must keep in mind when downloading soft fonts you want to use with WordStar is that they must be downloaded as permanent soft fonts. If you download a soft font as a temporary soft font, it will be erased from the LaserJet's memory by WordStar the first time you attempt to print a document.

Landscape Printing

If you want WordStar to print a document in Landscape mode, you must do two things. First, you should embed the dot command .pr=l on the first line of the document or page that you want to print in Landscape mode. Second, you should use the procedures we outlined in the previous section of this chapter to select a Landscape font.

FIGURE 7-51

When switching from a smaller to a **larger font,** **and** vice versa, you may experience problems with character spacing.

When you use fonts of different sizes on the same line, you may encounter problems with spacing.

Finally, as we pointed out in Chapter 1, the LaserJet cannot print in Landscape and Portrait mode on the same page. Therefore, you should not try to mix modes on a single page when using WordStar. However, when you have finished printing in Landscape mode, you can use the dot command .pr=p to switch back to Portrait mode. When WordStar encounters this command, the LaserJet will automatically eject any page that is currently being printed in Landscape mode before switching to Portrait mode.

Advanced Page Preview

One of the most interesting and useful features of WordStar is Advanced Page Preview. Advanced Page Preview allows you to view an on-screen WYSIWYG representation of any document. To access this feature, pull down the **Layout** menu and choose the **Page Preview** option, or type **[Ctrl]OP**. Figure 7-52 shows the view of the document shown in Figure 7-51 that Advanced Page Preview displays on an EGA monitor.

FIGURE 7-52

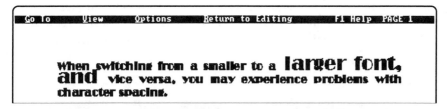

Advanced Page Preview can provide an on-screen representation of any document.

Now that we've looked at several issues related to formatting a document, let's send a document to the LaserJet. Whenever you want to print a document, you should begin by making sure it has been saved to disk. To do this, simply pull down the **File** menu and choose the **Save file, resume editing** command or press **[Ctrl]KS**.

Once you have saved a document to disk, you can issue a print command. To do this, pull down the **File** menu and select the **Print a file** command, or press **[Ctrl]KPP**. When you issue this command, the PRINT menu shown in Figure 7-53 will appear.

Printing a Document

FIGURE 7-53

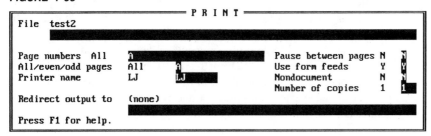

The PRINT menu will appear whenever you issue a print command.

As you can see in Figure 7-53, the PRINT menu allows you to specify the name of the file you want to print and the name of the PDF you want to use when printing the file. The PRINT menu also allows you to specify whether the document should include page numbers, as well as the number of copies of the document that WordStar should print. Finally, the PRINT menu allows you to specify the name of the port or disk file to which the document should be sent.

To make changes to a setting that appears on the PRINT menu, press the ↵ key to move the cursor to the setting, enter the appropriate value, then press ↵ to advance the cursor to the next setting. When you have finished making changes to the PRINT menu's settings, press **[F10]** to print the document. Likewise, if you do not want to make any changes to the default settings that appear on the PRINT menu, you should press **[F10]** to send the document to the LaserJet.

Addressing envelopes

Addressing envelopes with WordStar Professional Release 5 is a task that is made simple by the Merge Print command. To issue this command, pull down the **File** menu and select **Merge print a file**, or press **[Ctrl]KM**. When you do this, the MERGE PRINT menu shown in Figure 7-54 will appear on your screen.

FIGURE 7-54

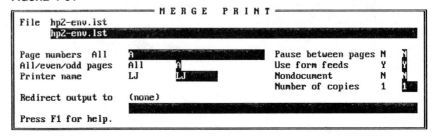

The MERGE PRINT menu will appear when you issue a Merge Print command.

When the MERGE PRINT menu appears, you must begin by entering the name of a merge print file. At this time, you should type **HP-ENV.LST** if you are using an original LaserJet, LaserJet Plus, or LaserJet 500 Plus. If you are using a LaserJet Series II or LaserJet IID, you should type **HP2-ENV.LST.**

Next, press **[F10]** to begin the process of addressing an envelope. When you do this, WordStar will display the message *PRINTING* in the top-right corner of the screen, you will hear a beep, and the message *PRINTING PAUSED* will appear. You should issue another Merge Print command. When you do this, you will be asked to enter all the information you want to print on an envelope. As you can see in Figure 7-55, once you have entered this information, you will be told to feed an envelope. Once you have done this, press ↵, and WordStar will print the information you have entered.

Merge printing

WordStar Professional Release 5 is shipped with a program called MailList that you can use to manage a mailing list. WordStar includes merge print files you can use to print envelopes and address labels using information stored in a MailList database.

If you have a LaserJet, LaserJet Plus, or LaserJet 500 Plus and want to address envelopes using information stored in a MAILLIST database, you should use the Merge Print command to print the merge print file HP-ENVMM.LST. If you have a LaserJet Series II, you should use the Merge Print command to print the merge print file HP2-ENVM.LST. When you print either of these files, messages will appear on the LaserJet's control panel prompting you to feed envelopes into the printer.

Finally, two merge print files that allow you to print labels using a MailList database are included with WordStar. If you want to print 1-inch by $2^3/_4$-inch labels

(33 per $8^1/_2$- by 11-inch sheet), you should use the Merge Print command to print the file HP-LAB3.LST. On the other hand, if you want to print 1-inch by $2^5/_8$-inch labels (30 per $8^1/_2$- by 11-inch sheet), you should use the Merge Print command to print the file LSRLABL3.LST.

FIGURE 7-55

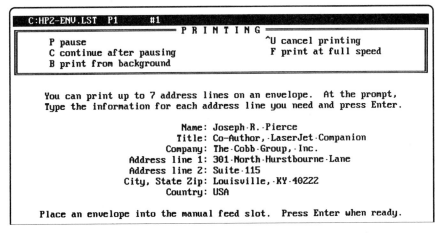

Once you have entered the information you want to print on an envelope, WordStar will prompt you to feed an envelope into the LaserJet.

CONCLUSION

In this chapter, we explained how to add support for a LaserJet to WordStar Professional Release 5. Then, we showed you how to use a LaserJet with WordStar. You are now ready to successfully use a LaserJet with WordStar.

MICROSOFT WORD 4.0 **8**

Microsoft Word is an extremely powerful and popular word processor that offers a great deal of support for the LaserJet. In this chapter, we'll show you how to install Word for the particular LaserJet and fonts you are using. Then, we'll show you how to include fonts in Word documents. Finally, we'll discuss two utility programs that allow you to add full support to Word for the specific set of fonts you are using.

In this section, we'll take a look at the procedure you must use to install support for your particular LaserJet and collection of internal, cartridge, and soft fonts. We'll begin by looking at the LaserJet printer description files that are included with Word or available from Microsoft Product Support, then we'll show you how to install printer files with the Word SETUP program. Once we've completed this task, we'll look at the procedure you must follow to use a printer description file.

INSTALLING LASERJET SUPPORT

Word's support for the LaserJet is contained within a collection of printer description (PRD) files. PRD files are data files that contain all of the PCL commands and information Word needs to use a specific set of LaserJet fonts. The PRD file you use will determine which fonts you can use in a document.

Choosing a Printer Description File

Word is shipped with a number of PRD files. Each file contains support for the LaserJet's Internal Courier 12 and Line Printer 8.5 fonts, as well as support for a specific set of cartridge or soft fonts. The names of these PRD files and the fonts supported by each are listed in Table 8-1. As we will show you later in this chapter, you can use the Microsoft Word SETUP program to install these PRD files.

Standard LaserJet PRD files

TABLE 8-1

Filename	Fonts supported
Portrait cartridge fonts	
HPLASER1.PRD	A, B, C, D, E, G, H, J, L, W, and X
HPLASER2.PRD	F, K, P, R, and U
HPLASER3.PRD	J, R, and Z
HPLASMS.PRD	Z
HPLASRMN.PRD	F
HPLASPS.PRD	B
HPLASTAX.PRD	T
HPPCCOUR.PRD	Y
Landscape cartridge fonts	
HPLASLAN.PRD	A, B, C, G, H, L, M, N, P, Q, U, and V
HPLASMSL.PRD	Z
Portrait soft fonts	
HPDWNCNP.PRD	SA
HPDWNGAP.PRD	RA
HPDWNHLP.PRD	UA
HPDWNLGP.PRD	DA
HPDWNPRP.PRD	EA
HPDWNSFP.PRD	AC and AE
HPDWNR8P.PRD	AD and AF
HPDWNZHP.PRD	TA
Landscape soft fonts	
HPDWNLGL.PRD	DA
HPDWNPRL.PRD	EA
HPDWNSFL.PRD	AC and AE
HPDWNR8L.PRD	AD and AF

Word is shipped with a number of PRD files that support most HP cartridge, soft, and internal fonts.

Revised LaserJet and LaserJet Plus PRD files

If you plan to use Landscape soft fonts with your LaserJet or LaserJet Plus, you should obtain a set of revised PRD files from Microsoft's Product Support department. These PRD files correct problems with many of the files shipped with Word and allow you to utilize the Landscape mode when using the legal-size paper tray with the LaserJet and LaserJet Plus. The names of these files, as well as the set of fonts each supports, are listed in Table 8-2. To obtain these files, contact Microsoft Product Support at 206-882-8089 and ask for the Word 4.0 Revised Print Drivers for the LaserJet and LaserJet Plus.

Unfortunately, you cannot use the Microsoft Word SETUP program to install support for these PRD files. Therefore, you should use the information presented in this table to choose the file(s) that contain(s) support for the specific set of fonts you plan to use with Word. Later in this chapter, we'll show you how to install the files you choose.

TABLE 8-2

Filename	Fonts supported
Landscape soft fonts	
HPDWNSFL.PRD	AC and AE
HPDWNR8L.PRD	AD and AF
HPDWNLGL.PRD	DA
HPDWNPRL.PRD	EA
Landscape soft fonts with legal-size paper tray	
HPLEGSFL.PRD	AC and AE
HPLEGR8L.PRD	AD and AF
HPLEGLGL.PRD	DA
HPLEGPRL.PRD	EA

These are the PRD files that let you utilize the Landscape mode with the LaserJet and LaserJet Plus.

LaserJet Series II PRD files

If you plan to use Landscape cartridge or soft fonts with your LaserJet Series II, you should obtain a set of Series II PRD files from Microsoft's Product Support department. These PRD files support the Series II's ability to draw lines, allow Landscape printing with legal-size paper, and correct problems with several of the PRD files shipped with Word. The names of these files and the set of fonts each supports are listed in Table 8-3.

Unfortunately, you cannot use the Microsoft Word SETUP program to install support for these PRD files. Therefore, you should use the information presented in this table to choose the file(s) that contain(s) support for the specific set of fonts you plan to use with Word. Later in this chapter, we'll show you how to install the files you choose.

TABLE 8-3

Filename	Fonts supported
Landscape soft fonts	
H2LASLAN.PRD	A, B, C, G, H, L, M, N, P, Q, U, and V
H2LASMSL.PRD	Z
H2DWNSFL.PRD	AC and AE
H2DWNR8L.PRD	AD and AF
H2DWNLGL.PRD	DA
H2DWNPRL.PRD	EA
Landscape soft fonts with legal-size paper tray	
H2LEGLAN.PRD	A, B, C, G, H, L, M, N, P, Q, U, and V
H2LEGMSL.PRD	Z
H2LEGSFL.PRD	AC and AE
H2LEGR8L.PRD	AD and AF
H2LEGLGL.PRD	DA
H2LEGPRL.PRD	EA

These PRD files support the LaserJet Series II's ability to draw lines, allow Landscape printing with legal-size paper, and correct problems with several of the PRD files shipped with Word.

DAT files

Every PRD file that supports a LaserJet soft font is accompanied by a file with the extension .DAT. For example, the PRD file HPLASLAN.PRD is accompanied by the file HPLASLAN.DAT. DAT files contain data and PCL commands Word can use to download soft fonts automatically to your LaserJet whenever you print a document. At this time, all you need to know about DAT files is that they exist. We'll discuss them in more detail later in this chapter.

Customizing Existing PRD Files

While the collection of PRD files shipped with Word and those available from Microsoft's Product Support department contain support for most of the fonts sold by HP, you'll find that none of these files contain support for all the fonts you can use. For example, suppose you are using a LaserJet Series II with the HP "Z" cartridge and AG soft fonts. Since none of the printer files shipped with Word contain support for this particular group of fonts, you must use the Word MERGE-PRD utility to build a PRD file for your system that contains support for the particular set of fonts you will be using. We'll show you how to use MERGEPRD later in this chapter.

If you plan to use fonts with your LaserJet that are not supported by any of the PRD files listed in Tables 8-1, 8-2, or 8-3, you must use a third-party utility to build a PRD file that supports them, or you must add support for those fonts to your PRD file manually. This is done by making entries in a text file that is converted into a PRD file by the Word MAKEPRD utility. We'll show you how to use MAKEPRD later in this chapter, and in Chapter 18, we'll discuss third-party utilities that can be used to create PRD files.

Building New PRD Files

In the previous section, we looked at each of the PRD files that are shipped with Word or available from Microsoft's Product Support department so that you could determine which file or files support the fonts you plan to use with your LaserJet. In this section, we'll show you how to use the Microsoft Word SETUP program to install support for the files that are shipped with Word, then we'll show you how to install support for other PRD files.

Installing a PRD File

The Microsoft Word SETUP program is versatile. You can use it to install support for a PRD file when you install Word for your system, or you can use it to install support for the LaserJet after you have installed Word. This makes it a bit different from other Microsoft SETUP programs, which allow you to install Laser-Jet support only when you are installing the main program.

Installing a PRD file with the Word SETUP program

To run the Word SETUP program, place the Word Utilities disk in drive A, type **SETUP**, then press ↵. When you do this, SETUP will display an introductory screen. When this screen appears on your monitor, press **C** to continue. The screen shown in Figure 8-1 will appear on your monitor.

Running SETUP

FIGURE 8-1

```
                        SETUP MENU
  ┌─────────────────────────────────────────────────────┐
  │  TO                                          PRESS   │
  ├─────────────────────────────────────────────────────┤
  │  Copy the Word program to the hard disk        W     │
  │                                                      │
  │  Copy the Learning Word program to the hard disk  L  │
  │                                                      │
  │  Copy the Spell program to the hard disk       S     │
  │                                                      │
  │  Copy Thesaurus program to the hard disk       T     │
  │                                                      │
  │  Copy printer information to the hard disk     P     │
  │                                                      │
  │  Copy mouse information to the hard disk        M     │
  │                                                      │
  │  Quit SETUP                                     Q     │
  └─────────────────────────────────────────────────────┘

  If you're using SETUP for the first time, do these in order.
```

The Microsoft Word SETUP program will display this screen on your monitor.

As you can see in the screen shown in Figure 8-1, Word's SETUP program allows you to install printer support separately from other parts of the package. Therefore, even if you've already installed some other printer, you can use SETUP at any time to add LaserJet support. On the other hand, if you have not installed Word on your system, you can install it and printer support at the same time.

Choosing a printer

To install the PRD that supports your LaserJet, select the Copy printer information to the hard disk or Copy printer information to system disk option by pressing **P**. When you press P, SETUP will ask you to enter the name of the directory into which it should copy printer information. After you have supplied the name of the appropriate directory, Word will display another screen that will ask if you want to continue, go back and change the directory specification, or quit. If you have entered the directory specification correctly, press **C** to continue.

After you have indicated that you have selected the correct directory specification into which you want printer support to be copied, Word will display the screen shown in Figure 8-2. As you can see, this screen contains a list of printers supported by Word. You can choose the appropriate LaserJet printer and font collection from this list.

FIGURE 8-2

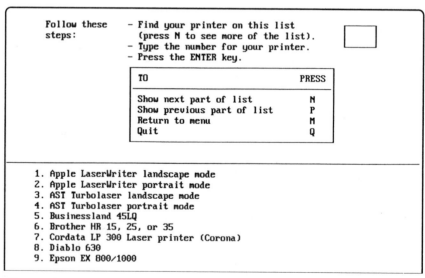

After you have supplied SETUP with the correct directory into which printer support can be copied, Word will ask you to pick a printer from the list shown in this figure.

To page through the list of printers that appear in Figure 8-2, press **N**. When you see the particular printer and font combination that best matches your system, type its number, and press ↵. For example, if you are using a LaserJet Series II that is equipped with the HP "Z" font cartridge, type **31**, and press ↵. Table 8-4 lists each of the HP LaserJet options that SETUP will display on your screen as you page through the list of printers shown in Figure 8-2.

TABLE 8-4

23. HP LaserJet with Landscape fonts on any cartridge
24. HP LaserJet & cartridges A, B, C, D, E, G, H, J, L, M, N, Q, W, X
25. HP LaserJet & cartridges F, K, P, R, U
26. HP LaserJet & cartridges J, R, and Z
27. HP LaserJet with TMS Proportional 1 cartridge (92286B)
28. HP LaserJet with TMS Proportional 2 cartridge (92286F)
29. HP LaserJet with Tax 1 cartridges (92286T)
30. HP LaserJet with PC Courier 1 cartridge (92286Y)
31. HP LaserJet with Microsoft cartridge (92286Z)
32. HP LaserJet with Microsoft cartridge, Landscape fonts (92286Z)
33. HP LaserJet+, Century Schoolbook Portrait download font set SA
34. HP LaserJet+, Garamond Portrait download font set RA
35. HP LaserJet+, Headline Portrait download font set UA
36. HP LaserJet+, LetterGothic Landscape download font set DA
37. HP LaserJet+, LetterGothic Portrait download font set DA
38. HP LaserJet+, Prestige Elite Landscape download font set EA
39. HP LaserJet+, Prestige Elite Portrait download font set EA
40. HP LaserJet+, HELV & TMSRMN Landscape download font sets AD & AF
41. HP LaserJet+, HELV & TMSRMN Portrait download font sets AD & AF
42. HP LaserJet+, HELV & TMSRMN Landscape download font sets AC & AE
43. HP LaserJet+, HELV & TMSRMN Portrait download font sets AC & AE
44. HP LaserJet+, Zapf Humanist Portrait download font set TA

When running the Microsoft Word SETUP program, you can install support for any of the fonts listed in this table.

Once you have entered the number that corresponds to the particular printer and font combination you are using, SETUP will display a screen that asks if you want to accept the selection, enter a different selection, or quit. If you respond by typing P to enter a different selection, SETUP will once again display the screen shown in Figure 8-2. If you choose to continue by pressing P, SETUP will prompt you to insert in drive A the diskette that contains support for the fonts you plan to use. For example, if you are installing support for a LaserJet Series II equipped with a "Z" cartridge, the screen shown in Figure 8-3 will appear on your monitor, asking you to insert the Printer1 diskette in drive A.

FIGURE 8-3

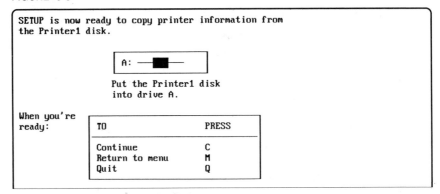

```
SETUP is now ready to copy printer information from
the Printer1 disk.

                    A: ——█——

                    Put the Printer1 disk
                    into drive A.

When you're
ready:        ┌─────────────────────────────────┐
              │ TO                      PRESS    │
              │─────────────────────────────────│
              │ Continue                C        │
              │ Return to menu          M        │
              │ Quit                    Q        │
              └─────────────────────────────────┘
```

SETUP will ask you to insert the diskette that contains support for the printer and fonts you are using.

Choosing a port

After you have inserted the proper disk in drive A, press ↵, and SETUP will proceed to copy support for the printer you select into the directory you have specified. When it has finished doing this, it will display the screen shown in Figure 8-4. This screen prompts you to select the port to which your LaserJet is connected. To select the port, simply choose the number associated with it. For example, to choose LPT1:, press **1**.

FIGURE 8-4

```
SETUP is copying the information about your printer onto
the hard disk...

You can now choose one of these output ports:
    1. LPT1:
    2. LPT2:
    3. LPT3:
    4. COM1:
    5. COM2:

Please enter a number (1-5) that corresponds to the port you want.
If you are not sure, enter 1.

    ┌───┐
    │   │
    └───┘
```

After it has copied the PRD that supports your printer into the directory you specified earlier, SETUP will ask you to specify the name of the port to which your LaserJet is connected.

If you are installing a PRD file that contains support for soft fonts, SETUP will ask you to place the Utilities disk in drive A after you have chosen the port to which your LaserJet is connected. As we pointed out earlier in the chapter, Word has the ability to download soft fonts automatically to the LaserJet. This capability is made possible by an external program called DOWN.EXE. This program is stored on the Utilities disk and is copied into your Word directory by the SETUP program whenever you install a PRD file that supports soft fonts.

Automatic soft font downloading

Once you have provided SETUP with the name of the port to which your LaserJet is connected, the screen shown in Figure 8-5 will appear. As you can see, this screen allows you to install support for another printer or additional LaserJet fonts. For example, if you plan to use the HP SA soft font package in addition to the "Z" cartridge we installed earlier, press P. As a result, the screen shown in Figure 8-2 will appear once more. Therefore, to choose the printer and/or fonts for which you want to install font support, type the appropriate number(s) and press ↵. For example, if you want to install support for the HP SA soft font package in addition to the "Z" cartridge, type **P** when the screen shown in Figure 8-5 appears on your monitor, then type **33**, and press ↵ to install it.

Installing more than one PRD file

FIGURE 8-5

```
If you want to use an additional printer, you can install it
now by copying information about that printer.

When you are ready to use this printer, you need to type its
PRD filename in the "printer" field of the
Print Options command.

When you're
ready:      ┌─────────────────────────────────────┐
            │ TO                    PRESS         │
            │                                     │
            │ Copy printer driver   P             │
            │ Return to menu        M             │
            │ Quit                  Q             │
            └─────────────────────────────────────┘
```

After you have installed support for the LaserJet, you may install support for another printer, or you may install support for additional soft fonts.

When you tell SETUP to install support for a second or third printer, it will copy the appropriate printer driver into the directory you have specified. If the PRD file you have selected is not on the disk in drive A, SETUP will prompt you to place the disk that contains the file in drive A.

Once SETUP has successfully installed a PRD file, it may prompt you to insert the Utilities disk in drive A so that SETUP may install the Word download utility. If you have previously installed a PRD file that contains support for a soft font, SETUP will skip this step.

Finally, after SETUP has installed an additional PRD file, it will again ask if you want to install support for additional printers or fonts. If you reply by pressing M, you will be returned to the main SETUP menu where you may install the Word program or program modules. If you do not want to install the Word program or other program modules, press **Q** to quit.

Manual PRD file installation

As we have just shown, you can use the Microsoft Word SETUP program to install the PRD files that are shipped with Word. However, if you want to install support for any other PRD file, you must do so manually.

To install support for a PRD file, you must begin by copying the file into the directory in which Word is installed. For example, if you want to install the PRD file CUSTOM.PRD for use with a copy of Word that is installed in the directory C:\WORD, copy CUSTOM.PRD into the C:\WORD directory.

Soft font support

If the PRD file you are installing contains support for soft fonts, it's possible that a download file may accompany it. As we pointed out earlier, a download file has the same file name as a PRD file, but has the extension DAT. Therefore, if the PRD file you are installing is accompanied by a DAT file, copy the DAT file into the directory in which Word is installed. If you are installing a PRD file that contains support for a soft font, but is not accompanied by a DAT file, you may want to create a DAT file. We'll show you how to do this later in this chapter.

Finally, if you are installing a PRD file that supports soft fonts and plan to take advantage of Word's ability to download soft fonts automatically, you must copy the program DOWN.EXE from the Word Utilities disk into the directory in which Word is installed.

Using a PRD File

Once you have used SETUP to install a PRD file or have manually copied a PRD file into your Word directory, you cannot use it until you enter its name in the printer field of Word's Print Options command. To do this, run Word by typing **Word** at the DOS prompt, then issue the Print Options command. When you do this, Word will display the menu shown in Figure 8-6. The printer field that appears on this menu allows you to specify the name of the PRD file Word should use.

To choose the PRD file you want to use, select the printer field, then type the name of the file. Alternatively, you can press **[F1]** to display a list of the PRD files stored in the directory in which Word is installed. When the list appears, select the name of the file you want to use, then press ↵ or the right button on your mouse. For example, we have all the PRD files shipped with Word plus a few others in our Word directory. Therefore, when we pressed [F1], the list shown in Figure 8-7 appeared on our screen. The list that appears on your screen will be similar.

FIGURE 8-6

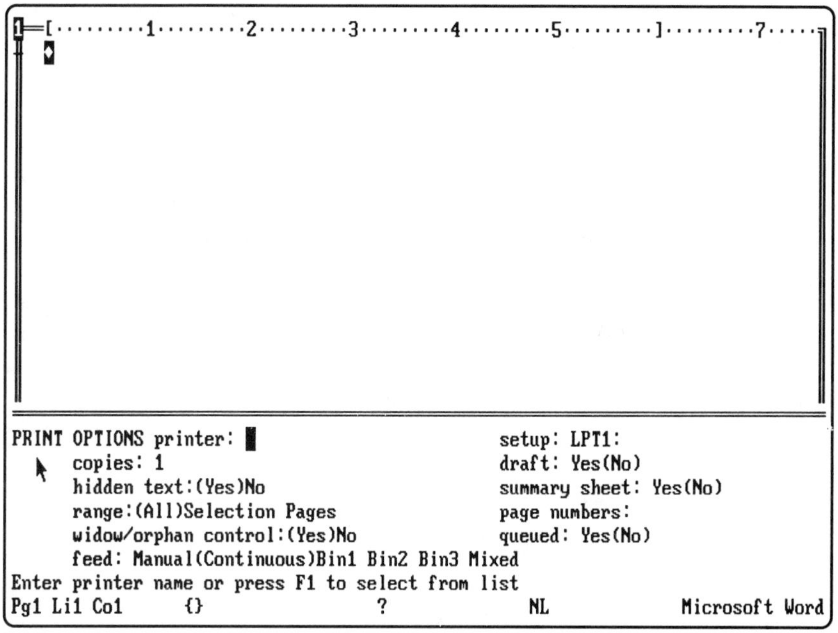

```
 ▯═[· · · · · · ·1· · · · · · · ·2· · · · · · · ·3· · · · · · · ·4· · · · · · · ·5· · · · · · · ·]· · · · · · · ·7· · · · ·
 ▯  ▯









PRINT OPTIONS printer: █                    setup: LPT1:
   ▶  copies: 1                              draft: Yes(No)
      hidden text:(Yes)No                    summary sheet: Yes(No)
      range:(All)Selection Pages             page numbers:
      widow/orphan control:(Yes)No           queued: Yes(No)
      feed: Manual(Continuous)Bin1 Bin2 Bin3 Mixed
Enter printer name or press F1 to select from list
Pg1 Li1 Co1      {}                ?            NL          Microsoft Word
```

You can use the printer field on the Print Options menu to choose a PRD file.

FIGURE 8-7

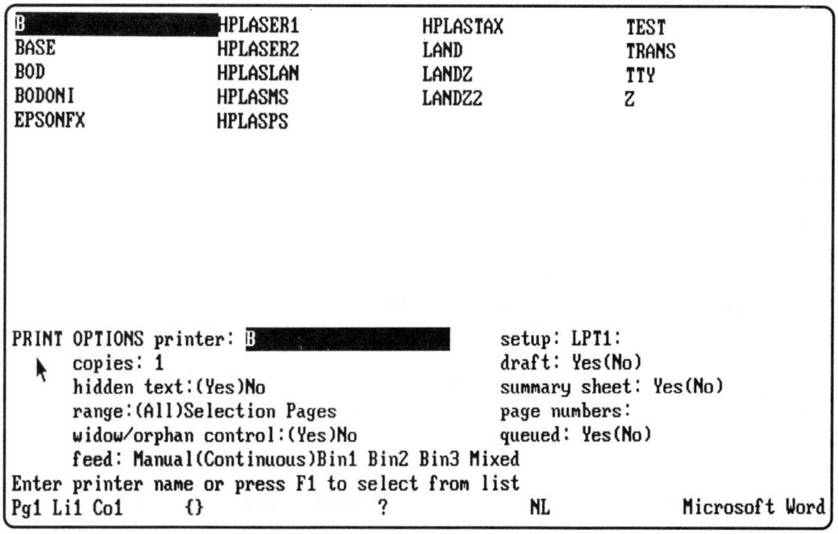

```
 ▊            HPLASER1        HPLASTAX        TEST
 BASE         HPLASER2        LAND            TRANS
 BOD          HPLASLAN        LANDZ           TTY
 BODONI       HPLASMS         LANDZ2          Z
 EPSONFX      HPLASPS




PRINT OPTIONS printer: ▊              setup: LPT1:
   ▶  copies: 1                       draft: Yes(No)
      hidden text:(Yes)No             summary sheet: Yes(No)
      range:(All)Selection Pages      page numbers:
      widow/orphan control:(Yes)No    queued: Yes(No)
      feed: Manual(Continuous)Bin1 Bin2 Bin3 Mixed
Enter printer name or press F1 to select from list
Pg1 Li1 Co1      {}                ?            NL          Microsoft Word
```

*If you press [F1] after selecting the printer field on the Print Options menu, Word
will list each PRD file stored in your Word directory.*

Changing
PRD files

As you may expect, you can use the Print Options command's printer field to change PRD files at any time. For example, if you normally use a PRD file that supports Portrait fonts, but want to print text using a Landscape font, simply issue a Print Options command and enter the name of the PRD file that supports those fonts in the printer field.

Choosing a port

If you haven't previously used the Word SETUP program to specify the name of the port to which your LaserJet is connected, you may use the Print Options command's setup field to do so. When you select the setup field, Word will display the message *Enter port name or press F1 to select from list.* At this prompt, type the name of the port to which your LaserJet is connected, or press **[F1]** to display a list of ports similar to the one shown in Figure 8-8. Once you press [F1] to display the list of available system ports, select the port to which your LaserJet is connected, then press ↵ or the right button on your mouse.

FIGURE 8-8

```
┌─────────────────────────────────────────────────────────────────────┐
│ COM1:              LPT1:            LPT2:            LPT3:            │
│ COM2:                                                                 │
│                                                                       │
│                                                                       │
│                                                                       │
│                                                                       │
│                                                                       │
│                                                                       │
│                                                                       │
│                                                                       │
│                                                                       │
│                                                                       │
│                                                                       │
│ PRINT OPTIONS printer: LANDZ              setup: COM1:                │
│      copies: 1                            draft: Yes(No)              │
│  ▸   hidden text:(Yes)No                  summary sheet: Yes(No)      │
│      range:(All)Selection Pages           page numbers:              │
│      widow/orphan control:(Yes)No         queued: Yes(No)            │
│      feed: Manual(Continuous)Bin1 Bin2 Bin3 Mixed                    │
│ Enter port name or press F1 to select from list                      │
│ Pg1 Li1 Co1       {}                    ?          NL    Microsoft Word │
└─────────────────────────────────────────────────────────────────────┘
```

If you press [F1] after selecting the setup field on the Print Options menu, Word will list the ports to which your LaserJet may be connected.

USING FONTS

Once you have used the Print Options command to specify the name of the PRD file that you want to use, you may use the fonts that PRD file supports. In this section, we'll discuss the process by which you can include fonts in a document.

You can use the Format Character command to specify which font Word will use to print a block of text before or after you enter the block of text. To choose a font before you enter a block of text, simply place the cursor at the point in the document where the block will begin, then issue the Format Character command. To choose a font after you have entered a block of text, highlight the block, then issue the Format Character command.

When you issue the Format Character command, the menu shown in Figure 8-9 will appear on your screen. The command fields that appear on this menu can be used to choose a font and point size. They can also be used to select attributes such as underlining.

The Format Character Command

FIGURE 8-9

```
╓═[·········1·········2····]····3·········4·········5·········6·········7·····╖
║  ▓&110←&181A¶
║  LaserJet·User¶
║  100·Main·Street¶
║  Anytown,·USA·55555¶
║  ::::::::::::::::::::::::::::::::::::::::::::::::::::::::::::::::::::::::::::::
║  ←&100¶
║  LaserJet·User¶
║  100·Main·Street¶
║  Anytown,·USA·55555¶
║  ¶
║  July·4,·1988¶
║  ¶
║  Dear·LaserJet·User,¶
║  ¶
║  →    As·we·are·sure·you·are·aware,·Hewlett·Packard's·
║  LaserJet·family·of·printers·is·extremely·versatile.··For·
║  example,·in·this·document·we·are·taking·advantage·of·the·
╟──────────────────────────────────────────────────────────────────────────
║FORMAT CHARACTER bold: Yes ▓No▓    italic: Yes(No)     underline: Yes(No)
║        strikethrough: Yes(No)     uppercase: Yes(No)   small caps: Yes(No)
║  ▸     double underline: Yes(No)  position:(Normal)Superscript Subscript
║        font name: modern b        font size: 12         hidden: Yes(No)
║Select option
║P1 D1 Li1 Co1     {e}              ?              NL         Microsoft Word
╙──────────────────────────────────────────────────────────────────────────
```

When you issue the Format Character command, this menu will appear on your screen.

To choose a font, use the cursor keys, [Tab] key, or mouse to select the font name command field. When you select this command field, Word will display the message *Enter font name or press F1 to select from list*. When this message appears on your screen, type the name of the font you want to use or press **[F1]** to display a list of available fonts. For example, if you press [F1] while support for a LaserJet Series II and the HP "Z" cartridge is installed, the list shown in Figure 8-10 will appear on your screen. To choose a font from the list Word displays, use the cursor keys, [Tab] key, or mouse to select its name.

Font name

FIGURE 8-10

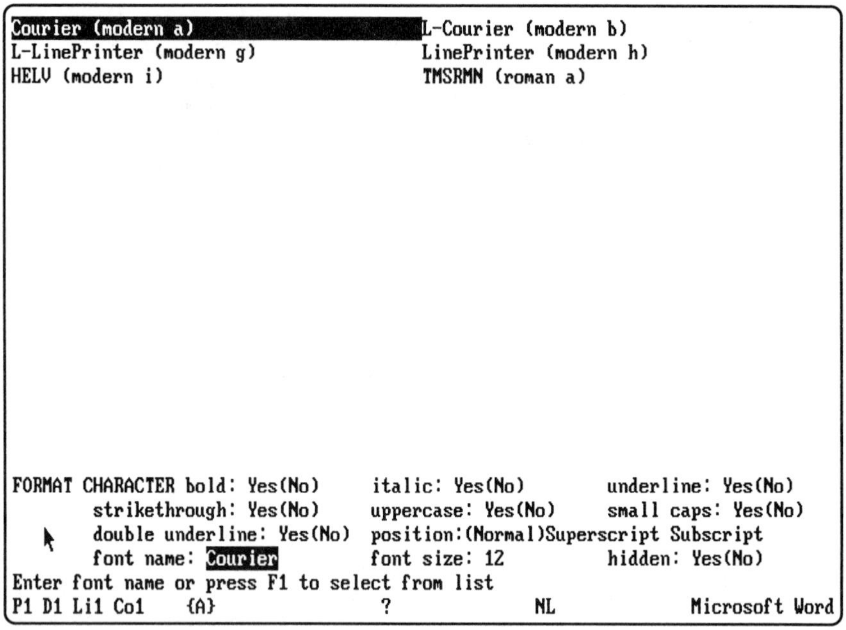

```
┌──────────────────────────────────────────────────────────────────┐
│Courier (modern a)                   L-Courier (modern b)           │
│L-LinePrinter (modern g)             LinePrinter (modern h)         │
│HELV (modern i)                      TMSRMN (roman a)               │
│                                                                    │
│                                                                    │
│                                                                    │
│                                                                    │
│                                                                    │
│                                                                    │
│                                                                    │
│                                                                    │
│                                                                    │
│                                                                    │
│                                                                    │
│ FORMAT CHARACTER bold: Yes(No)      italic: Yes(No)       underline: Yes(No) │
│           strikethrough: Yes(No)    uppercase: Yes(No)    small caps: Yes(No) │
│  ▶    double underline: Yes(No)  position:(Normal)Superscript Subscript │
│          font name: Courier         font size: 12        hidden: Yes(No) │
│ Enter font name or press F1 to select from list                    │
│ P1 D1 Li1 Co1    {A}                ?              NL      Microsoft Word │
└──────────────────────────────────────────────────────────────────┘
```

When the list of available fonts appears on your screen, use the cursor keys, [Tab] key, or mouse to select the font you want to use.

Font size

After you choose the name of the font you want to use, you may choose the specific size of the font you want to use. To do this, use the cursor keys, [Tab] key, or mouse to select the font size command field. When you do, Word will display the message *Enter font size or press F1 to select from list.* When this message appears on your screen, enter the value of the font size you want to use or press **[F1]** to display a list of possible sizes. For example, if you press [F1] after selecting the LaserJet's Internal Courier font, the list shown in Figure 8-11 will appear. To choose the size of the font from this list, use the cursor keys, [Tab] key, or mouse to select the font's size.

Other font attributes

In addition to allowing you to select a font and font size, the Format Character command allows you to print a block of text using bold or italic versions of the currently selected font. The Format Character command can also be used to underline, double underline, or strike through a block of text.

To underline, double underline, or strike through a block of text, highlight the block, issue the Format Character command, then set the corresponding command field to Yes. Likewise, you may define a block as bold or italic by setting the appropriate command to Yes or by pressing **[Alt]B** or **[Alt]I,** respectively.

FIGURE 8-11

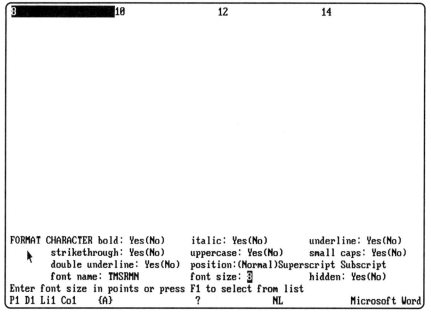

When a list of font sizes appears on your screen, use the cursor keys, [Tab] key, or mouse to select the font size you want to use.

Font Substitution

If you have used Word with a printer other than the LaserJet in the past, or if you use Word with different types of printers on a day-to-day basis, you probably will run into a situation where a document contains a block of text that is formatted for a font that is not supported by the LaserJet. For example, if you have recently upgraded to a LaserJet from an Epson FX-80, it's likely that your documents were formatted with the Epson Pica, Elite, or NLQ fonts.

When you print a document that contains fonts that are not supported by the LaserJet, Word will attempt to substitute a similar font. For example, if you send a document to the LaserJet that has been formatted with the Epson FX-80 Pica font, Word will automatically replace the Pica font with the LaserJet Courier font.

The key to Word's ability to substitute a similar font automatically for one that is not available is the generic name Word uses to identify each font. These names are based on the name of the family to which the font's typeface belongs.

When you use the Format Character command to assign a font to a specific block of text, Word allows you to choose the font on the basis of its commercial name. However, it identifies the font you choose internally with the generic name it has assigned to the font. Consequently, when you print a document that contains a block of text that has been formatted for a particular font, Word looks in the PRD file you are using for the font that matches the generic font name. If an exact match is not available, Word will use the closest possible match.

The format of the generic name Word uses to identify a font is quite simple. It consists of the name of the family to which the font's typeface belongs and a unique letter. The name of each typeface family name and the range of letters that Word may assign to a font are shown in Table 8-5.

TABLE 8-5

Family	Name
Modern	a through p
Roman	a through p
Script	a through h
Foreign	a through h
Decor	a through h
Symbol	a through h

Word will assign an internal name to each font that you use.

As we mentioned earlier, if you send a document to the LaserJet that contains text formatted with the Epson FX-80 Pica font, Word will substitute the LaserJet's Internal Courier font. It does this because both fonts are members of the Modern typeface family and are identified by the name Modern a.

Downloading Soft Fonts

As we discussed in Chapter 4, before you can use a LaserJet soft font to print text, you must download the font to the LaserJet. Fortunately, Word has the ability to download fonts automatically to the LaserJet when you send a document to the printer. We'll discuss this subject in greater detail in the next section of this chapter.

PRINTING

Once you have installed Word, you can print documents. In this section, we'll show you how to set up Word for your LaserJet, then we'll look at the commands you must issue to print a document. Finally, we'll take a look at several special types of printing.

Setting Up Word for the LaserJet

While the LaserJet is widely accepted as an industry standard, it has a few idiosyncrasies that must be addressed before you can use it to print a Word document. Specifically, you must make a few changes to Word's printer settings.

Margin settings

As we pointed out in Chapter 1, the LaserJet cannot print text on the entire area of a page. You must compensate for this limitation by adjusting Word's margins so that Word will not attempt to print text on the areas of the page on which the LaserJet cannot print.

To adjust the margins, you would issue the Format Division Margins command, then set the width to **8** inches, the length to **11** inches, and the running head position to a value equal to or greater than **0.25** inch.

Since all members of the LaserJet printer family can accept paper from more than one source, before you print a document with Word, you must select the proper Word paper bin setting. To choose a paper source for your LaserJet's, issue a Print Options command and select the Manual, Continuous, Bin1, Bin2, or Bin3 feed setting.

Paper bin setting

If you want to print text using paper fed from the single paper tray common to the LaserJet, LaserJet Plus, and LaserJet Series II, select the Continuous option. However, if you want to use the LaserJet 500 Plus' or LaserJet IID's second paper tray, you should select Bin2. You should select Bin3 if you want to use the LaserJet 2000's third paper tray. Finally, to feed paper manually into any LaserJet, select the Manual paper feed setting.

Microsoft Word has the ability to print documents in the background while you continue to edit documents in the foreground. To turn this feature on and off, issue the Print Options command, and select the queued setting. If you set the queued setting to No, Word will send documents directly to the printer—tying up your machine in the process. If you set the queued setting to Yes, you can continue to use Word as documents are printed in the background.

Queuing output

If you send a document to the LaserJet while the queued setting is No, you can stop printing at any time by pressing [Ctrl][Break]. If you send documents to the LaserJet while the queued option is set to Yes, you can stop printing by issuing the Print Queue Stop command. If you want to stop a document from printing, but want to continue printing it at a later time, issue the Print Queue Pause command. To allow Word to continue printing a document that has been paused, you must issue the Print Queue Continue command.

Once you've set up Word for the LaserJet and have formatted the document you want to print, you can send it to the LaserJet by issuing the Print Printer command. If you have used the method we described in the previous section to turn on the print queue, Word will send your documents to the print queue when you issue a Print Printer command. On the other hand, if the print queue is turned off when you issue a Print Printer command, Word will send the document directly to the printer.

Sending a Document to the LaserJet

When you print a document that contains text that will be printed with a soft font, Word will display the message *Enter Y to download fonts, N to skip, or Esc to cancel* if a DAT file that contains the commands and information Word needs to download the font is available. We'll discuss DAT files in greater detail later in this chapter. If this message appears on your screen, you should press Y if you want Word to download soft fonts to the LaserJet, N if you do not, or [Esc] if you want to abort the print operation and return to Word's Edit mode.

Sending a Document to a Disk File

From time to time, you may find it necessary to print a document to a disk file. Fortunately, Word's Print File command makes it possible to do so. When you issue the Print File command, Word will display the prompt *Enter filename*. At that time, you should enter the name of the file to which you want Word to write printer output, and press ↵.

When you use the Print File command to send a document to disk, Word will send the document to the disk file complete with any PCL commands that would normally be sent to the printer to produce the desired output. For example, if you instruct Word to print text using a specific font, the PCL command that instructs the LaserJet to use that font will be included in the document when you print it to disk.

Files printed to disk are commonly referred to as printer-ready files because they contain all the PCL commands required to produce the desired result when they are sent to the LaserJet. If you want to print a printer-ready file, you can copy it to the port to which the LaserJet is connected. For example, if you want to print the printer-ready file PRNTRDY.PRN from DOS, you should issue the command **COPY PRNTRDY.PRN LPT1: /B.**

Sending Text to the LaserJet from the Keyboard

Every now and then, you may run into an occasion where you need to print something in a hurry but do not want to create a new document. For example, addressing an envelope is something that you usually want to do right away. On such occasions, you can use Word's Print Direct command to send text directly to the LaserJet from the keyboard.

When you issue the Print Direct command, Word will display the prompt *Enter text*. At this time, any character that you type will be sent immediately to the LaserJet. Once you have entered the text that you want to print, press the **[Esc]** key to quit.

Since the [Esc] key instructs Word to exit the Print Direct mode, you must use the [Alt] key in conjunction with the numeric keypad on your keyboard to send the escape character to the LaserJet. This is extremely important if you want to send PCL commands to the LaserJet with the Print Direct command. Therefore, if you want to send the escape character to the LaserJet while in Print Direct mode, you must press the **[Alt]** key, type **27** on the numeric keypad, then release the [Alt] key.

Embedding PCL Commands in a Document

From time to time, you may find it necessary to send a PCL command directly to the LaserJet. For example, if you want to use any of the LaserJet's line drawing or shading capabilities, you must do so by sending PCL commands to the printer, because Word does not directly support these features.

If you want to send PCL commands directly to the LaserJet, you must embed them in the text of your documents. In other words, you must enter the PCL command in your document as if it were part of the document. The only special consideration that must be addressed when embedding PCL commands in a document is the escape character that precedes each PCL command. Since Word uses the [Esc] key to activate its menu system, you must use the [Alt] key in conjunction with the numeric keypad to place the escape character in your document. To enter the escape character, press the [**Alt**] key, type **27** on the numeric keypad, then release the [Alt] key.

While Word does not have the ability to give you an on-screen WYSIWYG representation of graphics in a document, it does have the ability to embed printer-ready graphics in a document. Printer-ready graphics are those that have been generated by printing a file to disk. For example, if you print a Microsoft Excel chart to disk, or send a Microsoft Chart chart to disk with the Print File command, you can embed those charts in a Word document.

Embedding Graphics in a Document

To embed a printer-ready graphics file in your document, you must place an entry in your document at the point where you want it to appear. The format of this entry is:

.P *.filename,height,<endmark>*

The first three characters of this entry tell Word that the parameters that follow should be used to send a printer-ready file to the LaserJet. These three characters (.P.) must appear at the beginning of a paragraph.

The first parameter that must appear after the .P. command is the file name of the printer-ready graphics file you want to embed. If the file you want to embed is not in your Word data directory, you should include the path name in this entry.

After you have supplied Word with the name of the printer-ready graphics file you want to embed, you must use the height parameter to specify the amount of space the graphic will occupy on the page. The height of a graphic is measured in the unit that is selected as the default with the Options command's measurement field. For example, if a graphic is 5 inches tall, you should use the value 5 as the height parameter.

Finally, you must conclude the entry with an endmark. This mark can be a semicolon, a paragraph mark, or a division sign. Once you've done this, highlight the entry, issue the Format Character command, and set the hidden option to **Y**es. Word then will recognize the entry as an embedded graphics entry and will send the data stored in the file to the LaserJet when you issue the Print Printer command.

As an example, suppose you have written a Microsoft Chart chart to a disk file named CHART.PRN and want to include it in a Word document. For the sake of this example, we'll assume that the chart is stored in the file C:\CHART\CHART and is 5 inches tall. To embed this chart in a Word document, you must move the cursor to the point in the document at which you want it to be printed and place the entry .P.C:\CHART.PRN,5; at that point. Consequently, whenever you issue the Print Printer command to send the document to the LaserJet, Word will automatically load CHART.PRN from disk and send it to the LaserJet.

Landscape Printing

Word PRD files cannot contain support for Landscape and Portrait fonts at the same time. Therefore, whenever you want to print text in Landscape mode, you must use a PRD file that supports only Landscape fonts, or you must manually select a Landscape font by embedding PCL commands in your document.

Using a PRD file that contains support for Landscape fonts

If you want to use a PRD file that contains support for a Landscape font, use one of the procedures we described earlier to install the file, then enter its name in the Print Options command's printer field. Once you have done this, you can use the Format Character command to choose the Landscape font you want to use. Subsequently, any text formatted with a Landscape font will be printed in Landscape mode when you issue the Print Printer command.

Embedding PCL commands to select and use Landscape fonts

If you want to print text in Landscape mode while using a PRD file that supports Portrait fonts, you must embed a PCL command in your document to select the Landscape mode. This method allows you to mix Portrait and Landscape text in a single document.

To print a block of text in Landscape mode while using a PRD file that supports Portrait fonts, you must begin by using the Format Character command to select the Portrait version of the font you want to use. For example, if you want to address an envelope using the Landscape version of the Courier font, you must use the Format Character command to assign the Portrait version of the Courier font to the block of text you want to print.

Once you have used the Format Character command to assign the appropriate Portrait font to the block of text you plan to print, you must place the PCL command $E_{s_c}\&\ell 1O$ on the line that immediately precedes the block. This command instructs the LaserJet to print any text that follows in Landscape mode. Likewise, you must place the PCL command $E_{s_c}\&\ell \emptyset O$ on the line that immediately follows the block. This command instructs the LaserJet to return to the Portrait mode.

Whenever you use this method to print a block of text in Landscape mode, you will find that the LaserJet will eject a blank page each time it switches between Portrait and Landscape modes. This occurs because the LaserJet cannot print Portrait and Landscape text on the same page.

Printing Envelopes

With the exception of the LaserJet 2000, all members of the LaserJet family let you print text on envelopes. Unfortunately, Word doesn't directly support this capability, but you can take advantage of it by using the proper margin settings and Landscape font. Next, we'll show you how to address envelopes with Word.

Choosing a Landscape font

To address an envelope with Word, you must use one of the procedures we described in the previous section of this chapter to select a Landscape font. As an example, let's assume you want to address envelopes without using a PRD file that directly supports Landscape fonts. To do this, you must embed PCL commands in your document to toggle the LaserJet between Portrait and Landscape modes. However, you must begin by using the Format Character command to select the Portrait version of the font you want to use to address the envelope. For example, if you want to print an envelope using the Landscape version of the Courier font, you first must select the Portrait version of the Courier font.

Once you have used the Format Character command to assign the appropriate Portrait font to the block of text you plan to print, you must place the PCL command $E_{s_c}\&\ell 1O$ on the line that immediately precedes the block. This command instructs the LaserJet to print any text that follows in Landscape mode. Likewise, you must place the PCL command $E_{s_c}\&\ell \emptyset O$ on the line that immediately follows the block. This command instructs the LaserJet to return to Portrait mode. As an example, the first three lines of the document shown in Figure 8-12 are encased by the PCL commands necessary to print them in Landscape mode.

FIGURE 8-12

```
[=[········1·········2····]····3·········4·········5·········6·········7····]
 ▓&110←&181A¶
 LaserJet·User¶
 100·Main·Street¶
 Anytown,·USA·55555¶
 ::::::::::::::::::::::::::::::::::::::::::::::::::::::::::::::::::::::::::::::
 ←&180¶
 LaserJet·User¶
 100·Main·Street¶
 Anytown,·USA·55555¶
 ¶
 July·4,·1988¶
 ¶
 Dear·LaserJet·User,¶
 ¶
 →    As·we·are·sure·you·are·aware,·Hewlett·Packard's·
 LaserJet·family·of·printers·is·extremely·versatile.··For·
 example,··in·this·document·we·are·taking·advantage·of·the·
 LaserJet's·ability·to·address·envelopes.¶
 ¶
                                                    =LETTER.DOC=
COMMAND: Copy Delete Format Gallery Help Insert Jump Library
  ▶       Options Print Quit Replace Search Transfer Undo Window
Edit document or press Esc to use menu
P1 D1 Li1 Co1    {e}            ?            NL        Microsoft Word
```

The first three lines of the document that appears on this Word screen are surrounded by PCL commands that select and deselect Landscape printing.

Setting margins

Regardless of the method you use to select the font you will use to address an envelope, you must use the Format Division Margins command to define the position at which the address will appear on the envelope. As you might expect, since the LaserJet can print text on four different types of envelopes, the margin settings you must use will vary. Table 8-6 lists the Top and Left margin settings you might use to address each of the envelopes that can be used with the LaserJet.

TABLE 8-6

	Series II and IID		LaserJet, Plus, and 500 Plus	
	Left	*Top*	*Left*	*Top*
Commercial	5.5in	4.5in	5.5in	6in
Monarch	4.0in	4.75in	4.0in	6.25in
DL	14cm	11cm	14cm	18cm
C5	14.5cm	14cm	15.5cm	21cm

These margin settings may be used to define the position at which Word will print an address on an envelope.

We found that the margin settings shown in Table 8-6 allow you to print an address at the appropriate position on each of the envelopes that can be used with the LaserJet. However, it is possible that you may want addresses to appear in a slightly different location from those listed above. Therefore, if the margin settings that appear in Table 8-6 do not satisfy your particular situation or taste, simply take a few minutes to increase or decrease the settings until you encounter a set that pleases you.

To set the margins for a particular block of text, highlight the block before issuing the Format Division Margins command. As a result, Word will insert a page break on the line that immediately follows the block. This page break will separate the margin settings for the envelope from those used to format the rest of your document.

Feeding envelopes

Once you are ready to address an envelope, feed it into your LaserJet. Figure 8-13 illustrates the proper methods for feeding an envelope into the LaserJet Series II and LaserJet IID, and into the original LaserJet, LaserJet Plus, and LaserJet 500 Plus. If you have a LaserJet Series II or LaserJet IID, you can feed envelopes into the manual feed slot by pulling the manual feed guides toward the center of the paper tray until there is enough room between them for the envelope you want to use. The LaserJet, LaserJet Plus, and LaserJet 500 Plus also require you to feed envelopes via the manual feed slot. Unfortunately, the manual feed slots on these printers do not have adjustable guides. Therefore, you must feed envelopes by placing them against the guide on the far right of the manual feed slot.

All members of the LaserJet family will automatically recognize the fact that an envelope is being fed through the manual feed slot. However, you may need to tell the LaserJet that it should request an envelope. For example, if you use the techniques we have described to address an envelope within a document that contains text that will be printed on normal paper, you should place a PCL command in the document that will instruct the LaserJet to request an envelope at the appropriate time.

FIGURE 8-13

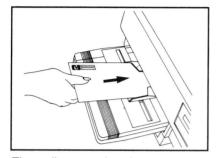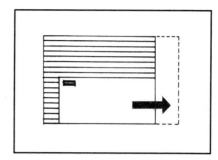

These diagrams show how envelopes may be fed into your LaserJet's manual feed slot.

The PCL command that instructs the LaserJet to request an envelope must be placed immediately below the line that contains the PCL command that switches the LaserJet into Landscape mode. The PCL commands that must be used to request each of the four envelopes that can be used by the LaserJet are listed in Table 8-7.

TABLE 8-7

Envelope Type	PCL Command
Commercial 10	$^E{}_{S_c}$&ℓ81A
Monarch	$^E{}_{S_c}$&ℓ8ØA
DL	$^E{}_{S_c}$&ℓ9ØA
C5	$^E{}_{S_c}$&ℓ91A

These PCL commands allow the LaserJet to prompt you to insert an envelope into the manual feed slot.

If you include one of these commands in your documents, the LaserJet, LaserJet Plus, and LaserJet 500 Plus will display the message *PE* on the control panel, while the LaserJet Series II and LaserJet IID will display the message *PE*, along with the name of the envelope you should feed manually into the LaserJet. When you see one of these messages on your LaserJet's control panel, feed the appropriate envelope, then press the LaserJet's CONTINUE key.

Printing on Legal-size Paper

If you plan to take advantage of the LaserJet's ability to use legal-size paper, you must do two things. First, you must change Word's page length setting to 13.5 inches. Second, you must place a PCL command on the first line of your document to inform the LaserJet that it should request legal-size paper.

To set the page length to 13.5 inches, issue a Format Division Margins command, select the page length field, type **13.5**, then press ↵ or the right mouse button to save the change. Once you have done this, you must place one of the PCL commands shown in Table 8-8 on the first line of your document.

TABLE 8-8

Printer	PCL Command	
	Manual Feed	*Legal Tray*
LaserJet, LaserJet Plus, and 500 Plus	$^{E}s_{c}\ell$84p2H	$^{E}s_{c}\ell$84pH
LaserJet Series II and LaserJet IID	$^{E}s_{c}\ell$3a2H	$^{E}s_{c}\ell$3A

If you are using legal-size paper with Word, you must place one of these PCL commands on the first line of your document.

When you send a document that contains one of the PCL commands listed in Table 8-8 to a LaserJet, LaserJet Plus, or LaserJet 500 Plus, the message *PF* will appear on the control panel, while the message *PF LL* will appear on the LaserJet Series II or LaserJet IID. When you see one of these messages on your LaserJet's control panel, insert the legal paper tray, or feed a sheet of legal-size paper into the manual feed slot, then press the LaserJet's CONTINUE key.

CUSTOMIZING PRD FILES

Earlier in this chapter, we mentioned that you can build PRD files that support the specific set of fonts you plan to use with Word. In this section, we'll begin by showing you how to use a Word utility called MERGEPRD to build custom PRD files using the font support provided within existing PRD files. Once we've done this, we'll show you how to use a Word utility called MAKEPRD to convert PRD files to and from a user-modifiable text format.

After we've shown you how to use MERGEPRD and MAKEPRD, we'll show you how to make changes and/or additions to a PRD file while it's in text format. Finally, we'll end this section by showing you how to create files that allow Word to download soft fonts automatically.

Using MERGEPRD

As we pointed out at the beginning of this chapter, Word is shipped with a number of PRD files, each of which supports a specific set of LaserJet fonts. However, as we stated, it's unlikely that any one of these files supports all of the fonts that you plan to use with Word. Fortunately, MERGEPRD allows you to use the PRD files shipped with Word as the RAM material for building your own PRD files. In other words, by extracting font support from the PRD files provided with Word, MERGEPRD allows you to build a PRD file that supports all the fonts you plan to use.

To run MERGEPRD, copy the file MERGEPRD.EXE from the Word Utilities disk into the directory in which your Word PRD files are stored. When this has been done, type **MERGEPRD** at the DOS prompt, press ↵, and MERGEPRD will display the menu shown in Figure 8-14.

FIGURE 8-14

```
MERGEPRD 1.10 - Microsoft Word Printer Description (.PRD) Merging Utility
Copyright (c) Intuition Systems Corporation, 1987.  All Rights Reserved.




        MERGEPRD - Microsoft Word .PRD Merging Utility

        P) Enter .PRD list
        C) List current .PRD list with available fonts
        E) Enter/edit desired font/size entries
        F) Display current font/size entries
        O) Create output .PRD file
        Q) Quit program

        Enter selection:
```

*When you run MERGEPRD from the DOS prompt, it will display this menu on
your screen.*

The first command on MERGEPRD's main menu allows you to enter the name of the PRD file(s) you want to modify. To select this command, type **P**. MERGEPRD will respond with the prompt *Enter Input .PRD Filename*. At this prompt, you should enter the name of a PRD file that contains support for the fonts you plan to use. Then, you should press ↵.

After you have entered the name of a PRD file that contains support for the fonts you want to use, MERGEPRD will load them into memory and will once again display the prompt *Enter Input .PRD Filename*. At this time, you may enter the name of another printer file, or you may press ↵ to return to the main menu.

*Entering a list
of PRD files*

The second command on MERGEPRD's menu lets you list the names of the PRD files you've loaded into memory. To select this command, type **C**. When you do this, MERGEPRD will display a list similar to the one shown in Figure 8-15.

*Listing currently
loaded PRDs
and fonts*

FIGURE 8-15

```
Font  PRD File  Generic    Font Name     Sizes
  #
  0   HPLASMS   Modern a   Courier       12
  1   HPLASMS   Modern h   LinePrinter   8.5
  2   HPLASMS   Modern i   HELV          8 10 12 14
  3   HPLASMS   Roman a    TMSRMN        8 10 12 14
Press a key to continue...
```

*MERGEPRD's main menu will display a list of all fonts supported by currently
loaded PRDs when you press C.*

As you can see in Figure 8-15, MERGEPRD supplies you with the name of each PRD file that is loaded, as well as the number assigned to each font supported by that file, the font's name, its internal Word name, and its available point sizes. You must use this information, particularly the font number, when adding support for particular fonts to the PRD file you will create with MERGEPRD.

Building a new PRD file

After you have loaded into memory the PRD files that contain support for the fonts you want to use, you can begin the process of creating a new PRD file. To do this, you must use the third command on the MERGEPRD's main menu. To execute this command, press **E**. The menu shown in Figure 8-16 will appear on your screen.

FIGURE 8-16

```
Enter/Edit Desired Font/Size Entries

A) Add new Font/Size Entry
D) Delete existing font/size entry
F) Display current font/size entries
L) Change linedraw font
R) Return to main menu

Enter selection:
```

When you issue an Enter/Edit Desired Font/Size Entries command, MERGEPRD will display this menu on your screen.

Adding fonts

The first command on the menu shown in Figure 8-16 allows you to add specific fonts to your new PRD file. To add a font to your PRD file, press **A**. When you do this, MERGEPRD will display the prompt *Add - Enter Font # (0-x):*. This prompt asks you to enter the number that MERGEPRD has assigned to each font you have loaded using the main menu's Enter .PRD list command. (As you may recall, you can display a list of currently loaded fonts, along with the number assigned to each, by pressing **C** at the main menu.)

When MERGEPRD prompts you to enter the number of a font you want to add to your new PRD file, type the number at the prompt, and press ↵. When you do this, MERGEPRD will display the number assigned to the font, the name of the PRD from which the font was extracted, the internal Word name associated with the font, the font's actual name, and available point sizes. Then, MERGEPRD will present you with a prompt at which you may enter the point sizes you want to install. If you want to install all available point sizes, simply type the word **ALL** at this prompt, and press ↵. If you want to install specific point sizes, type each size at the prompt, separating each with a space, then press ↵. When you do this, MERGEPRD will once again prompt you to enter the number of a font that you want to add to your PRD file. When this prompt appears, you may continue until you have added as many as 64 fonts to your PRD file. When you have finished adding fonts to your PRD file, press ↵ to return to the menu shown in Figure 8-16.

If you use the first command on the menu shown in Figure 8-16 to add support for a font to your PRD file, but later decide that you do not want to support that font, you can delete it by choosing the second command on the menu. To execute this command, press **D**. When you do this, MERGEPRD will display the prompt *Delete - Enter Font # (0-x):*. At this prompt, you should enter the number of the font you want to remove from your PRD file, and press ↵. When you use this command to delete a font, MERGEPRD will display that font's number, name, etc., along with a message confirming that it has been deleted.

Deleting fonts

The third command on the menu shown in Figure 8-16 allows you to display a list of the fonts you have added to your new PRD file. When you issue this command by pressing **F**, MERGEPRD will display a list similar to the one shown in Figure 8-17.

Listing fonts

FIGURE 8-17

```
Font  PRD File   Generic    Font Name     Selected Sizes
 #
 0    HPLASMS    Modern a   Courier       12
 1    HPLASMS    Modern h   LinePrinter   8.5
 2    HPLASMS    Modern i   HELV          8 10 12 14
 3    HPLASMS    Roman a    TMSRMN        8 10 12 14
Press a key to continue...
```

When you issue a Display current font/size entries command, MERGEPRD will display a list of all fonts that you have added to your PRD file.

The fourth command on the menu shown in Figure 8-16 allows you to specify which font Word will use to draw lines and boxes around text. For example, if you plan to use a font that contains line draw characters, such as the PC Courier font on the "Y" cartridge, you might want to use one of the characters in that font to draw boxes or lines. To execute this command, press **L**. When you do this, MERGEPRD will display the prompt *Change LineDraw - Enter Font # (0-x) (N=None)*. As you might expect, you should type the number of the font you want to use as a Line Draw font at this prompt, and press ↵. Likewise, if you do not want to use a Line Draw font, type **N**, then press ↵.

Choosing a Line Draw font

After you have finished adding fonts to your new PRD file, you can return to the MERGEPRD main menu by choosing the Return to main menu command. To execute this command, press **R**. When you do this, MERGEPRD will display the main menu shown in Figure 8-14.

Returning to the main MERGEPRD menu

The fourth command on the main MERGEPRD menu allows you to display a list of all fonts you have added to your PRD file. This command is identical to the Display current font/size entries command on the Enter/Edit Desired Font/Size Entries menu. To execute this command, press **F**. When you do this, MERGEPRD will display a list similar to the one shown in Figure 8-17.

Listing current font/size entries

Writing a new PRD file to disk

Once you have added support to your new PRD file for all the fonts you plan to use, you can write the file to disk. To do this, press **O** at the MERGEPRD main menu. As a result, MERGEPRD will display the prompt *Enter Output .PRD Filename (with .PRD extension):*. At this prompt, type the name you want to assign to your new PRD file, and press ↵.

Using a new PRD file

Finally, after you have used MERGEPRD to create a new PRD file, you can use the file with Word immediately by entering its name in the printer field of Word's Print Options command.

Using MAKEPRD

It is likely that you may want to use a font with Word that is not supported by one of the PRD files that is shipped with Word. For instance, if you purchase a soft font from a third party such as BitStream, you will find that it is not supported by Microsoft's PRD files. In such an instance, you must add support for the font to your PRD file manually. MAKEPRD is a utility that allows you to do this.

MAKEPRD is essentially a PRD file compiler and disassembler. It is a compiler because it converts text files that contain commands that build PRD files into actual PRD files. It's a disassembler because it will convert a PRD file into the text that contains the commands necessary to create it.

In this section, we'll show you how to run MAKEPRD. However, we won't discuss the format or structure of PRD files or the text files MAKEPRD acts upon. We'll save this topic for the next section of this chapter.

To run MAKEPRD, copy the file MAKEPRD.EXE from the Word Utilities disk into the directory in which your Word PRD files are stored. When this has been done, type **MAKEPRD** at the DOS prompt, and press ↵. After a moment, MAKEPRD will display the prompt *Name of PRD file :*. At this point, you should enter the name of the PRD file that you want to build or disassemble.

For example, if you want to convert the binary PRD file HPLASMSL.PRN to text format, you should type **HPLASMSL.PRD** when MAKEPRD displays the prompt *Name of PRD file :*. Likewise, if you want to build the binary PRD file HPLASMSL.PRD from a text file, you should type **HPLASMSL.PRD** at the *Name of PRD file :* prompt.

After you have entered the name of the binary PRD file you are building or converting to text format, MAKEPRD will display the prompt *Name of Text file :*. At this prompt, you should enter the name of the text file that MAKEPRD will use to build the PRD file you have specified, or the name of the file into which MAKEPRD will write information as it converts a binary PRD file into text format.

For example, if you want to convert the binary PRD file HPLASMSL.PRD into a text file named HPLASMSL.TXT, you should enter **HPLASMSL.TXT** at the *Name of Text file :* prompt. Likewise, if you want MAKEPRD to use the text file HPLASMSL.TXT to create the binary PRD file HPLASMSL.PRD, you should type **HPLASMSL.TXT** at the prompt.

Once you have entered the name of the PRD and text files, MAKEPRD will ask if you want to convert a text file to a PRD file, or if you want to convert a PRD file to a text file. If you want to convert a text file to a PRD file, type **P**, and press ↵. If you want to convert a PRD file to a text file, type **T**, and press ↵.

After you have instructed MAKEPRD to create a text or PRD file, it will begin the process of generating that file. Consequently, if the file names you have provided are the same as the ones MAKEPRD finds in the current path, it will ask you if you want to overwrite them before doing so. When it has finished converting a text file to a PRD file or vice versa, MAKEPRD will display the message *Conversion Complete* and return you to the DOS prompt.

Throughout this chapter, we have stated that if you plan to use LaserJet fonts other than those supported by the PRD files shipped with Word or available from Microsoft Product Support, you must add support for the font to one of those PRD files. In this section, we'll show you how to do this.

Making Changes or Additions to PRD Files

The key to creating a PRD file or making changes to an existing PRD file is a utility program called MAKEPRD. As we showed you in the previous section, MAKEPRD is a program that can be used to convert a binary PRD file into a text file, and vice versa. The ability to convert a PRD file from its normal binary form to a text format that you can edit makes it possible to make changes or additions to the file.

While MAKEPRD makes it possible to make changes or additions to a PRD file, you must understand the structure of the text files that MAKEPRD uses to create a binary PRD file. In this section, we'll show you a typical PRD file after it has been converted into a text file, then we'll discuss the components of this file. The information we will present will provide you with a frame of reference you can use to modify PRD files after they have been converted to text format.

As the basis for our example, we've used MERGEPRD to create a PRD file that contains support for the LaserJet's Internal Courier font and have used MAKEPRD to convert this PRD file to text format. This text file is shown in Figure 8-18. It contains examples of each of the five sections that you will find in any PRD text file. In the following paragraphs, we'll discuss each of these sections and will specifically address the changes you must make to them to add support for a third-party soft font to the file.

FIGURE 8-18

```
MAKEPRD 1.50
dxaMin:300 dyaMin:30 PrinterType:5
Microspace:0 SpecialFlags:0 SerialInterface:40960
WidthTSwap:1 DownloadFlag:1 LineDraw:64

{F0
CTP:T0
cPSDs:1

FontSize:24
Wtps:30 30 30 30
beginmod:0 "^[(8U^[(s3t12vpsb10H"
endmod:0
beginItalicmod:0
endItalicmod:0
beginBoldmod:0
endBoldmod:0
beginItalBoldmod:0
endItalBoldmod:0
DLF:0
FontName:Courier
}F

{T0
cCSD:3 chFirst:128 chLast:175
  128: "^0264 "    129: "^0317 "    130: "^0305 "    131: "^0300 "
  132: "^0314 "    133: "^0310 "    134: "^0324 "    135: "^0265 "
  136: "^0301 "    137: "^0315 "    138: "^0311 "    139: "^0335 "
  140: "^0321 "    141: "^0331 "    142: "^0330 "    143: "^0320 "
  144: "^0334 "    145: "^0327 "    146: "^0323 "    147: "^0302 "
  148: "^0316 "    149: "^0312 "    150: "^0303 "    151: "^0313 "
  152: "^0357 "    153: "^0332 "    154: "^0333 "    155: "^0277 "
  156: "^0273 "    157: "^0274 "    158: "^0257 "    159: "^0276 "
  160: " "     161: "^0325 "    162: "^0306 "    163: "^0307 "
  164: "^0267 "    165: "^0266 "    166: "^0371 "    167: "^0372 "
  168: "^0271 "    169: " "     170: " "     171: "^0370 "
  172: "^0367 "    173: "^0270 "    174: "^0373 "    175: "^0375 "

chFirst:225 chLast:225
  225: "^0336 "

chFirst:20 chLast:20
  20: "^0364 "

}T

{P
byte:0 mod:0 "^[&l6D^[&k12H"
byte:4 mod:0 "^[&l1H"
byte:8 mod:4 magic:0 value:0 "^[&l"
byte:14 mod:0 "p0e0o0L^[&a-3R"
byte:18 mod:4 magic:0 value:0 "^[&l"
byte:24 mod:0 "C"
byte:28 mod:8 magic:0 value:126 "^[&a+"
byte:34 mod:0 "H"
byte:38 mod:0 "^[&l1H"
byte:42 mod:0
byte:46 mod:0 "^[&l4H"
byte:50 mod:0
byte:54 mod:0
```

```
byte:58 mod:0
byte:62 mod:0
byte:66 mod:0
byte:70 mod:0  "^[&l5H"
byte:74 mod:0
byte:78 mod:0
byte:82 mod:0
byte:128 mod:0  "^[(s3B"
byte:132 mod:0  "^[(s0B"
byte:136 mod:0  "^[(s1S"
byte:140 mod:0  "^[(s0S"
byte:144 mod:0  magic:0 value:0  "^[&dD"
byte:150 mod:0  "^[&d@"
byte:154 mod:6  magic:0 value:0
byte:160 mod:0
byte:164 mod:6  magic:0 value:0
byte:170 mod:0
byte:174 mod:0  magic:0 value:0  "^[&a-45V"
byte:180 mod:0  "^[&a+45V"
byte:184 mod:0  magic:0 value:0  "^[&a+45V"
byte:190 mod:0  "^[&a-45V"

}P
E
```

This text file supports the LaserJet's Internal Courier font.

Header

The first section of a PRD text file is called the Header. The Header contains nine settings that describe the capabilities of the printer you are using. The only setting within the Header that you may have to change is `DownloadFlag`. If the file does not contain support for a soft font, `DownloadFlag` should be set to zero. On the other hand, if the file you are modifying contains or will contain support for a soft font, `DownloadFlag` should be set to 1. When `DownloadFlag` is set to 1, Word will attempt to download soft fonts automatically when they are used in a document. We'll discuss this topic in greater detail later.

Font descriptions

The second section of a PRD text file is called the font description section. This section contains all the information and PCL commands Word needs for selecting and using a particular font. To add support for a particular font to a PRD file, you must add a description of that font to the file.

Font number

Each font description must begin with the entry {F followed by a number that determines the generic name Word will use to identify the font within a document. As we pointed out, Word identifies fonts with an internal generic name so that it can substitute similar fonts for those that might not be supported by a particular PRD file. The number that is assigned to a font determines the generic name Word will assign to the font. Table 8-9 lists the number that may be assigned to a font within a font description and the internal generic Word name to which each corresponds.

TABLE 8-9

PRD font value	Generic font name
0-15	Modern (a-p)
16-31	Roman (a-p)
32-39	Script (a-h)
40-47	Foreign (a-h)
48-55	Decor (a-h)
56-63	Symbol (a-h)

The internal value assigned to a font within a PRD file determines the generic name Word will use to identify the font within a document.

As you can see in Figure 8-18, the Courier font's definition begins with the entry {FØ. This entry specifies that Word will assign the generic name *Modern a* to the Courier font. To determine the number you should use within a PRD file to identify a particular font, you should use the information provided in Table 8-10 to match the physical characteristics of the font to the appropriate family name.

TABLE 8-10

Family	Characteristics
Modern	Serif or sans serif fonts whose design is based on lines whose thickness is uniform
Roman	Serif fonts whose design is based on lines whose thickness varies
Script	Fonts whose design is based on continuous curved lines
Foreign	Fonts based on a foreign (non-US) alphabet
Decor	Decorative fonts
Symbol	Symbol fonts

You can assign a number to a font within a PRD file by matching its physical characteristics with the appropriate font family listed in this table.

Once you determine the family to which a font belongs, you may choose a number from the range of numbers that correspond to that family. For example, the font used to produce this text belongs to the Roman family. Therefore, if you were adding support for this font to a PRD file, you could choose any number in the range of 16 to 31 to identify it. Finally, when you choose a number for a font, you must be certain to choose one that is not currently assigned to another font. Otherwise, MAKEPRD will generate an error when you attempt to convert the text file into a binary PRD file.

The second entry that must appear in a font description is the Character Translation Pointer (CTP) entry. The `CTP` entry specifies the number of the character translation table that must be used when text is printed using this particular font. As we will show you later in this section, character translation tables may be used to resolve conflicts between the symbol set supported by the PC's screen font, and the symbol set supported by the LaserJet font you are using.

The format of a typical `CTP` entry is simple. For example, in Figure 8-18, the `CTP` entry within the Courier font description appears as `CTP:TØ`. This entry specifies that Word must use Character Translation Table Ø when using the Courier font. Likewise, if the entry appeared as `CTP:T1`, Word would use Character Translation Table 1 when using the Courier font.

Character Translation Pointer

The third entry that must appear in a font description is the `cPSDs` setting. This setting defines the number of individual font sizes that will be described within a font description. For example, the `cPSDs` setting that appears in Figure 8-18 indicates that only one size of the Courier font will be described within the Courier font's description. On the other hand, if three sizes of the Courier font were to be described within the font description, the `cPSDs` entry would appear as `cPSDs:3`.

Specifying the number of font sizes

The next entries that appear in a font description are components of a Printer Sequence Description (`PSD`). The 11 entries that constitute a PSD define the PCL commands that Word must send to the LaserJet to select and use specific styles of a font.

Printer Sequence Descriptions

The first component of a PSD is the `FontSize` entry. This entry specifies in half points the height of characters in the font you are defining. For example, the `FontSize` entry shown in Figure 8-18 specifies that the Courier font is 24 half points tall. Since the height of LaserJet characters is usually measured in points, you can calculate their height in half points by doubling the number of points. For example, a 12-point character is 24 half points tall. The height of a font in points is always listed in the documentation included with LaserJet cartridge and soft fonts.

Specifying a font's size

The second component of a PSD is the `Wtps` entry. This entry defines the width of the characters within the normal, italic, bold, and bold italic versions of the font that PSD describes. If the width of characters within the font being described is fixed, the `Wtps` entry will define the width of each of those characters in units equal to $1/_{300}$ inch. For example, in Figure 8-18, the entry `Wtps:30 30 30 30` indicates that the widths of the normal, italic, bold, and bold italic forms of the Courier font are $^{30}/_{300}$ inch wide.

On the other hand, if the widths of characters within the described font varies, the `Wtps` entry may be used to specify the name of a width table that defines the width of each character. For example, if the width of the characters in the font you

Specifying the width of characters

are using is defined with Width Table Ø, you should place the entry `Wtps:WØ WØ WØ WØ` in your font description. We'll discuss width tables in greater detail in a few moments.

Defining PCL commands to select a font

The next eight entries that appear in a PSD are settings that define the PCL commands that must be sent to the LaserJet to select the normal, italic, bold, and bold italic versions of the font being defined. For example, the `beginmod` setting shown in Figure 8-18 defines the PCL command that must be sent to the LaserJet to select the Internal Portrait Courier font. In the documentation that is included with the font, you can find the PCL command that you must send to the LaserJet to select a particular font.

As you may have noticed in Figure 8-18, the `beginItalicmod`, `begin-Boldmod`, and `beginItalBoldmod` settings are set to 0. The 0 value indicates that specific versions of the Courier font cannot be selected. Whenever a particular version of a font is not available, you should assign the value 0 to the setting that defines the PCL command that must be sent to the LaserJet to select it.

You may have also noticed that the `endmod`, `endItalicmod`, `end-Boldmod`, and `endItalBoldmod` settings shown in Figure 8-18 are set to 0. These settings are used to define the PCL command that must be sent to the LaserJet to reselect the LaserJet's default Courier font after a block of text has been printed using a particular version of another font. In this case, the 0 value indicates that it is not necessary to reselect the Courier font because the Courier font is the only font supported.

On the other hand, if you create a PSD that lets you use other versions of a specific font, the PCL command that must be sent to the LaserJet to reselect the Courier font is identical to the one defined by the `beginmod` setting in Figure 8-18.

Download flag

The final entry that must appear in a PSD is the `DLF` entry. The value associated with the `DLF` entry specifies whether the font defined by the PSD is a soft font. For example, the value 0 is associated with the `DLF` entry that appears in the Courier font's PSD. This indicates that the Courier font is not a soft font. Word will use the value assigned to the `DLF` entry to determine if it should automatically download a soft font when it is used in a document. We'll discuss this topic in the next section of this chapter.

If you create a PSD that supports a soft font, the value you must assign to the `DLF` entry will vary according to the forms of the font that are available and/or must be downloaded. To determine the value you should assign to the `DLF` entry in a particular PSD, add the values shown in Table 8-11 to 0. For example, if the normal version of a font is a soft font, you must assign the value 1 to `DLF`, while you must assign the value 3 to `DLF` if both the normal and italic versions of the font are soft fonts.

TABLE 8-11

Form	Value
Normal	1
Italic	2
Bold	4
Bold Italic	8

You must add these values to 0 when each specific form of a font is a soft font.

Additional PSDs

Since only one size of the Courier font is defined within the font description that appears in Figure 8-18, only one PSD is necessary. However, if other sizes of the Courier font are available, the PSDs that define the PCL commands required to use them would appear immediately below the one shown. Consequently, if you create a font description in which more than one size of a font is defined, the PSDs that define the PCL commands that must be sent to the LaserJet to select those sizes should appear one after another in ascending order—smallest size first, largest size last. Finally, the maximum number of font sizes that can be defined within a single font description is 255.

Font name

While the first entry of a font description defines the generic name Word will use to identify a font, the FontName entry defines the actual name of the font. As you can see in Figure 8-18, the FontName entry should appear immediately below a font description's last PSD and immediately above the entry }F, which marks the end of the font description. For example, in Figure 8-18, the FontName entry is associated with Courier. Consequently, you can assign any name you want to the FontName entry as long as its length does not exceed 16 characters.

Width tables

Earlier, we mentioned that width tables are used to define the width of each individual character in a proportional font. In this section, we'll discuss the format of the entries that appear in a typical width table.

Obtaining character width information

Before you create a width table, you must determine the width of each character in a font measured in units equal to $1/_{300}$ inch. If character width information is not present in the documentation that was included with a particular cartridge font that you plan to use, you can usually obtain it from the font's manufacturer. Likewise, if character width information is not present in the documentation that was included with a soft font that you want to use, it can be obtained from the font's manufacturer. However, if you want, you can write a program to extract width information directly from the soft font data file, or use a utility such as HP's FontLoad to extract the information. We'll discuss the format of soft font data files in Chapter 26. For instructions on using FontLoad, refer to Chapter 4.

Defining character widths

Each width table must begin with the entry {W followed by a number that identifies the table. This number should be between 0 and 128. The second entry that must appear in a width table is the FontSize entry. This entry defines the average width of characters defined in the width table in units equal to half points. You can see both of these entries in the width table shown in Figure 8-19.

FIGURE 8-19

```
{W0
FontSize:16 chFirst:32 chLast:255
 32:9   33:10   34:11   35:25   36:18   37:28   38:23   39:5
 40:11  41:11   42:16   43:28   44:9    45:10   46:9    47:16
 48:18  49:18   50:18   51:18   52:18   53:18   54:18   55:18
 56:18  57:18   58:10   59:10   60:28   61:28   62:28   63:18
 64:33  65:20   66:22   67:24   68:23   69:21   70:19   71:25
 72:24  73:8    74:17   75:21   76:18   77:28   78:24   79:26
 80:21  81:26   82:22   83:21   84:19   85:23   86:20   87:30
 88:20  89:21   90:20   91:12   92:16   93:12   94:16   95:18
 96:16  97:18   98:20   99:17  100:20  101:18  102:10  103:20
104:19 105:8   106:8   107:17  108:8   109:30  110:19  111:19
112:20 113:20  114:11  115:16  116:10  117:19  118:16  119:24
120:17 121:17  122:16  123:18  124:18  125:18  126:16  127:33
128:0  129:0   130:0   131:0   132:0   133:0   134:0   135:0
136:0  137:0   138:0   139:0   140:0   141:0   142:0   143:0
144:0  145:0   146:0   147:0   148:0   149:0   150:0   151:0
152:0  153:0   154:0   155:0   156:0   157:0   158:0   159:0
160:9  161:10  162:18  163:18  164:20  165:20  166:18  167:16
168:16 169:18  170:13  171:15  172:28  173:9   174:18  175:18
176:11 177:28  178:10  179:10  180:16  181:18  182:17  183:3
184:16 185:10  186:13  187:15  188:27  189:27  190:27  191:18
192:20 193:20  194:20  195:20  196:10  197:20  198:32  199:24
200:21 201:21  202:21  203:21  204:8   205:8   206:8   207:8
208:23 209:24  210:26  211:26  212:26  213:26  214:26  215:28
216:26 217:23  218:23  219:23  220:23  221:21  222:21  223:18
224:18 225:18  226:18  227:18  228:18  229:18  230:29  231:17
232:18 233:18  234:18  235:18  236:8   237:8   238:8   239:8
240:19 241:19  242:19  243:19  244:19  245:19  246:19  247:28
248:19 249:19  250:19  251:19  252:19  253:17  254:20  255:17

}W
```

Width tables such as this one are used to define the width of each character in a font.

The first entry that must appear following the FontSize entry is the chFirst entry. This entry defines the ASCII value associated with the first character whose width will be defined within the width table. For example, the chFirst entry that appears in Figure 8-19 indicates that the width of the character associated with the ASCII value 32 will be the first to be defined.

The next entry that must appear in a width table is the chLast entry. This entry defines the ASCII value associated with the last character whose width will be defined within the width table. For example, the chLast entry that appears in Figure 8-19 indicates that the width of the character associated with the ASCII value 255 will be the last to be defined.

After you have used `chFirst` and `chLast` to define the range of characters for which you want to define widths, you may assign widths to each character in that range by entering its ASCII value, a colon, and the width of the character measured in units equal to $1/_{300}$ inch. For example, the entry `32:9`, which appears in Figure 8-19, indicates that the character associated with ASCII value 32 is $9/_{300}$ inch wide. As you can see in Figure 8-19, you should never place more than eight entries on a single line, and you should separate each entry with a space. Finally, the entry `}W` must appear at the end of each width table.

Translation tables

In Chapter 4, we pointed out that the symbols supported by a font, as well as the values used to identify those symbols, constitute a symbol set. We also pointed out that conflicts may arise between the symbol set supported by the font that the IBM PC, PS/2, and compatible systems use to display text on screen, and the symbol set supported by LaserJet fonts.

For example, within the IBM PC symbol set, the symbol that represents British pounds sterling (£) is identified by the decimal code 156, while it is identified within the Roman-8 symbol set by the decimal code 187. Consequently, whenever a document contains a pound sign, the PC will tell the LaserJet to print the symbol associated with the decimal value 156.

Fortunately, you can resolve symbol set conflicts by including a translation table in your PRD file. Translation tables associate the values that represent individual symbols within the PC symbol set with the values that represent the same symbols within a LaserJet font's symbol set. As an example, a translation table that resolves conflicts between the PC symbol set and the Roman-8 symbol set is shown in Figure 8-18.

PC and Roman-8 conflicts

Since conflicts between the PC and Roman-8 symbol sets are the ones you are most likely to encounter, and a translation table that resolves them is present in all of the PRD files that are shipped with Word or available from Microsoft Product Support, you probably will never have to create a translation table. If you are adding support for a font to a Microsoft PRD file, you can include the proper entry in the font's description to use the Roman-8 translation table. This table is always identified within Microsoft PRD files as `TØ`. Finally, if you are creating a PRD file from scratch, you may use MAKEPRD to convert one of Microsoft's PRD files to text format, and copy the PC to the Roman-8 translation table into your PRD file.

Translating characters

As you can see in Figure 8-18, each translation table must begin with the entry `{T` followed by a number between 0 and 32. This number identifies the table. For example, the translation table shown in Figure 8-18 begins with the entry `{TØ`.

CSDs

The next entry that must appear in a translation table is the `cCSD` entry. This entry defines the total number of Character Sequence Definitions that will appear in the table. Character Sequence Definitions (CSDs) are essentially groups of consecutive characters whose values you want to translate. For example, if you want to translate the values of all the characters between the ranges of 32-127 and 128-255, your translation table must contain separate CSDs for each range.

Each CSD must begin with a `chFirst` entry. This entry defines the ASCII value associated with the first character that will be translated. For example, the first `chFirst` entry that appears in Figure 8-18 indicates that ASCII character 128 will be the first to be translated.

The next entry that must appear in a CSD is the `chLast` entry. This entry defines the ASCII value associated with the last character that will be translated. For example, the first `chLast` entry that appears in Figure 8-18 indicates that ASCII character 175 will be the last to be translated.

Translation table entry formats

After you have used `chFirst` and `chLast` to define the range of characters that you want to translate, you may include entries in the table that match the PC symbol set with the symbol set supported by the font you are using. The format of these entries consists of the ASCII value of the PC symbol, a colon, and the value that must be sent to the LaserJet to produce the matching symbol.

The ASCII value that represents PC symbols must be expressed in decimal form. For example, the pound sign (£) must be represented by the decimal value 156. On the other hand, the value that represents the symbol within the LaserJet font's symbol set may be expressed in octal, or by the PC character whose ASCII value is identical to the ASCII value that must be sent to the LaserJet to produce that symbol.

For example, in the translation table shown in Figure 8-18 the entry `156:"^0273 "` tells Word that it should send the ASCII decimal value represented by the octal value 0273 when the character represented by the value 156 appears in a document.

If you are not familiar with the octal numbering system, you may express the value that represents a LaserJet font's symbol by entering the PC character whose ASCII value is identical. For example, to generate the translation table entry that must be present if you want Word to send the decimal value 187 to the LaserJet each time the pound symbol (£) appears in a document, type **156:**, press the **[Alt]** key, type **187** on the numeric keypad, then release the [Alt] key. This will cause the PC to display the PC symbol represented by the ASCII value 187.

Finally, as you can observe in Figure 8-18, you should never place more than four translation entries on a single line, and you should separate each entry with a space. Finally, the entry `}T` must appear at the end of each translation table.

PCSD

The final component of your LaserJet PRD text files is the Printer Control Sequence Description (PCSD). The PCSD is a series of entries that define the commands and data that Word must use to print documents successfully with the LaserJet. As a rule, you should never have to make any changes to the PCSD.

Therefore, if you are modifying an existing Microsoft PRD file, you may ignore the PCSD. Likewise, if you are creating a new PRD file from scratch, you may use MAKEPRD to convert one of Microsoft's PRD files to text format, and copy its PCSD definitions in your PRD file.

Now that we've taken an in-depth look at the internal structure of a PRD file, we'll take a few moments to consider the task of adding support for a third-party soft font to a PRD file. As the basis for this example, let's assume that you have used MERGEPRD to create a PRD file that contains support for the LaserJet's Internal Courier font, and have used MAKEPRD to produce the text file that appears in Figure 8-18. Let's also assume you want to add support for BitStream's 14-point Broadway font to this text file. This font is part of the BitStream Headline Typeface 1 package.

Adding support for a third-party soft font to a PRD file

To make additions to the text file that appears in Figure 8-18, you must begin by loading it into Word with the Transfer Load command. Once you have done this, you may edit the file as you normally would.

The first thing you must change in the text file shown in Figure 8-18 is the `DownloadFlag` setting. Since the Broadway font is a soft font, you must set the `DownloadFlag` setting to `1`. This will allow Word to download the Broadway font automatically whenever you use it in a document.

The first addition you must make to the text file shown in Figure 8-18 is a font description that describes the 14-point Broadway font. Therefore, the first thing you must consider at this point is the number that you should assign to the font description. Since the Broadway font is a member of the Decor family, the number you assign to its description must be between 48 and 55. Since the text file shown in Figure 8-18 does not contain a font description that is identified by a number in this range, you should choose 48 and begin the font description with the entry {F48.

After you have assigned a number to the 14-point Broadway font's description, you must use the `CTP` (Character Translation Pointer) entry to define the number of the translation table that will be used to resolve conflicts with the PC symbol set. Since the Broadway font is based on the Roman-8 symbol set, you can use Character Translation Table Ø, which is already present in the text file. Therefore, the `CTP` entry should appear as `CTP:TØ`.

The next step is to use the `cPSDs` entry to define the number of sizes that will be defined within the Broadway font's description. Since we are adding support for a single size, this entry should appear as `cPSDs:1`.

Once you have defined the number of sizes that will be defined within the font description, you must use the `FontSize` entry to define the size of the font in half points. Since the Broadway font is 14 points tall, the `FontSize` entry should appear as `FontSize:28`.

After you have defined the size of the font, you must define the name of the width table that must be used with the font. We will discuss the process of creating a width table in a few moments. However, at this time, all you need to do is define the number that will be assigned to the table with the `Wtps` entry. Since the text file shown in Figure 8-18 does not contain a width table, you should choose 0. Therefore, the `Wtps` entry should appear as `Wtps: WØ WØ WØ WØ`.

The next step is to define the PCL command that Word must send to the LaserJet to select the 14-point Broadway font. You can find this command in the documentation that accompanies the Headline Typeface 1 package. The only consideration you must address when entering this PCL command is to recall that the escape character is represented by the characters ^[. Therefore, the entry that you must place in the font description to define the PCL command that must be sent to the LaserJet to select the 14-point Broadway font is `beginmod: Ø "^[(8U^[s1P^[(s14V^[sØS^[s3B^[s21T"`.

Once you have defined the PCL command that must be sent to the LaserJet to select the Broadway font, you must define the command that must be sent to the LaserJet to select the default Courier font after text has been printed with the Broadway font. The entry should appear in the font description as `endmod:Ø "^[(8U^[(s3t12vpsb1ØH"`.

After you have defined the PCL commands that must be sent to the LaserJet to select and deselect the Broadway font, you must add entries that define the commands required to select the bold, italic, and bold italic versions of the font. Since bold, italic, and bold italic versions of the Broadway font are not available, these entries should appear as they do within the Courier font's description that appears in Figure 8-18.

As we mentioned earlier, the Broadway font is a soft font. Therefore, you must assign the appropriate value to the `DLF` entry within the font description. Using the information that appears in Table 8-11, you should be able to determine that the `DLF` entry should appear as `DLF:1` since the normal version of the Broadway font is the only one that must be downloaded.

Next, you must use the `FontName` entry to define its name. Obviously, this entry should appear as `FontName: Broadway`. Once you have placed this entry in the font description, you should end the description with the entry `}F`. As a result, the font description you've created should be identical to the one in Figure 8-20.

After you have added the font description shown in Figure 8-20 to your printer file, you must add a width table to the file. As we mentioned earlier in this chapter, the only way to obtain the information needed to create a width table is to use HP's FontLoad utility, write a BASIC program that extracts it from the soft font data file, or contact the font manufacturer directly. Once you have obtained width information using one of these methods, you should create the width table shown in Figure 8-21 and add it to your text file.

FIGURE 8-20

```
{F48
CTP:T0
cPSDs:1

FontSize:28
Wtps:W0 W0 W0 W0
beginmod:0 "ˆ[(8Uˆ[s1Pˆ[s14Vˆ[s0Sˆ[s3Bˆ[s21T"
endmod:0 "ˆ[(8Uˆ[(s3t12vpsb10H"
beginItalicmod:0
endItalicmod:0
beginBoldmod:0
endBoldmod:0
beginItalBoldmod:0
endItalBoldmod:0
DLF:1
FontName:Broadway
}F
```

This font description provides support for BitStream's 14-point Broadway font.

FIGURE 8-21

```
{W0
FontSize:28 chFirst:0 chLast:255
  0:0    1:0    2:0    3:0    4:0    5:0    6:0    7:0
  8:0    9:0   10:0   11:0   12:0   13:0   14:0   15:0
 16:0   17:0   18:0   19:0   20:0   21:0   22:0   23:0
 24:0   25:0   26:0   27:0   28:0   29:0   30:0   31:0
 32:20  33:20  34:19  35:45  36:40  37:48  38:48  39:20
 40:19  41:19  42:24  43:48  44:20  45:30  46:20  47:29
 48:40  49:40  50:40  51:40  52:40  53:40  54:40  55:40
 56:40  57:40  58:20  59:20  60:48  61:48  62:48  63:32
 64:58  65:46  66:45  67:45  68:47  69:42  70:40  71:47
 72:48  73:25  74:39  75:43  76:40  77:58  78:47  79:47
 80:47  81:47  82:47  83:36  84:39  85:47  86:46  87:56
 88:45  89:44  90:40  91:19  92:29  93:19  94:40  95:29
 96:20  97:43  98:45  99:36 100:45 101:38 102:23 103:34
104:46  105:22  106:24  107:44  108:22  109:57  110:46  111:38
112:45  113:45  114:31  115:30  116:27  117:46  118:40  119:55
120:43  121:38  122:39  123:29  124:29  125:29  126:48  127:58
128:0  129:0  130:0  131:0  132:0  133:0  134:0  135:0
136:0  137:0  138:0  139:0  140:0  141:0  142:0  143:0
144:0  145:0  146:0  147:0  148:0  149:0  150:0  151:0
152:0  153:0  154:0  155:0  156:0  157:0  158:0  159:0
160:0  161:0  162:0  163:0  164:0  165:0  166:0  167:0
168:0  169:0  170:0  171:0  172:0  173:0  174:0  175:0
176:0  177:0  178:0  179:0  180:0  181:0  182:0  183:0
184:0  185:0  186:0  187:0  188:0  189:0  190:0  191:0
192:0  193:0  194:0  195:0  196:30 197:0  198:0  199:0
200:0  201:0  202:0  203:0  204:0  205:0  206:0  207:0
208:0  209:0  210:0  211:0  212:0  213:0  214:0  215:0
216:0  217:0  218:0  219:0  220:0  221:0  222:0  223:0
224:0  225:0  226:0  227:0  228:0  229:0  230:0  231:0
232:0  233:0  234:0  235:0  236:0  237:0  238:0  239:0
240:0  241:0  242:0  243:0  244:0  245:0  246:0  247:0
248:0  249:0  250:0  251:0  252:0  253:0  254:0  255:0

}W
```

This width table defines the widths of characters in the 14-point Broadway font.

Finally, after you have made all of the additions we have discussed to your printer file, you may use Word's Transfer Save command to write it to disk. Once you have done this, exit Word by issuing the Quit command, then use MAKEPRD to convert the text file into a binary PRD file.

After you have converted the text file into a PRD file, you should create a DAT file that contains the information Word needs to download the file automatically. For more information on this topic, see the discussion that follows this section.

Finally, after you've created a PRD and DAT file, run Word once again, issue a Print Options command, and type the name of the file in the printer field. You will now be able to use the 14-point Broadway font in your documents.

Building Soft Font DAT Files

Earlier in this chapter, we mentioned that Word has the ability to download soft fonts automatically when you print a document that contains text that should be printed using a soft font. We also mentioned that files containing the PCL commands and other information Word must use to download files should accompany each of the Microsoft-produced PRD files that support soft fonts. These files are officially known as DAT files because they carry the extension .DAT.

As we mentioned in the previous section of this chapter, if you add support for a third-party soft font to an existing PRD file, or create a PRD file that contains support for a third-party soft font, you must create a DAT file if you plan to take advantage of Word's ability to download that soft font automatically.

At this time, a utility that allows you to create DAT files easily is not shipped with Word. Since we feel that the absence of such a utility is a deficiency, not to mention an inconvenience, we have written such a utility in Microsoft GW-BASIC. This program is listed in Figure 8-22.

If the PRD file you are using contains support for a third-party soft font, run the Microsoft GW-BASIC interpreter, type in the program listed in Figure 8-22, and save it to disk with the command SAVE "DATMAKER". Next, run the program by typing RUN, and follow the prompts to create a DAT file.

When you run DATMAKER, it will prompt you to enter the name of the DAT file you want to create. It will then ask you to enter the name of the PRD file that contains the soft fonts you want to download. Next, it will ask you to enter the number assigned to each soft font within its font description and the name of the data file in which the soft font is stored. Once you have entered this information for each of the soft fonts your PRD file supports, DATMAKER will automatically create a DAT file that contains all of the information Word needs to download those fonts automatically. Finally, if you are interested in the internal structure of a DAT file, it is documented in Table 8-12 on page 350.

FIGURE 8-22

```
100 REM DATMAKER.BAS (C)
110 REM COPYRIGHT 1988 The Cobb Group, Inc.
120 REM Version 1.01 - August 1988 - JRP
130 CLS
140 DIM DN$(40),TN$(40),OU$(100)
150 PRINT "Enter name of DAT file (Include pathspec): ";:INPUT "",DN$
160 INPUT "How many soft fonts will this DAT file support";NS
170 OPEN "O",#1,DN$
175 PU$ = CHR$(NS)+CHR$(2)+CHR$(5)+CHR$(27)+"*c0F"+CHR$(0)
180 PRINT #1,PU$;
190 FOR X=1 TO NS
195 OU$="":TN$="":FI$=""
200 PRINT "Enter Soft Font number";X;"'s Word ID number: ";:INPUT "",ID
210 PRINT "Enter Soft Font number";X;"'s filename (Include pathspec): ";:INPUT "
",TN$
220 PRINT "Enter font's size in half points: ";:INPUT FS
225 PRINT "Enter Soft Font number";X;"'s PCL ID # :";:INPUT FI$
240 CL=4+LEN(FI$)
250 FL=LEN(TN$)
260 PL=CL+5
265 OU$ = CHR$(ID)+CHR$(FS)+CHR$(CL)+CHR$(27)+"*c"+FI$+"D"+CHR$(FL)+TN$+CHR$(PL)
+CHR$(27)+"*c"+FI$+"D"+CHR$(27)+"*c4F"
270 REM PRINT#1,ID;FS;CL;CHR$(27);"*c";FI$;"D";FL;TN$;PL;CHR$(27);"*c";FI$;"D";C
HR$(27);"*c4F";
271 PRINT#1,OU$;
275 NEXT X
280 CLOSE #1
```

This Microsoft GW-BASIC program will create DAT files for third-party soft fonts.

In this chapter, we've shown you how to add support for a LaserJet font to Word and how to use fonts in a document. We've also shown you how to build custom Word PRD files and how to take advantage of Word's ability to download soft fonts automatically. As a result, you should now be able to overcome almost any obstacle that the Word and LaserJet combination might produce.

CONCLUSION

TABLE 8-12

Byte(s)	Value	Purpose
DAT file header—appears at top of file		
1	Variable	Defines number of soft fonts supported by the DAT file.
1	2	Specifies the number of commands that must be sent to the LaserJet to download a soft font.
1	5	Defines length of PCL command that follows—this command must be sent to the LaserJet before any soft fonts are downloaded.
5	Esc*cØF	Deletes all soft fonts from LaserJet user memory.
1	Ø	Defines length of command that must be sent to LaserJet after font is downloaded. This value is always equal to zero since no command must be sent to the LaserJet after a font is downloaded.
Individual font entries—one for each soft font		
1	Variable	Word ID number of soft font as indicated within PRD file. Add 64 to this value if italic, 128 if bold, or 192 if bold italic.
1	Variable	Value equal to half-point size of font.
1	Variable	Value equal to length of PCL command that follows—this command assigns a unique LaserJet soft font ID number to each font.
Variable	Esc*#D	The # within this PCL command is the LaserJet soft font ID assigned to a font.
1	Variable	Value equal to the length of the file name in which soft font data is stored.
Variable	Variable	Name of soft font data file. May include directory specification.
1	Variable	Length of PCL command that follows— this command must be sent to the LaserJet after each soft font is downloaded.
Variable	Esc*c#DEsc*c4F	This command makes the soft font that has been downloaded a temporary soft font.

The format of the data stored in a DAT file is shown in this table.

DISPLAYWRITE 4 **9**

IBM's DisplayWrite 4 is a powerful word processing program that you can use to create, edit, and print a wide variety of letters and reports. Even though Display-Write 4 was designed to work with the IBM family of printers, you can use this program to generate attractive reports on an HP LaserJet printer. In this chapter, we'll take the mystery out of printing DisplayWrite 4 documents on your HP LaserJet printer.

To install a copy of DisplayWrite 4 (DW4) on a system that works with your LaserJet printer, you need two things: a copy of DW4 and a copy of the HP LaserJet Printer Function Table (PFT). If you've recently purchased a copy of DW4, you'll find a copy of the HP LaserJet Printer Function Table on the Printer Function Tables Supplement Diskette. If you've purchased an older copy of DW4 that does not contain the Printer Function Tables Supplement Diskette, contact the person from whom you purchased DW4 and ask for a copy of the disk (free of charge). If your software vendor cannot obtain the disk for you, and you are a registered user of DW4, contact an IBM sales office.

INSTALLING DW4 AND THE LASERJET PFT

DW4 uses a special file called a Printer Function Table to communicate with your printer. The Printer Function Table is similar to a human interpreter in that it translates the formatted documents you create with DW4 into command sequences your printer can understand. In order to perform this task, of course, the Printer Function Table must contain all of the printer commands necessary to activate your printer's various print attributes, including typestyles, pitches, line spacing, under-lining, and so forth.

The Printer Function Table

What's supported?

IBM's HPLASER.PFT file supports most of the printing features you'll want to use in your printed documents. Let's consider each set of features in detail.

Font cartridges

The IBM HP LaserJet Printer Function Table includes support for the following HP font cartridges:

A	-	Courier 1 (Part No. 92286A)
B	-	Tms Proportional 1 (Part No. 92286B)
C	-	International 1 (Part No. 92286C)
D	-	Prestige Elite (Part No. 92286D)
E	-	Letter Gothic (Part No. 92286E)
F	-	Tms Proportional 2 (Part No. 92286F)
G	-	Legal Elite (Part No. 92286G)
H	-	Legal Courier (Part No. 92286H)
J	-	Math Elite (Part No. 92286J)
K	-	Math Tms (Part No. 92286K)
L	-	Courier P&L (Part No. 92286L)
M	-	Prestige Elite P&L (Part No. 92286M)
N	-	Letter Gothic P&L (Part No. 92286N)
P	-	Tms Rmn P&L (Part No. 92286P)
Q	-	Memo 1 (Part No. 92286Q)
R	-	Presentations 1 (Part No. 92286R)
Y	-	PC Courier 1 (Part No. 92286Y)

In addition to using the fonts listed above, the LaserJet's PFT will allow you to boldface, underline, superscript, and subscript text. You can also select either automatic or manual sheet-feed modes. We'll show you how to do these things later in this chapter.

Line spacing and pitch sizes

IBM's HP LaserJet Printer Function Table provides support for the following vertical line spacing and pitch sizes:

- 5.3 lines per inch
- 6 lines per inch
- 24 lines per inch
- $1/_2$-line spacing
- $1^1/_2$-line spacing
- Proportional Spacing Mode (PSM)

- 5 pitch
- 8.55 pitch
- 10 pitch
- 12 pitch
- 15 pitch
- 17.1 pitch

Although the LaserJet's PFT supports the Proportional Spacing Mode, we have found it very difficult to create an attractive right margin when we use proportionally spaced text in our DW4 documents. When you print a document with the LaserJet's Tms Rmn font, for example, the right margin will be gappy and uneven, as shown in Figure 9-1. To fix the problem, you'll need to move several words in the document up or down a line. After making the changes and reprinting the document, you may need to reorganize it further to obtain a more even right margin. Since you'll have no idea how the document will look on printed paper while you are working with it on the screen, you may need to modify and reprint your document several times before you obtain a satisfactory report.

Notes on proportionally spaced fonts

FIGURE 9-1

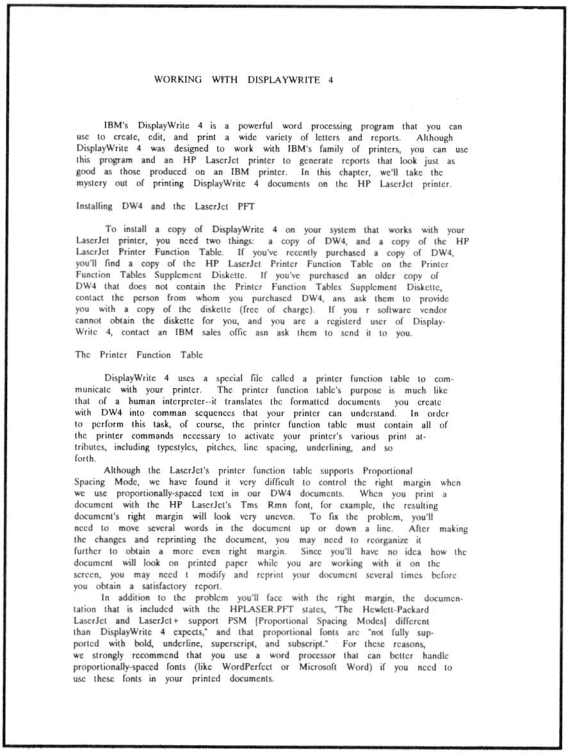

WORKING WITH DISPLAYWRITE 4

IBM's DisplayWrite 4 is a powerful word processing program that you can use to create, edit, and print a wide variety of letters and reports. Although DisplayWrite 4 was designed to work with IBM's family of printers, you can use this program and an HP LaserJet printer to generate reports that look just as good as those produced on an IBM printer. In this chapter, we'll take the mystery out of printing DisplayWrite 4 documents on the HP LaserJet printer.

Installing DW4 and the LaserJet PFT

To install a copy of DisplayWrite 4 on your system that works with your LaserJet printer, you need two things: a copy of DW4, and a copy of the HP LaserJet Printer Function Table. If you've recently purchased a copy of DW4, you'll find a copy of the HP LaserJet Printer Function Table on the Printer Function Tables Supplement Diskette. If you've purchased an older copy of DW4 that does not contain the Printer Function Tables Supplement Diskette, contact the person from whom you purchased DW4, ans ask them to provide you with a copy of the diskette (free of charge). If you r software vendor cannot obtain the diskette for you, and you are a registered user of Display-Write 4, contact an IBM sales offic asn ask them to send it to you.

The Printer Function Table

DisplayWrite 4 uses a special file called a printer function table to communicate with your printer. The printer function table's purpose is much like that of a human interpreter--it translates the formatted documents you create with DW4 into comman sequences that your printer can understand. In order to perform this task, of course, the printer function table must contain all of the printer commands necessary to activate your printer's various print attributes, including typestyles, pitches, line spacing, underlining, and so forth.

Although the LaserJet's printer function table supports Proportional Spacing Mode, we have found it very difficult to control the right margin when we use proportionally-spaced text in our DW4 documents. When you print a document with the HP LaserJet's Tms Rmn font, for example, the resulting document's right margin will look very uneven. To fix the problem, you'll need to move several words in the document up or down a line. After making the changes and reprinting the document, you may need to reorganize it further to obtain a more even right margin. Since you'll have no idea how the document will look on printed paper while you are working with it on the screen, you may need t modify and reprint your document several times before you obtain a satisfactory report.

In addition to the problem you'll face with the right margin, the documentation that is included with the HPLASER.PFT states, "The Hewlett-Packard LaserJet and LaserJet+ support PSM [Proportional Spacing Modes] different than DisplayWrite 4 expects," and that proportional fonts are "not fully supported with bold, underline, superscript, and subscript." For these reasons, we strongly recommend that you use a word processor that can better handle proportionally-spaced fonts (like WordPerfect or Microsoft Word) if you need to use these fonts in your printed documents.

Although you can print DW4 documents with proportionally spaced text, you'll find it very difficult to even up the right margin.

In addition to the problem you'll face with the right margin, the documentation that is included with the HPLASER.PFT file states "The Hewlett-Packard LaserJet and LaserJet+ support PSM [Proportional Spacing Mode] differently than Display-Write 4 expects," and says proportional fonts "are not fully supported with bold, underline, superscript, and subscript." For these reasons, we strongly recommend that you use a word processor that can better handle proportionally spaced fonts (like WordPerfect or Microsoft Word) if you need to use these fonts in your printed documents.

Installing DW4

To properly install DW4 on your system, you must do three things: run DW4's INSTALL program, copy IBM's HP LaserJet Printer Function Table into the \DW4 directory, and modify the DW4.BAT file.

Running INSTALL

To install DisplayWrite 4 on your computer, insert the DW4 Volume 1 diskette into drive A: and type **INSTALL** at the A> prompt. As soon as you press ↵, INSTALL will begin asking you questions about your system and copying the appropriate files onto your hard disk. After you answer the first few questions, INSTALL will ask you to select the type of printer you've connected to LPT1:, as shown in Figure 9-2. If your LaserJet is connected to LPT1:, you should type **10** to choose the Other option. As soon as you press ↵, INSTALL will present the screen shown in Figure 9-3, which asks if you have a Printer Function Table for your printer.

FIGURE 9-2

```
Choose the printer type attached to LPT1 from the
following list:

    1. IBM 5152-2 Graphics        5. IBM 3812 Pageprinter
    2. IBM 4201 Proprinter or     6. IBM 5140 PC Convertible System Printer
       IBM 4202 Proprinter XL     7. IBM 5216 Wheelprinter
    3. IBM 5201 Quietwriter or    8. IBM 5219 FFTDCA
       IBM 5201-2 Quietwriter     9. IBM 5223 Wheelprinter E
    4. IBM 3852 Model 2          10. Other
       Color Jetprinter          11. None

Type the number that describes the printer type on LPT1..[   ]


When finished, press Enter.
```

When the DW4 INSTALL program presents this list of printers, you should choose option 10 to install support for your LaserJet.

As we explained, you must obtain a copy of the HP LaserJet Printer Function Table in order to use DW4 with your LaserJet. If you have a copy of the LaserJet PFT, type **Y** and press ↵ in response to the screen in Figure 9-3. When you do this, INSTALL will ask you to type the name of your printer's Printer Function Table. If you've obtained IBM's version of the LaserJet PFT, you should type **HPLASER.PFT** and press ↵. INSTALL will then present the screen shown in Figure 9-4, which reminds you that after the DW4 installation is complete, you'll need to copy the file HPLASER.PFT into the directory containing the DW4 program files (we'll step through this procedure in a moment). To continue with the DW4 installation at this point, simply press ↵.

FIGURE 9-3

```
Your printer was not listed on the previous screen.  To
use your printer with DisplayWrite 4, you must have a
Printer Function Table that describes your printer to the
DisplayWrite 4 program.

Do you have a Printer Function Table already created
for your printer?

Type Y for yes or N for no..[ ]


When finished, press Enter.
```

Since DW4 does not provide a Printer Function Table for the LaserJet, you'll have to tell INSTALL that you'll provide your own PFT.

FIGURE 9-4

```
Since you are using your own Printer Function Table,
you must copy the table to the drive and directory
containing the DisplayWrite 4 program files before you can
print any DisplayWrite 4 documents.

Copy the table after Install is completed.


Press Enter to continue.

```

INSTALL reminds you to copy the LaserJet's PFT into the DW4 program directory.

After you've described the printer connected to LPT1:, INSTALL will bring up the same list shown in Figure 9-2 and ask you to describe the printer connected to LPT2:. If there is no printer connected to LPT2:, type **11** and press ↵ to choose the None option. If there is a printer connected to LPT2:, choose the appropriate option and press ↵. After you've defined both the LPT1: and LPT2: printers, INSTALL will ask if you've connected a printer to LPT3:. As before, choose the appropriate option from INSTALL's list and press ↵.

After you've defined the devices connected to LPT1:, LPT2:, and LPT3:, INSTALL will start copying files from the DW4 program disks onto your hard disk, prompting you to insert the additional DW4 disks along the way. When INSTALL is finished, it will remind you to store all of the original DW4 disk in a safe place and will return you to an A> prompt.

Installing the Printer Function Table

As we mentioned, you must copy the HP LaserJet's Printer Function Table (HPLASER.PFT) into the same directory as the DW4 program files (usually C:\DW4) after you run the DW4 INSTALL program. To do this, simply insert the disk containing the file HPLASER.PFT into drive A: and issue the DOS command **copy a:hplaser.pft c:/dw4**

Modifying DW4.BAT

The INSTALL program creates a file named DW4.BAT that you will use to load and run DW4. Unfortunately, this batch file contains a MODE command that will often prevent the computer from communicating with your LaserJet printer. To ensure that the computer and the LaserJet will communicate with each other once you load DW4, use any text processor to remove the line

MODE LPT1:,,,P

from the DW4.BAT file. Since the INSTALL program installs a copy of the DW4.BAT file in both the program directory (usually C:\DW4) and the root directory (C:\), be sure you modify both copies of the DW4.BAT files.

If you are running your LaserJet as a serial printer and have not inserted the appropriate MODE commands in your AUTOEXEC.BAT file, refer to the section entitled "Configuring Your LaserJet" in Chapter 2 and follow the instructions given there for modifying your AUTOEXEC.BAT file. Once you've entered the appropriate MODE commands in AUTOEXEC.BAT, you should remove all the MODE commands in your other batch files.

Loading DW4

After you copy the HPLASER.PFT file into the \DW4 directory, move into that directory, type **DW4**, then press ↵ to bring up DW4's main menu, which is shown in Figure 9-5. We'll use the commands on this menu to further customize DW4 for the LaserJet.

SETTING UP YOUR USER PROFILE

Before you begin composing and printing new documents with DW4, you need to change two groups of default settings in your user profile: the page layout and margin settings. To revise your user profile, choose the **9. Profiles** option from DW4's main menu, and then choose the **2. Revise Profile** option from the Profiles menu. When you do this, DW4 will present the screen shown in Figure 9-6. At this point, press ↵ to modify the profile named PROFILE.PRF. When DW4 brings up the Revise Profile menu, choose the **1. Text** option to bring up the Text Defaults menu, and then choose the **1. Document Format** option to bring up the Change Document Format menu shown in Figure 9-7 on page 358.

FIGURE 9-5

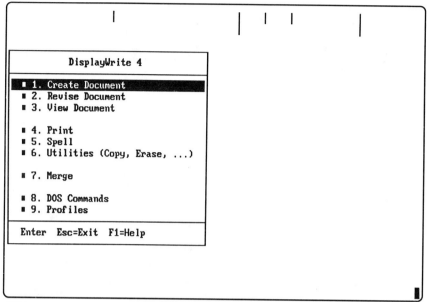

```
                ┌──────────────────────────────────────┐
                │          DisplayWrite 4              │
                ├──────────────────────────────────────┤
                │ ▪ 1. Create Document                 │
                │ ▪ 2. Revise Document                 │
                │ ▪ 3. View Document                   │
                │                                      │
                │ ▪ 4. Print                           │
                │ ▪ 5. Spell                           │
                │ ▪ 6. Utilities (Copy, Erase, ...)    │
                │                                      │
                │ ▪ 7. Merge                           │
                │                                      │
                │ ▪ 8. DOS Commands                    │
                │ ▪ 9. Profiles                        │
                ├──────────────────────────────────────┤
                │ Enter  Esc=Exit  F1=Help             │
                └──────────────────────────────────────┘
```

DW4's main menu appears as soon as you load DW4.

FIGURE 9-6

```
Revise Profile     |User Profile      |Repl|    |           |




                          ┌──────────────────────────────────────┐
                          │               Profile                │
                          ├──────────────────────────────────────┤
                          │ Profile Name..[C:\DW4\PROFILE.PRF   ] │
                          ├──────────────────────────────────────┤
                          │ Enter   Esc=Quit   F1=Help   F3=List  │
                          └──────────────────────────────────────┘
```

You'll need to modify a few settings in your default user profile before you can print your DW4 documents on the LaserJet.

FIGURE 9-7

```
┌─────────────────────────────────────────┐
│         Change Document Format            │
├─────────────────────────────────────────┤
│ ▄ 1. Margins and Tabs                     │
│ ▪ 2. Line Spacing/Justification           │
│ ▪ 3. Typestyle (Typeface and Pitch)       │
│                                           │
│ ▪ 4. Page Layout/Paper Options            │
│                                           │
│ ▪ 5. Footnote                             │
│ ▪ 6. Outline                              │
├─────────────────────────────────────────┤
│  Enter   Esc=Quit   F1=Help               │
└─────────────────────────────────────────┘
```

The Change Document Format menu lets you change the page layout and margin settings.

Adjusting the Page Layout Settings

When you choose **4. Page Layout/Paper Options** from the Change Document Format menu, the Page Layout/Paper Options menu shown in Figure 9-8 will appear on your screen. As you can see, the settings on this menu specify values for the first typing line for the first page, following pages, header and footer, and last typing line for each page.

FIGURE 9-8

```
┌─────────────────────────────────────────────────┐
│      Page Layout/Paper Options (1 of 2)           │
├─────────────────────────────────────────────────┤
│ First Typing Line for:                            │
│   First Page...........[7    ]                    │
│   Following Pages......[7    ]                    │
│   Header...............[3    ]                    │
│   Footer...............[63   ]                    │
│                                                   │
│ Last Typing Line......[60   ]                     │
├─────────────────────────────────────────────────┤
│  Enter   Esc=Quit   F1=Help   PgDn=More Options   │
└─────────────────────────────────────────────────┘
```

You need to change the default page layout settings to account for the LaserJet's unprintable regions.

Unfortunately, DW4's default page layout settings do not realize that the LaserJet will not print on the first and last three lines of a page. For this reason, you need to change DW4's default page layout values shown in Figure 9-8 to the values shown in Table 9-1. After you enter the new default values, press ↵ to return to the Change Document Format menu.

TABLE 9-1

First page:	4
Following pages:	4
Header:	2
Footer:	59
Last Typing Line:	57

Since DW4 does not account for the LaserJet's built-in top and bottom margins, you'll want to specify these page layout settings in your DW4 profile.

When you choose the **1. Margins and Tabs** option from the Change Document Format menu, the screen shown in Figure 9-9 will appear. As you can see in the ruler line at the top of the screen, DW4's default Left and Right margin settings are 15 and 75, respectively. Since there is a $1/_4$-inch unprintable region at the left and right edges of the page, however, the effective default Left and Right margin settings are 1.75 and 7.75 inches. When you print a document on the LaserJet using these default margin settings, the document will have a huge left margin and will not be centered on the page.

Adjusting the margin settings

FIGURE 9-9

```
Chg Document Format |User Profile          |    |    |          |
C:\DW4\PROFILE.PRF
     Enter=Return/Save  Esc=Quit  F1=Help  Ctrl+F2=Restore Margins and Tabs
◄....2...:...3...:...4....△....5...:...6...:...7....»....8....■....9....


         ┌─────────────────────────────────────────────────┐
         │                 Margins and Tabs                 │
         ├─────────────────────────────────────────────────┤
         │ CHANGE MARGINS: Move the cursor to the left (◄) or right (») margin
         │                 by pressing HOME or END.
         │                 Then press SPACE or BACKSPACE to change the margin.
         │
         │ CLEAR ALL TABS: Move the cursor to the left margin (◄); press DEL.
         │ CLEAR TAB:      Move the cursor to the tab setting; press DEL.
         │
         │ SET TAB:        Move the cursor to where you want a tab setting.  Then:
         │                 For a Flush Left Tab, press TAB
         │                 For a Decimal Tab, press .
         │                 For a Center Tab, press CENTER (Ctrl+C)
         │                 For a Flush Right Tab, press SHIFT+TAB
         └─────────────────────────────────────────────────┘
```

You will want to change the default left margin to 8 and the default right margin to 74.

To account for the LaserJet's unprintable region, you should follow the directions on the screen to change DW4's default Left and Right margin settings to 8 and 74, respectively. These new default margin settings will cause the LaserJet to leave approximately 1 inch of space at both the left and right edges of the page.

Saving your new user profile

After you change the default page layout and margin settings in your user profile, press **[Esc]** until you reach the End/Save menu, and then choose the **1. End and Save** option to save your changes. Since you revised DW4's active profile, you need not activate it after you've saved it. After you return to the Profiles menu, just press **[Esc]** to return to DW4's main menu.

FORMATTING DOCUMENTS

After you've installed DW4 and the LaserJet's Printer Function Table, and you've modified your user profile to account for the LaserJet's unprintable regions, you're ready to create and revise your DW4 documents. As you probably know, DW4 provides several formatting commands you can use to format your documents. Although most of DW4's commands do not affect the documents you'll print on the LaserJet any differently than documents you'll print on other printers, we need to discuss a few of DW4's formatting commands in some detail. In this section, we'll explain how to change your document's margins, page layout, and typeface; and we'll show you how to add boldfacing, underlining, and italicizing.

Changing the Margins

A moment ago, we showed you how to use the commands on DW4's Profiles menu to change the default margin settings for your DW4 documents. If you want, however, you can change the margin settings for the current document or for part of the document. To adjust the margins for the document, use the **2. Revise Document** command on DW4's main menu to bring the document up on the screen, press **[Ctrl][F7]** to bring up the Document Options menu, select the **1. Document Format** option, then choose the **1. Margins and Tabs** option to bring up a screen similar to the one shown in Figure 9-9. After you adjust the Left and Right margin settings, press ↵ to return to the Change Document Format menu, and then press **[Esc]** twice to return to the document. The new settings you define will affect every line from the beginning of the document to the first line that contains a format change code.

If you want to adjust the margin settings for only part of a document, position the cursor on the first line of the part you want to change, press **[F7]** to bring up the Format menu, then select the **1. Margins and Tabs** option to bring up the Margins and Tabs screen shown in Figure 9-9. After you adjust the margins and press ↵ to return to the document, DW4 will place a format change code on the appropriate line and change the ruler at the top of the screen to reflect the new margin settings. The new settings you define with the Format menu apply from the line containing the new format change code to the last line in the document, or to the line containing the next format change code.

Earlier in this chapter, we showed you how to use the commands on DW4's Profiles menu to change the default page layout settings for your DW4 documents. You'll find that the page layout settings we recommended in that section will almost always suit your printing needs. If you want, however, you can change the page layout settings while you are revising a document.

To adjust the document's page layout settings, you must use the **2. Revise Document** command on DW4's main menu to bring the document up on the screen, press **[F7]** to bring up the Format menu, and select **4. Page Layout/Paper Options** to bring up a screen like the one shown in Figure 9-8 on page 358. After you enter your new layout settings, press ↵ to return to the Format menu, and then press **[Esc]** to return to the document.

Keep in mind that DW4 does not realize that the LaserJet cannot print on the first or last three lines of the page. Consequently, if you specify a First Typing Line for Header setting of 1, the header line will actually appear $1^1/_2$ inches down the page. Similarly, if you specify a Last Typing Line setting of more than 60, DW4 will not break your pages in the proper locations.

Changing the Page Layout

As we mentioned, the HPLASER.PFT supports most LaserJet cartridge fonts. By default, DW4 will print your documents with the LaserJet's 10-pitch Internal Courier Medium font. If you want, however, you can tell DW4 to print your entire document in a different typestyle or to print parts of it in different typestyles.

Changing Typestyles

To print your entire document in a typestyle other than the default, you must use the **2. Revise Document** command on DW4's main menu to bring the document up on the screen, press **[Ctrl][F7]** to bring up the Document Options menu, choose the **1. Document Format** option, and finally choose **3. Typestyle (Typeface and Pitch)** to bring up the Typestyle box shown in Figure 9-10 on the next page. When this box appears, look up the typestyle code number that represents the font you want to use, and enter that number in the Typestyle box. Table 9-2 on page 363 lists the fonts supported by HPLASER.PFT, along with their associated codes.

Changing the typestyle of the entire document

After you change the code in the Typestyle box and return to the document, DW4 will change the typestyle code at the top of the screen to reflect the new typestyle you've defined. When you save the document and use DW4's Print command to print it, DW4 will instruct the LaserJet to use the new font you've defined instead of the default font. (We'll discuss the Print command in more detail later in this chapter.)

As an example, suppose you want to change the font used to print a particular document from 10-pitch Courier to 12-pitch Prestige Elite. To do this, you would open the document, bring up the Typestyle box shown in Figure 9-10, then look up the code number for the Prestige Elite typestyle in Table 9-2. As you can see in the table, you need to enter the number 86 or 76 in the Typestyle box, depending on which font cartridge you've installed in the LaserJet. If you've installed either the "D" or the "M" font cartridges, which contain fonts in the Roman-8 symbol set, you'll need to specify typestyle 86. However, if you've installed the "G" font cartridge, which contains fonts in the Legal 1 symbol set, you'll need to specify typestyle 76. After you save the document, return to the main menu, and issue the Print command, the LaserJet will print your entire document in 12-pitch Prestige Elite type.

FIGURE 9-10

```
┌──────────────────────────────────────────────────────────┐
│         Typestyle (Typeface and Pitch)                     │
├──────────────────────────────────────────────────────────┤
│                                                            │
│   Typestyle..[26 ]     1-65      (10 Pitch)                │
│                        66-153    (12 Pitch)                │
│                        154-200   (Proportional)            │
│                        211-239   (15 Pitch)                │
│                        240-249   (5 Pitch)                 │
│                        250-259   (17.1 Pitch)              │
│                        260-279   (8.55 Pitch)              │
│                                                            │
├──────────────────────────────────────────────────────────┤
│   Enter    Esc=Quit    F1=Help                             │
└──────────────────────────────────────────────────────────┘
```

To change the font used to print your document, you'll need to enter the appropriate typestyle code from Table 9-2 into the Typestyle box.

Changing the typestyle of a paragraph or page

If you want to change the typestyle for a paragraph or a page of a document, position the cursor on the first line of the part you want to change, press **[F7]** to bring up the Format menu, and then select the **3. Typestyle (Typeface and Pitch)** option to bring up a Typestyle screen like the one shown in Figure 9-10. After you enter the new typestyle code from Table 9-2 and press ↵, DW4 will place a format change code at the beginning of the line you specified and change the typestyle code at the top of the screen to reflect the new typestyle. The new typestyle you define with the Format menu applies from the line containing the format change code to the last line in the document, or to the next line that contains a format change code.

When you use the Format command to select a typestyle that has a different pitch from the rest of the document, DW4 automatically changes the margin values in the ruler line to reflect the new pitch. Fortunately, these new margin values keep the newly formatted text the same distance from the edges of the paper as the rest of the document. For this reason, you don't need to go back and adjust the margins in the sections that are assigned the new pitch.

TABLE 9-2

Typeface	Weight	Style	Pitch	Point	Symbol sets				
					Roman-8	USASCII	PC	Legal 1	Math 2
Courier	Medium	Upright	10	12	11	-----	53	50	-----
Courier	Medium	Italic	10	12	18	-----	54	51	-----
Courier	Light	Italic	10	12	18	-----	-----	-----	-----
P. Elite	Medium	Upright	12	10	86	-----	-----	76	115
P. Elite	Medium	Italic	12	10	92	-----	-----	77	-----
P. Elite	Medium	Upright	16.66	7	-----	259	-----	-----	-----
L. Gothic	Medium	Upright	12	12	87	-----	-----	-----	-----
L. Gothic	Medium	Italic	12	12	92	-----	-----	-----	-----
L. Gothic	Medium	Upright	10	14	-----	-----	-----	27	-----
Line Printer	Medium	Upright	16.66	8.5	257	-----	258	-----	-----
Line Printer	Light	Upright	16.66	8.5	257	-----	-----	-----	-----
Presentation	Bold	Upright	6.5	18	-----	244	-----	-----	-----
Presentation	Bold	Upright	8.1	16	-----	262	-----	-----	-----
Presentation	Bold	Upright	10	14	-----	-----	-----	52	-----
Tms Rmn	Medium	Upright	Prop	10	181	178	-----	-----	180
Tms Rmn	Medium	Italic	Prop	10	155	179	-----	-----	-----
Tms Rmn	Medium	Upright	Prop	8	184	183	-----	-----	-----
Tms Rmn	Light	Upright	Prop	8	-----	183	-----	-----	-----
Helv	Bold	Upright	Prop	14.4	-----	185	-----	-----	-----

You'll use these typestyle codes to change the fonts in your DW4 documents.

To return a section of a document to the Document Format, simply position the cursor on the first line you want to reformat, press **[F7]** to bring up the Format menu, select the **8. Reset Format** option, and then select either of the first two options on the Reset Format menu.

If you want to change the typestyle within a line of a document, position the cursor under the first letter that you want to appear in the new typestyle and press **[Ctrl]F** to bring up the Change Typeface box. After you enter the new typeface code from Table 9-2 and press ↵, DW4 will place a format change code just in front of the character you specified and will change the typestyle code at the top of the screen to reflect the change. The new typestyle you define applies to the area from the format change code to the last line in the document, or to the next format change code. We'll demonstrate the Change Typeface command when we explain how to italicize text.

Changing the typestyle within a line

Notes

You might have noticed that Table 9-2 does not include bold fonts for all of the HP typefaces. The HPLASER.PFT does not include bold fonts for Courier, Prestige Elite, and so forth, because DW4 uses a "backspacing" technique to boldface characters in a document. Consequently, this technique allows you to boldface any character in your document, regardless of whether you've installed bold fonts on your LaserJet printer.

Although DW4 accurately spaces all HP fonts with pitch sizes of 10, 12, and 14, it does not space fonts with pitch sizes of 6.5, 8.1, or 16.66 as you would expect. DW4 prints fonts that are listed as 6.5-pitch fonts on the font cartridge at 5 characters per inch; it prints 8.1-pitch fonts at 8.55 characters per inch; and it prints 16.66-pitch fonts at 17.1 characters per inch.

If you specify a typestyle code for a font whose cartridge is not currently installed, the LaserJet will substitute the available font that most closely resembles the requested font. If you specify a typestyle code that is not listed in Table 9-2, the LaserJet will print with its Internal Courier font but will maintain the typestyle code's associated pitch. For example, if you specify typestyle code 240 (which does not appear in Table 9-2), the LaserJet will print with the Courier font but will include large spaces between the characters since code 240 is reserved for a 5-pitch font. Similarly, code 250, which is reserved for a 17.1-pitch font, would cause the LaserJet to print Courier characters that overlap.

To change the typestyle that DW4 brings up as the default each time you create a new DW4 document, you'll need to change the default settings in your DW4 user profile.

Boldfacing and Underlining

To boldface or underline characters in a document, just use the Bold and Underline commands on DW4's Block menu. As we mentioned earlier, DW4 creates boldfacing by backing up and reprinting the appropriate characters. For this reason, you can boldface any character or group of characters, regardless of which bold fonts you've installed on your LaserJet.

As an example, suppose you want to boldface the word *immediately* in a document. To do this, just move the cursor below the first letter in the word, press **[F4]** to bring up the Block menu, and choose the **7. Bold** option. At this point, DW4 will prompt you to move the cursor to the end of the block you want to boldface. You should now use either the ➡ key or the [Spacebar] to highlight the entire word *immediately*, then press ↵. When you save the document and print it, the word *immediately* will appear in bold type.

Italicizing

Unfortunately, it's not as easy to italicize characters in your document as it is to boldface or underline them. Unlike boldfacing and underlining, which DW4 can perform on any characters in your document, italicizing can be performed only when you've installed an italic font on your LaserJet printer. As you can see in Table 9-2, the LaserJet's Printer Function Table supports italic fonts in several typestyles, including Courier and Prestige Elite.

To italicize characters in a DW4 document, you must position the cursor under the first character you want to italicize, then use the Change Typeface command ([Ctrl]F) to assign the italic typestyle to that portion of the document. After you've changed the typestyle at the beginning of the block you want to italicize, you must move the cursor to the end of the block and use the Change Typeface command again to reassign the upright font to the remainder of the document.

As an example, let's assume your LaserJet is equipped with an "A" font cartridge, which contains the Courier Italic font in the Roman-8 symbol set. Now, suppose you've created the document shown in Figure 9-11, whose default font is Courier Upright (typestyle 11), and you want the words *LaserJet Companion* in the fifth line of body text to appear in italic type.

FIGURE 9-11

```
Revise Document        |              |Ins |    |      |Pg  1
SAMPLE.DOC             |              |Typestyle 178  (PSM) |Ln  12
   F2=End/Save  F4=Block  F5=Functions  F6=Search  F7=Format  F8=Instructions
«....:....2....:....3....:....4....:...∆5....:....6...█:....7....:....8....:..»
                WORKING WITH DISPLAYWRITE 4


     IBM's DisplayWrite 4 is a powerful word processing program that you can
use to create, edit, and print a wide variety of letters and reports.  Although
DisplayWrite 4 was designed to work with IBM's family of printers, you can use
DW4 and an HP LaserJet printer to generate reports that look just as good as
those produced on an IBM printer.  In this chapter of LaserJet Companion,
we'll take the mystery out of printing DisplayWrite 4 documents on the HP
LaserJet printer.

Installing DW4 and the LaserJet PFT

     To install a copy of DisplayWrite 4 on your system that works with your
LaserJet printer, you need two things:  a copy of DW4, and a copy of the HP
LaserJet Printer Function Table.  If you've recently purchased a copy of DW4,
you'll find a copy of the HP LaserJet Printer Function Table on the Printer
Function Tables Supplement Diskette.  If you've purchased an older copy of
DW4 that does not contain the Printer Function Tables Supplement Diskette,
```

We'll use this sample document to show you how to italicize words in your document.

To italicize the words *LaserJet Companion*, position the cursor below the letter *L* in *LaserJet* and press **[Ctrl]F** to bring up the Typestyle box shown in Figure 9-10. Since Table 9-2 indicates that the Courier Italic font in the Roman-8 symbol set is represented by typestyle code 18, you should type **18** in the Typestyle box, and press ↵ to return to the document. Now, move the cursor below the space following the last letter in the word *Companion*, press **[Ctrl]F** again to bring up the Typestyle box, and enter typestyle code **11** to reassign the Courier Upright font to the rest of the document. When you print this document, the LaserJet will use the Courier Italic font to print the words *LaserJet Companion* and will use the Courier Upright font to print the rest of the document.

Headers and Footers

As you probably know, a document's header and footer are always printed in the document's default typestyle. If you want to change the typestyle used to print your document's header and footer, you'll have to change the default typestyle for the entire document. To do this, press **[Ctrl][F7]** to bring up the Document Options menu, select the **1. Document Format** option, and then select the **3. Typestyle (Typeface and Pitch)** option from the Change Document Format menu to bring up the Typestyle box shown in Figure 9-10. When the Typestyle box appears, type the new document typestyle (using the codes in Table 9-2), and press ↵.

As you might guess, the document's default margin settings also determine where the header and footer will be positioned on the page. To learn how to change the document's default margin settings, refer to the section entitled "Changing the Margins" that appears on page 360.

Paginating

Before you can print a DW4 document, you need to paginate it. Paginating organizes your document into pages that conform to the format settings you've assigned, including the margin settings, layout settings, footnotes, outlines, and page numbers. To paginate your document after you've finished revising it, simply press **[F2]** to bring up the End/Save menu, and choose the **4. Paginate, End, and Save** option. When the Paginate Document screen appears, define the appropriate settings, and press ↵. After DW4 paginates the entire document, it will return to the main menu.

PRINTING DOCUMENTS

Fortunately, printing DW4 documents on a LaserJet is not much different from printing documents on any other printer. After we explain how to use DW4's Print command to print standard documents on the LaserJet, we'll explain how to print Landscape-oriented documents, legal documents, and envelopes.

Printing Standard-size Documents

The Print command on DW4's main menu is the tool you'll use to print your DW4 documents. When you choose the **4. Print** option from the main menu, and then choose the **1. Print Document** option, DW4 will bring up the Print Document box shown in Figure 9-12.

As you can see, the settings in this box let you specify the document name, the range of pages to be printed, and the number of copies. After you've defined the appropriate settings, press ↵ to send the document to the printer. While DW4 is sending the document to the printer, it will present the screen shown in

Figure 9-13. To cancel the print job, press **[Ctrl][Break]**. If the LaserJet is in the process of printing a page when you cancel the Print command, it won't stop printing immediately. Instead, the LaserJet will finish printing all the information that DW4 sent before you pressed [Ctrl][Break].

FIGURE 9-12

```
┌────────────────────────────────────────────────────────────────┐
│                    Print Document (1 of 2)                       │
├────────────────────────────────────────────────────────────────┤
│ Document Name.....[SAMPLE.DOC                               ]    │
│                                                                  │
│ From Page.........[        ]    Blank = First Page               │
│                                 1-9999                           │
│ Through Page......[        ]    Blank = Last Page                │
│                                 1-9999                           │
│ Number of Copies..[1 ]          1-99                             │
├────────────────────────────────────────────────────────────────┤
│ Enter    Esc=Quit   F1=Help   F3=List        PgDn=More Options   │
└────────────────────────────────────────────────────────────────┘
```

You'll use the Print command to print your DW4 documents.

FIGURE 9-13

```
┌────────────────────────────────────────────────────────────────┐
│              Foreground Processing for Print                     │
├────────────────────────────────────────────────────────────────┤
│                                                                  │
│ To temporarily suspend Print processing and perform             │
│ one of the following tasks, press Ctrl+Break.                   │
│                                                                  │
│      -    Print Document                                         │
│      -    Options for Printer                                    │
│      -    List or Reorder Print Jobs                             │
│      -    Cancel Print Jobs                                      │
│                                                                  │
└────────────────────────────────────────────────────────────────┘
```

DW4 presents this box while it is sending your document to the printer.

Unfortunately, the LaserJet will eject a blank sheet of paper after it prints each page in your document. If you are like most DW4 users, you'll want to "recycle" these blank sheets by removing them from your documents and reloading them into the paper tray after you've built up a sizable stack.

Figure 9-14 shows the first and second page of a document we printed using the LaserJet's Internal Courier font and the margin and page layout settings we recommended earlier in the section "Setting Up Your User Profile." As you can see, there is approximately 1 inch of white space on all four sides of the document, and DW4 has broken the pages in the proper locations.

FIGURE 9-14

We printed this document using the default print settings we recommended earlier in this chapter.

Printing Landscape Documents

If you want to print a document in Landscape orientation, you must first make sure that your LaserJet has access to the appropriate Landscape font. If you're using a LaserJet, LaserJet Plus, or LaserJet 500 Plus, this means you'll need to install a font cartridge that contains the Landscape font you want to use. If you're using a LaserJet Series II or LaserJet IID, you can either use the Internal Courier or Line Printer Landscape fonts, or install a font cartridge that contains a different Landscape font.

Once you've equipped your LaserJet with the appropriate Landscape fonts, you can tell DW4 to print the document in Landscape orientation by changing a few of the document's page layout settings. You'll also want to adjust the Right margin setting.

Changing the page layout settings

To change the document's page layout settings, issue the **2. Revise Document** command on DW4's main menu to bring the appropriate document up on your screen. When the document appears on your screen, press **[Ctrl][F7]**, select **1. Document Format** and **4. Page Layout/Paper Options**, then define the page layout settings shown in Figure 9-15.

After you enter the settings shown in Figure 9-15, press the **[Pg Dn]** key to bring up the second part of the Page Layout/Paper Options box, and enter the settings shown in Figure 9-16. Notice that we've swapped the Paper Width and Paper Length settings so that the paper is now 11- by $8^1/_2$-inch instead of $8^1/_2$- by 11-inch.

Also notice that we've selected Manual Feed as the paper source. (Unfortunately, DW4 doesn't print Landscape documents on the LaserJet properly unless you select Manual Feed.)

FIGURE 9-15

```
┌─────────────────────────────────────────────────────────┐
│         Page Layout/Paper Options (1 of 2)              │
├─────────────────────────────────────────────────────────┤
│  First Typing Line for:                                 │
│    First Page..........[4   ]                           │
│    Following Pages......[4   ]                           │
│    Header..............[2   ]                           │
│    Footer..............[45  ]                           │
│                                                         │
│  Last Typing Line......[43  ]                           │
├─────────────────────────────────────────────────────────┤
│  Enter   Esc=Quit   F1=Help   PgDn=More Options         │
└─────────────────────────────────────────────────────────┘
```

You need to define these page layout settings to print Landscape documents.

FIGURE 9-16

```
┌─────────────────────────────────────────────────────────────────┐
│              Page Layout/Paper Options (2 of 2)                  │
├─────────────────────────────────────────────────────────────────┤
│  Paper Options:                                                  │
│    Paper Width..........[11  ]    .1-45.5 Inches                 │
│    Paper Length.........[8.5 ]    .1-45.5 Inches                 │
│                                                                  │
│    Printing Paper Source                                         │
│      for Cut Paper Only....[M]    T = Top        M = Manual Feed │
│                                   B = Bottom     E = Envelope Feed│
│                                   O = Bottom, This Page Only     │
│    Print Header On........[A]     A = All Pages  F = Following Pages│
│    Print Footer On........[A]     A = All Pages  F = Following Pages│
├─────────────────────────────────────────────────────────────────┤
│  Enter   Esc=Quit   F1=Help                  PgUp=More Options   │
└─────────────────────────────────────────────────────────────────┘
```

After you select the settings shown in Figure 9-15, press [Pg Dn], then define these settings.

After you've defined all of the page layout settings shown in Figures 9-15 and 9-16 (except the Print Header On and Print Footer On settings), press ↵ to return to the Change Document Format menu.

Adjusting the Right margin setting

Once you've defined the new page layout settings, select the **1. Margins and Tabs** option from the Change Document Format menu, and change the Right margin setting to **98** in order to leave about 1 inch of white space along the right edge of the page.

Printing the document

After you adjust the page layout and Right margin settings, press **[Esc]** until you exit the menus, press the **[F2]** key, and choose the **4. Paginate, End, and Save** option to return to the main menu. When you use the Print command to send the document to the printer, the LaserJet will prompt you to manually insert sheets of paper until it has printed the entire document. Figure 9-17 shows page 1 of a sample document we printed in Landscape orientation.

FIGURE 9-17

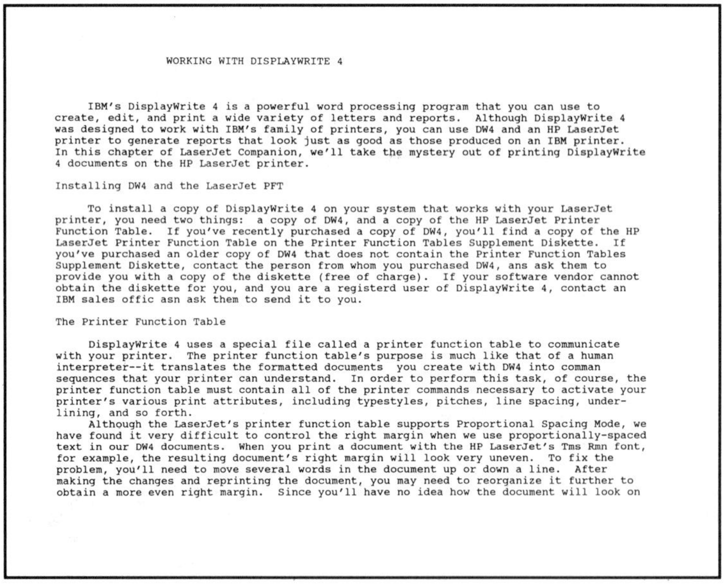

DW4 can easily print Landscape-oriented documents on your LaserJet printer.

Printing Legal-size Documents

To print a document on legal-size paper, you need to modify a few of the document's page layout settings. After you use the Revise Document command to bring the document up on your screen, press **[Ctrl][F7]**, choose **1. Document Format,** and **4. Page Layout/Paper Options**, then define the page layout settings shown in Figure 9-18.

FIGURE 9-18

```
┌─────────────────────────────────────────────────────┐
│                                                       │
│        Page Layout/Paper Options (1 of 2)             │
├─────────────────────────────────────────────────────┤
│   First Typing Line for:                              │
│     First Page..........[4    ]                       │
│     Following Pages......[4    ]                       │
│     Header...............[2    ]                       │
│     Footer...............[78   ]                       │
│                                                       │
│   Last Typing Line......[76   ]                       │
│                                                       │
├─────────────────────────────────────────────────────┤
│   Enter   Esc=Quit   F1=Help   PgDn=More Options      │
└─────────────────────────────────────────────────────┘
```

You need to define these page layout settings to print legal-size documents.

FIGURE 9-19

```
┌─────────────────────────────────────────────────────────────┐
│            Page Layout/Paper Options (2 of 2)                 │
├─────────────────────────────────────────────────────────────┤
│  Paper Options:                                               │
│   Paper Width............[8.5 ]     .1-45.5 Inches            │
│   Paper Length...........[14  ]     .1-45.5 Inches            │
│                                                               │
│   Printing Paper Source                                       │
│    for Cut Paper Only....[M]    T = Top      M = Manual Feed  │
│                                 B = Bottom   E = Envelope Feed│
│                                 O = Bottom, This Page Only    │
│   Print Header On........[A]    A = All Pages  F = Following Pages│
│   Print Footer On........[A]    A = All Pages  F = Following Pages│
├─────────────────────────────────────────────────────────────┤
│  Enter   Esc=Quit   F1=Help              PgUp=More Options    │
└─────────────────────────────────────────────────────────────┘
```

After you enter the settings shown in Figure 9-18, press [Pg Dn], then define these settings.

After you enter the settings shown in Figure 9-18, press the **[Pg Dn]** key to bring up the rest of the page layout options, and enter a Paper Width of **8.5** and a Paper Length of **14**, as shown in Figure 9-19. If you do not have a legal-size paper tray for your LaserJet, make sure you change the Printing Paper Source for Cut Paper Only setting to **M** for Manual Feed.

Once you've defined all of the appropriate page layout settings, press ↵ to return to the Change Document Format menu, and then press **[Esc]** until you exit the menus. Now, press the **[F2]** key, choose the **4. Paginate, End, and Save** option to return to the main menu. You can then use the Print command to send the document to the printer. If you do not have a legal-size paper tray, the LaserJet will prompt you to manually insert sheets of paper after you send the document.

Printing Envelopes

To print envelopes in Courier (10-pitch) typestyle on your LaserJet printer with DW4, you must first create a document like the one in Figure 9-20 that contains the name and address you want to print on the envelope. After you've created the document, you'll need to adjust the page layout and margin settings, then paginate and save your document. You must also select automatic feed on the Options for Printer menu before you send the document to the printer. Let's work through an example to demonstrate this process.

FIGURE 9-20

```
┌─────────────────────────────────────────────────────────────────────────┐
│Revise Document      |                    |Ins |    |          |Pg  1      │
│C:\ENVELOPE.DOC                            |Typestyle 26  (10p) |Ln  25     │
│    F2=End/Save  F4=Block  F5=Functions  F6=Search  F7=Format  F8=Instructions│
│▓....6....:....7....:....◊....:....9....:...10....:»..1▪....:...12....:...13...│
│Mr. and Mrs. W.E. Crane                                                     │
│506 Westerham Court                                                         │
│Louisville, KY  40222                                                      │
└─────────────────────────────────────────────────────────────────────────┘
```

We'll use this sample document to print an envelope on the LaserJet with DW4.

Changing the page layout settings

To define the page layout settings that will let you print envelopes, bring the envelope document up on your screen, press **[Ctrl][F7]**, select **1. Document Format**, and then select **4. Page Layout/Paper Options** to bring the Page Layout/Paper Options box up on your screen. At this point, you should enter the page layout settings shown in Table 9-3. Notice that the First Typing Line value depends on which LaserJet printer you're using.

TABLE 9-3

Setting	LJet or LJet Plus	LJet Series II or LJet IID
First Typing Line for First Page:	10	25
Last Typing Line:	45	45

You'll need to define these page layout settings when you want to print envelopes.

After you enter the settings shown in Table 9-3, press the **[Pg Dn]** key to display the second part of the Page Layout/Paper Options box, and enter the settings shown in Figure 9-21. Notice that we've swapped the Paper Width and Paper Length settings so that the paper is now 11- by $8^1/_2$-inch instead of $8^1/_2$- by 11-inch. Also notice that we've selected envelope feed as the paper source.

FIGURE 9-21

```
┌──────────────────────────────────────────────────────────────────────┐
│Chg Document Format |                    |Repl|   |        |Pg  1       │
│C:\ENVELOPE.DOC                          |Typestyle 26  (10p)  |Ln  25   │
├──────────────────────────────────────────────────────────────────────┤
│▓....6....:....7....:....◬....:....9....:....10....:▸.1▪....:....12....:....13....│
│Mr. and Mrs. W.E. Crane                                                 │
│506 Westerham Court                                                     │
│Louisville, KY  40222                                                   │
│                                                                        │
│   ┌──────────────────────────────────────────────────────────────┐    │
│   │           Page Layout/Paper Options (2 of 2)                 │    │
│   ├──────────────────────────────────────────────────────────────┤    │
│   │  Paper Options:                                              │    │
│   │   Paper Width...........[11  ]     .1-45.5 Inches            │    │
│   │   Paper Length..........[8.5 ]     .1-45.5 Inches            │    │
│   │                                                              │    │
│   │   Printing Paper Source                                      │    │
│   │    for Cut Paper Only....[E]     T = Top       M = Manual Feed│    │
│   │                                  B = Bottom    E = Envelope Feed│  │
│   │                                  0 = Bottom, This Page Only   │    │
│   │   Print Header On........[A]     A = All Pages  F = Following Pages│
│   │   Print Footer On........[A]     A = All Pages  F = Following Pages│
│   ├──────────────────────────────────────────────────────────────┤    │
│   │  Enter   Esc=Quit  F1=Help               PgUp=More Options    │    │
│   └──────────────────────────────────────────────────────────────┘    │
└──────────────────────────────────────────────────────────────────────┘
```

After you enter the settings shown in Table 9-3, press [Pg Dn], then define these settings.

After you've defined all of the page layout settings shown in Table 9-3 and Figure 9-21, press ↵ to return to the Change Document Format menu.

Adjusting the margin settings

After you define the new page layout settings, select the **1. Margins and Tabs** option from the Change Document Format menu, then follow the directions on the screen to define a left margin of **55** and a right margin of **106**.

Printing the document

After you adjust the page layout and margin settings, press **[Esc]** until you exit the menus, press the **[F2]** key, and choose the **4. Paginate, End, and Save** option to return to the main menu. To print the envelope, choose the **4. Print** option from DW4's main menu, then choose the **2. Options for Printer** option, and select the appropriate printer from the Options for Printer menu to bring up the screen shown in Figure 9-22. When this screen appears, type an **A** in the Paper Handling box to select automatic paper feed, and press ↵ to save your new setting. After you select automatic feed, print your document in the usual way. When the LaserJet prompts you to insert an envelope into the printer, insert the envelope as shown in Figure 9-23. If you're using a LaserJet or LaserJet Plus printer, insert the envelope as shown in Figure 9-24. The resulting envelope is shown in Figure 9-25.

FIGURE 9-22

```
┌─────────────────────────────────────────────────────────────────┐
│                     Options for Printer 1                         │
├─────────────────────────────────────────────────────────────────┤
│  Draft Mode..............[Y]    Y = Yes      N = No               │
│                                                                   │
│  Paper Handling..........[A]    C = Continuous Paper              │
│                                 A = Automatic Feed (Cut Paper)    │
│                                 M = Manual Feed (Cut Paper)       │
│                                 P = Prompted Manual Feed (Cut Paper)│
│  Collate Copies..........[D]    D = By Document (pg1pg2 pg1pg2)   │
│                                 P = By Page (pg1pg1 pg2pg2)       │
│  Pause at Document Start.: N    Y = Yes      N = No               │
├─────────────────────────────────────────────────────────────────┤
│  Enter    Esc=Quit    F1=Help                                     │
└─────────────────────────────────────────────────────────────────┘
```

You must select automatic paper feed before you can print envelopes with DW4.

FIGURE 9-23

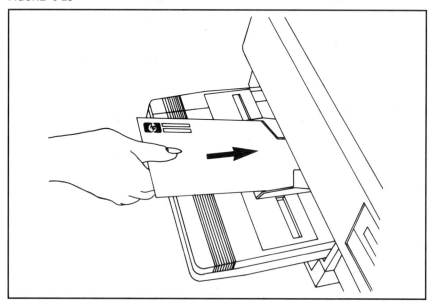

When the LaserJet Series II or LaserJet IID printer prompts you to insert an envelope, make sure you insert the correct end first.

FIGURE 9-24

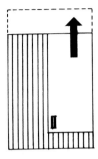

When the LaserJet or LaserJet Plus printer prompts you to insert an envelope, make sure you insert the correct end first.

FIGURE 9-25

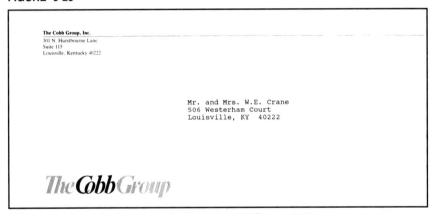

The Cobb Group, Inc.
301 N. Hurstbourne Lane
Suite 115
Louisville, Kentucky 40222

Mr. and Mrs. W.E. Crane
506 Westerham Court
Louisville, KY 40222

We printed this envelope from the document in Figure 9-20.

CONCLUSION

In this chapter, we've explained how to print documents on an HP LaserJet printer using IBM's DisplayWrite 4 word processor. After we explained how to install DW4 and the HP LaserJet's Printer Function Table, we showed you how to adjust some settings in your DW4 user profile to account for the LaserJet's unprintable regions. Next, we showed you how to use DW4's formatting commands to change the margins, page layout, typestyle, and so forth. Finally, we showed you how to use DW4 to print standard-size documents, legal-size documents, Landscape-oriented documents, and envelopes on the LaserJet.

dBASE III PLUS 10

Ashton-Tate's dBASE III Plus is the most popular database manager on the market today. If you own a copy of dBASE III Plus and an HP LaserJet printer, you can create and print professional-looking custom reports and mailing labels from the information stored in your databases.

In this chapter, we'll show you how to take advantage of the LaserJet's printing capabilities with dBASE III Plus. After we show you how to configure your serial port and select a printer, we'll demonstrate the use of dBASE's command language to select special print features that will help you format reports and mailing labels. We'll also show you how to use the LaserJet to print addresses directly onto envelopes. Finally, we'll discuss some programming techniques you can use to turn the LaserJet's special printing effects on and off in the middle of material you are printing.

HARDWARE SETUP

As we said in Chapter 1, you can run the LaserJet Series II or the LaserJet Plus printer as either a parallel or serial printer. Since most PC systems are set up to print to a parallel printer connected to the LPT1: printer port, dBASE sends print data to the LPT1: port by default. If you want to send print data to a different printer port, adjust dBASE's printer settings with a combination of dBASE and DOS commands.

Configuring a Serial Port

If you intend to use the LaserJet as a serial printer, then the first thing you need to do is set the baud rate, parity, data bits, and stop bits for the serial interface connected to your LaserJet. Together, these settings constitute the communications protocol that your PC will use to communicate with the LaserJet. You can use

DOS's MODE command to establish these settings. The MODE command runs a DOS utility program called MODE.COM that sets the protocol for a specified printer device. For example, the DOS command

MODE COM1:9600,N,8,1,P

defines the protocol settings for the primary serial interface (COM1:). The number 9600 sets the baud rate for the COM1: interface to 9600 bits per second. The *N* argument sets the parity to "none." This MODE command also sets the number of data bits to 8 and the number of stop bits to 1. The *P* at the end of the command tells DOS that the serial device connected to the COM1: interface is a printer.

You can issue the MODE command in DOS before loading dBASE or from within dBASE. To use the MODE command from within dBASE, you must embed the DOS command in the dBASE command RUN. The RUN command executes a specified DOS command as if you had typed that command at the DOS prompt. For example, to issue the MODE command that we discussed above, you would type this command

RUN MODE COM1:9600,N,8,1,P

at the dBASE dot prompt. Of course, dBASE can successfully issue the MODE command only if the MODE.COM file is in the current directory, or if your DOS path includes the directory in which that file is located. If neither of these conditions is true, then DOS will display the error message *Bad command or file name* and return you to dBASE. The simplest solution to this problem is to include the directory path to the MODE.COM file in the RUN MODE command. For example, if the MODE.COM file is in the \DOS directory and dBASE is in a different directory, you can use the RUN command

RUN \DOS\MODE COM1:9600,N,8,1,P

to issue the MODE command from the dBASE dot prompt.

The dBASE III Plus manual suggests using the dBASE command SET PATH to set the directory path to the MODE.COM file before issuing the RUN MODE command. However, this approach will not work because the SET PATH command changes the path that dBASE uses to find files, but does not affect the path that DOS uses to search for the MODE.COM file.

You may also be tempted to try changing the DOS path by embedding DOS's PATH command in a RUN command. However, before dBASE processes any RUN command, it creates a new DOS environment nested inside the environment in which dBASE is running, then issues the RUN-embedded command in the new environment. A PATH command embedded in a RUN command changes the path for the new DOS environment, but when dBASE resumes operation, that new environment and its directory path cease to exist. Though you could exit dBASE and use a PATH command to change the DOS path from the DOS prompt, it is easier and quicker to include the directory path in the RUN MODE command.

Whether you intend to use the LaserJet as a parallel or a serial printer, the dBASE command SET PRINTER lets you select the appropriate printer interface. (As we said earlier, you don't need to worry about setting the printer if you are using the LaserJet as a parallel printer hooked up to the LPT1: interface.) The SET PRINTER command has this syntax

Selecting a Printer

SET PRINTER TO *<DOS printing device>*

The *<DOS printing device>* that you specify in the command must be one of the five printer interfaces: LPT1:, LPT2:, LPT3:, COM1:, or COM2:. Also, dBASE will only accept the SET PRINTER command if you have a printer connected to the port that you specify in the command.

For example, suppose your HP LaserJet is connected to the parallel printer port LPT3:. Before trying to send a report to the LaserJet, you would type **SET PRINTER TO LPT3** at the dBASE dot prompt, then press ↵. If the LaserJet was connected and ready to print, dBASE would then send all printer output from that point on to the LaserJet. If the printer was not connected, then dBASE would present an error message like the one shown in Figure 10-1.

FIGURE 10-1

```
. SET PRINTER TO LPT1
Printer is either not connected or turned off.
                    ?
SET PRINTER TO LPT1
Do you want some help? (Y/N)
```

dBASE warns you if the printer you selected is not ready.

If you installed your LaserJet as a serial printer connected to the COM1: interface, then you would select the LaserJet by typing the command **SET PRINTER TO COM1** and pressing ↵. Before you can select a serial printer with the SET PRINTER command, you must set up the protocol for the serial printer's interface, as we discussed above. After you've set the printer, you are ready to begin printing.

**PRINTING
REPORTS**

    Special files called report forms let you design and print reports based on information in databases. The REPORT command is the tool that you use to print dBASE reports. The REPORT command has this syntax

    REPORT FORM *<report form>* TO PRINT

    If you omit the TO PRINT option in the command, dBASE will present the report on the screen without sending it to the printer. Before you can print a report, you need to design the report form. The CREATE REPORT and MODIFY REPORT commands place you in a menu-driven subsystem of dBASE that you use to design report forms. The two commands have the same function. Either command will let you modify a specified report form for the current database if that form already exists, or create a new report form if the specified form does not exist. The commands also have the same syntax:

    CREATE REPORT *<report form>*
    MODIFY REPORT *<report form>*

    Let's look at an example of a report designed specifically to be printed on a LaserJet. For our sample reports in this chapter, we'll use fields from a database called LISTINGS. The LISTINGS database contains information on the houses currently for sale through a fictitious real estate company. Figure 10-2 shows the structure of the LISTINGS database.

FIGURE 10-2

```
. USE LISTINGS
. DISPLAY STRUCTURE
Structure for database: C:LISTINGS.dbf
Number of data records:     65
Date of last update   : 08/11/88
Field  Field Name  Type        Width   Dec
    1  ADDRESS     Character      20
    2  TOWN        Character      10
    3  OWNER       Character      10
    4  LISTDATE    Date            8
    5  TERM        Numeric         4
    6  STYLE       Character      10
    7  PRICE       Numeric        14     2
    8  SQFT        Numeric        10
    9  BRS         Numeric         5
   10  BATHS       Numeric         5     1
   11  NOTES       Character      40
** Total **                     137
```

The LISTINGS database lists information about houses being sold by a real estate company.

Let's suppose you want to design a report called HOUSES for the LISTINGS database. First, open the LISTINGS database by issuing the command **USE LISTINGS**. Then, issue the command **MODIFY REPORT HOUSES**. After you issue the MODIFY REPORT command, dBASE will place you in the menu-driven report form system, and your screen will look like Figure 10-3. The Groups, Columns, and Locate selections on this menu are the tools that let you define and organize the data that is included in the report. The Options submenu lets you specify a page title for the report, define the page layout, and tell the printer to form feed before and/or after printing the report.

FIGURE 10-3

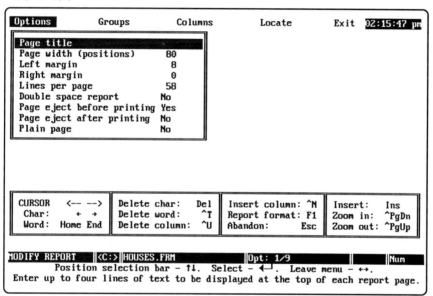

dBASE displays this menu system when you issue the CREATE REPORT or MODIFY REPORT command.

Printing Basics

As you can see, dBASE automatically selects the Options submenu when it enters the report form design system. The default values that dBASE assigns to the settings on the Options menu will create attractive reports on most printers. However, because the LaserJet cannot print in a small area around the edge of the page, these settings will produce an off-center report if used with the LaserJet.

As we mentioned in Chapter 1, every LaserJet printer is unable to print at the extreme top, bottom, left, and right edges of the page. This unprintable area occupies about $1/4$ inch on each edge of the page, and there is absolutely no way to make dBASE or any other software print in the unprintable area. The LaserJet also sets default margins that extend the unprintable area to cover the top and bottom $^1/_2$ inch of the page. The default margins and the unprintable area combined take up the first three and last three lines of the page and the first $2^1/_2$ and last $2^1/_2$ character spaces on each row.

It is the $2^1/_2$ characters that the LaserJet adds to the beginning of each row that move the report off the center of the page. Fortunately, this problem is easily fixed by changing the default settings.

As you can see in Figure 10-3, dBASE assigns a default Left margin setting of 8 character spaces to each new report form. Adding this margin to the $2^1/_2$ character spaces in the unprintable area creates an actual margin of $10^1/_2$ characters. Since the default Page width is 80 characters (this value includes both left and right margins), and the default Right margin is 0, a report printed on the LaserJet with these default settings seems to slide toward the right side of the page. Figure 10-4 shows the printed HOUSES report using dBASE's default settings. As you can see, the left margin is much wider than the right margin.

FIGURE 10-4

Using default page settings with the LaserJet produces an off-center report.

You can easily balance the left and right margins by decreasing the Left margin setting. The LaserJet will print a more balanced-looking report if you change the Left margin setting to 5. This new value, which is 3 less than the default margin, compensates for the $2^1/_2$ characters in the unprintable area along the left edge of the page. To change the Left margin setting, press the ↓ key until that setting is highlighted on the Options submenu, then press ↵ to lock onto the Left margin setting. After you press ↵, a triangle will appear next to the Left margin value, as shown in Figure 10-5, to indicate that you can now change that setting. To change the setting from 8 to 5, press ↓ three times, then press ↵ to save the new value.

Changing the default Left margin and Page width settings

FIGURE 10-5

Options	
Page title	Head Sta
Page width (positions)	80
Left margin	**▶ 8**
Right margin	0
Lines per page	58
Double space report	No
Page eject before printing	Yes
Page eject after printing	No
Plain page	No

The triangle indicates that you can now change the Left margin setting.

As a rule of thumb, always set the left margin to a value that is three characters less than the actual margin that you want to use on the page. For instance, if you want a $1/_2$-inch left margin (six characters with the Courier 12 font), then you should set the Left margin setting to 3.

If you change the left margin before you define the columns in the report, then you may also want to change either the default Page width setting (80 characters) or the default Right margin setting (0 characters). The page width includes both the left and right margins, as well as the columns that appear in the report. For instance, the default settings of 80 characters for the page width, 8 for the left margin, and 0 for the right margin leave you with 72 characters in which you can place columns of data. When you decrease the left margin without changing the other settings, you add the number of characters that you deleted from the margin to the number of characters that you can use for columns. Since the whole idea behind shrinking the Left margin setting is to balance it with the right margin, you'll probably want to add to the right margin the character spaces that you deleted from the left margin. You can do this in either of two ways. You can add the number of characters that you removed from the Left margin to the Right margin setting, or you can leave the Right margin setting at 0 and subtract from the page width the same number of characters that you deleted from the left margin.

For example, to make up for the three characters that we deleted from the left margin in the HOUSES report, you could change the page width from 80 to 77, or you could change the Right margin setting from 0 to 3. Either way, the actual left and right margins on the printed page will be closer to the same size, giving the report a more balanced look.

The Lines per page setting

Though the default Lines per page setting of 58 will work just fine in reports printed on the LaserJet, there is one thing that you should keep in mind about the Lines per page setting. While most printers print a maximum of 66 lines per page, the unprintable area along each edge of the page limits the LaserJet to a maximum of 60 lines per page. However, because dBASE prints one blank line at the top of each report page, the highest value that you should select for the Lines per page setting is 59. If you set the lines per page to a value greater than 59, the LaserJet will not break the pages in the report correctly.

Aligning the page

As with most other printers, you must make sure that the paper in the LaserJet is aligned at the top of a page before you send a report to be printed. The Options submenu gives you one tool to make sure that the paper in the LaserJet is aligned before dBASE sends the report to the printer, and another tool to make sure that the LaserJet ejects the last page of the report.

The Page eject before printing option tells dBASE to eject the current page in the LaserJet before it sends the report to the printer. If the Page eject before printing setting is Yes, then dBASE will automatically issue a form feed before sending the report to the LaserJet. If the Page eject before printing setting is No, then dBASE will send the report to the LaserJet without sending a form feed first. The default setting for Page eject before printing is Yes.

The Page eject after printing option determines whether dBASE ejects a page after the report is finished printing. The default setting is No, but we recommend changing it to Yes. If you leave the setting at No, the LaserJet will not eject the last page of a report unless every line of that page is filled with data. Unlike most printers, the LaserJet does not even begin printing a page that is only partially filled with data. Instead, the LaserJet leaves the blank page in the paper tray until the PC sends a form feed or additional data to the printer. You can tell when the LaserJet is holding data from a partially full page because the orange light above the FORM FEED key on the LaserJet's control panel will light up. To be sure you don't overlook the FORM FEED light and forget the last page of a report, we recommend changing the Page eject after printing setting to Yes in most cases. Later, we'll show you how to write dBASE programs that set up the LaserJet for specific reports, activating selected printing options. Since these programs automatically issue form feeds before and after printing a report, you will want to set both the Page eject before printing and the Page eject after printing to No for the reports that you print with these programs.

Since dBASE is a character-based product, it can display only fixed-space characters on your screen, and it expects your printer to use only fixed-space characters in printed reports. For this reason, you'll find it impractical to print dBASE reports with proportionally spaced fonts.

As we said in Chapter 4, the LaserJet's internal fonts include Courier 12 (Medium and Bold) and Line Printer Compressed. Both of these fonts look nice in dBASE reports. The LaserJet Series II contains these fonts in both Portrait and Landscape orientations, but the LaserJet and LaserJet Plus printers contain these fonts in Portrait orientation only. If you use one of the older LaserJet models, you will need to buy an additional font cartridge to print in Landscape orientation. The catalog in Apendix 2 lists HP's current font cartridge offerings. You should identify the fonts you need most, then select the cartridge or cartridges that best meet your needs.

Although it is possible to print dBASE reports using soft fonts that you have downloaded to your LaserJet, we do not recommend using soft fonts with dBASE. Most soft fonts are proportionally spaced and, for the reasons we stated above, do not work well with dBASE. Most of the fixed-space fonts that are available as soft fonts are also available in font cartridges.

To save a modified report form after you have changed the Left margin and any other Options settings, press ➜ four times to move to the Exit submenu, and then press ↵ to select the Save option. Now, you can print the report by issuing the command **REPORT FORM HOUSES TO PRINT**. Figure 10-6 on the following page shows the printed HOUSES report with the new left margin.

By default, the LaserJet uses the Courier 12 font. This font occupies six lines per inch vertically and ten characters per inch horizontally. However, the LaserJet can also print more lines per inch, print in boldface or italics, print in Portrait or Landscape orientation, and even print in completely different fonts. You can select one or more of the LaserJet's printing options by sending a setup string to the printer before you print the report. Setup strings consist of a series of escape codes and regular characters. The LaserJet interprets setup strings as instructions to change fonts, toggle the orientation, or turn various printing capabilities on and off.

The particular print options that are available to you depend on the LaserJet model you use and the fonts you have installed. The setup string doesn't import any special features; it simply turns existing features on and off. For example, you cannot use a setup string to create italic type unless you've installed a font cartridge or soft font that provides italic type. Table 4-2 on page 141 lists the built-in fonts for each LaserJet model, and the catalog in Appendix 2 lists the font options that are available for each printer.

Table 10-1 on pages 387-389 shows the common setup strings that you can use in dBASE to control LaserJet printers. All these strings have a similar form. All setup strings begin with CHR(27). The dBASE function CHR() converts a number into the character or keystroke that the number represents in the ASCII code system. Since the ASCII code for the [Esc] key is 27, CHR(27) represents this unprintable character, which is called an escape code. In addition to the introductory escape code, each setup string includes a series of characters, the last of which is a capital letter. For example, the string that activates boldface printing is CHR(27) + "(s3B", while the string that activates condensed printing is CHR(27) + "(s16.66H". When you send any setup string to the printer, you should type the appropriate string exactly as it appears in Table 10-1. Make sure to distinguish the number Ø from the letter O, and the number 1 from the letter *ℓ*. If you accidentally transpose these letters and numbers, your setup strings will not produce the expected results.

FIGURE 10-6

```
Page No.      1
09/22/88
                            Head Start Realty Company

                            Current Listings

Address                Town        Style        Bedrooms Baths      Price
---------------------  ----------  ----------   -------- -----  ------------

  123 Abby Ct.         Louisville  Ranch            3    1.0      32950.00
  426 St. James Ct.    Louisville  Ranch            2    1.0      19500.00
  766 Baird St.        Louisville  Colonial         4    2.5     139950.00
  222 Big Ben Dr.      Louisville  Other            3    1.5      53500.00
  666 Montana Ave.     Louisville  Cape Cod         3    1.0      55000.00
  589 Morocco Dr.      E'Town      Cape Cod         3    1.5      62500.00
  987 Allan Dr.        Louisville  Cape Cod         4    2.0      60000.00
  549 Billtown Rd.     Louisville  Ranch            3    2.0      72500.00
  343 Market St.       Louisville  Ranch            3    1.0      42900.00
  198 Main St.         J'Town      Other            3    1.0      27500.00
  885 Jefferson St.    J'Town      Ranch            3    1.0      55000.00
  913 Whitney Dr.      North Hill  Cape Cod         4    2.0      99500.00
  363 Dower Ct.        North Fork  Cape Cod         4    2.0     109000.00
  620 Windsong Ct.     Louisville  Colonial         6    3.5     250000.00
 4500 Hempstead Dr.    Louisville  Colonial         4    2.5     150000.00
 #6 Brandon Way        Louisville  Ranch            4    1.5      67000.00
 6610 Vermin Dr.       Louisville  Ranch            3    1.5      75000.00
  712 Clifton Ct.      Louisville  Ranch            3    1.0      30000.00
 5432 Miller Rd.       Louisville  Other            2    1.0      17500.00
 #12 Circle Ct.        Louisville  Other            2    1.0      10000.00
 1222 Dee Rd.          South Fork  Ranch            3    1.0      22950.00
  222 Earl Ave.        J'Town      Ranch            3    1.0      51000.00
 9827 Rowan St.        J'Town      Ranch            3    1.0      47950.00
 3355 Bank St.         J'Town      Ranch            3    1.0      37500.00
   77 Portland Ave.    North Hill  Ranch            3    1.0      20000.00
   99 Cardinal Hill Rd. North Hill Cape Cod         3    1.5      70000.00
 #10 Old Mill Rd.      Louisville  Ranch            3    1.5      75000.00
 5532 Mud Creek Dr.    Louisville  Ranch            2    1.0      12000.00
 4444 Normie Ln.       Louisville  Cape Cod         5    2.5     120000.00
 3498 Bold Rd.         Louisville  Colonial         5    3.5     275000.00
 #82 Rudd Rd.          Louisville  Cape Cod         4    2.0      88950.00
 6712 Shelby St.       Louisville  Ranch            4    2.0      92500.00
 7235 Shiloh Dr.       E'Town      Ranch            4    2.5      95000.00
 8989 Big D Ln.        South Fork  Ranch            2    1.0      17000.00
 1001 Spring St.       North Hill  Other            3    1.5      45000.00
 6935 Shiloh Dr.       E'Town      Cape Cod         3    2.0      81000.00
 4989 Adler Way        Louisville  Cape Cod         3    1.5      76500.00
 5678 Beech St.        Louisville  Cape Cod         3    1.5      65950.00
 #62 Billy Bone Ct.    Louisville  Ranch            3    1.0      34500.00
 3323 Mt. Holly Dr.    Louisville  Ranch            3    1.0      22100.00
 9909 Midway Rd.       Louisville  Ranch            3    2.0      61250.00
  435 Oxted Ln.        Louisville  Ranch            3    1.0      53790.00
   22 N. Ridge Ct.     Louisville  Colonial         5    3.0     200000.00
  654 Nora Ln.         Louisville  Cape Cod         3    1.0      40000.00
  659 Ridge Rd.        Louisville  Ranch            3    1.0      30000.00
   14 Short Rd.        Louisville  Ranch            3    1.0      52300.00
  721 Zabel Way        Louisville  Ranch            3    1.0      47950.00
  581 Yale Dr.         Louisville  Ranch            4    1.5      78000.00
```

Changing the Left margin setting centers the report on the page.

Table 10-1 also lists suggested Lines per page and Page width settings for the various setup strings. These numbers are the maximum values that you should enter on the Options submenu when designing a report form to be printed with the setup strings. The actual page lengths and widths that the LaserJet uses when you use the setup strings are greater than the settings listed in the table, but the listed values will produce the most attractive report possible.

TABLE 10-1

	Setup string	Lines per page	Page width
Portrait			
Letter-size paper			
60 lines per page			
10 cpi	CHR(27) + "E"	59	77
12 cpi	CHR(27) + "(sØp12H"	59	93
16.66 cpi	CHR(27) + "(s16.66H"	59	129
66 lines per page			
10 cpi	CHR(27) + "&ℓ7.27C"	65	77
12 cpi	CHR(27) + "&ℓ7.27C" + CHR(27) + "(sØp12H"	65	93
16.66 cpi	CHR(27) + "&ℓ7.27C" + CHR(27) + "(s16.66H"	65	129
89 lines per page			
10 cpi	CHR(27) + "&ℓ5.39C"	88	77
12 cpi	CHR(27) + "&ℓ5.39C" + CHR(27) + "(sØp12H"	88	93
16.66 cpi	CHR(27) + "&ℓ5.39C" + CHR(27) + "(s16.66H"	88	129
Legal-size paper (legal tray)			
78 lines per page			
10 cpi	CHR(27) + "E"	77	77
12 cpi	CHR(27) + "(sØp12H"	77	93
16.66 cpi	CHR(27) + "(s16.66H"	77	129
104 lines per page			
10 cpi	CHR(27) + "&ℓ8D"	103	77
12 cpi	CHR(27) + "&ℓ8D" + CHR(27) + "(sØp12H"	103	93
16.66 cpi	CHR(27) + "&ℓ8D" + CHR(27) + "(s16.66H"	103	129
150 lines per page			
16.66 cpi	CHR(27) + "&ℓ4.16C" + CHR(27) + "(s16.66H"	149	129

	Setup string	Lines per page	Page width
Portrait			
Legal-size paper (manual feed)			
78 lines per page			
10 cpi	CHR(27) + "&ℓ84p2H"	77	77
12 cpi	CHR(27) + "&ℓ84p2H" + CHR(27) + "(sØp12H"	77	93
16.66 cpi	CHR(27) + "&ℓ84p2H" + CHR(27) + "(s16.66H"	77	129
104 lines per page			
10 cpi	CHR(27) + "&ℓ84p2hØo8D"	103	77
12 cpi	CHR(27) + "&ℓ84p2hØo8D" + CHR(27) + "(sØp12H"	103	93
16.66 cpi	CHR(27) + "&ℓ84p2hØo8D" + CHR(27) + "(s16.66H"	103	129
150 lines per page			
16.66 cpi	CHR(27) + "&ℓ84p2hØo4.16C" + CHR(27) + "(s16.66H"	149	129
Landscape			
Letter-size paper			
45 lines per page			
10 cpi	CHR(27) + "&ℓ1O"	44	103
12 cpi	CHR(27) + "&ℓ1O" + CHR(27) + "(sØp12H"	44	124
16.66 cpi	CHR(27) + "&ℓ1O" + CHR(27) + "(s16.66H"	44	173
66 lines per page			
10 cpi	CHR(27) + "&ℓ1o5.45C"	65	103
12 cpi	CHR(27) + "&ℓ1o5.45C" + CHR(27) + "(sØp12H"	65	124
16.66 cpi	CHR(27) + "&ℓ1o5.45C" + CHR(27) + "(s16.66H"	65	173

	Setup string	Lines per page	Page width
Landscape			
Legal-size paper (legal tray)			
45 lines per page			
10 cpi	CHR(27) + "&ℓ1O"	44	133
12 cpi	CHR(27) + "&ℓ1O" + CHR(27) + "(sØp12H"	44	160
16.66 cpi	CHR(27) + "&ℓ1O" + CHR(27) + "(s16.66H"	44	223
66 lines per page			
10 cpi	CHR(27) + "&ℓ1o5.45C"	65	133
12 cpi	CHR(27) + "&ℓ1o5.45C" + CHR(27) + "(sØp12H"	65	160
16.66 cpi	CHR(27) + "&ℓ1o5.45C" + CHR(27) + "(s16.66H"	65	223
Legal-size paper (manual feed)			
45 lines per page			
10 cpi	CHR(27) + "&ℓ84p2h1O"	44	133
12 cpi	CHR(27) + "&ℓ84p2h1O" + CHR(27) + "(sØp12H"	44	160
16.66 cpi	CHR(27) + "&ℓ84p2h1O" + CHR(27) + "(s16.66H"	44	223
66 lines per page			
10 cpi	CHR(27) + "&ℓ84p2h1o5.45C"	65	133
12 cpi	CHR(27) + "&ℓ84p2h1o5.45C" + CHR(27) + "(sØp12H"	65	160
16.66 cpi	CHR(27) + "&ℓ84p2h1o5.45C" + CHR(27) + "(s16.66H"	65	223

You can use these common setup strings to activate your printer's special print features. The page width and page length values in this table represent the recommended settings for reports printed with the setup strings.

The easiest way to activate certain print options for a report is to use a ? command to send the correct setup string to the LaserJet before you print the report. The ? command advances the cursor to the next line of the screen or printer page and then displays the data defined in the command's argument. The command

? "Enter any value"

displays the string *Enter any value* on the next line of the screen or printer. The ?? command displays data beginning at the current cursor location without moving the cursor to the next line. For example, the command ?? "Enter any value" displays the string *Enter any value* on the screen beginning at the current cursor location.

Before you can use a ? command to send a setup string to the printer, you must issue a SET PRINT ON command. This command tells dBASE to send all displayed data to the printer as well as to the screen. If you don't issue a SET PRINT ON command before sending a setup string in a ? command, the string will appear on the screen but never make it to the printer. (The SET PRINT ON command actually affects all data except information displayed by @...SAY commands. We'll show you how to send @...SAY commands to the printer later in this chapter.)

Although you can issue the SET PRINT ON command and subsequent ? commands at the dot prompt, we recommend that you incorporate the commands into short programs for two reasons. After a SET PRINT ON command, dBASE sends everything that appears on the screen to the printer, including the commands that you enter through the keyboard. If you write a program that issues the commands for you, dBASE never displays the commands on the screen and, therefore, never sends them to the printer. Only the setup strings embedded in ? commands and the report that you want to print go to the printer. In addition, automating the commands that set up the LaserJet and the REPORT command that prints the report in a program can save you a great deal of time. Instead of typing one command to redirect data to the printer, another command to set up the printer, and another to print the report, type one command to run the program.

The Printer not ready prompt

All the sample programs that we present in this chapter send different types of setup strings to the LaserJet. Since the LaserJet needs a few moments to process some of these setup strings, dBASE will sometimes present you with the prompt *Printer not ready. Retry (Y/N)* when the sample program attempts to send more data to the LaserJet. It is important that you always respond to this prompt by pressing **Y**. If you press N, then the program will continue without trying again to send the data that did not reach the printer. If the program continues without sending that data, then the setup string will be incomplete, or some printed data will be lost.

Printing in Landscape

Setup strings are especially useful for changing the size and orientation of your printed reports. For example, Figure 10-7 shows the Options settings for a report based on the LISTINGS database. The report, called HOUSE2, is 100 characters wide. A report of this size would not fit on a letter-size ($8\frac{1}{2}$- by 11-inch) page in Portrait orientation, but it will fit on a letter-size page in Landscape orientation.

Before you can print in Landscape orientation, you need to make a few other changes to the report form's settings. As you can see in Figure 10-7, we've changed the Lines per page setting in the HOUSE2 report form to 44, the number of lines that fit on a page turned sideways. (The LaserJet actually prints up to 45 lines on a page in Landscape orientation, but, as we mentioned earlier, dBASE inserts a blank line at the top of each report.) Also, we changed the Page eject before printing setting to No because the program that sets up the LaserJet to print in Landscape orientation also forces form feeds before and after it sends the report to the printer. In addition, we decreased the Left margin setting to compensate for the unprintable area along the left edge of the page.

FIGURE 10-7

```
 Options 

 Page title              Head Sta
 Page width (positions)  100
 Left margin             5
 Right margin            0
 Lines per page          44
 Double space report     No
 Page eject before printing No
 Page eject after printing No
 Plain page              No
```

The page settings for this report form will fit nicely on a letter-size page in Landscape orientation.

Figure 10-8 shows the program that sets up the LaserJet and sends the report to the printer. We named the program HOUSE2 so that it would have the same name as the report form that it sends to the printer.

FIGURE 10-8

```
Edit: C:house2.prg                    Num
USE LISTINGS                                    <
SET PRINT ON                                    <
? CHR(27) + "E" + CHR(27) + "&l10"              <
REPORT FORM HOUSE2                              <
? CHR(27) + "E"                                 <
SET PRINT OFF                                   <
USE                                             <
```

The HOUSE2 program prints our sample report in Landscape orientation.

Let's look at each line of the program to see how it works. The first line uses the dBASE command USE to open the LISTINGS database in the current work area. The SET PRINT ON command on the second line tells dBASE to send all output to the printer, as well as to the screen.

The ? command on the third line of the program sends a setup string to the LaserJet. The setup string consists of two elements. The first element, CHR(27) + "E", resets the printer to its default settings. The LaserJet will automatically eject a page when it receives this reset command. Then, the second element, CHR(27) + "&ℓ1O", sets the LaserJet to print in Landscape orientation.

The command REPORT FORM HOUSE2 generates a report based on the HOUSE2 report form and sends it to the screen and the LaserJet. (The TO PRINT option is not necessary because dBASE is still sending all output to the printer.) When the LaserJet is finished printing the report, the next line of the program sends another reset command, again resetting the LaserJet to its default settings and forcing another form feed. Then, the sixth line tells dBASE to stop sending output to the printer, and the USE command on the final line of the program removes the LISTINGS database from the the work area.

To print a copy of the report defined in the HOUSE2 report form, all you have to do is play the HOUSE2 program by entering the command **DO HOUSE2** at the dot prompt. Figure 10-9 shows the first page of the printed report.

FIGURE 10-9

```
Page No.      1
09/22/88
                              Head Start Realty Company

                                  Current Listings

Address                Town        Style       Square Feet Bedrooms Baths        Price List Date
--------------------   ----------  ----------  ----------- -------- -----  ------------- ---------

   123 Abby Ct.        Louisville  Ranch          1500        3     1.0      32950.00 06/16/88
   426 St. James Ct.   Louisville  Ranch           950        2     1.0      19500.00 06/19/88
   766 Baird St.       Louisville  Colonial       2600        4     2.5     139950.00 06/22/88
   222 Big Ben Dr.     Louisville  Other          1900        3     1.5      53500.00 06/22/88
   666 Montana Ave.    Louisville  Cape Cod       1900        3     1.0      55000.00 06/23/88
   589 Morocco Dr.     E'Town      Cape Cod       1875        3     1.5      62500.00 06/24/88
   987 Allan Dr.       Louisville  Cape Cod       1900        4     2.0      60000.00 06/26/88
   549 Billtown Rd.    Louisville  Ranch          2000        3     2.0      72500.00 06/28/88
   343 Market St.      Louisville  Ranch          1675        3     1.0      42900.00 06/29/88
   198 Main St.        J'Town      Other           800        3     1.0      27500.00 06/29/88
   885 Jefferson St.   J'Town      Ranch          1500        3     1.0      55000.00 07/02/88
   913 Whitney Dr.     North Hill  Cape Cod       1800        4     2.0      99500.00 07/04/88
   363 Dower Ct.       North Fork  Cape Cod       2100        4     2.0     109000.00 07/05/88
   620 Windsong Ct.    Louisville  Colonial       4000        6     3.5     250000.00 07/06/88
  4500 Hempstead Dr.   Louisville  Colonial       2600        4     2.5     150000.00 06/18/88
    #6 Brandon Way     Louisville  Ranch          2250        4     1.5      67000.00 07/22/88
  6610 Vermin Dr.      Louisville  Ranch          2100        3     1.5      75000.00 07/24/88
   712 Clifton Ct.     Louisville  Ranch          1500        3     1.0      30000.00 07/24/88
  5432 Miller Rd.      Louisville  Other           800        2     1.0      17500.00 07/29/88
   #12 Circle Ct.      Louisville  Other           800        2     1.0      10000.00 08/02/88
  1222 Dee Rd.         South Fork  Ranch           950        3     1.0      22950.00 08/02/88
   222 Earl Ave.       J'Town      Ranch          1200        3     1.0      51000.00 08/05/88
  9827 Rowan St.       J'Town      Ranch          1100        3     1.0      47950.00 08/18/88
  3355 Bank St.        J'Town      Ranch          1500        3     1.0      37500.00 08/17/88
    77 Portland Ave.   North Hill  Ranch          1500        3     1.0      20000.00 08/19/88
    99 Cardinal Hill Rd. North Hill Cape Cod      2000        3     1.5      70000.00 08/19/88
   #10 Old Mill Rd.    Louisville  Ranch          2150        3     1.5      75000.00 08/21/88
  5532 Mud Creek Dr.   Louisville  Ranch           950        2     1.0      12000.00 08/24/88
  4444 Normie Ln.      Louisville  Cape Cod       2400        5     2.5     120000.00 08/25/88
  3498 Bold Rd.        Louisville  Colonial       3800        5     3.5     275000.00 08/29/88
   #82 Rudd Rd.        Louisville  Cape Cod       2800        4     2.0      88950.00 08/30/88
  6712 Shelby St.      Louisville  Ranch          2400        4     2.0      92500.00 08/30/88
  7235 Shiloh Dr.      E'Town      Ranch          2750        4     2.5      95000.00 08/31/88
  8989 Big D Ln.       South Fork  Ranch          1200        2     1.0      17000.00 09/01/88
```

The HOUSE2 program will print a report on letter-size paper in Landscape orientation.

Other sample reports

The HOUSE2 program can serve as a model for other programs that send different setup strings to the LaserJet. For example, suppose that you want to print a report that is wider than the HOUSE2 report. Figure 10-10 shows the page settings for such a report form. The settings for this report form, called HOUSE3, are identical to those for the HOUSE2 report form, except the Page width is 30 character spaces wider to accommodate field columns we added to the body of the report. This page width is too large for an $8^1/_2$- by 11-inch page, even in Landscape orientation. However, you could print the report in Landscape orientation on a legal-size page.

FIGURE 10-10

```
Options
┌─────────────────────────────────────────┐
│ Page title                    Head Sta   │
│ Page width (positions)        130        │
│ Left margin                   5          │
│ Right margin                  0          │
│ Lines per page                44         │
│ Double space report           No         │
│ Page eject before printing    No         │
│ Page eject after printing     No         │
│ Plain page                    No         │
└─────────────────────────────────────────┘
```

This HOUSE3 report form is too wide for Landscape printing on a letter-size page, but it will fit on a legal-size page.

Figure 10-11 shows a program called HOUSE3. In addition to changing the printing orientation to Landscape, the HOUSE3 program also sets the LaserJet to accept manually fed legal-size pages. When you run the HOUSE3 program, the LaserJet will display the message *PF FEED LEGAL*, indicating that you need to insert a legal-size page through the guides on top of the paper tray. Figure 10-12 on the following page shows the printed HOUSE3 report.

FIGURE 10-11

```
Edit: C:house3.prg                    Num
USE LISTINGS                                          <
SET PRINT ON                                          <
? CHR(27) + "E" + CHR(27) + "&l84p2h10"               <
REPORT FORM HOUSE3                                    <
? CHR(27) + "E"                                       <
SET PRINT OFF                                         <
USE                                                   <
```

The HOUSE3 program sets the LaserJet to print in Landscape orientation on legal-size pages.

By using the appropriate setup string, you can print a report even wider than the HOUSE3 report. Figure 10-13 on the next page shows the Options settings for another report form that includes additional fields from the LISTINGS database. This report form, called HOUSE4, has a Page width setting of 170. You can fit the HOUSE4 report on a letter-size page by printing in Landscape orientation with the compressed Line Printer font. Figure 10-14 on page 395 shows the HOUSE4 program, which installs the Line Printer font and changes the printing orientation to Landscape.

FIGURE 10-12

```
Page No.     1
09/22/88
                                          Head Start Realty Company

                                              Current Listings

Address              Town       Style        Square Feet Bedrooms Baths     Price Notes
-------------------- ---------- -----------  ----------- -------- -----  ------------- ----------------------------------------

  123 Abby Ct.       Louisville Ranch            1500      3      1.0      32950.00 New roof, carpet, remodeled kitchen
  426 St. James Ct.  Louisville Ranch             950      2      1.0      19500.00 Lovely all brick exterior
  766 Baird St.      Louisville Colonial         2600      4      2.5     139950.00 w/w carpet, built-ins
  222 Big Ben Dr.    Louisville Other            1900      3      1.5      53500.00
  666 Montana Ave.   Louisville Cape Cod         1900      3      1.0      55000.00 All brass plumbing
  589 Morocco Dr.    E'Town     Cape Cod         1875      3      1.5      62500.00 Upgrades throughout
  987 Allan Dr.      Louisville Cape Cod         1900      4      2.0      60000.00 Kitchenette alcove, new plush carpet
  549 Billtown Rd.   Louisville Ranch            2000      3      2.0      72500.00
  143 Market St.     Louisville Ranch            1675      3      1.0      42900.00 Pool
  198 Main St.       J'Town     Other             800      3      1.0      27500.00
  885 Jefferson St.  J'Town     Ranch            1500      3      1.0      55000.00 Security system
  913 Whitney Dr.    North Hill Cape Cod         1800      4      2.0      99500.00
  363 Dower Ct.      North Fork Cape Cod         2100      4      2.0     109000.00
  620 Windsong Ct.   Louisville Colonial         4000      6      3.5     250000.00 Lighted tennis court
 4500 Hempstead Dr.  Louisville Colonial         2600      4      2.5     150000.00 Fishing pond in front yard, tennis court
   #6 Brandon Way    Louisville Ranch            2250      4      1.5      67000.00 Lots of airport noise
 6610 Vermin Dr.     Louisville Ranch            2100      3      1.5      75000.00 Two car garage in basement
  712 Clifton Ct.    Louisville Ranch            1500      3      1.0      30000.00
 5432 Miller Rd.     Louisville Other             800      2      1.0      17500.00 Patio with adjoining redwood deck
  #12 Circle Ct.     Louisville Other             800      2      1.0      10000.00
 1222 Dee Rd.        South Fork Ranch             950      3      1.0      22950.00
  222 Earl Ave.      J'Town     Ranch            1200      3      1.0      51000.00 Hot tub built into patio
 9827 Rowan St.      J'Town     Ranch            1100      3      1.0      47950.00
 3355 Bank St.       J'Town     Ranch            1500      3      1.0      37500.00
   77 Portland Ave.  North Hill Ranch            1500      3      1.0      20000.00
   99 Cardinal Hill Rd. North Hill Cape Cod      2000      3      1.5      70000.00
  #10 Old Mill Rd.   Louisville Ranch            2150      3      1.5      75000.00
 5532 Mud Creek Dr.  Louisville Ranch             950      2      1.0      12000.00
 4444 Normie Ln.     Louisville Cape Cod         2400      5      2.5     120000.00
 3498 Bold Rd.       Louisville Colonial         3800      5      3.5     275000.00
  #82 Rudd Rd.       Louisville Cape Cod         2800      4      2.0      88950.00
 6712 Shelby St.     Louisville Ranch            2400      4      2.0      92500.00
 7235 Shiloh Dr.     E'Town     Ranch            2750      4      2.5      95000.00
 8989 Big D Ln.      South Fork Ranch            1200      2      1.0      17000.00
```

The HOUSE3 program prints a report that is centered on legal-size paper.

FIGURE 10-13

```
┌─────────┐
│ Options │
└─────────┘
┌──────────────────────────────────────────┐
│ Page title                     Head Sta   │
│ ▐Page width (positions)         170     ▌ │
│ Left margin                     5         │
│ Right margin                    0         │
│ Lines per page                  44        │
│ Double space report            No         │
│ Page eject before printing     No         │
│ Page eject after printing      No         │
│ Plain page                     No         │
└──────────────────────────────────────────┘
```

These are the Options settings for the HOUSE4 report.

Figure 10-15 shows the printed HOUSE4 report. As you can see, the compressed Line Printer font greatly increases the number of columns that you can fit on a page.

You could use the Line Printer font to print the HOUSE2 report shown in Figure 10-7 in Portrait rather than Landscape orientation, or, if you need to print an especially wide report, you could use the Line Printer font in Landscape orientation on a legal-size page. This combination of print options can accommodate reports up to 226 characters wide.

FIGURE 10-14

```
Edit: C:house4.prg                              Num
USE LISTINGS                                                    <
SET PRINT ON                                                   <
? CHR(27) + "E" + CHR(27) + "&l10" + CHR(27) + "(s0p16.66h8.5v0s0b0T"   <
REPORT FORM HOUSE4                                             <
? CHR(27) + "E"                                               <
SET PRINT OFF                                                  <
USE                                                           <
```

The HOUSE4 program uses the Line Printer font in Landscape orientation.

FIGURE 10-15

The HOUSE4 program prints a report in compressed type.

As you have seen, the LaserJet can print your reports in many different formats. The format and the setup string that you choose will depend as much on your personal preference as it does on the size of the report you are printing. We hope our examples will give you an idea of the options the LaserJet provides.

PRINTING LABELS

Many people use dBASE to manage mailing lists and to print mailing labels. Just as the CREATE REPORT and MODIFY REPORT commands let you design report forms, the CREATE LABEL and MODIFY LABEL commands let you create label forms that format data for output as printed labels. The latter two commands have the same function. Either command will let you modify an existing label form for the current database or create a new label form if the specified form does not exist. The commands also have the same syntax:

CREATE LABEL *<report form>*
MODIFY LABEL *<report form>*

When you issue either of these commands, dBASE presents the menu system shown in Figure 10-16. The main menu has three selections: Options, Contents, and Exit. When you highlight the Contents selection, dBASE presents a column of blank lines, one for each line on the label that you are using. You can then fill the lines with the names of fields from the active database or literal strings enclosed in quotation marks. Your dBASE III Plus manual includes detailed instructions on defining label contents.

FIGURE 10-16

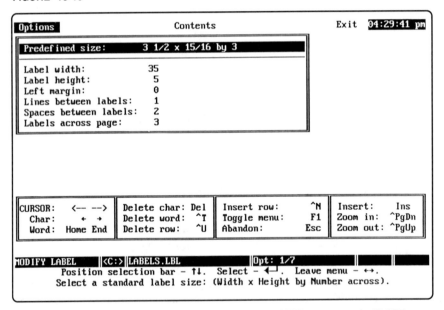

When you issue the CREATE LABEL or MODIFY LABEL command, dBASE
presents this menu system.

When you highlight the Options selection, dBASE presents a submenu with settings that describe the labels you are using. The Options submenu lets you specify the width and height of each label, the left margin on the label page, the number of lines and spaces between labels, and the number of labels in each row across the page. The Options submenu also includes a Predefined size selection that lets you set all the label dimensions by choosing one of five common types of mailing labels. If you want to print labels on an HP LaserJet, you will not be able to use any of the Predefined size settings. Even if you use one of the five predefined label sizes, you'll need to change some of the label dimension settings.

Label Problems

Printing labels is much more difficult with a LaserJet than with most printers. When dBASE begins printing labels, it assumes that you have aligned the page in the printer at the top of a label. Of course, you can use vertical positioning commands to set the LaserJet to begin printing on any line on the page. However, dBASE also assumes that every two rows of labels are the same number of lines apart. For instance, suppose you specify a Lines between labels setting of 1. In this case, dBASE assumes that it should skip one line after finishing a label in order to position the printer at the first line of the next label, whether the new label is at the beginning, middle, or end of the page. This logic works on most printers because they process pages of labels as continuous forms. However, the unprintable area around the edge of the LaserJet's page prevents the printer from being able to print on every label on the page. Even if you use a vertical placement command to align the first label printed, the LaserJet will not print the entire last label on the page if part of that label is in the unprintable area. The LaserJet will print any lines left over from the last label at the top of the next page, probably in the bottom half of a label whose top half is in the unprintable area.

The only solution to the problem is to use a setup string to redefine the logical page on which the LaserJet can print. This new page should exclude any row of labels completely or partially covered by the unprintable area. The new page must include every line on all the labels that are a part of the page. As a result, the number of lines on this logical page will be a multiple of the number of lines on each label. Since this new page begins and ends with a row of complete labels, dBASE will move from one page of labels to the next without splitting the data on the last labels of the first page.

An Example Setup String

Let's suppose that you want to print on labels that are 1 inch high by $2^7/_8$ inches wide (six lines of 28 characters each, with the LaserJet's default font and Vertical Motion Index). Labels this size are usually arranged three across and 11 deep on each page. Figure 10-17 shows a page of these labels. Since about half of the top row of labels on each page is in the unprintable area, you'll want the top margin to completely exclude this row of labels from the logical page. The area where the LaserJet can print should begin with the second row of labels. Since the last row on the page also partially occupies the unprintable area, the new logical page should end with the second-to-last row of labels. Removing the first and last row from the physical page leaves nine rows of labels on the LaserJet's logical page. Since each label is six lines high, the page length of the logical page is 54 lines.

FIGURE 10-17

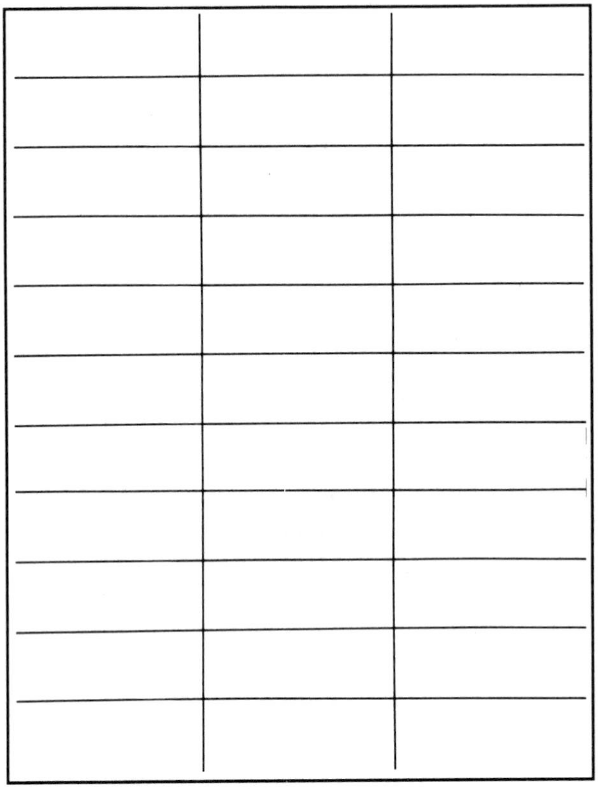

The top and bottom rows on this page of commonly used mailing labels would be excluded from the logical page.

The setup string that sets the LaserJet's top margin has the form

CHR(27) + "&ℓ#E"

where the # value equals the number of the first line on which the LaserJet will print. The setup string that sets the number of lines on the LaserJet's logical page is

CHR(27) + "&ℓ#F"

where the # value equals the number of lines on the logical page.

In this case, the second row of labels begins on the fourth line of the LaserJet's printable area. (You'll probably have to experiment a little to determine the correct top margin if you use a different size label.) The setup string that sets the top margin to begin printing on line 4 is

CHR(27) + "&ℓ4E"

The setup string that sets the number of lines in the logical page to 54 is

CHR(27) + "&ℓ54F"

You can combine these two setup strings into a single setup string

CHR(27) + "&ℓ4e54F"

which tells the LaserJet to print on a logical page that begins on line 4 and is 54 lines long.

Formatting the labels

Before you can use the setup string to print labels, you need to create a label form defining the format for the labels. For this example, we'll print labels based on names and addresses in a database called NAMELIST. Figure 10-18 shows the structure for the NAMELIST database. To design a label form called ELEVNROW for the NAMELIST database, you must first issue the command **USE NAMELIST** to open the database in the current work area, then issue the command **MODIFY LABEL ELEVNROW.** Assuming that you've used the Contents selection of the label form design system to format the names and addresses in the NAMELIST database on the first four lines of each label, let's look at the label dimensions that you should specify under the Options submenu.

FIGURE 10-18

```
. USE NAMELIST
. DISPLAY STRUCTURE
Structure for database: C:NAMELIST.dbf
Number of data records:      33
Date of last update   : 08/15/88
Field  Field Name  Type      Width    Dec
    1  FIRST_NAME  Character    15
    2  LAST_NAME   Character    15
    3  ADDRESS     Character    20
    4  CITY        Character    15
    5  STATE       Character     2
    6  ZIP         Character    10
** Total **                    78
```

The NAMELIST database has this structure.

There are a few things you should keep in mind when you are entering the dimensions for labels that you will print on the LaserJet. First of all, the unprintable area will prevent the LaserJet from printing in the first $2^1/_2$ character spaces of the first column of labels on each page. Therefore, the actual printing space of these labels is $2^1/_2$ characters less than the width of the label. To prevent material from the first row of labels from spilling over onto the second row of labels, we recommend using a Label width setting that is 3 less than the width of the label. To compensate for this subtraction in the spacing between labels, we recommend adding 3 to the Spaces between labels setting.

For some reason, the LaserJet will not print the last line of the logical page when it is printing labels. To prevent dBASE from losing the last line of the last label on each page, you should enter a value of at least 1 for the Lines between labels setting, even if there are no lines between the labels you are using. Setting Lines between labels to a value greater than 0 ensures that the lost line at the bottom of the page will be a blank line between labels rather than a line of data.

Figure 10-19 shows the Options settings that we recommend for the 1-inch by $2^7/_8$-inch labels that we are using in our example. Although the labels are 28 character spaces wide, we advise using a Label width setting of 25 characters, with a Spaces between labels setting of 3. In addition, even though the labels are six lines in height with no lines between labels, we advise using a Label height setting of 5, with a Lines between labels setting of 1. The Labels across page setting is 3.

To save the ELEVNROW label form after you have entered the Options settings, press → twice to select the Exit option on the main menu, and then press ↵ to select the Save option from the Exit submenu.

FIGURE 10-19

Options

Predefined size:	3 1/2 x 15/16 by 3
Label width:	25
Label height:	5
Left margin:	0
Lines between labels:	1
Spaces between labels:	3
Labels across page:	3

These are the recommended Options settings for 1-inch by $2^7/_8$-inch labels.

Writing the setup program

After creating the label form, you are ready to write a program that sets up the LaserJet and sends the labels to the printer. Figure 10-20 shows a program called ELEVNROW. The ELEVNROW program works just like the report setup programs that we discussed earlier in this chapter. The program sends a setup string that sets the top line of the LaserJet's logical page to the first line of the second row of labels. The setup string also sets the length of the logical page to 54 lines, then the program sends the labels to the LaserJet and resets the printer after it has finished printing the labels.

FIGURE 10-20

```
Edit: C:elevnrow.prg                              Num
USE NAMELIST                                                    <
SET PRINT ON                                                    <
? CHR(27) + "E" + CHR(27) + "&l4e54F"                           <
LABEL FORM ELEVNROW                                             <
? CHR(27) + "E"                                                 <
SET PRINT OFF                                                   <
USE                                                             <
```

The ELEVNROW program sets up the printer, prints the labels, and resets the printer after it has finished.

If you load the LaserJet with the labels and issue the command **DO ELEVNROW**, the LaserJet will eject one page of blank labels (when dBASE sends the first reset string), and then print the labels. Figure 10-21 on the following page shows one page of the printed labels.

Using Forms to Print on Envelopes

The LaserJet is capable of printing addresses directly on envelopes, which you can load either with an envelope tray or manually through the paper guides on top of the printer's regular paper tray. With the correct setup string, you can use a label form to print addresses from a database on envelopes fed either manually or with an envelope tray.

Designing a label form for envelopes

The key to using a label form to print on envelopes is designing a form that includes only one label on each page and sending the LaserJet a setup string that makes the printer treat each envelope as a separate logical page. This setup string must define the logical page in a way that ensures the LaserJet will place each address in the correct location on the envelope.

Figure 10-22 shows the Options settings for a sample label form designed for printing on envelopes. This label form is called, appropriately enough, ENVE-LOPE. As you can see, the Labels across page setting for the ENVELOPE label form is 1. The Label width setting of 40 provides ample room for any line of data that you might want to print, and the Label height setting of 5 gives you up to five lines for each address. The Lines between labels setting is 1 to prevent the LaserJet from losing the last line of the address. As we mentioned, the LaserJet does not print the last line on each page. Since the LaserJet will treat each envelope as a separate page, it will not print the last line on each envelope. Making that last line a line between labels causes the printer to lose that blank line, rather than an actual line of data.

FIGURE 10-21

Don Ripley 1234 Elm St. Louisville, KY 40214	Joe Johnson 2345 Smokey Rd. Elizabethtown, KY 40898	Joe Smith 776 3rd St. Louisville, KY 40213
Mark Pierce 7823 Glue Rd. Louisville, KY 40222	Doug King 9876 Majecsty Ct. Shively, KY 040216	Tom Nottingham 3248 Sherwood Dr. St. Matthews, KY 40442
Steve McDaniel 2354 2nd St. Louisville, KY 40214	Tony Robey 1256 Lambert Ct. Louisville, KY 40218	Frank Miozza 8766 Clarks Ln. Louisville, KY 40213
Jack Metzmeier 234 Mary Lou Ct. Shively, Ky 40216	Raquel Lampley 8725 Grant Dr. Floyds Knobs, IN 47119	Mary Jane Wren 8687 Ham Rd. Louisville, KY 40222
Susan Smith 1248 Jones Rd. New Albany, IN 47150	Jerry Montano 2368 Jamestown Rd. St. Matthews, KY 40224	Joe Crane 7230 Grape Vine Dr. Louisville, KY 40218
Danny Metcalf 5400 Rolling Rdg Rd. Louisville, KY 40214	John Drees 896 Pulaski Ct. Louisville, KY 40217	Victor Koslowski 823 Reed Ave. Louisville, KY 40212
Jan Embry 9347 Furman Rd. Louisville, KY 40224	Dan Blake 8463 Strathmoor Blvd Louisville, KY 40223	Marty Ryan 8277 Whipps Mill Rd. St. Matthews, KY 40224
Steve Yocom 8238 Hauser Ave Shively, KY 40223	Beth Fitsimmons Rt. 2, Box 345-J Floyds Knobs, IN 47119	James Beck 8984 Catfish Rd. New Albany, IN 47150
Steve Young 255 Baker St. Louisville, KY 40213	Joe Drake 8923 Mallard Dr. Gooseville, KY 40289	Jim Flannegan 845 Green St. Shively, KY 40216

We printed these labels with the ELEVNROW program.

FIGURE 10-22

```
Options
```

Predefined size:	4 x 1 7/16 by 1
Label width:	40
Label height:	5
Left margin:	0
Lines between labels:	1
Spaces between labels:	0
Labels across page:	1

The Options settings for the ENVELOPE form create a label format you can use to print envelopes.

The setup string you'll use to print envelopes with dBASE depends on the method you'll use to feed envelopes into the printer. First, we'll show you a program that prints envelopes with an envelope tray. Then, we'll show you how to modify that program to print envelopes without an envelope tray.

The setup program for an envelope tray

When you insert the envelope tray into the LaserJet, the printer automatically displays its Envelope size setting and gives you the opportunity to change that setting if it does not match the type of envelope you have loaded in the tray. The LaserJet is capable of printing on four sizes of envelopes: Business, Letter, International DL, and International C5. Chapter 2 includes detailed instructions on how to set the envelope size when you load the printer with envelopes.

Since you specify the envelope size when you load the paper tray, there is no need to set the envelope size again in the setup string. (The setup string will need to set the envelope size if you feed the envelopes manually, as we'll explain later.) However, even if you use an envelope tray, you need to send a setup string that sets the printing orientation to Landscape and defines a logical page that will place your address on the envelope correctly. To define this logical page, the setup string must set a top margin and a left margin that place the first character correctly on the envelope. The new logical page should also have a page length that is equal to the total number of lines (including blank lines between labels) specified in the label form that you will use to print the envelopes.

Figure 10-23 shows a program called ENVELOPE that sets the LaserJet to print in Landscape orientation on the logical page that we described above. In addition to the page formatting commands that set the print orientation, top margin, and page length, the setup string in the ENVELOPE program also uses the setup string CHR(27) + "&a42L" to set the left margin of the page.

FIGURE 10-23

```
Edit: C:envelope.prg                    Num
USE NAMELIST                                              <
SET PRINT ON                                             <
? CHR(27) + "E" + CHR(27) + "&l1o8e6F" + CHR(27) + "&a42L"  <
LABEL FORM ENVELOPE                                      <
? CHR(27) + "E"                                          <
SET PRINT OFF                                            <
USE                                                     <
                                                        <
```

The ENVELOPE program prints envelopes loaded in an envelope tray.

When you run the ENVELOPE program by issuing the **DO ENVELOPE** command, the LaserJet will eject one blank envelope (due to the program's reset command) and then print as many envelopes as remain in the envelope tray. Figure 10-24 shows an envelope printed by the ENVELOPE program. If the tray empties before the LaserJet finishes printing all the envelopes, you can reload the tray and continue printing by pressing **Y** at the *Printer not ready. Retry (Y/N)* prompt.

FIGURE 10-24

The ENVELOPE program prints envelopes that look like this.

The ENVELOPE program sets the LaserJet to print addresses on business-size envelopes. If you use a different size, you will have to adjust the values in the program's setup string to make the logical page fit the size of the envelopes you are using. Making this adjustment may require a little experimentation, but it should not prove to be much trouble if you use the same basic format of the ENVELOPE program in your setup program.

Printing envelopes without an envelope tray

The MANFEED program shown in Figure 10-25 (a slightly modified version of the ENVELOPE program) uses the ENVELOPE label form to print addresses on manually fed envelopes. The MANFEED program adds two elements to the setup string in the ENVELOPE program. Since you don't manually set the LaserJet's envelope type if you load the envelopes manually, the setup string in the MANFEED program sets the envelope type for you with the setup string CHR(27) + "&ℓ81A". This setup string sets the envelope size to business size. Table 10-2 shows the setup strings for the four sizes of envelopes on which the LaserJet is capable of printing.

FIGURE 10-25

```
Edit: C:manfeed.prg                              Num
USE NAMELIST                                                    <
SET PRINT ON                                                    <
? CHR(27) + "E" + CHR(27) + "&l81a2h1o8e6F" + CHR(27) + "&a42L" <
LABEL FORM ENVELOPE                                             <
? CHR(27) + "E"                                                 <
SET PRINT OFF                                                   <
USE                                                            <
                                                              <
                                                              <
```

The MANFEED program prints on manually fed envelopes.

TABLE 10-2

Envelope Name	Size	Setup string
Letter	$3^7/_8$" x $7^1/_2$"	CHR(27) + "&ℓ80A"
Business	$4^1/_8$" x $9^1/2$"	CHR(27) + "&ℓ81A"
International DL	110mm x 220mm	CHR(27) + "&ℓ90A"
International C5	162mm x 229mm	CHR(27) + "&ℓ91A"

These are the setup strings you use to set the LaserJet's envelope size.

The setup string in the MANFEED program also sets the LaserJet for manual paper feed with the setup string CHR(27) + "2H". When you run the MANFEED program by issuing the command **DO MANFEED**, the LaserJet will eject one page from the paper tray and then display the message *PF FEED COM-10*. Since COM-10 represents a business-size envelope, this message means that you should adjust the paper guide on top of the paper tray and feed the printer a business-size envelope. Be sure to feed each envelope into the printer face up, with the left edge of the envelope facing away from the printer. After the LaserJet prints the first envelope, it will display the message *PF FEED COM-10* again until you feed another envelope. This process will continue until the LaserJet has printed an envelope for each record in the NAMELIST database. Actually, the last envelope that you insert into the LaserJet will come out blank because the printer will eject it when the MANFEED program sends the last reset command. After the LaserJet resets to its default settings and ejects the blank envelope, the printer will display the message *ØØ READY* (or simply *ØØ* if you have a LaserJet Plus).

dBASE PROGRAMS

dBASE report forms and label forms are handy tools for printing information in your databases, but both are limited in the flexibility they provide in formatting your data. As you become more experienced with dBASE, you will probably begin to write more complex programs to format your data on printed pages. We don't have room in this chapter to cover the basics of dBASE programming, but we will offer a few programming tips that will help you take advantage of the LaserJet's capabilities in your programs.

Embedded Setup Strings

The dBASE command @...SAY displays data at a specified position on the screen or current page. @...SAY commands have the syntax

@*row,col* SAY *<expression>*

where the *row* value defines a screen or printer row, and the *col* value specifies a column on the page or screen. An @...SAY command moves the cursor to the page or screen position specified by these coordinates and then displays the expression defined in the command. This expression can be a number, a string, a memory variable, or a database field. By default, dBASE sends data in @...SAY commands to the screen. You can tell dBASE to direct this data to the printer by issuing the command **SET DEVICE TO PRINT.** The command SET DEVICE TO SCREEN tells dBASE to resume sending @...SAY commands to the screen only.

By embedding setup strings in @...SAY commands, you can tell the LaserJet to turn various print features on and off while printing anywhere on the page. Italic printing, underlining, and bold printing are among the features that you can turn on and off with embedded setup strings. Table 10-3 shows several setup strings that activate and deactivate some commonly used print features.

TABLE 10-3

Feature	Setup string
Underline On	CHR(Ø27) + "&dD"
Underline Off	CHR(Ø27) + "&d@"
Boldface On	CHR(Ø27) + "(s3B"
Boldface Off	CHR(Ø27) + "(sØB"
Italic On	CHR(Ø27) + "(s1S"
Italic Off	CHR(Ø27) + "(sØS"
Printer Reset	CHR(Ø27) + "E"

You might want to embed these setup strings in your dBASE programs.

To embed a setup string in an @...SAY command, simply use a + sign to insert the setup string in the printed data as you would insert any other string. Figure 10-26 shows a program called PRNTEST that demonstrates the use of embedded setup strings.

FIGURE 10-26

```
Edit: C:prntest.prg                          Num
*** PRNTEST:  Using embedded setup strings                      <
SET DEVICE TO PRINT                                             <
@0,0 SAY CHR(27) + "E"                                          <
@1,4 SAY "dBASE says to " + CHR(27) + "(s3B" + "boldface" +
CHR(27) + "(s0B" + " this word."                               <
@3,4 SAY "dBASE says to " + CHR(27) + "&dD" + "underline" +
CHR(27) + "&d@" + " this word."                                <
@5,4 SAY "dBASE says to " + CHR(27) + "(s1S" + "italicize" + CHR(27) + "(s0S"
+ " this word."                                                <
@6,0 SAY CHR(27) + "E"                                         <
SET DEVICE TO SCREEN                                           <
                                                               <
```

The PRNTEST program uses setup strings to turn print features on and off in the middle of printed sentences.

The PRNTEST program first issues a SET DEVICE TO PRINT command to tell dBASE to send data from the program's @...SAY commands to the printer. Next, the program uses the command @0,0 SAY CHR(27) + "E" to send a reset command to the LaserJet.

The program then sends the string *dBASE says to **boldface** this word.* to the printer, using an @...SAY command to place the first character of the string on the first line and fourth column of the page. The program activates the bold printing feature by sending the appropriate setup string just after the last blank space in the string *dBASE says to* that is included in the @1,4 SAY command. After the program sends the string **boldface** to the printer, it sends a setup string to turn bold printing off before sending the rest of the sentence. The rest of the program uses the same method to activate underlining and italic printing in the middle of two other sentences. After the program prints all three sentences, it sends the printer another reset command, which resets the printer's default settings and ejects the page. Figure 10-27 shows the page printed by the PRNTEST program.

FIGURE 10-27

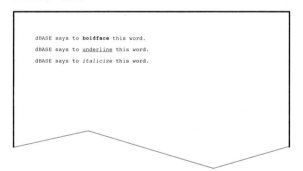

dBASE says to **boldface** this word.
dBASE says to <u>underline</u> this word.
dBASE says to *italicize* this word.

The PRNTEST program prints this page.

You can set off large blocks of text on a printed page by activating a print feature with an @...SAY command, and then leaving the feature turned on while subsequent @...SAY commands print data on several lines. Figure 10-28 shows a program called ITALICS. The @...SAY command on the third line of the ITALICS program positions the cursor at the fifth row and fourth column on the page, then prints the string *dBASE says to italicize the next two lines.* The next @...SAY command in the program moves the cursor down two lines on the page, sends the setup string to turn italic printing on, and then prints the string *That includes this line....* The next @...SAY command moves the cursor to the next line on the page and prints the string *...and this line too.* Since the @...SAY command that turns italic printing on does not turn it off, the LaserJet should print both of these lines in italics. Then, another @...SAY command moves the cursor two more lines down the page, turns italic printing off and prints the string *Now, it's back to normal print.*

Setting off large blocks of text

FIGURE 10-28

```
Edit: C:italics.prg                          Ins
*** PRNTEST:  Using embedded setup strings                        <
SET DEVICE TO PRINT                                               <
@0,0 SAY CHR(27) + "E"                                            <
@5,4 SAY "dBASE says to italicize the next two lines."           <
@7,4 SAY CHR(27) + "(s1S" + "That includes this line..."         <
@8,4 SAY "...and this line too."                                 <
@10,4 SAY CHR(27) + "(s0S" + "Now, it's back to normal print."   <
@11,0 SAY CHR(27) + "E"                                           <
SET DEVICE TO SCREEN                                             <
                                                                 <
```

The ITALICS program prints two lines of text in Italics.

Figure 10-29 shows the page that the LaserJet prints when you run the ITALICS program. As you can see, the LaserJet prints both the second and third lines of text in italics.

FIGURE 10-29

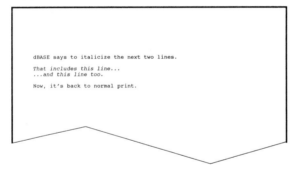

The ITALICS program prints this page.

The underlining problem

Although you can leave most print features activated for several @...SAY commands, any @...SAY command that turns underlining on should also turn that feature off. If you don't turn underlining off before the end of the @...SAY command, dBASE will underline the entire line that the next @...SAY command prints, even if the *col* value in the command positions the cursor in the middle of the line. Figure 10-30 shows a program called MISTAKE that uses several @...SAY commands to print two lines of text. The program uses one @...SAY command to print the string *dBASE says to*, uses another command to send the "underline on" setup string, and then uses another command to print the string *underline the rest of this line....* Then, without turning underlining off, another @...SAY command moves the cursor down a line on the page and sends the string *...and the next line too.* The last @...SAY command in the program sends a reset command to the LaserJet, which turns off underlining and forces a form feed.

FIGURE 10-30

```
Edit: C:mistake.prg                         Ins
*** PRNTEST:  Using embedded setup strings                          <
SET DEVICE TO PRINT                                                 <
@0,0 SAY CHR(27) + "E"                                              <
@3,4 SAY "dBASE says to "                                           <
@3,18 SAY CHR(27) + "&dD"                                           <
@3,18 SAY "underline the rest of this line..."                     <
@4,4 SAY "...and the next line too."                               <
@5,0 SAY CHR(27) + "&d@"                                            <
@6,0 SAY CHR(27) + "E"                                             <
SET DEVICE TO SCREEN                                                <
                                                                   <
```

The MISTAKE program leaves the underline feature turned on between @...SAY commands.

Figure 10-31 shows the page that the MISTAKE program produces. As you can see, the underlining for both lines of text begins in column 0, the first column on the page, even though the two @...SAY commands positioned the cursor in different columns before sending underlined data to the LaserJet. This quirk is not unique to the LaserJet; dBASE affects the underlining capabilities of all printers in this manner. However, you can avoid the problem by turning the underline feature off in every @...SAY command that turns the feature on.

FIGURE 10-31

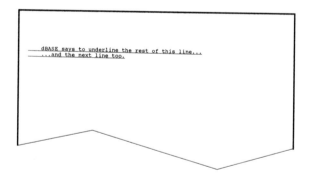

The MISTAKE program prints this page.

Most of the problems you will encounter while using setup strings in dBASE programs will probably result from typographical errors in the setup strings. As we said earlier, setup strings must be entered in precisely the correct form for them to work as expected. You can reduce the chances of a typing error in setup strings in your programs by saving the setup strings in memory variables. After you save a setup string in a variable, you can send the setup string to the LaserJet by including the variable in an @...SAY command (or a PRINT command) directed to the printer.

Saving setup strings in variables

For example, you can save the LaserJet's reset command setup string in the variable *lj_reset* with this command:

lj_reset = CHR(27) + "E"

Then, as long as the *lj_reset* variable remains in memory, you can reset the LaserJet by sending this command to the printer:

@0,0 SAY lj_reset

You can initialize several variables as setup strings at the beginning of your program, and then use these variables in the program whenever you want to send one of the setup strings to the printer. However, it is usually more efficient to write one program that stores several setup strings in variables and then uses a SAVE command to save the variables in a memory file. Then, you can use a RESTORE command in another program to restore all the "setup variables" into memory.

For example, Figure 10-32 shows a program called LJ_VARS, which stores several setup strings in memory variables. As you can see, each variable name begins with the letters *lj* (for LaserJet). The rest of the variable name describes what the setup string does. For example, the variable that turns on the underline feature is named *lj_ul_on*. After the program stores the setup strings in the variables, the command SAVE ALL LIKE lj* TO LJ_VARS saves all variables that begin with the letters *lj* to a memory file called LJ_VARS. The last command in the program releases all the setup variables from memory.

FIGURE 10-32

```
Edit: C:lj_vars.prg                              Num
*** LJ_VARS:  Saving setup strings in variables          <
*                                                         <
* Underline setup strings                                 <
   lj_ul_on = CHR(27) + "&dD"                             <
   lj_ul_off = CHR(27) + "&d@"                            <
* Boldface setup strings                                  <
   lj_bf_on = CHR(27) + "(s3B"                            <
   lj_bf_off = CHR(27) + "(s0B"                           <
* Italic setup strings                                    <
   lj_ita_on = CHR(27) + "(s1S"                           <
   lj_ita_off = CHR(27) + "(s0S"                          <
* Printer reset string                                    <
   lj_reset = CHR(27) + "E"                               <
SAVE ALL LIKE lj* TO LJ_VARS                              <
RELEASE ALL LIKE lj*
```

The LJ_VARS program saves setup strings as variables in a memory file.

Figure 10-33 shows a modified version of the PRNTEST program that restores the setup variables from the LJ_VARS memory file and then uses the variables to activate bold, underlining, and italic printing. The new program, called PRNTEST2, prints a page like the one shown in Figure 10-27 (the page produced by the PRNTEST program). The only difference between the two programs is that the PRNTEST2 program replaces all the setup strings in the PRNTEST program with memory variables. When PRNTEST2 finishes printing the three sentences, the last command in the program releases all the setup variables from memory.

FIGURE 10-33

```
Edit: C:prntest2.prg                    Ins    Num
*** PRNTEST3:  Using variables as embedded setup strings          <
*                                                                 <
RESTORE FROM LJ_VARS                                              <
SET DEVICE TO PRINT                                               <
@0,0 SAY lj_reset                                                 <
@1,4 SAY "dBASE says to " + lj_bf_on + "boldface" + lj_bf_off
+ " this word."                                                   <
@3,4 SAY "dBASE says to " + lj_ul_on + "underline" + lj_ul_off
+ " this word."                                                   <
@5,4 SAY "dBASE says to " + lj_ita_on + "italicize" + lj_ita_off
+ " this word."                                                   <
@6,0 SAY lj_reset                                                 <
SET DEVICE TO SCREEN                                              <
RELEASE ALL LIKE lj*                                              <
```

The PRNTEST2 program uses memory variables as setup strings.

dBASE IV

As *LaserJet Companion* went to press, Ashton-Tate was developing a new version of dBASE, called dBASE IV. We expect this new version to enhance dBASE's ability to take advantage of the LaserJet's full range of printing capabilities. Although this book was printed before technical details on dBASE IV were available, The Cobb Group is planning to publish *LaserJet Companion TechNotes for dBASE IV*—a special publication full of tips and suggestions to help you maximize dBASE IV's printing capabilities with the HP LaserJet printer. If you are interested in learning how dBASE IV works with a LaserJet, contact The Cobb Group at the address listed in the front of this book.

CONCLUSION

You can access many of the Hewlett-Packard LaserJet's printing capabilities with dBASE III Plus, but it is rarely easy. With a little bit of work and experimentation, you can use the LaserJet to produce attractive dBASE reports and mailing labels. We've given you dozens of tips that should help you take advantage of the LaserJet's capabilities with dBASE III Plus. As your dBASE programming expertise grows, so will your ability to take full advantage of your HP LaserJet.

VENTURA PUBLISHER 11

Ventura Publisher is a powerful desktop publishing package that provides an exceptional level of support for the HP LaserJet. In this chapter, we'll show you how to install Ventura Publisher for use with standard and PostScript-equipped Laser-Jets. Once we've done that, we'll show you the procedures you must follow to install the various fonts that Ventura Publisher supports. Finally, we'll explain how to print a document with Ventura Publisher and the LaserJet.

The process of installing LaserJet support for Ventura Publisher is automated by a program called VPPREP. If you have not previously installed Ventura Publisher on your hard disk, you can use VPPREP to install LaserJet support as you install the main program. Likewise, if you have previously used VPPREP to install Ventura Publisher, you can use VPPREP to add LaserJet support to the installed version of the program.

INSTALLING LASERJET SUPPORT

VPPREP is shipped on Ventura Publisher Application Disk #1. To run VPPREP, place Application Disk #1 in drive A, type **VPPREP** at the DOS prompt, and press ↵.

Running VPPREP

VPPREP will immediately prompt you to enter the letter that identifies your hard disk, then ask you if you are installing a particular version of Ventura Publisher for the first time. If you are, you should respond by typing **Y**. If you have previously installed Ventura Publisher and your goal is to use VPPREP to install LaserJet support, you should respond by typing **N**.

Choosing a
printer

Next, VPPREP will ask you to identify the type of display system and mouse you are using. Once you've provided this information, VPPREP will display the screen shown in Figure 11-1, which asks you to identify your printer.

FIGURE 11-1

```
Which printer do you have?

A    EPSON MX/FX
B    HP LJ, w/92286F Font
C    HP LJ+, 150dpi
D    HP LJ+, 300dpi
E    POSTSCRIPT
F    INTERPRESS
G    JLASER
H    CORDATA
I    AST TURBO
J    XEROX 4045, 150dpi
K    XEROX 4045, 300dpi
L    XEROX 4020

Type the letter of the of printer you have:
```

VPPREP will ask you to identify the type of printer you will be using with Ventura Publisher.

When the screen shown in Figure 11-1 appears on your screen, you should type the letter that corresponds to the particular LaserJet configuration you plan to use. You should choose **B HP LJ, w/92286F Font** only if you plan to use an original LaserJet equipped with the HP "F" font cartridge. If you choose this option, you will be able to use the LaserJet's Internal Courier font, as well as all of the fonts supported by the "F" cartridge. You will also be able to print full-page 75 dpi graphics.

If you plan to use a LaserJet Plus, Series II, IID, or 2000 and want to print full-page graphics at 150 dpi, choose **C HP LJ+, 150dpi**. Likewise, if you plan to use a LaserJet Plus, Series II, IID, or 2000 and want to print full-page graphics at 300 dpi, you should choose **D HP HL+, 300dpi**. When you choose either of these options, you will be able to use the LaserJet's Internal Courier font and three soft fonts that are supplied with the Ventura package. As we will show you later in this chapter, if you choose either of these options, you may use any HP soft font with Ventura Publisher.

Finally, if your LaserJet is equipped with JetScript or a similar device that provides Adobe Systems Inc.'s PostScript page description language, you should choose **E POSTSCRIPT**. When you do, you may print full-page 300 dpi graphics and use any of the PostScript fonts resident in a LaserJet PostScript system, such as JetScript. As we will show you later, you may also use PostScript soft fonts with Ventura Publisher if you choose the E POSTSCRIPT option.

Finally, while it is possible to install support for more than one printer or LaserJet option, Ventura Publisher will consider whichever printer you install first to be the default printer. Therefore, if you plan to install support for several printers or LaserJet options, you should choose the one that you plan to use most often.

After you have chosen the printer that you plan to use with Ventura Publisher, VPPREP will display a list of ports on your screen. When this list, which is shown in Figure 11-2, appears on your screen, you should choose the port that your computer will use to communicate with your LaserJet. For example, if your LaserJet is connected to LPT1:, choose A **Printer Parallel Port #1**.

Choosing a port

FIGURE 11-2

```
Which printer port are you using?
A    Printer Parallel Port #1
B    Printer Parallel Port #2
C    Printer Parallel Port #3
D    Printer Serial Port #1
E    Printer Serial Port #2

Type the letter of the printer port you are using:
```

After you have chosen the printer you plan to use with Ventura Publisher, VPPREP will ask you to choose the port to which it is connected.

Once you have provided VPPREP with the name of the printer that you plan to use with Ventura Publisher and have specified the name of the port to which it is connected, VPPREP will ask you if you want to select another printer. If you want to install support for one of the other LaserJet options, or for a completely different printer, you may do so by typing **Y** at this prompt. If you do not want to install support for another printer, you should type **N**.

There are several reasons why you might install support for more than one printer. For example, if you have a LaserJet Plus, 500 Plus, Series II, IID, or 2000,

Choosing additional printers

you might install all three LaserJet options. This would allow you to print full-page graphics at 75, 150, and 300 dpi and give you access to the LaserJet's Internal Courier font, the fonts supported by the "F" cartridge, the three soft fonts shipped with Ventura Publisher, and any other soft font. Also, if your LaserJet is equipped with JetScript or a similar PostScript option, you might want to take advantage of the ability to install support for the LaserJet as a PCL and PostScript printer.

If you choose to install support for another printer, VPPREP will once again display the list of printers shown in Figure 11-1 and will ask you to make a selection. Once you have chosen a printer from this list, VPPREP will display the list shown in Figure 11-2 and will ask you to choose the port to which your printer is connected. Finally, after you have chosen the printer and port, VPPREP will ask whether you want to install support for yet another printer.

Completing the installation process

Once you have installed support for all of the printers that you plan to use with Ventura Publisher, VPPREP will display a summary screen that lists the display, mouse, and printer(s) you have chosen. For example, Figure 11-3 shows the summary screen that would appear if you told VPPREP that you have an IBM EGA video system, a Microsoft Bus Mouse, and a 300 dpi LaserJet Plus. When VPPREP displays a summary screen similar to this one, you may accept the choices you have made and continue the installation process by typing **Y**, or you may make new choices by typing **N**.

FIGURE 11-3

```
Your screen device choices are:

IBM Enhanced Card / Enhanced Display (640x350)
     Xerox, AT&T, Microsoft Buss Mouse ( Uses MOUSE.COM )
     No communication port selected

Your printer device choices are:

HP LJ+, 300dpi
     LPT1:
POSTSCRIPT
     LPT2:

Are these the correct screen and printer choices? Y
```

Before completing the installation process, VPPREP will display a summary of the hardware devices you have chosen.

Finally, VPPREP will install Ventura Publisher and/or support for the devices you have chosen. When the installation process has been completed, VPPREP will return you to the DOS prompt from which you can run Ventura Publisher by typing **VP**.

FONTS

The key to Ventura Publisher's ability to produce quality documents is its support for LaserJet fonts. Therefore, in this section, we'll discuss the mechanism Ventura Publisher uses to manage fonts, and we'll take a brief look at the level of font support that is provided when you use VPPREP to install support for your particular LaserJet. Once we've done this, we'll discuss Ventura Publisher screen fonts, and we'll show you how to choose the font that you want to use to print a block of text or a paragraph. Finally, we'll show you how to add support for PCL and PostScript soft fonts and how to match Ventura Publisher screen fonts.

LaserJet Font Support

When you use VPPREP to install support for a printer, it will copy into the \VENTURA directory on your hard disk a data file that contains information Ventura Publisher will use to access a specific set of fonts supported by that printer. These data files are called width tables.

First, we'll take a look at the width tables VPPREP will copy into your \VENTURA directory when you install support for a LaserJet. Then, we'll discuss the set of fonts each of these width tables support.

PCL font support

When you install support for a LaserJet equipped with an "F" cartridge, VPPREP will copy the width table HPF.WID into the \VENTURA directory on your hard disk. This width table will allow you to use the LaserJet's Internal Courier font, as well as the fonts available on the "F" cartridge.

On the other hand, if you use VPPREP to install support for a 150 or 300 dpi LaserJet Plus, it will copy the width table HPLJPLUS.WID into the \VENTURA directory on your hard disk. This width table will allow you to use the LaserJet's Internal Courier font, but you will not be able to use any cartridge fonts. HPLJPLUS.WID will also allow you to use any of the three PCL LaserJet soft fonts—Dutch (Times Roman), Swiss (Helvetica), and Symbol—that are included with Ventura Publisher. We'll show you how to install support for other HP soft fonts later in this section.

PostScript font support

When you install support for a PostScript-equipped LaserJet, VPPREP will copy the width table POSTSCPT.WID into the \VENTURA directory on your hard disk. This width table will allow you to use any of 41 PostScript fonts. A complete list of these fonts appears in Table 11-1. As you can see, POSTSCPT.WID supports all of the fonts resident in an Apple LaserWriter-compatible LaserJet PostScript system, such as HP's JetScript accessory kit, as well as a number of Adobe PostScript soft fonts.

TABLE 11-1

Font name (**R**=*Resident* **S**=*Soft font*)	
Helvetica (R)	Glypha (S)
Times (R)	Goudy (S)
Courier (R)	Helvetica Light (S)
Symbol (R)	Helvetica Black (S)
ITC Avant Garde (R)	Helvetica Condensed Light (S)
ITC Bookman (R)	Helvetica Condensed (S)
Helvetica Narrow (R)	Helvetica Condensed Black (S)
Palatino (R)	ITC Korinna (S)
Century Schoolbook (R)	Letter Gothic (S)
Zapf Chancery (R)	Lubalin Graph (S)
Zapf Dingbats (R)	ITC Machine (S)
American Typewriter (S)	Melior (S)
ITC Benguiat (S)	New Baskerville (S)
Bodoni (S)	Optima (S)
Bodoni Poster (S)	Orator (S)
Century Old Style (S)	Park Avenue (S)
Cheltenham (S)	Prestige Elite (S)
Franklin Gothic (S)	Sonata (S)
Franklin Gothic Heavy (S)	ITC Souvenir (S)
Friz Quadrata (S)	Trump Mediaeval (S)
ITC Galliard (S)	

Ventura Publisher supports these PostScript fonts.

Screen Fonts

While Ventura Publisher can print text using PCL and PostScript fonts, it cannot use PCL and PostScript fonts to display text on your screen. Instead, it uses screen fonts. For example, if you print a block of text using the Dutch PCL soft font included with Ventura Publisher, then Ventura Publisher will use a Dutch screen font to represent the block of text on your screen.

A base set of three screen fonts—Dutch (Times Roman), Swiss (Helvetica), and Symbol—are included with Ventura Publisher. The Dutch and Swiss screen fonts allow Ventura Publisher to provide you with an on-screen representation of any text that you print using the Dutch and Swiss PCL soft fonts, the "F" font cartridge's Times Roman and Helvetica fonts, or PostScript's Times and Helvetica fonts. The Symbol screen font matches the PCL Symbols soft font that is included with Ventura Publisher.

If you instruct Ventura Publisher to print a block of text using a PCL or PostScript font in a document for which a matching screen font is not available, Ventura Publisher will not be able to provide you with an on-screen WYSIWYG representation of that block of text. Instead, Ventura Publisher will compensate by representing it with an available screen font. This process is called screen font substitution.

While screen font substitution makes it possible to use LaserJet fonts that are not accompanied by a matching screen font in a Ventura Publisher document, it is always desirable to have screen fonts that match any PCL or PostScript fonts that you use. Therefore, later in this section, we'll show you how to obtain and install screen fonts that match many PCL and PostScript fonts.

Finally, if you'd like to know more about the concepts behind screen fonts and WYSIWYG, be sure to read the discussion that appears in Chapter 4.

Choosing Fonts

Now that we've looked at the font support that is provided with Ventura Publisher, it's time to look at the commands you issue to choose the font you want to use to print a block of text or a paragraph.

To choose the font that you want to use to print a specific block of text, select the Text icon that appears in the upper-left corner of the Ventura Publisher display. Once you have done this, highlight the block of text for which you want to choose a font, then select the Set Font button that appears immediately below the Text icon. The Text icon and the Set Font button are shown in Figure 11-4.

FIGURE 11-4

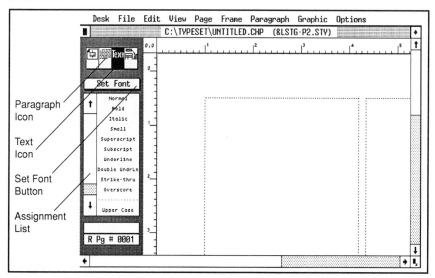

These icons and attributes may be used to select the fonts you want to use in a document.

To choose the font that you want to use to print a specific paragraph, select the Paragraph icon that appears just to the left of the Text icon. This icon is shown in Figure 11-4. Once you have selected the Paragraph icon, highlight the paragraph for which you want to choose a font, pull down the Paragraph menu, and select the Font command.

When you select the Text icon and the Set Font button, or the Paragraph icon and the Paragraph menu's Font command, Ventura Publisher will display a dialog box that allows you to select a particular font. This dialog box will be similar to the one shown in Figure 11-5 if you are using a PCL LaserJet, while it will be similar to the one shown in Figure 11-6 if you are using a PostScript-equipped LaserJet.

As you can see in Figures 11-5 and 11-6, Ventura Publisher allows you to choose the font that you want to use, as well as its size and style. You can also specify if the block of text you have highlighted should be shifted up or down, and you can reduce the amount of space reserved between characters by entering an appropriate value in the Kern: field. Finally, while Ventura Publisher does allow you to assign a particular color to a font, the only color you may use when printing text with a standard LaserJet is black. However, if your LaserJet is equipped with PostScript, you may use a white font on a black background.

Finally, as you can see in Figure 11-4, when the Text icon is selected, you may assign text attributes to a highlighted block of text by selecting them from the assignment list. For example, if you highlight a block of text and select Underline from the assignment list, Ventura Publisher will underline that block of text.

FIGURE 11-5

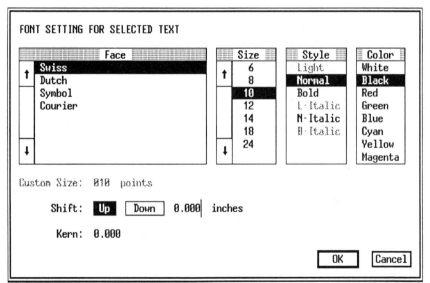

When you highlight a block of text and select Set Font, Ventura Publisher will display a dialog box like this one on your screen if you are using a PCL LaserJet.

FIGURE 11-6

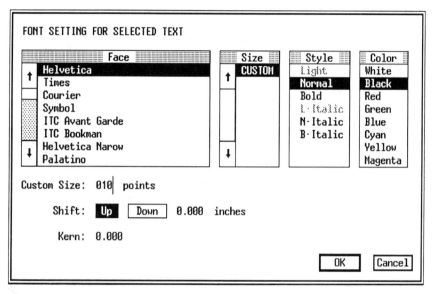

When you highlight a block of text and select Set Font, Ventura Publisher will display a dialog box similar to this one on your screen if you are using a PostScript-equipped LaserJet.

Adding Support for PCL Soft Fonts

While Ventura Publisher is shipped with three PCL soft fonts, chances are you will want to use other soft fonts as well. Therefore, in this section, we'll show you how to use utilities that are included with Ventura Publisher to add support for a PCL soft font.

Choosing a soft font directory

If you want to use a PCL soft font with Ventura Publisher, you must copy that soft font into the appropriate directory. If you do not place soft font data files in the proper directory, you will not be able to use them with Ventura Publisher. By default, soft font data files must be placed in the \VENTURA directory, or in the directory you've chosen by adding a downpath entry to your HPLJPLUS.CNF file.

HPLJPLUS.CNF is a text file that contains information concerning the location and ID numbers assigned to a soft font. You may make changes to HPLJPLUS.CNF with any editor that will produce pure ASCII text files. The entry you must place on the first line of HPLJPLUS.CNF to specify the name of the directory in which soft font data files are stored must be in the following format:

```
downpath (Drivespec:\Directoryname)
```

For example, if you plan to store soft font data files in the directory C:\HPSFONTS, you must place the entry downpath (C:\HPSFONTS) on the first line of your HPLJPLUS.CNF file.

Renaming soft font data files

After you have copied soft font data files into the directory specified within HPLJPLUS.CNF, you must rename those files using the extension .SFP for Portrait fonts and .SFL for Landscape fonts. For example, HP-produced Portrait soft fonts carry the extension .R8P, while HP-produced Landscape soft fonts carry the extension .R8L. Therefore, if you want to use an HP soft font, you must rename the data files in which they are stored by issuing the commands **REN *.R8P *.SFP** and **REN *.R8L *.SFL** at the DOS prompt.

Creating Landscape fonts

If a Landscape version of the soft font you are installing is not available, the next step is to create a Landscape version. You may do this with a utility called PORTOLAN, which is shipped on Ventura Publisher Utilities Disk #11. To use PORTOLAN, begin by copying the file PORTOLAN.EXE from Ventura Publisher Utilities Disk #11 into the directory on your hard disk in which your soft fonts are located. Next, type **PORTOLAN**, the name of the Portrait soft font for which you want to create a Landscape soft font, and press ↵ at the DOS prompt. For example, if you want to create a Landscape version of the soft font stored in the file BROADWAY.SFP, type **PORTOLAN BROADWAY.SFP** at the DOS prompt, and press ↵.

Finally, if you must create several Landscape fonts, you may use standard DOS wildcard conventions when invoking PORTOLAN. For example, if you want to create Landscape fonts for all of the Portrait fonts stored in a directory, type **PORTOLAN *.SFP** at the DOS prompt, and press ↵.

Building a font metrics file

After you have created Landscape versions of the soft fonts you want to use with Ventura Publisher, you must build a font metrics file for each Portrait soft font. A font metrics file contains all of the information needed to create a width table, which, as we pointed out earlier, is used by Ventura Publisher to manage a font.

The process of building a font metrics file is automated by a utility called HPLTOVFM, which is shipped in the /HPLJPLUS directory of Ventura Publisher Utilities Disk #11. To use HPLTOVFM, start by copying the file HPLTOVFM.EXE from the /HPLJPLUS directory of Ventura Publisher Utilities Disk #11 into the directory on your hard disk in which your soft fonts are located. Once you have done this, you may run HPLTOVFM from the DOS prompt. However, when you invoke HPLTOVFM, you must provide it with such information as the name of the soft font data file for which you are creating a font metrics file, the name of the font, a typeface ID, the point size, and the weight of the font. To do this, you must use a series of switches on the command line. Table 11-2 summarizes these switches.

TABLE 11-2

Switch	Purpose
/F=Font name	Specifies commercial name of font
/N=Face Id	Must be unique value between 15 and 255
/P=Point size	Specifies point size (two characters)
/W=Weight	Specifies weight (one character)
	N=Normal, B=Bold, I=Italic, T=Bold Italic

When you use HPLTOVFM to create a font metrics file, you must use these switches on the command line to provide HPLTOVFM with information it needs to build the file.

The /F=Font name switch must be included on the command line when you invoke HPLTOVFM to provide Ventura Publisher with the commercial name of the font for which you are creating a font metrics file and, ultimately, a width table. For example, if you are creating a font metrics file for BitStream's Broadway font, you should include the switch /F=Broadway on the command line when you invoke HPLTOVFM.

Choosing a font name

The /N=Face Id switch must be included on the command line when you invoke HPLTOVFM to provide Ventura Publisher with the internal value it will use to identify the font. The Face Id you specify must be a unique value between 15 and 255 and may be determined by examining the table that begins on page K-15 of your *Ventura Publisher Reference Guide.*

Choosing a Face Id

When you examine this table of Face Ids, you will see that Face Id values are assigned from a range based on the physical characteristics of the font in question. For example, the standard fonts that may be used when you install Ventura Publisher are identified by Face Ids 1 through 14, while serif fonts are identified by Face Ids 20 through 49, sans serif fonts are identified by Face Ids 50 through 99, fixed-space fonts are identified by Face Ids 100 through 127, and all other fonts are identified by Face Ids 128 through 255.

Notice, too, that Face Ids have already been assigned to a number of fonts. For example, the Face Id number 21 has been assigned to the Palatino typeface. Therefore, when you use the /N=Face Id switch to assign a Face Id to a font, you should check this table to determine if an Id has already been assigned to that font. If not, you should choose an unused Id number from the appropriate range.

For example, if you create a font metrics file for a Palatino soft font, you must use the switch /N=21 to assign the Face Id 21 to the font. You must do so because this Face Id has been reserved for Palatino within the table that begins on page K-15 of the *Ventura Publisher Reference Guide.* On the other hand, if a Face Id has not been reserved for a font, you must choose an unused Id number from the appropriate range. For example, if the font for which you are creating a font metrics file has serifs, you must choose a Face Id between 40 and 49. If it is a sans serif font, you must choose a Face Id between 61 and 99. If it is a fixed-space font, choose a Face Id between 106 and 127. Finally, if it is a decorative or symbol font, choose a Face Id between 131 and 255.

Specifying point size

To specify the point size of the font for which you are creating a font metrics file, you must include the switch /S=Point size on the command line when you invoke HPLTOVFM. For example, if you are creating a font metrics file for a 10-point font, you should include the switch /S=10 on the command line.

Specifying font weight

The last switch that you must include on the command line when you invoke HPLTOVFM is the /W=Weight switch. This switch must be used to specify the weight or style of the font for which you are creating a font metrics file. If you are creating a font metrics file for a Normal font, you should use the switch /W=N, while you should use the switch /W=B for a Bold font, /W=I for an Italic font, or /W=T for a Bold Italic font.

An example

Now that you know how to include switches on the command line when you invoke HPLTOVFM to create a font metrics file, let's consider a simple example. Suppose you want to create a font metrics file for a 12-point Italic Palatino file stored in the soft font file PALAI12.SFP. To do this, you must issue the command **HPLTOVFM PALAI12.SFP /N=Palatino /N=21 /P=12 /W=I** at the DOS prompt. When you issue this command, HPLTOVFM will create the font metrics file PALAI12.VFM.

Converting a font metrics file into a width table

After you have created a font metrics file for each soft font that you plan to use, you may create a width table that supports any single font or group of fonts. To specify the font or group of fonts for which you want to build a width table, list the name of the font metrics file that you have created for each font in an ASCII text file. Next, you must use a utility called VFMTOWID, which is shipped on Ventura Publisher Utilities Disk #11, to convert the font metrics files listed in this ASCII text file into a single width table. This width table will allow you to use each of the fonts on which the font metrics files were based.

As an example, let's assume that you have created the font metrics files PALAN10.VFM, PALAI10.VFM, and PALAB10.VFM and want to create a width table that supports the fonts on which these font metrics files are based. To create this width table, you must begin by listing the names of these font metrics files on individual lines in a text file. For this example, we'll assume that this text file is named PALATINO.TXT.

Once you have created the text file that contains the names of the font metrics files that VFMTOWID will use to create a width file, you may run VFMTOWID.

To do this, begin by copying VFMTOWID from Ventura Publisher Utilities Disk #11 to the directory in which the font metrics files are stored, then issue the command **VFMTOWID PALATINO.TXT** at the DOS prompt. As a result, VFMTOWID will create the width table PALATINO.WID.

Once you have created a width table that supports a PCL soft font, you must merge that width table with the width table that was installed by VPPREP before you can use those fonts in a Ventura Publisher document. We'll show you how to do this in the "Managing Fonts" section of this chapter.

Using a PCL soft font width table

As we pointed out earlier, the width table that is copied into the \VENTURA directory on your hard disk when you install support for a PostScript printer contains support for 41 PostScript fonts. Thirty of these fonts are soft fonts, which cannot be used in a Ventura Publisher document unless you purchase them from Adobe Systems, Inc.

Adding Support for PostScript Soft Fonts

If you purchase one of these 30 soft fonts from Adobe Systems, Inc., you must copy it into the appropriate directory on your hard disk before it can be used with Ventura Publisher. By default, soft fonts must be copied into the directory \PSFONTS. However, if you want to use another directory, you may do so by changing the *psfonts* entry within the file POSTSCPT.CNF.

POSTSCPT.CNF is a text file that contains configuration information that Ventura Publisher will use when dealing with PostScript. This file is always stored in your \VENTURA directory, and the entries within it may be changed with any editor that will produce pure ASCII text files. The format of the *psfonts* entry, which should always appear on the first line of POSTSCPT.CNF, is:

```
psfonts(Drivespec:\Directoryname)
```

For example, if you plan to store soft font data files in the directory C:\POSTSOFT, you must place the entry `downpath (C:\POSTSOFT)` on the first line of your POSTSCPT.CNF file.

Once you have specified the directory in which PostScript soft fonts will be stored, you must copy the soft font data file into that directory. As an example, let's assume that you have purchased the Bodoni soft font from Adobe Systems, Inc., and you want to use it with Ventura Publisher. If you have specified that PostScript soft fonts will be stored in the directory C:\POSTSOFT, you must copy the soft font data file BDR____ into that directory. Once you have done this, you can use the Bodoni font in a Ventura Publisher document.

**Installing Screen
Fonts**

Once you have added support for a PCL or PostScript font to Ventura Publisher, you may want to add support for a matching screen font. In this section, we'll show you how to obtain and install screen fonts.

*Installing screen
fonts that match
PCL fonts*

Screen fonts that match PCL internal, cartridge, or soft fonts must be purchased from a commercial source or created with a utility program such as SoftCraft's WYSIfonts! or BitStream's FontWare. We'll discuss these utilities in detail in Chapter 18.

The procedure you must follow to install a screen font that matches a PCL font is quite simple. First, you must be sure that the screen font you want to install has been designed for the particular video system you are using. You can make this determination by examining the extension of the soft font's file name. Screen fonts that have the extension .EGA may be used with all of the video systems supported by Ventura Publisher with the exception of the IBM Color Graphics Adapter. As you might expect, screen fonts that may be used with the Color Graphics Adapter will carry the extension .CGA.

Once you are certain that the screen font you want to install has been designed for use with your video system, you must copy the screen font data file into your \VENTURA directory. For example, if you want to install the soft font stored in the file A:BROADWAY.EGA, you must copy that file into your \VENTURA directory by issuing the command COPY A:BROADWAY.EGA C:\VENTURA at the DOS prompt. After you copy a screen font data file into the \VENTURA directory, Ventura Publisher will automatically recognize its presence and will use it to represent the matching PCL font on your display.

*Installing screen
fonts that match
PostScript fonts*

Adobe Systems, Inc., sells a number of PostScript screen fonts that match PostScript printer fonts. However, before you can use any of these fonts with Ventura Publisher, you must convert them into a format Ventura Publisher can understand. Also, because the format into which you must convert PostScript screen fonts differs from the format of the screen fonts that are shipped with Ventura Publisher, you cannot use them at the same time.

This fact presents one problem that is easily overcome. Ventura Publisher will not run properly unless a version of the Times Roman (Dutch) and Helvetica (Swiss) screen fonts are available. Therefore, if you plan to use PostScript screen fonts, you must purchase and install the Times and Helvetica PostScript screen fonts.

Converting an Adobe PostScript screen font into Ventura Publisher format is a relatively simple process. To do this, you must use a utility program called ABFTOFNT.EXE. This program is shipped in the \VENTURA directory of Ventura Publisher Utilities Disk #11.

To use ABFTOFNT.EXE, begin by copying it into the \VENTURA directory on your hard disk. Once you have done this, copy the PostScript screen fonts that you want to use into your \VENTURA directory and rename them so that they will carry the extension ABF. For example, if you copy the screen font file BDR_____ into your \VENTURA directory, rename it with the command **REN BDR____ BDR_____.ABF**.

Once you have renamed all PostScript screen font files so that they carry the extension .ABF, you may convert them to Ventura Publisher format. To do this, type **ABFTOFNT *.ABF** at the DOS prompt, then press ↵. After ABFTOFNT has converted a PostScript screen font to Ventura Publisher format, you may delete the PostScript screen font data file from your hard disk.

Finally, to use a PostScript screen font after it has been converted to Ventura Publisher format, run Ventura Publisher, then issue a **Set Printer Info...** command from the Options menu. When the dialog box shown in Figure 11-7 on the next page appears on your screen, press **[Backspace]** three times, type **PSF** at the *Screen Fonts:* prompt, then select **OK**, or press ↵.

Managing Fonts

Earlier in this chapter, we pointed out that when you install support for your LaserJet, VPPREP will copy a width table into your \VENTURA directory that provides you with the ability to use a specific set of fonts. We also pointed out that if you want to use any additional fonts, you must create a width table that provides support for those fonts. Therefore, in this section, we'll show you how to merge a width table that you have created with one that was installed by VPPREP.

To make changes to the width table that you are currently using, you must pull down the Options menu and select the **Add/Remove Fonts...** command. This command will produce an ADD/REMOVE FONTS dialog box that lists each font supported by the currently loaded width table. For example, the ADD/REMOVE FONTS dialog box in Figure 11-7 lists each of the fonts that may be used with Ventura Publisher when you install support for a LaserJet Plus with VPPREP.

As you can see, the file name OUTPUT.WID is displayed at the top of the ADD/REMOVE FONTS dialog box. This is the name of the width table that contains support for the set of fonts that can be used with the printer that has been installed as the default printer. VPPREP automatically copies this width table into the \VENTURA directory on your hard disk when you install support for your default printer.

Merging width tables

If you have created a width table that supports a PCL or PostScript soft font, you may want to merge it with the width table that was automatically installed by VPPREP. To do this, choose the **Merge Width Tables...** option, then select the name of the width table that you want to merge with the currently loaded width table. As a result, Ventura Publisher will load into memory the width table you have created and will list the fonts it supports along with those supported by the currently loaded width table.

FIGURE 11-7

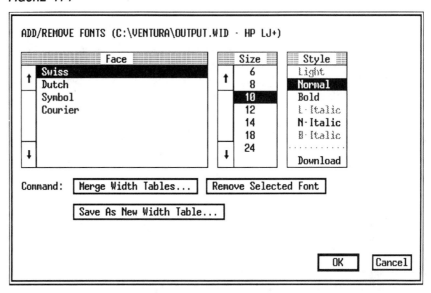

```
ADD/REMOVE FONTS (C:\VENTURA\OUTPUT.WID · HP LJ+)

       Face              Size        Style
   Swiss             ↑    6        Light
↑  Dutch                  8        Normal
   Symbol                 10       Bold
   Courier                12       L·Italic
                          14       N·Italic
                          18       B·Italic
↓                    ↓    24
                                   Download

Command:   Merge Width Tables...     Remove Selected Font

           Save As New Width Table...

                                          OK    Cancel
```

This dialog box will appear when you pull down the Options menu and select the Add/Remove Fonts... command.

As an example, let's assume that you have created a width table that supports BitStream's PCL University Roman soft font and want to merge this width table into the OUTPUT.WID width table that supports the Courier, Dutch, Swiss, and Symbol fonts that may be used with a LaserJet Plus. To do this, issue the **Merge Width Tables...** command. This command will produce an item selector box from which you can choose the name of the file in which the width table that supports the University Roman soft font is stored. Once you have selected the width table from this box, Ventura Publisher will read the width table into memory and will add the fonts it supports to the list of fonts supported by OUTPUT.WID.

Once you have merged a width table, you can select OK and immediately use any of the fonts listed in the ADD/REMOVE FONTS dialog box. If you want to save a merged width table to disk for future use, you may do so by issuing the ADD/REMOVE FONTS dialog box's Save As New Width Table... command.

Removing a font from a width table

The ADD/REMOVE FONTS dialog box also allows you to remove support for a font from a dialog box. To do this, highlight the name, size, and style of the font, then choose the Remove Selected Font option. When you do this, the font you have selected will disappear from the dialog box. After you have removed a font from your width table, you can select OK and immediately use any of the fonts listed in the ADD/REMOVE FONTS dialog box, or save the modified width table to a disk file for future use by issuing the ADD/REMOVE FONTS dialog box's Save As New Width Table... command.

Automatic soft font downloading

Ventura Publisher has the ability to download soft fonts automatically. You may use the ADD/REMOVE FONTS dialog box's download/resident flag to control this feature.

The main advantage of allowing Ventura Publisher to download soft fonts automatically is convenience. This eliminates the need to download fonts yourself before you run Ventura Publisher.

On the other hand, the main disadvantage of allowing Ventura Publisher to download soft fonts automatically is the amount of time it takes. When Ventura Publisher downloads a PCL soft font, it downloads it as a temporary soft font. As a result, each time a particular soft font is used in a document, Ventura Publisher must download it to the LaserJet. This can often take a long time since the amount of data that must be sent to the LaserJet when a font is downloaded is usually large.

Likewise, if you use soft fonts with several applications, you may want to download them before you run Ventura Publisher. For example, if you want to use a PostScript font with Microsoft Word and Ventura Publisher, you should download it with an external utility before running either program.

PCL soft fonts

When you find that the amount of time Ventura Publisher takes to download PCL LaserJet soft fonts as temporary fonts is lengthy, you may download them as permanent soft fonts using a download utility such as HP's FontLoad. To use a soft font that has been downloaded to the LaserJet as a permanent soft font, you must begin by toggling its download/resident flag in order to download.

To toggle the download/resident flag for a particular font, select the font's name, size, and style, then select the download/resident flag that appears at the bottom of the style list. As you can see in Figure 11-7, the 10-point Normal Swiss font is flagged as downloadable.

After you have flagged a font as downloadable or resident, you may select OK and immediately use any of the fonts listed in the ADD/REMOVE FONTS dialog box, or save the modified width table to a disk file for future use by issuing the ADD/REMOVE FONTS dialog box's Save As New Width Table... command.

Once you have set a soft font's download/resident flag, you must specify the Soft Font Id number you assigned to the font when it was downloaded by placing an entry in your HPLJPLUS.CNF file. The format of this entry is:

```
permfont(Font Id number  Soft font filename)
```

As we pointed out earlier in this chapter, HPLJPLUS.CNF is an ASCII text file that contains settings Ventura Publisher will use when it sends a document to a PCL LaserJet. If you download a soft font stored in the file UNIV.SFP to the LaserJet as a permanent soft font with the Face Id number 1, you must place the entry `permfont(1 UNIV.SFP)` in your HPLJPLUS.CNF file.

PostScript soft fonts

You can download PostScript fonts with an external utility such as the JETFONTS utility that is included with the HP JetScript Accessory Kit. However, if you choose to do this, you should set the font's download/resident flag to resident.

To toggle the download/resident flag for a particular font, select the font's name, size, and style, then select the download or resident flag that appears at the bottom of the style list. After you have flagged a font as downloadable or resident, you may select OK and immediately use any of the fonts listed in the ADD/REMOVE FONTS dialog box, or save the modified width table to a disk file for future use by issuing the ADD/REMOVE FONTS dialog box's Save As New Width Table… command.

PRINTING

In this section, we'll explain the process of printing a document. Once we've done this, we'll show you how to change printers within Ventura Publisher, and we'll address a few special considerations you must keep in mind when printing a document with the LaserJet.

The To Print... Command

To send a document to the LaserJet, pull down the File menu, and select the To Print… command. When you do, the dialog box shown in Figure 11-8 will appear on your screen. This dialog box is called the PRINT INFORMATION dialog box.

FIGURE 11-8

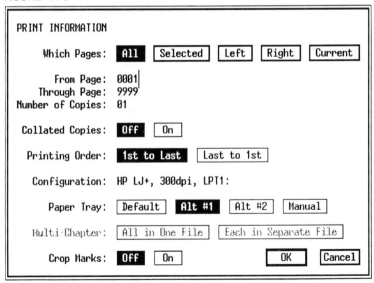

This dialog box will appear on your screen when you issue a To Print… command from Ventura Publisher's File menu.

The PRINT INFORMATION dialog box that will appear on your screen when you issue a To Print… command provides you with a great deal of information about your printer and document. It also allows you to change a number of settings that may be used to affect the printing process. Once you have made any necessary changes to these settings, you may send the document to the LaserJet by selecting OK, or by pressing ↵.

If you are using a LaserJet, LaserJet Plus, or LaserJet 500 Plus, then you are probably aware that the LaserJet stacks documents in reverse order as they are printed. You may also be aware that rearranging extremely long documents into proper order can be a tedious process. Fortunately, Ventura Publisher allows you to avoid this situation.

Choosing the print order

If you are using a LaserJet, LaserJet Plus, or LaserJet 500 Plus and want to print a document in reverse order, select the **Last to 1st** option in the PRINT INFORMA-TION dialog box. If you are using a LaserJet Series II, IID, or 2000, or do not want to print a document in reverse order, select the **1st to Last** option.

The PRINT INFORMATION dialog box's Paper Tray setting may be used to specify the paper source Ventura Publisher will use when it prints a document. You should select the **Default** option if you want to feed paper via the LaserJet's internal paper tray, while you should select the **Manual** option if you want to feed paper via the LaserJet's manual feed slot.

Choosing the paper source

The LaserJet 500 Plus and LaserJet IID each supports a second paper tray. If you want to feed paper from this tray, select the **Alt #1** option. Finally, if you want to feed paper from the LaserJet 2000's third paper tray, select the **Alt #2** option.

If you use VPPREP to install support for more than one LaserJet option, you must choose the one you want to use within Ventura Publisher before you print a document. You can do this by pulling down the Options menu and selecting the Set Printer Info… command. When you select this command, Ventura Publisher will display on your screen the SET PRINTER INFO dialog box shown in Figure 11-9.

Changing Printers within Ventura Publisher

When the SET PRINTER INFO dialog box appears on your screen, you can choose the printer to which Ventura Publisher will send output, the port to which the printer is connected, the name of the width file that supports the set of fonts you want to use with the printer, and the set of screen fonts that match the fonts you want to use with the printer. Once you have made any changes to the settings in the SET PRINTER INFO dialog box, select **OK** or press ↵ to continue.

FIGURE 11-9

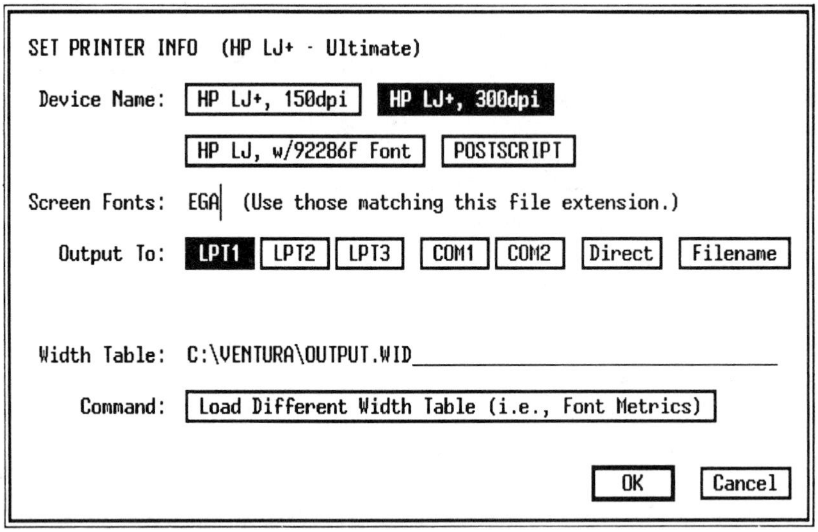

```
┌─────────────────────────────────────────────────────────────────┐
│                                                                   │
│  SET PRINTER INFO   (HP LJ+ - Ultimate)                           │
│                                                                   │
│   Device Name:   ┌─────────────────┐  ┌──────────────────┐        │
│                  │ HP LJ+, 150dpi  │  │  HP LJ+, 300dpi  │        │
│                  └─────────────────┘  └──────────────────┘        │
│                  ┌──────────────────┐  ┌─────────────┐            │
│                  │ HP LJ, w/92286F Font │ │ POSTSCRIPT │         │
│                  └──────────────────┘  └─────────────┘            │
│   Screen Fonts:  EGA│  (Use those matching this file extension.)  │
│                                                                   │
│     Output To:  ┌────┐ ┌────┐ ┌────┐ ┌────┐ ┌────┐ ┌──────┐ ┌──────────┐ │
│                 │LPT1│ │LPT2│ │LPT3│ │COM1│ │COM2│ │Direct│ │ Filename │ │
│                 └────┘ └────┘ └────┘ └────┘ └────┘ └──────┘ └──────────┘ │
│                                                                   │
│   Width Table:  C:\VENTURA\OUTPUT.WID_____     │
│                                                                   │
│      Command:   ┌────────────────────────────────────────────┐   │
│                 │ Load Different Width Table (i.e., Font Metrics) │ │
│                 └────────────────────────────────────────────┘   │
│                                                                   │
│                                          ┌────┐   ┌────────┐      │
│                                          │ OK │   │ Cancel │      │
│                                          └────┘   └────────┘      │
└─────────────────────────────────────────────────────────────────┘
```

Ventura Publisher will display this dialog box on your screen when you issue a Set Printer Info... command.

Choosing a printer

As you can see in Figure 11-9, Ventura Publisher will list the device name of each printer for which support has been installed in the SET PRINTER INFO dialog box. The first time you issue a Set Printer Info... command subsequent to the installation process, the printer that you install as your default printer will be selected. For example, in Figure 11-9, the HP LJ+, 300dpi option is selected, indicating that it was installed as the default printer. You can choose the particular printer that you want to use at any one moment by clicking on the button within the SET PRINTER INFO dialog box that contains its name.

Choosing an output destination

Just as you can change the printer to which Ventura Publisher will send documents, you can also change the port that Ventura Publisher will use to communicate with your printer by clicking on the button within the SET PRINTER INFO dialog box that contains its name. If you have installed support for a LaserJet equipped with an "F" font cartridge, a 150 dpi LaserJet Plus, a 300 dpi LaserJet Plus, or PostScript, you may choose any of the ports listed in the SET PRINTER INFO dialog box. Likewise, you may also choose the Filename option.

When you choose Filename as the output destination, Ventura Publisher will send documents to a disk file whose name you must specify. We'll discuss this subject in more detail later in this chapter. Finally, while you can send PostScript output to a JetScript-equipped LaserJet via LPT1:, LPT2:, or LPT3:, it is possible that you may run into a PostScript system that requires you to choose the Direct option. The Direct option allows Ventura Publisher to send output directly to an external PostScript device driver.

Choosing a width table and screen fonts

After you have chosen the printer to which you want Ventura Publisher to send printer output, you must specify the name of the width table that supports the fonts you want to use with that printer. You also must specify the file extension that identifies the screen fonts that match the fonts you plan to use with the printer.

For example, consider the SET PRINTER INFO dialog box shown in Figure 11-9. As you can see, the HP LJ+, 300dpi is selected as the printer to which Ventura Publisher will send documents, while screen fonts with the extension EGA and the printer fonts supported by the width table OUTPUT.WID will be used.

With this situation in mind, suppose that you select POSTSCRIPT as the printer to which Ventura Publisher will send documents. Now, you must also specify the name of the width table that supports PostScript fonts. To do this, you must select the Load Different Width Table (i.e., Font Metrics) command. This command will produce a dialog box similar to the one shown in Figure 11-10. From this dialog box, you may choose the name of the width table that supports the fonts you want to use. In this case, you should choose **POSTSCPT.WID**.

FIGURE 11-10

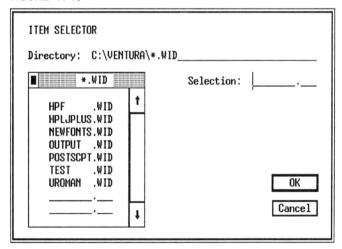

This dialog box allows you to choose the width file that supports the fonts that may be used with the printer you have chosen within the SET PRINTER INFO dialog box.

Once you have chosen the width table that supports the fonts that may be used with the printer you have chosen, you must specify the file extension that identifies the screen fonts that match the printer fonts. For example, as we pointed out earlier in this chapter, PostScript screen fonts carry the extension .PSF. Therefore, if you want to use PostScript screen fonts, you should type .PSF in the Screen Fonts: field.

Speeding up PostScript Printing

Each time you instruct Ventura Publisher to send a document to a LaserJet that is equipped with PostScript, it will send a setup file to the PostScript interpreter. As you might expect, this adds a few seconds to the amount of time it takes to print a document.

Technically, it is not necessary to send a setup code to the PostScript interpreter each time you print a document. Therefore, if you want, you can set up the PostScript interpreter once before you run Ventura Publisher, and avoid the procedure each time you print a document thereafter.

To take advantage of the ability to set up the PostScript interpreter before you run Ventura Publisher, you must begin by copying the file PERMVP.PS from the \POSTSCPT directory of Ventura Publisher Utilities Disk #11 to the \VENTURA directory on your hard disk. Once you have done this, you should delete the file PS2.PRE from your \VENTURA directory.

After you have copied PERMVP.PS into your \VENTURA directory, you may use the DOS copy command to send it to the PostScript interpreter. For example, if your computer communicates with your LaserJet's PostScript interpreter via LPT2:, you may send PERMVP.PS to the PostScript interpreter by issuing the command **COPY \VENTURA\PERMVP.PS LPT2:** at the DOS prompt. If you want, you may add this command to your AUTOEXEC.BAT file, or to the VP.BAT file that you use to run Ventura Publisher.

CONCLUSION

In this chapter, we've discussed aspects of Ventura Publisher that pertain to the LaserJet. For example, we've shown you how to install the LaserJet support that is provided with Ventura Publisher, and we've shown you how to make additions to this support. As a result, you should now be able to perform any printing task using Ventura Publisher with your LaserJet.

OTHER DOS APPLICATIONS 12

We haven't counted them, but there are literally thousands of applications available for the IBM PC, PS/2, and compatible systems, such as those produced by Compaq, Tandy, and Dell. This situation has its good and bad points.

Having so many applications from which to choose is beneficial because it's likely that one of them will offer the specific set of features you need. On the other hand, weeding through all the applications to find the ones that fit your needs is not an easy task.

When we decided to write *LaserJet Companion*, we realized that we couldn't include every DOS application. Therefore, we limited our discussion of DOS applications to the seven most widely used products.

While we were satisfied that a discussion of seven applications—WordPerfect, 1-2-3, WordStar, DisplayWrite 4, Microsoft Word, dBASE III Plus, and Ventura Publisher—would meet the needs of the majority of *LaserJet Companion* readers, we wanted to explain other popular applications as well. Our solution is *LaserJet Companion TechNotes*.

Each edition of *LaserJet Companion TechNotes* is comparable to a chapter in *LaserJet Companion,* and each discusses the procedures for using a product such as Paradox, Quattro, or XyWrite III Plus.

Since products are constantly being upgraded and released, we will frequently publish updated *LaserJet Companion TechNotes*. To find out if an edition of *LaserJet Companion TechNotes* has been released or is planned for a specific application, call The Cobb Group at 800-223-8720 (502-425-7756 in Kentucky).

In this chapter, we'll briefly discuss the applications for which we have written *LaserJet Companion TechNotes*. In addition, we'll outline of the content *LaserJet Companion TechNotes* for each application.

PARADOX

Borland International's Paradox is a powerful database management system that offers an exceptional amount of support for the LaserJet family of printers. *LaserJet Companion TechNotes for Paradox* discusses everything you need to know to get the most out of Paradox and your LaserJet.

For example, we explain how to install LaserJet support and how to access LaserJet features that are not directly supported by Paradox. In addition, we show you how to print labels and how to use any LaserJet font when printing reports.

QUATTRO

Borland International's Quattro is currently the premier low-cost DOS spread-sheet. One of Quattro's most attractive features is its support for the LaserJet family of printers.

In *LaserJet Companion TechNotes for Quattro*, we show you how to install support for a LaserJet and how to print worksheets and graphs. We also explain how to overcome problems with margins and how to improve the quality of output by embedding PCL commands directly in a worksheet.

XYWRITE III PLUS

XyQuest's XyWrite III Plus is a powerful word processor that supports the LaserJet family of printers. In *LaserJet Companion TechNotes for XyWrite III Plus*, we show you how to install and use the LaserJet printer files that are provided with XyWrite III Plus or are available from XyQuest. In addition, we show you how to build a printer file that supports any collection of LaserJet internal, cartridge, or soft fonts. Finally, we discuss the use of LaserJet fonts in a XyWrite III Plus document and look at special considerations, such as printing envelopes.

IMPENDING RELEASES

At the time *LaserJet Companion* went to press, several of the products we discussed were due for major upgrades. Specifically, Lotus had announced 1-2-3 Release 3.0, Xerox was showing Ventura Publisher 2.0 to weekly trade magazines, and Ashton-Tate was putting the finishing touches on dBASE IV. As these upgrades (or upgrades to any of the other products discussed in *LaserJet Companion*) become available, we will publish *LaserJet Companion TechNotes* written specifically for them. Whenever one of the products discussed in *LaserJet Companion* is upgraded, you can contact The Cobb Group for information concerning the availability of an edition of *LaserJet Companion TechNotes* for that product.

CONCLUSION

If you are using a DOS application that is not discussed in *LaserJet Companion*, you should contact The Cobb Group to determine if an edition of *LaserJet Companion TechNotes* for that product has been published.

Microsoft Windows

Section Three

Using the LaserJet
with Microsoft Windows

Section Three shows you how to use a LaserJet with Microsoft Windows and applications that run under Windows. We'll begin in Chapter 13 by showing you how to add support for a normal and PostScript-equipped LaserJet to Microsoft Windows/286 and Windows/386 version 2.1. We'll also show you how to configure this support for the specific set of LaserJet fonts and features that you want to use.

Additionally, we'll discuss the problem of matching Windows screen fonts with LaserJet fonts, and we'll walk through the process of printing a document with a Windows application.

In Chapters 14 through 16, we'll show you how to use Aldus PageMaker, Microsoft Excel, and Microsoft Write with the LaserJet. These chapters discuss LaserJet-related issues that are specific to each application. For example, in Chapter 15, we'll show you how to select and use LaserJet fonts in a Microsoft Excel worksheet.

Finally, in Chapter 17, we will discuss *LaserJet Companion TechNotes* that provide all the information you need to use your LaserJet with Windows-based applications not covered in *LaserJet Companion*.

MICROSOFT WINDOWS 13

In this chapter, we'll explain how to use a LaserJet with Microsoft Windows 286 and 386 Version 2.1, including installing and configuring Windows for the LaserJet and applying Windows to LaserJet fonts. Then, we'll take a brief look at the process of printing a document with a Windows application.

As you make your way through the sections of this chapter that are related to installation, configuration, and fonts, it will be encouraging to keep one fact in mind: Windows is a unified environment. As a result, once you have installed and configured support for your LaserJet and its fonts, there will be no need to re-install or reconfigure printer support as you add Windows applications to your system in the future.

As we mentioned earlier, this chapter was written for users of Microsoft Windows 286 and 386 Version 2.1. If you are using a previous version of Microsoft Windows, you can upgrade for a minimal cost by contacting Microsoft Corporation at the address or telephone number listed in Appendix 2.

In this section, we'll show you how to install LaserJet support as you install Windows with the Microsoft Windows SETUP program. Once we've done this, we'll take a look at how you can use the control panel to add LaserJet support subsequent to the initial Windows installation process. Finally, we'll discuss the technical issues related to the process of adding LaserJet support to Microsoft Windows.

ADDING LASERJET SUPPORT TO WINDOWS

Using SETUP to Install LaserJet Support

The Microsoft Windows SETUP program will ask you several questions about your system and will install Windows according to the answers you provide. SETUP also allows you to install support for a LaserJet.

To run SETUP, place the Microsoft Windows Setup, Build and Displays 1 disk in drive A, and type **SETUP** at the DOS prompt. SETUP will evaluate your system and will then ask you to verify that it has detected the correct type of computer, display adapter, keyboard, and mouse you are using. Once you have provided answers to these questions, SETUP will ask you if you want to install support for a printer. Figure 13-1 shows the screen that will appear when SETUP asks this question.

FIGURE 13-1

```
Setup will allow you to install a printer or plotter.


     ┌──────────────────────────────────────────────────┐
     │ WHEN YOU'RE READY TO                     PRESS    │
     ├──────────────────────────────────────────────────┤
     │ Install a printer or plotter               █ I   │
     │ Continue Setup                               C    │
     ├──────────────────────────────────────────────────┤
     │ Exit without completing Setup           CONTROL+X │
     └──────────────────────────────────────────────────┘
```

The Microsoft Windows SETUP program will ask you if you want to install support for a printer.

When SETUP asks you if you want to install a printer, respond by typing **I** or by pressing ↵. Then, SETUP will display a list of printer names similar to the one shown in Figure 13-2 and ask you to choose the printer you want to install.

To select a printer for installation, use the ↑ and ↓ keys to move the highlight bar through the list of printer names that SETUP displays on your screen. When the name of the printer you want to install is highlighted, press ↵.

Installing support for a standard PCL LaserJet

The name of each member of the LaserJet printer family appears on the list of printer names displayed by SETUP. Therefore, if you want to install support for one of these printers, use the procedure we have just described. For example, if you want to install support for a LaserJet Series II, use the ↑ and ↓ keys to move through the list of printer names until the name HP LaserJet Series II [PCL / HP LaserJet] is highlighted, then press ↵.

Installing support for a PostScript-equipped LaserJet

The list of printer names displayed by SETUP does not include an entry for a PostScript-equipped LaserJet. Therefore, if you want to install support for a PostScript-equipped LaserJet, you must choose the name of a compatible PostScript printer from the list.

FIGURE 13-2

```
Select an output device (printer, plotter, etc.) from the following list.

 - Use the DIRECTION (↑,↓) keys to move the highlight to your selection.

HP DeskJet
HP DraftPro [HP Plotter]
HP DraftMaster I [HP Plotter]
HP DraftMaster II [HP Plotter]
HP LaserJet [PCL / HP LaserJet]
HP LaserJet Plus [PCL / HP LaserJet]
HP LaserJet 500+ [PCL / HP LaserJet]
HP LaserJet Series II [PCL / HP LaserJet]
HP LaserJet 2000 [PCL / HP LaserJet]
HP PaintJet
HP ThinkJet
IBM Color Printer (B/W only)
IBM Graphics

            (To see more of the list, press the DOWN(↓) key.)

    ┌─────────────────────────────────────────────────────┐
    │ WHEN YOU'RE READY TO                          PRESS  │
    ├─────────────────────────────────────────────────────┤
    │ Confirm your choice                           ENTER │
    │ Exit without completing Setup            CONTROL+X   │
    └─────────────────────────────────────────────────────┘
```

SETUP will display a list of printer names from which you can install any member of the LaserJet printer family.

The manual that is included with your PostScript system may list the names of the PostScript printers with which it is compatible. If not, you must obtain this information from the manufacturer before trying to install support for your printer.

For example, the manual that is included with the QMS JetScript system states that a LaserJet Series II equipped with JetScript is compatible with the Apple LaserWriter Plus and the QMS-PS 800 Plus. Therefore, if you want to install support for a JetScript-equipped Series II, use the ↑ and ↓ keys to move through the list of printer names until the name Apple LaserWriter Plus [PostScript Printer] or QMS-PS 800 Plus [PostScript Printer] is highlighted, then press ↵.

After you have selected the name of the specific LaserJet you want to install, SETUP will display the list of port names shown in Figure 13-3 on the following page. From this list, you should select the port to which your LaserJet is connected. For example, if your LaserJet is connected to LPT1:, use the ↑ and ↓ keys to move through the list of port names until LPT1: is highlighted, then press ↵.

The port that you choose at this time is not the port to which your LaserJet must always be connected. You can change it at any time after the installation process by using the Connections... command on the control panel's Setup menu. We'll show you how to do this later in this chapter.

Choosing a printer port

FIGURE 13-3

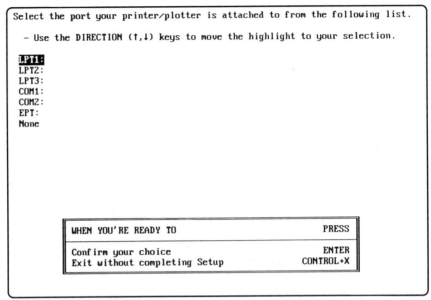

After you have selected a LaserJet from the list shown in Figure 13-2, SETUP will prompt you to choose the port to which your printer is connected.

Installing support for more than one printer

If your LaserJet is equipped with both PCL and PostScript, you may want to install support for both. Fortunately, SETUP allows you to do this. After you have selected the port that Windows will use to communicate with your printer, SETUP will ask you if you want to install support for another printer. The screen that asks this question is shown in Figure 13-4.

FIGURE 13-4

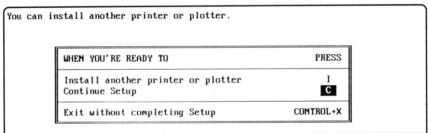

After you have selected a printer and the port Windows will use to communicate with that printer, SETUP will ask you if you want to install another printer.

If you want to install support for another printer, you should respond to this question by typing **I** or by pressing ↵. Since the process of installing support for additional printers is identical to the process you use to install the first printer, you can refer to the previous discussion for specific details.

Finally, if you choose not to install support for another printer, press **C**, and SETUP will complete the remainder of the Windows installation process.

Helpful hints

After SETUP has completed the process of installing support for PCL- and/or PostScript-equipped LaserJets, it will copy a file named READMEHP.TXT and/or a file named READMEPS.TXT into the directory in which you are installing Windows. These text files contain information concerning the use of your LaserJet. Although we will discuss the topics covered in these files later in this chapter, you can read them by issuing the commands **TYPE READMEHP.TXT** and/or **TYPE READMEPS.TXT** at the DOS prompt, or by loading them into a text editor that can handle pure ASCII files.

Adding LaserJet Support with the Control Panel

If you did not install support for the LaserJet while running the Microsoft Windows SETUP program, or if you installed a different printer, it is possible to add support for the LaserJet without having to re-install the package completely. You can do this by using the Add New Printer command on the control panel's Installation menu.

The control panel is a Desktop accessory that is automatically installed when you run SETUP. Therefore, you can run it with the Microsoft Windows MS-DOS Executive by selecting the file name CONTROL.EXE. The control panel is shown in Figure 13-5.

FIGURE 13-5

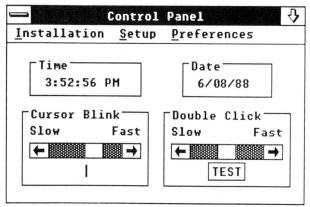

You can run the control panel from the MS-DOS Executive by selecting the file name CONTROL.EXE.

If you pull down the control panel's Installation menu and select the Add New Printer command, the control panel will display the dialog box shown in Figure 13-6. This dialog box prompts you to specify the directory in which the printer device driver files can be found.

FIGURE 13-6

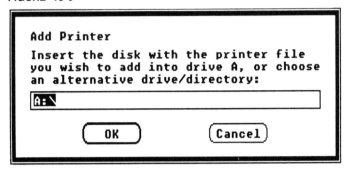

The Add New Printer command on the control panel's Installation menu will produce this dialog box.

After you specify the directory in which the control panel can find printer device drivers, the control panel will search that directory and list the drivers that it finds. If you select one of these drivers, Windows will copy the file into your Windows directory or onto your Windows boot disk. It will also update your WIN.INI file to reflect the fact that a new printer has been installed.

Adding support for a standard PCL LaserJet

As an example, suppose that you want to add Windows support for a LaserJet Series II. To do this, pull down the control panel's Installation menu and select the Add New Printer command. When the control panel prompts you to insert the disk that contains the printer file you want to install, place the disk in drive A, and choose **OK**. As a result, the control panel will display a dialog box similar to the one shown in Figure 13-7.

FIGURE 13-7

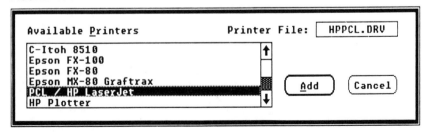

When a dialog box similar to this one appears on your screen, you can choose the printer for which you want to install support.

When the dialog box shown in Figure 13-7 appears on your screen, choose the **PCL / HP LaserJet** option from the list of available printers. Then, issue the <u>A</u>dd command to install support for the LaserJet Series II.

If you want to add support for a PostScript-equipped LaserJet to Windows, pull down the control panel's <u>I</u>nstallation menu, and select the Add <u>N</u>ew Printer command. When the control panel prompts you to insert the disk that contains the printer file you want to install, place the disk in drive A, and choose **OK**. As a result, the control panel will display a dialog box similar to the one shown in Figure 13-8.

Adding support for a PostScript-equipped LaserJet

FIGURE 13-8

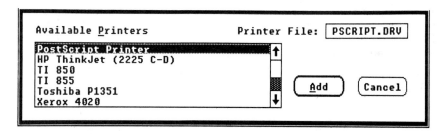

This dialog box will appear when you are adding support for a PostScript printer.

When the dialog box shown in Figure 13-8 appears on your screen, choose the **PostScript Printer** option from the list of available printers, then issue the <u>A</u>dd command to install support for PostScript.

When you use the Windows SETUP program to install support for a particular printer, you are asked to specify the MS-DOS device (port) to which the printer is connected. However, when you use the Add Printer command on the control panel's Installation menu to install support for a printer, you are not asked to specify the port to which the printer is connected. In this section, we'll show you how to assign a port to a printer that has been installed by the control panel. We'll also show you how to change the port to which a printer has been assigned.

Choosing a printer port

To define or change the port to which a printer is connected, pull down the control panel's Setup menu and select the Connections command. As a result, the control panel will display the dialog box shown in Figure 13-9 on the next page.

When this dialog box appears, use the mouse or Printer command to select the name of the printer whose port specification you want to change or define. Next, use the mouse or Connections command to select the port to which the printer is connected, and choose OK.

As an example, let's walk through the process of changing the port specification for a LaserJet from LPT1: to COM1:. To do this, pull down the control panel's

Setup Menu and select the Connections command. When the dialog box shown in Figure 13-9 appears on your screen, choose **PCL / HP LaserJet on LPT1:** from the Printer list and choose **COM1:** from the Connection list. Finally, choose **OK** to complete the process.

FIGURE 13-9

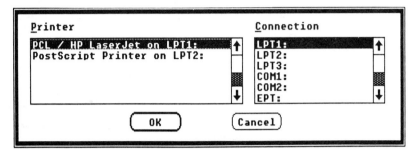

This dialog box allows you to define or change the port to which a particular printer is connected.

Technical Issues

When you add support for a standard or PostScript-equipped LaserJet to Microsoft Windows, several things happen below the surface. Specifically, changes are made to WIN.INI, and files called device drivers are copied into the directory in which Microsoft Windows is installed.

Device drivers

When you add support for a PCL LaserJet to Microsoft Windows, the HPPCL.DRV file is copied into the directory in which Windows is installed. Likewise, when you add support for a PostScript-equipped LaserJet, the file PSCRIPT.DRV is copied into the directory in which Windows is installed.

HPPCL.DRV and PSCRIPT.DRV are device drivers. In other words, they are program modules that have been designed for the specific purpose of allowing Windows to send output to a PCL- or PostScript-equipped LaserJet.

Consequently, whenever you instruct a Windows application to print a document, the document will be sent to the PCL or PostScript device driver. These drivers will then convert the document into PCL or PostScript code, which will then be sent to the Windows Spooler or directly to the LaserJet. We'll make references to device drivers throughout the remainder of this chapter.

WIN.INI

When you add support for a LaserJet to Microsoft Windows, the Microsoft Windows SETUP program or the control panel will make several additions and changes to a text file called WIN.INI.

WIN.INI is the Microsoft Windows equivalent of AUTOEXEC.BAT and CONFIG.SYS. In other words, just as MS-DOS uses the information stored in AUTOEXEC.BAT and CONFIG.SYS to configure itself, WIN.INI is a text file that contains a great deal of information that Windows uses to configure itself.

Chances are good that you will never have to make additions or changes to the information stored in WIN.INI. However, at various points throughout this chapter, we will point out instances when it is necessary to do so.

Now that we've shown you how to add support for a LaserJet to Windows, we'll show you how to remove it. If you installed support for a printer during the initial Windows installation procedure, or if you added support later using the methods outlined in the previous section, you can use the Delete Printer command on the control panel's Installation menu to remove it.

If you pull down the control panel's Installation menu and select the Delete Printer command, the control panel will display a dialog box similar to the one shown in Figure 13-10. This dialog box contains a list of printers presently installed, from which you can select and delete the printer of your choice.

REMOVING PRINTER SUPPORT

FIGURE 13-10

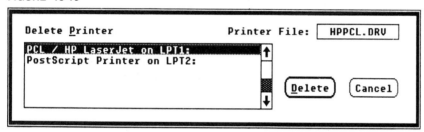

The Delete Printer command on the control panel's Installation menu will produce this dialog box.

After you specify the printer that you want to delete, the control panel will display a dialog box similar to the one shown in Figure 13-11 on the next page. This dialog box asks you if you want to delete the device driver (printer file) in addition to the entries in WIN.INI that tell Windows that a device is installed. If you choose to delete the device driver, the control panel will remove it from the directory specified in the dialog box. If you choose not to delete the device driver, Windows will remove the device driver and port specifications from just your WIN.INI file.

As an example, let's walk through the process of deleting support for a LaserJet that is connected to LPT1:. To begin, pull down the control panel's Installation menu and select the Delete Printer command. When the dialog box shown in Figure 13-10 appears on your screen, choose **PCL / HP LaserJet on LPT1:** from the Delete Printer list, then issue the Delete command to delete it. Next, when the dialog box shown in Figure 13-11 appears on your screen, choose Yes if you want to delete the printer file, choose No if you do not want to delete the printer file, or choose **Cancel** to end the process.

FIGURE 13-11

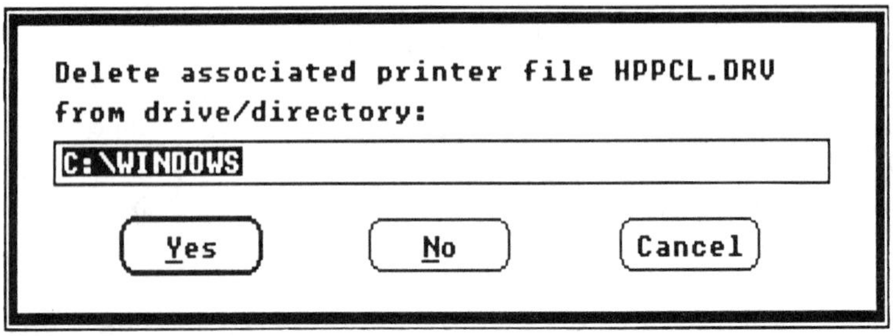

```
┌─────────────────────────────────────────────┐
│  ┌───────────────────────────────────────┐  │
│  │                                       │  │
│  │  Delete associated printer file HPPCL.DRV │
│  │  from drive/directory:                │  │
│  │  ┌─────────────────────────────────┐  │  │
│  │  │C:\WINDOWS                       │  │  │
│  │  └─────────────────────────────────┘  │  │
│  │                                       │  │
│  │  ┌────────┐  ┌────────┐  ┌──────────┐ │  │
│  │  │  Yes   │  │   No   │  │  Cancel  │ │  │
│  │  └────────┘  └────────┘  └──────────┘ │  │
│  │                                       │  │
│  └───────────────────────────────────────┘  │
└─────────────────────────────────────────────┘
```

After you select the printer you want to delete, the control panel will ask
if you want to delete the device driver file associated with that printer.

SETTING UP

After you have used the Microsoft Windows SETUP program or the control panel to install support for your LaserJet, there are several issues that must be addressed before you can actually print a document. For example, if you have installed support for more than one printer, you must choose a default printer. Also, now is the time to add support to Windows for any fonts that you want to use with your LaserJet. In this section, we'll discuss the issues you must address before you can use your LaserJet with Windows.

Configuring the Serial Port for a Serial LaserJet

If your LaserJet is connected to a serial port, you must configure the port so that Windows can use it. To do this, you can use the Communications Port command on the control panel's Setup menu.

To configure your serial port for a serial LaserJet, pull down the control panel's Setup menu and select the Communications Port option. When you do this, the dialog box shown in Figure 13-12 will appear on your screen.

When this dialog box appears, use the Port command or the mouse to select the serial port to which your LaserJet is connected (**COM1:** or **COM2:**). After you have done this, set the Baud Rate to **9600**, Word Length to **8**, Parity to **None**, Stop Bits to **1**, and Handshake to **None**. Finally, select **OK** to end the process of configuring the serial port.

Choosing a Default Printer

When you use the Windows SETUP program or control panel to install support for more than one printer, Windows will treat the first printer installed as the default printer. In other words, whenever you instruct a Windows application to print a document, it will automatically send the document to the first printer that was installed. You can use the Printer command on the control panel's Setup menu to change the default printer setting.

When you pull down the Setup menu and select the Printer command, the control panel will display the dialog box shown in Figure 13-13. As you can see, this box lists the printers that are presently available.

FIGURE 13-12

```
Communications Settings

Baud Rate:      9600

Word Length  ○ 4    ○ 5    ○ 6    ○ 7    ● 8

Parity       ○ Even    ○ Odd    ● None

Stop Bits    ● 1       ○ 1.5    ○ 2

Handshake    ○ Hardware  ● None

Port         ● COM1:    ○ COM2:

        (      OK      )    (   Cancel   )
```

This dialog box allows you to configure your serial port for a serial LaserJet.

FIGURE 13-13

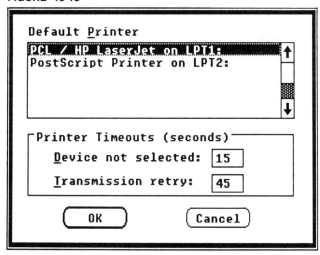

You can use the Printer command on the control panel's Setup menu to select the default Windows printer.

When you select a printer from the list shown in Figure 13-13, the control panel will display a dialog box you can use to change a number of settings specific to that printer. For example, if you select PCL / HP LaserJet on LPT1: from the list shown in Figure 13-13, the dialog box shown in Figure 13-14 will appear on your screen.

FIGURE 13-14

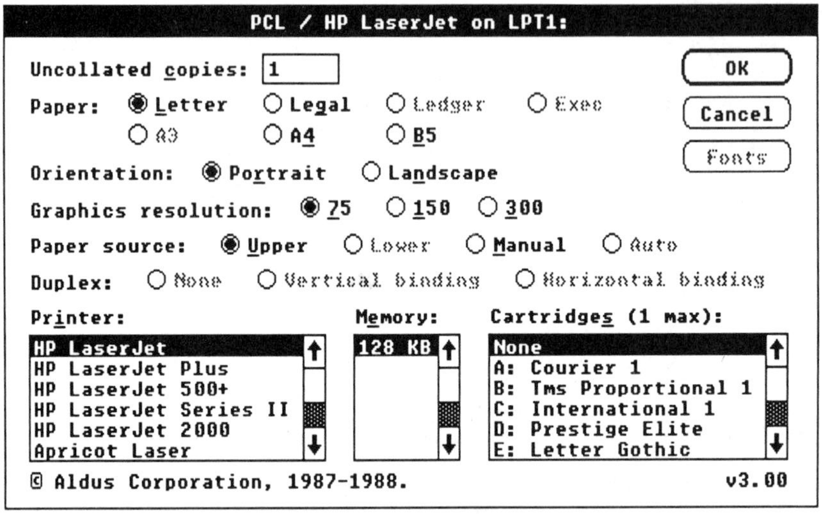

```
╔══════════════════════════════════════════════════════════╗
║           PCL / HP LaserJet on LPT1:                     ║
╠══════════════════════════════════════════════════════════╣
║  Uncollated copies: [1        ]          ┌──────────┐    ║
║                                          │    OK    │    ║
║  Paper:  ◉ Letter  ○ Legal  ○ Ledger  ○ Exec          ║
║          ○ A3      ○ A4     ○ B5         ┌──────────┐    ║
║                                          │  Cancel  │    ║
║  Orientation:  ◉ Portrait  ○ Landscape                  ║
║                                          ┌──────────┐    ║
║  Graphics resolution:  ◉ 75  ○ 150  ○ 300  │  Fonts  │  ║
║                                                          ║
║  Paper source:  ◉ Upper  ○ Lower  ○ Manual  ○ Auto      ║
║                                                          ║
║  Duplex:  ○ None   ○ Vertical binding  ○ Horizontal binding ║
║                                                          ║
║  Printer:              Memory:      Cartridges (1 max):  ║
║  ┌──────────────────┐  ┌────────┐  ┌──────────────────┐ ║
║  │HP LaserJet      ↑│  │128 KB ↑│  │None             ↑│ ║
║  │HP LaserJet Plus  │  │        │  │A: Courier 1      │ ║
║  │HP LaserJet 500+  │  │        │  │B: Tms Proportional 1│║
║  │HP LaserJet Series II│ │       │  │C: International 1 │ ║
║  │HP LaserJet 2000  │  │        │  │D: Prestige Elite │ ║
║  │Apricot Laser    ↓│  │       ↓│  │E: Letter Gothic ↓│ ║
║  └──────────────────┘  └────────┘  └──────────────────┘ ║
║  © Aldus Corporation, 1987-1988.              v3.00     ║
╚══════════════════════════════════════════════════════════╝
```

When you select a PCL LaserJet as your default printer, this dialog box will appear on your screen.

Once you have selected a printer from the list shown in Figure 13-13, and a dialog box such as the one shown in Figure 13-14 has appeared on your screen, you can select that printer as the default by choosing the OK option. We'll discuss the printer-specific settings that appear in this box shortly.

As an example, let's assume that you used the Windows SETUP program to install support for a PCL LaserJet on LPT1:, and later used the control panel to add support for a PostScript-equipped LaserJet on LPT2:. As a result, Windows recognizes the PCL / HP LaserJet on LPT1: as the default printer.

To make the PostScript-equipped LaserJet installed on LPT2: the default printer, pull down the control panel's Setup menu and select the Printer command. When the dialog box shown in Figure 13-13 appears on your screen, select **PostScript Printer on LPT2:**, and choose **OK** to make this the default printer.

Specifying Timeout Values

While the LaserJet is an extremely reliable printer, things will go wrong from time to time. For example, you might try to print a document while the LaserJet is off-line, or you may run out of paper while printing an extremely long document.

To change the period of time Windows will wait before informing you that an error has occurred, use the Printer command on the control panel's Setup menu. Immediately below the Default Printer list that appears in the dialog box shown in Figure 13-13 are two printer timeout settings that determine the number of seconds Windows will wait for the LaserJet to respond before generating an error message.

FIGURE 13-15

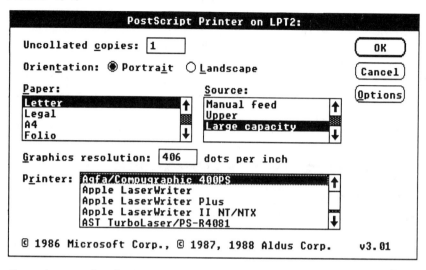

If you choose a PostScript-equipped LaserJet as your default printer, this dialog box will appear on your screen.

The Device not selected setting specifies the number of seconds Windows will wait before alerting you that the LaserJet is not responding to an initial print request. For example, if you tell Windows to print a document and the LaserJet is not turned on or is off-line, Windows will continue its attempt to print the document until the amount of time specified by this setting has passed. At that time, an error message will be displayed on your screen. By default, Windows will wait 15 seconds before generating an error message when the LaserJet does not respond to an initial print request.

The Transmission retry setting specifies the number of seconds Windows will wait before alerting you that a problem has occurred as a document is being printed. For example, if your LaserJet runs out of paper or jams while printing a document, Windows will continue its attempt to print the document until the number of seconds specified by this setting has passed. At that time, an error message will be displayed on your screen. By default, Windows will wait 45 seconds before generating an error message when an error occurs as a document is being printed.

Timeout settings are not dependent on the printer you have selected as the default printer. In other words, once you specify the amount of time Windows should wait before generating an error message, Windows will use these settings regardless of the printer you are using.

**Setting Up the
PCL Device
Driver**

Once you have installed support for a PCL LaserJet and have addressed the issues we discussed in the previous section of this chapter, you're ready to set up the PCL device driver so that it can take full advantage of your printer's capabilities. In this section, we'll show you how to to do this from the control panel.

If you use the Printer command on the control panel's Setup menu to select a PCL LaserJet as your default printer, the dialog box shown in Figure 13-16 will appear on your screen. For the sake of convenience, we'll refer to this dialog box as the PCL settings box throughout the remainder of this discussion.

FIGURE 13-16

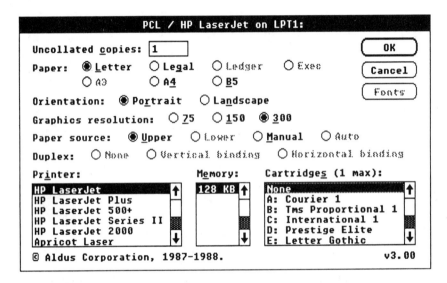

You can use the PCL settings box to tell the PCL device driver about your LaserJet.

The settings that appear in the PCL settings box tell the PCL device driver about your printer. For example, they define the type of LaserJet you are using, as well as the resolution at which you want to print graphics.

Choosing the settings that match the capabilities of your LaserJet is an extremely important process. Therefore, in this section, we'll take a look at each of the PCL settings that can be changed and discuss the significance of each.

*How to select
a setting*

Before we discuss each of the settings in the PCL settings box, we'll give you a quick overview of the methods you can use to select them. If you have a mouse, you can select any of the settings in the PCL settings box by clicking on them. If you do not have a mouse, you can select the settings by using the [Alt] key in conjunction with the underlined character in the name of the setting. For example, the Printer command can be issued by pressing **[Alt] R**. After you have selected all of the PCL settings that you want to select, you must save them to your WIN.INI file. To do this, press ↵ or select **OK**.

Several of the settings that appear in the PCL settings box may be changed only once. For example, once you tell the PCL device driver that you are using an HP LaserJet Series II, it is unlikely you will need to change this setting in the future. On the other hand, settings such as the one that allows you to specify the font cartridges you are using at a particular time may need to be changed quite frequently.

When to select a setting

Most Windows applications, such as Aldus PageMaker and Microsoft Excel, give you the ability to change the settings that appear in the PCL settings box without running the control panel. Likewise, since Windows is a multitasking environment, you can use the control panel to change these settings when running an application that does not provide you with the ability to change them directly. We'll discuss this subject in more detail later in this chapter when we take a look at the process of printing with a Windows application. We'll also discuss it when we look at specific Windows applications in subsequent chapters.

The most important setting that you can alter using the PCL settings box is the Printer setting. This setting allows you to specify which member of the LaserJet printer family you plan to use. As you can see in Figure 13-16, the PCL settings box lists all of the members of the LaserJet family, as well as several LaserJet/PCL-compatible printers available from other manufacturers. You should choose from this list the name of the particular LaserJet you are using.

Choosing a printer

The printer that you select will directly affect the availability of many of the other settings in the PCL settings box. For example, if you choose the HP LaserJet 2000, you can access the Auto Paper source option. You cannot access this option if you choose any other LaserJet.

The Printer setting also provides the PCL driver with information concerning the fonts that are resident in your printer. For example, if you choose the LaserJet Series II, the PCL driver will allow you to include any of the fonts resident in the Series II in documents produced by a Windows application. We'll show you how to tell the PCL driver about cartridge and soft fonts later in this chapter.

Finally, at the time *LaserJet Companion* went to press, the list of printers that appears in the PCL settings box did not include an HP LaserJet IID option. Therefore, if you want to use a LaserJet Series IID with Windows, you should choose the HP LaserJet 2000 option. Of course, if the PCL settings box that was included with the version of Windows you are using does offer an HP LaserJet Series IID option, you should select it if you want to use a LaserJet Series IID.

Specifying the amount of printer memory

Once you have selected the particular LaserJet you are using, you must select the appropriate Memory setting. As you might expect, the list of memory options that appear in the PCL settings box will change according to the particular LaserJet that is selected. For example, if you select the HP LaserJet Series II, the memory settings that appear in the PCL settings box shown in Figure 13-16 will be available. You should choose the amount of memory that is installed in your LaserJet.

Specifying the number of uncollated copies

The PCL settings box's Uncollated copies setting allows you to specify the number of copies that will be printed when a Windows application prints a document. For example, if you set the number of Uncollated copies to 5, the PCL driver will tell the LaserJet to print five copies of any document printed by a Windows application. If you want to print multiple copies of documents on a regular basis, it is worthwhile to take advantage of the Uncollated copies setting. Whenever you instruct Windows to print a document, a certain amount of time is spent converting it to a data format that the LaserJet will recognize. Additional time is then spent transmitting this data to the LaserJet.

If you use the Uncollated copies setting, Windows will begin by converting documents from Windows format to LaserJet format. It will then send this data to the LaserJet along with a command telling the LaserJet to print the number of copies you have specified. Therefore, to print multiple copies of a document, Windows does not have to send the same data to the LaserJet several times. In many instances, particularly when your document contains graphics, this will save a significant amount of time.

Duplex printing

The LaserJet 2000 and LaserJet Series IID have the ability to print documents on both sides of a page. Therefore, if you have selected the LaserJet 2000 from the Printer list, the PCL settings box will allow you to access the Duplex options. Otherwise, the Duplex options are not available.

If you do not want to print text on both sides of a page, you should choose the None option. On the other hand, you should choose the Vertical binding option if you want to print text on both sides of a page so that you can bind your document along the long edge of each page. Finally, you should choose the Horizontal binding option if you want to print text on both sides of a page so that you can bind your document along the short edge of each page. If you'd like to know more about the duplex printing capability of the LaserJet 2000 and Series IID, see the discussions that appear in Chapters 2 and 21.

Choosing paper

Each member of the LaserJet family can use a number of types of paper stock. You can use the PCL settings box to choose the type of paper you plan to use with the LaserJet when printing with a Windows application.

While the PCL driver supports seven types of paper, no member of the LaserJet family can handle all seven. Table 13-1 lists each member of the LaserJet family supported by the PCL driver that was being shipped with Windows 286 and 386 Version 2.1 at the time *LaserJet Companion* went to press, along with the types of paper each can use.

TABLE 13-1

Printer	Types of paper supported
LaserJet	Letter, Legal, A4, B5
LaserJet Plus	Letter, Legal, A4, B5
LaserJet 500 Plus	Letter, Legal, A4, B5
LaserJet Series II	Letter, Legal, Exec, A4, B5
LaserJet 2000	Letter, Legal, Exec, A3, A4

This table lists the types of paper that can be used by each member of the LaserJet family supported by the Windows PCL driver.

Orientation

As you learned in Chapter 4, the LaserJet can print documents using Portrait or Landscape orientation if the appropriate fonts are available. When Portrait orientation is used, text is printed across what you normally consider to be the x-axis of a page. When Landscape orientation is used, text is printed across what you normally consider to be the y-axis of a page. You can change the orientation the LaserJet will use when printing any document by selecting the Portrait or Landscape setting from the PCL's setting box.

Graphics resolution

The LaserJet family of printers is based on Canon laser engines that can print graphics at a maximum resolution of 300 dots per inch (dpi). All LaserJets can also print graphics at resolutions of 75 and 150 dpi. You can specify the resolution at which you want Windows to print graphics on the LaserJet by selecting the 75, 150, or 300 options in the PCL settings box.

As we pointed out in Chapter 4, the number of dpi directly affects the quality of graphics. Therefore, if quality is important, you should choose the option that allows you to print graphics using the highest number of dpi your LaserJet supports. On the other hand, if speed is the only concern, you may want to choose one of the lower settings.

Choosing a paper source

Each member of the LaserJet printer family can accept paper from a variety of sources. The PCL settings box allows you to choose the source of paper that Windows will use when you print a document.

Windows supports four sources of paper. However, no member of the LaserJet family supports all four. Table 13-2 lists each member of the LaserJet family supported by the PCL driver being shipped with Microsoft Windows 286 and 386 Version 2.1 at the time *LaserJet Companion* went to press, along with the paper sources each supports.

TABLE 13-2

Printer	Paper sources supported
LaserJet	Upper, Manual
LaserJet Plus	Upper, Manual
LaserJet 500	Upper, Lower, Manual
LaserJet Series II	Upper, Manual
LaserJet 2000	Upper, Lower, Auto

This table lists each member of the LaserJet family supported by the Windows PCL driver, and the paper sources each printer supports.

Adding support for HP font cartridges

The easiest way to add fonts to the LaserJet is to add a font cartridge. The Windows PCL driver currently supports 24 Hewlett-Packard font cartridges that can be selected using the Cartridges command from the PCL settings box. If you do not have a font cartridge, you should select the None option that appears at the top of the cartridge list.

As you can see in Figure 13-16, Windows displays just above the Cartridges list in the PCL settings box the maximum number of cartridges you can select. This number is determined by the LaserJet you are using. For example, if you are using a LaserJet, LaserJet Plus, or LaserJet 500 Plus, you can select one cartridge. If you are using a LaserJet Series II, you can select two cartridges, and you can select three cartridges if you are using a LaserJet 2000.

If you are using a LaserJet that supports more than one font cartridge, you must select these cartridges from the list that appears in the PCL settings box. If you have a mouse, you can select the first cartridge by clicking on its name. However, to select the second and third cartridges, you must hold down the Shift key while clicking on their names.

If you do not have a mouse, selecting more than one cartridge is more complex. To select the first cartridge, press **[Alt]S** to activate the Cartridges List, then use the ↑ and ↓ keys to highlight the name of the cartridge. To select the second and/or third cartridge, hold down the **[Ctrl]** key while using the ↑ and ↓ keys to highlight the name(s), then press **[Spacebar]**.

Finally, if you want to remove support for all font cartridges, use the mouse or keyboard to select the **None** option. If you want to remove support for a single font cartridge while preserving support for another, hold down the **[Shift]** key and select the name of the font cartridge you want to remove.

Adding support for PCL soft fonts

As we pointed out in Chapter 4, all members of the LaserJet printer family, with the exception of the original LaserJet, support soft fonts. Fortunately, the procedure you must use to add support for soft fonts to Microsoft Windows 286 and 386 Version 2.1 is quite simple.

To add support for soft fonts to Microsoft Windows, select the Fonts option from the PCL settings box. When you do this, the Soft Font Installer dialog box shown in Figure 13-17 will appear on your screen.

FIGURE 13-17

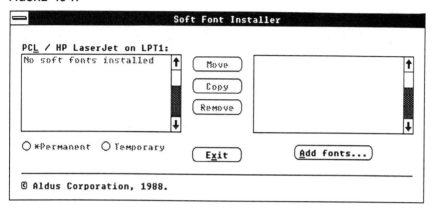

PCL / HP LaserJet on LPT1:

No soft fonts installed

Move
Copy
Remove

○ *Permanent ○ Temporary

Exit

Add fonts...

© Aldus Corporation, 1988.

The Soft Font Installer dialog box simplifies the process of adding soft font support to Microsoft Windows.

When the Soft Font Installer dialog box appears on your screen, you can add support for a soft font by choosing the Add fonts... option. When you choose this option, the Add fonts dialog box shown in Figure 13-18 will appear. When the Add fonts dialog box appears, you can enter the name of the directory in which the soft fonts you want to install are stored. For example, if the soft fonts you want to install are stored in the directory A:\, press ↵ when the Add fonts dialog box appears.

FIGURE 13-18

Add fonts   OK

Insert the disk with the soft font files   Cancel
you wish to add in drive A, or choose an
alternative drive/directory:

A:\

When the Add fonts dialog box appears, you should enter the name of the directory containing the soft fonts you want to install.

After you have entered the name of the appropriate directory, the names of each of the fonts stored there will be listed in the Drive list of the Soft Font Installer dialog box. For example, as you can see in Figure 13-19, the Drive list of the Soft Font Installer dialog box contains the names of each soft font stored in A:\ .

FIGURE 13-19

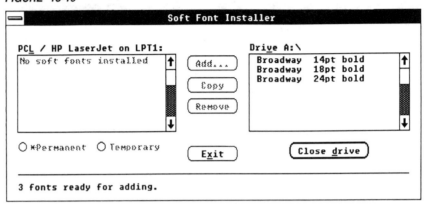

The Soft Font Installer dialog box will list each of the fonts stored in the directory that you specify.

Once the Drive list contains the names of soft fonts, you can select the fonts for which you want to add support to Microsoft Windows. If you have a mouse, you can do this by clicking on the name of the individual font. If you want to select more than one font at a time, click on the first font name, then press the **[Shift]** key as you click on successive font names.

If you do not have a mouse, you can select a font with the keyboard. To do this, press **[Alt]V**, then use the ↑ and ↓ keys to scroll through the list of font names until the cursor is highlighting the one that you want to select. If you want to select more than one font at a time, use the ↑ and ↓ keys to select the first font name, press the **[Ctrl]** key, use the ↑ and ↓ keys to highlight successive font names, then press the **[Spacebar]** to select them.

When you have selected the font(s) for which you want to add support to Microsoft Windows, you should choose the A̲dd... option. When you do this, the Add fonts dialog box shown in Figure 13-20 will appear on your screen.

As you can see, this dialog box prompts you to enter the name of the directory in which soft fonts should be installed. At this time, you should enter the name of the directory in which you want to install soft fonts, or you should press ↵ to accept the default directory C:\PCLFONTS.

Once you have supplied the Soft Font Installer with the name of the directory in which it should install soft fonts, all of the soft fonts you have selected will be installed, and their names will be listed in the PCL list of the Soft Font Installer dialog box. Now, you can select the Add… option to add more fonts, the Remove option to delete fonts, or the Exit option to return to the PCL settings box. You can also change the download status of installed fonts from temporary to permanent, or you can enable the Edit button to make changes to a font's font metrics.

FIGURE 13-20

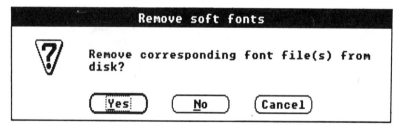

The Soft Font Installer will present this dialog box, which prompts you to enter the name of the directory in which it should install soft fonts.

Just as you can use the Soft Font Installer to install support for a soft font, you can use it to remove support for a soft font by choosing the Remove option. To remove support for a soft font, highlight its name in the Soft Font Installer dialog box's PCL list, then choose <u>R</u>emove. When you do this, the dialog box shown in Figure 13-21 will appear.

Removing support for a soft font

FIGURE 13-21

```
┌──────────────────────────────────────────────────────┐
│               Remove soft fonts                        │
├──────────────────────────────────────────────────────┤
│   ┌──┐                                                 │
│   │?/│   Remove corresponding font file(s) from        │
│   └──┘   disk?                                          │
│                                                        │
│      ( Yes )      ( No )      ( Cancel )                │
└──────────────────────────────────────────────────────┘
```

The Soft Font Installer will ask you to verify that you want to remove support for a soft font.

As you can see in Figure 13-21, the Soft Font Installer will ask you if you want to remove the actual data file in which a soft font is stored, in addition to Windows' support for that font. Therefore, when this dialog box appears on your screen, choose <u>Y</u>es if you want to remove support for a font and delete the data file in which the font is stored. If you want to remove support for a font, but do not want to delete the data file in which it is stored, choose <u>N</u>o. Finally, if you want to abort the operation, choose **Cancel**.

**Changing a font's
download status**

One of the most important settings that can be altered by the Soft Font Installer is a soft font's download status. When you use a soft font in a document, the PCL device driver will check its download status. If a font's download status is permanent, the PCL driver will assume that it has already been downloaded and will print the document in question.

On the other hand, if a font's download status is temporary, the PCL driver will immediately download the font to the LaserJet. Once the document that contains the font has been printed, the PCL driver will delete all temporary soft fonts from the LaserJet's memory. As a result, each time you use a soft font whose download status is temporary, the PCL driver must download it to the LaserJet.

If you plan to use a soft font several times during a Windows session, you should use the Soft Font Installer to change its download status to permanent. To do this, highlight the name of the font whose status you want to change in the PCL list, then select the Permanent option.

The first time you change a font's download status from temporary to permanent, the Soft Font Installer will display a dialog box that explains the ramifications of the change. Once you have read the explanation that appears in this dialog box, choose **Continue** to return to the Soft Font Installer dialog box.

After you change the status of a font or group of fonts from temporary to permanent and choose Exit to return to the PCL settings box, the Download options dialog box shown in Figure 13-22 will appear. As you can see, the purpose of this dialog box is to allow you to specify when and if the font(s) whose status has been changed to permanent should be downloaded.

FIGURE 13-22

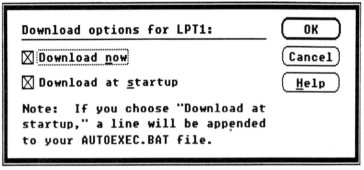

*The Download options dialog box allows you specify when and if
permanent soft fonts should be downloaded.*

If you want the soft font(s) whose status has been changed to permanent to be downloaded automatically when you turn on your computer, select the Download at startup option, then choose **OK**. When you do this, the Soft Font Installer will add a line to your AUTOEXEC.BAT file. Consequently, whenever you turn on or reboot your computer, you will be asked if you want to download PCL fonts to the port to which your LaserJet is connected.

If you want to want to use the soft font(s) whose download status you have changed from temporary to permanent during the current Windows session, select the Download now option, then choose **OK**. When you do this, the Soft Font Installer will download all fonts whose download status has been changed to permanent.

Finally, to download all soft fonts with a utility such as HP's FontLoad, deselect both options, then choose **OK**. If you want all soft fonts to be downloaded each time you turn on your computer, and you want to use soft fonts during the current Windows session, select both options, then choose **OK**.

Editing font metrics

Font metrics is a term that refers to the information that identifies the character-istics of a font. A font's name and point size, as well as the ID number you can use to select a font once it has been downloaded to the LaserJet, are prime examples of this type of information.

When you add support for a font to Microsoft Windows, the Soft Font Installer will create a data file in which it will store font metrics information. If you need to change the information stored in this file, you can do so by enabling the Soft Font Installer's Edit button.

To enable the Soft Font Installer's Edit button, use the mouse or press **[Alt][Spacebar]** to pull down the control menu shown in Figure 13-23, then select the Enable edit button option.

FIGURE 13-23

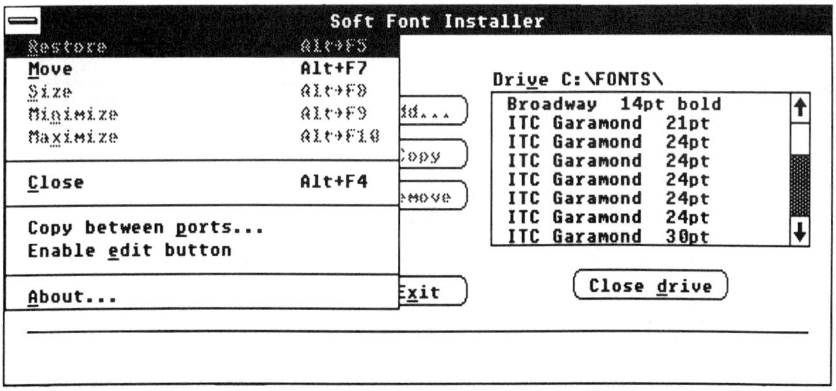

The Enable edit button option lets you to enable the Soft Font Installer's Edit button.

When you select the Enable edit button option on the Soft Font Installer's control menu, the Edit button will appear in the Soft Font Installer dialog box between the Remove and Exit buttons. As an example, the Edit button has been enabled in the Soft Font Installer dialog box shown in Figure 13-24.

FIGURE 13-24

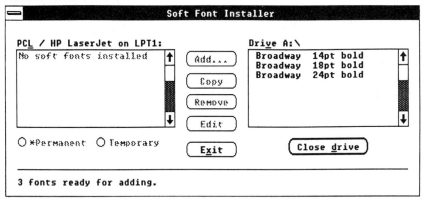

The Edit button allows you to make changes to font metrics.

Once you have enabled the Edit button, you can use it to make changes to the font metrics associated with any installed soft font. To select a font whose font metrics information you want to change, highlight its name in the PCL list box, then press **[Alt]E** or click on the Edit button. When you do this, a Font metrics dialog box similar to the one shown in Figure 13-25 will appear.

FIGURE 13-25

```
┌──────────────────────────────────────────────────────────────┐
│  ┌──────────────────────────────────────────────────────────┐ │
│  │  Font metrics                                  (  OK  )   │ │
│  │  Description:  Broadway   14pt bold            (Cancel)   │ │
│  │     Font file: BW140BPX.USP                               │ │
│  │         Name: [Broadway]                                  │ │
│  │       Font ID: [1  ]                                      │ │
│  │       Status: ○ *Permanent ● Temporary                   │ │
│  │       Family: ○ Roman    ○ Modern    ● Decorative         │ │
│  │               ○ Swiss    ○ Script    ○ Don't care         │ │
│  │   Edit mode: ☐ Changes apply to all selected fonts        │ │
│  └──────────────────────────────────────────────────────────┘ │
└──────────────────────────────────────────────────────────────┘
```

The Font metrics dialog box allows you to make changes to the information that identifies a font.

As you can see in Figure 13-25, the Font metrics dialog box shows a description of a font and the name of the file in which it is stored. In addition, the Font metrics dialog box will allow you to change a font's name, ID number, status, and family. For more information on each of these topics, see the discussions that appear in Chapter 4.

If you want to change the name Windows will use to identify a font, enter the name you want to use in the Name text box. If you want to change the soft font ID number that Windows will use to select a font once it has been downloaded to the LaserJet, enter a number between 0 and 999 in the Font ID text box.

If you need to change a font's download status from temporary to permanent, select the Permanent option. If you need to change a font's status from permanent to temporary, select the Temporary option. Finally, if you want to change a font's family setting, simply select the appropriate Family option.

Once you have made any necessary changes to the information in the Font metrics box, choose **OK** to save those changes and to return to the Soft Font Installer dialog box. If you do not want to save the changes you have made, or simply want to return to the Soft Font Installer dialog box, choose **Cancel**.

Copying soft font support

If your computer has access to more than one LaserJet, you can use the Soft Font Installer to copy or move support for soft fonts to any or all of them. To do this, use the mouse or press **[Alt][Spacebar]** to pull down the control menu, then select the Copy between ports option. When you do this, the Copy between ports dialog box shown in Figure 13-26 will appear.

FIGURE 13-26

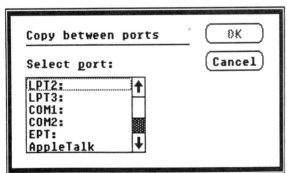

If you choose the control menu's Copy between ports option, this dialog box will ask you to identify the port to which you want to download soft fonts.

When the Copy between ports dialog box appears on your screen, select the port to which your LaserJet is connected from the Select port list, then choose OK. For example, if you want to copy or move soft font support from your default LaserJet to a LaserJet connected to an LPT2:, select **LPT2:**, then choose **OK**.

Once you have chosen the port to which the LaserJet is connected, the Soft Font Installer dialog box will undergo a few changes, as shown in Figure 13-27.

FIGURE 13-27

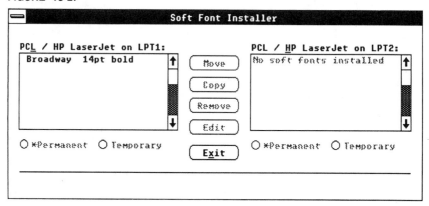

The Soft Font Installer dialog box will change while the Copy between ports option is enabled.

As you can see, the Drive list shown on the Soft Font Installer box that appears in Figure 13-19 on page 460 is replaced by a list that represents the fonts supported by the LaserJet connected to the port you specified. In addition, the Add... button shown in Figure 13-19 is now the Move button.

To copy support for a soft font from one LaserJet to another, highlight the name of the font in either font list, then choose Copy. To move support from one LaserJet to another, select the font, then choose Move.

Once you have completed the task of moving or copying support for soft fonts from one printer to another, use the mouse or press **[Alt][Spacebar]** to pull down the control menu and select the End between ports option.

PCL font summary file

After you have added Windows support for PCL LaserJet internal, cartridge, and soft fonts by making changes to your WIN.INI file, the PCL device driver will create a file in your Windows directory called the PCL font summary file. The name of this file will consist of the letters *FS*, followed by the name of the port to which your LaserJet is connected and the extension .PCL. For example, if you have a LaserJet connected to LPT1:, the PCL driver will create a PCL font summary file called FSLPT1.PCL.

The PCL font summary file contains printer font metrics information for all internal and cartridge fonts, along with the PCL commands necessary to select them. If you have installed any soft fonts, the PCL font summary file will contain the names of the printer font metrics (PFM) files associated with each of those fonts.

When you print a document that contains a LaserJet font, the PCL driver will interrogate the PCL font summary file for the printer font metrics and PCL information the driver needs to select and use that font. If you use the LaserJet's

Internal Courier font in a document, the PCL driver will extract the PCL command it needs, then use the Courier font from your PCL font summary file. If you include a LaserJet PCL or PostScript device font in a document when a matching Windows screen font is not available, Windows will use the printer font metrics information in the PCL font summary to pick an appropriate screen substitute for the PCL or PostScript device font. It will then use this screen font as a substitute to represent the LaserJet PCL or PostScript device font on your screen.

The PCL device driver keeps track of the location of your PCL font summary file in the PCL section of your WIN.INI file. For example, if Windows is installed on your hard disk in the directory C:\WINDOWS, and you have a LaserJet connected to LPT1:, the PCL driver will place the line `Fontsummary=C:\WINDOWS\FSLPT1.PCL` in your WIN.INI file.

Whenever you print a document, the PCL driver will look for the PCL font summary file specified by the Fontsummary setting in the PCL section of your WIN.INI file. If the file is not found, a new one will be automatically created based on the information stored in the PCL section of your WIN.INI file.

If you add a font to your LaserJet and make the appropriate changes in your WIN.INI file to reflect the addition, the PCL driver will not immediately update your PCL font summary file. Instead, the first time you print a document using a new font, the PCL device driver will search the existing PCL font summary file for the information it requires. If this information is not found, the PCL font summary file will be updated to reflect the current status of your system as indicated by the settings in the PCL section of your WIN.INI file.

On the other hand, if you remove a font from your LaserJet and make the appropriate changes to WIN.INI, your PCL font summary file will never be changed to reflect the fact. Therefore, whenever you remove Windows support for a LaserJet font, always delete the PCL font summary file and allow the PCL driver to re-create it the next time you print a document.

Once you have installed support for a PostScript LaserJet and have addressed the setup issues we discussed earlier, you must set up the PostScript device driver so that it can take full advantage of your printer's capabilities. In this section, we'll show you how to to do this with the control panel.

Setting Up the PostScript Driver

If you use the Printer command on the control panel's Setup menu to select a PostScript-equipped LaserJet as your default printer, the dialog box shown in Figure 13-28 will appear on your screen. For convenience, we'll refer to this dialog box as the PostScript settings box throughout the remainder of this discussion.

The settings that appear in the PostScript settings box tell the PostScript device driver about your printer. For example, they define the type of PostScript printer you are using, as well as the resolution at which you want to print graphics.

FIGURE 13-28

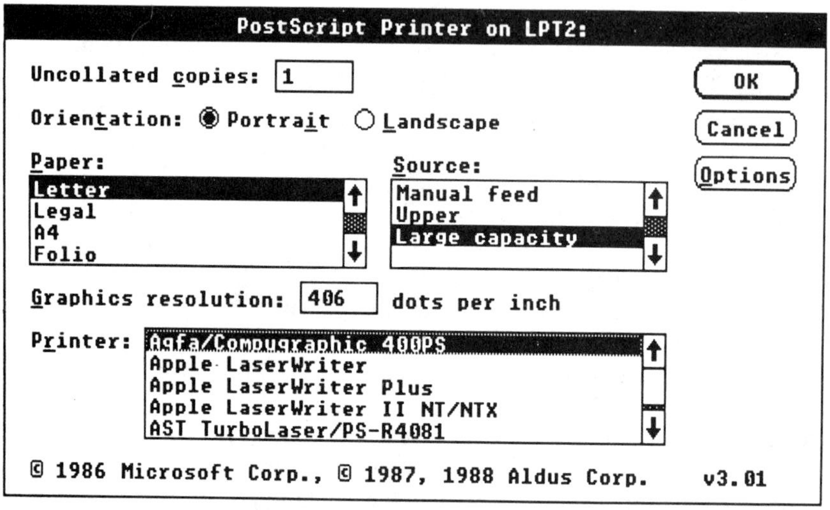

```
┌──────────────────────────────────────────────────────────┐
│             PostScript Printer on LPT2:                  │
│                                                          │
│  Uncollated copies: │1    │              ╭─────────╮     │
│                                          │   OK    │     │
│  Orientation: ◉ Portrait  ○ Landscape    ╰─────────╯     │
│                                          ╭─────────╮     │
│  Paper:                   Source:        │ Cancel  │     │
│  ┌─────────────────┬─┐   ┌─────────────┬─┐╰─────────╯    │
│  │Letter           │↑│   │Manual feed  │↑│╭─────────╮    │
│  │Legal            │▓│   │Upper        │ ││Options  │    │
│  │A4               │ │   │Large capacity│ ╰─────────╯    │
│  │Folio            │↓│   │             │↓│              │
│  └─────────────────┴─┘   └─────────────┴─┘              │
│                                                          │
│  Graphics resolution: │406  │  dots per inch            │
│                                                          │
│  Printer: ┌────────────────────────────────┬─┐          │
│           │Agfa/Compugraphic 400PS         │↑│          │
│           │Apple LaserWriter               │ │          │
│           │Apple LaserWriter Plus          │ │          │
│           │Apple LaserWriter II NT/NTX     │ │          │
│           │AST TurboLaser/PS-R4081         │↓│          │
│           └────────────────────────────────┴─┘          │
│                                                          │
│  © 1986 Microsoft Corp., © 1987, 1988 Aldus Corp.  v3.01│
└──────────────────────────────────────────────────────────┘
```

You can use the PostScript settings box to tell the PostScript device driver about your LaserJet.

Choosing the settings that match the capabilities of your LaserJet is an important process. In this section, we'll take a look at each of the PostScript settings that can be changed and discuss the significance of each.

How to select a setting

Before we discuss each of the settings in the PostScript settings box, we'll give you a quick overview of the methods you may use to select them. If you have a mouse, you can select any of the settings in the PCL settings box by clicking on them. If you do not have a mouse, you can select the settings by using the [Alt] key in conjunction with the underlined character in the name of the setting. For example, the P̲rinter command can be issued by pressing **[Alt]R**. After you have selected all the PCL settings that you want to select, you must save them to your WIN.INI file. To do this, press ↵ or select **OK**.

When to select a setting

Several of the settings that appear in the PostScript settings box must be changed only once. For example, once you tell the PCL device driver that you are using an Apple LaserWriter Plus, it is unlikely that you will need to change this setting in the future. On the other hand, settings such as the one that allows you to specify the number of uncollated copies may need to be changed frequently.

Most Windows applications, such as Aldus PageMaker and Microsoft Excel, give you the ability to change the settings that appear in the PostScript settings box without running the control panel. Likewise, since Windows is a multitasking environment, you can use the control panel to change these settings when you are running an application that does not provide you with the ability to change them directly. We'll discuss this subject in more detail later in this chapter when we take a look at the process of printing with a Windows application. We'll also discuss it when we look at specific Windows applications in subsequent chapters.

The most important setting on the PostScript settings box is the Printer setting. The purpose of this setting is to tell the PostScript driver which PostScript printer you are using.

Choosing a printer

While the names of 13 PostScript printers are listed in the PostScript settings box, a PostScript-equipped LaserJet is not among them. Therefore, if you want to install support for a PostScript-equipped LaserJet, you must choose the name of a compatible PostScript printer from the list.

The manual that is included with your PostScript system may list the names of the PostScript printers with which your system is compatible. If not, you must obtain this information from the manufacturer before trying to install support for your printer.

For example, the manual that is included with the QMS JetScript system states that a LaserJet Series II equipped with JetScript is compatible with the Apple LaserWriter Plus and the QMS-PS 800 Plus. Therefore, if you want to install support for a JetScript-equipped Series II, use the Printer command to select the **Apple LaserWriter Plus** or **QMS-PS 800 Plus**.

The availability of other settings in the PostScript settings box will be affected by the capabilities of the printer you select with the Printer setting. For example, neither the Apple LaserWriter Plus nor the QMS-PS 800 Plus supports a lower paper tray. Therefore, if you tell the PostScript driver that you are using either of these printers, the Lower tray settings will not be available.

The Printer setting also provides the PostScript driver with information concerning the fonts that are resident in your printer. For example, if you choose the Apple LaserWriter Plus or the QMS-PS 800 Plus, the PostScript driver will allow you to include in documents produced by a Windows application any of the 35 fonts resident in these printers.

The PostScript settings box's Uncollated copies setting allows you to specify the number of copies that will be printed when a Windows application prints a document. For example, if you set the Uncollated copies setting to 5, the PostScript driver will tell the LaserJet to print five copies of any document printed by a Windows application.

Specifying the number of uncollated copies

Unfortunately, the Uncollated copies settings is volatile. In other words, it is not stored in WIN.INI when you press ↵ or select OK. As a result, whenever you run Windows, the Uncollated copies setting is always set to 1. If you want to take advantage of the ability to print multiple copies of a document automatically, you must change the Uncollated copies setting each time you run Windows.

If you want to print multiple copies of documents on a regular basis, it is worthwhile to take advantage of the Uncollated copies setting. Whenever you instruct Windows to print a document, a certain amount of time is spent converting it to PostScript code. Additional time is spent transmitting this code to the PostScript interpreter, which, in turn, must convert it into data that will produce the desired output when it is sent to the LaserJet. If you use the Uncollated copies setting to print multiple copies of a document, Windows will convert the document to PostScript code. It will then send this code to the PostScript interpreter along with a command specifying the number of copies that should be printed. Therefore, to print multiple copies of a document, Windows does not have to send the same PostScript code to the LaserJet several times. In many instances, particularly when your document contains graphics, this will save a significant amount of time.

Choosing paper

The PostScript device driver allows you to use any one of six types of paper with a PostScript-equipped LaserJet. The six types of paper are listed in the PostScript settings box. You can make a paper selection by using the mouse or issuing the Paper command. For example, if you want to use letter-size paper, use the mouse or Paper command to select the **Letter** option.

Choosing a paper source

The PostScript device driver allows you to feed paper from the LaserJet's internal paper tray and manual feed slot. To choose the source from which you want to feed paper, use the mouse or Source command to select it. For example, if you want to feed paper from the LaserJet's manual feed slot, use the mouse or Source command to select the **Manual feed** option.

Orientation

As you learned in Chapter 4, the LaserJet can print documents using Portrait or Landscape orientation if the appropriate fonts are available. When Portrait orientation is used, text is printed across what you normally consider to be the x-axis of a page. On the other hand, when Landscape orientation is used, text is printed across what you normally consider to be the y-axis of a page. You can change the orientation the LaserJet will use when printing any document by selecting the Portrait or Landscape setting in the PostScript settings box.

Graphics resolution

The LaserJet family of printers is based on Canon laser engines that can print graphics at a maximum resolution of 300 dots per inch (dpi). With PostScript installed, the LaserJet can print graphics at 75, 100, 150, and 300 dpi. You can specify the resolution at which you want Windows to print graphics on the LaserJet by selecting the Graphics resolution option and entering the appropriate value. For example, if you want to print graphics at 300 dpi, select the Graphics resolution option, then type **300**.

As we pointed out in Chapter 2, the number of dpi directly affects the quality of graphics. Therefore, if quality is important, you should choose the option that allows you to print graphics using the highest number of dpi your LaserJet supports. On the other hand, if speed is the only concern, you may want to choose one of the lower settings.

In addition to the options and settings that you can change directly via the PostScript settings box, there are a number of PostScript-specific settings and options that can be changed by choosing Options. When you choose Options, the PostScript printer options dialog box shown in Figure 13-29 will appear.

FIGURE 13-29

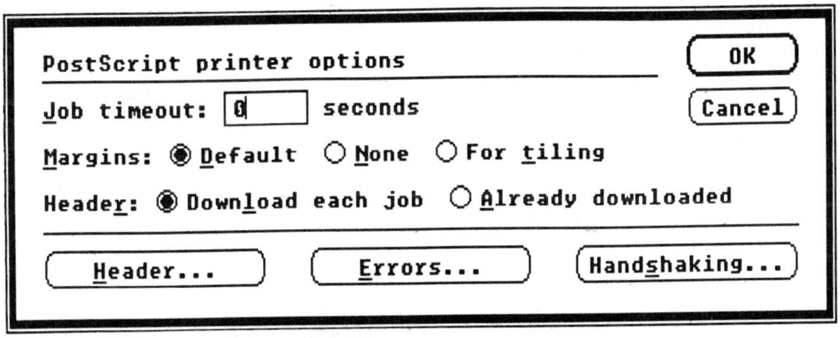

```
┌─────────────────────────────────────────────────────────┐
│  PostScript printer options              ( OK )          │
│  Job timeout: [0]    seconds            ( Cancel )       │
│  Margins: ● Default  ○ None  ○ For tiling                │
│  Header: ● Download each job  ○ Already downloaded       │
│  ─────────────────────────────────────────────────────  │
│  ( Header... )   ( Errors... )   ( Handshaking... )      │
└─────────────────────────────────────────────────────────┘
```

The PostScript printer options dialog box provides access to a number of PostScript-specific settings and options.

Job timeout

The first setting that can be changed via the PostScript printer options dialog box is the Job timeout setting. This option allows you to specify the number of seconds the PostScript interpreter will wait before generating a timeout error that will be detected by the Windows PostScript device driver. By default, the Job timeout setting is zero. Therefore, whenever a printer error occurs, the PostScript interpreter will generate an error message immediately.

If you want to change this setting, enter a new value in the Job timeout text box. For example, if you want the PostScript interpreter to wait ten seconds before generating a timeout error, type **10** in the Job timeout text box.

Margins

The second setting that can be changed via the PostScript printer options box is the Margins setting. As you can see in Figure 13-29, this setting is normally set to Default, which means that the PostScript driver will not attempt to print text or graphics in the LaserJet's unprintable region. On the other hand, if you select the None option, the PostScript driver will attempt to print text and graphics in the unprintable region. (As you might expect, if you choose the None option, any text or graphics that the PostScript driver attempts to print in the unprintable region will not be printed.)

Finally, if you want to print a PostScript document that is larger than the type of paper you are using, you can choose the For tiling option to inform the PostScript driver that it should print the document on several sheets of paper. Then, you can tape these sheets of paper together to construct the document.

Header

Each time you tell Windows to print a document, the PostScript driver will send a setup code to the PostScript interpreter. This adds a few seconds to the amount of time it takes to print a document.

Technically, it is not necessary to send a setup code to the PostScript printer each time you print a document. Therefore, you can set up the printer once at the beginning of your session, and Windows will bypass the setup procedure each time you print a document thereafter.

To take advantage of this capability, select the Header... option in the PostScript printer options dialog box. When you do this, the dialog box shown in Figure 13-30 will appear. Now, select the File option, then type **C:\WINDOWS\PSPREP.TXT** and press ↵. When you do, the PostScript driver will write to disk the setup code normally sent at the beginning of every print job.

FIGURE 13-30

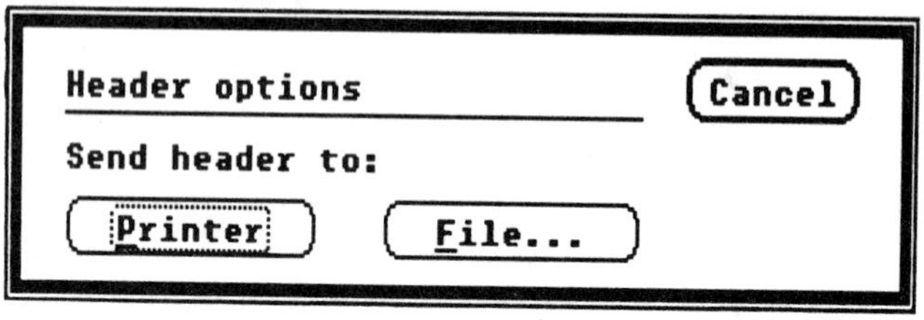

```
┌─────────────────────────────────────────────┐
│  ┌───────────────────────────────────────┐  │
│  │  Header options            ( Cancel )  │  │
│  │  ───────────────────────               │  │
│  │  Send header to:                       │  │
│  │  ( Printer )      ( File... )          │  │
│  └───────────────────────────────────────┘  │
└─────────────────────────────────────────────┘
```

This dialog box allows you to write PostScript setup code to a disk file.

Once the PostScript driver has written the PostScript setup code to disk, you will be returned to the PostScript printer options dialog box. At this time, select the Already downloaded option, then choose **OK**.

After you have written PostScript setup code to disk and have selected the Already downloaded option, you must add a line to your AUTOEXEC.BAT file that will send the file to the PostScript interpreter automatically each time you boot your system. For example, if your PostScript-equipped LaserJet is connected to LPT2:, add the line COPY PSPREP.TXT LPT1: to your AUTOEXEC.BAT file.

Error handling

The next option on the PostScript printer options dialog box—Errors...— allows you to download an error handler to the PostScript interpreter. The error handler is a PostScript program that will instruct the PostScript interpreter to print an error message when a PostScript error has occurred. This is a feature you may want to use if you are developing a Windows application that communicates with a PostScript-equipped LaserJet.

To download the PostScript error handler, select the Errors... option. When you do this, a dialog box will appear that will allow you to send the error directly to the PostScript interpreter or to a disk file. Therefore, you should select the Printer option if you want to send it to the PostScript interpreter, while you should choose the File option if you want to send it to a disk file (whose name you will then be asked to specify).

The final option on the PostScript printer options dialog box is the Handshaking... option. This option allows you to specify whether your computer should use hardware- or software-driven handshaking when communicating with a PostScript printer that interfaces via a serial RS-232 port.

Handshaking

For example, if you have a LaserJet or LaserJet Plus that is equipped with a PostScript lid, and you plan to use it with Windows without using the Windows Spooler, you must use hardware handshaking. To do this, select the Handshaking... option, choose the Hardware option, then choose **OK** when the PostScript driver asks you if you want to permanently alter your printer's handshaking.

To install an Adobe PostScript soft font for use with Windows, you must use an external utility program to download it from your computer's hard disk to your printer. In addition, you must copy the Windows printer font metrics (PFM) file that is included with every Adobe PostScript soft font into the directory in which the actual soft font data files are stored. Finally, you must add at least two entries to the section of your WIN.INI file that contains PostScript settings.

Adding support for PostScript soft fonts

To add these entries to your WIN.INI file, run the Microsoft Windows Notepad and load WIN.INI. When the file has been loaded, scroll through it until you find the section that contains PostScript settings. For example, if your PostScript-equipped LaserJet is connected to LPT2:, the beginning of the section of your WIN.INI file that contains PostScript settings should be marked by the header `[PostScript,LPT2]`. After you have added all necessary entries to this section of your WIN.INI file, pull down the Notepad's File menu and issue a Save command to save the changes.

The first entry that must be added to your WIN.INI file provides the PostScript device driver with the total number of soft fonts that are installed. Therefore, if you have one soft font installed, the line `softfonts=1` should appear in the section of your WIN.INI file that contains the PostScript settings.

Once you have added the `softfonts` setting to your WIN.INI file, you must add an entry that specifies the location of that font's printer font metrics (PFM) file. The format of such an entry is:

Softfont[*Soft font ID number*]=[*PFM file name*]

As you can see, there are two essential components in each soft font's WIN.INI entry. The first component is the *Soft font ID number*. As we pointed out in Chapter

4, when you download a PostScript soft font to the LaserJet, you must assign a discrete number to it. Therefore, to use a soft font with Windows successfully, you must include its Soft font ID number in its WIN.INI entry.

The second component of each soft font's WIN.INI entry is the PFM file name. This file name should specify the name of the soft font's printer font metrics file.

As an example, let's assume that you want to use Adobe's Bodoni font with Windows. The name of the PFM file included with the Bodoni font is BDR_____.PFM, and its typeface ID is 36. Therefore, to use this font with Windows, you should place the entry `Softfont36=BDR_____.PFM` in your WIN.INI file.

As you might expect, if you want to remove support for a PostScript soft font, simply remove from your WIN.INI file the entry that corresponds to the font you want to delete. When you have removed a soft font's entry from your WIN.INI file, the font will no longer be recognized by Windows; however, the actual file in which the font is stored will remain. Therefore, if you plan to re-install support for a font in the near future, it may be a good idea to leave such font files alone. On the other hand, if you do not plan to re-install support in the near future, or if you need to free up some disk space, you can delete the font file. To delete a soft font data file, highlight its name with the MS-DOS Executive, pull down the File menu, and choose Delete.

SCREEN FONTS

The ability to display different fonts on the screen is the most useful aspect of Microsoft Windows. Therefore, in this section, we'll provide the information you need about installing and using Windows screen fonts.

We'll begin by taking a look at the types of screen fonts that Windows supports. Next, we'll move on to show you how to install and use LaserJet screen fonts with Windows. Finally, we'll discuss the problem of matching Windows screen fonts with the fonts your LaserJet will use to print text.

GDI Fonts

Because they are meant to be used with the Microsoft Windows Graphics Device Interface (GDI), screen fonts are officially referred to as GDI fonts. There are two types of GDI fonts—raster fonts and stroke fonts. While the LaserJet cannot print text using GDI raster (bit-mapped) fonts, it is technically possible for the LaserJet to print text using GDI stroke fonts, although the latter ability is often limited by particular applications.

For example, you will find that Microsoft Windows Write does not allow you to include stroke fonts in a document. Instead, it limits the fonts that you can use in a document to those installed as LaserJet device fonts. For instance, if the only LaserJet device font you have installed for use with Windows is the 12-point Internal Courier font, this is the only font Write will allow you to use in a document.

On the other hand, applications such as Aldus PageMaker will allow you to include any GDI font in a document, regardless of whether a matching LaserJet PCL or PostScript font is available. As a result, PageMaker will print stroke fonts by shifting the LaserJet into graphics mode, while it will substitute an available LaserJet PCL or PostScript font for GDI raster fonts. We'll take a closer look at the process of font substitution in the next section.

To print text using a GDI stroke font, you must shift the LaserJet into graphics mode. As a result, it takes much longer to print a document that contains a GDI stroke font than it does to print one that contains only device fonts.

Likewise, if you include a GDI raster font in a document and a matching printer font is not available, the concept of WYSIWYG (What You See Is What You Get) is violated when another printer font is used in its place.

As a result of these two considerations, applications developers will often trade the advantage of being able to use GDI fonts in the document for the advantages of faster printing and true WYSIWYG operation.

Installing Screen Fonts with SETUP

Earlier in this chapter, we discussed the process of using the Microsoft Windows SETUP program to install Windows on your system. Another operation that SETUP performs is the installation of a base set of GDI fonts. In this section, we'll take a brief look at the fonts installed by SETUP when you install Windows on your system.

When you run the Microsoft Windows SETUP program to install Windows on your system, SETUP will automatically install a set of GDI fonts that were specifically designed for use with the display hardware you are using. For example, if you tell SETUP that you have an EGA video system, it will automatically install a base set of three GDI raster fonts specifically designed for use with the EGA.

Regardless of the video system you are using, the base set of GDI raster fonts installed by SETUP includes versions of the Courier, Tms Rmn, and Helv fonts. A sample of each of these fonts is shown in Figure 13-31. A base set of three GDI stroke fonts is also installed by SETUP whenever you install Windows on your system. This base set includes the Roman, Script, and Modern fonts. A sample of each of these fonts is also shown in Figure 13-31.

These six fonts support the Microsoft Windows ANSI symbol set and are stored in data files that carry the extension .FON. For example, the file that contains the EGA version of the Tms Rmn GDI raster font is stored in a file named TMSRB.FON. Whenever you use one of these fonts in an application, Windows will load it into memory from disk. We'll refer to this class of GDI fonts as external fonts throughout the remainder of this discussion.

In addition to the six external GDI raster and stroke fonts installed by SETUP, two raster fonts are built directly into the Windows environment. These are the System and Terminal fonts. The System font is used by Windows in menus, dialog boxes, and system alert boxes and supports the ANSI standard symbol set. The Terminal font is used by the Windows Terminal application and supports the standard IBM PC symbol set. Windows often refers to the PC symbol set as the OEM, or ASCII, symbol set. A sample of these fonts is shown in Figure 13-31.

FIGURE 13-31

```
This is a sample of the System font

This is a sample of the Terminal font

This is a sample of the COURIER font

This is a sample of the Tms Rmn font

This is a sample of the Helv font

This is a sample of the Roman font

This is a sample of the Script font

This is a sample of the Modern font
```

The Microsoft Windows SETUP program automatically installs a base set of six GDI fonts, in addition to the two GDI fonts that are built into Windows.

Installing Screen Fonts with the Control Panel

As we mentioned earlier, when you use the Windows SETUP program to install Windows for use with a LaserJet, several GDI fonts are automatically installed. However, it is possible that you will eventually want to install additional GDI fonts. In this section, we'll show you how to use the control panel to install GDI fonts.

To install a GDI font, pull down the control panel's Installation menu and select the Add New Font command. When you do this, the control panel will display the dialog box shown in Figure 13-32. This dialog box allows you to specify the directory containing the font files you want to install.

FIGURE 13-32

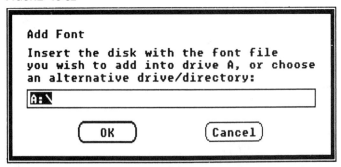

```
Add Font
Insert the disk with the font file
you wish to add into drive A, or choose
an alternative drive/directory:

A:\

     OK            Cancel
```

If you issue the Add New Font command on the control panel's Installation menu, you must tell the control panel where the FON files you want to install are located.

Once you have specified the directory in which FON files can be found, the control panel will search that directory and display a list of fonts that can be installed. To install one of these fonts, select it and choose <u>A</u>dd. The control panel will then copy the file to the appropriate directory and automatically update WIN.INI to reflect the installation of a new GDI font.

FIGURE 13-33

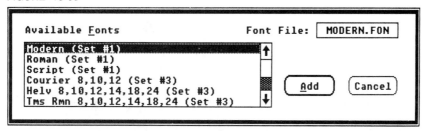

Once you have told the control panel where the FON files you want to install are located, you can select and install them from a list similar to the one shown here.

If you use the Add New Font command on the control panel's Installation menu to install GDI fonts, it is important to note that the number of font files this command can recognize is limited. If there are more than 40 font files stored in the directory you specify when the dialog box shown in Figure 13-32 appears, only the first 40 will be recognized when the control panel lists them in the dialog box shown in Figure 13-33.

If you have more than 40 font files stored in a directory, there is a way to install them. Simply copy the specific files you want to install to a directory where the total number of font files is within the limit, then use the Add New Font command to install them normally.

Deleting Screen Font Support

To delete support for a GDI font, pull down the control panel's <u>I</u>nstallation menu and select the <u>D</u>elete Font command. When you do this, the control panel will immediately display a dialog box similar to the one shown in Figure 13-34 on the following page, which lists the fonts presently installed.

Select the font you want to delete and choose <u>D</u>elete. The control panel will then display a dialog box similar to the one shown in Figure 13-35. This dialog box asks whether you want to delete the font file in which the font you have selected is stored. If you select Yes, the file in which the font is stored will be deleted along with the corresponding font entry in your WIN.INI file. If you respond No, only the font entry in your WIN.INI file will be removed.

FIGURE 13-34

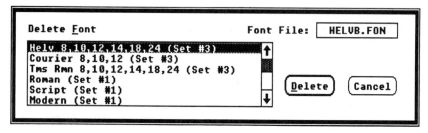

This dialog box lists the first 40 GDI fonts presently installed. From this list, you can select and delete the font of your choice.

FIGURE 13-35

```
Delete associated font file HELVB.FON
from drive/directory:

C:\WINDOWS

    Yes          No          Cancel
```

Once you have selected a GDI font for deletion, the control panel will ask if you also want to delete the font file in which the font is stored.

When you issue the Delete Font command, the control panel will only display the first 40 fonts that are installed. Therefore, if you have more than 40 fonts installed, and the control panel does not list a particular font that you want to delete when you issue the Delete Font command, you must delete it manually by removing its entry from your WIN.INI file.

To do this, run the Microsoft Windows Notepad and load WIN.INI. Next, scroll through the file until you find the location of the section that contains GDI font settings. This section is identified by an entry containing the header [fonts].

Once you have located the fonts section of your WIN.INI file, delete the entry that corresponds to the font that you want to delete. For example, the first entry in the [fonts] section shown in Figure 13-36 indicates that an external font identified as Helv 8,10,12,14,18, 24 (Set #3) is installed and is stored in the file HELVB (the extension .FON is assumed). To delete support for this font, you should delete the entry from this WIN.INI file. After you remove the entry that corresponds to the font you want to delete, pull down the Notepad's File menu, and issue the Save command to save the change.

Once you have removed a GDI font's entry from your WIN.INI file, the font will no longer be recognized by Windows. However, the actual file in which the font is stored will remain. Therefore, if you plan to re-install support for a font in the near future, it may be a good idea to leave such font files alone. On the other hand, if you do not plan to re-install support in the near future, or if you need to free up some disk space, you can delete the font file. For example, to delete the file in which the Helv font is stored, as indicated by the entry in Figure 13-36, select the file name **HELVB.FON**, then pull down the Windows MS-DOS Executive File menu, and select Delete.

FIGURE 13-36

```
[fonts]
Helv 8,10,12,14,18,24 (Set #3)=HELVB
Courier 8,10,12 (Set #3)=COURB
Tms Rmn 8,10,12,14,18,24 (Set #3)=TMSRB
Roman (Set #1)=ROMAN
Script (Set #1)=SCRIPT
Modern (Set #1)=MODERN
```

You can delete support for GDI fonts by removing entries from the fonts section of your WIN.INI file.

Font Substitution

At some point, you will run into a situation where you will use a GDI font in a document and later realize that you do not have a matching LaserJet PCL or PostScript font. It is also possible that you will tell Windows to include a LaserJet PCL or PostScript font in a document when a matching GDI font is not available.

In either case, Windows will solve the conflict created when matching fonts are not available by substituting fonts according to their characteristics. In other words, if a particular font is not available, Windows will look at the list of available fonts and substitute the one that most closely matches the one not available.

For example, if you tell Windows to display text using the 14-point Broadway LaserJet soft font that is available from HP and Bitstream, Windows will try to find a matching GDI font. If a matching font is not available, Windows will then look at each of the available GDI fonts until one is found that closely matches the physical characteristics of the Broadway font. In this case, if the default set of GDI fonts is installed, Windows will substitute bold 14-point Tms Rmn type for 14-point Broadway type.

Matching Screen Fonts with LaserJet Fonts

Windows applications allow you to use GDI and/or LaserJet PCL and Post-Script device-specific fonts in documents. However, if you include a GDI font in a document, a matching LaserJet PCL or PostScript device font must be installed if you want the document printed by the LaserJet to be identical to what you see on the screen. Likewise, if you include a LaserJet PCL or PostScript device font in a document, and a matching GDI font is not available, Windows will substitute a GDI font with similar characteristics when representing it on the screen.

In this section, we'll show you how to obtain matching GDI and device fonts. Once you have obtained these fonts and have installed using the procedures we have outlined throughout this chapter, you will finally be able to take advantage of Windows' ability to produce accurate, on-screen representations of a document.

Obtaining screen fonts that match PCL fonts

At this time, there is no commercial source for GDI fonts that match most cartridge and internal LaserJet PCL fonts. Therefore, if you plan to use cartridge or internal fonts with Windows, often you will have to live without true WYSIWYG operation.

However, BitStream's Fontware Installation Kit for Microsoft Windows and SoftCraft's WYSIfonts! will create Windows GDI fonts for any LaserJet soft font. You can obtain these utilities by contacting your local software dealer or by contacting BitStream or SoftCraft directly at the addresses and/or phone numbers listed in Appendix 2. The Fontware Installation Kit for Microsoft Windows and WYSIfonts! is discussed in greater detail in Chapter 18.

Obtaining screen fonts that match PostScript fonts

If you have a CompuServe account, you can download Windows GDI fonts to match the PostScript printer fonts resident in PostScript products such as JetScript. These fonts are stored in DL 7 of the Adobe Systems Special Interest Group. Table 13-3 lists the file names you must download to match each set of GDI fonts corresponding to the PostScript fonts resident in a JetScript-equipped LaserJet Series II.

If you don't have access to CompuServe, you can obtain these fonts directly from Adobe Systems using the address and/or phone number listed in Appendix 2.

TABLE 13-3

PostScript font	CIS file containing GDI font
New Century Schoolbook	NC-WIN.ARC
ITC Zapf Chancery®	ZC-WIN.ARC
ITC Zapf Dingbats®	ZD-WIN.ARC
Helvetica®Narrow	HN-WIN.ARC
ITC Avant Garde®	AG-WIN.ARC
ITC Bookman®	BO-WIN.ARC
Helvetica®	Included with Windows
Palatino®	PO-WIN.ARC
Symbol	SY-WIN.ARC
Courier	Included with Windows
Times®	Included with Windows

These files, which are available from Adobe System's SIG on CompuServe, contain GDI fonts that match the fonts resident in a JetScript-equipped LaserJet.

Because PCL LaserJets can print GDI stroke fonts by shifting into graphics mode, it is not necessary to obtain LaserJet PCL device fonts that match the default set of Windows GDI stroke fonts. However, PCL LaserJets cannot print text using GDI raster fonts. It is necessary to acquire LaserJet PCL device fonts that match the default set of Windows' GDI raster fonts if you want to use them in a document.

Obtaining PCL fonts that match the default set of screen fonts

Table 13-4 lists each GDI raster font's name, style, and point size, along with a commercial source for a matching PCL font. If a commercial source for a particular font is not available, you can create it manually using a utility such as the SoftCraft Font Editor. We'll take a look at that program in Chapter 18.

TABLE 13-4

Helv (Helvetica)			
Size	**Style**	**Font cartridge(s)**	**Soft font(s)**
8	Normal	HP 92286Z Microsoft®1A	HP 33412AD
8	Bold	n/a	HP 33412AD
8	Italic	n/a	HP 33412AD
10	Normal	HP 92286Z Microsoft®1A	HP 33412AD
10	Bold	HP 92286Z Microsoft®1A	HP 33412AD
10	Italic	HP 92286Z Microsoft®1A	HP 33412AD
12	Normal	HP 92286Z Microsoft®1A	HP 33412AD
12	Bold	HP 92286Z Microsoft®1A	HP 33412AD
12	Italic	HP 92286Z Microsoft®1A	HP 33412AD
14	Normal	n/a	HP 33412AD
14	Bold	HP 92286Z Microsoft®1A	n/a
14	Italic	n/a	HP 33412AD
18	Normal	n/a	HP 33412AD
18	Bold	n/a	HP 33412AD
18	Italic	n/a	HP 33412AD
24	Normal	n/a	HP 33412AD
24	Bold	n/a	HP 33412AD
24	Italic	n/a	HP 33412AD

TmsRmn (Times Roman)

Size	Style	Font cartridge(s)	Soft font(s)
8	Normal	HP 92286Z Microsoft®1A	HP 33412AD
8	Bold	n/a	HP 33412AD
8	Italic	n/a	HP 33412AD
10	Normal	HP 92286Z Microsoft®1A	HP 33412AD
10	Bold	HP 92286Z Microsoft®1A	HP 33412AD
10	Italic	HP 92286Z Microsoft®1A	HP 33412AD
12	Normal	HP 92286Z Microsoft®1A	HP 33412AD
12	Bold	HP 92286Z Microsoft®1A	HP 33412AD
12	Italic	HP 92286Z Microsoft®1A	HP 33412AD
14	Normal	n/a	HP 33412AD
14	Bold	HP 92286Z Microsoft®1A	n/a
14	Italic	n/a	HP 33412AD
18	Normal	n/a	HP 33412AD
18	Bold	n/a	HP 33412AD
18	Italic	n/a	HP 33412AD
24	Normal	n/a	HP 33412AD
24	Bold	n/a	HP 33412AD
24	Italic	n/a	HP 33412AD

Courier

Size	Style	Font cartridge(s)	Soft font(s)
8	Normal	n/a	n/a
8	Bold	n/a	n/a
8	Italic	n/a	n/a
10	Normal	Internal	n/a
10	Bold	92286Q	n/a
10	Italic	92286Q	n/a
12	Normal	n/a	n/a
12	Bold	n/a	n/a
12	Italic	n/a	n/a

n/a = Not available

This table lists the default set of GDI fonts shipped with Windows 2.03, along with a source for a LaserJet version of each font if one is available.

Versions of Windows' Helv, Tms Rmn, and Courier fonts are resident in all the PostScript products available for the LaserJet. Therefore, if your LaserJet is equipped with PostScript, it isn't necessary to obtain PostScript fonts that match the default set of Windows' GDI raster fonts. Likewise, since a PostScript printer can print GDI stroke fonts by shifting into graphics mode, it is not necessary to obtain PostScript fonts that match the default set of Windows' GDI stroke fonts.

On the other hand, if you want to use the System or Terminal GDI font, it will be necessary to obtain a matching PostScript font. Unfortunately, a commercial source for PostScript versions of these fonts is not currently available. Therefore, it will be necessary to design them manually using a font design utility such as the SoftCraft Font Editor. We'll discuss this program in Chapter 18.

Obtaining PostScript fonts that match the default set of screen fonts

Now that we have shown you how to install and configure a device driver that will allow Windows to print documents on a PCL- or PostScript-equipped LaserJet, it's time to discuss the process of printing. In this section, we'll take a look at the command you must issue to print a document, as well as all of the other considerations you must address when you tell a Windows applications to print a document.

PRINTING

Microsoft Windows is a unique combination of technology and philosophy. Technically, it is nothing more than a set of subroutines that programmers can use in their programs. Philosophically, it is a set of rules that programmers must follow when they write programs.

Issuing a Print Command

This combination of technology and philosophy forms a consistent user interface that allows you to associate specific or similar operations with specific commands. The command you must issue to tell a Windows application to print a document is an excellent example of this concept.

If a Windows application is written according to the rules specified by Microsoft, the process of printing should always be initiated by pulling down the File menu and selecting the Print command. For example, this is the command you must use to print a document with Microsoft Windows Write, Microsoft Excel, and Aldus PageMaker.

Once you pull down the File menu and select the Print command, many Windows applications will display a dialog box that will allow you to change a number of settings related to the process of printing. For example, when you select the Print command from Microsoft Windows Write's File menu, the dialog box shown in Figure 13-37 on the next page will appear on your screen. As you can see, this dialog box allows you to specify the range of pages and the number of copies you want to print.

After the dialog box shown in Figure 13-37 has been displayed on your screen and you have made any necessary changes to the settings, select OK to print your document or Cancel to abort the process. If you choose OK, your application will send the document to the printer. Normally, this is done by sending it to the Spooler. However, if you have turned off the Spooler, documents will be sent directly to your printer. We'll show you how to turn the Spooler on and off a bit later in this chapter.

FIGURE 13-37

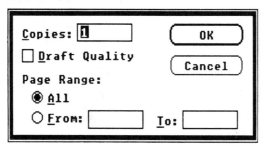

When you issue the Print command, many Windows applications will display this dialog box.

As a document is being sent to the Spooler or directly to your printer, you will usually see a dialog box similar to the one shown in Figure 13-38. This dialog box allows you to abort the process of printing.

FIGURE 13-38

This dialog box allows you to abort the process of printing a document.

When Windows has finished sending the document, the dialog box shown in Figure 13-38 will disappear from your screen. You can then continue to use the application that printed the document, or any other Windows application.

Changing the Default Printer and Printer Settings within an Application

Earlier in this chapter, we showed you how to use the Printer command on the control panel's Setup menu to choose and configure a default printer. At that time, we pointed out that the many Windows applications provide you with the opportunity to change these settings.

The implications of being able to change the default printer specification and printer settings are extremely important. For example, if you are using a PCL LaserJet, you may use particular font cartridges with particular applications. In such a case, it will be necessary to change the setting that specifies which font cartridges you are using before printing a document with a particular application.

As an example of how the ability to change the default printer specification and printer settings can be used, let's suppose that you have a LaserJet Series II equipped with a JetScript board and have installed Windows support for both a PostScript and PCL printer. More importantly, you have installed the PCL printer as the default printer on LPT1: but want to print a particular Microsoft Windows Write document using PostScript on LPT2:.

Before Microsoft Windows Write can send your document to the PostScript interpreter on the JetScript board, you must pull down the File menu and select the Change Printer command. As a result, the dialog box shown in Figure 13-39 will appear on your screen.

FIGURE 13-39

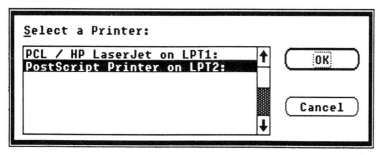

When you change target printers within an application, this dialog box will appear on your screen.

When this dialog box appears, select **PostScript Printer on LPT2:**. Write will display the PostScript settings box that was shown in Figure 13-28 on page 468. After you change any of the settings in this box, all subsequent Write output will be sent to the JetScript board's PostScript interpreter when you issue a Print command.

As this example has illustrated, the ability to change target printers within an application is an extremely handy feature. However, if a particular application you are using does not offer this capability directly, you can take advantage of Windows' multitasking environment by using the control panel to change the default printer and/or printer settings.

The Spooler

The Spooler is a Windows application whose sole purpose is to print documents in the background as you continue to use your machine. In this section, we'll take a look at the Spooler and discuss the things you must know about it to print documents successfully on a LaserJet. We'll also show you how to turn the Spooler off in the event that you are running Windows on a floppy-based system or network.

Running the Spooler

Whenever you tell a Windows application to print a document, one of three things will occur. First, if the Spooler is not running, it will be run automatically, and your document will be sent directly to the Spooler's queue where it will remain until it can be printed. Since the Spooler is nothing more than an ordinary Windows application, you can run it at any time with the Windows MS-DOS Executive. To run the Spooler, highlight the file name **SPOOLER.EXE**, pull down the File menu, and select Run.

Second, if the Spooler is running when you issue the Print command, your application will send the document to the Spooler, which will handle the actual task of sending it to the printer. As the Spooler sends the document to your printer in the background, you may use any Windows application in the foreground.

Third, after a document has been sent to the Spooler, you can simply allow it to print the document, or you can interfere in the process by activating the Spooler's main window. You can do this by clicking on the Spooler icon or by pressing [Alt][Tab]. The Spooler icon is shown in Figure 13-40.

FIGURE 13-40

You can activate the Spooler as it is printing a document by clicking on the Spooler icon or by pressing [Alt][Tab].

The Spooler is an independent Windows application. Therefore, it may appear on your screen in a resizable window, or it may occupy the entire screen. The appearance of the Spooler on your screen does not affect its operation.

Whenever the Spooler is activated, it displays a list of the printers presently installed on your system. Below the names of each of these printers, the Spooler will then display a list of any documents that are presently being printed or are waiting in the queue. An example is shown in Figure 13-41.

Controlling the queue

As you can see, when the Spooler's main window is activated, the Spooler displays a list of all the documents that are printing or waiting to be printed.

Terminating a document

At some point, you may want to stop printing a document that is presently being printed, or you may want to remove a document from the Spooler's queue. To do this, activate the Spooler, and select the document that you want to terminate by clicking on its name with the mouse or by using the ↓ and ↑ keys. Once you have selected the name of the document, pull down the Queue menu, and select Terminate. As a result, the Spooler will display the dialog box shown in Figure 13-42. This dialog box gives you the opportunity to cancel your decision to terminate the document. If you want to terminate the document, choose **OK**. If you do not want to terminate the document, choose **Cancel**.

FIGURE 13-41

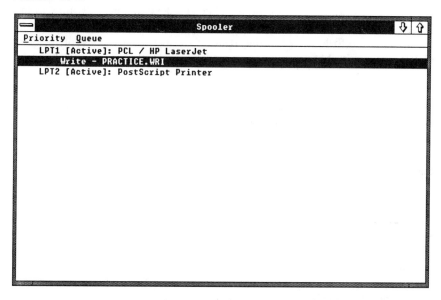

When it is activated, the Spooler displays a list of the currently installed printers, as well as a summary of files that are printing or waiting in the queue.

FIGURE 13-42

When you terminate a document, the Spooler will display this dialog box.

Pausing

If you notice a problem developing with your printer, you may want to pause the Spooler temporarily. For example, if your LaserJet has a problem, such as an exhausted toner cartridge, you may want the Spooler to stop sending additional output until the problem has been corrected. To do this, activate the Spooler, and select the printer to which output should be halted by clicking on its name with the mouse or by using the ↓ and ↑ keys. Then, pull down the Queue menu and select Pause. When you are ready to allow the Spooler to resume sending output, select the printer once again, pull down the Queue menu, and select Resume.

Setting priority

If you have plenty of CPU time to spare, you may want to take advantage of the ability to increase the speed of the Spooler. To devote more CPU time to the Spooler, pull down the Priority menu and select Hi. As a result, the Spooler will devote more time to the task of sending data to the printer at the expense of the speed of any other applications that may be running.

Receiving messages from the Spooler

If an error occurs as the Spooler is printing a document, it will not immediately display an error message. Instead, it will flash the title bar of the currently active application to alert you that an error has occurred. When you see this flash, you should activate the Spooler by double-clicking on its icon or by pressing [Alt][Tab]. Once it has been selected, it will immediately display a message explaining the error that has occurred.

Turning off the Spooler

While most users will always want to use the Spooler, there are instances when it should not be used. For example, if you are running Windows on a floppy-based system, you may want to turn off the Spooler to conserve disk space and to speed operation. Likewise, if your computer is connected to a network that offers print spooling, it is usually advantageous to turn the Spooler off. Otherwise, you will end up spooling output twice. However, if you find that the Windows Spooler is faster than the network spooler, you may want to turn off the network spooler instead.

You can turn the Spooler on and off by changing the Spooler setting in the windows section of your WIN.INI file. For example, if you do not want to spool output, change the `spooler` entry in your WIN.INI file to `spooler=no`.

To change the Spooler setting, run the Microsoft Windows Notepad and load WIN.INI. When you have done this, scroll through the file until you locate the section that contains generic Windows settings. You can identify this section by looking for a line containing the header `[windows]`.

When you have found the `[windows]` section of your WIN.INI file, look for the Spooler entry, make the necessary change, then pull down the File menu and issue the Save command to save the change.

CONCLUSION

In this chapter, we have discussed the aspects of Windows that apply to printing with the LaserJet. While it may seem that there a number of concepts you must understand, and an even larger number of settings that must be addressed, you should not be discouraged. As we discuss specific Windows applications in the chapters that follow, you'll find that setting up Windows frees you from the task of setting up each individual application.

ALDUS PAGEMAKER 14

Aldus Corporation defined the term "desktop publishing" when it introduced PageMaker for the Apple Macintosh computer. Using PageMaker on the Mac, along with an Apple LaserWriter printer, made it possible to create publications with integrated text and graphics on the Desktop without using scissors and glue. A few years later, Aldus unveiled a copy of PageMaker for the IBM PC family of computers. It is now possible for PC users to produce publications that look as good as those produced with a Mac.

In this chapter, we'll show you how to get the most out of your HP LaserJet printer with PageMaker. After we show you how to install PageMaker on your computer, we'll cover the basics of printing a PageMaker publication. Next, we'll talk about PageMaker's advanced printing features, including its ability to print thumbnails and spot color overlays. Finally, we'll point out a couple of traps to avoid when printing publications with PageMaker on a PCL LaserJet.

INSTALLING PAGEMAKER

As you already know, Aldus PageMaker runs under the Microsoft Windows operating environment. In order to run PageMaker, you must either purchase and install a copy of Microsoft Windows, or install the run-time version of Microsoft Windows that is shipped along with PageMaker. Although the run-time version of Windows works just fine, you cannot use it to run any other Windows applications, like Microsoft Paint or Microsoft Excel. Using a full-fledged version of Microsoft Windows allows you to transfer data between your Windows applications and to control DOS tasks from the Windows environment. If you don't own a copy of Microsoft Windows, we recommend that you install PageMaker with the run-time version of Windows now, and then purchase and install the full version of Microsoft Windows as soon as possible.

Regardless of which version of Windows you install, almost all of the information we presented in Chapter 13 is important to know if you are installing PageMaker on your computer. For this reason, we highly recommend that you at least skim through that chapter before reading this section on installing PageMaker.

Installing Only PageMaker Program Files

If you've already installed Microsoft Windows on your hard disk, you can install Aldus PageMaker on your machine by inserting PageMaker's Install disk into drive A:, typing **INSTALL** at DOS's A> prompt, and pressing ↵. The INSTALL program will take it from there, prompting you for information about your computer system, telling you when to change disks, and copying the appropriate files from each of the floppy disks to your hard disk.

When INSTALL is finished, it will return you to an A> prompt. If you've already customized Windows to work with your LaserJet printer as we described in Chapter 13, you do not need to perform any additional installation procedures.

Installing PageMaker and Run-time Windows

As we have said, if you have not installed a copy of Microsoft Windows on your system, you'll have to install PageMaker's run-time version of Windows before you can install PageMaker. To do this, insert the Windows run-time Setup/Build Disk into drive A:, type **SETUP** at DOS's A> prompt, and press ↵. As soon as you press ↵ to install run-time Windows, PageMaker's SETUP program will ask you several questions about your computer system. For example, it will ask you to define the type of computer, display adapter, keyboard, and mouse you are using.

After asking you several questions about your equipment, SETUP will present the screen shown in Figure 14-1, which asks if you want to install a printer or plotter. When you see this screen, you should respond by either typing an **I** or pressing ↵.

FIGURE 14-1

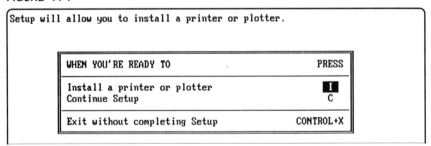

This SETUP screen marks the beginning of the printer installation process.

After you tell SETUP that you want to install a printer, it will present a list of printers similar to the list shown in Figure 14-2. To choose the printer you want to install, use the ↑ or ↓ key to move the highlight bar through the list of printer names, then press ↵ when the bar appears over the name of the printer you want to install.

FIGURE 14-2

```
┌────────────────────────────────────────────────────────────────────┐
│ Select an output device (printer, plotter, etc.) from the following list. │
│                                                                      │
│   - Use the DIRECTION (↑,↓) keys to move the highlight to your selection. │
│                                                                      │
│  ███████████                                                         │
│  No selection                                                        │
│  Apple LaserWriter [Postscript printer]                              │
│  Apple LaserWriter Plus [Postscript printer]                         │
│  Apricot Laser [PCL / HP LaserJet]                                   │
│  C-Itoh 8510                                                         │
│  Dataproducts LZR 2665 [Postscript printer]                          │
│  Digital LN03R ScriptPrinter [Postscript printer]                    │
│  Digital LPS PrintServer 40 [Postscript printer]                     │
│  HP DeskJet [HP DeskJet]                                             │
│  Epson LQ Printers [Epson 24 Pin]                                    │
│  Epson MX,FX,LX Printers [Epson 9 Pin]                               │
│  Epson JX,EX,RX Printers [Epson 9 Pin]                               │
│  AMT Office Printer [AMT]                                            │
│                                                                      │
│           (To see more of the list, press the DOWN(↓) key.)          │
│    ┌──────────────────────────────────────────────────┐             │
│    │ WHEN YOU'RE READY TO                      PRESS   │             │
│    ├──────────────────────────────────────────────────┤             │
│    │ Confirm your choice                       ENTER   │             │
│    │ Exit without completing Setup          CONTROL+X  │             │
│    └──────────────────────────────────────────────────┘             │
│                                                                      │
└────────────────────────────────────────────────────────────────────┘
```

When this list of printers appears, press the [Pg Dn] key to display the HP LaserJet printers.

Installing a PCL LaserJet

If you press the [Pg Dn] key to move down the list in Figure 14-2, the names of a few LaserJet family members will appear, as shown in Figure 14-3 on the next page. To install support for your LaserJet, simply use the ↑ or ↓ key to highlight the LaserJet model you use, and press ↵.

Installing a PostScript-equipped LaserJet

Although SETUP does not include an entry for a PostScript-equipped LaserJet printer, you can make PageMaker work with this type of LaserJet by selecting one of the other PostScript printers from the SETUP list. The manual that comes with your LaserJet's PostScript system should list the names of the printers with which that system is compatible. If it doesn't, contact the manufacturer and request this information.

For example, if you've installed the QMS JetScript system on your computer and LaserJet, you'll notice that the manual included with that system states that the LaserJet is compatible with the Apple LaserWriter Plus and with the QMS-PS 800 Plus. Consequently, you should highlight either the Apple LaserWriter Plus or the QMS-PS 800 Plus option, and press ↵.

FIGURE 14-3

```
Select an output device (printer, plotter, etc.) from the following list.

  - Use the DIRECTION (↑,↓) keys to move the highlight to your selection.

AMT Office Printer [AMT]
MT910 Laser Printer [MT910]
Digital LA50/75 Driver
HP LaserJet [PCL / HP LaserJet]
HP LaserJet Plus [PCL / HP LaserJet]
HP LaserJet 500+ [PCL / HP LaserJet]
HP LaserJet Series II [PCL / HP LaserJet]
HP LaserJet 2000 [PCL / HP LaserJet]
IBM Color Printer (B/W only)
IBM Graphics
IBM Personal Pageprinter [Postscript printer]
IBM Proprinter [IBM Proprinters]
IBM Proprinter II [IBM Proprinters]

          (To see more of the list, press the DOWN(↓) key.)

    ┌─────────────────────────────────────────────────────┐
    │ WHEN YOU'RE READY TO                          PRESS  │
    ├─────────────────────────────────────────────────────┤
    │ Confirm your choice                           ENTER  │
    │ Exit without completing Setup            CONTROL+X   │
    └─────────────────────────────────────────────────────┘
```

When this list appears, highlight the type of LaserJet printer you use.

Choosing a port

After you've selected the name of the printer you want to install, SETUP will display the list of the port names shown in Figure 14-4. Simply use the ↑ or ↓ key to select the port to which you've connected your LaserJet printer, and press ↵ to save your selection. (As we mentioned in Chapter 13, you can use the Connections… command on the control panel's Setup menu if you need to change the LaserJet's printer port assignment after you run the SETUP program.)

Installing both a PCL and a PostScript LaserJet

If your LaserJet printer is equipped with both PCL and PostScript, you will probably want to install support for both. Fortunately, SETUP allows you to do this. After you have selected the port that is connected to your LaserJet printer, SETUP will present the screen in Figure 14-5, which asks if you would like to install another printer.

FIGURE 14-4

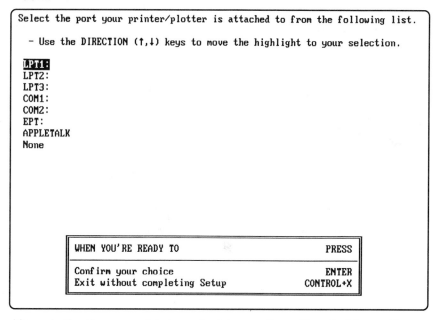

After selecting the appropriate type of printer, you'll need to select the port to which your printer is connected.

FIGURE 14-5

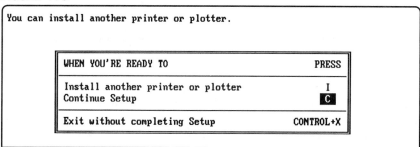

After you install support for your LaserJet printer, SETUP will allow you to install support for a second printer.

To install support for a second printer, simply type **I** (or use the ↑ key to highlight the letter *I*) and press ↵. At this point, SETUP will redisplay the screen shown in Figure 14-2 and repeat the printer installation process we described earlier.

**Completing
the Printer
Installation**

After you install all the printers that are connected to your system, and SETUP presents the screen in Figure 14-5, finish the installation by typing a C. When you do this, SETUP will continue asking questions and copying the appropriate Windows files over to your hard disk.

**Installing
PageMaker**

After the SETUP program finishes installing the run-time version of Windows, it will present the screen shown in Figure 14-6, which instructs you to insert PageMaker's Install disk into your machine. From this point, the SETUP program will prompt you for some additional information, telling you when to change disks and copying the appropriate files from each of the floppy disks to your hard disk. When SETUP is finally finished, it will return you to the A> prompt.

FIGURE 14-6

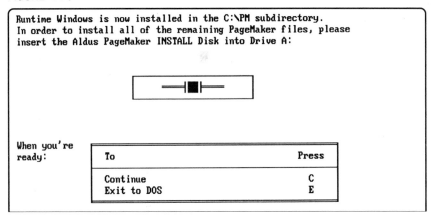

*After SETUP installs run-time Windows, it will install PageMaker onto your
system.*

A note

After SETUP has completed the installation process, it will copy a file named READMEHP.TXT and/or a file named READMEPS.TXT into the directory where it has installed Windows. These two text files contain information about using your LaserJet with Windows applications. Although we'll discuss all of the topics covered in these files, you might want to browse through them, either by loading them into a text processor that handles pure ASCII files or by typing the command **TYPE READMEHP.TXT** (or **TYPE READMEPS.TXT**) at the A> prompt.

**Setting Up Your
LaserJet's
Device Driver**

After you've used the INSTALL or SETUP program to install PageMaker, you need to load PageMaker and set up the device driver that will communicate with your printer. In other words, you need to tell Windows exactly which fonts and features you've installed on your LaserJet so that PageMaker can take full advantage of your LaserJet's printing capabilities.

To set up your LaserJet's device driver, first load PageMaker, then select the Printer Setup... command from PageMaker's File menu. When you do this, PageMaker will present a dialog box similar to the one shown in Figure 14-7 that includes all of the printers you installed with the SETUP or INSTALL program. When this box appears, simply select a printer name from the Printer box, then choose the Setup... option to bring up a larger dialog box that lets you define some specific information about the selected printer.

FIGURE 14-7

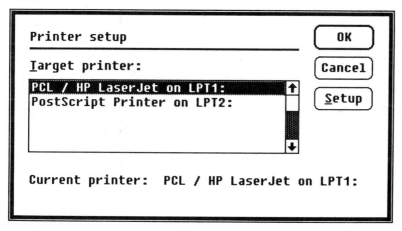

PageMaker presents a dialog box like this when you select the Printer Setup... command from the File menu.

Setting up a PCL LaserJet

To set up the device driver for a PCL LaserJet printer, select **PCL / HP LaserJet on LPT1:** from the dialog box shown in Figure 14-7, then choose the Setup... option. When you do this, PageMaker will present the dialog box shown in Figure 14-8 on the next page.

This is the same dialog box that appears when you use the Printer command on the control panel's Setup menu to set up a PCL LaserJet printer. Refer to the section entitled "Setting up the PCL Device Driver" in Chapter 13 to learn the significance of each setting in this dialog box, then use that information to define the appropriate settings for your LaserJet printer. After you've defined the appropriate settings, choose **OK** to return to the dialog box in Figure 14-7, then choose **OK** again to return PageMaker to ready mode.

FIGURE 14-8

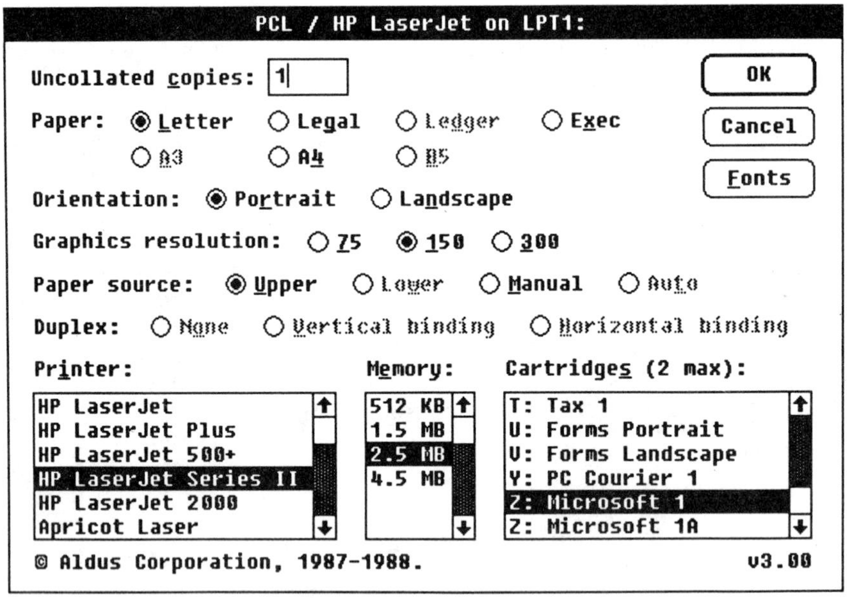

```
┌────────────────────────────────────────────────────────────┐
│          PCL / HP LaserJet on LPT1:                         │
├────────────────────────────────────────────────────────────┤
│                                                 ┌────────┐   │
│  Uncollated copies: │1│                         │   OK   │   │
│                                                 └────────┘   │
│  Paper: ⦿ Letter  ○ Legal  ○ Ledger  ○ Exec    ┌────────┐   │
│           ○ A3      ○ A4     ○ B5                │ Cancel │   │
│                                                 └────────┘   │
│  Orientation:  ⦿ Portrait  ○ Landscape          ┌────────┐   │
│                                                 │ Fonts  │   │
│  Graphics resolution:  ○ 75  ⦿ 150  ○ 300       └────────┘   │
│                                                              │
│  Paper source:  ⦿ Upper  ○ Lower  ○ Manual  ○ Auto          │
│                                                              │
│  Duplex:  ○ None  ○ Vertical binding  ○ Horizontal binding   │
│                                                              │
│  Printer:               Memory:      Cartridges (2 max):     │
│  ┌─────────────────┬─┐  ┌────────┬─┐ ┌────────────────────┬─┐│
│  │HP LaserJet      │▲│  │512 KB  │▲│ │T: Tax 1            │▲││
│  │HP LaserJet Plus │ │  │1.5 MB  │ │ │U: Forms Portrait   │ ││
│  │HP LaserJet 500+ │ │  │2.5 MB  │ │ │U: Forms Landscape  │ ││
│  │HP LaserJet Series II│  │4.5 MB  │ │ │Y: PC Courier 1     │ ││
│  │HP LaserJet 2000 │ │  │        │ │ │Z: Microsoft 1      │ ││
│  │Apricot Laser    │▼│  │        │▼│ │Z: Microsoft 1A     │▼││
│  └─────────────────┴─┘  └────────┴─┘ └────────────────────┴─┘│
│  © Aldus Corporation, 1987-1988.                    v3.00    │
└────────────────────────────────────────────────────────────┘
```

This dialog box lets you tell PageMaker which options you've installed on your PCL LaserJet.

Setting up a PostScript-equipped LaserJet

To set up the device driver for a PostScript-equipped LaserJet printer, select **PostScript Printer on LPT2:** from the dialog box shown in Figure 14-7, and then choose the Setup... option. When you do this, PageMaker will present the dialog box shown in Figure 14-9.

The dialog box shown in Figure 14-9 is the same one that appears when you use the Printer command on the control panel's Setup menu to set up a PostScript printer. Refer to the section entitled "Setting up the PostScript Driver" in Chapter 13 to learn the significance of each setting in this dialog box, and then use that information to define the settings for your LaserJet printer. After you've defined the appropriate settings, choose **OK** to return to the dialog box shown in Figure 14-7, then choose **OK** again to return PageMaker to ready mode.

Installing Fonts

Now that you've installed PageMaker and set up your LaserJet's device drivers, you need to install the fonts you'll use with PageMaker. As with all applications that run under Microsoft Windows, Aldus PageMaker can display a variety of fonts on the screen and can take full advantage of your LaserJet's font capabilities. As we explained in Chapter 13, you need two kinds of fonts to compose publications on your LaserJet with a Windows application: GDI fonts (fonts you can display on your screen) and device fonts (fonts you can print on your printer).

FIGURE 14-9

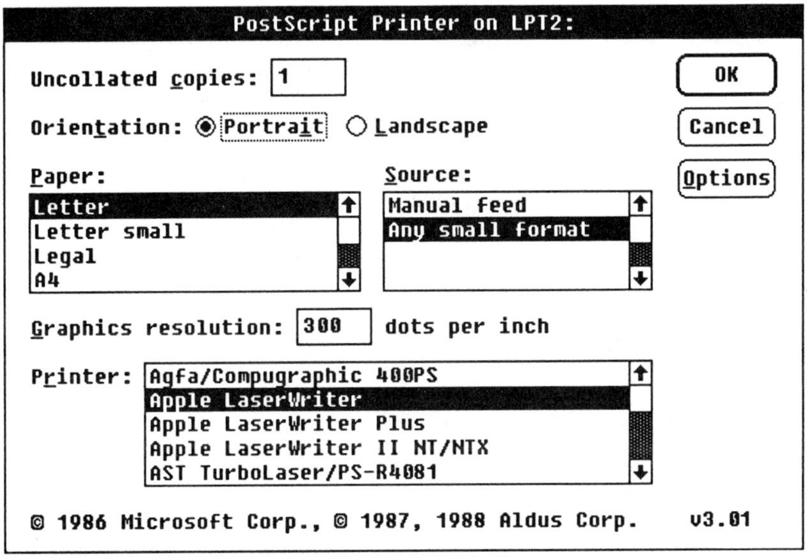

```
┌──────────────────────────────────────────────────────────────┐
│            PostScript Printer on LPT2:                        │
│                                                              │
│  Uncollated copies: │1      │              ┌────────┐        │
│                                            │   OK   │        │
│  Orientation: ◉ Portrait  ○ Landscape      └────────┘        │
│                                            ┌────────┐        │
│  Paper:                  Source:           │ Cancel │        │
│  ┌──────────────────┐▲   ┌──────────────────┐▲  └────────┘    │
│  │Letter            │   │Manual feed       │   ┌────────┐    │
│  │Letter small      │   │Any small format  │   │Options │    │
│  │Legal             │   │                  │   └────────┘    │
│  │A4                │▼  │                  │▼                │
│  └──────────────────┘   └──────────────────┘                │
│                                                              │
│  Graphics resolution: │300  │  dots per inch                 │
│                                                              │
│  Printer: ┌──────────────────────────────────┐▲             │
│           │Agfa/Compugraphic 400PS            │              │
│           │Apple LaserWriter                  │              │
│           │Apple LaserWriter Plus             │              │
│           │Apple LaserWriter II NT/NTX        │              │
│           │AST TurboLaser/PS-R4081            │▼             │
│           └──────────────────────────────────┘              │
│                                                              │
│  © 1986 Microsoft Corp., © 1987, 1988 Aldus Corp.   v3.01   │
└──────────────────────────────────────────────────────────────┘
```

When you use the Printer Setup... command to set up a PostScript printer, PageMaker presents this dialog box.

You should first decide which printer fonts you want to use in your printed publications, then install the matching screen fonts into your Windows system. If you install matching sets of printer fonts and screen fonts, your PageMaker publications will look almost the same on paper as they do on the screen. (This concept is often referred to as WYSIWYG, which stands for What You See Is What You Get.) If you install unmatched sets of printer fonts and screen fonts, however, you won't be able to take advantage of Windows' WYSIWYG capabilities.

Installing PCL printer fonts

You can add additional fonts to your LaserJet by installing font cartridges, downloadable soft fonts, or both. You'll most likely want to start off using some basic font types (like Helv, Tms Rmn, and Courier), and purchase additional fonts as your needs grow.

Installing font cartridges

If you are like most PageMaker users, you'll want to install HP's "Z" font cartridge (HP Part No. 92286Z) in your LaserJet printer when you are printing with PageMaker. The "Z" font cartridge was specifically designed for Microsoft Windows applications, and it includes several variations of the two most popular typefaces: Tms Rmn (similar to Times Roman), and Helv (similar to Helvetica). You can purchase a "Z" font cartridge (or any other HP font cartridge) from your local computer vendor or from HP Direct Marketing (800-538-8787).

After you've plugged your font cartridge(s) into your LaserJet, you need to bring up the dialog box in Figure 14-8 with PageMaker's Printer Setup... command and select the cartridge(s) you've installed in the Cartridges list box. After you've selected the appropriate font cartridge(s), choose **OK** to lock in your selections. (For more information on installing font cartridges, refer to the section entitled "Adding Support for HP Font Cartridges" in Chapter 13.)

Installing soft fonts

If you use an HP LaserJet printer other than the original LaserJet, you can use soft fonts in addition to cartridge fonts to give your printer access to optional typefaces. Like cartridge fonts, there are dozens of soft fonts available for LaserJet printers. To learn how to install soft fonts into your Windows system, refer to the sections entitled "Adding Support for PCL Soft Fonts" and "Adding Support for Postscript Soft Fonts" in Chapter 13.

New versions of PageMaker include a copy of Bitstream's Fontware installation kit for Windows. You can use the Fontware package to create an assortment of printer fonts ranging from 6 points to 72 points. For more information on Fontware, either refer to the *Fontware for PageMaker* manual that is included with PageMaker, or read the section entitled "Bitstream Fontware" in Chapter 18.

Managing fonts and memory

As you already know, the memory installed in your LaserJet printer is used to store both soft fonts and bit-mapped graphics. Of course, the more memory you've installed in your printer, the more soft fonts you can use and the higher the resolution of the graphics you can print on a page. Table 14-1 shows the fractions of a page each LaserJet printer can cover using different print resolutions.

TABLE 14-1

Printer	Memory	75 dpi	150 dpi	300 dpi
LaserJet	128K	full page	quarter page	sixteenth page
LaserJet Plus &	512K	full page	full page	half page
LaserJet 500 Plus	2MB	full page	full page	full page
LaserJet Series II	512K	full page	full page	half page
	1.5MB	full page	full page	full page
	2.5MB	full page	full page	full page
	4.5MB	full page	full page	full page

By installing more memory in your LaserJet printer, you can increase the resolution of your printed graphics.

Since downloaded soft fonts use the same printer memory as bit-mapped graphics, the LaserJet might run out of memory if you print a publication that uses a few soft fonts and contains large, high-resolution graphics images. If the LaserJet runs out of memory, it will display an out of memory error message (20 or 21).

If you are continually running into memory problems when printing with PageMaker, try to reduce the number and size of the soft fonts in your publication. One way to conserve memory is to use a cartridge font for your publication's body text and soft fonts only for headlines and special effects. If reducing the number and size of your soft fonts does not resolve your LaserJet's memory problems, you'll have to purchase a memory upgrade. For information on memory options for the LaserJet printer, refer to Chapter 1.

Like PCL soft fonts, PostScript soft fonts must be downloaded from your computer's hard disk to your printer. To learn how to install PostScript soft fonts into your Windows system, refer to the section entitled "Adding Support for PostScript Soft Fonts" in Chapter 13.

Installing Post-Script printer fonts

Just as you need to install cartridge fonts and soft fonts to let your LaserJet print in a variety of typestyles, you need to install screen fonts to let Microsoft Windows applications *display* a variety of typestyles. Fortunately, Windows' SETUP program automatically installs a base set of screen fonts that are specifically designed for the display hardware you are using. For example, if you are using an EGA video system, SETUP will automatically install a base set of three screen fonts that are specifically designed for use with the EGA.

Installing screen fonts

No matter which video system you use, SETUP always installs versions of the Tms Rmn, Helv, and Courier raster screen fonts. In addition, SETUP installs the Roman, Script, and Modern stroke fonts. Finally, two additional raster screen fonts are built directly into the Windows environment: the System font and the Terminal font. Figure 14-10 on the next page shows a sample of all eight basic screen fonts.

If you want to install additional screen fonts on your LaserJet printer, you'll have to use the Add New Font... command on the control panel's Installation menu. For a detailed explanation of this procedure, refer to the section entitled "Installing Screen Fonts with the Control Panel" in Chapter 13.

At some point, you may assign a screen font to a section of a PageMaker publication that does not have a matching LaserJet PCL or PostScript font. On the other hand, you may assign a printer font to a section of a publication that has no matching screen font. In either case, PageMaker will do just what you'd expect: substitute the font that most closely matches the font you've assigned.

Matching printer fonts with screen fonts

FIGURE 14-10

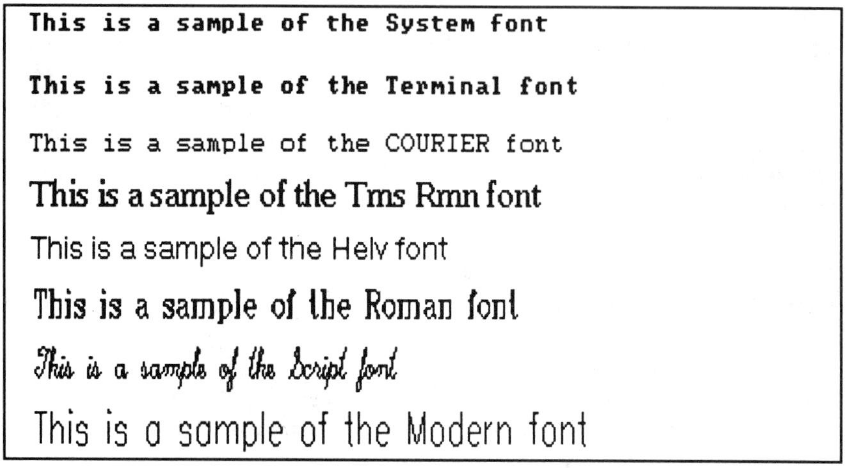

```
This is a sample of the System font

This is a sample of the Terminal font

This is a sample of the COURIER font

This is a sample of the Tms Rmn font

This is a sample of the Helv font

This is a sample of the Roman font

This is a sample of the Script font

This is a sample of the Modern font
```

The Windows SETUP program automatically installs these eight screen fonts when you install Windows on an EGA computer system.

The sections entitled "Obtaining Screen Fonts that Match PCL Fonts" and "Obtaining Screen Fonts that Match PostScript Fonts" in Chapter 13 explain how to obtain matching printer and screen fonts for your Windows applications. If you read those sections carefully, you'll know how to take full advantage of Windows' ability to produce great-looking publications both on your screen and on your LaserJet printer.

Bitstream Fontware

New versions of Aldus PageMaker include a copy of Bitstream's Fontware Installation Kit for Windows. This powerful font package allows you to create a wide assortment of matching printer and screen fonts from 6 points to 72 points. You'll find Fontware's ability to create different size screen fonts a real advantage if you often display your publication at different page views (actual size, 200%, 75%, and 50%), since you can create a font that matches each view. For example, after you use Fontware to create a 10-point printer font, you can also create screen fonts in 10 point (actual size), 7.5 point (75% of actual size), and 20 point (200% of actual size). For more information on Bitstream's Fontware package, either refer to the *Fontware for PageMaker* manual that is included with PageMaker, or read the section entitled "Bitstream Fontware" in Chapter 18.

A note

If you've installed matching printer fonts and screen fonts into your Windows system, and you still can't make PageMaker print your publications as they appear on your screen, the problem might be related to the font summary file (FSLPT1.PCL) in your Windows directory. As we explained in Chapter 13, the font summary file contains printer font metrics information for all internal, cartridge, and soft fonts, along with the PCL commands necessary to select them. If you erase your old font summary file, then begin a new Windows session, Windows will automatically create a new font summary file based on the current settings in your WIN.INI file. For additional information on the font summary file, refer to the section entitled "PCL Font Summary File" in Chapter 13.

SETTING UP THE PAGE

When you select the New... command on PageMaker's File menu to create a new publication, the Page setup dialog box shown in Figure 14-11 will appear. When you see this dialog box, you should enter the appropriate settings and choose OK to begin composing your publication. If you later want to change some of the Page setup settings, you can call up the Page setup dialog box with the Page setup... command on the File menu.

As you can see in Figure 14-11, the Page setup dialog box lets you select the page size and orientation, specify the range of pages to print, change the margins, and select the Double-sided printing and Facing pages options. Let's consider how each of these settings affect the publications you'll be printing on the LaserJet.

FIGURE 14-11

```
┌──────────────────────────────────────────────────────────┐
│  Page setup                                  ( OK )        │
│                                                            │
│  Page size: ◉ Letter  ○ Legal  ○ Tabloid    (Cancel)      │
│                                                            │
│             ○ A4  ○ A3  ○ A5  ○ B5                         │
│                                                            │
│             ○ Custom:  [8.5    ] x [11      ]  inches      │
│                                                            │
│  Orientation: ◉ Tall  ○ Wide                              │
│                                                            │
│  Start page #: [1    ]   # of pages: [1      ]            │
│                                                            │
│  Options: ⊠ Double-sided  ⊠ Facing pages                 │
│                                                            │
│  Margin in inches:  Inside [1     ]  Outside [0.75  ]     │
│                                                            │
│                     Top [0.75  ]    Bottom [0.75  ]      │
│                                                            │
│  Target printer: PCL / HP LaserJet on LPT1:              │
└──────────────────────────────────────────────────────────┘
```

PageMaker's Page setup dialog box lets you control the layout of your publications.

Page Size

The group of buttons near the top of the dialog box lets you select the page size the LaserJet will use when it prints your publication. If you need to compose a publication that is larger than the paper in your printer, read the section entitled "Printing Oversize Pages" later in this chapter.

Orientation

The Orientation setting tells PageMaker to print the pages of your publication in either Tall (Portrait) or Wide (Landscape) orientation. If you want to mix tall and wide pages in a single publication, you'll have to create two separate publications (one tall and one wide), then manually collate the printed pages.

Start Page # and # of Pages

If you want PageMaker to begin numbering your pages with a value other than 1, you should type the new start value in the Start page #: edit bar. (PageMaker can number pages from 1 to 9999.) In addition, you should type the number of pages you plan to include in your publication in the # of pages: edit bar. Don't worry if you're not sure how many pages you'll need to create—you can insert or remove pages later with PageMaker's Insert pages... and Remove pages... commands on the Page menu. (PageMaker can create up to 128 pages in a single publication. If you need to create more than 128 pages, just create two separate publications with a break between major sections.)

Double-sided and Facing Pages

If your publication will be printed on both sides of the paper, you should select the Double-sided checkbox in the Page setup dialog box. Selecting the Double-sided option causes PageMaker to shift the inside margin from the left to the right side of the page as it moves from a right-hand (odd-numbered) page to a left-hand (even-numbered) page.

If you select the Double-sided checkbox and you want PageMaker to display facing pages (both left-hand and right-hand pages at the same time), you should select the Facing pages checkbox. If you want PageMaker to display only one page at a time, however, simply deselect the Facing pages checkbox.

Margins

The Margin in inches setting in the Page setup dialog box lets you define the top, bottom, inside, and outside margins of your report. As we mentioned in Chapter 1, HP LaserJet printers are unable to print to a small region along the outside edges of a page. This unprintable region occupies approximately $\frac{1}{4}$ inch of space at the top and bottom edges of the page, as well as $\frac{1}{4}$ inch of space at the left and right edges. For this reason, even if you specify a margin setting of less than $\frac{1}{4}$ inch, the LaserJet will print that report with $\frac{1}{4}$ inch of blank space along that edge.

Closing the Dialog Box

After you've defined all the appropriate settings in the Page setup dialog box, choose the **OK** option to close the dialog box and complete the command. As we mentioned earlier, you can go back and modify the page setup at any time by selecting the Page setup... command on PageMaker's File menu.

PRINTING

You'll use the Print... command to print your PageMaker publications on the HP LaserJet printer. Before you attempt to send your publication to the printer, however, you must use the Printer setup... command on the File menu to specify the target printer.

When you issue the Printer setup command on PageMaker's File menu, a dialog box like the one shown in Figure 14-12 will appear. When this dialog box appears, you should select the printer you will use to print your publication, then choose **OK**. If your LaserJet printer does not appear in the list of target printers, refer to Chapter 13 to find out how to install the appropriate printer driver to your Windows system.

Choosing a Target Printer

FIGURE 14-12

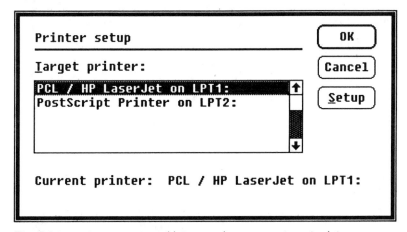

The Printer setup... command lets you choose your target printer.

After you've set up and composed your publication, and you've chosen a target printer, you're ready to print. When you issue the Print... command on the File menu, PageMaker presents the dialog box shown in Figure 14-13 on the next page.

Printing the Publication

As you can see, the Print dialog box contains several options that affect the way the LaserJet prints your publication. In this section, we'll discuss the basic print options. In the next section, we'll talk about the options that let you perform some special printing tasks, like the Thumbnails and Spot color overlays options.

PageMaker always prints to the destination printer you select in the Printer list box that appears at the bottom of the Print dialog box. The first time you issue the Print... command, the destination printer in the Printer list box will be the same as the target printer you selected with the Printer Setup... command. If you want to specify a different destination printer, just highlight the appropriate printer in the Printer list box before you choose OK to complete the Print... command.

Choosing a destination printer

FIGURE 14-13

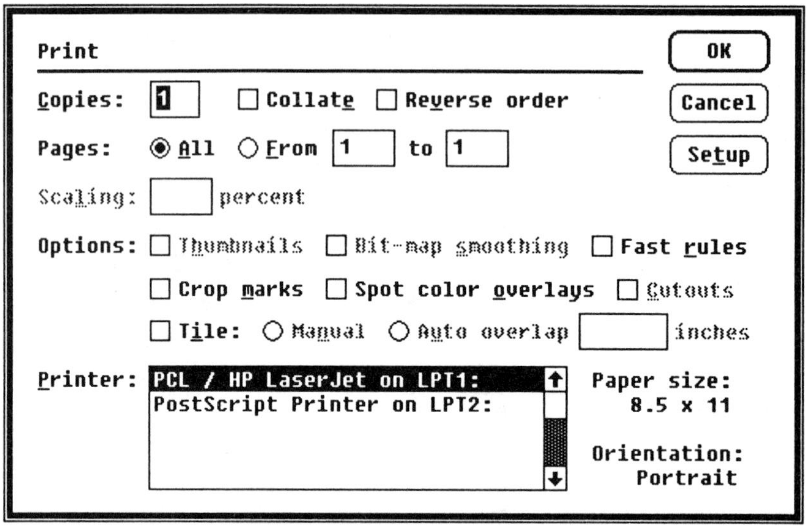

You'll use the Print... command to print your PageMaker publications.

To understand why PageMaker lets you select both a target printer (with the Printer Setup... command) and a destination printer (with the Print... command), consider the following situation. Suppose you use both a LaserJet Series II printer and a Linotronic typesetter. Since the Linotronic typesetter takes a long time to print a document compared to the LaserJet printer, you'll most likely want to print your drafts on the LaserJet and print your final copies on the Linotronic typesetter. The easiest way to do this is to use the Printer Setup... command to specify the Linotronic typesetter as the target printer and the Print... command to specify the LaserJet as the destination printer. After you've printed drafts of your publication on the LaserJet and are ready to send the document to the Linotronic typesetter, just issue the Print... command and select the Linotronic device from the list of printers in the Printer list box.

If you print drafts on any printer other than the target printer, make sure that the draft printer can use the same fonts as the target printer. If your draft printer and your target printer do not share the same set of installed fonts, your publications may not look the same when they are printed on both printers.

The Copies setting

To print multiple copies of a publication on your LaserJet printer, simply change the Copies setting in the Print dialog box from 1 to the number of copies you want to print (you can print up to 99 copies).

By default, PageMaker will print the specified number of copies of page 1, then the same number of copies of page 2, and so forth. If you want PageMaker to print each copy of the document in its entirety before starting on the next copy, you'll want to select the Collate checkbox. Although the Collate option will eliminate the need to manually collate your documents after they print, collated publications print much more slowly than uncollated publications (this is because PageMaker formats each page only once under the uncollated method). You'll most likely want to print your publications uncollated, and then collate them manually after they print.

Since some LaserJet printers stack the documents face up, while others stack them face down, PageMaker lets you specify the order in which the pages of your publication will be printed. By default, PageMaker prints page 1 of your publication first, then prints the remaining pages. This works out fine if you are printing on a LaserJet Series II or a LaserJet IID printer. However, since the LaserJet and LaserJet Plus printers stack documents face up, you'll want to select the Reverse order checkbox in the Print dialog box so that page 1 is printed last and ends up on top of the printed stack.

The Pages setting in the Print dialog box tells PageMaker which pages of the publication to print. The default setting, All, instructs PageMaker to print every page in the publication. If you want to print only part of a multiple-page publication, type the number of the first page in the From edit bar, and then type the number of the last page in the To edit bar.

The Pages setting

The Bit-map smoothing option (which is available only on PostScript-equipped LaserJet printers) tells PageMaker to use dots to fill in the ragged edges of a publication's paint-type graphics. To select Bit-map smoothing, simply select the Bit-map smoothing checkbox before you choose OK to complete the Print... command. Although bit map smoothing usually improves the appearance of graphics, it sometimes darkens the image and makes it look worse. Typically, you'll want to use bit map smoothing only in publications that contain large, ragged graphics. Of course, bit map smoothing always increases the amount of time that it takes to print the publication.

The Bit-map smoothing option

If your publication contains only simple, nonoverlapping objects, you can print the publication much faster on a PCL LaserJet printer by selecting the Fast rules option. The Fast rules option tells PageMaker to send the dimensions of the rules and boxes in your publication instead of the bit-mapped representations of those images. You should not select this option when you are printing spot color overlays with cutouts—if you do, the printed publication will not contain the   correct shapes.

The Fast rules option

*The Crop
marks option*

Crop marks are short, thin lines that indicate where the paper should be trimmed to match the page size (see Figure 14-14). If you've selected a page size that is smaller than your paper size, you can print the crop marks in your publication by selecting the Crop marks checkbox. After the LaserJet prints the publication, just trim the paper along the crop marks.

FIGURE 14-14

*Crop marks show you
where to trim the pages
in a document.*

*Sending the
publication*

After you're satisfied with all of your print settings, you can send the report to the printer by choosing OK in the Print dialog box. As soon as PageMaker begins sending the publication, it will display a Printing status box like the one shown in Figure 14-15, which lets you know the current status of the print job. After the entire publication has been printed, the status box will disappear, and PageMaker will exit from the menus.

FIGURE 14-15

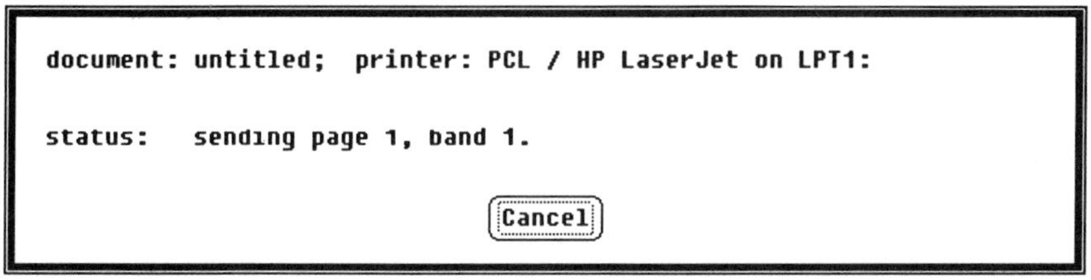

```
document: untitled;  printer: PCL / HP LaserJet on LPT1:

status:   sending page 1, band 1.

                    [ Cancel ]
```

The Printing status box lets you know the current status of the print job.

Of course, you can cancel the print job at any time by choosing the Cancel option in the Printing status box. If the LaserJet is in the process of printing a page when you choose the Cancel option, it won't stop printing immediately. Instead, the LaserJet will finish printing all the information PageMaker sent before you issued the Cancel command.

Special Print Topics

PageMaker offers some extremely powerful printing features that allow you to print publications in a variety of ways. For instance, no matter which LaserJet model you use, you can create oversize pages by breaking the publication into smaller sections called tiles, then manually pasting those tiles together to create the page. In addition, you can print spot color overlays for a multicolor publication. If your LaserJet is equipped with PostScript capabilities, you can print thumbnails (miniature copies) of the publication, or you can print enlarged or reduced pages.

Printing spot color overlays

When commercial printers create a two-color publication, they must prepare two separate printing plates. One printing plate will contain only the items in the publication that will appear in one color, while the other will contain the items that will appear in a different color. When the print images created from these two plates are superimposed, an attractive, two-color publication results.

Fortunately, PageMaker lets you indicate which parts of a publication should appear in one color, and which parts should appear in another color. When you are ready to send the master pages of the publication to your local printer, you can tell PageMaker to print a page for each color you've used in the publication, and your commercial printer can then create the printing plates directly from the pages you've printed.

To tell PageMaker to print color overlays for your publication, select the Spot color overlays option in the Print dialog box. If you want PageMaker to print the overlays with cutouts (see Figure 14-16), select the Cutouts option in the Print dialog box as well. When you choose OK, PageMaker will print a separate page for each color in your publication. If the image area of an overlay does not occupy the entire area of the printed page, PageMaker automatically prints the name of the color outside the image area on each printed overlay. For more information on creating color overlays in your publications, refer to your *PageMaker User Manual*.

FIGURE 14-16

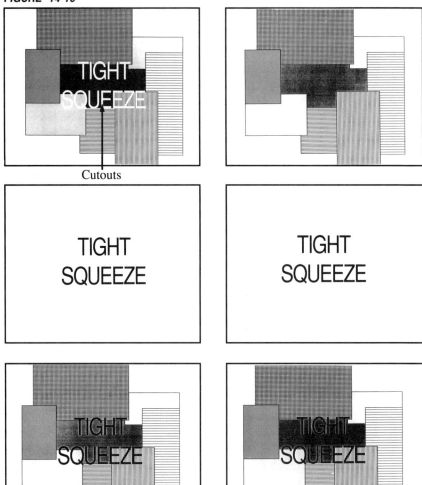

Cutouts

PageMaker lets you print color overlays with or without cutouts.

Printing enlarged or reduced pages

If you're using a PostScript-equipped LaserJet printer, you can scale the size of your publication from 25 to 1,000 percent. To scale your publication, simply type the scaling value in the Scaling edit bar. For example, to make your publication appear half as short and wide as it appears at actual size, just type 50 in the Scaling edit bar. When you choose OK to send the publication to the printer, the LaserJet will print the publication at half-size in the center of the page. As you might guess, it takes more time to print scaled pages than it does to print regular-size pages.

If you want to enlarge your publication, you can do so by entering a large scaling value in the Scaling edit bar. For example, if you want a one-page publication to appear three pages high by three pages wide, just type 300 in the Scaling edit bar.

If you need to create a publication that is larger than the paper you'll use in the LaserJet printer, you can use the Tile option in the Print dialog box to print the oversize page. Tiling a publication simply involves dividing your printed page into seperate tiles, and then printing each tile on a separate sheet of paper. Figure 14-17 on the following page shows an oversize page that has been broken into four tiles. After you print all the tiles that make up the publication, you can manually assemble the tiles on a paste-up board to create the oversize page.

Printing oversize pages

You'll use the Tile option in the Print dialog box to tile the pages in your publication. As the options on the right of the Tile checkbox indicate, you can tile pages either automatically or manually. If you let PageMaker tile your publication automatically, your publication may be broken in undesirable locations, or it may be broken into too many tiles. For this reason, you'll usually want to manually tile the pages in your publication.

When you tile your publications automatically, PageMaker uses the overlap value you specify in the Auto overlap edit bar to determine where each tile begins. After PageMaker breaks the publication into tiles, it prints all of the first page's tiles, then all of the next page's tiles, and so forth.

Tiling automatically

To tell PageMaker you want to tile your publication automatically, just choose the Tile checkbox in the Print dialog box. By default, PageMaker selects the Auto option and presents a default overlap value of 0.65 inches. Since the LaserJet printer cannot print to a region along the edges of the page, you should maintain an overlap value no lower than 0.5 inches. After you specify the desired overlap value, choose **OK** to send the publication to the printer. If PageMaker breaks the publication in undesirable locations, you'll want to reissue the Print... command and tile the publication manually.

When you tile your publication manually, you first move PageMaker's zero point (the point where the zeros on the rulers intersect) to the place where you want the first tile to begin. Next, you select the Print... command on the File menu, select the Tile checkbox, then select the Manual option next to the Tile checkbox. When you choose **OK** to complete the Print... command, PageMaker will print the tile you've defined for every page in the publication. After PageMaker prints the first set of tiles, reposition the zero point to the place where the next tile should begin, then reissue the Print... command to print the second set of tiles. After you've

Tiling manually

printed tiles that cover the entire publication, you can cut and paste the tiles together on a paste-up board. For more information on manual tiling, refer to your *PageMaker User Manual*.

FIGURE 14-17

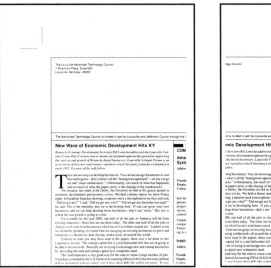
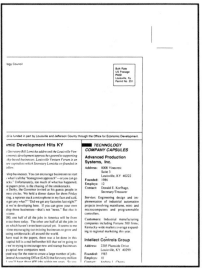

If you create a publication that is too large to fit on a single page, you can use the Tile option to break it up into smaller tiles that you can assemble on a paste-up board.

The Thumbnails option (which is available only on PostScript-equipped LaserJet printers) lets you print miniature copies (thumbnails) of your publication. To print thumbnails instead of regular-size pages, just select the Thumbnails checkbox before your choose **OK** to complete the Print… command. Figure 14-18 shows a publication printed with the Thumbnails checkbox selected. As you might expect, the LaserJet takes longer to print thumbnails than it does to print regular-size pages.

Printing thumbnails

FIGURE 14-18

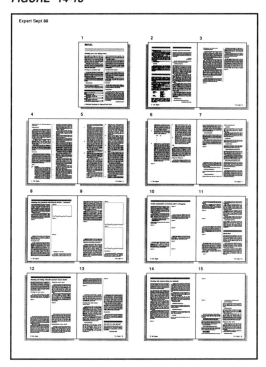

The Thumbnails option lets you print miniature copies of the pages in your publication on a PostScript-equipped LaserJet printer.

As you already know, a PCL LaserJet cannot perform all the same functions that a PostScript-equipped LaserJet can. One shortcoming of a PCL LaserJet is its inability to print white text on a black background. Only PostScript printers can print inverse text in a PageMaker publication. If you attempt to send a publication with inverse text to a PCL LaserJet printer, you'll see solid black images where the white text should appear. Unfortunately, there is nothing you can do to resolve this problem—it is simply a limitation of the LaserJet's PCL language.

A note

In this chapter, we've covered the issues that are important when printing PageMaker publications on an HP LaserJet printer. With a little practice, you can use PageMaker to create all kinds of attractive publications on your LaserJet.

CONCLUSION

MICROSOFT EXCEL 15

Microsoft Excel best represents the newest generation of spreadsheet software. Since this spreadsheet program runs under the Microsoft Windows operating environment, it offers many advanced features not found on most other spreadsheet products, including pull-down menus, dialog boxes, and easy-to-use icons. In short, Excel is bigger, faster, and stronger than other spreadsheet products, yet its intuitive graphical interface lets you learn the program quickly and easily.

Although Excel offers tremendous performance without tremendous complexity, the one feature that sets it apart from other spreadsheet programs is its report-generating capabilities. When you use Excel with an HP LaserJet printer, you can produce worksheet reports attractive enough for the company's annual report.

In this chapter, we'll show you how to get the most out of your HP LaserJet printer with Microsoft Excel. After we show you how to install support for the HP LaserJet, we'll cover the basics of printing an Excel worksheet. Then, we'll talk about Excel's formatting options, including margin settings, font variations, and shading, and we'll present a few sample reports that show off the LaserJet's printing capabilities. Finally, we'll discuss some important concepts related to printing charts on an HP LaserJet.

INSTALLING EXCEL

As you already know, Microsoft Excel runs under the Microsoft Windows operating environment. In order to run Excel, you must either purchase and install a copy of Microsoft Windows, or use the run-time version of Microsoft Windows that is packaged along with Excel. Although the run-time version of Windows works just fine with Excel, you cannot use it to run any other Windows applications, like Aldus PageMaker or Microsoft Write. Using a full-fledged version of

Microsoft Windows allows you to transfer data between Microsoft Excel and other Windows applications, and it allows you to control DOS tasks from the Windows environment. If you don't own a copy of Microsoft Windows, we recommend that you install Excel with the run-time version of Windows now, then purchase and install the full version of Microsoft Windows as soon as possible.

Regardless of which version of Windows you install, almost all of the information we presented in Chapter 13 is important if you are installing Excel on your computer. For this reason, we highly recommend that you skim through Chapter 13 before reading this section on installing Excel.

Running SETUP

To install Microsoft Excel on your machine, insert Excel's Setup Disk (Disk 1) into drive A:, type **SETUP** at the DOS A> prompt, and press ↵. The SETUP program will take it from there, prompting you for information about your computer system, telling you when to change disks, and copying the appropriate files from each of the floppy disks to your hard disk.

Installing Excel files only

If you've already installed Microsoft Windows on your hard disk, Excel's SETUP program will copy only the necessary Excel files onto your disk. When SETUP is finished, it will return you to an A> prompt. If you've already customized Windows to work with your LaserJet printer as we described in Chapter 13, you do not need to perform any additional installation procedures after running Excel's SETUP program. To start Excel, simply load Windows, choose the **EXCEL.EXE** file from the MS-DOS Executive window, and then press ↵. If you're using a mouse, just double-click on the file EXCEL.EXE.

Installing Excel and run-time Windows

If SETUP cannot find an installed copy of Windows on your hard disk, it will present the screen shown in Figure 15-1 before it completes the Excel installation. As this screen indicates, you can either press ↵ to install the run-time version of Windows on your disk, or you can press [Ctrl]X to exit Excel's SETUP program and install a full version of Windows before you install Excel.

As soon as you press ↵ to install run-time Windows, Excel's SETUP program will ask you several questions about your computer system. For example, it will ask you to define the type of computer, display adapter, keyboard, and mouse you are using. Once you've answered all of those questions, SETUP will present the screen shown in Figure 15-2, which asks if you want to install support for a printer. When you see this screen, you should respond by either typing an **I**, or by pressing ↵.

FIGURE 15-1

```
Now do one of the following:

*If you haven't yet purchased Microsoft Windows,
 version 2.0 or higher, press ENTER to install
 the "run-time" windows.

*If you've already purchased Microsoft Windows, version
 2.0 or higher:

    -Exit SETUP.
    -Run the Microsoft Windows 2.0 SETUP and install
     Windows in your Microsoft Excel directory.


 ╔══════════════════════════════════════════════╗
 ║ WHEN YOU'RE READY TO                  PRESS   ║
 ╠══════════════════════════════════════════════╣
 ║ Install the "run-time" Windows         I      ║
 ║ Quit                                   Q      ║
 ╚══════════════════════════════════════════════╝
```

When this screen appears during SETUP, just press ↵ to install the run-time version of Microsoft Windows.

FIGURE 15-2

```
Setup will allow you to install a printer or plotter.


    ╔═══════════════════════════════════════════════╗
    ║ WHEN YOU'RE READY TO                  PRESS   ║
    ╠═══════════════════════════════════════════════╣
    ║ Install a printer or plotter           I      ║
    ║ Continue Setup                         C      ║
    ╠═══════════════════════════════════════════════╣
    ║ Exit without completing Setup      CONTROL+X  ║
    ╚═══════════════════════════════════════════════╝
```

This SETUP screen marks the beginning of the printer installation process.

After you tell SETUP that you want to install a printer, SETUP will present a list of printers similar to the one shown in Figure 15-3 on the following page. To choose the printer you want to install, use the ↑ or ↓ key to move the highlight bar through the list of printer names, and press ↵ when the bar appears over the name of the printer you want to install.

Installing a PCL LaserJet

If you press the [Pg Dn] key twice to move down the list in Figure 15-3, the names of a few LaserJet family members will appear, as shown in Figure 15-4 on the next page. To install support for your LaserJet, simply use the ↑ or ↓ key to highlight the LaserJet model you own, and press ↵.

FIGURE 15-3

```
┌──────────────────────────────────────────────────────────────────┐
│ Select an output device (printer, plotter, etc.) from the following list. │
│                                                                    │
│   - Use the DIRECTION (↑,↓) keys to move the highlight to your selection. │
│                                                                    │
│ ▌No selection▐                                                     │
│ Apple LaserWriter                                                  │
│ Apple LaserWriter Plus                                             │
│ Apricot Laser                                                      │
│ C-Itoh 8510                                                        │
│ Dataproducts LZR 2665                                              │
│ Digital LN03R ScriptPrinter                                        │
│ Digital LPS PrintServer 40                                         │
│ Epson FX-80                                                        │
│ Epson LQ800                                                        │
│ Epson LQ850                                                        │
│ Epson LQ1000                                                       │
│ Epson LQ1050                                                       │
│                                                                    │
│          (To see more of the list, press the DOWN(↓) key.)         │
│        ┌──────────────────────────────────────────────┐           │
│        │ WHEN YOU'RE READY TO                    PRESS │           │
│        ├──────────────────────────────────────────────┤           │
│        │ Confirm your choice                     ENTER │           │
│        │ Exit without completing Setup       CONTROL+X │           │
│        └──────────────────────────────────────────────┘           │
└──────────────────────────────────────────────────────────────────┘
```

When this list of printers appears, press the [Pg Dn] key twice to display the HP LaserJet printers.

FIGURE 15-4

```
┌──────────────────────────────────────────────────────────────────┐
│ Select an output device (printer, plotter, etc.) from the following list. │
│                                                                    │
│   - Use the DIRECTION (↑,↓) keys to move the highlight to your selection. │
│                                                                    │
│ HP 7586B                                                           │
│ HP ColorPro                                                        │
│ HP ColorPro with GEC                                               │
│ HP DraftPro                                                        │
│ HP DraftMaster I                                                   │
│ HP DraftMaster II                                                  │
│ HP LaserJet                                                        │
│ HP LaserJet Plus                                                   │
│ HP LaserJet 500+                                                   │
│ ▌HP LaserJet Series II▐                                            │
│ HP LaserJet 2000                                                   │
│ HP ThinkJet (2225 C-D)                                             │
│ IBM Color Printer (B/W only)                                       │
│                                                                    │
│          (To see more of the list, press the DOWN(↓) key.)         │
│        ┌──────────────────────────────────────────────┐           │
│        │ WHEN YOU'RE READY TO                    PRESS │           │
│        ├──────────────────────────────────────────────┤           │
│        │ Confirm your choice                     ENTER │           │
│        │ Exit without completing Setup       CONTROL+X │           │
│        └──────────────────────────────────────────────┘           │
└──────────────────────────────────────────────────────────────────┘
```

When this screen appears, highlight the type of LaserJet printer you will be using.

Although SETUP does not include an entry for a PostScript-equipped LaserJet printer, you can make Excel work with this type of LaserJet by selecting one of the other PostScript printers from SETUP's list. The manual that comes with your LaserJet's PostScript system should list the names of the printers with which that system is compatible. If not, contact the manufacturer and request this information.

Installing a Post-Script-equipped LaserJet

For example, if you've installed the QMS JetScript system on your computer and LaserJet, you'll notice that the manual included with that system states that the LaserJet is compatible with the Apple LaserWriter Plus and with the QMS-PS 800 Plus. Consequently, you should use the ↑ or ↓ key to highlight either the Apple LaserWriter Plus or the QMS-PS 800 Plus option, and press ↵.

After you've selected the name of the printer you want to install, SETUP will display the list of the port names shown in Figure 15-5. Simply use the ↑ or ↓ key to select the port to which you've connected your LaserJet printer, and press ↵ to save your selection. (As we mentioned in Chapter 13, you can use the Connections... command on the control panel's Setup menu if you need to change the LaserJet's printer port assignment after you run the SETUP program.)

Choosing a port

FIGURE 15-5

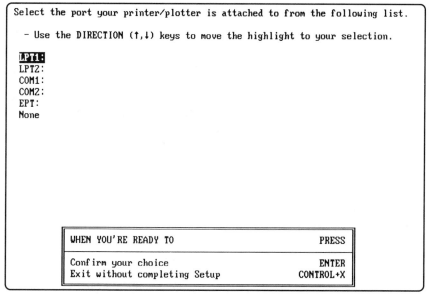

After selecting the appropriate type of printer, you'll need to select the port to which your printer is connected.

Installing both a PCL and a PostScript LaserJet

If your LaserJet printer is equipped with both PCL and PostScript, you will probably want to install support for both. Fortunately, SETUP allows you to do this. After you have selected the port that is connected to your LaserJet printer, SETUP will present the screen in Figure 15-6, which asks if you want to install support for another printer.

FIGURE 15-6

```
You can install another printer or plotter.


   ┌─────────────────────────────────────────────────────┐
   │ WHEN YOU'RE READY TO                      PRESS       │
   ├─────────────────────────────────────────────────────┤
   │ Install another printer or plotter          I        │
   │ Continue Setup                             █C█       │
   ├─────────────────────────────────────────────────────┤
   │ Exit without completing Setup           CONTROL+X    │
   └─────────────────────────────────────────────────────┘
```

After you install support for your LaserJet printer, SETUP will allow you to install support for another printer.

To install support for another printer, simply type **I** (or use the ↑ key to highlight the letter **I**) and press ↵. At this point, SETUP will bring up the screen shown in Figure 15-3 again and repeat the printer installation process we described earlier.

Completing the printer installation

After you've installed all the printers available to your system, and SETUP presents the screen in Figure 15-6, finish the installation by typing a C. When you do this, SETUP will continue copying files over to your hard disk and will eventually finish the installation and return you to an A> prompt.

A note

After SETUP has completed the installation process, it will copy a file named README HP.TXT and/or a file named READMEPS.TXT into the directory where it has installed Windows. These two text files contain information about using your LaserJet with Windows applications. Although we'll discuss all of the topics covered in that file in this chapter (as we did in Chapter 13), you might want to browse through the file by either loading it into a text processor that handles pure ASCII files or by typing the command **TYPE READMEHP.TXT** (or **TYPE READMEPS.TXT**) at the DOS prompt.

Setting Up Your LaserJet's Device Drivers

After you've used Excel's SETUP program to install Excel (and, if necessary, a run-time version of Windows), you need to load Excel and set up the device driver that will communicate with your printer. In other words, you need to tell Windows exactly which fonts and features you've installed on your LaserJet so that Excel can take full advantage of your LaserJet's printing capabilities.

To set up your LaserJet's device driver, first load Excel, and then select the Printer Setup... command from Excel's File menu. When you do this, Excel will present a dialog box similar to the one shown in Figure 15-7 that includes all of the printers you installed with the SETUP program. When this box appears, simply select a printer name from the Printer box, then choose the Setup... option to bring up a larger dialog box that lets you specify more detailed information about the selected printer.

FIGURE 15-7

Excel presents a dialog box like this when you select the Printer Setup... command from the File menu.

To set up the device driver for a PCL LaserJet printer, select **PCL / HP LaserJet on LPT1:** from the dialog box shown in Figure 15-7, then choose the Setup... option. When you do this, Excel will present the dialog box shown in Figure 15-8 on the following page.

Setting up a PCL LaserJet

The dialog box shown in Figure 15-8 is the same one that appears when you use the Printer command on the control panel's Setup menu to set up a PCL LaserJet printer. Refer to the section entitled "Setting up the PCL Device Driver" in Chapter 13 to learn the significance of each setting in this dialog box, and then use that information to define the appropriate settings for your LaserJet printer. After you've defined the appropriate settings, choose **OK** to return to the dialog box in Figure 15-7, and then choose **OK** again to return Excel to Ready mode.

FIGURE 15-8

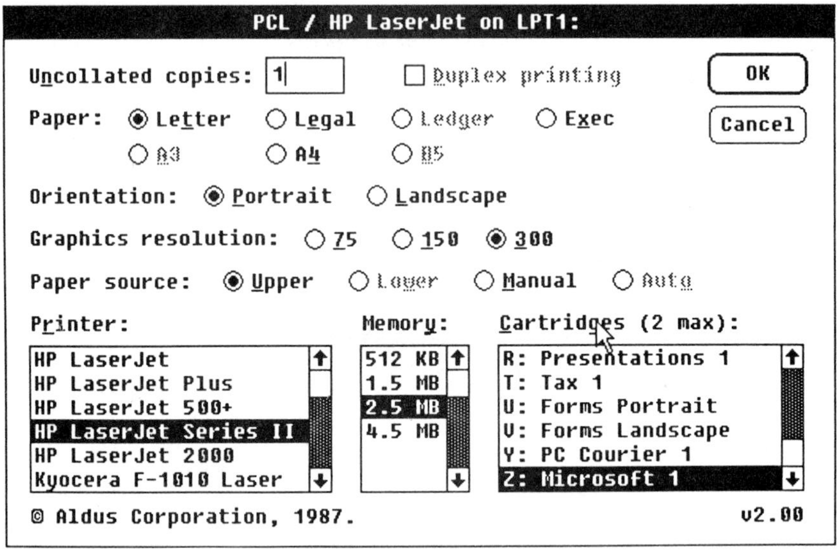

```
┌─────────────────────────────────────────────────────────────────┐
│              PCL / HP LaserJet on LPT1:                          │
│                                                                   │
│  U̲ncollated copies: [1│    ]    ☐ D̲uplex printing     ╭─────────╮ │
│                                                         │   OK    │ │
│  Paper:  ◉ Le̲tter   ○ L̲egal   ○ L̲edger   ○ E̲xec       ╰─────────╯ │
│          ○ A̲3       ○ A̲4      ○ B̲5                     ╭─────────╮ │
│                                                         │ Cancel  │ │
│  Orientation:  ◉ P̲ortrait   ○ L̲andscape               ╰─────────╯ │
│                                                                   │
│  Graphics resolution:  ○ 7̲5   ○ 1̲50   ◉ 3̲00                      │
│                                                                   │
│  Paper source:  ◉ U̲pper   ○ L̲ower   ○ M̲anual   ○ A̲uto           │
│                                                                   │
│  Pr̲inter:              Memor̲y:        Cartridg̲es (2 max):        │
│  ┌──────────────────┐  ┌─────────┐   ┌─────────────────────────┐ │
│  │HP LaserJet      ↑│  │512 KB ↑│   │R: Presentations 1      ↑│ │
│  │HP LaserJet Plus  │  │1.5 MB  │   │T: Tax 1                 │ │
│  │HP LaserJet 500+  │  │2.5 MB  │   │U: Forms Portrait        │ │
│  │HP LaserJet Series II│ │4.5 MB │   │V: Forms Landscape       │ │
│  │HP LaserJet 2000  │  │        │   │Y: PC Courier 1          │ │
│  │Kyocera F-1010 Laser↓│ │     ↓│   │Z: Microsoft 1          ↓│ │
│  └──────────────────┘  └─────────┘   └─────────────────────────┘ │
│  © Aldus Corporation, 1987.                            v2.00     │
└─────────────────────────────────────────────────────────────────┘
```

This dialog box lets you tell Excel which options you've installed on your LaserJet.

Setting up a PostScript-equipped LaserJet

To set up the device driver for a PostScript-equipped LaserJet printer, select **PostScript Printer on LPT2:** from the dialog box shown in Figure 15-7, and then choose the S̲etup… option. When you do this, Excel will present the dialog box shown in Figure 15-9.

The dialog box shown in Figure 15-9 is the same one that appears when you use the Printer command on the control panel's Setup menu to set up a PostScript printer. Refer to the section entitled "Setting up the PostScript Driver" in Chapter 13 to learn the significance of each setting in this dialog box, and then use that information to define the appropriate settings for your LaserJet printer. After you've defined the appropriate settings, choose **OK** to return to the dialog box in Figure 15-7, and then choose **OK** again to return Excel to Ready mode.

Installing Fonts

Now that you've installed Excel and set up your LaserJet's device drivers, you need to install the fonts you'll use with Excel. Like all applications that run under Microsoft Windows, Microsoft Excel can display a variety of fonts on the screen and can take full advantage of your LaserJet's font capabilities. As we explained in Chapter 13, you need two different kinds of fonts to compose documents on your LaserJet printer with a Windows application: GDI fonts (fonts you can display on your screen) and device fonts (fonts you can print on your printer).

FIGURE 15-9

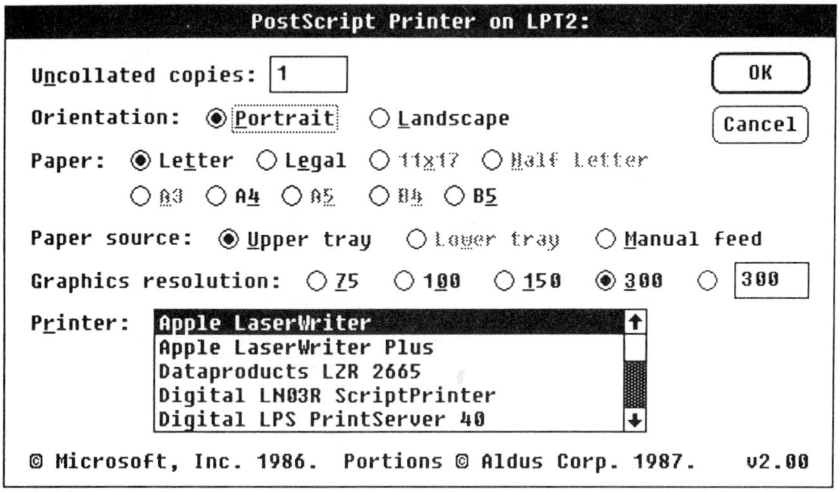

```
┌────────────────────────────────────────────────────────────┐
│                PostScript Printer on LPT2:                  │
│                                                             │
│  Uncollated copies: │1     │            ┌───────────┐       │
│                                         │    OK     │       │
│  Orientation:  ◉ Portrait   ○ Landscape └───────────┘       │
│                                         ┌───────────┐       │
│  Paper:  ◉ Letter  ○ Legal  ○ 11x17  ○ Half Letter          │
│          ○ A3  ○ A4  ○ A5  ○ B4  ○ B5   │  Cancel   │       │
│                                         └───────────┘       │
│  Paper source:  ◉ Upper tray  ○ Lower tray  ○ Manual feed   │
│                                                             │
│  Graphics resolution:  ○ 75  ○ 100  ○ 150  ◉ 300  ○ │300 │  │
│                                                             │
│  Printer:  ┌─────────────────────────────────────┬──┐      │
│            │ Apple LaserWriter                    │▲ │      │
│            │ Apple LaserWriter Plus               │  │      │
│            │ Dataproducts LZR 2665                │██│      │
│            │ Digital LN03R ScriptPrinter          │██│      │
│            │ Digital LPS PrintServer 40           │▼ │      │
│            └─────────────────────────────────────┴──┘      │
│  © Microsoft, Inc. 1986.  Portions © Aldus Corp. 1987.  v2.00 │
└────────────────────────────────────────────────────────────┘
```

When you use the Printer Setup... command to set up a PostScript printer, Excel presents this dialog box.

Your task as an Excel user is first to install the printer fonts you want to use in your printed worksheets, then to install the matching screen fonts into your Windows system. If you install matching sets of printer fonts and screen fonts, your Excel worksheets will look the same on paper as they do on the screen. (This concept is often referred to as WYSIWYG, which stands for What You See Is What You Get.) If you install unmatched sets of printer fonts and screen fonts, however, you won't be able to take advantage of Windows' WYSIWYG capabilities.

Installing PCL printer fonts

As you probably know, you can add additional fonts to your LaserJet by installing font cartridges, downloadable soft fonts, or both. You'll most likely want to start off using some basic font types (like Helv, Tms Rmn, and Courier), then purchase additional fonts as you gain a clearer understanding of which fonts look best in your printed worksheets.

Installing font cartridges

If you are like most Excel users, you'll want to install the HP "Z" font cartridge (HP Part No. 92286Z) in your LaserJet when you are printing with Excel. The "Z" font cartridge was specifically designed for Microsoft Windows applications and includes several variations of the three most popular spreadsheet typefaces: Tms Rmn (a variation of Times Roman), Helv (a variation of Helvetica), and Line Printer (a compressed, fixed-pitch font that is well-suited for printing large spreadsheets). You can purchase a "Z" font cartridge (or any other HP font cartridge) from your local computer vendor or from HP Direct Marketing (800-538-8787).

After you've plugged your font cartridge(s) into your LaserJet, you need to bring up the dialog box shown in Figure 15-8 with Excel's Printer Setup... command, and select the cartridge(s) you've installed in the Cartridges list box. After you've selected the font cartridge(s), choose OK to lock in your selections.

Installing soft fonts

If you use any HP LaserJet printer other than the original LaserJet, you can use soft fonts in addition to font cartridges to give your printer access to optional typefaces. Like font cartridges, there are dozens of soft fonts available for HP LaserJet printers.

After you copy the optional soft fonts onto your hard disk, you'll need to tell Windows where you've installed the new soft fonts in order to use them with Excel. To learn how to install soft fonts into your Windows system, refer to the section entitled "Adding Support for PCL Soft Fonts" in Chapter 13.

Installing PostScript printer fonts

Like PCL soft fonts, PostScript soft fonts must be downloaded from your computer's hard disk to your printer. To learn how to install PostScript soft fonts into your Windows system, refer to the section entitled "Adding Support for PostScript Soft Fonts" in Chapter 13.

Installing screen fonts

Just as you need to install font cartridges and soft fonts to let your LaserJet print in a variety of typestyles, you need to install screen fonts to let Microsoft Windows applications *display* a variety of typestyles. Fortunately, the SETUP program automatically installs a base set of screen fonts that are specifically designed for the display hardware you are using. For example, if you are using an EGA video system, SETUP will automatically install a base set of three screen fonts that are specifically designed for use with the EGA.

No matter which video system you use, SETUP always installs versions of the Tms Rmn, Helv, and Courier raster screen fonts. In addition, SETUP installs the Roman, Script, and Modern stroke fonts. Finally, two additional raster screen fonts are built directly into the Windows environment: the System font and the Terminal font. Figure 15-10 shows a sample of all eight of these basic screen fonts.

If you want to install additional screen fonts on your LaserJet printer, you'll have to use the Add New Font... command on the control panel's Installation menu. For a detailed explanation of this procedure, refer to the section entitled "Installing Screen Fonts with the Control Panel" in Chapter 13.

Matching printer fonts with screen fonts

Somewhere down the road, you will assign a screen font to an entry in an Excel worksheet that does not have a matching LaserJet PCL or PostScript font. On the other hand, you may also assign a printer font to a worksheet entry that has no matching screen font. In either case, Excel will substitute the font that most closely matches the font you've assigned. We'll look at an example that illustrates this problem a little later in this chapter.

FIGURE 15-10

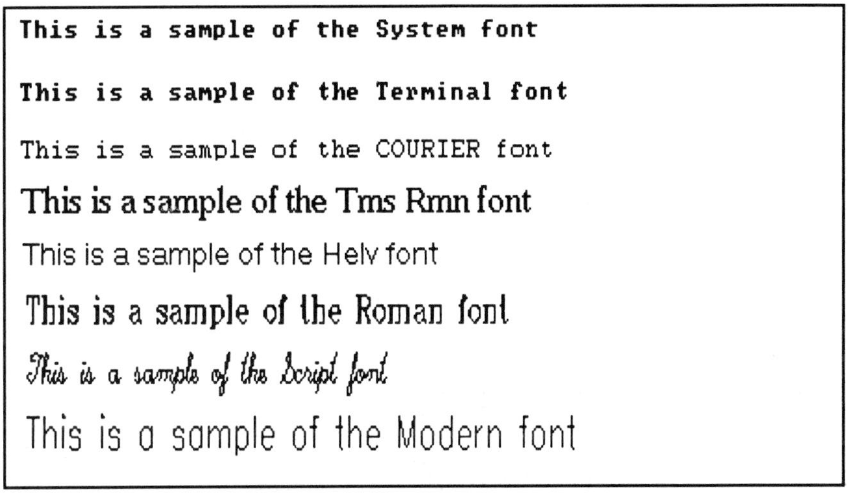

```
This is a sample of the System font

This is a sample of the Terminal font

This is a sample of the COURIER font

This is a sample of the Tms Rmn font

This is a sample of the Helv font

This is a sample of the Roman font

This is a sample of the Script font

This is a sample of the Modern font
```

Microsoft Windows automatically installs these eight screen fonts when you install Windows on an EGA computer system.

The section entitled "Matching Screen Fonts with LaserJet Fonts" in Chapter 13 explains how to obtain matching printer and screen fonts for your Windows applications. If you carefully read that section, you'll know how to take full advantage of Windows' ability to produce great-looking documents both on your screen and on your LaserJet printer.

If you've installed matching printer fonts and screen fonts into your Windows system, and you still can't make Excel print your worksheets as they appear on your screen, the problem might be related to the font summary file (FSLPT1.PCL) in your Windows directory. As we explained in Chapter 13, the font summary file contains printer font metrics information for all internal, cartridge, and soft fonts, along with the PCL commands necessary to select them. If you erase your old font summary file, then begin a new Windows session, Windows will automatically create a new font summary file based on the current settings in your WIN.INI file. For additional information on the font summary file, refer to the section entitled "PCL Font Summary File" in Chapter 13.

PRINTING WORKSHEETS

As we mentioned earlier, Microsoft Excel possesses the most powerful formatting capabilities of any spreadsheet program currently on the market. When you combine the formatting power of Excel with the sharp print quality of the LaserJet printer, you can easily create polished, professional-looking reports from your worksheet. After we introduce you to the basics of printing worksheets, we'll discuss a few formatting concerns related to the LaserJet, and then we'll present a few sample reports that really show off the LaserJet's capabilities.

Basics

The tool you'll use to print Excel worksheet reports is the Print... command on the File menu. Before you print your worksheet, however, you'll want to use the Page Setup... command on the File menu, which lets you control the layout of your printed reports.

The Page Setup...
command

When you select the Page Setup... command from the File menu, Excel presents a dialog box like the one shown in Figure 15-11. As you can see, this box lists all of your page-layout options. You can create a header across the top of the page and a footer across the bottom, change the page margins, and indicate whether row and column headers and gridlines should appear on your printed report. Let's consider how each of these settings affect a report printed on a LaserJet printer.

FIGURE 15-11

```
┌──────────────────────────────────────────────────┐
│  Page Setup              ┌──────────────┐         │
│                          │      OK      │         │
│  Header: █&f          █  └──────────────┘         │
│                          ┌──────────────┐         │
│  Footer: │Page &p     │  │   Cancel     │         │
│                          └──────────────┘         │
│  ┌─Margins──────────────────────────────────┐    │
│  │ Left: │0.75   │    Right: │0.75   │       │    │
│  │ Top:  │1      │    Bottom:│1      │       │    │
│  └──────────────────────────────────────────┘    │
│  ☒ Row & Column Headings   ☒ Gridlines            │
└──────────────────────────────────────────────────┘
```

Excel's Page Setup... command lets you control the layout of your printed reports.

The Header and Footer settings

As you might guess, the Header and Footer settings in the Page Setup dialog box create a single line of text that appears at the top or bottom of each page of a report. The LaserJet always prints the text in the header line and in the footer line $1/_2$ inch from the top or bottom of each page.

By default, Excel creates both a header and a footer for your report. The default header, &f, tells Excel to print the name of the document at the top of each page. The default footer, Page &p, instructs Excel to print the word *Page*, followed by the page number, at the bottom of each page. Excel centers headers and footers unless you tell it to do otherwise. If you want to print a report without a header or footer, simply highlight the appropriate edit bar, and press the [**Delete**] key.

The symbols &f and &p that appear in the default header and footer are among the 12 special codes you can use in headers and footers. Table 15-1 summarizes these codes and their associated meanings.

TABLE 15-1

Code	Action
&l	Left-aligns subsequent characters
&c	Centers subsequent characters (the default)
&r	Right-aligns subsequent characters
&p	Includes page number
&p+*number*	Includes page number and adds *number* to it (allows you to change starting page numbers)
&p-*number*	Includes page number and subtracts *number* from it (allows you to change starting page numbers)
&d	Includes current date in mm/dd/yy format
&t	Includes current time in hh:mm AM/PM format
&f	Includes document name
&&	Includes single ampersand
&b	Prints subsequent characters in bold type
&i	Prints subsequent characters in italic type

You can insert these special codes into your header and footer.

In addition to entering special values into your headers and footers, like the date, time, and page number, the codes in Table 15-1 let you control the alignment and style (bold or italics) of your headers and footers. To assign special attributes to words in your header and footer, simply precede the appropriate portion of the text in the header or footer with the special code. For example, to print the words *The Cobb Group* at the top of each page in bold type and aligned at the left margin, you would enter the header line **&b&lThe Cobb Group**. Similarly, to create a header that looks like this:

1/6/89 **The Cobb Group** *9:08 AM*

you would enter the header line **&l&i&d&c&bThe Cobb Group&r&i&t.**

Since Excel prints the header and footer with Font 1 in the Format Font dialog box, you'll have to use the Format Font... command to change Font 1 if you want to change the size or typeface of the header or footer. We'll explain how to use the Format Font... command when we talk about fonts later in this chapter.

The Margins settings

The Margins settings in the Page Setup dialog box let you define the top, bottom, left, and right margins of your report in inches. As you might expect, the LaserJet printer will leave exactly the amount of blank space you specify in the Top and Left margin box at the top and left edges of the page. Since the worksheet data doesn't always coincide with the page's bottom and right edges, the Bottom and Right margin settings define the minimum amount of space the LaserJet should reserve along those edges of the printed report.

As we mentioned in Chapter 1, every LaserJet printer is physically unable to print to a small region along the outside edges of a page. This unprintable region occupies approximately $\frac{1}{4}$ inch of space at the top and bottom edges of the page, as well as $\frac{1}{4}$ inch of space at the left and right edges. For this reason, if you specify a margin setting of less than $\frac{1}{4}$ inch, the LaserJet will still print that report with $\frac{1}{4}$ inch of blank space along that edge.

In the previous section, we explained that header and footer lines always appear $\frac{1}{2}$ inch from the top and bottom edges of the page. If you define a header line in a report whose Top margin setting is less than $\frac{1}{2}$ inch, the LaserJet will print the header line on top of the worksheet data, resulting in an unsightly mess. Similarly, reports containing footers that are printed with a Bottom margin setting of less than $\frac{1}{2}$ inch will contain overlapping data in the footer line. Consequently, when you print a worksheet report that contains a header and a footer, you should specify a Top and Bottom margin setting larger than $\frac{1}{2}$ inch.

The Row & Column Headings and Gridlines options

The last two options that appear in the Page Setup dialog box are the Row & Column Headings option and the Gridlines option. As you might expect, selecting these options tells the LaserJet to include the worksheet's gridlines and its row and column headings in the printed report.

Typically, you'll want to print your rough drafts with both of these options active so that you can easily identify the location of any entry in the worksheet. When you print your final version, however, you'll probably want to turn these options off to produce a clean, professional-looking report. Figure 15-12 shows a worksheet that has been printed with both options selected, while Figure 15-13 shows the same worksheet printed with both options deselected.

FIGURE 15-12

	A	B	C	D	E	F	G	H
1								
2					SALES FORECAST			
3								
4				QTR 1	QTR 2	QTR 3	QTR 4	Total
5		Product 1						
6		Units	2%	3,500	3,570	3,641	3,714	
7		Dollars	$12.95	$45,325	$46,232	$47,156	$48,099	$186,812
8		Product 2						
9		Units	1%	3,000	3,030	3,060	3,091	
10		Dollars	$14.95	$44,850	$45,299	$45,751	$46,209	$182,109
11		Product 3						
12		Units	1%	2,800	2,828	2,856	2,885	
13		Dollars	$16.95	$47,460	$47,935	$48,414	$48,898	$192,707
14								
15		Totals		$137,635	$139,465	$141,322	$143,206	$561,627

This worksheet was printed with both the Row & Column Headings and the Gridlines options selected.

FIGURE 15-13

		SALES FORECAST				
		QTR 1	QTR 2	QTR 3	QTR 4	Total
Product 1						
Units	2%	3,500	3,570	3,641	3,714	
Dollars	$12.95	$45,325	$46,232	$47,156	$48,099	$186,812
Product 2						
Units	1%	3,000	3,030	3,060	3,091	
Dollars	$14.95	$44,850	$45,299	$45,751	$46,209	$182,109
Product 3						
Units	1%	2,800	2,828	2,856	2,885	
Dollars	$16.95	$47,460	$47,935	$48,414	$48,898	$192,707
Totals		$137,635	$139,465	$141,322	$143,206	**$561,627**

This worksheet was printed with both the Row & Column Headings and the Gridlines options deselected.

In addition to the Printer Setup… and Page Setup… commands on Excel's File menu, three commands on the Options menu affect the way your worksheet reports are printed: Set Print Area, Set Print Titles, and Set Page Break.

By default, the Print… command tells Excel to print the entire area of the worksheet that contains entries. If you want to print only selected areas of the worksheet, you can highlight the appropriate areas, and choose the Set Print Area command on the Options menu. The next time you issue the Print… command, Excel will print only the areas you've defined.

The Set Print Titles command helps you make sense of a multiple-page report that would be impossible to decipher without seeing the row and column headings on each page. The Set Print Titles command simply tells Excel to print the contents of one or more rows, one or more columns, or a combination of rows and columns on every page of a report. To define the rows and/or columns to be printed on each page, simply highlight the appropriate rows and/or columns of the worksheet, then choose the Set Print Titles command on the Options menu.

You'll frequently want to specify where to divide a report into pages, rather than leave the decision to Excel. Fortunately, you can do this with Excel's Set Page Break command. To force a horizontal page break in your worksheet, simply highlight the row that you want to begin the next page, place the cell pointer in column A of that row, and choose the Set Page Break command on the Options menu. Similarly, to force a vertical page break, highlight the column that you want to begin the next page, place the cell pointer in row 1 of that column, and choose the Set Page Break command.

The Set Print Area, Set Print Titles, and Set Page Break commands

The Print...
command

After you've set up your printer, defined your page layout, specified the print area, and adjusted any other relevant settings, you're ready to print. The Print... command on the File menu is the tool you'll use to print reports in Excel. When you issue the Print... command, Excel presents the dialog box shown in Figure 15-14. As you can see, this dialog box contains five settings that control the way Excel prints the document: Copies, Pages, Draft Quality, Preview, and Print. Let's consider how each of these settings affects the way the LaserJet prints your Excel worksheet reports.

FIGURE 15-14

```
┌──────────────────────────────────────────┐
│ PCL / HP LaserJet on LPT1:                │
│ ┌──────────────────────────────────────┐ │
│ │                          ┌─────────┐  │ │
│ │ Copies: [1   ]           │   OK    │  │ │
│ │                          └─────────┘  │ │
│ │                          ┌─────────┐  │ │
│ │ Pages: ◉ All             │ Cancel  │  │ │
│ │                          └─────────┘  │ │
│ │        ○ From: [    ]  To: [    ]     │ │
│ │                                       │ │
│ │ ☐ Draft Quality      ☐ Preview        │ │
│ │ ┌Print──────────────────────────────┐ │ │
│ │ │ ◉ Sheet    ○ Notes    ○ Both      │ │ │
│ │ └───────────────────────────────────┘ │ │
│ └──────────────────────────────────────┘ │
└──────────────────────────────────────────┘
```

The Print... command is the tool you'll use to print your Excel worksheets.

The Copies setting

To print multiple copies of a worksheet on your LaserJet printer, simply change the Copies setting in the Print dialog box from 1 to the number of copies you want to print. When Excel prints multiple copies of a document, it prints the first copy in its entirety, then the second copy, and so forth.

As we explained in Chapter 13, you can speed up the process of printing multiple copies of your Windows documents by using the Uncollated copies setting in the Printer Setup dialog box. Using the Uncollated copies setting instead of the Copies setting tells the LaserJet to first print multiple copies of page 1, then multiple copies of page 2, and so forth. Because the LaserJet formats each page only once when you use the Uncollated copies setting, the Uncollated copies method is much faster. The only drawback to using the Uncollated copies setting is that you'll have to manually collate your documents after they print.

The Pages setting

The Pages setting in the Print dialog box tells Excel which pages of the worksheet report to print. The default setting, All, instructs Excel to print every page of the defined print area. If you want to print only part of a multiple-page worksheet report, type the number of the first page in the From edit bar, and then type the number of the last page in the To edit bar.

The Draft Quality option is intended to allow an Excel user to quickly print drafts of an Excel worksheet that do not reflect all of the worksheet's formatted options. Although this option can save you considerable time when printing a report on a dot-matrix printer, it doesn't affect the printing of a report on a LaserJet printer in any way. Consequently, you can ignore the Draft Quality option in the Print dialog box altogether when printing with your LaserJet.

The Draft Quality option

Selecting the Preview option in Excel's Print dialog box tells Excel to show you a picture of the printed report before it sends the report to the printer. Because the fonts Excel displays on your screen are only representations of the LaserJet's printable fonts, the printed report will sometimes differ from the picture on your screen in several ways. In most cases, however, the Preview option allows you to determine whether you need to go back and change something in your worksheet before you send that worksheet to the printer.

The Preview option

The Print options at the bottom of the Print dialog box let you tell Excel to print the worksheet, to print any notes attached to the worksheet, or to print both the worksheet and the notes.

The Print options

After you're satisfied with all of your print settings, you can send the report to the printer by choosing OK in the Print dialog box. (If you've entered the Preview window, just choose the Print option from the menu bar.) As soon as Excel begins printing the document, it will display a Printing status box like the one shown in Figure 15-15 that lets you know which page of the document is currently being printed. After the entire document (or the specified number of pages) has been printed, the status box will disappear and Excel will return to Ready mode.

Printing the document

FIGURE 15-15

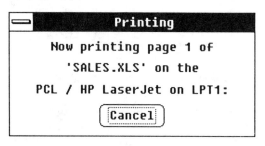

The Printing status box lets you know which page of the document is currently being printed.

Of course, you can cancel the print job at any time by choosing the Cancel option in the Printing status box. If the LaserJet is in the process of printing a page when you choose the Cancel option, it won't stop printing immediately. Instead, the LaserJet will finish printing all the information that Excel had already sent before you issued the Cancel command.

**Formatting
Reports**

As we said earlier, Excel's powerful formatting capabilities place it head and shoulders above all other spreadsheet programs. Although we cannot explain how to use every formatting tool Excel offers, we should at least discuss a couple of formatting commands that really take advantage of your LaserJet's printing capabilities: the Format Font... command and the Format Border... command.

*The Format
Font... command*

Excel's Font... command on the Format menu lets you assign different fonts to a range of entries in your Excel worksheet. The first time you highlight a cell or range and select the Font... command from the Format menu, Excel presents the dialog box shown in Figure 15-16. As you probably know, choosing one of the other three fonts in this dialog box and then choosing OK tells Excel to assign that font to the range of cells you highlighted before you issued the command.

FIGURE 15-16

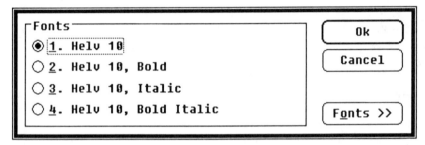

The Format Font... command lets you use up to four fonts in your worksheet.

An example

As an example of the Font... command, suppose you want to change the font of the entries in cells A5 and A22 of the worksheet in Figure 15-17 from Helv 10 (Font 1) to Helv 10, Bold (Font 2). To do this, highlight cells **A5** and **A22**, and then select the Font... command from the Format menu to bring up the dialog box shown in Figure 15-16. When the dialog box appears, choose option 2 (Helv 10, Bold) and choose **OK**. The resulting worksheet is shown in Figure 15-18.

**Using the
Fonts>> option**

Excel lets you use only four different fonts in any one worksheet. As you can see in Figure 15-16, the four default fonts are Helv 10; Helv 10, Bold; Helv 10, Italic; and Helv 10, Bold Italic. If you want to use a font that is not in this set, you'll need to use the Fonts>> option to swap one of the default fonts for the font you want.

When you choose the Fonts>> option in the Fonts dialog box, Excel expands the Font dialog box, as shown in Figure 15-19 on page 532. You can now use the options in the Font, Size, and Style boxes to define a different font for use in the worksheet. After you've defined the font, size, and style for the new font, you can choose the Replace option to replace the font selected at the top of the dialog box with the font you've defined at the bottom. In order to assign the new font to the highlighted range and complete the Font... command, choose the **Ok** option.

FIGURE 15-17

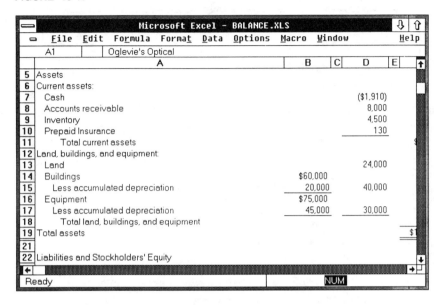

We'll use this worksheet to demonstrate the Format Font... command.

FIGURE 15-18

Microsoft Excel - BALANCE.XLS					
File Edit Formula Format Data Options Macro Window					Help
A1	Oglevie's Optical				
A	B	C	D	E	
5 Assets					
6 Current assets:					
7 Cash			($1,910)		
8 Accounts receivable			8,000		
9 Inventory			4,500		
10 Prepaid Insurance			130		
11 Total current assets					
12 Land, buildings, and equipment:					
13 Land			24,000		
14 Buildings	$60,000				
15 Less accumulated depreciation	20,000		40,000		
16 Equipment	$75,000				
17 Less accumulated depreciation	45,000		30,000		
18 Total land, buildings, and equipment					
19 Total assets				$	
21					
22 Liabilities and Stockholders' Equity					

Ready   NUM

Cells A5 and A22 of this worksheet have been assigned the Helv 10, Bold font.

FIGURE 15-19

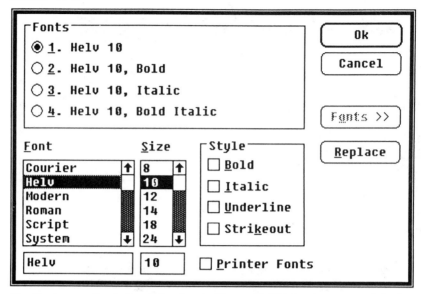

The Fonts>> option in the dialog box in Figure 15-16 lets you swap a default font for the font of your choice.

The fonts that appear in the Font and Size boxes are the screen fonts (GDI fonts) that are currently installed in Windows. As we said earlier, the LaserJet doesn't always have access to the printer fonts that match the screen fonts you've installed. To display only the fonts that can be printed by your printer in the Font and Size list boxes, select the Printer Fonts checkbox at the bottom of the Fonts dialog box. After you use the new Font, Size, and Style options to define a new font from the list of printer fonts, choose the **Ok** option to assign that new font to the range you've highlighted.

If you assign a printer font to some cells in the worksheet for which there is no matching screen font, Excel will substitute an installed screen font that is approximately the same size and shape as the printer font. For example, Figure 15-20 shows a worksheet containing three entries that have been assigned three different fonts: Helv 12, University Roman 24, and Cooper Black 30. Figure 15-21 shows the printed report that we generated from the worksheet in Figure 15-20. As you can clearly see, only the Helv font looks the same on both the screen and on the printed page. Because we installed the printer fonts University Roman 24 and Cooper Black 30 without installing their matching screen fonts, Excel had to use other screen fonts to approximate the display of these printer fonts in the worksheet. For more information on matching screen fonts and printer fonts, refer to the section entitled "Matching GDI Fonts with Device Fonts" in Chapter 13.

FIGURE 15-20

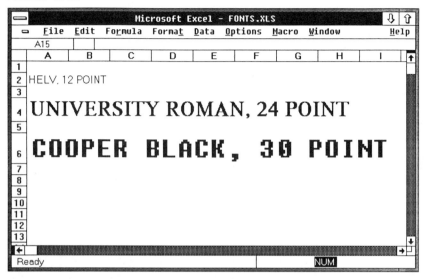

When you assign a printer font to a cell for which there is no matching screen font, Excel substitutes the font that most closely resembles that printer font.

FIGURE 15-21

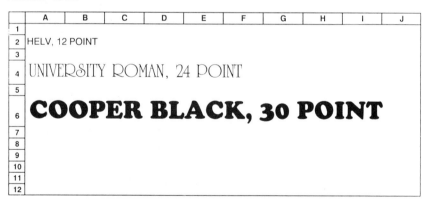

This is how the worksheet in Figure 15-20 looks when printed on our HP LaserJet Series II printer.

The Format Border… command lets you draw a border around any edge of a cell or group of cells in your worksheet. In addition, this command lets you shade any cell or group of cells. To use this command, simply highlight the cells you want to shade or draw a border around, then select the Border… command on the Format menu. When you do this, Excel will present the dialog box shown in Figure 15-22.

The Format Border… command

FIGURE 15-22

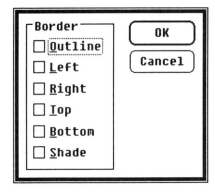

The Format Border... command lets you draw lines and add shading in your Excel worksheets.

As you can see, there are six types of borders that Excel can create for the cells of your worksheet. Outline, Left, Right, Top, Bottom, and Shade. As you might guess, selecting the Outline option tells Excel to draw a line around all four sides of the range of cells you've highlighted. Similarly, selecting the Left, Right, Top, or Bottom option tells Excel to draw a line along the respective edge of the highlighted cells. The last option, Shade, tells Excel to add shade to the cells you have selected.

An example

As an example of how to use the Border... command effectively, suppose you want to draw lines below the column headings and above the totals in the worksheet shown in Figure 15-23. To do this, first highlight cells **D4..H4** and cells **D13..H13**, then select the Border... command from the Format menu. When the dialog box in Figure 15-22 appears, select the Bottom checkbox and choose **OK**. The resulting worksheet is shown in Figure 15-24.

To draw a box around the entire worksheet, highlight cells **A1..H15**, select the Border... command from the Format menu, and select the Outline checkbox from the Border dialog box. When you choose **OK** to complete the command, Excel will draw a box around the cells highlighted, as shown in Figure 15-25 on page 536.

As a final example, suppose you want to use shading to add a "drop shadow" effect to the worksheet in Figure 15-25. To do this, first highlight cells **B16..I16** and cells **I2..I15**. Next, select the Border... command from the Format menu, select the Shade checkbox, and choose **OK** to complete the command. Figure 15-26 on page 536 shows the resulting worksheet.

FIGURE 15-23

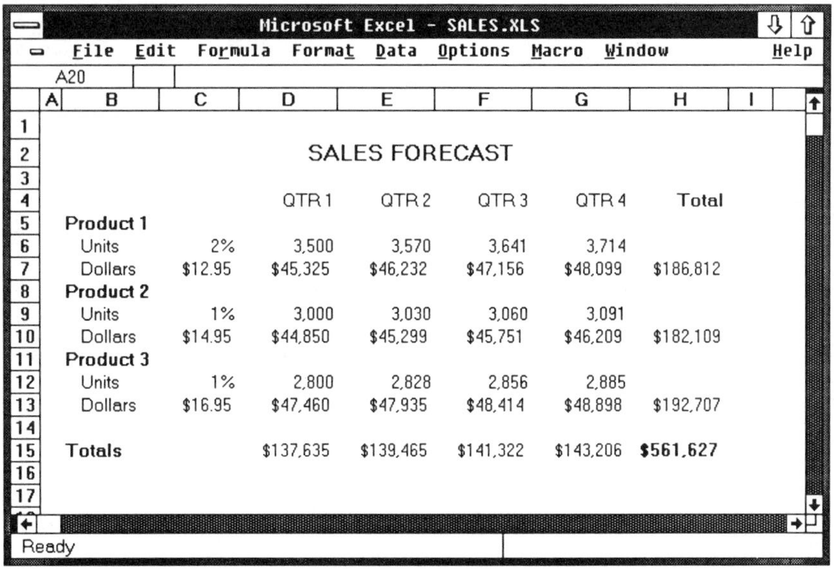

We'll use this worksheet to demonstrate the Format Border... command.

FIGURE 15-24

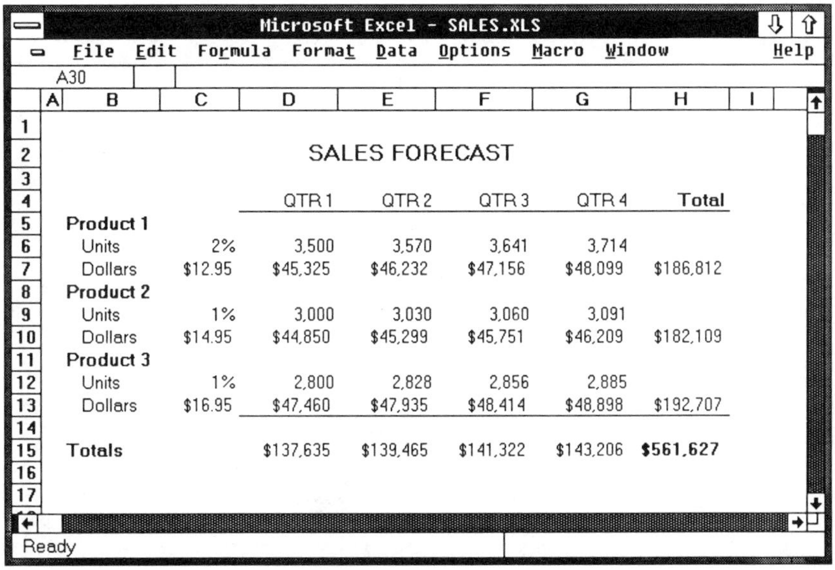

As you can see, borders help draw attention to the important locations in the worksheet.

FIGURE 15-25

	A	B	C	D	E	F	G	H	I	

Microsoft Excel – SALES.XLS

File Edit Formula Format Data Options Macro Window   Help

A30

		QTR 1	QTR 2	QTR 3	QTR 4	Total
Product 1						
Units	2%	3,500	3,570	3,641	3,714	
Dollars	$12.95	$45,325	$46,232	$47,156	$48,099	$186,812
Product 2						
Units	1%	3,000	3,030	3,060	3,091	
Dollars	$14.95	$44,850	$45,299	$45,751	$46,209	$182,109
Product 3						
Units	1%	2,800	2,828	2,856	2,885	
Dollars	$16.95	$47,460	$47,935	$48,414	$48,898	$192,707
Totals		$137,635	$139,465	$141,322	$143,206	**$561,627**

SALES FORECAST

Ready

The Outline option in the Border dialog box lets you draw a box around data in your worksheet.

FIGURE 15-26

Microsoft Excel – SALES.XLS

File Edit Formula Format Data Options Macro Window   Help

A30

	A	B	C	D	E	F	G	H	I	J

		QTR 1	QTR 2	QTR 3	QTR 4	Total
Product 1						
Units	2%	3,500	3,570	3,641	3,714	
Dollars	$12.95	$45,325	$46,232	$47,156	$48,099	$186,812
Product 2						
Units	1%	3,000	3,030	3,060	3,091	
Dollars	$14.95	$44,850	$45,299	$45,751	$46,209	$182,109
Product 3						
Units	1%	2,800	2,828	2,856	2,885	
Dollars	$16.95	$47,460	$47,935	$48,414	$48,898	$192,707
Totals		$137,635	$139,465	$141,322	$143,206	**$561,627**

SALES FORECAST

Ready

The Shade option in the Border dialog box lets you create "drop shadow" effects in your worksheets.

When you print the worksheet shown in Figure 15-26 on an HP LaserJet Series II printer, the resulting report looks like the one shown in Figure 15-27. This printed worksheet looks good enough for the company's annual report, and it clearly demonstrates the LaserJet's ability to create rich, vivid reports in just a few seconds.

FIGURE 15-27

		SALES FORECAST				
		QTR 1	QTR 2	QTR 3	QTR 4	Total
Product 1						
Units	2%	3,500	3,570	3,641	3,714	
Dollars	$12.95	$45,325	$46,232	$47,156	$48,099	$186,812
Product 2						
Units	1%	3,000	3,030	3,060	3,091	
Dollars	$14.95	$44,850	$45,299	$45,751	$46,209	$182,109
Product 3						
Units	1%	2,800	2,828	2,856	2,885	
Dollars	$16.95	$47,460	$47,935	$48,414	$48,898	$192,707
Totals		$137,635	$139,465	$141,322	$143,206	$561,627

It doesn't take long to "dress up" an Excel worksheet with the Border… command.

After you've used Excel's Format Border… command to "dress up" your worksheet, and you send that worksheet to the printer, Excel and your LaserJet will automatically work together to draw the lines and shading in the appropriate places in your worksheet. If you are printing on an original LaserJet or a LaserJet Plus printer, it will take a little longer to print the borders and shading than it will on a LaserJet Series II or LaserJet IID printer. In addition, the newer LaserJets print a finer shade pattern than the older LaserJets. An improved Printer Command Language (PCL) is the reason the newer LaserJet printers can handle borders and shading more easily than the older LaserJets.

Notes

Advanced uses of the Font... and Border... commands

With a little practice and some common sense, you can use Excel's Font... and Border... commands to create reports that look polished and professional when printed on a LaserJet printer. Although we can't explain how to master these commands in this chapter, Figure 15-28 should give you an idea of how much these commands can improve the appearance of your plain Excel worksheets. Take time to experiment with the Font... and Border... commands. These two commands truly unlock the power of your LaserJet printer.

FIGURE 15-28

Fun & Games, Inc.

Variance Analysis

Six Month Shipping Total		Jan	Feb	Mar	Apr	May	Jun	Total
Baseball Bats	Actual units	1,253	1,580	2,600	2,487	1,865	1,398	11,183
	Forecast units	1,400	1,600	2,400	2,000	1,600	1,400	10,400
	Actual revenue	$3,759	$4,740	$7,800	$7,461	$5,595	$4,194	$33,549
	Forecast revenue	$4,200	$4,800	$7,200	$6,000	$4,800	$4,200	$31,200
	Variance	$441	$60	($600)	($1,461)	($795)	$6	($2,349)
	%	10.50%	1.25%	-8.33%	-24.35%	-16.56%	0.14%	-7.53%
Roller Skates	Actual units	356	487	754	1,380	1,278	1,245	5,500
	Forecast units	400	500	800	1,200	1,200	1,200	5,300
	Actual revenue	$1,068	$1,461	$2,262	$4,140	$3,834	$3,735	$16,500
	Forecast revenue	$1,200	$1,500	$2,400	$3,600	$3,600	$3,600	$15,900
	Variance	$132	$39	$138	($540)	($234)	($135)	($600)
	%	11.00%	2.60%	5.75%	-15.00%	-6.50%	-3.75%	-3.77%
Water Skis	Actual units	312	319	327	589	692	1,087	3,326
	Forecast units	300	350	400	700	1,000	1,200	3,950
	Actual revenue	$936	$957	$981	$1,767	$2,076	$3,261	$9,978
	Forecast revenue	$900	$1,050	$1,200	$2,100	$3,000	$3,600	$11,850
	Variance	($36)	$93	$219	$333	$924	$339	$1,872
	%	-4.00%	8.86%	18.25%	15.86%	30.80%	9.42%	15.80%
Baseball Mitts	Actual units	89	387	412	976	567	589	3,020
	Forecast units	200	300	500	1,000	800	700	3,500
	Actual revenue	$267	$1,161	$1,236	$2,928	$1,701	$1,767	$9,060
	Forecast revenue	$600	$900	$1,500	$3,000	$2,400	$2,100	$10,500
	Variance	$333	($261)	$264	$72	$699	$333	$1,440
	%	55.50%	-29.00%	17.60%	2.40%	29.13%	15.86%	13.71%
Tennis Rackets	Actual units	879	876	1,134	1,876	1,965	1,432	8,162
	Forecast units	800	900	1,200	2,000	1,800	1,300	8,000
	Actual revenue	$2,637	$2,628	$3,402	$5,628	$5,895	$4,296	$24,486
	Forecast revenue	$2,400	$2,700	$3,600	$6,000	$5,400	$3,900	$24,000
	Variance	($237)	$72	$198	$372	($495)	($396)	($486)
	%	-9.88%	2.67%	5.50%	6.20%	-9.17%	-10.15%	-2.03%
Totals	Actual units	2,889	3,649	5,227	7,308	6,367	5,751	31,191
	Forecast units	3,100	3,650	5,300	6,900	6,400	5,800	31,150
	Actual revenue	$8,667	$10,947	$15,681	$21,924	$19,101	$17,253	$93,573
	Forecast revenue	$9,300	$10,950	$15,900	$20,700	$19,200	$17,400	$93,450
	Variance	$633	$3	$219	($1,224)	$99	$147	($123)
	%	6.81%	0.03%	1.38%	-5.91%	0.52%	0.84%	-0.13%

With a little practice, you can use Excel's Font... and Border... commands to create worksheets that look good enough for the company's annual report.

PRINTING CHARTS

Now that you're familiar with the concepts related to printing Excel worksheets on a LaserJet printer, let's consider Excel charts. For the most part, printing Excel charts is the same as printing Excel worksheets. However, there are a few minor differences that we need to point out. Specifically, let's consider the two commands you'll use to lay out and print your Excel charts: the Page Setup... command and the Print... command.

Before you print an Excel chart, you'll want to select the Page Setup... command on the File menu to adjust the layout of your printed chart. When you issue the Page Setup... command, Excel presents the dialog box shown in Figure 15-29.

**The Page
Setup...
Command**

FIGURE 15-29

```
┌────────────────────────────────────────────────┐
║ Page Setup                      ┌──────────────┐ ║
║                                 │      OK      │ ║
║ Header: [&f                ]    └──────────────┘ ║
║                                 ┌──────────────┐ ║
║ Footer: [Page &p          ]    │    Cancel    │ ║
║                                 └──────────────┘ ║
║ ┌─Margins────────────────────────────────────┐ ║
║ │ Left: [0.75]      Right: [0.75]            │ ║
║ │                                            │ ║
║ │ Top:  [1   ]      Bottom: [1  ]            │ ║
║ └────────────────────────────────────────────┘ ║
║ ┌─Size───────────────────────────────────────┐ ║
║ │ ○ Screen Size  ◉ Fit to Page  ○ Full Page │ ║
║ └────────────────────────────────────────────┘ ║
└────────────────────────────────────────────────┘
```

*Excel presents this dialog box when you issue the Page Setup...
command from the chart environment.*

Although the Header, Footer, and Margins options are the same in both the chart and worksheet environments, the Row & Column Headings and Gridlines options that appear in the worksheet Page Setup dialog box are replaced in the chart dialog box by three new options: Screen Size, Fit to Page, and Full Page.

The default Size setting, Fit to Page, tells Excel to print the chart as large as possible while maintaining the height-to-width ratio shown on the screen. If you want to control the dimensions of your printed chart manually, you can do so by choosing the Screen Size option, and then resizing the chart window (just as you would resize a worksheet or macro sheet window). The Full Page option instructs Excel to fill the entire page with the chart, regardless of the chart's height-to-width ratio displayed on the screen.

After you use the Page Setup... command to define the layout of your Excel chart, you'll select the Print... command on Excel's File menu to send the chart to the printer. When you issue the Print... command from the chart environment, Excel presents the dialog box shown in Figure 15-30. As you can see, the only difference between this dialog box and the one you see when you issue the Print... command in the worksheet environment is that the Worksheet and Notes options do not appear at the bottom of the chart environment's Print dialog box.

**The Print...
Command**

FIGURE 15-30

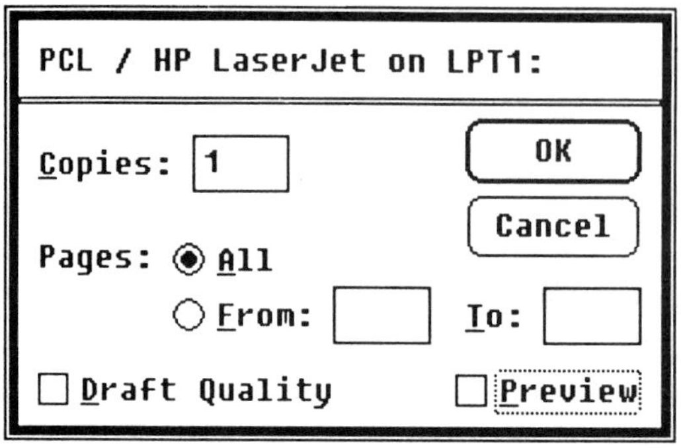

```
┌─────────────────────────────────────────┐
│ ┌───────────────────────────────────┐    │
│ │  PCL / HP LaserJet on LPT1:        │    │
│ ├───────────────────────────────────┤    │
│ │                      ╭─────────╮   │    │
│ │  Copies: │1        │ │   OK    │   │    │
│ │                      ╰─────────╯   │    │
│ │                      ╭─────────╮   │    │
│ │                      │ Cancel  │   │    │
│ │  Pages: ◉ All        ╰─────────╯   │    │
│ │         ○ From: │      │ To: │    ││    │
│ │  ☐ Draft Quality     ☐ Preview    │    │
│ └───────────────────────────────────┘    │
└─────────────────────────────────────────┘
```

This Print dialog box appears in the chart environment.

Because all of your charts will be one page long, you'll never need to use the Pages option when you print from the chart environment. You'll also find the Draft Quality checkbox useless when you're printing charts on a LaserJet printer. If you select the Draft Quality checkbox and then choose OK to print the chart on your LaserJet, Excel will present the message *Can't print chart in draft quality*. The only way you can tell the LaserJet to use a different resolution when it prints charts is to select the Printer Setup... command on the File menu. (Refer to Chapter 13 for more information on setting up your LaserJet printer.)

You'll notice that it sometimes takes quite awhile for Excel to print a chart on a LaserJet printer. For this reason, you'll find the Preview option in the Print dialog box extremely helpful. Like the Preview option in the worksheet environment, this option tells Excel to display a "picture" of the chart as it will appear when it is printed on the page. Once you've entered Preview mode, you can zoom in on selected parts of the chart to get a full-scale view of the finished product. By previewing your charts before sending them to the printer, you'll save a significant amount of time.

CONCLUSION

Like all applications that are designed to run under Microsoft Windows, Microsoft Excel lets you fully unlock the powerful capabilities of an HP LaserJet printer. In this chapter, we've shown you how to install support for the LaserJet printer with Excel's SETUP program, and we've discussed some ideas and techniques that will allow you to easily create impressive reports and charts from your Excel worksheets.

MICROSOFT WINDOWS WRITE 16

Microsoft Write is a simple word processing program that is included with every copy of Microsoft Windows. Although it does not possess the powerful features found in many other word processors, you can use Write to create a vivid, professional-looking report that takes full advantage of Windows' WYSIWYG (What You See Is What You Get) capabilities. In addition, Microsoft Write allows you to paste information or graphics from other Windows applications, such as Microsoft Excel or Microsoft Paint, directly into a Write document.

In this chapter, we'll discuss how Write's printing and formatting commands affect your HP LaserJet printer. However, you need to follow the instructions in Chapter 13 to install and configure Windows before you can effectively use Write to print documents on your HP LaserJet.

BASICS

Before we explain how to format and print Write documents on the HP LaserJet printer, we need to discuss a couple of basic ideas that we touched on in the other Windows applications chapters. After we explain how to install and load Microsoft Write, we'll briefly discuss how you will use optional LaserJet fonts with Write.

Installing and Loading Write

The Microsoft Write program file (WRITE.EXE) is installed automatically when you use Microsoft Windows' SETUP program to install Windows onto your computer's hard disk. For information on installing and configuring Microsoft Windows for your equipment, refer to Chapter 13.

After you've installed Windows on your computer, you can use any of three methods to load Microsoft Write. First, you can move into the Windows directory, type **win write**, and press ↵. Alternatively, you can move into the Windows directory, type **win**, press ↵ to bring up Windows' MS-DOS Executive, highlight the file **WRITE.EXE**, and select the <u>R</u>un… command from the <u>F</u>ile menu. Finally, you can type **win** and press ↵ to bring up the MS-DOS Executive, then use the mouse to double-click on the file **WRITE.EXE**. After a brief pause, the Microsoft Write screen shown in Figure 16-1 will appear.

FIGURE 16-1

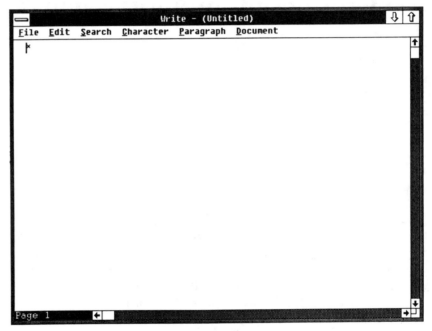

This is the screen that appears when you first load Microsoft Write.

Installing Fonts

Like all applications that run under Microsoft Windows, Microsoft Write can display a variety of fonts on the screen and can take full advantage of your LaserJet's font capabilities. As we explained in Chapter 13, you need two kinds of fonts to compose documents on your HP LaserJet printer with a Windows application: GDI fonts (fonts you can display on your screen) and device fonts (fonts you can print on your printer).

The best approach to take when installing fonts for Microsoft Write (or for any Windows application) is to first install the device (printer) fonts you want to use in your printed documents, then install the matching GDI (screen) fonts into your Windows system. After installing matched sets of printer fonts and screen fonts, your Write documents will look almost the same on paper as they do on the screen. If you install unmatched sets of printer fonts and screen fonts, however, you won't be able to take advantage of Windows' WYSIWYG capabilities.

As you probably know, you can add additional fonts to your LaserJet by installing font cartridges, downloadable soft fonts, or both. You'll most likely want to start off using some basic font types (like Helv, Tms Rmn, and Courier), and then purchase additional fonts later.

Installing PCL printer fonts

If you are like most Write users, you'll want to install the HP "Z" font cartridge (HP Part No. 92286Z) in your LaserJet printer when you are printing with Write. The "Z" font cartridge was specifically designed for Microsoft Windows applications, and it includes several variations of the three most popular typefaces: Tms Rmn (a variation of Times Roman), Helv (a variation of Helvetica), and Line Printer (a compressed, fixed-pitch font that is well suited for printing large documents). You can purchase a "Z" font cartridge (or any other HP font cartridge) from your local computer vendor, or from HP Direct Marketing (800-538-8787).

After you've plugged the optional font cartridge(s) into the LaserJet, tell Windows that you've equipped the LaserJet with some additional fonts. Follow the instructions in the section in Chapter 13 entitled "Setting up."

Installing font cartridges

If you use any HP LaserJet printer other than the original LaserJet, you can use soft fonts in addition to font cartridges to give your printer access to optional typefaces. Like font cartridges, there are dozens of soft fonts available for HP LaserJet printers.

After you copy the optional soft fonts onto your hard disk, you'll need to tell Windows where you've installed the new soft fonts in order to use them with Write. To learn how to install soft fonts into your Windows system, refer to the section in Chapter 13 entitled "Adding Support for PCL Soft Fonts."

Installing soft fonts

Like PCL soft fonts, PostScript soft fonts must be downloaded from your computer's hard disk to your printer. After you install the PostScript soft font onto your hard disk, you must tell Windows that you've installed the optional font. To learn how to install PostScript soft fonts into your Windows system, refer to the section in Chapter 13 entitled "Adding Support for PostScript Soft Fonts."

Installing PostScript printer fonts

Just as you need to install font cartridges and soft fonts to let your LaserJet print in a variety of typestyles, you need to install screen fonts to let Microsoft Windows applications *display* a variety of typestyles. Fortunately, the SETUP program automatically installs a base set of screen fonts that are specifically designed for the display hardware you are using. For example, if you are using an EGA video system, SETUP will automatically install a base set of three screen fonts that are specifically designed for use with the EGA.

No matter which video system you use, SETUP always installs versions of the Tms Rmn, Helv, and Courier raster screen fonts. In addition, SETUP installs the Roman, Script, and Modern stroke fonts. Finally, two additional raster screen fonts

Installing screen fonts

are built directly into the Windows environment: the System font and the Terminal font. Figure 16-2 shows a sample of all eight basic screen fonts.

FIGURE 16-2

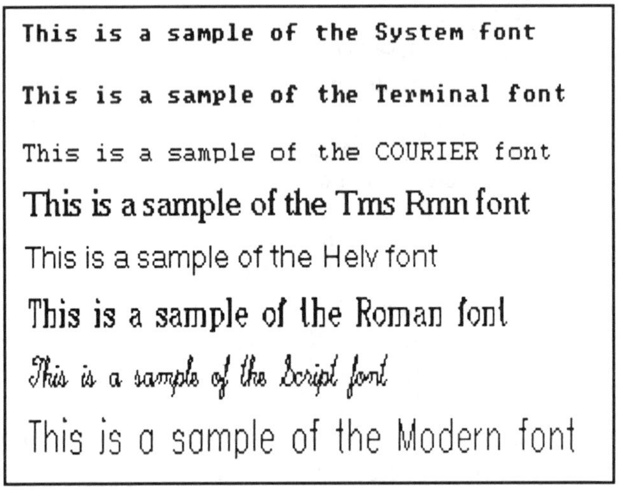

This is a sample of the System font

This is a sample of the Terminal font

This is a sample of the COURIER font

This is a sample of the Tms Rmn font

This is a sample of the Helv font

This is a sample of the Roman font

This is a sample of the Script font

This is a sample of the Modern font

Microsoft Windows automatically installs these eight screen fonts when you install Windows on an EGA computer system.

If you want to install additional screen fonts on your LaserJet printer, you'll have to use the Add New Font... command on the control panel's Installation menu. For a detailed explanation of this procedure, refer to the section in Chapter 13 entitled "Installing Screen Fonts with the Control Panel."

Matching printer fonts with screen fonts

If you assign a LaserJet PCL or PostScript font to text in a Write document that does not have a matching screen font, Write will substitute the screen font that most closely matches the printer font you've assigned.

The section in Chapter 13 entitled "Matching Screen Fonts with LaserJet Fonts" explains how to obtain matching screen and printer fonts for your Windows applications. Read this section carefully to take full advantage of Windows' ability to produce great-looking documents both on your screen and on your LaserJet.

PRINTING DOCUMENTS

As we mentioned earlier, Microsoft Write possesses some very powerful formatting capabilities. The formatting power of Write, combined with the sharp print quality of the HP LaserJet printer, makes it easy to create polished, professional-looking reports.

Basics

The tool you'll use to print Write documents is the Print... command on the File menu. Before you print your document, you'll want to use the Change Printer... command to select the target printer, and the Page Layout... command on the

Document menu to control the layout of your printed reports. You'll also want to use the Header... or Footer... command to add a header or footer to your document.

Selecting a printer

If you installed support for more than one printer when you installed Microsoft Windows, you can use Write's Change Printer... command to choose the printer that will receive and print your Write documents. When you select the Change Printer... command from the File menu, Write will present a dialog box that lists all the printers you've installed, as shown in Figure 16-3. To specify the HP LaserJet as the target printer, highlight the **PCL / HP LaserJet** option (or, if you've installed a PostScript board on your printer, the **PostScript Printer** option), and choose **OK**. If the PCL / HP LaserJet option (or the PostScript Printer option) does not appear in the list when you issue the Change Printer... command, or if you want to change the interface (LPT) assignments in the Change Printer dialog box, read the section in Chapter 13 entitled "Adding LaserJet Support with the Control Panel."

FIGURE 16-3

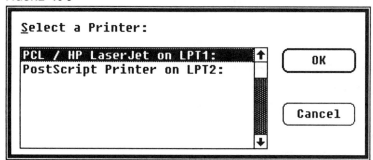

You'll use the Change Printer... command to tell Write where to send your documents.

Working with headers and footers

The Header... and Footer... commands on Write's Document menu create a single line of text that appears at the top or bottom of each page in the printed report. When you issue the Header... command, Write presents a blank header document and the dialog box shown in Figure 16-4 on the following page. At this point, simply type the header text in the document portion of the screen, and choose the Return to Document option in the Page Header dialog box.

By default, Write prints the document's header line $^3/_4$ inch from the top of the page. To change the distance between the header line and the top of the page, just change the Distance from Top setting in the Page Header dialog box. If you change the Distance from Top setting, make sure the new setting you define falls between the LaserJet's minimum value (0.3 inches) and the value you've defined for the top margin.

The Page Footer dialog box contains a Distance from Bottom setting in place of the Distance from Top setting. As you might guess, any new Distance from

Bottom setting you define should fall between the minimum value (0.46 inches) and the value you've specified for the bottom margin.

FIGURE 16-4

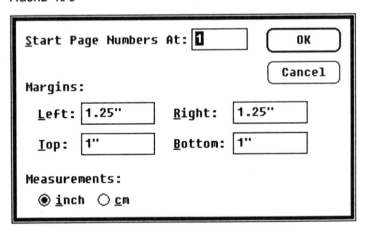

The Header... command lets you create a line of text that appears at the top of every page of the printed report.

Defining the margins

When you select the Page Layout... command from the Document menu, Write presents a dialog box like the one shown in Figure 16-5. As you can see, this box lets you do two things: change the page margins and specify the document's starting page number.

FIGURE 16-5

Write's Page Layout... command lets you control the layout of your printed reports.

The Margins settings in the Page Layout dialog box let you define in inches the top, bottom, left, and right margins of your report. As you might expect, the LaserJet printer will leave at the top and left edges of the page exactly the amount of blank space you specify in the Top and Left margin boxes. Since the document doesn't always fill to the page's bottom and right edges, the Bottom and Right margin settings define the minimum amount of space the LaserJet will reserve along those edges of the printed report.

As we mentioned in Chapter 1, all HP LaserJet printers are unable to print to a small region along the outside edges of a page. Fortunately, when you specify a low margin setting that would cause Write to print in the LaserJet's unprintable region, Write will present the dialog box shown in Figure 16-6 when you choose OK to lock in your settings. When this dialog box appears, choose OK to return to the Page Layout dialog box, then change your margin settings so that they meet the constraints shown in Figure 16-6.

FIGURE 16-6

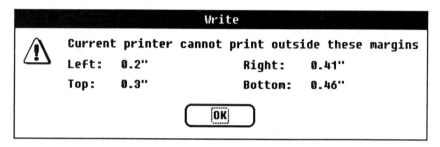

Write will not let you define margin settings that tell it to print in the LaserJet's unprintable region.

As we explained in the previous section, the Page Header's Distance from Top setting is 0.75 inch. If you define a header line in a document and change the top margin to a value less than 0.75 inch, Write will print the header line on top of the document's body text, resulting in an unsightly mess. Similarly, documents containing footers that are printed with a Bottom margin setting of less than 0.75 inch will have footers that overlap the document's body. For this reason, when you print a document that contains a header and a footer, you should specify a Top and Bottom margin setting larger than 0.75 inch.

If you want to define your margin settings in centimeters instead of in inches, simply select the cm button in the bottom of the dialog box. When you define your margins in units of centimeters instead of inches, the minimum margin values you can define are:

Left:	0.5 cm	Right:	1.04 cm
Top:	0.75 cm	Bottom:	1.17 cm

After you've selected the target printer, defined a header or footer, and defined your page layout, you're ready to print. The Print... command on the File menu is the tool you'll use to print Write documents. When you issue the Print... command, Write will present the dialog box shown in Figure 16-7. As you can see, this dialog box lets you specify the number of copies and the range of pages you want Write

Printing the document

to print. (Since the LaserJet printer does not have a "draft" mode, however, the Draft Quality option in the Print dialog box is useless.)

FIGURE 16-7

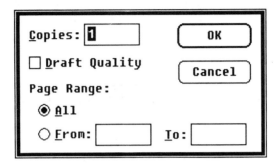

When you issue the Print... command, this dialog box will appear.

The Copies setting

To print multiple copies of a report on your LaserJet printer, simply change the Copies setting in the Print dialog box from 1 to the number of copies you want to print. When Write prints multiple copies of a document, it prints the first copy in its entirety, then the second copy, and so forth.

As we explained in Chapter 13, you can speed up the process of printing multiple copies of your Windows documents by using the Uncollated copies setting in Windows' Printer Setup dialog box. Using the Uncollated copies setting instead of the Copies setting tells the LaserJet to first print multiple copies of page 1, then multiple copies of page 2, and so forth. Since Write formats each page only once when you use the Uncollated copies setting, the Uncollated copies method is much faster than printing each document in its entirety multiple times. The only drawback to using the Uncollated copies setting is that you'll have to manually collate your documents after they print.

The Page Range setting

The Page Range setting in the Print dialog box tells Write which pages of the document to print. The default setting, All, instructs Write to print every page in the entire document. If you want to print only part of a document, type the number of the first page of the section you want to print in the From edit bar, then type the number of the last page you want to print in the To edit bar.

The Draft Quality checkbox

The Draft Quality checkbox is intended to allow you to quickly print drafts that do not reflect all the formatted options. Although this option can save you considerable time when you're printing a report on a dot-matrix printer, it doesn't affect the printing of a document on an HP LaserJet printer. Consequently, you can ignore the Draft Quality option in the Print dialog box when you're printing to your LaserJet.

When you're satisfied with all your print settings, you can send the document to the printer by choosing OK in the Print dialog box. As soon as Write begins printing the document, it will display a Printing status box like the one shown in Figure 16-8. After the entire document (or the specified number of pages) has been printed, the status box will disappear, and the LaserJet will print your report.

Sending the document

FIGURE 16-8

Write presents this status box while it is printing your document.

Of course, you can cancel the print job at any time by choosing the Cancel option in the Printing status box. If the LaserJet is in the process of printing a page when you choose the Cancel option, it won't stop printing immediately. Instead, the LaserJet will finish printing all the information already sent by Write before you issued the Cancel command.

Pagination is the process of breaking a document into pages. Fortunately, Write automatically uses the margin settings in the Page Layout dialog box to paginate your documents when you issue the Print... command.

Paginating Documents

Although Write's page breaks will usually fall in acceptable places in the document, you may sometimes print a report whose page breaks occur erratically or in undesirable locations. When this happens, first select the Page Layout... command on Write's Document menu and check the document's margin settings. If the margin settings seem reasonable for the paper you're using, browse through your document and remove all your manual page breaks. After you've removed all the manual page breaks in the printed document, issue Write's Repaginate... command on the File menu, select the Confirm Page Breaks checkbox in the Repaginate dialog box, and choose **OK** to begin repagination. After you've reviewed and confirmed all of Write's page breaks, reissue the Print... command to re-send your document to the LaserJet.

As we said earlier, Write's powerful formatting capabilities allow you to create vivid, professional-looking documents with your HP LaserJet printer. Although a complete discussion of Write's formatting tools is beyond the scope of this book, we should at least discuss a few formatting commands that let you take full advantage of the LaserJet's printing capabilities—the commands on Write's Character menu.

Formatting Characters

These commands, which are shown in Figure 16-9, let you assign different attributes or different fonts to the characters in your Write document. As you probably know, choosing one of the items from the Character menu tells Write to assign that particular attribute or font to the characters you highlighted before issuing the command.

FIGURE 16-9

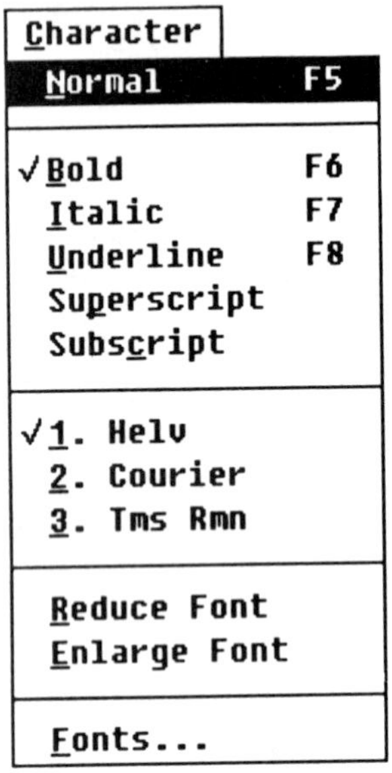

```
 Character
 Normal          F5

√Bold            F6
 Italic          F7
 Underline       F8
 Superscript
 Subscript

√1. Helv
 2. Courier
 3. Tms Rmn

 Reduce Font
 Enlarge Font

 Fonts...
```

The commands on Write's Character menu let you assign different attributes and different fonts to characters in your Write document.

An example

Suppose you want to assign the Bold attribute to the title of the document shown in Figure 16-10. To do this, simply highlight the words in the title, then select the Bold command from the Character menu. The resulting document is shown in Figure 16-11 on page 552.

You can use this technique to assign any of the five attributes listed at the top of the Character menu (Bold, Italic, Underline, Superscript, and Subscript) to a group of characters. The next time you highlight those characters and pull down the Character menu, a check mark will appear next to the attributes you've assigned to those characters.

To remove an attribute from a group of characters, simply highlight the appropriate group and reselect the attribute from the Character menu. When you do this, Write will remove the appropriate attribute and the check mark indicator next to that attribute in the Character menu. To remove simultaneously all the attributes you've assigned to a group of characters, highlight the appropriate group and choose the Normal command from the Character menu.

FIGURE 16-10

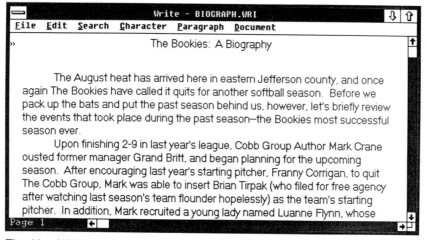

The title of this sample document appears in regular type.

If you want to decrease or increase the point size of some characters in your document, just highlight those characters and select the Reduce Font or the Enlarge Font command from the Character menu. These commands will automatically adjust the size of the characters you've highlighted down or up to the next available point size in that particular font.

Reducing and enlarging fonts

As you can see in Figure 16-9, three default fonts appear on Write's Character menu: Helv, Courier, and Tms Rmn. If you want to assign one of these three fonts to characters in your document, just highlight those characters, then select the desired font from the Character menu. Sooner or later, however, you'll want to use a font other than these three. When that happens, you'll have to issue the Fonts... command on the Character menu.

The Fonts... command

When you issue the Fonts... command, Write will present a dialog box like the one shown in Figure 16-12. The font names and sizes that appear in the Fonts and Sizes list boxes are the printer fonts you've installed in your Windows system. When this dialog box appears, just choose the name and size of the font you want to use, then choose the OK option to complete the command.

FIGURE 16-11

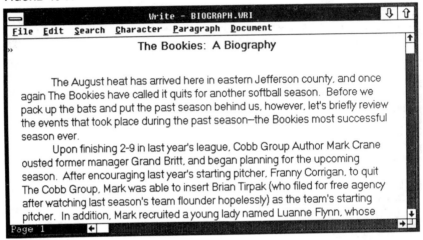

We've used Write's Bold command to boldface the title of this document.

FIGURE 16-12

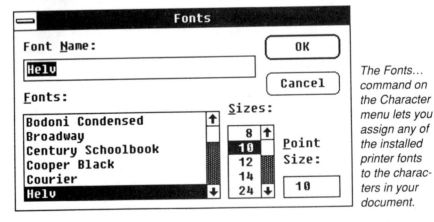

The Fonts... command on the Character menu lets you assign any of the installed printer fonts to the characters in your document.

A note

If you assign a printer font to some text in the document for which there is no matching screen font, Write will substitute an installed screen font that is approximately the same size and shape as the printer font. For more information on matching screen fonts and printer fonts, refer to the section in Chapter 13 entitled "Matching Screen Fonts with LaserJet Fonts."

CONCLUSION

Like all applications that run under Microsoft Windows, Microsoft Write allows you to create polished, professional-looking documents on your HP LaserJet printer. In this chapter, we've shown you how to use Write's printing and formatting commands to take full advantage of your LaserJet's printing capabilities.

OTHER WINDOWS APPLICATIONS 17

Because we could not include every application that runs under Microsoft Windows in *LaserJet Companion*, we limited our discussion of Windows applications to three that are widely used—Microsoft Excel, Aldus PageMaker, and Microsoft Windows Write.

To supplement the information in this book, we have covered additional Windows applications in *LaserJet Companion TechNotes*. Each edition of *LaserJet Companion TechNotes* is comparable to a chapter in *LaserJet Companion*.

The release of several applications that run under Microsoft Windows was pending at the time *LaserJet Companion* went to press, so it was impossible to predict all the programs for which we could write *LaserJet Companion TechNotes*. Therefore, to determine if an edition of *LaserJet Companion TechNotes* is available or is being planned for a specific product, call The Cobb Group at 800-223-8720 (502-425-7756 in Kentucky).

IMPENDING RELEASES

The only Windows-based product discussed in this book that had not been recently upgraded when *LaserJet Companion* went to press was Microsoft Excel. However, when a Microsoft Excel upgrade becomes available, we will publish *LaserJet Companion TechNotes* written specifically for it.

Likewise, whenever one of the Windows-based products discussed in *LaserJet Companion* is upgraded, you can contact The Cobb Group for information concerning the availability of an edition of *LaserJet Companion TechNotes* for that product.

CONCLUSION

If you are using a Windows-based application that is not discussed in *LaserJet Companion*, you should contact The Cobb Group to determine whether an edition of *LaserJet Companion TechNotes* for that product has been published.

THE COBB GROUP

The Best

GUARANTEED

Enhancements

Section Four

Enhancing the LaserJet

While LaserJet printers are incredibly powerful, it is often necessary to use a utility program to tap that power. Also, there may be instances when you want to increase the power of your LaserJet by adding enhancements such as Adobe's PostScript page description language. The purpose of Section Four is to introduce you to the BitStream Fontware Installation Kit, the JetScript Accessory Kit, WYSIFonts! and other products that you can use to enhance the performance of your LaserJet.

UTILITIES AND ENHANCEMENTS 18

Throughout the previous 13 chapters of *LaserJet Companion*, we have shown you how to use specific business applications with the HP LaserJet printer. In this chapter, we will shift gears and look at utility programs you can use to create, modify, and install soft fonts. We'll also show you how to turn a LaserJet Series II into an Apple LaserWriter-compatible PostScript printer.

Before we proceed, it's important to note that we have limited the discussions in this chapter to the utilities and enhancements we found to be the most useful while writing *LaserJet Companion*. A capsule discussion of several other utility programs and enhancements appears in Appendix 2.

Finally, the structure of this chapter is a bit different from that of the rest of *LaserJet Companion*. Each section of this chapter is devoted to a specific utility or enhancement. In each of these sections, we will discuss the capabilities of a product and, when necessary, walk you through installing and using the product.

BITSTREAM FONTWARE

As we mentioned in Chapter 4, the size of standard PCL fonts is fixed. In other words, the bit-mapped data that describes the pattern of dots the LaserJet must print to form characters on a page cannot be manipulated to produce smaller or larger versions of a font. Consequently, whenever you want to use a specific size of a certain font, you must install a font cartridge that contains the appropriate size, or you must download it to the LaserJet as a soft font.

While the fixed size of PCL fonts is a major limitation and inconvenience, a solution is available from BitStream, Inc., which offers the Fontware Typeface Library and a line of Fontware Installation Kits.

The BitStream Fontware Typeface Library is a collection of fonts that are based on outlines. A font that is based on an outline can be scaled—that is, automatically increased or decreased according to your specifications.

Before you can use a BitStream Fontware Typeface with the LaserJet, you must use a BitStream Fontware Installation Kit to convert a BitStream Fontware Typeface outline into a standard PCL soft font that can be downloaded to the LaserJet. In this section, we'll take a look at a BitStream Fontware Installation Kit, and we'll discuss the process of using it to create PCL soft fonts.

Fontware Installation Kits

Several versions of the BitStream Fontware Installation Kit are available. Each version is designed for use with a specific software application. For example, at the time *LaserJet Companion* went to press, versions of the Fontware Installation Kit were available for use with WordPerfect 5, Microsoft Word 4, Microsoft Windows, Ventura Publisher, Lotus Manuscript, and several other products.

When we say that these Fontware Installation Kits are customized for use with a specific application, we mean they all have the ability to automatically install support for any soft font created by the Installation Kit. For example, if you use the Fontware Installation Kit for Microsoft Word 4 to build a 12-point Dutch font, it will automatically create the .PRD file needed to use that font with Word.

In addition to installing soft fonts, several versions of the Fontware Installation Kit can create screen fonts that match those soft fonts. For instance, if you use the Fontware Installation Kit for Microsoft Windows to build a 12-point Dutch font, you can also instruct the Installation Kit to create a Windows GDI screen font that matches the Dutch font.

Running a Fontware Installation Kit

As a rule, all versions of the Fontware Installation Kit are essentially identical. However, each version usually will contain a few special features that are required by the specific application for which it is designed. One prime example of such a feature is the capability of the Installation Kit for Microsoft Windows to create screen fonts.

Since each version of the Fontware Installation Kit is similar to every other version, we won't look at each of them individually. Instead, we'll walk through a sample session with the FontWare Installation Kit for Microsoft Windows that is included with Aldus PageMaker 3.0.

Installation

Installing a Fontware Installation Kit is simple. For example, to install the Installation Kit for Microsoft Windows, just place the Installation disk in drive A and type **FONTWARE**. When you do this, a screen similar to the one shown in Figure 18-1 will appear. As you can see, the purpose of this screen is to determine if you are using a color display.

FIGURE 18-1

When you run a Fontware Installation Kit from drive A, you will see this prompt.

Once you tell the Fontware Installation Kit whether you are using a color display, the Fontware Main Menu shown in Figure 18-2 on the following page will appear. Four options—Set Up Fontware, View Control Panel, Add/Delete Fontware Typefaces, and Make Fonts—appear on the Fontware Main Menu, but the only one you can access at this point is the Set Up Fontware option. To choose this option, press ↵.

When you choose the Set Up Fontware option from the Fontware Main Menu, the Fontware Control Panel will appear on your screen, and you will be asked to accept or enter the name of the directory in which the Fontware Installation Kit is to be installed. You will also be asked to accept or enter the name of the directory containing the product for which the Installation Kit was designed, as well as the name of the directory in which PCL soft font data files created by the Fontware Installation Kit should be stored. As an example, Figure 18-3 on the next page shows the Fontware Installation Kit for Microsoft Windows' Fontware Control Panel as it will appear after you have accepted the name of each directory.

As you can see in Figure 18-3, once you have accepted or entered the name of each directory, you can continue the installation process by pressing Y, or you can press N to re-enter the names of the directories in which Fontware, the product in question, and PCL soft fonts are stored. When you verify that the directory names you have provided are correct, the Fontware Installation Kit program and associated files will be copied into the appropriate directory.

FIGURE 18-2

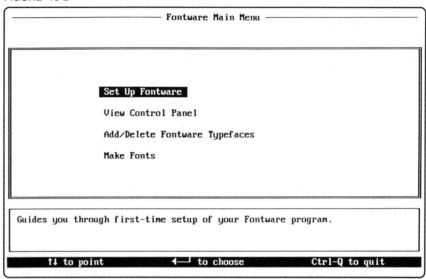

The Fontware Main Menu's Set Up Fontware option allows you to install a Fontware Installation Kit on your system.

FIGURE 18-3

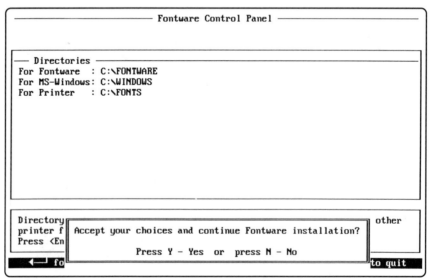

The Fontware Control Panel will ask you to accept or enter the name of the directories in which the Fontware Installation Kit, Fontware Typefaces, and PCL soft fonts should be installed.

If the particular version of the Fontware Installation Kit you are using can create screen fonts, you will be asked to identify the type of video system you are using. For example, the Fontware Installation Kit for Microsoft Windows will prompt you to select one of the video systems shown in the display models list that appears in Figure 18-4. To choose a display from this list, use the ↑ or ↓ key to highlight your video system, then press ↵.

Screen fonts

FIGURE 18-4

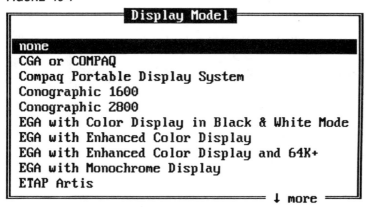

```
┌──────────────┤ Display Model ├──────────────┐
│                                              │
│ none                                         │
│ CGA or COMPAQ                                │
│ Compaq Portable Display System              │
│ Conographic 1600                             │
│ Conographic 2800                             │
│ EGA with Color Display in Black & White Mode│
│ EGA with Enhanced Color Display             │
│ EGA with Enhanced Color Display and 64K+    │
│ EGA with Monochrome Display                 │
│ ETAP Artis                                   │
└════════════════════════════════ ↓ more ════┘
```

The Fontware Installation Kit for Microsoft Windows will ask you to choose a display model.

Once you have chosen the type of display system you are using, you must choose the character (symbol) set on which screen fonts should be based. For example, the Fontware Installation Kit for Microsoft Windows will display the list of character sets shown in Figure 18-5. To choose a character set from this list, use the ↑ or ↓ key to highlight it, then press ↵.

FIGURE 18-5

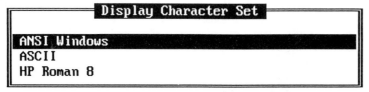

```
┌──────┤ Display Character Set ├──────┐
│                                     │
│ ANSI Windows                        │
│ ASCII                               │
│ HP Roman 8                          │
└─────────────────────────────────────┘
```

The Fontware Installation Kit for Microsoft Windows will ask you to choose a character set for screen fonts.

As a rule, you should always choose the same character set for both screen and printer fonts. For example, if you plan to create printer fonts based on the

Roman-8 character set, you should choose that set when the list shown in Figure 18-5 appears on your screen. If you need more information on how to choose a character set, refer to the discussion of the topic in Chapter 4.

Printer fonts

The next step in the Fontware Installation Kit installation process is choosing a printer model. When it is time to do this, a list of printer models similar to the one shown in Figure 18-6 will appear on your screen. To select a printer from this list, use the ↑ or ↓ key to highlight the appropriate model, then press ↵.

FIGURE 18-6

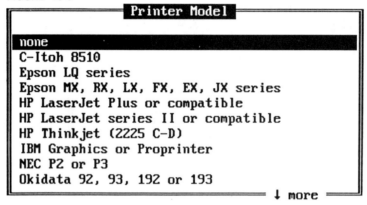

A list of printers similar to the one shown here will appear when it's time to choose the printer for which you want to create fonts.

If you have a LaserJet Plus or LaserJet 500 Plus, you should choose the HP LaserJet Plus or compatible option from the list of printers shown in Figure 18-6. If you have a LaserJet Series II, IID, or 2000, you should choose the HP LaserJet series II or compatible option.

Once you have provided the Fontware Installation Kit with the name of the printer for which you want to create fonts, it will display the list of orientation options shown in Figure 18-7. When this list appears, use the ↑ or ↓ key to highlight the type (orientation) of fonts you want to create, then press ↵.

FIGURE 18-7

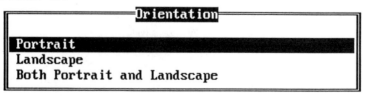

Once you have chosen a printer, you will be asked to choose the orientation mode(s) for which fonts will be created.

If you have a LaserJet Plus, LaserJet 500 Plus, or LaserJet Series II and want to create and use fonts in both Portrait and Landscape modes, choose the Both Portrait and Landscape option. If you have a LaserJet IID or LaserJet 2000, it is not necessary to create Landscape and Portrait versions of each soft font because both printers can automatically rotate fonts. Consequently, if you choose the Portrait option, you can use all the Portrait fonts the Fontware Installation Kit will create in Portrait and Landscape modes.

Once you have designated the type of printer and desired font orientation, the Fontware Installation Kit will ask you to choose the character set it will use when creating those fonts. For example, the Fontware Installation Kit for Microsoft Windows will display the list of character sets shown in Figure 18-8. To choose a character set from this list, use the ↑ or ↓ key to highlight your selection, then press ↵.

FIGURE 18-8

```
╔═══════════ Printer Character Set ═══════════╗
║                                             ║
║  ANSI Windows                               ║
║  ASCII                                      ║
║  HP Roman 8                                 ║
║                                             ║
╚═════════════════════════════════════════════╝
```

The Fontware Installation Kit for Microsoft Windows will ask you to choose a character set for printer fonts.

As we mentioned earlier, if you are using a version of the Fontware Installation Kit that can create screen fonts for the particular application for which it was designed, you should choose the same character set for both screen and printer fonts. For example, if you specified that all screen fonts should be based on the Roman-8 character set, you should choose the HP Roman 8 option when the list of character sets shown in Figure 18-8 appears on your screen.

After you have chosen a character set, the Fontware Installation Kit will display a list of printer ports similar to the one shown in Figure 18-9 on the following page. Use the ↑ or ↓ key to highlight the name of the port to which your LaserJet is connected, then press ↵.

When you have selected the appropriate port, the Fontware Control Panel will appear on your screen and will display a summary of all of the information you have provided about your system and printer. For example, the Fontware Control Panel shown in Figure 18-10 on the next page lists all of the information we provided when we installed the Fontware Installation Kit for Microsoft Windows.

As you can see in Figure 18-10, you should press **[F10]** if you want to save all the information shown on the Fontware Control Panel to disk as defaults. If you want to change this information, you can press **[Esc]** to step back through the installation process. Finally, if you want to abort the entire installation process, you can press **[Ctrl]Q** to quit.

FIGURE 18-9

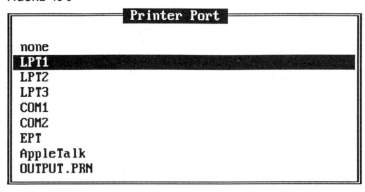

When this list appears, choose the port to which your LaserJet
is connected.

FIGURE 18-10

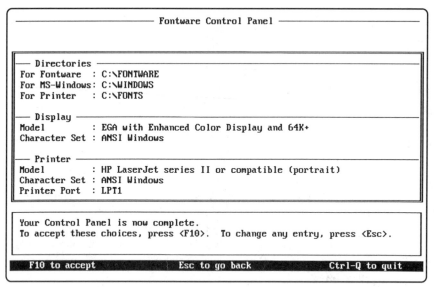

The Fontware Control Panel summarizes all of the information you have provided
about your system and printer.

*Adding
Fontware
Typefaces*

After you have saved the Fontware Control Panel settings to disk, the Fontware
Installation Kit will display the Fontware Typefaces menu, shown in Figure 18-11,
which informs you that you must install a Fontware Typeface before you can make
a font. At this time, you should press **[F3]**.

FIGURE 18-11

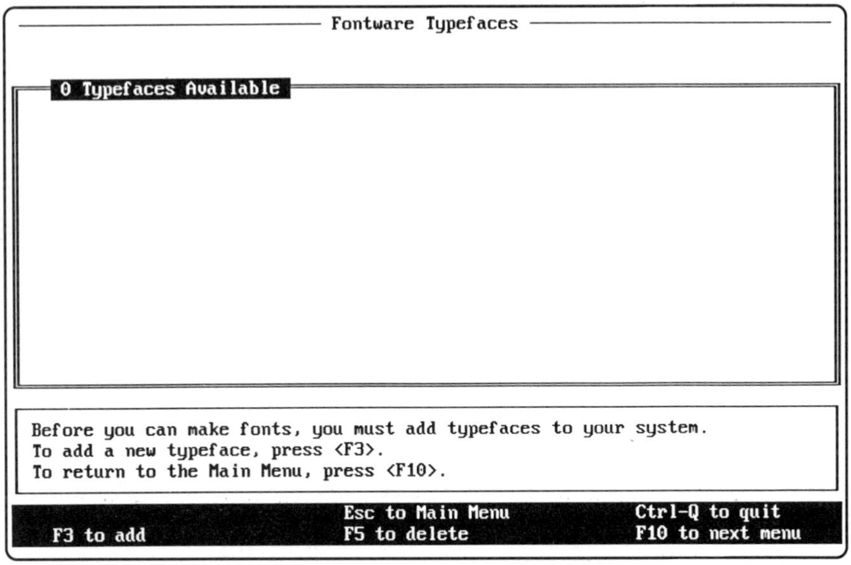

```
┌──────────────── Fontware Typefaces ─────────────────┐
│                                                      │
│ ┌─ 0 Typefaces Available ──────────────────────────┐ │
│ │                                                  │ │
│ │                                                  │ │
│ │                                                  │ │
│ │                                                  │ │
│ │                                                  │ │
│ │                                                  │ │
│ │                                                  │ │
│ │                                                  │ │
│ │                                                  │ │
│ │                                                  │ │
│ └──────────────────────────────────────────────────┘ │
│ ┌──────────────────────────────────────────────────┐ │
│ │ Before you can make fonts, you must add typefaces to your system. │ │
│ │ To add a new typeface, press <F3>.               │ │
│ │ To return to the Main Menu, press <F10>.         │ │
│ └──────────────────────────────────────────────────┘ │
│                       Esc to Main Menu      Ctrl-Q to quit │
│   F3 to add           F5 to delete          F10 to next menu │
└──────────────────────────────────────────────────────┘
```

Before you can make a font, you must install a Fontware Typeface.

The Fontware Installation Kit will then prompt you to insert Fontware Typeface Disk #1 into drive A. This disk, which usually includes the Dutch, Swiss, and Courier Typeface outlines, is included with every version of the Fontware Installation Kit, regardless of the specific application for which it was designed. Once you have placed Fontware Typeface Disk #1 in drive A, press ↵ to continue.

The Fontware Installation Kit will now display the list of typefaces shown in Figure 18-12 on the following page. Use the ↑ or ↓ key to highlight the name of the typefaces you want to install, then press ↵. After you have chosen all of the desired typefaces, press **[F10]** to initiate the process.

When the Fontware Installation Kit has completed the task of installing the typeface(s) you have selected, it will display a list of all presently installed typefaces. For example, if you install the Dutch Roman, Italic, Bold, and Bold Italic typefaces, the list shown in Figure 18-13 on the next page will appear on your screen.

When this screen appears, press [F3] to install other Fontware typefaces, [F5] to delete an installed Fontware Typeface, or [F10] to build a PCL soft font.

Finally, if you want to add typefaces to the Fontware Installation Kit after you have completed the initial installation process, you can do so by choosing the Fontware Main Menu's Add/Delete Fontware Typefaces option. The Fontware Main Menu, which is shown in Figure 18-14 on page 569, will appear on your screen whenever you run the Fontware Installation Kit from the DOS prompt subsequent to the initial installation process.

FIGURE 18-12

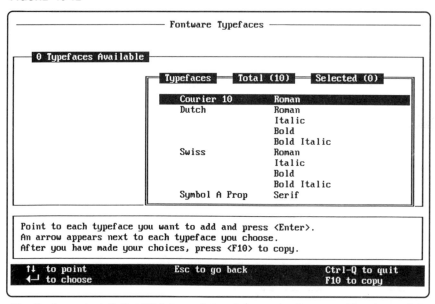

The Fontware Installation Kit lists each typeface on the Fontware Typefaces disk.

FIGURE 18-13

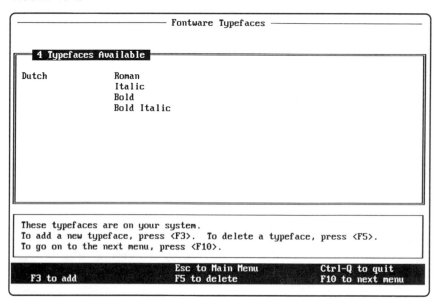

Once you have installed a typeface, the Fontware Installation Kit will display a list of all installed Fontware Typefaces.

FIGURE 18-14

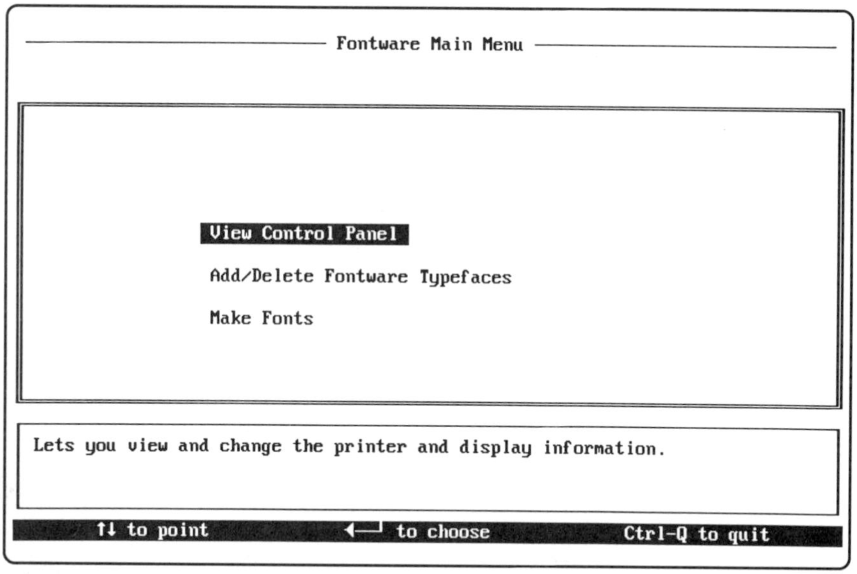

```
┌──────────────────────────────────────────────────────────────┐
│ ────────────────── Fontware Main Menu ──────────────────      │
│                                                                │
│  ┌──────────────────────────────────────────────────────┐    │
│  │                                                        │    │
│  │                                                        │    │
│  │          ▐ View Control Panel ▌                        │    │
│  │                                                        │    │
│  │           Add/Delete Fontware Typefaces                │    │
│  │                                                        │    │
│  │           Make Fonts                                   │    │
│  │                                                        │    │
│  │                                                        │    │
│  └──────────────────────────────────────────────────────┘    │
│  ┌──────────────────────────────────────────────────────┐    │
│  │ Lets you view and change the printer and display       │    │
│  │ information.                                            │    │
│  │                                                        │    │
│  └──────────────────────────────────────────────────────┘    │
│  ▐ ↑↓ to point ▌      ▐ ←┘ to choose ▌   ▐ Ctrl-Q to quit ▌   │
└──────────────────────────────────────────────────────────────┘
```

To add a typeface, you should choose the Fontware Main Menu's Add/Delete Fontware Typefaces option.

When you select the Add/Delete Fontware Typefaces option from the Fontware Main Menu, the Fontware Installation Kit will display a list of all currently installed Fontware Typefaces similar to the one shown in Figure 18-13. When this list appears, you can install additional Fontware Typefaces by pressing [F3].

Making a font

There are two ways to access the section of the Fontware Installation Kit that allows you to create fonts. First, when you have completed the process of adding Fontware typefaces, the menu shown in Figure 18-13 will appear on your screen. At this time, you can begin the process of creating fonts by pressing [F10].

Second, whenever you run the Fontware Installation Kit after the initial installation process, the Fontware Main Menu shown in Figure 18-14 will appear on your screen. Consequently, you can begin the process of creating fonts by choosing the Make Fonts option from this menu. To choose this option, use the ↑ or ↓ key to highlight it, then press ←┘.

Printer fonts

Regardless of the method you use to initiate the process of creating fonts, the menu shown in Figure 18-15 on the following page will appear on your screen. As you can see, this menu lists each installed Fontware Typeface.

To make a font, begin by highlighting a typeface with the ↑ or ↓ key, then press ←┘. When you do this, you will be allowed to enter the point sizes you want to create in the Point Size Selection field to the right of the typeface name. You may enter as many as 16 sizes in this field by separating each entry with a space. If you have a LaserJet Series II, IID, or 2000, the sizes you choose must be no smaller than 2 points and no larger than 144 points. If you have a LaserJet Plus or LaserJet 500 Plus, the sizes you choose must be no smaller than 2 points and no larger than 32 points.

FIGURE 18-15

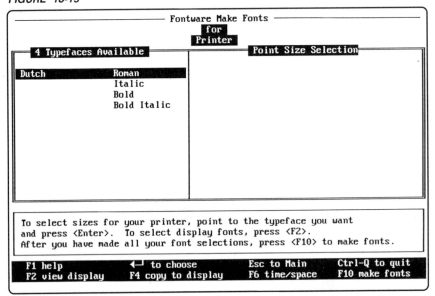

The Fontware Make Fonts for Printer menu lists each installed Fontware Typeface.

For example, if you want to make 9-, 10-, 11-, and 12-point versions of the Dutch Roman typeface listed in Figure 18-15, use the ↑ or ↓ key to highlight the **Dutch Roman** typeface entry, press ↵, type **9 10 11 12** in the Point Size Selection field, then press ↵ to accept the sizes. After you do this, the Fontware Make Fonts for Printer menu should be identical to the one shown in Figure 18-16.

Once you have chosen all the desired fonts, you can create them by pressing [F10]. However, if the Fontware Installation Kit you are using can create screen fonts, you must issue instructions to create them, by pressing [F2] or [F6].

Screen fonts

When you press [F2], the Fontware Make Fonts for Display menu shown in Figure 18-17 will appear on your screen. To make a screen font, highlight a typeface with the ↑ or ↓ key, then press ↵. When you do this, you will be allowed to enter the point sizes you want to create in the Point Size Selection field to the right of the typeface name. You may enter as many as 16 sizes in this field by separating each entry with a space.

FIGURE 18-16

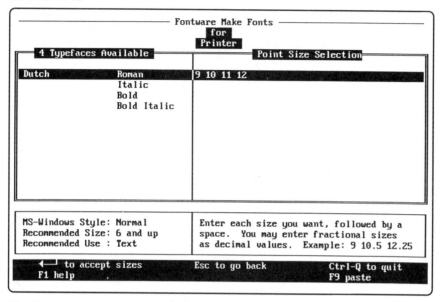

The Fontware Make Fonts for Printer menu will display the size(s) of fonts you want to create in the Point Size Selection field to the right of the typeface name.

FIGURE 18-17

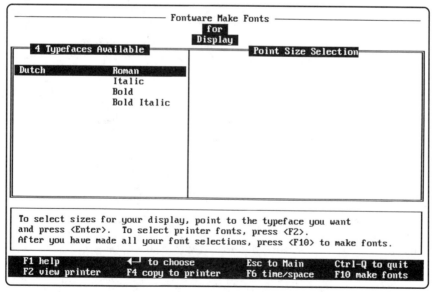

The Fontware Make Fonts for Display menu allows you to create screen fonts.

For example, if you want to make 9-, 10-, 11- and 12-point versions of the Dutch Roman typeface listed in Figure 18-17, use the ↑ or ↓ key to highlight the **Dutch Roman** typeface entry, press ↵, type **9 10 11 12** in the Point Size Selection field, then press ↵ to accept the sizes. As a result, the Fontware Make Fonts for Display menu should be identical to the one shown in Figure 18-18.

FIGURE 18-18

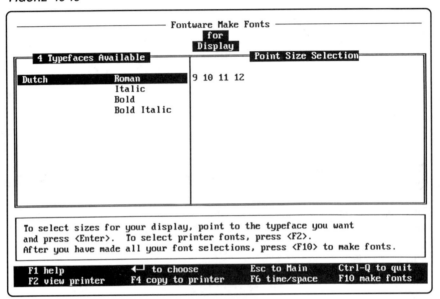

The Fontware Make Fonts for Display menu will show the size(s) of fonts you want to create in the Point Size Selection field to the right of the typeface name.

On the other hand, if you simply want to create screen fonts that match each of the printer fonts you have selected, use the ↑ or ↓ key to highlight the font, then press **[F4]**. The Fontware Installation Kit will then display a message box similar to the one shown in Figure 18-19 and will automatically update the Fontware Make Fonts for Display menu.

Finally, after you have selected all of the printer and/or display fonts that you want to create, you can press [F6] to display a message box that will tell you if the amount of free disk space needed to create the fonts is available . This message box will also display an estimate of the amount of time required to create the fonts. For example, the message box shown in Figure 18-20 indicates that it will take 39 minutes to create printer and display versions of the Dutch Roman 9-, 10-, 11-, and 12-point fonts.

FIGURE 18-19

```
┌─────────────────────────────────────────────┐
│       - Printer Sizes to Display Sizes -     │
│   Copied:                                     │
│   ███████████████████████████████████████████ │
│   9 10 11 12                                   │
│                                               │
│   Please press any key to continue...        │
└─────────────────────────────────────────────┘
```

When you press [F4], the Fontware Installation Kit will create display versions of the printer fonts you have selected and then will display a message box similar to this one.

FIGURE 18-20

```
┌─────────────────────────────────────────────┐
│          - Time and Space Estimates -        │
│     4 printer fonts, 4 display fonts          │
│     Time needed:  39 minutes                  │
│     Available disk space is okay.             │
│                                               │
│     Please press any key to continue...      │
└─────────────────────────────────────────────┘
```

Fontware Installation Kits can estimate the amount of time needed to create fonts as well as tell you if enough disk space is available.

Once you have chosen the fonts you want to create, you may initiate the process of creating them by pressing [F10]. The Fontware Installation Kit will display a message box similar to the one shown in Figure 18-20, and will ask you to press Y to make fonts or N to abort the procedure. If you respond by typing Y, it will then display a screen similar to the one shown in Figure 18-21 on the following page as the font is created.

After it has created all of the fonts you have chosen, the Fontware Installation Kit will install them for use with the product for which it was designed and will return you to the DOS prompt. For example, the Fontware Installation Kit for Microsoft Windows will automatically create .PFM files for each soft font and will update WIN.INI.

Summary

BitStream's Fontware Installation Kits are extremely useful tools for LaserJet users. Not only can they create a soft font of any size you specify between 2 and 144 points, but they also manage the task of installing each font they create so that the fonts can be used with the application for which the Fontware Installation Kit was designed. If you need to create various sizes of fonts, BitStream Fontware Installation Kits might be just what you need.

FIGURE 18-21

```
┌─────────────────────────────────────────────────────────────┐
│ BITSTREAM FONTWARE INSTALLATION KIT FOR MICROSOFT WINDOWS     │
│ Version 2.03                    (c) Copyright 1987, 1988      │
│                                                               │
│ Font 1 of 1                                                   │
│ Dutch Roman     9.0 Point                                     │
│ ANSI Windows Character Set                                    │
│ HP LaserJet series II or compatible                           │
│                                                               │
│ Making PCL Font Metric Files (PFMs)                           │
│                                                               │
│ Making PCL Fonts                                              │
│                                                               │
│ Installing Fonts                                              │
│                                                               │
│                                                               │
│                                                               │
│ Bitstream Fontware Installation Completed.                    │
│                                                               │
│ No warnings or errors reported.                               │
│                                                               │
│                                                               │
│                                                               │
│ C:\FONTWARE                                                   │
│                                                               │
└─────────────────────────────────────────────────────────────┘
```

Fontware Installation Kits display a screen similar to this one as they create PCL soft fonts.

FONT EFFECTS

When it comes to font design, font manufacturers have taken the Henry Ford approach. In other words, you can have a font in any color you want as long as it's black. Fortunately, SoftCraft's Font Effects makes it possible to jazz up any standard PCL soft font.

Capabilities

While Font Effects can't add blazing color to your fonts, it does allow you to radically alter their appearance. For example, in Figure 18-22 you can see a line of text printed with BitStream's ITC Garamond font as it appears normally. In the same figure, you can also see a version of the ITC Garamond font that was created with the help of Font Effects.

FIGURE 18-22

ABCD   ABCD
Normal   Outline

This figure shows how Font Effects can radically alter the appearance of a font.

Modifying the appearance of a font with Font Effects is as easy as choosing the particular effect you want to use. For example, the second version of the ITC Garamond font shown in Figure 18-22 was created with the assistance of the Thin Outline effect.

While only 14 standard effects are shipped with Font Effects, it is possible to create a number of custom effects. For example, if you want to fill characters with a pattern other than the ones included with Font Effects, you can use a graphics editor such as Z-Soft's PC Paintbrush to create the pattern. Once you have created the pattern, you can use a utility program called IMGXFORM.EXE, which is included with Font Effects, to convert it into a Tagged Image File Format (TIFF) file that can be used by Font Effects. For example, the ITC Garamond characters shown in Figure 18-23 are filled with a TIFF-based lattice pattern.

FIGURE 18-23

Lattice

These ITC Garamond characters are filled with a TIFF-based lattice pattern.

In addition to the ability to fill characters with various patterns, Font Effects allows you to add shadows to characters. For example, we used the standard light drop shadow with separation effect included with Font Effects to create the ITC Garamond characters shown in Figure 18-24.

FIGURE 18-24

Shadow

A shadow has been added to these ITC Garamond characters.

As we pointed out in Chapter 4, each character in a font exists within a conceptual box called a cell. In most cases, this box is conceptually white, and characters are formed within it by printing small areas of black. However, Font Effects makes it possible to invert the image of a character and the box in which it exists. Font Effects also allows you to fill the background of a character box with a pattern of your choice. As an example, ITC Garamond characters are shown inverted in Figure 18-25.

FIGURE 18-25

Inverted

The background of these ITC Garamond characters has been inverted by Font Effects.

Finally, in addition to modifying the patterns used to fill a character or the background on which the character exists, Font Effects can scale the vertical and horizontal size of a font. This is a useful capability if you want to create an extremely large font, or if you want to make a font appear tall and thin, or short and fat. An example of ITC Garamond characters whose width has been decreased is shown in Figure 18-26.

FIGURE 18-26

Width

The width of these ITC Garamond characters has been decreased by Font Effects.

Running Font Effects

Font Effects is an extremely easy program to install and run. If you plan to use Font Effects on a system that has a hard disk, begin by issuing the command **md fontfx** at the DOS prompt to create a directory into which the Font Effects program will be installed. Once you have done this, place the Font Effects disk into drive A and issue the command **copy a:*.* c:\fontfx*.*** at the DOS prompt. If you plan to use Font Effects on a floppy-based system, simply place the Font Effects disk in drive A.

Interactive mode

Font Effects can be run and used in interactive mode or in command line mode. Let's look first at the interactive mode. To run Font Effects in interactive mode from a hard disk, type **cd fontfx** at the DOS prompt to move into the FONTFX directory, then type **font fx**. To run Font Effects in interactive mode from a floppy disk, simply type **font fx** at the DOS prompt. When you do this, the Font Effects main menu shown in Figure 18-27 will appear on your screen. You can use the commands on this menu to make changes to the appearance of a soft font.

FIGURE 18-27

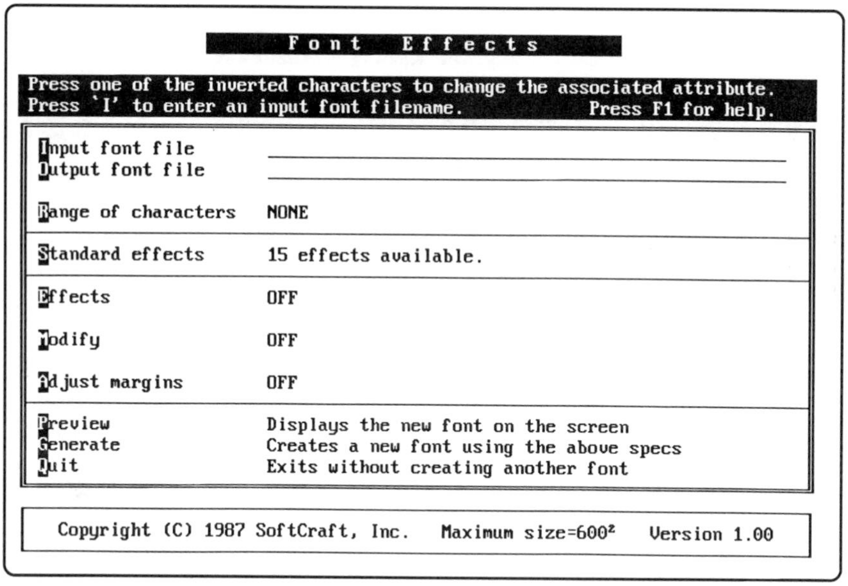

```
┌─────────────────────────────────────────────────────────────────────┐
│              ███████ Font    Effects ███████                          │
│  Press one of the inverted characters to change the associated attribute. │
│  Press 'I' to enter an input font filename.        Press F1 for help. │
│  ┌─────────────────────────────────────────────────────────────────┐  │
│  │ Input font file        _____        │  │
│  │ Output font file       _____        │  │
│  │                                                                    │  │
│  │ Range of characters    NONE                                        │  │
│  │                                                                    │  │
│  │ Standard effects       15 effects available.                       │  │
│  │                                                                    │  │
│  │ Effects                OFF                                         │  │
│  │                                                                    │  │
│  │ Modify                 OFF                                         │  │
│  │                                                                    │  │
│  │ Adjust margins         OFF                                         │  │
│  │                                                                    │  │
│  │ Preview                Displays the new font on the screen         │  │
│  │ Generate               Creates a new font using the above specs    │  │
│  │ Quit                   Exits without creating another font         │  │
│  └─────────────────────────────────────────────────────────────────┘  │
│  ┌─────────────────────────────────────────────────────────────────┐  │
│  │  Copyright (C) 1987 SoftCraft, Inc.  Maximum size=600²  Version 1.00 │  │
│  └─────────────────────────────────────────────────────────────────┘  │
└─────────────────────────────────────────────────────────────────────┘
```

When you run Font Effects in interactive mode, the main menu will appear.

To demonstrate how Font Effects can be used in interactive mode to modify the appearance of a soft font, we'll walk through the process of adding a light drop shadow to BitStream's ITC Garamond font.

To begin this process, press **I** to issue an Input font file command, then type the name of the data file in which its bit map is stored. For example, if your goal is to modify the 30-point version of the ITC Garamond font stored in the file GA300RPN.USP, type **GA300RPN.USP** when Font Effects prompts you to enter the name of the input file.

Once you have specified the name of the soft font file you want to modify, you must choose a name for the file into which the modified version of the font will be written. To do this, press **O** to issue an Output font file command, then enter a file name at the prompt.

After you have specified the names of the input and output files, it's time to modify the input file by choosing a pattern. To add a shadow to the ITC Garamond font, press **S** to issue a Standard effects command, then press **U** to select the Use option. When you do this, the list of effects shown in Figure 18-28 will appear on your screen.

To choose an effect from this list, use the ↑ or ↓ key to highlight your selection, then press ↵. For example, to add a shadow to the ITC Garamond font, highlight the light drop shadow with separation effect, then press ↵.

FIGURE 18-28

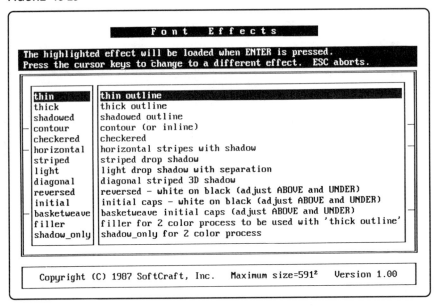

```
┌─────────────────────────────────────────────────────────────────┐
│              ▓▓▓▓▓  F o n t    E f f e c t s  ▓▓▓▓▓               │
│  ┌───────────────────────────────────────────────────────────┐  │
│  │ The highlighted effect will be loaded when ENTER is pressed.│ │
│  │ Press the cursor keys to change to a different effect. ESC aborts.│
│  └───────────────────────────────────────────────────────────┘  │
│  ┌────────────┬──────────────────────────────────────────────┐  │
│  │ thin       │ thin outline                                  │  │
│  │ thick      │ thick outline                                 │  │
│  │ shadowed   │ shadowed outline                              │  │
│ ─┤ contour    │ contour (or inline)                           ├─ │
│  │ checkered  │ checkered                                      │  │
│ ─┤ horizontal │ horizontal stripes with shadow                │  │
│  │ striped    │ striped drop shadow                           │  │
│  │ light      │ light drop shadow with separation             │  │
│  │ diagonal   │ diagonal striped 3D shadow                    │  │
│  │ reversed   │ reversed - white on black (adjust ABOVE and UNDER)│
│  │ initial    │ initial caps - white on black (adjust ABOVE and UNDER)│
│ ─┤ basketweave│ basketweave initial caps (adjust ABOVE and UNDER)├─│
│  │ filler     │ filler for 2 color process to be used with 'thick outline'│
│  │ shadow_only│ shadow_only for 2 color process               │  │
│  └────────────┴──────────────────────────────────────────────┘  │
│  ┌───────────────────────────────────────────────────────────┐  │
│  │ Copyright (C) 1987 SoftCraft, Inc.  Maximum size=591²  Version 1.00│
│  └───────────────────────────────────────────────────────────┘  │
└─────────────────────────────────────────────────────────────────┘
```

This list of effects will appear on your screen when you issue a Standard effects command and choose the Use option.

After you have chosen this effect, you can preview the appearance of the modified font on the screen by pressing **P** to issue a Preview command. When you do this, you will be prompted to enter the range of characters you want to preview in the Range of characters field. For example, if you want to preview characters A through Z, type **A** and **Z** in the Range of characters field.

Once you have provided Font Effects with the range of characters you want to preview, you will be prompted to continue or to abort the process. If you press Y to continue, Font Effects will display the first character in the range on your screen. Figure 18-29 shows the ITC Garamond character *A* as it will appear in Preview mode after a light drop shadow has been added.

Once Font Effect's Preview mode is active, you may advance through the range of characters you have specified in the Range of characters field by pressing **[Space]**. If you want to exit Preview mode, press **[Esc]**.

Finally, once you have added a shadow to the ITC Garamond font and have previewed the result on screen, you can write the actual soft font data to a disk file by pressing **G** to issue a Generate file command. When you do this, Font Effects will begin the task of generating the soft font. Finally, when Font Effects has finished the task of generating a soft font, you may exit by pressing **Q**.

FIGURE 18-29

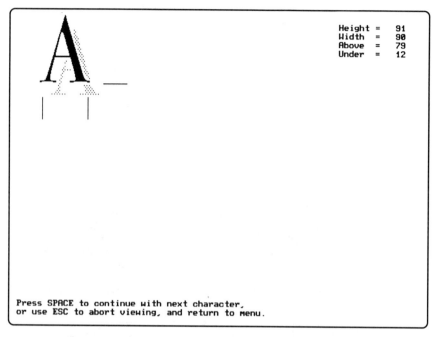

This figure shows an ITC Garamond character as it appears in Preview mode after a light drop shadow has been added.

Command line mode

In the previous section, we showed you how to use Font Effects in interactive mode. However, this is not the only mode in which Font Effects can be used. By including parameters on the command line when you invoke Font Effects from the DOS prompt, you can bypass the main menu shown in Figure 18-27. This makes it possible to run Font Effects from a batch file. As an example, the command used to invoke Font Effects for the purpose of creating a light drop shadow version of the ITC Garamond font is:

FONT FX GA300RPN.USP GASHADOW.USP -SULIGHT -G

For more information on the various switches that can be used to invoke Font Effects in command line mode, consult the manual that was included with the Font Effects package.

Summary

Font Effects is an extremely powerful, useful, and well-designed product. If your goal is to enhance or modify the appearance of an existing soft font with a minimal amount of work, Font Effects is the perfect choice for the task.

FONTLOAD

Hewlett-Packard's FontLoad is a utility program that is now included with most HP soft fonts. Its main purpose, as we explained in Chapter 4, is to automate the process of downloading soft fonts to the LaserJet. FontLoad also has the ability to produce a report that lists the width of each character in a soft font.

To produce this character width table, run FontLoad from the DOS prompt by typing **fload**. When you do this, the screen shown in Figure 18-30 will appear. Press **[F1]** to issue a NEW SETUP command, then type the name of the directory in which your soft fonts are stored. FontLoad will then list each of those fonts on the screen and prompt you to enter the name of the port to which your LaserJet is connected. When this prompt appears, press ↵ if your LaserJet is connected to LPT1: or type the name of the port.

FIGURE 18-30

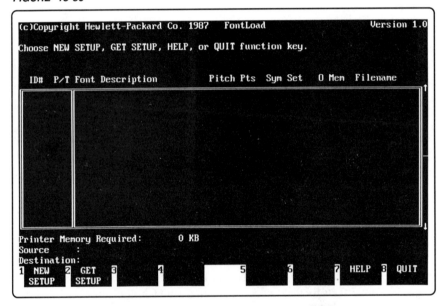

This screen will appear when you run FontLoad from the DOS prompt.

Once you have provided FontLoad with SETUP information, each soft font found in the directory you specified will be listed on the screen. For example, Figure 18-31 shows a list of soft fonts stored in the directory \PCLFONTS.

When FontLoad displays a list of fonts similar to the one shown in Figure 18-31, you can use the WIDTH TABLES command to produce a report that lists the width of each character in a specific soft font. To do this, use the ↑ or ↓ key or mouse to position the cursor to the left of the soft font for which you want to create a width table, then press **[F1]** to issue a SELECT FONT command.

FIGURE 18-31

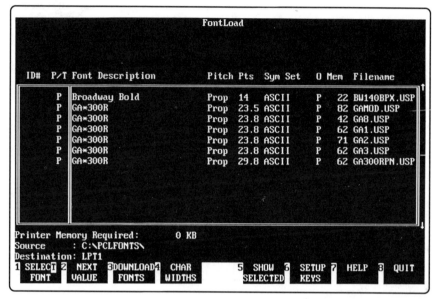

FontLoad will list each font found in the directory you specify.

After you have selected the font for which you want to create a width table, press **[F4]** to issue a WIDTH TABLE command. When you do this, FontLoad will generate a report that lists the width of each character in the font. For example, Figure 18-32 on the following page shows the width table that FontLoad generated for BitStream's 14-point Broadway font.

Summary

In this section, we've taken a brief look at FontLoad's ability to generate a character width table that can be used when adding support for soft fonts to applications such as Microsoft Word and WordPerfect. If you are interested in learning more about FontLoad's ability to automatically download soft fonts, see the discussion that appears in Chapter 4.

JETSCRIPT ACCESSORY KIT

The JetScript Accessory Kit is a software and hardware package that adds support for Adobe's PostScript page description language to the LaserJet Series II. Designed and manufactured by QMS, Inc., the JetScript Accessory Kit contains a circuit board that requires one standard 8-bit PC slot. This board contains a 16MHz 68000 CPU and 3MB of RAM. In addition, the JetScript Accessory Kit includes a circuit board that plugs into the LaserJet Series II's optional I/O slot, and a PostScript interpreter that includes support for all of the fonts found in the Apple LaserWriter Plus and LaserWriter II. Utilities that allow you to configure and communicate with the PostScript interpreter and to download PostScript soft fonts are also included.

FIGURE 18-32

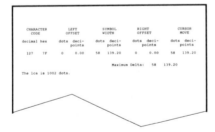

FontLoad has the ability to generate a character width table that can be used to add support for a soft font to an application such as Microsoft Word or WordPerfect.

Installation

Installation of the JetScript Accessory Kit is extremely simple. However, if you're not the type of person who likes to pull the cover off your PC, it might be a good idea to allow your HP dealer to handle the process.

The major component of the JetScript Accessory Kit is the Motorola 68000-based PostScript controller. This board, which plugs into any full-length standard 8-bit PC expansion slot, handles the task of converting the PostScript code generated by an application program into data that instructs the LaserJet to produce a document.

The JetScript PostScript controller communicates with the LaserJet Series II via a shielded cable connected to a small circuit board that you must plug into the optional I/O slot located to the left of the serial port on the back of the unit.

Once you have completed the process of installing the JetScript hardware, you must install the software. To do this, place the JetScript Installation Disk in drive

A, type **JETINSTL** and follow the prompts. JETINSTL will ask you to choose the port through which you want to communicate with the PostScript controller and will install all of the software required to initialize and use JetScript in a directory called \QMSJS. Your AUTOEXEC.BAT and CONFIG.SYS files will be modified so that support for JetScript will be loaded automatically each time you turn on your PC.

Capabilities

The JetScript Accessory Kit includes 35 fonts that are identical to the fonts supported by the Apple LaserWriter Plus and the Apple LaserWriter II family of printers. In addition, any Adobe PostScript soft font can be used with the JetScript Accessory Kit. We'll discuss this topic in more detail a bit later.

One of PostScript's most widely hailed features is the ability to automatically scale fonts. PostScript can adjust the size of each of the 11 fonts included with the JetScript Accessory Kit. For example, if you want to use a 7-, 29- or 113-point version of the Palatino font, PostScript will automatically create those sizes.

In addition to the ability to automatically scale fonts, PostScript offers several other features, including the ability to rotate fonts and manage special effects such as shading. As an example of the capabilities of JetScript, Figure 18-33 on the following page shows the startup page JetScript will produce when you power up your PC and load the PostScript interpreter onto the PostScript controller. Figure 18-33 also shows three documents that illustrate the capabilities of the JetScript Accessory Kit and PostScript.

The last, and perhaps most important, feature of the JetScript Accessory Kit is speed. Since it was introduced to the marketplace in the original Apple LaserWriter, PostScript has been criticized for the amount of time it requires to process and produce a document. However, since the JetScript Accessory Kit is based on a 16MHz 68000 CPU, and it interfaces with your computer via the PC bus and a high-speed video interface (while other PostScript printers interface via slow serial or parallel interfaces), a JetScript-equipped LaserJet Series II is one of the fastest PostScript printers on the market.

Using JetScript

When you turn on your PC with JetScript installed, your AUTOEXEC.BAT file will invoke a program called JETSTART. This program will transfer more than 1MB of PostScript code and fonts from your hard disk to the JetScript PostScript controller. If you are using a standard 8MHz 80286-based PC, you can expect this task to take approximately one minute. Fortunately, once you have initialized the PostScript controller, there will be no need to re-initialize it unless you turn off your PC. In other words, if you reset your PC by pressing [Ctrl][Alt][Del], the JETSTART program that initializes the PostScript controller will recognize the fact that the initialization process has been completed and will display a message informing you of this.

FIGURE 18-33

These pages illustrate some of the most impressive capabilities of PostScript.

The JetScript Accessory Kit is designed so that it is possible to use the LaserJet in native PCL mode as well as in PostScript mode. For example, if you connect the LaserJet's parallel port to your PC via LPT1: and communicate with the PostScript controller LPT2:, you can use the LaserJet in standard PCL mode by sending data to LPT1:, or you can use it in PostScript mode by sending PostScript code to LPT2:. As we mentioned earlier, you can choose the port that your computer will use to communicate with the JetScript PostScript controller during the installation procedure.

Finally, while a JetScript-equipped LaserJet Series II is one of the fastest PostScript printers available, it's not a speed demon. Therefore, you may notice that the amount of time it takes to print a document with the JetScript Accessory Kit will be longer than the amount of time it takes to print the same document using the LaserJet's native PCL mode. However, the benefits of PostScript normally outweigh the few extra seconds it requires to print a document.

Running JETSET

As we mentioned earlier, a utility that allows you to communicate with the PostScript controller is included with the JetScript Accessory Kit. This utility, which is called JETSET, allows you to determine the status of the PostScript controller, download PostScript files, turn manual feed on and off, communicate with the PostScript interpreter interactively, change the printer's name, set timeout, and reset alignment.

To run JETSET, type **jetset** at the DOS prompt, then press ↵. When you do this, the menu shown in Figure 18-34 will appear in the upper-right corner of your screen.

FIGURE 18-34

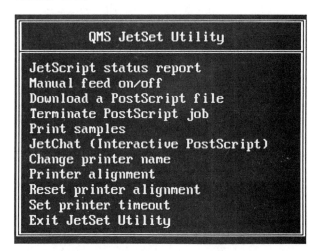

```
┌──────────────────────────────────────┐
│     QMS JetSet Utility               │
├──────────────────────────────────────┤
│ JetScript status report              │
│ Manual feed on/off                   │
│ Download a PostScript file           │
│ Terminate PostScript job             │
│ Print samples                        │
│ JetChat (Interactive PostScript)     │
│ Change printer name                  │
│ Printer alignment                    │
│ Reset printer alignment              │
│ Set printer timeout                  │
│ Exit JetSet Utility                  │
└──────────────────────────────────────┘
```

Commands on JETSET's menu allow you to determine the status of the JetScript system and much more.

As you can see, this menu contains commands that provide access to each of the functions we mentioned earlier. For example, to determine the status of the JetScript system, press **J**, or use the ↑ or ↓ key to highlight the JetScript status report option, then press ↵. When you do this, JETSET will display the list of settings shown in Figure 18-35.

FIGURE 18-35

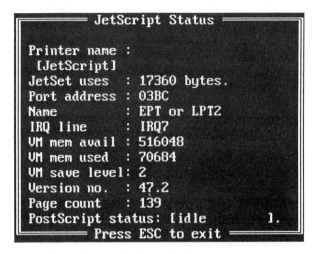

JETSET will display
this list of settings
when you choose the
JetScript status
report option from
the menu shown in
Figure 18-34.

Finally, once you have used JETSET to display a status report, download a PostScript file, and so forth, you may return to the DOS prompt by selecting the Exit JetSet Utility option.

Running JETFONTS

If you want to download PostScript soft fonts to the JetScript Accessory Kit's PostScript controller, you must use the utility program called JETFONTS, which is included with the JetScript Accessory Kit.

Before you run JETFONTS, you must copy any PostScript soft font file you want to download into a directory called \PSFONTS. Otherwise, JETFONTS will display an error message. Once you have copied PostScript soft font files into the \PSFONTS directory, type **jetfonts** at the DOS prompt, then press ↵. JETFONTS will display a list of each PostScript soft font stored in the \PSFONTS directory. To select a font that appears on this list for downloading , use the ↑ or ↓ key to highlight your selection, then press the **[Spacebar]**. Once you have selected all of the fonts you want to download, press ↵ to send them to the JetScript PostScript controller. Finally, to exit JETFONTS, press the **[Esc]** key.

Summary

The JetScript Accessory Kit is a powerful addition to any LaserJet Series II for two reasons. First, it provides access to Adobe's PostScript Page Description Language. Second, it maintains compatibility with the LaserJet's native PCL mode, thereby allowing you to access the ever-growing library of PCL-based software products. If you use your LaserJet in an environment that requires a great deal of flexibility when printing text, the JetScript Accessory Kit is an ideal companion.

Although a vast and rapidly growing number of soft fonts are now available for the LaserJet, it's possible you may need to create a font from scratch. When you do, SoftCraft's Font Editor is a good candidate for the task. However, creating new fonts is not the only task for which the SoftCraft Font Editor is suited.

For example, you can use the SoftCraft Font Editor to make changes to any existing PCL soft font. In addition, the SoftCraft Font Editor can import graphics images produced by products such as Z-Soft's PC Paintbrush. This is an extremely useful capability that can be used to import corporate logos or other symbols into a font so that they can be printed by the LaserJet.

In this section, we'll show you how to install and run the SoftCraft Font Editor. Once we've done this, we'll show you how to access the SoftCraft Font Editor's many features and commands, and we'll discuss the process of creating or editing a soft font.

SOFTCRAFT FONT EDITOR

The SoftCraft Font Editor requires a CGA, EGA, VGA, or Hercules graphics board, MS-DOS 2.11 or later, and at least 450K of available memory. In addition, while it is not an absolute necessity, a mouse makes using the SoftCraft Font Editor a much more pleasant experience.

Before you can use the SoftCraft Font Editor to create or edit a font, you must install it for use with your system. If you have a hard disk, you should begin the installation process by using the DOS MD command to create a directory into which SoftCraft Font Editor will be installed. Once you have done this, use the DOS CD command to move into that directory, then copy each of the three SoftCraft Font Editor disks into that directory. If you plan to use the SoftCraft Font Editor on a floppy-based system, simply place SoftCraft Font Editor Disk 1 into drive A.

Once you have copied all three SoftCraft Font Editor disks into the \SCFE directory on your hard disk, or you have placed SoftCraft Font Editor Disk 1 in drive A, type **ffconfig** at the DOS prompt. The SoftCraft configuration program will display the menu shown in Figure 18-36 on the next page.

When this menu appears, press **p** to choose the type of printer you are using. Next, choose **o** to choose the port to which your printer is connected. Then, press **f** to enter the name of the directory in which the soft fonts you want to edit or create are (or will be) stored. Finally, choose **s** to save this information to disk, then press **q** to return to the DOS prompt.

Once you have have used FFCONFIG to configure the SoftCraft Font Editor for your system, you're ready to go. However, if you have a mouse, you should load your mouse device driver before you run the SoftCraft Font Editor. For example, if you have a Microsoft mouse, you should run MOUSE.COM or modify your CONFIG.SYS file so that it will automatically load the MOUSE.SYS device driver each time your system is booted.

Finally, to run the SCFE, type **scfe** at the DOS prompt. When you do this, the dialog box shown in Figure 18-37 will appear on your screen.

Running the SoftCraft Font Editor

FIGURE 18-36

```
Ffconfig:  SoftCraft configuration program, version 3.0Laser
Copyright (C) 1987  SoftCraft, Inc.




                    SoftCraft Configuration
                          Main Menu
          (p)  Printer type is HP LaserJetII +2M
          (o)  Output Port is lpt1 (IBM Compatible)
          (f)  Font location is "C:\PCLFONTS\"
          (r)  Portrait printer font file (prf File) is not defined
               (R) for fast listing of prf files.
          (l)  Landscape printer font file (prf File) is not defined
               (L) for fast listing of prf files.
          (t)  Terminal characteristics
          (d)  Display terminal characteristics

          (s)  Save
          (q)  Quit

Change one of the above, Save, or Quit (one of: p,d,o,f,r,R,l,L,t,s,q)>
```

The SoftCraft configuration program allows you to set up the SoftCraft Font Editor for your system.

FIGURE 18-37

```
Enter a font to edit
Press ENTER to create a new
font.
To pick from a list click [R]
or type a wildcard name


->

Enter file name to READ
```

When you run the SoftCraft Font Editor, this dialog box will appear on your screen.

When this dialog box appears, enter the name of the font you want to modify, or press ↵ if you want to create a new soft font. You can also display a list of the soft fonts stored in your default soft font directory by entering a file name that includes standard DOS wildcards or by pressing the right mouse button.

Once you provide the SoftCraft Font Editor with the name of the soft font you want to edit, or press ↵ to indicate that you want to create a new soft font, the dialog box shown in Figure 18-38 will appear on your screen. At this time, you should enter the character you want to edit or create. For example, if you want to edit the character *A*, type **A**, then press ↵.

FIGURE 18-38

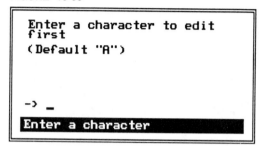

After you have entered the name of the soft font, you must specify which character you want to edit or create.

After you have specified the character you want to edit or create, the main SoftCraft Font Editor screen shown in Figure 18-39 will appear. As you can see, this screen features two edit windows, a help window, and a menu bar from which you can select commands.

FIGURE 18-39

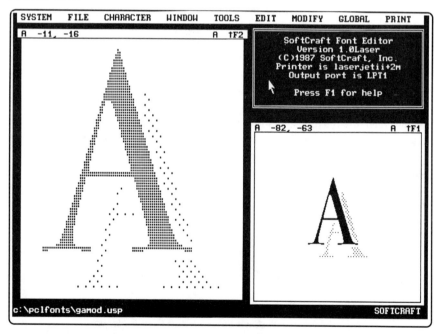

The SoftCraft Font Editor's graphical user interface should be familiar to anyone who uses Microsoft Windows, GEM, or Macintosh.

As you can see in Figure 18-39, the character *A* is shown in both edit windows. However, as we mentioned earlier, it is possible to open as many as five edit windows at once, with each containing a different character. Regardless of the actual number of edit windows that are active, or the characters displayed within them, you can use the mouse cursor and the commands available via the SoftCraft Font Editor's pull-down menus to change a character in an edit window.

For example, the main SoftCraft Font Editor screen shown in Figure 18-39 features two edit windows that contain different views of the character *A*. Each of these windows is divided into a grid, and each square on this grid is equal to one LaserJet dot unit ($\frac{1}{300}$ inch by $\frac{1}{300}$ inch).

You can make changes to the character shown in these windows by manipulating the pattern of dots that form the character on the grid. If you want to turn on a dot (change it from white to black), use the mouse or cursor-movement keys to move the pointer into either edit window, then press ↵ or the left mouse button. If you want to turn off a dot (change it from black to white), use the mouse or cursor-movement keys to move the pointer into either edit window, then press **[Ins]** or the right mouse button.

If the process of designing characters by toggling individual dots on and off seems tedious, you can take advantage of the SoftCraft Font Editor's graphics tools, which are accessible via the TOOLS menu. For example, you can use the TOOLS menu to automatically draw circles, boxes, ellipses, and splines. In addition, the SoftCraft Font Editor allows you to fill an area and rotate, enlarge, reduce, slant, and invert any portion of a character.

To pull down a menu from the menu bar at the top of the SoftCraft Font Editor's main screen, use the mouse to move the pointer to the menu name, or type the first letter of the menu name. For example, to pull down the TOOLS menu, highlight **TOOLS**, then press the left mouse button or press **T**. When you do this, the menu shown in Figure 18-40 will appear.

FIGURE 18-40

TOOLS
Line
Spline
Fill
Circle
Ellipse
Box

You can pull down the SoftCraft Font Editor's TOOLS menu with the mouse or keyboard.

After you have pulled down a menu, you can use the keyboard or the mouse to highlight the command or option you want to select. For example, to use the keyboard to select the Circle option from the TOOLS menu shown in Figure 18-40, press the ↓ key four times to highlight Circle, then press ↵. If you want to select the Circle option with the mouse, hold down the left mouse button after you pull down the TOOLS menu, move the pointer over the Circle option, then release the left mouse button.

Finally, once you have used the SoftCraft Editor to create or make changes to a font, you can use the SYSTEM menu's Exit & Save option to save the font to a disk file and return to the DOS prompt. Once you have saved a font to disk, you can use it with any application that supports soft fonts.

Summary

In this section, we've taken a brief look at the SoftCraft Font Editor. We've shown that it is based on a graphical user interface that should be familiar to anyone who has used a product such as Microsoft Windows, GEM, or the Macintosh. We've also mentioned that the SoftCraft Font Editor has a wide array of features and capabilities. The SoftCraft Font Editor deserves serious consideration if you need to edit or create a LaserJet soft font.

WYSIFONTS!

If you've ever used Ventura Publisher or a Microsoft Windows application such as PageMaker, it's probably safe to assume that you've encountered the problem of matching the fonts these applications use to display text on the screen with the fonts the LaserJet uses to print text. For example, if you install BitStream's Broadway font, which is part of the Headline Typefaces 1 soft font package marketed by Hewlett-Packard, you'll find that Windows and Ventura Publisher will display a substitute font on the screen.

At the time *LaserJet Companion* went to press, the only solution for the problem of matching screen fonts to LaserJet soft fonts was SoftCraft's WYSIfonts!. WYSIfonts! is a software package that allows you to create screen fonts for Microsoft Windows and Ventura Publisher that match any PCL soft font. In addition, WYSIfonts! automates the process of installing PCL and screen fonts for both products.

Running WYSIfonts!

You must install WYSIFonts! on a hard disk before you can begin creating screen fonts. To begin the installation process, use the DOS MD command to create a directory on your hard disk in which the version of WYSIfonts! you want to use will be installed. Once this is done, use the CD command to access that directory, and copy all of the files from WYSIfonts! Disk 1 and Disk 2. For example, if you have created a directory called \WIP in which you want to install WYSIfonts!, issue the command **CD WIP**, place the WYSIfonts! Disk 1 in drive A, and type **copy a:*.***. After you have done this, place the WYSIfonts! Disk 2 in drive A, and type **copy a:*.*** once again.

The WYSIfonts! package includes two versions of the same program. One of these versions is designed for Microsoft Windows, while the other is designed for Ventura Publisher. Therefore, to complete the installation process, you should delete from your hard disk the version of WYSIfonts! you do not want to use.

If you want to use the version of WYSIfonts! that was designed for Microsoft Windows, you should issue the command **del vip*.*** at the DOS prompt to delete the version designed for Ventura Publisher. Likewise, if you want to use the version that was designed for Ventura Publisher, issue the command **del wip*.*** at the DOS prompt to delete the version that was designed for Microsoft Windows.

Once you have installed the WYSIfonts! package and have removed the version you do not want to use, you can run the desired version. To run the version of WYSIfonts! designed for Microsoft Windows, type **wip** at the DOS prompt. When you do this, you will be prompted to enter the name of the directory in which you have installed Microsoft Windows. Once you supply the appropriate directory name at this prompt, the menu shown in Figure 18-41 will appear on your screen.

FIGURE 18-41

```
          Windows WYSIFonts (version 1.1)
   Font Installation for PageMaker and Microsoft Windows
           Copyright (C) 1988 SoftCraft, Inc.

 Action:  Install                               Font Directory:
                                                C:\WIP
 Orientation:  Portrait
                                    ┌────────┐   √ OLDE20.FON
 Screen Fonts:  ON                  │   OK   │
                                    └────────┘
   Windows Font Version:  >= 2.0    ┌────────┐
   Screen Font Size:  Min 10pt. Max 36pt. │ CANCEL │
   Display Type:  EGA/Hercules      └────────┘
   Resolution:  Horiz 96/300   Vert 72/300  ┌────────┐
                                    │ CONFIG │
 Kern Tables:  AUTO                 └────────┘
                                    ┌────────┐
 Windows Directory:  C:\WINDOWS     │ TAG ALL │
                                    ├────────┤
 Printer:  HP LaserJet+             │UnTAG ALL│
                                    └────────┘

 Click left mouse button or ◄┘ to select a new action.
```

This menu will appear when you run the version of WYSIfonts! that was designed for Microsoft Windows.

If you want to run the version of WYSIfonts! designed for Ventura Publisher, type **vip** at the DOS prompt. As you can see in Figure 18-42, the menu that appears on your screen when you run the Ventura Publisher version of WYSIfonts! is almost identical to the one that appears when you run the version designed for Microsoft Windows.

Since both versions of WYSIfonts! are essentially identical, we won't discuss the operation of each one in great detail. Instead, we'll walk you through an example in which we will create screen fonts for Microsoft Windows.

FIGURE 18-42

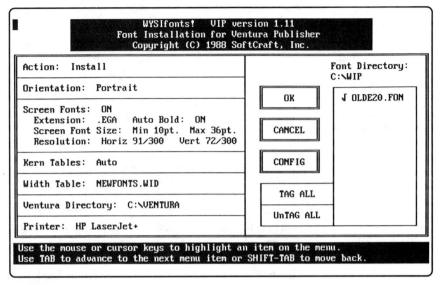

This menu will appear when you run the version of WYSIfonts! designed for Ventura Publisher.

When the menu shown in Figure 18-41 appears on your screen after you run WYSIFonts!, it's likely that you'll have to make several changes to the settings that appear on the menu. For example, you may have to change the Display Type: setting so that WYSIfonts! will create screen fonts for the specific type of video system you are using.

You can use the mouse or keyboard to make changes to any of the settings on the menu shown in Figure 18-41. For example, if you want to select a setting with the keyboard, press the [Tab] key to move forward through the list of settings until the one you want to change is highlighted. To move backward through the list of settings, press [Shift][Tab]. If you have a mouse, use it to highlight the setting you want to change.

Once you have highlighted a setting, press ↵ or the left mouse button to select it. When you do this, a list of possible alternative settings will appear. For example, if you select the Display Type: setting, the list of displays shown in Figure 18-43 on the following page will appear on your screen.

When a list of alternative settings similar to the one shown in Figure 18-43 appears on your screen, use the mouse or the ↑ or ↓ key to highlight the setting you want to choose, then press ↵ or the left mouse button to select it.

Once you have used this procedure to make any necessary changes to the settings that appear on the menu shown in Figure 18-41, it's time to select the PCL font for which you want to create a matching screen font. Begin by using the mouse or keyboard to select the Font Directory: setting and enter the name of the directory in which the soft font for which you want to create a screen font is stored. When you do this, a list of all screen fonts in that directory will appear below the Font Directory: setting.

FIGURE 18-43

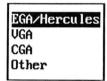

This list of displays will appear if you select the Display Type: setting.

When WYSIfonts! lists each of the fonts stored in your soft font directory, all of the fonts in that list will automatically be tagged. In other words, WYSIfonts! will assume that you want to create screen fonts for each of them. Therefore, if you do not want to create screen fonts for each font in your soft font directory, use the mouse or keyboard to highlight those fonts, then press ↵ or the left mouse button to remove the tag.

After you have removed the tag from the fonts for which you do not want to create a matching screen font, use the mouse or keyboard to select the OK command to the left of the font list, then press ↵ or the left mouse button. When you do this, WYSIfonts! will create a screen font that matches all the selected soft fonts, and will automatically install the screen font for use with Microsoft Windows (or Ventura Publisher).

Finally, once WYSIfonts! has created a screen font that matches each tagged soft font, you can exit to DOS by selecting the CANCEL command to the left of the font list. At this time, you can run Microsoft Windows or Ventura Publisher and immediately begin to use any screen font that was created and installed by WYSIfonts!. For example, Figure 18-44 shows the Microsoft Windows screen font WYSIfonts! created to match the version of the ITC Garamond font we modified with SoftCraft's Font Effects.

Summary

WYSIfonts! is well designed, well documented, easy to use, and relatively inexpensive. If you are an avid user of Ventura Publisher or of any product that runs under Microsoft Windows, and you want to take full advantage of that product's ability to provide WYSIWYG representations of a document, WYSIfonts! is a program you should consider.

FIGURE 18-44

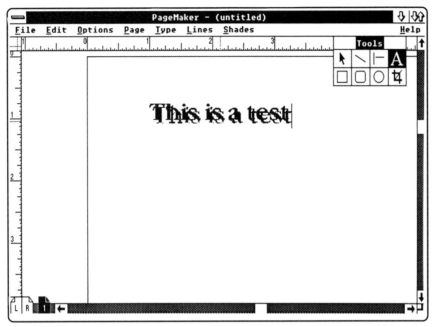

Once you have used WYSIfonts! to create a screen font, you can begin to use it immediately.

CONCLUSION

In this chapter, we've taken a look at products you can use to dramatically affect the appearance of documents produced by the LaserJet. We've discussed the JetScript Accessory Kit, BitStream Fontware, SoftCraft Font Editor Font Load and WYSIfonts. In these discussions, we've also suggested how each product might be used to solve specific problems.

As we pointed out at the beginning of this chapter, we've limited our discussion to the products we found most useful while we were writing *LaserJet Companion.* However, we'd like to emphasize that each of these products has competitors in the marketplace. Consequently, since we did not have room to discuss every competing product in great detail, we provide a brief look at several products in Appendix 2.

THE COBB GROUP

The
Best

· GUARANTEED ·

Programming

Section Five

Programming
the LaserJet

Section Five documents Hewlett-Packard's Printer Command Language (PCL). As we have mentioned throughout *LaserJet Companion*, PCL is a collection of commands you can use to access and control the LaserJet's features.

We'll begin in Chapter 19 by introducing the levels of PCL and the process of sending PCL commands to the LaserJet. In Chapters 20 through 25 we'll examine in detail each PCL command supported by the LaserJet printer family. Throughout these chapters, we'll show you the form of each PCL command, and we'll provide you with a practical discussion of how and when you should use these commands. Finally, in Chapter 26, we'll document the structure of a PCL soft font.

PCL BASICS 19

In this chapter, we'll take a look at Hewlett-Packard's Printer Command Language (PCL) from a conceptual viewpoint. We'll discuss the history of PCL, the level of PCL support provided by each member of the LaserJet family, and the structure of PCL commands. Once we've done this, we'll consider the task of sending PCL commands to the HP LaserJet printer, and we'll look at a few commands that can simplify the task of debugging programs that communicate with the LaserJet.

CAPABILITIES

PCL was developed by Hewlett-Packard as a standard interface through which software can communicate with all HP printers. Although it has been implemented across the HP product line, PCL is best known as the language you must use to communicate with the LaserJet family of printers.

PCL is essentially a collection of commands. Each of these commands instructs a printer to perform a specific operation. For example, each member of the LaserJet printer family supports a PCL command that allows you to explicitly instruct it to print text using the page orientation that you specify.

At the time *LaserJet Companion* went to press, there were four different levels of PCL. Each of these levels supports a different set of commands and capabilities. Levels I, II, and III are supported by all members of the LaserJet printer family, while Level IV is supported by all members of the LaserJet printer family except the original LaserJet.

Each PCL level is a superset of the previous level. Therefore, you can assume that PCL Level IV incorporates all commands supported by PCL Levels I, II, and III. Also, all levels of PCL have the ability to ignore PCL commands they do not support. This allows you to use, with some degree of success, software written for newer PCL printers, such as the LaserJet Series II, with older PCL printers, such as the original LaserJet.

PCL Level I

PCL Level I is known in HP lingo as Print and Space PCL and is supported by all members of the LaserJet printer family. PCL Level I provides support for standard control codes, such as carriage returns and line feeds, as well as support for a small set of commands. The control codes and PCL commands supported by PCL Level I are listed in Table 19-1. We'll take an in-depth look at each of these commands throughout the next seven chapters.

TABLE 19-1

Control code	Description
CR	Carriage Return
LF	Line Feed
SP	Space
SO	Shift Out
SI	Shift In
ESC	Escape

PCL command	Description
E_{s_c}Y	Enables display functions mode
E_{s_c}Z	Disables display functions mode
E_{s_c}&d∅D	Enables underlining
E_{s_c}&d@	Disables underlining
E_{s_c}&k∅S	Sets primary and secondary font pitch to 10 cpi
E_{s_c}&k2S	Sets primary and secondary font pitch to 16.66 cpi
E_{s_c}&ℓ1L	Enables perforation skip mode
E_{s_c}&ℓ∅L	Disables perforation skip mode
E_{s_c}*r#A	Sets left margin in raster graphics mode
E_{s_c}*b#W [data]	Transfers raster graphics data
E_{s_c}*rB	Exits raster graphics mode

Legend

E_{s_c}	= Escape (ASCII 27 decimal, 1B hexadecimal)
ℓ	= Lowercase l (ASCII 108 decimal, 6C hexadecimal)
#	= User-definable parameter

These control codes and commands are supported by PCL Level I.

PCL Level II is known as EDP/Transaction PCL because it was intended for use in printers designed for transaction processing. It is supported by all members of the LaserJet printer family. PCL Level II supports all of the commands and control codes found in PCL Level I in addition to a number of new commands and a new control code. These new commands are listed in Table 19-2. We'll look at each of these commands throughout the next seven chapters.

PCL Level II

TABLE 19-2

Control code	Description
BS	Backspace
PCL command	**Description**
$E_{s_c}9$	Clears left and right margins
E_{s_c}&a#L	Sets left margin
E_{s_c}&a#M	Sets right margin
E_{s_c}&a#R	Moves cursor to row
E_{s_c}&a#C	Moves cursor to column
E_{s_c}&ℓ6D	Sets line spacing to 6 lpi
E_{s_c}&ℓ8D	Sets line spacing to 8 lpi
E_{s_c}&ℓ#F	Sets text length
E_{s_c}&ℓ#P	Sets page length
E_{s_c}([10]	Designates primary symbol set
E_{s_c})[10]	Designates secondary symbol set
E_{s_c}(s#H	Designates primary font pitch
E_{s_c})s#H	Designates secondary font pitch
E_{s_c}&p#X [data]	Transparent print data transfer command

Legend

E_{s_c} = Escape (ASCII 27 decimal, 1B hexadecimal)

ℓ = Lowercase l (ASCII 108 decimal, 6C hexadecimal)

= User-definable parameter

These control codes and commands are supported by PCL Level II.

PCL Level III is known as Office Word Processing PCL because it was designed for printers used for word processing. As you might expect, PCL Level III is supported by all members of the LaserJet printer family. In addition to a number of new commands, PCL Level III supports all of the commands and control codes found in PCL Levels I and II. The new commands offered by PCL Level III are listed in Table 19-3. We'll look at each of these commands throughout the next seven chapters.

PCL Level III

TABLE 19-3

PCL command	Description
E_{s_c}(s#P	Designates primary font spacing
E_{s_c})s#P	Designates secondary font spacing
E_{s_c}(s#S	Designates primary font style
E_{s_c})s#S	Designates secondary font style
E_{s_c}(s#B	Designates primary stroke weight
E_{s_c})s#B	Designates secondary stroke weight
E_{s_c}(s#T	Designates primary typeface
E_{s_c})s#T	Designates secondary typeface
E_{s_c}=	Sends half-line feed
E_{s_c}&k#H	Sets horizontal motion index
E_{s_c}&ℓ#C	Sets vertical motion index
E_{s_c}&a#H	Sets horizontal cursor position in decipoints
E_{s_c}&a#V	Sets vertical cursor position in decipoints

Legend

E_{s_c}	=	Escape (ASCII 27 decimal, 1B hexadecimal)
ℓ	=	Lowercase l (ASCII 108 decimal, 6C hexadecimal)
#	=	User-definable parameter

These control codes and commands are supported by PCL Level III.

PCL Level IV

PCL Level IV is known as Page Formatting PCL because it is intended for use in printers designed for desktop publishing. PCL Level IV is supported by all members of the LaserJet family except the original LaserJet. The most important new feature to PCL provided by PCL Level IV is support for soft fonts.

In addition to a substantial number of new commands and a new control code, PCL Level IV includes all of the commands and control codes found in PCL Levels I, II, and III. The new commands offered in PCL Level IV are listed in Table 19-4. We'll look at these commands throughout the next seven chapters.

TABLE 19-4

PCL command	Description
$^{E}s_c$(s#V	Designates primary font height
$^{E}s_c$)s#V	Designates secondary font height
$^{E}s_c$&ℓ#O	Sets page orientation
$^{E}s_c$&ℓ#E	Sets top margin
$^{E}s_c$*c#D	Assigns ID number to soft font
$^{E}s_c$*c#E	Specifies character code
$^{E}s_c$*c#F	Font and character control
$^{E}s_c$(s#W [data]	Downloads character command
$^{E}s_c$)s#W[data]	Downloads font descriptor command
$^{E}s_c$(s#X	Designates soft font as primary font
$^{E}s_c$)s#X	Designates soft font as secondary font
$^{E}s_c$*p#X	Positions horizontal cursor in dots
$^{E}s_c$*p#Y	Positions vertical cursor in dots
$^{E}s_c$*c#A	Specifies horizontal size of rule or pattern in dots
$^{E}s_c$*c#B	Specifies vertical size of rule or pattern in dots
$^{E}s_c$*c#H	Specifies horizontal size of rule or pattern in decipoints
$^{E}s_c$*c#V	Specifies vertical size of rule or pattern in decipoints
$^{E}s_c$*c#G	Specifies pattern ID or gray scale percentage
$^{E}s_c$*c#P	Fill rectangular area command
$^{E}s_c$&f#S	Push/pop cursor position command
$^{E}s_c$&f#X	Macro control command
$^{E}s_c$&f#Y	Assigns ID number to a macro

Legend

$^{E}s_c$	= Escape (ASCII 27 decimal, 1B hexadecimal)
ℓ	= Lowercase 1 (ASCII 108 decimal, 6C hexadecimal)
#	= User-definable parameter

These control codes and commands are supported by PCL Level IV.

PCL Extensions

The basic levels of PCL have extensions that take advantage of specific printer features. For example, several commands were added to the LaserJet 2000 and LaserJet IID version of PCL to take advantage of their ability to print on both sides of a page. All of the commands that have been added to the versions of PCL supported by the LaserJet printer family are listed in Table 19-5. We'll discuss these commands throughout the next seven chapters.

TABLE 19-5

Control code	Description
LaserJet Series II, IID, and 2000	
SP	Definable space character
HT	Horizontal tab

PCL command	Description
All LaserJets	
E_{s_c}&ℓ#D	Sets line spacing
E_{s_c}&a#R	Moves cursor to row
E_{s_c}&a#V	Moves cursor to column
E_{s_c}*r#R	Sets graphics resolution
E_{s_c}&k#G	Line termination command
E_{s_c}&sØC	Enables end-of-line wrap
E_{s_c}&s1C	Disables end-of-line wrap
E_{s_c}&ℓ#X	Sets number of copies
E_{s_c}&ℓ#H	Paper input control command
E_{s_c}&ℓ#E	Sets top margin
E_{s_c}(s#V	Designates primary font height
E_{s_c})s#V	Designates secondary font height
LaserJet 500 Plus and 2000	
E_{s_c}&ℓ1T	Job separation command
LaserJet Series II, IID, and 2000	
E_{s_c}&ℓ#A	Paper size command
E_{s_c}&d3D	Enables flexible underline
LaserJet IID and 2000	
E_{s_c}&ℓ#S	Simplex/Duplex print command
E_{s_c}&ℓ#U	Left offset registration command
E_{s_c}&ℓ#Z	Top offset registration command
E_{s_c}&a#G	Duplex page side selection command
E_{s_c}&*rF	Selects graphics presentation

Control code	Description
LaserJet 2000	
$^{E}s_c$&ℓ5H	PDX bin select command

Legend

$^{E}s_c$	=	Escape (ASCII 27 decimal, 1B hexadecimal)
ℓ	=	Lowercase l (ASCII 108 decimal, 6C hexadecimal)
#	=	User-definable parameter

These extensions to PCL provide access to, and control of, features supported by specific LaserJet printers.

PCL COMMAND STRUCTURE

Now that we've taken a brief look at each PCL command supported by the LaserJet printer family, we will discuss the three types of PCL commands—control codes, escape sequences, and parameterized escape sequences.

Control Codes

Control codes are ASCII codes that instruct the LaserJet to perform specific operations. For example, a form feed (ASCII 12 decimal, 0C hexadecimal) is a control code. Consequently, whenever you send a form feed to the LaserJet, it will eject a page. We'll discuss each control code supported by the LaserJet printer family in more detail in the following chapters.

Escape Sequences

Escape sequences begin with an escape character (ASCII 27 decimal, 1B hexadecimal) and are followed by a character that instructs the LaserJet to perform a specific operation. The LaserJet reset command, $^{E}s_c$E, is a typical example of an escape sequence. We'll look at the escape sequences supported by the LaserJet printer family in Chapters 20 through 26.

Parameterized Escape Sequences

The last and most prominent form of PCL command is the parameterized escape sequence. Parameterized escape sequences begin with an escape character that is followed by a number of characters that instruct the LaserJet to perform a specific operation. The PCL underline command, $^{E}s_c$&dØD, is an example of a parameterized escape sequence.

Parameterized escape sequences must contain user-specified parameters. For example, when you send a parameterized escape sequence to the LaserJet to set the left margin, you must include a parameter in the command that specifies the location at which the margin should be set. The form of a parameterized escape sequence is shown in Figure 19-1.

FIGURE 19-1

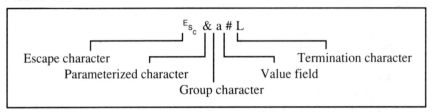

Parameterized escape sequences may contain parameters that allow you to perform a specific function.

Parameterized character

The parameterized character must be associated with ASCII codes 33 through 47 decimal. When a character associated with this range of ASCII codes follows an escape character, PCL will automatically assume that the command it is about to receive contains parameters. The parameterized character also defines the type of operation the command will perform.

Group character

The group character must be associated with ASCII codes 96 through 126 decimal. Its purpose is to identify the specific command or operation that an escape sequence will perform. For example, commands that contain the group character *s* are font-selection commands.

Value field

The value field is a user-definable parameter. In other words, the value you place in this field will be used by the LaserJet to perform a specific operation. For example, when you issue the command ᴱs_c&a1ØL, the LaserJet will set the left margin to the tenth column because the value field contains the value 10.

Many PCL commands allow or require you to place signed and/or fractional values in the value field. If you must place a negative value in the value field, you should indicate that it is a negative value by placing a minus sign (-) before it. Likewise, if you must specify a fractional value, you should use a decimal point (.) to mark the point between whole and fractional digits.

Termination character

The termination character must be associated with ASCII codes 64 through 94. The purpose of the termination character is to mark the end of an escape sequence and to identify the specific command or operation that will be performed. As we will show you in the next section, the termination character must be changed if you merge two or more PCL commands into a single command.

Merging Escape Sequences

If you want to send a series of escape sequences to the LaserJet, you may be able to merge them into a single command. Merging escape sequences allows you to save time and improve performance by eliminating unnecessary escape codes and group characters.

The only rule you must follow when merging commands is quite simple. If you want to merge two or more commands, the parameterized and group characters in those commands must be identical.

Once you have determined that the parameterized and group characters that appear in a series of commands are identical, you must change the termination character to lowercase in all but the last command that will appear in the merged command. You also must remove the parameterized character and group character from all but the first command that will appear in the merged command.

As an example, let's assume that you want to change page orientation from Portrait to Landscape and set the top margin to 10. To do this, you normally would send the commands $^E s_c \& \ell$ 1O and $^E s_c \& \ell$ 1ØE to the LaserJet. However, since the parameterized and group characters in each command match, you can merge them into a single command.

To merge the landscape and set top margin commands into a single command, change the landscape command's terminating character O to o, and remove the parameterized character & and group character ℓ from the set top margin command. The result is the command $^E s_c \& \ell$ 1o1ØE.

Most PCL commands instruct the LaserJet to perform a specific operation. For example, the set left margin command instructs the LaserJet to set its left margin to a value you specify. However, many PCL commands act as headers that tell the LaserJet it is about to receive bit-mapped data. The transfer raster data command is a prime example of this type of command.

The format of commands that act as headers to inform the LaserJet it is about to receive bit-mapped data is identical to that of any parameterized escape sequence. However, the value field in these commands is used to specify the number of bytes of data that will follow the command. For example, if you send the transfer raster data command, $^E s_c$*b512W, to the LaserJet, it will expect 512 bytes of bit-mapped data to follow.

Transferring Data with an Escape Sequence

Whenever the LaserJet receives an escape character, it will automatically assume that it is about to receive a PCL command. That's why it's very easy to send PCL commands to the LaserJet.

If you are writing a program in BASIC, C, Pascal, or any other language, you can send PCL commands to the LaserJet by sending them to the port to which the LaserJet is connected. For example, if your LaserJet is connected to LPT1:, you can send PCL commands to the LaserJet by sending them to LPT1:. Also, as we have illustrated in earlier chapters that show you how to use the LaserJet with applications software, it's possible to send PCL commands to the LaserJet by embedding them in a document or any batch of data that will be sent to the LaserJet.

SENDING PCL COMMANDS TO THE LASERJET

**PCL Command
Execution**

When you send a PCL command to the LaserJet, it will attempt to perform the operation specified by that command. If the command is valid, meaning that it is a command your LaserJet's PCL can execute, the command will be executed. If the command is not valid, the LaserJet will ignore it.

Debugging

While the capability to ignore invalid PCL commands makes it possible to use software written for new PCL printers on older PCL printers, it also creates problems when a PCL command contains a bug.

Just as any program you write will have a few bugs, it's probable that bugs will creep into PCL commands. Therefore, whenever you find that the results you are getting are not the results you expect, you can take advantage of two PCL commands that simplify the process of finding and removing PCL bugs. The first of these features allows you to instruct the LaserJet to print, rather than execute, PCL commands. The second feature allows you to print a report of current settings if you have a LaserJet Series II, LaserJet IID, or LaserJet 2000.

*Printing PCL
commands*

If you find that a PCL command you are sending to the LaserJet is not producing the results you expect, it's usually safe to assume that the command contains an invalid parameterized character, group character, value field, or termination character. The easiest way to determine if there is an error in a PCL command is to instruct the LaserJet to print it. Do this by issuing a display functions command.

The display functions command instructs the LaserJet to print all PCL commands it receives except the command necessary to turn the display functions option off. This command allows you to determine if commands are being sent to the LaserJet in the proper format. To turn the display functions option on, you should send the command $^{E}s_{c}$Y to the LaserJet. Send the command $^{E}s_{c}$Z to turn it off.

*Running a
self-test*

When you are programming the LaserJet Series II, IID, or 2000, you sometimes may find it useful to run a self-test. When you send a self-test command to your LaserJet, it will perform an internal check of all printer memory, fonts, and so forth, and will print a self-test page similar to the one shown in Figure 19-2.

As you can see in Figure 19-2, the LaserJet Series II self-test command will produce a printout that provides you with a summary listing the number of pages your LaserJet has printed, the version of the internal program and font ROM installed, and the amount of RAM installed in your LaserJet. It also provides you with the current status of the user-selectable default settings.

This information can be very helpful if you are trying to determine if a PCL command or series of PCL commands you have sent to the LaserJet have produced the results you desire. If you need to determine if the proper symbol set is currently selected, you can use the reset command to make such a determination.

FIGURE 19-2

```
Page Count=6743
Program ROM Datecode=19861203, Internal Font ROM Datecode=19860611
Auto Continue=ON
Installed Memory=2560 Kbytes
Symbol Set=ROMAN-8
Menu Items:
   Copies=1, Manual Feed=OFF, Font Source=I, Font Number=00,
   Form=60 Lines
Parallel I/O


 !"#$%&'()*+,-./0123456789:;<=>?@ABCDEFGHIJKLMNOPQRSTUVWXYZ[\]^_`abcdefghijklmno
!"#$%&'()*+,-./0123456789:;<=>?@ABCDEFGHIJKLMNOPQRSTUVWXYZ[\]^_`abcdefghijklmnop
"#$%&'()*+,-./0123456789:;<=>?@ABCDEFGHIJKLMNOPQRSTUVWXYZ[\]^_`abcdefghijklmnopq
#$%&'()*+,-./0123456789:;<=>?@ABCDEFGHIJKLMNOPQRSTUVWXYZ[\]^_`abcdefghijklmnopqr
$%&'()*+,-./0123456789:;<=>?@ABCDEFGHIJKLMNOPQRSTUVWXYZ[\]^_`abcdefghijklmnopqrs
%&'()*+,-./0123456789:;<=>?@ABCDEFGHIJKLMNOPQRSTUVWXYZ[\]^_`abcdefghijklmnopqrst
&'()*+,-./0123456789:;<=>?@ABCDEFGHIJKLMNOPQRSTUVWXYZ[\]^_`abcdefghijklmnopqrstu
'()*+,-./0123456789:;<=>?@ABCDEFGHIJKLMNOPQRSTUVWXYZ[\]^_`abcdefghijklmnopqrstuv
()*+,-./0123456789:;<=>?@ABCDEFGHIJKLMNOPQRSTUVWXYZ[\]^_`abcdefghijklmnopqrstuvw
)*+,-./0123456789:;<=>?@ABCDEFGHIJKLMNOPQRSTUVWXYZ[\]^_`abcdefghijklmnopqrstuvwx
*+,-./0123456789:;<=>?@ABCDEFGHIJKLMNOPQRSTUVWXYZ[\]^_`abcdefghijklmnopqrstuvwxy
+,-./0123456789:;<=>?@ABCDEFGHIJKLMNOPQRSTUVWXYZ[\]^_`abcdefghijklmnopqrstuvwxyz
,-./0123456789:;<=>?@ABCDEFGHIJKLMNOPQRSTUVWXYZ[\]^_`abcdefghijklmnopqrstuvwxyz{
-./0123456789:;<=>?@ABCDEFGHIJKLMNOPQRSTUVWXYZ[\]^_`abcdefghijklmnopqrstuvwxyz{|
./0123456789:;<=>?@ABCDEFGHIJKLMNOPQRSTUVWXYZ[\]^_`abcdefghijklmnopqrstuvwxyz{|}
/0123456789:;<=>?@ABCDEFGHIJKLMNOPQRSTUVWXYZ[\]^_`abcdefghijklmnopqrstuvwxyz{|}~
0123456789:;<=>?@ABCDEFGHIJKLMNOPQRSTUVWXYZ[\]^_`abcdefghijklmnopqrstuvwxyz{|}~▪
123456789:;<=>?@ABCDEFGHIJKLMNOPQRSTUVWXYZ[\]^_`abcdefghijklmnopqrstuvwxyz{|}~▪ 
23456789:;<=>?@ABCDEFGHIJKLMNOPQRSTUVWXYZ[\]^_`abcdefghijklmnopqrstuvwxyz{|}~▪ !
3456789:;<=>?@ABCDEFGHIJKLMNOPQRSTUVWXYZ[\]^_`abcdefghijklmnopqrstuvwxyz{|}~▪ !"
456789:;<=>?@ABCDEFGHIJKLMNOPQRSTUVWXYZ[\]^_`abcdefghijklmnopqrstuvwxyz{|}~▪ !"#
56789:;<=>?@ABCDEFGHIJKLMNOPQRSTUVWXYZ[\]^_`abcdefghijklmnopqrstuvwxyz{|}~▪ !"#$
6789:;<=>?@ABCDEFGHIJKLMNOPQRSTUVWXYZ[\]^_`abcdefghijklmnopqrstuvwxyz{|}~▪ !"#$%
789:;<=>?@ABCDEFGHIJKLMNOPQRSTUVWXYZ[\]^_`abcdefghijklmnopqrstuvwxyz{|}~▪ !"#$%&
89:;<=>?@ABCDEFGHIJKLMNOPQRSTUVWXYZ[\]^_`abcdefghijklmnopqrstuvwxyz{|}~▪ !"#$%&'
9:;<=>?@ABCDEFGHIJKLMNOPQRSTUVWXYZ[\]^_`abcdefghijklmnopqrstuvwxyz{|}~▪ !"#$%&'(
:;<=>?@ABCDEFGHIJKLMNOPQRSTUVWXYZ[\]^_`abcdefghijklmnopqrstuvwxyz{|}~▪ !"#$%&'()
;<=>?@ABCDEFGHIJKLMNOPQRSTUVWXYZ[\]^_`abcdefghijklmnopqrstuvwxyz{|}~▪ !"#$%&'()*
<=>?@ABCDEFGHIJKLMNOPQRSTUVWXYZ[\]^_`abcdefghijklmnopqrstuvwxyz{|}~▪ !"#$%&'()*+
 ÀÂÈÊËÎÏ´`ˆ¨˜ÙÛ£¯Ýý°ÇçÑñ¡¿¤£¥§ƒ¢âêôûáéóúàèòùäëöüÅîØÆåíøæÄìÖÜÉïßÔÁÃãĐđÍÌÓÒÕõŠšÚŸÿ
ÀÂÈÊËÎÏ´`ˆ¨˜ÙÛ£¯Ýý°ÇçÑñ¡¿¤£¥§ƒ¢âêôûáéóúàèòùäëöüÅîØÆåíøæÄìÖÜÉïßÔÁÃãĐđÍÌÓÒÕõŠšÚŸÿÞ
ÂÈÊËÎÏ´`ˆ¨˜ÙÛ£¯Ýý°ÇçÑñ¡¿¤£¥§ƒ¢âêôûáéóúàèòùäëöüÅîØÆåíøæÄìÖÜÉïßÔÁÃãĐđÍÌÓÒÕõŠšÚŸÿÞþ
ÈÊËÎÏ´`ˆ¨˜ÙÛ£¯Ýý°ÇçÑñ¡¿¤£¥§ƒ¢âêôûáéóúàèòùäëöüÅîØÆåíøæÄìÖÜÉïßÔÁÃãĐđÍÌÓÒÕõŠšÚŸÿÞþ·
ÊËÎÏ´`ˆ¨˜ÙÛ£¯Ýý°ÇçÑñ¡¿¤£¥§ƒ¢âêôûáéóúàèòùäëöüÅîØÆåíøæÄìÖÜÉïßÔÁÃãĐđÍÌÓÒÕõŠšÚŸÿÞþ·µ
ËÎÏ´`ˆ¨˜ÙÛ£¯Ýý°ÇçÑñ¡¿¤£¥§ƒ¢âêôûáéóúàèòùäëöüÅîØÆåíøæÄìÖÜÉïßÔÁÃãĐđÍÌÓÒÕõŠšÚŸÿÞþ·µ¶
ÎÏ´`ˆ¨˜ÙÛ£¯Ýý°ÇçÑñ¡¿¤£¥§ƒ¢âêôûáéóúàèòùäëöüÅîØÆåíøæÄìÖÜÉïßÔÁÃãĐđÍÌÓÒÕõŠšÚŸÿÞþ·µ¶¾
Ï´`ˆ¨˜ÙÛ£¯Ýý°ÇçÑñ¡¿¤£¥§ƒ¢âêôûáéóúàèòùäëöüÅîØÆåíøæÄìÖÜÉïßÔÁÃãĐđÍÌÓÒÕõŠšÚŸÿÞþ·µ¶¾—
´`ˆ¨˜ÙÛ£¯Ýý°ÇçÑñ¡¿¤£¥§ƒ¢âêôûáéóúàèòùäëöüÅîØÆåíøæÄìÖÜÉïßÔÁÃãĐđÍÌÓÒÕõŠšÚŸÿÞþ·µ¶¾—¼
`ˆ¨˜ÙÛ£¯Ýý°ÇçÑñ¡¿¤£¥§ƒ¢âêôûáéóúàèòùäëöüÅîØÆåíøæÄìÖÜÉïßÔÁÃãĐđÍÌÓÒÕõŠšÚŸÿÞþ·µ¶¾—¼½
ˆ¨˜ÙÛ£¯Ýý°ÇçÑñ¡¿¤£¥§ƒ¢âêôûáéóúàèòùäëöüÅîØÆåíøæÄìÖÜÉïßÔÁÃãĐđÍÌÓÒÕõŠšÚŸÿÞþ·µ¶¾—¼½ª
¨˜ÙÛ£¯Ýý°ÇçÑñ¡¿¤£¥§ƒ¢âêôûáéóúàèòùäëöüÅîØÆåíøæÄìÖÜÉïßÔÁÃãĐđÍÌÓÒÕõŠšÚŸÿÞþ·µ¶¾—¼½ªº
˜ÙÛ£¯Ýý°ÇçÑñ¡¿¤£¥§ƒ¢âêôûáéóúàèòùäëöüÅîØÆåíøæÄìÖÜÉïßÔÁÃãĐđÍÌÓÒÕõŠšÚŸÿÞþ·µ¶¾—¼½ªº«
ÙÛ£¯Ýý°ÇçÑñ¡¿¤£¥§ƒ¢âêôûáéóúàèòùäëöüÅîØÆåíøæÄìÖÜÉïßÔÁÃãĐđÍÌÓÒÕõŠšÚŸÿÞþ·µ¶¾—¼½ªº«■
Û£¯Ýý°ÇçÑñ¡¿¤£¥§ƒ¢âêôûáéóúàèòùäëöüÅîØÆåíøæÄìÖÜÉïßÔÁÃãĐđÍÌÓÒÕõŠšÚŸÿÞþ·µ¶¾—¼½ªº«■»
£¯Ýý°ÇçÑñ¡¿¤£¥§ƒ¢âêôûáéóúàèòùäëöüÅîØÆåíøæÄìÖÜÉïßÔÁÃãĐđÍÌÓÒÕõŠšÚŸÿÞþ·µ¶¾—¼½ªº«■»±
¯Ýý°ÇçÑñ¡¿¤£¥§ƒ¢âêôûáéóúàèòùäëöüÅîØÆåíøæÄìÖÜÉïßÔÁÃãĐđÍÌÓÒÕõŠšÚŸÿÞþ·µ¶¾—¼½ªº«■»± 
Ýý°ÇçÑñ¡¿¤£¥§ƒ¢âêôûáéóúàèòùäëöüÅîØÆåíøæÄìÖÜÉïßÔÁÃãĐđÍÌÓÒÕõŠšÚŸÿÞþ·µ¶¾—¼½ªº«■»± À
ý°ÇçÑñ¡¿¤£¥§ƒ¢âêôûáéóúàèòùäëöüÅîØÆåíøæÄìÖÜÉïßÔÁÃãĐđÍÌÓÒÕõŠšÚŸÿÞþ·µ¶¾—¼½ªº«■»± ÀÂ
```

The LaserJet will print a self-test page similar to this one whenever you send it a self-test command.

The command you must issue to perform a self-test is $^{E}s_{c}z$. If you send this command to the LaserJet, LaserJet Plus, or LaserJet 500 Plus, it will not provide you with a summary of internal settings. Instead, it will provide you with a page of characters similar to those that appear below the settings in the printout produced by the LaserJet Series II. Consequently, the self-test command is not a useful debugging tool if you are using a LaserJet, LaserJet Plus, or LaserJet 500 Plus.

Finally, if you send a self-test command to the LaserJet after you have sent text and/or graphics data, the LaserJet will print that text and/or graphics data before executing the self-test. For example, if you send a half-page of text to the LaserJet and then send a self-test command, the LaserJet will print that half-page of text before performing the self-test. Once the self-test is complete, the LaserJet will automatically place itself on-line and will be ready to accept print data or PCL commands from your computer.

CONCLUSION

After reading this chapter, you should have a basic idea of what PCL is, what it can do, and how it works. You should now be ready to tackle the discussions of specific PCL commands that we will explain throughout the next seven chapters.

CURSOR MOVEMENT **20**

While the HP LaserJet printer is not a video monitor, the technology on which both are based is very similar. Just as a video monitor is divided into a grid on which it displays an image by arranging dots in a specific pattern, the LaserJet produces images by printing a specific pattern of dots on a conceptual grid. Consequently, just as computer monitors often have cursors that indicate the position at which a dot or character will appear, the LaserJet has an internal cursor that does the same.

In this chapter, we'll begin by discussing the system that defines the method you must use to address each dot on a page. After we've done this, we'll look at the PCL commands you must use to position the cursor on a page.

PCL COORDINATE SYSTEM

PCL treats a page as if it were a sheet of graph paper. In other words, each page is divided into a grid. In this grid, each square, which is called a dot, is $^1/_{300}$ inch tall and $^1/_{300}$ inch wide. The PCL Coordinate System defines the units and methods you must use to address each point on this grid.

Each dot on a page can be addressed using standard (x,y) coordinates. Therefore, as you might expect, the coordinate of the dot located at the top-left corner of a page is (0,0). This concept is illustrated in Figure 20-1.

FIGURE 20-1

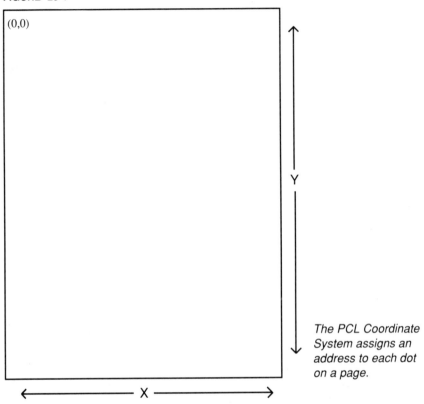

(0,0)

Y

X

The PCL Coordinate
System assigns an
address to each dot
on a page.

Physical Page

The term physical page refers to the dimensions of an actual sheet of paper. The physical size of each type of paper that can be used with the LaserJet family of printers is shown in Table 20-1. As we will explain shortly, LaserJet printers cannot address, and therefore cannot print on, the entire physical page.

Logical Page

The term logical page refers to the area of a page that can be addressed with the PCL Coordinate System. As you can see in Table 20-2, the length of the logical page is equal to that of the physical page, but the width is shorter because LaserJet printers cannot print in regions along the left and the right borders of a page. The width of each of these regions is 50 dots.

TABLE 20-1

Paper type	Width (dots)	Length (dots)
Letter	2550	3300
Executive	2175	3150
Legal	2550	4200
Ledger	3300	5100
A4	2480	3507
A3	3507	4960
B5	2151	3036

This table shows the physical size of each type of paper that may be used with the LaserJet family of printers.

TABLE 20-2

Paper type	Width (dots)	Length (dots)
Letter	2450	3300
Executive	2075	3150
Legal	2450	4200
Ledger	3200	5100
A4	2380	3507
A3	3407	4960
B5	2051	3036

This table shows the logical size of each type of paper that may be used with the LaserJet family of printers.

Printable Area

The printable area is the most important area of a page because, as its name implies, it is the area of a page on which you can actually print. Since the LaserJet cannot print in regions along each border of a page, the printable area will always be smaller than the physical page. The printable area of each type of paper you can use with the LaserJet printer family is shown in Table 20-3.

TABLE 20-3

Paper type	Width (dots)	Length (dots)
Letter	2450	3200
Executive	2075	3050
Legal	2450	4100
Ledger	3200	5000
A4	2380	3407
A3	3407	4860
B5	2051	2936

This table shows the printable area of each type of paper that may be used with the LaserJet family of printers.

Dealing with the Unprintable Area

The area in which the LaserJet cannot print is known as the unprintable area and extends 50 dots from each border. Whenever you set the left, right, top, or bottom margin when printing with the LaserJet, you always must consider the fact that those margins will be set in relation to the area of the page in which you can print, not in relation to the physical size of the page. For example, if you want to set a 1-inch left margin, you must set it in relation to the unprintable region. In other words, to set a 1-inch left margin, you must tell the LaserJet to set it 250 dots from the left edge of the printable area of the page. When added to the 50-dot unprintable region, this will produce a 1-inch margin.

Finally, whenever you issue a command to print text or graphics in the unprintable region, the LaserJet will simply ignore the command. However, if only a portion of a graphic falls outside the printable area, the LaserJet will print the portion that is within the boundaries of the printable area.

If you attempt to print a portion of a character in the unprintable region, the LaserJet (with the exception of the LaserJet 2000) won't print the character at all. The LaserJet 2000 will print only the portion of the character that falls inside the printable area.

MOVING THE CURSOR

When you position the cursor along the horizontal axis of a page, you may use dots, decipoints, or columns. Likewise, you may specify the position of the cursor along the vertical axis of a page using dots, decipoints, or rows.

As we pointed out earlier, each dot is $1/300$ inch tall and $1/300$ inch wide. Each decipoint is equal to $1/720$ inch. The size of a column, however, will vary.

If you are using a fixed-pitch font such as the LaserJet's Internal Courier font, the width of a column will be equal to the pitch of the font. For example, if you use the LaserJet's 10-pitch Internal Courier font, each column will be $^{30}/_{300}$ inch wide. You can adjust the width of columns when using fixed-pitch fonts by setting the Horizontal Motion Index (HMI). We'll show you how to do this in Chapter 22.

If you are using a proportionally spaced font, the width of a column is determined by the HMI setting. The HMI is automatically set to reflect the width of the space character whenever you select a proportionally spaced font. For example, if you use a proportionally spaced font whose space character is $^{30}/_{300}$ inch wide, the cursor will move $^{30}/_{300}$ inch each time you instruct it to move one column.

Finally, the size of each row depends on the height of the specific font you are using, as well as the amount of leading (white space) that is reserved between lines of text. If you can print eight lines per inch and instruct the LaserJet to move the cursor eight rows down or up, the cursor will move one inch. We'll show you how to use this information to modify the size of a row in Chapter 22.

Specifying the Horizontal Cursor Position

You may use any one of three commands to specify the position of the cursor along the horizontal axis of the logical page. The first of these commands, $^{E}s_{c}$&a#C, allows you to specify the horizontal position of the cursor using columns. The second command, $^{E}s_{c}$&a#H, may be used to specify the horizontal position of the cursor using decipoints. Finally, the third command, $^{E}s_{c}$*p#X, may be used to specify the horizontal position of the cursor using dots.

When you send any of these three commands to the LaserJet, replace the character # with a value equal to the absolute or relative position of the cursor. If you place a plus sign (+) before the cursor value, the cursor will be moved to the right of the current cursor position. The cursor will be moved to the left of the current cursor position if you place a minus sign (-) before the cursor value. We'll discuss relative cursor positioning in more detail in a few moments.

Carriage return

In Chapter 19, we mentioned that certain characters, known as control codes, may be used to instruct the LaserJet to perform specific operations. A carriage return is such a character. Its purpose is to move the cursor from the current horizontal position to the left margin boundary when you are printing text.

To execute a carriage return, you must send the ASCII code 12 decimal, 0C hexadecimal to the LaserJet. When the LaserJet receives this code, it will automatically return the cursor to the presently selected left margin. We'll show you how to set the left margin in Chapter 22.

Space

The space character is a control code that may be used to move the cursor along the horizontal axis of a page when you are printing text. It is represented by ASCII code 32 decimal, 20 hexadecimal. When the LaserJet receives this ASCII code, it will automatically advance the cursor one column to the right. As we pointed out earlier, the exact amount of space the cursor will move when it receives a space character is determined by the Horizontal Motion Index (HMI) setting.

Backspace

The backspace character is a control code that moves the cursor to the left. The backspace character is represented by the ASCII code 8 decimal, 08 hexadecimal. When it receives this ASCII code, the LaserJet will automatically move the cursor one column to the left. As you might expect, the exact amount of space the cursor will move when it receives a backspace character is determined by the Horizontal Motion Index (HMI) setting.

Horizontal tab

The last control code that may be used to move the cursor along the horizontal axis of a page is the horizontal tab character. When it receives a horizontal tab, the LaserJet will automatically move the cursor to the next tab stop. Tab stops begin at the left margin and are located at every eighth column. To execute a horizontal tab, you must send the ASCII code 9 decimal, 09 hexadecimal to the LaserJet.

Specifying the Vertical Cursor Position

Three commands may be used to specify the vertical position of the cursor on the logical page. The first command, E_{s_c}&a#R, allows you to specify the position of the cursor using rows. The second command, E_{s_c}&a#V, may be used to specify the vertical position of the cursor using decipoints. Finally, the third command, E_{s_c}*p#Y, allows you to specify the vertical position of the cursor using dots.

When you send any of these three commands to the LaserJet, replace the character # with a value equal to the absolute or relative position of the cursor. If you place a plus sign (+) before the cursor value, the cursor will be moved up in relation to the current cursor position. The cursor will be moved down if you place a minus sign (-) before the cursor value.

Line feed

Just as other control codes allow you to move the cursor along the horizontal axis of a page when printing text, the line feed control code allows you to move the cursor along the vertical axis. The line feed is represented by the ASCII code 10 decimal, 0A hexadecimal.

When the LaserJet receives a line feed, it will automatically move the cursor down the logical page. However, the amount of space it will move is controlled by the setting that determines the number of lines per inch the LaserJet will print. For example, by default, the LaserJet can print six lines per inch. Therefore, a line feed will cause the LaserJet to move the cursor $\frac{1}{6}$ inch down a page. Later in this chapter, we'll show you how to change the number of lines your LaserJet will print in an inch.

Half-line feed

At some point, you might find it helpful to send a half-line feed to the LaserJet. To do this, send the command E_{s_c}= to the LaserJet. When the LaserJet receives this command, it will move the cursor down the logical page.

Just as in the case of a normal line feed, the amount of space the cursor will move when the LaserJet receives a half-line feed command is determined by the number of lines per inch the LaserJet will print. Therefore, if the LaserJet prints six lines per inch by default, a half-line feed command will move the cursor down $\frac{1}{12}$ inch.

The last control code we will discuss is the form feed. When the LaserJet receives a form feed, it will immediately eject the page that is currently being printed. The form feed is represented by the ASCII code 12 decimal, 0C hexadecimal.

Form feed

As we pointed out in Chapter 2, all LaserJet printers will eject a page if you attempt to print more lines than will fit on that page. If the number of lines you want to print is less than the number that can be printed on a page, you must send a form feed control code to the LaserJet.

Whenever your LaserJet receives a carriage return, it will return the cursor to the start of the current line. Likewise, whenever the LaserJet receives a line feed, it will immediately advance one line without changing the position of the cursor on the x-axis of the page. Finally, whenever the LaserJet receives a form feed, it will automatically print and eject whatever page is currently being printed.

Line Termination

At some point, you may encounter a situation where it will be necessary to modify the way in which the LaserJet reacts to a line feed, carriage return, or form feed. It is possible to do this by sending a line termination command.

The format of the line termination command is $^E s_c$&k#G. To specify how the LaserJet should translate carriage returns, line feeds, and form feeds, simply send this command to the LaserJet—replacing the character # with one of the values listed in Table 20-4.

TABLE 20-4

Value	Control code translation		
	CR	**LF**	**FF**
Ø	CR	LF	FF
1	CR+LF	LF	FF
2	CR	CR+LF	CR+FF
3	CR+FF	CR+FF	CR+FF

By including the appropriate value in the line termination command, you may determine how your LaserJet will react when it receives a carriage return, line feed, or form feed.

In addition to being able to specify the position of the cursor in dots, decipoints, rows, and columns, you may specify the position in absolute or relative terms. When you specify the position of the cursor in absolute terms, you must specify the coordinate of the position on the logical page. However, when you specify the position of the cursor in relative terms, you must do so in relation to the position at which the cursor is currently located.

Absolute vs. Relative Cursor Positioning

For example, let's assume that the cursor is positioned at the dot located at coordinate (100,100), and you want to move it to coordinate (200,200). To move the cursor to (200,200) in absolute terms, you must explicitly instruct the LaserJet to move it to that point by issuing the commands $^E s_c$*p2ØØX and $^E s_c$*p2ØØY. However, to move it to (200,200) in relative terms, you merely have to tell the LaserJet to move 100 dots in the appropriate direction along the x-axis and y-axis by issuing the commands $^E s_c$*p+1ØØX and $^E s_c$*p+1ØØY.

While absolute cursor positioning is useful, you will find that relative cursor positioning is more flexible because it provides you with the ability to print text or graphics regardless of the orientation of the page on which you are printing.

Storing the Cursor Position on the Stack

All common microprocessors support a construct known as a stack. A stack is essentially a place where you can store values by piling them on top of one another. Stacks are LIFO (Last In, First Out) devices—meaning that when you place several values on a stack, you must retrieve them in reverse order.

PCL supports a stack on which you may place as many as 20 cursor positions. You may find this to be an extremely useful tool whenever you use relative cursor positioning. For example, if you want to move the cursor from a specific location but plan to return to that position later, you may store it on the PCL stack and retrieve it when it is needed.

To place (push) the current position of the cursor on the stack, you must issue the command $^E s_c$&fØS. To remove (pop) a value from the stack, you must issue the command $^E s_c$&f1S.

For example, let's suppose that the cursor is located at coordinate (100,100) and you want to move it to coordinate (200,200) before returning to (100,100). To do this using relative cursor positioning, you should begin by issuing the command $^E s_c$&fØS to place the position (100,100) on the stack. Once you have done this, issue the commands $^E s_c$*p+1ØØX and $^E s_c$*p+1ØØY to move the cursor to (200,200), then issue the command $^E s_c$&f1S to pop the coordinate (100,100) from the stack. When you pop the value (100,100) from the stack, the cursor will automatically be placed at that coordinate.

CONCLUSION

In this chapter, we've discussed the PCL Coordinate System, and we've looked at the PCL commands that allow you to position the cursor on a page. Once you understand the PCL Coordinate System, you're ready for Chapters 21 through 24, in which we look at the commands that format a page, print text, and print graphics.

JOB CONTROL 21

Before you send text or graphics to the LaserJet, you must issue several job control commands. These commands prepare the LaserJet to print the series of pages that will follow and allow you to take advantage of features specific to particular members of the LaserJet printer family. We'll look at these commands in this chapter.

JOB CONTROL

The term job is used to refer to a specific series of pages that are considered to be a single entity. For example, if you send a ten-page term paper to the LaserJet, the ten pages will be considered a single job.

The commands we will look at in this chapter are called job control commands because they affect and control the LaserJet's operation when a job is processed. An example of a job control command is the number of copies command. As we will discuss shortly, this command allows you to specify how many copies should be printed when you send a specific document to the LaserJet.

RESETTING THE LASERJET

Just as you can reset your PC by pressing [Ctrl][Alt][Del], you can reset your LaserJet by issuing a reset command. When you send this command to the LaserJet, several things will occur. First, all temporary soft fonts and/or macros that were stored in the LaserJet's RAM will be deleted. Second, all job control and page settings will be restored to their default state. Finally, if the LaserJet has received any text and/or graphics data before receiving a reset command, it will print that text and/or graphics data before executing the reset command.

As a rule, you should send a reset command to the LaserJet at the beginning and end of each print job. This command, $^E_{s_c}$E, will ensure that any changes you make to job control or page settings while printing one document will not infringe upon another document.

PRINTING MULTIPLE COPIES

All members of the LaserJet family have the ability to print up to 99 copies of any document automatically. In other words, once you send to the LaserJet the data necessary to produce a document, it is possible to produce as many as 99 copies of that document without resending data for each copy.

By default, the LaserJet will print only one copy of each page. However, whenever you send a number of copies command to the LaserJet, the number that you specify in that command will become the default value until you issue another number of copies command or reset the LaserJet.

You must use the number of copies command to specify the number of copies that should be printed when you send a document to the LaserJet. The format of this command is $^E_{s_c}$&ℓ#X. However, when you send this command to the LaserJet, you must replace the # character with a value between 1 and 99.

As an example, let's assume that you want the LaserJet to print two copies of a document. To do this, send the command $^E_{s_c}$&ℓ2X to the LaserJet before you send the actual text and/or graphics data that will be printed.

DUPLEX PRINTING

As we pointed out in Chapter 19, the versions of PCL supported by the LaserJet IID and LaserJet 2000 contain commands that allow you to take advantage of each printer's ability to automatically print text on both sides of a page (duplex mode).

To tell your LaserJet IID or LaserJet 2000 that it should print in duplex mode, you must issue a simplex/duplex command. The format of this command is $^E_{s_c}$&ℓ#S. However, when you send the simplex/duplex command to your LaserJet, you must replace the # character with a value that selects the print mode.

For example, the command $^E_{s_c}$&ℓØS tells the LaserJet that it should print in normal simplex mode, while the command $^E_{s_c}$&ℓ1S tells the LaserJet that it should print in vertical binding duplex mode. Finally, the command $^E_{s_c}$&ℓ2S tells the LaserJet that it should print in horizontal binding duplex mode.

Binding Modes

While the LaserJet IID and LaserJet 2000 cannot actually bind pages together, they can print a series of pages suitable for binding. When you use the duplex capabilities of the LaserJet IID and LaserJet 2000 to print a series of pages, you must specify how you want to bind those pages. The LaserJet IID and LaserJet 2000 will then print that series of pages so that you can bind them as you have specified.

Vertical binding

The vast majority of printed matter, including *LaserJet Companion*, is bound along the long edge of each page. This is known as vertical binding. To tell your LaserJet IID or LaserJet 2000 to print a series of pages so that they can be bound vertically, issue the simplex/duplex command $^E_{s_c}$&ℓ1S.

When you use the vertical binding mode while printing in Portrait mode, your LaserJet will automatically shift to the right text and graphics printed on the front of the pages, while it will shift to the left text and graphics printed on the back of the pages. This shifting results in extra white space along the appropriate edge of each page. This space allows pages to be bound vertically without obstructing a portion of the printed area.

If you are printing in Landscape mode and use the vertical binding mode, your LaserJet IID or LaserJet 2000 will automatically shift the position of text and graphics down as it prints the front and back of each page. This provides extra white space along the long edge of each page, which allows the pages to be bound without obstructing a portion of the printed area. Also, whenever you use the vertical binding mode while printing in Landscape mode, the LaserJet IID and LaserJet 2000 will automatically rotate text and graphics printed on the back of each page 180 degrees. It does this so that the text and/or graphics on the back of the page will be readable once a series of pages are bound.

Horizontal binding

While most documents are bound along the long edge of each page, some are bound along the short edge. This type of binding is referred to as horizontal binding. To tell your LaserJet IID or LaserJet 2000 to print a series of pages so that they may be horizontally bound, issue the simplex/duplex command $^E{}_{s_c}\&\ell\,2S$.

When you use the horizontal binding mode while printing in Portrait mode, your LaserJet IID or LaserJet 2000 will automatically shift the position of text and graphics down as it prints the front and back of each page. This provides extra white space along the appropriate edge of each page, which allows pages to be bound horizontally without obstructing a portion of the printed area. Also, whenever you use the horizontal binding mode while printing in Portrait mode, the LaserJet IID and LaserJet 2000 will automatically rotate text and graphics printed on the back of each page 180 degrees. It does this so that the text and/or graphics on the back of the page will be readable once a series of pages is bound.

When you use the horizontal binding mode while printing in Landscape mode, your LaserJet will automatically shift to the right text and graphics printed on the front of pages, while it will shift to the left text and graphics printed on the back of pages. The result of this shift is extra white space along the appropriate edge of each page. This space allows pages to be bound horizontally without obstructing a portion of the printed area.

Choosing the appropriate binding mode

Now that we've discussed the basic concepts of vertical and horizontal binding, it's time to consider when to use each mode. You should use the vertical binding mode whenever you are printing in Portrait mode and want to bind a series of pages so that they can be flipped from left to right. You should also use the vertical binding mode whenever you are printing in Landscape mode and want to bind a series of pages so that they can be flipped from top to bottom. Figure 21-1 shows examples of vertical binding.

FIGURE 21-1

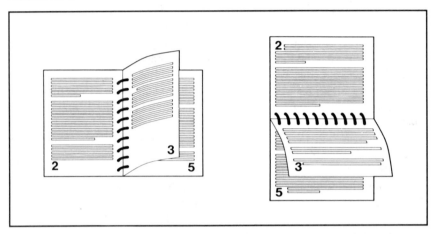

You should tell your LaserJet IID or LaserJet 2000 to use vertical binding whenever you want to bind documents along the long edge of a page.

If you want to print a series of pages in Portrait mode and want to bind them so that they can be flipped from top to bottom, you should use the horizontal binding mode. You should also use the horizontal binding mode whenever you are printing in Landscape mode and want to bind a series of pages so that they can be flipped from left to right. Figure 21-2 on the next page illustrates horizontal binding.

Left and Top Offset Registration

As we mentioned earlier, when you use the ability of the LaserJet IID and LaserJet 2000 to print text on both sides of a page, the position of any text or graphics printed will be shifted away from the edge of the page that will be bound. You can control the actual distance the text or graphics will be shifted with the left and top offset registration commands.

You can specify the distance between the left edge of a page and your text and/or graphics by issuing a left offset registration command. The format of this command is $^E s_c \& \ell \#U$. When you send this command to the LaserJet, replace the # character with a value equal to the number of decipoints between your data and the left edge of the page.

Likewise, you may specify the distance your LaserJet will shift text and/or graphics away from the top edge of a page by issuing a top offset registration command. The format of the top offset registration command is $^E s_c \& \ell \#Z$.   When you send this command to the LaserJet, replace the # character with a value equal to the number of decipoints between the text and/or graphics and the top edge of a page.

FIGURE 21-2

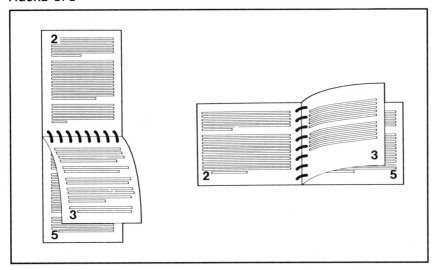

You should tell your LaserJet IID or LasetJet 2000 to use horizontal binding whenever you want to bind documents along the short edge of a page.

Finally, the value that determines the amount of space between text or graphics and the left or top edge of a page when printing in duplex mode can be negative or positive, depending on the direction in which you want your LaserJet IID or LaserJet 2000 to move text and graphics in relation to the default position of the logical page. It also may include as many as four decimal places. For example -704.2342, 403.0292, 310, and 0.25 are all values that can be used in the left and top offset registration commands.

Page Side Selection

Sometimes when you are printing a series of pages using the duplex option, you may find it necessary to skip a page. In other words, you may run into a situation where you want to print on the front of a page, but not on the back.

To skip a page, you may issue a page side selection command. The format of this command is ^{E}s$_c$&a#G. When you send a page side selection command to the LaserJet, replace the # character with a value that selects the side of a page on which you want to print.

If you want to print on the next side of a page, regardless of whether it is the front or back, issue the command ^{E}s$_c$&aØG. If the next side of a page on which you want to print must be the front side, issue the command ^{E}s$_c$&a1G. If the next side of a page on which you want to print must be the back side, issue the command ^{E}s$_c$&a2G.

JOB SEPARATION

The LaserJet 500 Plus and LaserJet 2000 both have the ability to separate documents as they are stacked in the output tray. This ability is made possible by the job separation command, ^{E}s$_c$&ℓ1T, which should be included at the beginning of each job immediately following the reset command. If you send a job separation command to any member of the LaserJet printer family other than the LaserJet 500 Plus or LaserJet 2000, the command will be ignored.

The LaserJet 500 Plus separates jobs by stacking pages in one of two positions. By default, it will stack pages in what is considered to be the normal position. However, once it receives a job separation command, the LaserJet 500 Plus will begin stacking pages in the offset position. A subsequent job separation command will instruct the LaserJet 500 Plus to stack pages in the normal position.

The LaserJet 2000 separates jobs by ejecting an extra page each time it receives a job separation command. A heavy black bar is printed on the front edge of that page to further simplify the task of determining where one job ends and another begins.

USING JOB CONTROL COMMANDS

Now that we've had a chance to look at the PCL commands that allow you to reset the LaserJet, select the number of copies, and set the appropriate duplex print mode, it is a good time to consider how these commands might be sent to the LaserJet.

As we pointed out in Chapter 19, you can send PCL commands to the LaserJet by embedding them in a stream of text data. PCL commands can also be sent to the LaserJet directly by programs written in BASIC, C, Pascal, or any other computer language. As an example, we'll show you a small Microsoft GW-BASIC program that sends PCL job control commands to the LaserJet.

Each line of the Microsoft GW-BASIC program shown in Figure 21-3 sends a particular PCL job control command to the LaserJet. For example, line 10 sends a reset command to the LaserJet. As we pointed out earlier, this command instructs the LaserJet to reset all settings controlled by job and page control commands to their default values. Line 20 sends a number of copies command that instructs the LaserJet to print two copies of each page. Finally, line 30 instructs a LaserJet IID or LaserJet 2000 to print documents using the duplex vertical binding mode.

FIGURE 21-3

```
10 LPRINT CHR$(27);"E"
20 LPRINT CHR$(27);"&l2X"
30 LPRINT CHR$(27);"&l1S"
```

This Microsoft GW-BASIC program is a typical example of a program that uses PCL job control commands, such as those that allow you to reset the LaserJet and to specify the number of copies of each page to be printed.

In this chapter, we've discussed the PCL commands you can use to reset the LaserJet or define the number of copies the LaserJet will print. We've also looked at the PCL commands you can use to take advantage of the ability of the LaserJet IID and LaserJet 2000 to print text on both sides of a page. Therefore, you now should be able to write software that will communicate with the LaserJet using these commands.

CONCLUSION

PAGE CONTROL 22

Each member of the HP LaserJet printer family supports a number of PCL commands that allow you to manipulate the position of text and graphics on a page. With these commands, you can define the size of the area on a page in which you want to print text and graphics. In this chapter, we'll show you how you use page formatting commands to set page margins and define the length of a page.

The first, and probably most important, page control command is the paper source command. This command allows you to select the actual source from which the LaserJet will feed paper when you print a document.

All members of the LaserJet printer family have the ability to feed paper from at least two sources—the internal paper tray and the manual feed slot. Several members of the LaserJet family also have the ability to feed paper from other paper trays. To specify the source from which your LaserJet will feed paper, you must issue a paper source command.

The format of the paper source command is $^E_{s_c}$&ℓ#H. When you send this command to the LaserJet, replace the # character with the value associated with the paper source from which you want to feed paper. All seven paper sources and the values associated with each are listed in Table 22-1.

Each of the values that appear in Table 22-1 represents a possible LaserJet paper source. Therefore, whenever you include one of these values in the paper source command, the LaserJet will feed paper from the source associated with the command. Finally, while values 1 through 6 are associated with specific paper sources, the value Ø is not. When included in a paper source command, this value instructs the LaserJet to feed paper from the currently selected paper source.

TABLE 22-1

Value	Paper source	LaserJet model
Ø	Current source	All LaserJets
1	Upper tray	All LaserJets
2	Manual feed	All LaserJets
3	Manual envelope input	All LaserJets
4	Lower tray	LaserJet 500 Plus, IID, 2000
5	Paper Deck (PDX)	LaserJet 2000 (optional)
6	Envelope feeder	LaserJet IID (optional)

By including the appropriate value in the paper input control command, you can select the source from which your LaserJet will feed paper.

CHOOSING THE TYPE OF PAPER

After you have chosen the source from which your LaserJet will feed paper, you must tell the LaserJet what type of paper you plan to use. For example, if you want to print a document on legal-size paper, you must tell the LaserJet to use that size. Otherwise, the LaserJet will always assume that you are using standard letter-size paper.

Using the Page Length Command

The page length command can be used to select the type of paper you want to use, regardless of which LaserJet you are using. Therefore, if compatibility with the entire LaserJet printer family is your goal, you should always use this command to select the type of paper you will need.

The page length command's format is $E_{s_c}\&\ell\#P$. When you send this command to the LaserJet, replace the # character with a value equal to the total number of lines your LaserJet will be able to print on a page.

Vertical Motion Index

To determine the number of lines your LaserJet can print on a page, you must consider the Vertical Motion Index (VMI). The VMI defines the number of lines your LaserJet can print in one inch. By default, the VMI is set to $^8/_{48}$ inch, which allows you to print six lines per inch. The format of the command you must use to change the VMI is $E_{s_c}\&\ell\#C$. When you send this command to the LaserJet, replace the # character with the appropriate value. For example, if you want to set the VMI so that it will allow the LaserJet to print eight lines per inch, you must issue the command $E_{s_c}\&\ell6C$, where the 6 represents $^6/_{48}$ inch.

Selecting paper with the page length command

Now that we've shown you how to specify the number of lines your LaserJet will print in one inch, we'll show you how to use the page length command to select the type of paper you want to use. First, you must determine the number of lines the LaserJet can print on the type of paper you want to use by multiplying the number of inches your LaserJet will print in an inch by the length of the page. For example, if the current VMI specifies that your LaserJet will print six lines per inch, and you want to use letter-size paper that is 11 inches long, the LaserJet will be able to print 66 lines on that page.

Once you have determined the total number of lines the LaserJet can print on the type of paper you want to use, you should send that value to the LaserJet within a page length command. For example, to select standard letter-size paper, you should send the command $^E\!s_c\&\ell66P$ to the LaserJet.

Finally, the length of each type of paper that can be used with the LaserJet printer family while in Portrait mode is listed in Table 22-2. As you can see, lengths are provided for the LaserJet's standard VMI setting, which allows it to print six lines per inch, as well as for a VMI setting that allows the LaserJet to print eight lines per inch.

TABLE 22-2

Paper	Value	
	6 lpi	**8 lpi**
Default	Ø	Ø
Letter	66	88
Legal	84	112
Executive	63	84
A4	70	93
B5	60	80

You can select any of these types of paper while in Portrait mode by sending the appropriate page length to the LaserJet with the page length command.

If you want to use the page length command to select a particular type of paper for Landscape printing, you should switch the LaserJet into Landscape mode by issuing the command $^E\!s_c\&\ell1O$ immediately before you issue a page length command. Table 22-3 shows the values you can include in a page length command to select each type of paper that can be used with the LaserJet printer family while in Landscape mode.

Finally, when you issue a page length command that selects a type of paper other than the one currently being used, the LaserJet will display a message on the control panel. This message will prompt you to feed into the LaserJet the type of paper you specified with the page length command. Once you have fed the appropriate type of paper, you must press the CONTINUE button on the control panel before the LaserJet will be able to print a document.

TABLE 22-3

Paper	Value	
	6 lpi	8 lpi
Default	Ø	Ø
Letter	51	68
Legal	84	112
Executive	43	58
A4	49	66
B5	41	46

You can select any of these types of paper while in Landscape mode by sending the appropriate page length to the LaserJet with the page length command.

Using the Page Size Command

If you use a LaserJet Series II, LaserJet IID, or LaserJet 2000, you can use the page size command to tell the LaserJet which type of paper you are using or to tell it that you are using an envelope. The format of the page size command is $E_{s_c}\&\ell\#A$. To choose a specific type of paper or envelope with this command, replace the # character with one of the values listed in Table 22-4.

TABLE 22-4

Value	Paper	Value	Envelopes
1	Executive	8Ø	Monarch
2	Letter	81	Commercial 10
3	Legal	9Ø	International DL
26	A4	91	International C5

By including the appropriate value in a page size command, you can select the size of paper or envelope your LaserJet will use to print a document.

If your LaserJet has received any text and/or graphics data before it receives a page size command, it will print that text and/or graphics data before executing the page size command. For example, if you send a half-page of text to the LaserJet and then send a page size command, the LaserJet will print that half page of text before executing the page size command.

In addition, whenever you issue a page size command, the LaserJet will automatically reset all margins to their default values, and any macro that has been overlayed will be disabled. We'll discuss macros in detail in Chapter 25.

Finally, when you issue a page size command that selects a size of paper or envelope other than the one currently being used, the LaserJet will display a message on the control panel. This message will prompt you to feed into the

LaserJet the size of paper or type of envelope the page size command specifies. Once you have done this, you must press the CONTINUE button on the control panel before the LaserJet will be able to print the document that follows the page size command.

SETTING MARGINS

In Chapter 20, we explained that the area on a page in which the LaserJet can print text is called the printable area. We also pointed out that you can limit and/or adjust the boundaries of this area by adjusting the LaserJet's internal margin settings. Now, we'll show you how to make changes to these margin settings.

Defining Line and Character Spacing

Before you can define the length of a page or a margin setting, you must specify the number of lines and characters your LaserJet will print in an inch. To define the number of characters that can be printed in one inch, you must use the Horizontal Motion Index (HMI) command. You can define the number of lines that can be printed in one inch by issuing a Vertical Motion Index (VMI) command. However, if you have a LaserJet Plus, 500 Plus, Series II, IID, or 2000, you can use the line spacing command to achieve the same result.

Horizontal Motion Index

The Horizontal Motion Index (HMI) defines the amount of space your LaserJet will reserve between columns when it is printing fixed-space text. By default, the HMI is set to $^{12}/_{120}$ inch, which is equivalent to ten characters per inch.

The format of the command you must use to define the HMI is $^{E}s_c$&k#H. When you issue this command, replace the # character with a value equivalent to the width of each column in increments of $^{1}/_{120}$ inch. For example, if you want to set the HMI so that it will allow the LaserJet to print 12 characters per inch, send the command $^{E}s_c$&k1ØH to the LaserJet.

When you use a proportionally spaced font, the HMI setting is automatically set to reflect the width of the space character. For example, if you use a proportionally spaced font whose space character is $^{1}/_{10}$ inch wide, the HMI setting will be set to $^{12}/_{120}$ inch. If you change the HMI setting while using a proportionally spaced font, the amount of space the cursor will move when you send a space or backspace control code to the LaserJet will be affected.

Vertical Motion Index

We showed you how to set the VMI on page 630. We also pointed out that the LaserJet's default VMI setting allows you to print six lines per inch. For example, to change the LaserJet's default VMI setting so you can print only six lines per inch, you must issue the command $^{E}s_c$&ℓ8C.

**Using the
line spacing
command**

If you have a LaserJet Plus, 500 Plus, Series II, IID, or 2000, you can use the line spacing command to specify the number of lines that will be printed in one inch. However, if compatibility with the entire LaserJet printer family is your goal, you should always use the Vertical Motion Index command to specify the number of lines that will be printed in one inch.

The format of the line spacing command is E_{s_c}&ℓ#D. When you send this command to the LaserJet, replace the # character with the value 1, 2, 3, 4, 6, 8, 12, 16, 24, or 48. Each of these values defines the number of lines per inch that your LaserJet will print.

Setting the Top Margin

You can specify the amount of space the LaserJet will reserve at the top of the page by issuing a top margin command. The format of this command is E_{s_c}&ℓ#E. When you issue a top margin command, replace the # character with a value equal to the number of lines between the top of the logical page and the point at which you want to print text.

As we mentioned earlier, the number of lines your LaserJet will print in one inch is defined by the VMI. Therefore, if your VMI is set to its default value, which allows the LaserJet to print six lines per inch, you should issue the command E_{s_c}&ℓ6E if you want to leave a one-inch margin at the top of a page.

Setting the Bottom Margin

To define the amount of space the LaserJet will leave at the bottom of a page when you print text, you must issue a text length command. The format of this command is E_{s_c}&ℓ#F. When you send this command to the LaserJet, replace the # character with a value equal to the number of lines that will be printed between the top margin and the bottom margin.

The easiest way to calculate the number of lines that will be printed between the top and bottom margins is to subtract the size of the top and bottom margins (in inches) from the length of the logical page. The resulting value should then be multiplied by the number of lines your LaserJet will print in one inch to produce the number of lines that will be printed between the top and bottom margins.

As an example, let's assume that you have used the top margin command to specify a top margin of one inch, and you are using standard $8^1/_2$- by 11-inch letter-size stationery. Therefore, if you want to leave a one-inch margin at the top and bottom of a page while the VMI is set to default (six lines per inch), the text area will be 54 lines long. To tell the LaserJet that the text area is 54 lines long, you should issue the command E_{s_c}&ℓ54F.

Setting the Left Margin

You can define the amount of space reserved along the left side of each page by issuing a left margin command. The format of this command is E_{s_c}&a#L. When you send a left margin command to the LaserJet, replace the # character with a value equivalent to a column number.

As we showed you earlier, the width of each column is defined by the Horizontal Motion Index (HMI) command. Therefore, if the HMI has been set so that the LaserJet will print ten characters per inch and you want to leave a $^1/_2$-inch margin along the left edge of the logical page, you must issue the command ^{E}s$_c$&ℓ5L.

Setting the Right Margin

You can define the amount of space reserved along the right edge of a page by issuing a right margin command. The format of this command is ^{E}s$_c$&a#M. When you issue a right margin command, replace the # character with a value equivalent to a column number.

As we showed you earlier, the width of each column is defined by the HMI command. Therefore, if the HMI has been set so that the LaserJet will print ten characters per inch, a standard letter-size page will contain 80 column positions. As a result, if you want to leave a $^1/_2$-inch margin along the right edge of the logical page, you must issue the command ^{E}s$_c$&ℓ75M.

Clearing Left and Right Margins

If you ever find it necessary to return left and right margin settings to their default values, you can do so by issuing the command ^{E}s$_c$9. This command will tell the LaserJet that the left margin is set to the left edge of the logical page, while the right margin is set to the right edge of the logical page. If you recall the discussion of the logical page that appeared in Chapter 20, you know that these positions are equivalent to the leftmost and rightmost positions at which it is possible for the LaserJet to print text.

End-of-line Wrapping

The end-of-line-wrap command tells the LaserJet what it should do when it reaches the right margin of a page. When end-of-line wrapping is enabled, the LaserJet will automatically wrap text to the next line whenever the right margin boundary is reached. When end-of-line wrapping is disabled, the LaserJet will simply clip any text received after it reaches the right margin of a page.

To enable end-of-line wrapping, you should send the command ^{E}s$_c$&s$\emptyset$C to the LaserJet. You should send the command ^{E}s$_c$&s1C to the LaserJet if you want to disable end-of-line wrapping.

SKIPPING THE PERFORATION REGION

If you attempt to print text or graphics in the area along the bottom edge of a page that falls within the unprintable region or bottom margin, the LaserJet will refuse to print the text or graphics. However, it is possible to avoid this situation by issuing a perforation skip command.

When the perforation skip feature is activated, the LaserJet will automatically print any data that falls outside the printable or text area of a page at the top of the next page. The command you must send to the LaserJet to activate the perforation skip feature is ^{E}s$_c$&ℓ1L, while the command you must send to the LaserJet to de-activate the perforation skip feature is ^{E}s$_c$&$\ell$$\emptyset$L.

USING PAGE CONTROL COMMANDS

Now that we've looked at the PCL commands that allow you to select paper and adjust the dimensions of the area of a page on which the LaserJet will print text, let's consider how these commands might be sent to the LaserJet.

As we pointed out in Chapter 19, you can send PCL commands to the LaserJet by embedding them in a stream of text data. PCL commands can also be sent to the LaserJet directly by programs written in BASIC, C, Pascal, or any other computer language. Therefore, as an example, we'll show you a short Microsoft GW-BASIC program that sends PCL page control commands to the LaserJet.

Each line of the Microsoft GW-BASIC program shown in Figure 22-1 sends a particular PCL page control command to the LaserJet. Line 10 sends a paper source command that instructs a LaserJet Series II to feed letter-size paper from the manual feed slot, while line 20 sends a page size command that selects letter-size paper. Line 30 sets the left margin to column 10; line 40 sets the right margin to column 75; and line 50 sets the top margin to one inch. Finally, line 60 instructs the LaserJet to automatically wrap each line at the right margin boundary, while line 70 enables the perforation skip mode.

FIGURE 22-1

```
10 LPRINT CHR$(27);"&l2H"
20 LPRINT CHR$(27);"&l2A"
30 LPRINT CHR$(27);"&a1ØL"
40 LPRINT CHR$(27);"&a75M"
50 LPRINT CHR$(27);"&l8E"
60 LPRINT CHR$(27);"&sØC"
70 LPRINT CHR$(27);"&l1L"
```

This sample Microsoft GW-BASIC program uses PCL page control commands to select paper and adjust the area of a page on which the LaserJet will print text.

CONCLUSION

In this chapter, we've looked at the PCL commands that allow you to choose the source and type of paper you want to use, as well as the margins your LaserJet will use when printing text. We've also looked at the commands that allow you to specify both the width of columns and the number of lines the LaserJet can print on a page. As a result, you should now be ready to move on to the next two chapters in which we will examine the commands and procedures you must use to print text and graphics.

USING FONTS 23

In this chapter, we'll begin by looking at the process by which the HP LaserJet prints text. Once we've done this, we'll look at the PCL commands that allow you to select, manage, and use PCL fonts.

Before we take a look at the procedures you can use to select a font, it is important that you understand the process by which the LaserJet uses the fonts to print text. The LaserJet is essentially an ASCII device. In other words, to print text, you must send it to the LaserJet in ASCII format. Consequently, when you send an ASCII code to the LaserJet, it will print the symbol associated with that ASCII value. For example, if you send the ASCII code 65 decimal, 41 hexadecimal to the LaserJet while the Internal Courier font is selected, it will print the character A.

PRINTING TEXT

The LaserJet considers all of the characters associated with ASCII codes 0 through 31 to be control codes. Therefore, the LaserJet will not print a character when it receives one of these codes. This is not a problem when you are printing text while using a font based on the Roman-8 symbol set, or another font in which characters are not associated with codes 0 through 31. However, it is a problem when you are using a font based on the IBM PC symbol set or another symbol set in which characters are associated with codes 0 through 31.

Printing Special Characters

To print a character that is associated with codes 0 through 31, you must send a transparent print data command to the LaserJet. This command tells the LaserJet to ignore whatever operation might normally be associated with a control code. For example, if you send a transparent print data command to the LaserJet that instructs it to print the character associated with ASCII code 12 decimal, 0C hexadecimal, it will print that character. If you send the ASCII code 12 decimal, 0C hexadecimal to the LaserJet without issuing a transparent print data command, the LaserJet will execute a form feed.

The format of the transparent data command is ^{E}s$_c$&p#X. When you send this command to the LaserJet, substitute for the # character a value equal to the number of bytes that follow the command that should be treated as transparent data. For example, if you want to print the character associated with the ASCII code 8 decimal, 08 hexadecimal, send the command ^{E}s$_c$&p1X to the LaserJet. This command tells the LaserJet to print the character associated with the next ASCII code value it receives.

UNDERLINING

LaserJets have the ability to automatically underline any block of text regardless of the font used to print that block of text. This is made possible by the underline command. To enable underlining, you should send the command ^{E}s$_c$&dØD to the LaserJet before you send the text you want to underline.

When you instruct the LaserJet to underline a block of text, it will place a line that is three dots thick five dots below the imaginary line on which the characters stand. This imaginary line is called the baseline.

The LaserJet Series II, LaserJet IID, and LaserJet 2000 each support the ability to print a floating underline. When the LaserJet prints a floating underline, the position of the underline will not be fixed five dots below the baseline. Instead, it will be placed at the lowest possible position below the baseline. This position will vary according to the font you are using. To print a floating underline, send the command ^{E}s$_c$&d3D to the LaserJet before you send the actual block of text you want to underline.

Finally, to disable underlining after you have printed a block of text, send the command ^{E}s$_c$&d@ to the LaserJet.

SELECTING FONTS

Until you specify otherwise, the LaserJet will use the 12-point Internal Courier font to print all text. However, by using one of the methods we will describe, you can select and use any LaserJet internal, cartridge, or soft font to print text.

Selecting Primary and Secondary Fonts

PCL allows you to choose one font as a primary font and another as a secondary font. Therefore, you may select the font defined as the primary font by sending a Shift Out control code (ASCII code 15 decimal, 0F hexadecimal) to the LaserJet, while you may select the secondary font by sending a Shift In control code (ASCII code 14 decimal, 0E hexadecimal).

The commands you send to the LaserJet to specify the characteristics of the primary font must begin with an ^{E}s$_c$ code followed by the left parenthesis character, while the commands you send to the LaserJet to specify the characteristics of the secondary font always begin with an ^{E}s$_c$ code followed by the right parenthesis character.

If you want to ensure compatibility across the entire LaserJet product line, you must select fonts by specifying their characteristics. The LaserJet will then compare the characteristics you specify to the characteristics of all currently installed internal, cartridge, and soft fonts. When a match is found, the appropriate font will be selected.

When you tell the LaserJet to select a font based on a set of characteristics, it will do so by assigning priority to specific characteristics. For example, the first characteristic the LaserJet will consider is the orientation of the font you are trying to select. The characteristics you can define when selecting a font are listed by priority in Table 23-1.

Selecting a Font by Specifying Its Characteristics

TABLE 23-1

Characteristic	Priority
Orientation	1
Symbol Set	2
Spacing	3
Pitch	4
Height	5
Style	6
Stroke Weight	7
Typeface	8

The LaserJet will select a font based on the priority of characteristics shown in this table.

If, after comparing the characteristics you specify with those supported by currently installed fonts, the LaserJet finds that more than one font matches those criteria, it will select a font based on its form and location. The priority assigned to fonts according to their form and location is listed in Table 23-2.

TABLE 23-2

Location	Priority
Soft Fonts (Lowest ID—Highest ID)	1
Left Cartridge Fonts	2
Center Cartridge Fonts (LaserJet 2000)	3
Right Cartridge Fonts	4
Internal Fonts	5

When it cannot select a font based on the characteristics you have specified, the LaserJet will use the location of a font as a criterion for selection.

Now that you have learned to select a font by specifying its characteristics, we'll take a look at the commands you must send to the LaserJet to select a font. These commands may be sent to the LaserJet individually or as part of a merged command. For more information on sending PCL commands to the LaserJet and on how the LaserJet handles combined commands, see Chapter 19.

Orientation

To specify the orientation of the font you want to select, you must send the orientation command to the LaserJet. If you want to select a Portrait font, you should issue the command ^{E}s$_c$&ℓØO, while you should issue the command ^{E}s$_c$&ℓ1O if you want to select a Landscape font.

When you issue an orientation command, all members of the LaserJet printer family, with the exception of the LaserJet 2000, will attempt to select a font that was designed for the orientation you specify. If the font you specify is not available, the Internal Courier font will be selected.

The LaserJet 2000 has the ability to automatically rotate any font. Therefore, if you send an orientation command to a LaserJet 2000 to select a Landscape font, it will automatically create that font by rotating the Portrait version of the font.

Finally, when you issue an orientation command, page length, text length, the Horizontal Motion Index, the Vertical Motion Index, and the top, right, and left margins will be reset to their respective default values. The orientation command will also disable any auto overlay macro that is active. We'll discuss macros in Chapter 25.

Symbol set

The symbol set command allows you to specify which symbol set you want to use with the LaserJet's primary and secondary fonts. In Chapter 4, we pointed out that the term "symbol set" is used to define the actual symbols represented by a font, as well as the values that represent those symbols. The symbol set that you can select is determined by the specific font and LaserJet you are using.

All LaserJet fonts support a specific symbol set. For example, most HP fonts support the HP Roman-8 symbol set. However, many fonts support other symbol sets that have been designed for specific uses. To select one of these symbol sets, you must send a symbol set command to the LaserJet. The format of the symbol set command you must send to the LaserJet to select the symbol set you want to use with the primary font is ^{E}s$_c$(followed by an ID number that identifies the symbol set. Similarly, the format of the symbol set command you must send to the LaserJet to select the secondary font is ^{E}s$_c$) followed by an ID number that identifies the symbol set. A list of HP-approved symbol sets and their respective ID numbers is shown in Table 23-3.

TABLE 23-3

Symbol set	ID number
HP Math-7	ØA
HP Line Draw	ØB
ISO 60: Norwegian Version 1	ØD
ISO 61: Norwegian Version 2	1D
HP Roman Extension	ØE
ISO 4: United Kingdom	1E
ISO 25: French	ØF
ISO 69: French	1F
HP German	ØG
ISO 21: German	1G
HP Greek-8	8G
ISO 15: Italian	ØI
ISO 14: JIS ASCII	ØK
ISO 57: Chinese	2K
HP Math7	ØM
Technical-7	1M
HP Math-8	8M
HP Math-8a	ØQ
HP Math-8b	1Q
ISO 100: ECMA-94 (Latin 1)	ØN
OCR A	ØO
OCR B	1O
ISO 11: Swedish	ØS
HP Spanish	1S
ISO 17: Spanish	2S
ISO 10: Spanish	3S
ISO 16: Portuguese	4S
ISO 84: Portuguese	5S
ISO 85: Spanish	6S
USASCII	ØU
ISO 6: ASCII	ØU
HP Legal	1U
ISO 2: International Reference Version	2U
OEM-1	7U
HP Roman-8	8U
PC-8	10U
PC-8(D/N)	11U
HP Pi Font	15U
HP Pi Fonta	2Q

These symbol sets have been officially defined by Hewlett-Packard and assigned the ID numbers listed in this table.

Finally, the LaserJet Series II, LaserJet IID, and LaserJet 2000 can create various symbol sets on the fly by rearranging the order of symbols within the Roman-8 symbol set. These symbol sets are based on standards set by the the International Standards Organization (ISO) and appear in Table 23-3 with the prefix ISO.

If you have a LaserJet Series II, LaserJet IID, or LaserJet 2000, you may use any ISO symbol set whenever you are using a font that is based on the Roman-8 symbol set. On the other hand, you cannot use an ISO symbol with a LaserJet, LaserJet Plus, or LaserJet 500 Plus.

Spacing

To determine if the amount of space between characters supported by the font you want to select is proportional or fixed, you must send a spacing command to the LaserJet. If you want to select a fixed-space font as your primary font, you should issue the command $^E s_c$(sØP, while you should issue the command $^E s_c$(s1P if you want to select a proportionally spaced font. Likewise, if you want to select a fixed-space font as your secondary font, you should issue the command $^E s_c$)sØP, while you should issue the command $^E s_c$)s1P if you want to select a proportionally spaced font.

Pitch

To specify the width of a fixed-space font, you must send a pitch command to the LaserJet. This command allows you to specify the pitch of a font in units equal to the number of characters that may be printed in one inch. The format of the pitch command that allows you to specify the pitch of the primary font is $^E s_c$(s#H, while the format of the pitch command that allows you to specify the pitch of the secondary font is $^E s_c$)s#H. When you send either command to the LaserJet, replace the # character with a value equal to the number of characters per inch. This value may include as many as two decimal places. For example, the command $^E s_c$(s16.66H instructs the LaserJet to select a 16.66 cpi fixed-space font as the primary font.

Height

To specify the height of a font in points, you must send a height command to the LaserJet. As we pointed out in Chapter 4, one point is equivalent to $\frac{1}{72}$ inch.

The format of the command that allows you to specify the height of the primary font is $^E s_c$(s#V, while the format of the command that allows you to specify the height of the secondary font is $^E s_c$)s#V. When you send these commands to the LaserJet, replace the # character with a value equal to the height of the font. This value may include as many as two decimal places. For example, the command $^E s_c$(s10.25V instructs the LaserJet to select a font that is 10.25 points tall.

Finally, whenever you specify a point size that is not available, the LaserJet will select the font whose height is closest. For example, if a 10.25-point font is not available, the LaserJet will select a 10-point font, if one is available.

Style

To specify if you are selecting a normal upright or italic font, you must use the style command. The format of the style command that allows you to select the style of the primary font is ^{E}s$_c$(s#S, while the format of the style command that allows you to specify the style of the secondary font is ^{E}s$_c$)s#S. When you send these commands to the LaserJet, replace the # character with the value 0 if you want to select a normal upright font, or with the value 1 if you want to select an italic font. If you try to select an italic font when one is not available, the LaserJet will ignore the style command.

Stroke weight

The stroke weight command specifies the stroke weight of a font. The format of the stroke weight command that allows you to select the stroke weight of the primary font is ^{E}s$_c$(s#B, while the format for specifying the stroke weight of the secondary font is ^{E}s$_c$)s#B. When you send these commands to the LaserJet, replace the # character with the value that represents the desired stroke weight. These values are listed in Table 23-4. If you try to select a particular stroke weight that is not available, the LaserJet will ignore the stroke weight command.

TABLE 23-4

Stroke	Weight value
Ultra thin	-7
Thin	-5
Light	-3
Medium	0
Bold	3
Black	5
Ultra Black	7

These values are associated with standard LaserJet stroke weights.

Typeface

To specify the typeface on which the design of a font is based, you must use the typeface command. The format of the typeface command that allows you to select the typeface of the primary font is ^{E}s$_c$(s#T, while the format for specifying the typeface of the secondary font is ^{E}s$_c$)s#T. In each command, you must replace the # character with the value that represents a typeface. At the time *LaserJet Companion* went to press, HP had assigned values to 15 typefaces. These values and typefaces are listed in Table 23-5. If you try to select a particular typeface that is not available, the LaserJet will ignore the typeface command.

TABLE 23-5

Typeface name	Value
Line Printer	0
Courier	3
Helv	4
Tms Rmn	5
Letter Gothic	6
Prestige	8
Presentations	11
Optima	17
Garamond	18
Cooper Black	19
Coronet Bold	20
Broadway	21
Bauer Bodoni Black Condensed	22
Century Schoolbook	23
University Roman	24

When you send a typeface command to the LaserJet, specify a typeface by inserting its corresponding value.

Using Font ID Numbers to Select a Soft Font

Once you have assigned a font Id number to a specific soft font, you can use the font Id select command to select the primary and/or secondary font. The format of the command for choosing a soft font as the primary font is ^{E}s$_c$(#X, while the format of the command for choosing the secondary font is ^{E}s$_c$)#X. When you send these commands to the LaserJet, replace the # character with the appropriate font ID number. For example, to select soft font 12 as the primary font, you should send the command ^{E}s$_c$(12X to the LaserJet. We'll show you how to assign ID numbers to a soft font in the next section of this chapter.

Reselecting the Default Font

When you turn your LaserJet on, the Internal Courier font, or another font you specify using the control panel, will be considered the default font. Certain font cartridges also support fonts that will become default fonts when they are plugged into the LaserJet.

If, during a session, you issue the commands necessary to select a font other than the default font, you can reselect the default font as the primary font at any time by issuing the command ^{E}s$_c$(3@. Likewise, you can reselect the default font as the secondary font by issuing the command ^{E}s$_c$)3@.

SOFT FONT MANAGEMENT

If you have any LaserJet except the original LaserJet, then you can use soft fonts. As you might expect, a special series of PCL commands that allow you to select, manage, and use soft fonts has been included in each of these printers. Therefore, we'll take a look at these commands in this section.

As we mentioned in Chapter 4, when you download a soft font, you must assign it a font ID number. You may then use a soft font's ID number to select or delete it. To assign a font ID number to a soft font, you must send a font Id command to the LaserJet immediately before you download the font.

The format of the font Id command is $^{E}s_{c}$*c#D. When you send a font Id command to your LaserJet, replace the # character with a value between 0 and 32767. For example, if you want to assign the font ID number 1 to a font, you should send the command $^{E}s_{c}$*c1D to the LaserJet before you download the font.

Assigning a Font ID Number to a Soft Font

When you download a soft font to the LaserJet, it will be treated as a temporary soft font. This means that the font will be deleted from the LaserJet's RAM whenever you issue a reset command. If you want to make a soft font resistant to a reset command, you must make it a permanent soft font. To do this, you must use the font control command in combination with the font Id select command.

The format of the command you must issue to make a soft font permanent is $^{E}s_{c}$*c#d5F. When you send this command to your LaserJet, replace the # character with the ID number of the appropriate soft font. For instance, if you want to make the soft font associated with the font ID number 10 permanent, you should send the command $^{E}s_{c}$*c1Ød5F to the LaserJet.

Just as you might want to make a temporary soft font permanent, it is possible that you might want to make a permanent soft font temporary. The format of the command you must issue to do this is $^{E}s_{c}$*c#d4F. As you might expect, whenever you send this command to your LaserJet, you must replace the # character shown here with the ID number of the soft font you want to make temporary. If, for example, you want to make the soft font associated with the font ID number 12 temporary, you should send the command $^{E}s_{c}$*c12d4F to the LaserJet.

Temporary vs. Permanent Soft Fonts

Since soft fonts are stored in RAM, it is possible to delete them. This is an extremely useful capability if you are using a LaserJet Plus or LaserJet Series II equipped with only 512K of memory. It's also useful when you share a LaserJet, because each user can take advantage of the soft fonts he or she must use without taking RAM away from other users.

To delete soft fonts, you must use the font control command. If you want to delete all soft fonts regardless of their temporary or permanent status, you should issue the command $^{E}s_{c}$*cØF. You should issue the command $^{E}s_{c}$*c1F if you want to delete all temporary fonts.

You can delete a permanent soft font by combining the font Id select command with the font control command. The format of this combined command is $^{E}s_{c}$*c#d2F. When you send this command to the LaserJet, replace the # character with the ID number of the soft font you want to delete. For example, to delete soft font 12, you should send the command $^{E}s_{c}$*c12d2F to the LaserJet.

Deleting Soft Fonts

CONCLUSION   The commands and concepts we've discussed in this chapter allow you to take advantage of the LaserJet's ability to use a variety of fonts. Now that we've taken an in-depth look at each of these commands and concepts, you should be able to put them to use when writing programs that send text to the LaserJet. Likewise, you can use these concepts and commands with applications that require you to select fonts by sending PCL commands directly to the LaserJet.

USING GRAPHICS 24

The ability to print high quality bit-mapped graphics is one of the most important features of the LaserJet printer family. In this chapter, we'll begin by discussing how you must send graphics to the LaserJet. Then, we'll look at the PCL commands you must use to print graphics, and we'll offer some advice that can make printing graphics more efficient.

As we pointed out in Chapter 19, the LaserJet prints text and graphics on a page **CONCEPTS** by printing a specific pattern of dots. The bit maps that define the pattern of dots—which must be printed to form a specific character—are stored in ROM or RAM and are associated with a specific ASCII code. Therefore, when you send an ASCII code to the LaserJet, it will print the pattern of dots associated with that code.

When you print graphics on the LaserJet, you must place the cursor at the point **Bit Maps** on the printable area of the page and define the specific pattern of dots you want to print at that position by transferring a bit map. A bit map is a series of bits whose values determine if the LaserJet will print a dot. Specifically, if a bit is set to 1, the LaserJet will print a dot; if a bit is set to 0, it won't.

You must send a bit map to the LaserJet one byte at a time. Therefore, even if you want to print only one or two dots, you must send at least one byte (eight bits) of data to the LaserJet. A typical LaserJet bit map is shown in Figure 24-1.

FIGURE 24-1

```
11111111 00000000 11111111 00000000
11111111 00000000 11111111 00000000
11111111 00000000 11111111 00000000
11111111 00000000 11111111 00000000
00000000 11111111 00000000 11111111
00000000 11111111 00000000 11111111
00000000 11111111 00000000 11111111
00000000 11111111 00000000 11111111
11111111 00000000 11111111 00000000
11111111 00000000 11111111 00000000
11111111 00000000 11111111 00000000
11111111 00000000 11111111 00000000
```

This is a typical LaserJet graphics bit map.

If you examine this bit map, you can see that the arrangement of ones and zeros forms a checkerboard pattern. If you send this bit map to the LaserJet, it will print the pattern of dots the bit map represents.

Resolution

Since you must transfer one bit to the LaserJet to print a single dot, the amount of data you must transfer to print an entire page at 300 dpi is quite large. To be more specific, there are a total of 7,840,000 dots that can be printed on a standard sheet of letter-size stationery. Therefore, the bit map of an entire 300 dpi page is 980,000 bytes long.

This means you must have at least 980,000 bytes of RAM installed in your LaserJet to hold an entire 300 dpi page. However, to actually print a 300 dpi page, you must have at least 1.5MB of RAM installed in your LaserJet.

If you do not have enough RAM to print an entire page of 300 dpi graphics, you can print only part of a page, or you may choose to use a lower resolution. If you have an original LaserJet, you can print 85.9 square inches at 75 dpi, 48.3 square inches at 100 dpi, 21.5 square inches at 150 dpi, and 5.4 square inches at 300 dpi. Therefore, if you need crisp, high quality graphics, the original LaserJet is not the perfect choice for the task.

With 512K of RAM installed, the LaserJet Plus, 500 Plus, Series II, and IID can print 30 to 32 square inches at 300 dpi, or an entire letter-size page of graphics at 75, 100, and 150 dpi. While the quality of full-page 150 dpi graphics is not very good, it is acceptable in many situations. As an example, Figure 24-2 shows output produced by the LaserJet at 75, 100, 150, and 300 dpi. Later, we'll take a look at the PCL command you must issue to specify resolution.

FIGURE 24-2

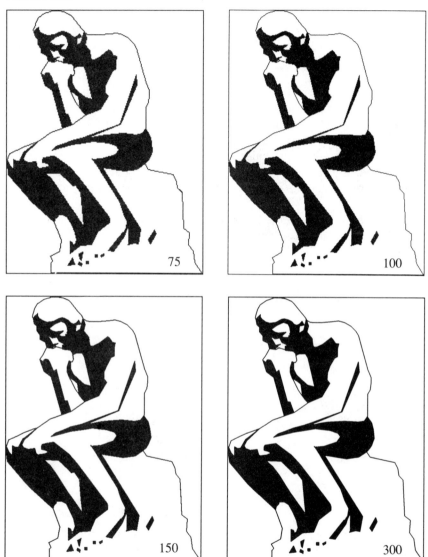

This figure shows an example of 75, 100, 150, and 300 dpi LaserJet graphics.

PRINTING RASTER GRAPHICS

Now that we've discussed the concepts behind PCL graphics, it's time to look at the PCL commands you must send to the LaserJet to print raster (bit-mapped) graphics. We'll begin with the commands that can be used to transfer bit maps, then we'll consider advanced PCL graphics commands that can be used to draw and fill rectangles.

Specifying Resolution

As we pointed out earlier, the quality of the LaserJet's output is determined by the resolution at which you print. We also pointed out that the resolutions you can use are determined by the amount of memory installed in your LaserJet.

You can specify the resolution at which your LaserJet will print graphics by issuing a raster graphics resolution command. The format of this command is E_{s_c}*t#R. When you send a raster graphics resolution command to the LaserJet, replace the # character with the value that specifies the resolution at which you want to print.

All members of the LaserJet printer family can print graphics at 75, 100, 150, and 300 dpi. Therefore, if you include the values 75, 100, 150, or 300 in a raster graphics resolution command, the corresponding resolution will be selected.

When you change the resolution at which the LaserJet will receive bit maps, you are actually changing the size of the dots the LaserJet will print. The conceptual size of the dot the LaserJet will use at each resolution is illustrated in Figure 24-3.

FIGURE 24-3

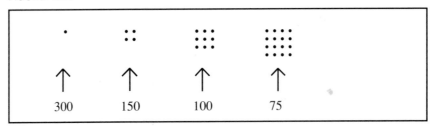

The size of the dot with which the LaserJet prints will vary according to the resolution you select.

Starting Raster Graphics

Once you have specified the resolution at which you want to print graphics, you must issue a start raster graphics command to specify the left raster graphics margin. This is the margin to which the LaserJet will return after each transfer of raster data (a bit map). To set the left raster graphics margin to the current cursor position, send the command E_{s_c}*r1A to the LaserJet. If you want to set the left raster graphics margin to position zero on the logical page, send the command E_{s_c}*rØA to the LaserJet.

To transfer raster data to the LaserJet, you must issue the transfer raster data command. This command, whose format is $^E s_c$*b#W [raster data], specifies the number of bytes of raster data that will follow the command. When you send this command to the LaserJet, replace the # character with a value equal to the number of bytes that you want to transfer. For example, if you plan to transfer a four-byte bit map, you should send the command $^E s_c$*b4W to the LaserJet.

Each byte of raster data that you transfer to the LaserJet must be expressed in the form of a decimal value, between 0 and 255, that corresponds to the pattern of bits being transferred. To determine the decimal value that represents a specific bit pattern, total the values that represent each bit in the pattern that is set to 1. For example, the bit pattern 01000000 is associated with the value 64, while the bit pattern 01010101 is associated with the value 85. The values associated with each bit in a byte are shown in Figure 24-4.

Transferring Raster Data to the LaserJet

FIGURE 24-4

Bit	7	6	5	4	3	2	1	0
Value	128	64	32	16	8	4	2	1

This table shows all possible bit patterns that can be sent to the LaserJet, along with the decimal value that represents them.

Once you have transferred a bit map, you must issue the command $^E s_c$*rB to inform the LaserJet that it should exit the raster graphics transfer mode. This command, which is called the end raster graphics command, informs the LaserJet that all raster transfer operations have been completed. Therefore, upon receipt of this command, the LaserJet will return to text mode.

Ending Raster Graphics Transfer

As an example, let's assume that you want to transfer the bit map shown in Figure 24-1 to the LaserJet. To do this, you must begin by specifying the resolution at which you want to print and the position of the left raster graphics margin. Once this is done, you must send each row of the bit map to the LaserJet individually. Therefore, since the bit map shown in Figure 24-1 has 12 rows, you must send the 12 transfer raster data commands shown in Table 24-1 to the LaserJet. Finally, after you have transferred all 12 rows of bit-mapped data, you must inform the LaserJet that it can return to text mode by issuing an end raster graphics command.

An Example

TABLE 24-1

PCL command	Data bytes that must follow command			
E_{s_c}*b4W	255	0	255	0
E_{s_c}*b4W	255	0	255	0
E_{s_c}*b4W	255	0	255	0
E_{s_c}*b4W	255	0	255	0
E_{s_c}*b4W	0	255	0	255
E_{s_c}*b4W	0	255	0	255
E_{s_c}*b4W	0	255	0	255
E_{s_c}*b4W	0	255	0	255
E_{s_c}*b4W	255	0	255	0
E_{s_c}*b4W	255	0	255	0
E_{s_c}*b4W	255	0	255	0
E_{s_c}*b4W	255	0	255	0

These commands and data bytes must be sent to the LaserJet to transfer the image shown in Figure 24-1 to the LaserJet.

RECTANGLES AND AREA FILLS

Now that we've discussed the PCL commands you must use to print raster graphics, it's time to look at a group of PCL commands that can be used to draw rectangles and lines on a page. However, before we proceed, it is important to note that these commands are not supported by the original LaserJet.

Positioning a Rectangle

Before you can print a rectangle, you must position the cursor at some point on the printable area of the page. This point will become the upper-left corner of the rectangle. For example, if you move the cursor to coordinate (300,300), this point will be treated as a home value when you specify the horizontal and vertical size of the rectangle. For more information on how to position the cursor, see Chapter 20.

Defining the Horizontal Size of a Rectangle

The first step in the process of drawing a rectangle is to specify its horizontal size. There are two commands you can use to do this. The first command allows you to specify the size in dots, while the second command allows you to specify the size in decipoints.

The format of the command you must use to define the horizontal size of a rectangle in dots is E_{s_c}*c#A. When you send this command to the LaserJet, replace the # character with a value equal to the horizontal size of the rectangle in dots. For example, if you want to draw a rectangle whose horizontal size is 100 dots, you should send the command E_{s_c}*c100A to the LaserJet.

The format of the command you must use to define the horizontal size of a rectangle in decipoints is $^E{s_c}$*c#H. When you send this command to the LaserJet, replace the # character with a value equal to the horizontal size of the rectangle in decipoints. For example, if you want to draw a rectangle whose horizontal size is 100 decipoints, you should send the command $^E{s_c}$*c100H to the LaserJet.

Defining the Vertical Size of a Rectangle

Once you have defined the horizontal size of a rectangle, you must specify its vertical size. As you might expect, there are two commands that you can use to do this. The first command allows you to specify the size in dots, while the second command allows you to specify the size in decipoints.

The format of the command you must use to define the vertical size of a rectangle in dots is $^E{s_c}$*c#B. When you send this command to the LaserJet, replace the # character with a value equal to the vertical size of the rectangle in dots. For example, if you want to draw a rectangle whose vertical size is 300 dots, you should send the command $^E{s_c}$*c300B to the LaserJet.

The format of the command you must use to define the vertical size of a rectangle in decipoints is $^E{s_c}$*c#V. When you send this command to the LaserJet, replace the # character with a value equal to the vertical size of the rectangle in decipoints. For example, if you want to draw a rectangle whose vertical size is 100 decipoints, you should send the command $^E{s_c}$*c100V to the LaserJet.

Area Fill Id

Once you have specified the horizontal and vertical size of a rectangle, you can choose a pattern or level of shading that will be used to fill that rectangle. To specify the pattern or shade you want to use, you must send an area fill Id command to the LaserJet. The format of this command is $^E{s_c}$*c#G. When you send an area fill Id command to the LaserJet, replace the # character with a value that represents the level of shading or the type of pattern you want to use.

You can use any value between 1 and 100 to define the level of shading that the LaserJet will use when filling a rectangle. For example, if you send the command $^E{s_c}$*c50G to the LaserJet, it will fill 50% of the area within the rectangle, while if you send the command $^E{s_c}$*c20G, only 20% of the area within a rectangle will be filled.

Finally, if you want to fill a rectangle with a pattern, you must use a value between 1 and 6 to specify which pattern you want to use. The patterns you can use to fill a rectangle are shown in Figure 24-5.

FIGURE 24-5

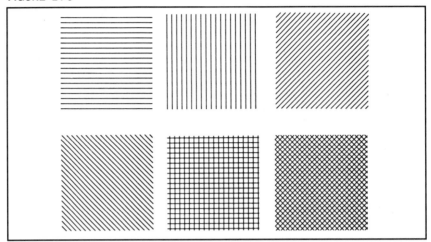

You can fill rectangles with any of these patterns by specifying the appropriate value when you send an area fill Id command to the LaserJet.

Filling a Rectangle

Once you have specified the horizontal and vertical size of a rectangle, and have chosen the pattern or level of shading that will be used to fill the rectangle, you must send a fill rectangular area command to the LaserJet. The format of the fill rectangular area command is E_{s_c}*c#P. When you send this command to the LaserJet, replace the # character with a value that specifies whether the rectangle is to be filled with a pattern, a shade, or solid black.

For example, to fill a rectangle with the level of shading you have specified with the area fill Id command, send the command E_{s_c}*c2P to the LaserJet. You must send the command E_{s_c}*c3P to the LaserJet if you want to fill a rectangle with the pattern you specified with the area fill Id command. Finally, if you want to fill a rectangle with black, you should send the command E_{s_c}*cØP to the LaserJet.

TIPS AND TECHNIQUES

Now that we've taken a look at the PCL commands you can use to print raster graphics, it's time to consider a few issues that you will run into when you print raster graphics. In addition, we'll provide you with a few tips and techniques that can substantially improve the performance of any program you design that prints raster graphics.

Rotating Graphics

With the exception of the LaserJet IID and LaserJet 2000, all members of the LaserJet family will address a page in Portrait mode even if Landscape mode has been selected. Therefore, if you want to rotate the position of graphics on a page, you must do so manually.

For example, if you want to print a vertical line 16 dots wide and 160 dots tall in Portrait mode, you must begin by specifying the appropriate resolution, then you must specify the position of the cursor at which you want to print. Once you have done this, you must issue 160 transfer raster data commands. Each of these commands must transfer 16 bits of raster data to the LaserJet.

On the other hand, if you want to print a vertical line 16 dots wide and 160 dots tall while using Landscape mode, you must begin by selecting Landscape mode. Once you have done this, you must select the appropriate resolution setting and position the cursor at the point at which you want to print. Finally, you must issue 16 transfer raster data commands, each of which must transfer 160 bits of raster data to the LaserJet.

If you have a LaserJet IID or LaserJet 2000, you can take advantage of the ability of your LaserJet to automatically rotate graphics. To do this, you must send a raster graphics presentation mode command to the LaserJet before you issue a start raster graphics command.

For example, if you want to print a vertical line 16 dots wide and 160 dots tall in Landscape mode, issue a resolution command, then issue the raster graphics presentation mode command E_{s_c}*r3F. Once you have done this, you must issue 160 transfer raster data commands. Each of these commands must transfer 16 bits of raster data to the LaserJet.

Optimization

When you transfer bit maps to the LaserJet, you must keep an eye on the amount of white space in the bit map. If, at any time, you find that more than 34 consecutive bytes are being used to transfer the bit map of white space to the LaserJet, you should exit graphics mode, position the cursor at the point at which dots will be printed subsequent to the white space in question, then re-enter graphics mode and transfer the appropriate data.

Since the process of transferring a bit map of a vertical line to the LaserJet requires an extremely large number of transfer raster data commands, you should always use rectangular area fill commands to draw vertical lines. Finally, whenever you are printing a black space whose bit map is greater than 18 bytes, you should use rectangular area fill commands to define and fill the space.

CONCLUSION

In this chapter, we've considered the process of sending raster graphics to the LaserJet and looked at the PCL commands you must issue to transfer raster data to the LaserJet. In addition, we've discussed the LaserJet's ability to print and fill rectangles and considered a few issues that can improve or hinder the LaserJet's performance when you are printing graphics.

USING MACROS 25

Macros are an extremely useful, yet underused, capability of HP LaserJet printers. In a nutshell, they allow you to download a group of PCL commands to the LaserJet and assign a number to each of them. You can then execute this series of commands by issuing a single macro command, or you can have the LaserJet automatically execute the macro each time it prints a page. In this chapter, we'll discuss the PCL commands you must use to create, manage, and delete macros.

To create a macro, you must send a macro control command to the LaserJet before you actually send the series of commands you want to define as a macro. When you have finished sending the series of commands, you must issue another macro control command to inform the LaserJet that the macro definition has ended.

Before you inform the LaserJet that you want to record a macro, you must assign an ID number to that macro. To do this, issue a macro Id command. The format of the macro Id command is $^E s_c$&f#Y. When you send this command to the LaserJet, replace the # character with the ID number you want to assign to the macro you are about to define. For example, to assign the macro ID number 12 to a macro, issue the command $^E s_c$&f12Y.

After you have assigned an ID number to a macro, send the command $^E s_c$&fØX to the LaserJet. Once you have done this, the LaserJet will automatically record any commands it receives until it receives the command $^E s_c$&f1X. This command informs the LaserJet that the macro definition has ended.

CREATING A MACRO

There are three methods you can use to run a macro. In this section, we'll look at each of these methods, and we'll discuss why you might want to use one method in lieu of another.

RUNNING MACROS

Calling Macros

If you run a macro by calling it, the macro will not destroy any job or page control settings you may have specified. For example, if you set the left margin to 10 and call a macro that sets it to 20, the macro will return the margin to 10 once its execution has been completed.

To call a macro, you must specify its ID number by issuing a macro Id command. Once you have done this, send the command E_{s_c}&f3X to the LaserJet. For example, if you want to call macro 1, send the command E_{s_c}&f1Y to select its ID number, then issue the command E_{s_c}&f3X.

Executing Macros

If you run a macro by executing it, the macro may destroy page and job control settings. For example, if you set the left margin to 10 and execute a macro that sets it to 20, the margin setting will remain at 20 once the macro's execution is completed.

To execute a macro, you must specify its ID number by issuing a macro Id command. Once you have done this, you must send the command E_{s_c}&f2X to the LaserJet. For example, if you want to execute macro 1, send the command E_{s_c}&f1Y to select its ID number, then issue the command E_{s_c}&f2X.

Overlaying Macros

If you want to execute a macro each time the LaserJet prints a page, you may do so by overlaying the macro. Unlike executed macros, overlayed macros will not corrupt current job or page control settings.

To overlay a macro, you must specify its ID number by issuing a macro Id command. Once you have done this, send the command E_{s_c}&f4X to the LaserJet. For example, if you want to overlay macro 1, send the command E_{s_c}&f1Y to select its ID number, then issue the command E_{s_c}&f4X.

MANAGING MACROS

Just as you can specify the status of soft fonts as permanent or temporary, you can specify the status of macros. In this section, we'll take a look at the commands that allow you to specify the status of macros. Then, we'll look at the commands you can use to delete macros.

Temporary vs. Permanent Macros

When you record a macro, it will be treated as a temporary macro. This means that the macro will be deleted from the LaserJet's RAM whenever you issue a reset command. If you want to make a macro resistant to a reset command, you must make it permanent. To do this, you must use a macro control command in combination with a macro Id command.

To make a macro permanent, use a macro Id command to select it, then issue the command E_{s_c}&f1ØX. For example, if you want to make the macro associated with the font ID number 10 permanent, you should send the commands E_{s_c}&f1ØY and E_{s_c}&f1ØX to the LaserJet.

Just as you may want to make a temporary macro permanent, it is possible you may want to make a permanent macro temporary. To do this, you must use the macro Id command to select a macro, then you must send the command $^E s_c$&f9X to the LaserJet. For example, if you want to make the macro associated with the font ID number 12 temporary, you should send the commands $^E s_c$&f12Y and $^E s_c$&f9X to the LaserJet.

Deleting Macros

Since macros are stored in RAM, it is possible to delete them. This is a very useful capability when you are using a LaserJet Plus or LaserJet Series II equipped with only 512K of memory. It's also helpful when you share a LaserJet, because it allows each user to take advantage of the macros he or she must use without taking RAM away from other users.

To delete macros, you must use the macro control command. If you want to delete all macros regardless of their temporary or permanent status, you should issue the command $^E s_c$&f6X, while you should issue the command $^E s_c$&f7X if you want to delete all temporary macros.

You can delete a permanent macro by combining a macro Id command with a macro control command. For example, to delete macro number 12, you should send the commands $^E s_c$&f12Y and $^E s_c$&f8X to the LaserJet.

USING MACROS

Now that we've looked at the PCL commands you must use to record and use a macro, it's time to consider some of their potential uses. The first and most obvious use of macros is to replay a series of often used commands. For example, if you are printing a document that contains a series of lines, you should record the commands required to print a line, then replay them whenever necessary by using the macro control command's execute or run options.

Perhaps the most exciting use of macros is for printing letterheads on stationery. It's possible to use the macro control command's overlay option to print a letterhead (even one that contains a logo) on every page.

CONCLUSION

In this chapter, we explained how to record a series of PCL commands as a macro. We also showed you how to execute and manage macros. You should now be ready to put macros to use when you are writing programs that communicate with the LaserJet.

CREATING SOFT FONTS 26

All members of the HP LaserJet printer family, with the exception of the original LaserJet, can print text using soft fonts. As we pointed out in Chapter 4, soft fonts are fonts whose bit-mapped image is stored in a data file that must be downloaded to the LaserJet's on-board RAM.

In this chapter, we'll take a look at the procedures you can use to create a soft font and send it to the LaserJet. As we do this, we'll discuss the format of the data that must be sent to the LaserJet to create a soft font, and we'll point out situations where this data may be used for other purposes.

Before we move on, it's important to note that the information presented in this chapter is highly technical in nature and is intended for those who have a high degree of technical and programming skill. Therefore, if high-powered programming is not your cup of tea, you should use a soft font editor, such as the one we discussed in Chapter 18, to create soft fonts.

As we mentioned earlier, soft fonts exist in the form of data files that must be downloaded to the LaserJet's on-board RAM. These data files contain several PCL commands, the actual bit map that defines the pattern of dots the LaserJet must print to form a specific character, and a great deal of information that describes the physical characteristics of the font.

CONCEPTS, TERMS, AND PROCEDURES

The font descriptor is the first chunk of data you will find in a soft font file. Its purpose is to provide the LaserJet with a summary of the physical characteristics of a font. For example, a typical font descriptor will contain information defining a

Font Descriptor

variety of characteristics, including the height and width of a font, the symbol set on which it is based, its stroke weight, and its pitch. We'll take an in-depth look at the font descriptor later in this chapter.

To download a font descriptor, you must send a font descriptor command to the LaserJet. Therefore, all soft font data files must begin with the font descriptor command E_{s_c})s#W. When you send this command to the LaserJet, replace the # with a value equal to the number of bytes in the font descriptor that follows the command. For example, if a soft font's font descriptor is 64 bytes long, send the command E_{s_c})s64W to the LaserJet before transferring the font descriptor.

Character Descriptor and Data

The character descriptor is a block of data that describes the physical characteristics of each character in a soft font. This block of data always precedes the actual bit-mapped data that defines the pattern of dots that must be printed to form a specific character.

Each character in a font has its own character descriptor and bit map. Therefore, as many as 255 character descriptors and bit maps may exist in a single soft font file. Each of these character descriptors and bit maps must be preceded by a character code command. This command assigns a unique ASCII decimal value to the character being defined. The format of the character code command is E_{s_c}*c#E. When you send this command to the LaserJet, replace the # with a unique value between 0 and 255. For example, to associate a character descriptor and bit map with the ASCII code 128, send the command E_{s_c}*c128E to the LaserJet before transferring a character descriptor and character bit map.

Downloading a Soft Font Data File

In Chapter 4, we discussed the procedures you must use to download soft font data files to the LaserJet. We pointed out that all soft fonts may be given a font ID number before they are downloaded. To give a soft font an ID number, you must use the soft font Id command. This command and the concept of font ID numbers are discussed in detail in Chapter 23.

FONT DESCRIPTOR FORMAT

Now that we've taken a look at the components of a PCL soft font data file and have discussed the PCL commands that must be included in the file to transfer the various components to the LaserJet, it's time to discuss the actual format of the font descriptor. Before we begin this discussion, however, we should take a few moments to consider Table 26-1, which presents the whole format of the font descriptor.

Font Descriptor Size

A font descriptor must be at least 26 bytes long; however, you will find that most are 64 bytes long. While HP recommends that the length of a font descriptor not exceed 64 bytes, several commercial soft fonts sport font descriptors whose length approaches 256 bytes. Technically, a font descriptor may be 65,535 bytes long, although at this time there is no reason for one ever to reach that length.

TABLE 26-1

Offset Byte	Purpose	
	Most significant byte	| *Least significant byte*
0	Font descriptor size (UI)	
2	Reserved for future use (Ø)	| Font type (UB)
4	Reserved for future use (Ø)	
6	Distance of baseline from top of cell (UI)	
8	Width of cell (UI)	
10	Height of cell (UI)	
12	Orientation (UB)	| Character spacing (B)
14	Symbol set (UI)	
16	Pitch (UI)	
18	Font height (UI)	
20	xHeight (UI)	
22	Proportional width type (SB)	| Style (UB)
24	Stroke weight (SB)	| Typeface (UB)
26	Reserved for future use (Ø)	| Serif style (UB)
28	Reserved for future use (Ø)	
30	Distance of underline from baseline (SB)	| Underline height (UB)
32	Text height (UI)	
34	Text width (UI)	
36	Reserved for future use (Ø)	
38	Reserved for future use (Ø)	
40	Pitch extended (UI)	| Height extended (UI)
42	Reserved for future use (Ø)	
44	Reserved for future use (Ø)	
46	Reserved for future use (Ø)	
48-63	Name of font (ASCII)	

Legend: UI: Unsigned Integer (0..65535)
SB: Signed Byte (-128..127)
UB: Unsigned Byte (0..255)
B: Boolean value (0,1)
Ø: Byte(s) must contain the value zero
ASCII: ASCII text

This table shows the format of the font descriptor of a PCL soft font.

To define the length of a font descriptor, place a value in bytes 0 and 1. This value should be an unsigned integer—meaning that byte 1 should contain the least significant byte (lsb), while byte 0 should contain the most significant byte (msb).

For example, let's assume that you are creating a font descriptor that is 64 bytes long. Therefore, you must use bytes 0 and 1 to express the value 64. To do this, byte 0 should contain the value 0 while byte 1 must contain the value 64.

Font Type

Byte 3 in the font descriptor specifies the type of font described. You must place the value 0 in byte 3 if the font described is one in which only characters associated with ASCII codes 32 to 127 can be printed, while you must use the value 1 when the font is one in which characters 32 to 127 and 160 to 255 are printable. You must place the value 2 in byte 3 if the font is one in which all characters except those associated with ASCII codes 0, 7, 15, and 27 can be printed.

Baseline Distance

The value stored in bytes 6 and 7 of the font descriptor defines the distance in dots from the top of a character cell to the bottom of the baseline. This value must be no smaller than 0, and no larger than the height of a character cell minus one dot. For example, if a character cell is 300 dots tall, 0 through 299 are valid baseline distance values.

The baseline distance value must be expressed in binary form as an unsigned integer. For example, if the baseline distance is 299, byte 6 should contain the value 41, while byte 7 should contain the value 1.

Cell Width

Bytes 8 and 9 in the font descriptor specifies the width in dots of character cells. For example, if the font described by a font descriptor is a fixed font, and all cells are 128 dots wide, you must place the value 128 in byte 8 and 0 in byte 9.

The maximum value you may use to define cell width varies according to the specific member of the LaserJet printer family you are using. It must not exceed 255 if you are using a LaserJet Plus or LaserJet 500 Plus, while it must not exceed 4200 if you are using a LaserJet Series II or LaserJet IID. This value is required by all members of the LaserJet printer family, with the exception of the LaserJet 2000, and must be expressed as an unsigned integer.

Cell Height

Bytes 10 and 11 specify the height of character cells in dots. For example, if the font described by a font descriptor is a fixed font, and all cells are 128 dots tall, you must place the value 128 in byte 10 and the value 0 in byte 11.

Finally, the maximum value you may use to define cell height varies according to the specific member of the LaserJet printer family you are using. It must not exceed 255 if you are using a LaserJet Plus or LaserJet 500 Plus, while it must not exceed 4200 if you are using a LaserJet Series II or LaserJet IID. This value is required by all members of the LaserJet printer family, with the exception of the LaserJet 2000, and must be expressed as an unsigned integer.

Byte 12 specifies the orientation for which a font is designed. You should set this byte to 0 if the font is being designed for Portrait mode. You should set it to 1 if the font is being designed for Landscape mode.

Orientation

Byte 13 specifies whether the space between characters in a font is fixed or proportional. If you use fixed spacing, you should set this value to 0, while you should set it to 1 if you use proportional spacing.

Spacing

Bytes 14 and 15 specify the symbol set a font supports. To determine the value you must place in this field, you must multiply by 32 the PCL ID number associated with the symbol set, then add the ASCII value of the termination character associated with the symbol set, and subtract 64. For example, as you can see in Table 26-2, the HP Roman-8 symbol set is associated with the PCL ID 8U. Therefore, if you multiply 8 by 32, add the decimal ASCII value of U (85) to that total, then subtract 64, you will produce the symbol set value 277. This is the value you must place in bytes 14 and 15 to specify that a font is based on the Roman-8 symbol set.

Symbol Set

At the time *LaserJet Companion* went to press, the symbol set values listed in Table 26-2 were the only ones in use by HP. However, HP reserves the right to use symbol set values 0 through 1023 and has set aside values 1024 through 2047 for use by third-party developers. Therefore, you may have to use the method we described in the previous paragraph to use the PCL ID to calculate the symbol set value. Regardless of the method you use to obtain the symbol set value, it must be expressed in bytes 14 and 15 as an unsigned integer.

Bytes 16 and 17 specify the default pitch of a font. This value must be expressed as an unsigned integer in units equal to one-quarter dot. For example, if you are dealing with a 10-pitch (10 characters per inch) font, you may assume that each character is $^{30}/_{300}$ inch or 120 quarter dots wide. Therefore, you must place the value 120 in byte 16 and the value 0 in byte 17.

Pitch

Bytes 18 and 19 specify the default height of a font. This value must be expressed as an unsigned integer in units equal to one-quarter dot. For example, if you are dealing with a font that is 72 points high, you may assume that the font is 300 dots or 1,200 quarter dots high. Therefore, you must place the value 4 in byte 18 and the value 176 in byte 19.

Height

Bytes 20 and 21 specify the height of the character x. This value must be expressed as an unsigned integer in units equal to one-quarter dot. For example, if you are dealing with an x character that is 18 points high, you may assume that the font is 75 dots or 300 quarter dots high. Therefore, you must place the value 1 in byte 20 and the value 44 in byte 21.

xHeight

TABLE 26-2

Symbol set	PCL ID	Value
HP Math-7	ØA	1
HP Line Draw	ØB	2
ISO 60: Norwegian Version 1	ØD	4
ISO 61: Norwegian Version 2	1D	36
HP Roman Extension	ØE	5
ISO 4: United Kingdom	1E	37
ISO 25: French	ØF	6
ISO 69: French	1F	38
HP German	ØG	7
ISO 21: German	1G	39
HP Greek-8	8G	263
ISO 15: Italian	ØI	9
ISO 14: JIS ASCII	ØK	11
ISO 57: Chinese	2K	75
HP Math7	ØM	13
Technical-7	1M	45
HP Math-8	8M	269
HP Math-8a	ØQ	17
HP Math-8b	1Q	49
ISO 100: ECMA-94 (Latin 1)	ØN	14
OCR A	ØO	15
OCR B	1O	47
ISO 11: Swedish	ØS	19
HP Spanish	1S	51
ISO 17: Spanish	2S	83
ISO 10: Spanish	3S	115
ISO 16: Portuguese	4S	147
ISO 84: Portuguese	5S	179
ISO 85: Spanish	6S	211
USASCII	ØU	21
ISO 6: ASCII	ØU	21
HP Legal	1U	53
ISO 2: International Reference Version	2U	85
OEM-1	7U	245
HP Roman-8	8U	277
PC-8	10U	341
PC-8(D/N)	11U	373
HP Pi Font	15U	501
HP Pi Fonta	2Q	32

Hewlett-Packard has defined these symbol sets and assigned them these ID numbers.

xHeight is not currently required by any member of the LaserJet printer family, but you should include it to ensure compatibility with future printers.

Byte 22 specifies the width type of a font. The value you place in this field must be one of those listed in Table 26-3. Although this field is not currently required by any member of the LaserJet printer family, you should include it to ensure future compatibility.

Width Type

TABLE 26-3

Width type	Value
Condensed	-2
Semi-condensed	-1
Normal	0
Semi-expanded	1
Expanded	2

Hewlett-Packard has defined these width types.

Byte 23 specifies the style of a font. In other words, it specifies whether a font is upright or italic. If a font is upright, you should set this value to 0. You should set it to 1 if the font is italic.

Style

Byte 24 specifies a font's stroke weight. The value you place in this field must be one of those listed in Table 26-4. For example, if a font's stroke weight is medium, you should place the value 0 in the stroke weight field.

Stroke Weight

TABLE 26-4

Stroke Weight	Value
Ultra Thin	-7
Thin	-5
Light	-3
Medium	0
Bold	3
Black	5
Ultra Black	7

To specify the stroke weight of a font, you must specify the appropriate value in the font descriptor's stroke weight field.

Byte 25 specifies a font's typeface. The value you place in this field must be one of those listed in Table 26-5. For example, if a font's design is based on the Courier typeface, you should place the value 3 in the typeface field.

Typeface

TABLE 26-5

Typeface	Value
Line Printer	0
Courier	3
Helv	4
Tms Rmn	5
Letter Gothic	6
Prestige	8
Presentations	11
Optima	17
Garamond	18
Cooper Black	19
Coronet Bold	20
Broadway	21
Bauer Bodoni Black Condensed	22
Century Schoolbook	23
University Roman	24

To specify a font's typeface, you must specify the appropriate value in the font descriptor's typeface field.

Serif Style

Byte 27 specifies a font's serif style. The value you place in this field must be one of those listed in Table 26-6. For example, if a font's serif style is sans serif square, you should place the value 0 in the serif style field.

TABLE 26-6

Serif style	Value
Sans Serif Square	0
Sans Serif Round	1
Serif Line	2
Serif Triangle	3
Serif Swath	4
Serif Block	5
Serif Bracket	6
Rounded Bracket	7
Flair Stroke	8

To specify a font's serif style, you must specify the appropriate value in the font descriptor's serif style field.

Byte 30 is used to define the distance from a character's baseline to the top of an underline. This value must be specified in dots. A negative value represents a position below the baseline, while a positive value represents a position above the baseline. For example, if you want to place the underline four dots below the baseline, you should place the value -4 in byte 30.

Underline Distance

Byte 31 is used to specify the thickness of the underline in dots. However, since all current members of the LaserJet printer family always print underlines that are three dots thick, they will ignore any value you place in this field.

Underline Height

Bytes 32 and 33 are used to specify the ideal amount of line spacing that should be used with a font. This value must be expressed as an unsigned integer in units equal to one-quarter dot. For example, if you are dealing with a font whose ideal line spacing would be one dot, you must place the value 4 in the font descriptor's text height field.

Finally, while text height is not currently required by any member of the LaserJet printer family, you should include it in the font descriptor to ensure compatibility with future PCL-based products.

Text Height

Bytes 34 and 35 of the font descriptor are used to specify the ideal amount of space that should be reserved between characters. This value must be expressed as an unsigned integer in units equal to one-quarter dot. For example, if you are dealing with a font where the ideal space between characters would be four dots, you must place the value 16 in the font descriptor's text width field.

Finally, while text width is not currently required by any member of the LaserJet printer family, you should include it in the font descriptor to ensure compatibility with future PCL-based products.

Text Width

Byte 40 is used to extend the value you can express when defining a font's pitch. The values you must express in this field are equal to $^1/_{1024}$ dot. Therefore, if you have placed the value 120 in the pitch field and 512 in the pitch extended field, you are specifying that the pitch of the font is 10.5 cpi.

Pitch Extended

Byte 41 is used to extend the value you can express when defining a font's height. The values you must express in this field are equal to $^1/_{1024}$ dot. If you have placed the value 1200 in the height field and 512 in the height extended field, you are specifying that the height of the font is 72.5 points.

Height Extended

Bytes 48 through 63 are reserved for a 16-character ASCII font name. For example, if the descriptor specifies a Courier font, the name Courier could appear in this field. All members of the LaserJet printer family ignore this field, but its main purpose is to provide a space for font manufacturers to post a copyright notice.

Font Name

CHARACTER DESCRIPTOR FORMAT

As we pointed out earlier in this chapter, the character descriptor contains information that describes the physical characteristics of a character as well as the length of the bit-mapped data that defines the pattern of dots that must be printed to form the character. In this section, we'll discuss the format of the character descriptor and the bit-mapped data you must transfer to the LaserJet to form a character. Refer to Table 26-7 as we discuss these character descriptor formats.

TABLE 26-7

Byte	Purpose	
	Most significant byte	I *Least significant byte*
Ø	Format (UB)	I Continuation (B)
2	Descriptor size (UB)	I Class (UB)
4	Orientation (UB)	I Reserved (Ø)
6	Left Offset (SI)	
8	Top Offset (SI)	
10	Character Width (UI)	
12	Character Height (UI)	
14	Delta X (SI)	
16	Character Data	

Legend: UI: Unsigned Integer (0..65535)
SI: Signed Integer (-32768..32767)
SB: Signed Byte (-128..127)
UB: Unsigned Byte (0..255)
B: Boolean value (0,1)
Ø: Byte(s) must contain the value zero
ASCII: ASCII text

This table shows the format of a PCL soft font character descriptor.

Format Number

Byte 0 must contain a value that identifies the format of the character descriptor. The current family of LaserJet printers requires the value 4 in this byte. Any other value produces an error when you download the character descriptor to the LaserJet.

Continuation

The value of byte 1 specifies whether a character descriptor is a continuation of a previous character descriptor or an independent character descriptor. If you have previously transferred as much of a bit map as allowed by the 32,767-byte limit imposed by PCL, and you want to continue transferring data, byte 1 must contain the value 0. If you are defining an entirely new character, byte 1 must contain the value 1.

The value stored in byte 2 specifies the length of the descriptor. The current family of LaserJet printers requires that the value 14 be stored in this byte. Any other value will produce an error when you download the character descriptor to the LaserJet.

Descriptor Size

The value stored in byte 3 specifies the format of the character data you are about to transfer. The current family of LaserJet printers requires the value 1 in this byte. Any other value will produce an error when you download the character descriptor to the LaserJet.

Class

The value stored in byte 4 specifies the orientation of the character data the descriptor describes. If the character is being designed for Portrait mode, you should set this value to 0, while you should set it to 1 if the character is being designed for Landscape mode.

Orientation

Bytes 6 and 7 are used to store a value equal to the distance between the position one dot to the left of the baseline and the left border of the cell in which the character exists. This distance must be expressed in dots. The value you place in the left offset field must be -128 to 127 if you are using a LaserJet Plus or LaserJet 500 Plus, -4200 to 4200 if you are using a LaserJet Series II or LaserJet IID, or -16384 to 16384 if you are using a LaserJet 2000.

Left Offset

Bytes 8 and 9 are used to store a value equal to the distance between the baseline and the top border of the cell in which the character exists. This distance must be expressed in dots. The value you place in the top offset field must be -128 to 127 if you are using a LaserJet Plus or LaserJet 500 Plus, -4200 to 4200 if you are using a LaserJet Series II or LaserJet IID, or -16384 to 16384 if you are using a LaserJet 2000.

Top Offset

Bytes 10 and 11 are used to specify the width of a character in dots. As we have mentioned, this value must be used to calculate appropriate line endings whenever you print justified text using a proportionally spaced font. The value you place in the character width field must be 0 to 128 if you are using a LaserJet Plus or LaserJet 500 Plus, 1 to 4200 if you are using a LaserJet Series II or LaserJet IID, or 1 to 16384 if you are using a LaserJet 2000.

Character Width

Bytes 12 and 13 of the character descriptor are used to specify the height of a character in dots. This value must be used to adjust line spacing whenever you print text using a variety of fonts on a single line. The value you place in the character height field must be 0 to 128 if you are using a LaserJet Plus or LaserJet 500 Plus, 1 to 4200 if you are using a LaserJet Series II or LaserJet IID, or 1 to 16384 if you are using a LaserJet 2000.

Character Height

Delta X

Bytes 14 and 15 of the character descriptor are used to specify the amount of space the cursor will be moved across the horizontal axis after you print the character you have defined. This value must be expressed in one-quarter dot units. For example, if you want to move the cursor $^1/_{300}$ inch after printing a character, you must place the value 4 in this field.

The value you place in the Delta X field must be 0 to 4200 if you are using a LaserJet Plus or LaserJet 500 Plus, 0 to 16800 if you are using a LaserJet Series II or LaserJet IID, or 0 to 32767 if you are using a LaserJet 2000.

Character Data

Bytes 16 through 32767 contain the bit-mapped representation of the dot pattern you must print to form a particular character. To send a character bit map to the LaserJet, you must send it one byte at a time. Therefore, even if you only want to print one or two dots, you must send a total of eight bits to the LaserJet. Figure 26-1 shows a typical LaserJet character bit map.

FIGURE 26-1

```
11111111 00000000 11111111 00000000
11111111 00000000 11111111 00000000
11111111 00000000 11111111 00000000
11111111 00000000 11111111 00000000
00000000 11111111 00000000 11111111
00000000 11111111 00000000 11111111
00000000 11111111 00000000 11111111
00000000 11111111 00000000 11111111
11111111 00000000 11111111 00000000
11111111 00000000 11111111 00000000
11111111 00000000 11111111 00000000
11111111 00000000 11111111 00000000
```

This is a typical LaserJet character bit map.

If you examine the character bit map shown in Figure 26-1, you can see that the arrangement of ones and zeros forms a checkerboard pattern. Therefore, if you send this bit map to the LaserJet, it will print a checkerboard pattern.

CONCLUSION

In this chapter, we've explored the format of the data you must send to the LaserJet to create a soft font, and we've looked at the PCL commands that control the process. However, as we pointed out earlier, it is important to remember that the information presented in this chapter is highly technical in nature and is intended for those who like to "hack." If you don't enjoy high-powered programming, you will probably be better off using a soft font editor to design your soft fonts.

ASCII SYMBOL TABLE A1

Roman 8	PC - 8	Decimal	Hexadecimal	Octal
		0	0	0
	☺	1	1	1
	☻	2	2	2
	♥	3	3	3
	♦	4	4	4
	♣	5	5	5
	♠	6	6	6
	·	7	7	7
	◘	8	8	10
	○	9	9	11
	◙	10	A	12
	♂	11	B	13
	♀	12	C	14
	♪	13	D	15
	♫	14	E	16
	☼	15	F	17
	►	16	10	20
	◄	17	11	21
	↕	18	12	22
	‼	19	13	23
	¶	20	14	24
	§	21	15	25
	▬	22	16	26
	↨	23	17	27
	↑	24	18	30
	↓	25	19	31
	→	26	1A	32
	←	27	1B	33
	∟	28	1C	34
	↔	29	1D	35
	▲	30	1E	36
	▼	31	1F	37

Roman 8	PC - 8	Decimal	Hexadecimal	Octal
		32	20	40
!	!	33	21	41
"	"	34	22	42
#	#	35	23	43
$	$	36	24	44
%	%	37	25	45
&	&	38	26	46
'	'	39	27	47
(	(	40	28	50
)	)	41	29	51
*	*	42	2A	52
+	+	43	2B	53
,	,	44	2C	54
–	–	45	2D	55
.	.	46	2E	56
/	/	47	2F	57
0	0	48	30	60
1	1	49	31	61
2	2	50	32	62
3	3	51	33	63
4	4	52	34	64
5	5	53	35	65
6	6	54	36	66
7	7	55	37	67
8	8	56	38	70
9	9	57	39	71
:	:	58	3A	72
;	;	59	3B	73
<	<	60	3C	74
=	=	61	3D	75
>	>	62	3E	76
?	?	63	3F	77

Roman 8	PC - 8	Decimal	Hexadecimal	Octal
@	@	64	40	100
A	A	65	41	101
B	B	66	42	102
C	C	67	43	103
D	D	68	44	104
E	E	69	45	105
F	F	70	46	106
G	G	71	47	107
H	H	72	48	110
I	I	73	49	111
J	J	74	4A	112
K	K	75	4B	113
L	L	76	4C	114
M	M	77	4D	115
N	N	78	4E	116
O	O	79	4F	117
P	P	80	50	120
Q	Q	81	51	121
R	R	82	52	122
S	S	83	53	123
T	T	84	54	124
U	U	85	55	125
V	V	86	56	126
W	W	87	57	127
X	X	88	58	130
Y	Y	89	59	131
Z	Z	90	5A	132
[	[	91	5B	133
\	\	92	5C	134
]	]	93	5D	135
^	^	94	5E	136
—	—	95	5F	137

Roman 8	PC - 8	Decimal	Hexadecimal	Octal
`	`	96	60	140
a	a	97	61	141
b	b	98	62	142
c	c	99	63	143
d	d	100	64	144
e	e	101	65	145
f	f	102	66	146
g	g	103	67	147
h	h	104	68	150
i	i	105	69	151
j	j	106	6A	152
k	k	107	6B	153
l	l	108	6C	154
m	m	109	6D	155
n	n	110	6E	156
o	o	111	6F	157
p	p	112	70	160
q	q	113	71	161
r	r	114	72	162
s	s	115	73	163
t	t	116	74	164
u	u	117	75	165
v	v	118	76	166
w	w	119	77	167
x	x	120	78	170
y	y	121	79	171
z	z	122	7A	172
{	{	123	7B	173
|	|	124	7C	174
}	}	125	7D	175
~	~	126	7E	176
▓	▓	127	7F	177

Roman 8	PC - 8	Decimal	Hexadecimal	Octal
	Ç	128	80	200
	ü	129	81	201
	é	130	82	202
	â	131	83	203
	ä	132	84	204
	à	133	85	205
	å	134	86	206
	ç	135	87	207
	ê	136	88	210
	ë	137	89	211
	è	138	8A	212
	ï	139	8B	213
	î	140	8C	214
	ì	141	8D	215
	Ä	142	8E	216
	Å	143	8F	217
	É	144	90	220
	æ	145	91	221
	Æ	146	92	222
	ô	147	93	223
	ö	148	94	224
	ò	149	95	225
	û	150	96	226
	ù	151	97	227
	ÿ	152	98	230
	Ö	153	99	231
	Ü	154	9A	232
	¢	155	9B	233
	£	156	9C	234
	¥	157	9D	235
	₧	158	9E	236
	ƒ	159	9F	237

Roman 8	PC - 8	Decimal	Hexadecimal	Octal
À	á	160	A0	240
Â	í	161	A1	241
È	ó	162	A2	242
Ê	ú	163	A3	243
Ë	ñ	164	A4	244
Î	Ñ	165	A5	245
Ï	ª	166	A6	246
´	º	167	A7	247
`	¿	168	A8	250
^	⌐	169	A9	251
¨	¬	170	AA	252
~	½	171	AB	253
Ù	¼	172	AC	254
Û	¡	173	AD	255
£	«	174	AE	256
	»	175	AF	257
Ý		176	B0	260
ý		177	B1	261
°	▓	178	B2	262
Ç	│	179	B3	263
Ç	┤	180	B4	264
Ñ	╡	181	B5	265
ñ	╢	182	B6	266
¡	╖	183	B7	267
¿	╕	184	B8	270
¤	╣	185	B9	271
£	║	186	BA	272
¥	╗	187	BB	273
§	╝	188	BC	274
f	╜	189	BD	275
¢	╛	190	BE	276
	┐	191	BF	277

Roman 8	PC - 8	Decimal	Hexadecimal	Octal
â	└	192	C0	300
ê	┴	193	C1	301
ô		194	C2	302
û	├	195	C3	303
á	─	196	C4	304
é	┼	197	C5	305
ó		198	C6	306
ú	╞	199	C7	307
à		200	C8	310
è		201	C9	311
ò	╓	202	CA	312
ù	╥	203	CB	313
ä	╥	204	CC	314
ë	═	205	CD	315
ö	╧	206	CE	316
ü	╨	207	CF	317
Å	╨	208	D0	320
î	╤	209	D1	321
Ø	╥	210	D2	322
Æ		211	D3	323
å	╘	212	D4	324
í	╒	213	D5	325
ø		214	D6	326
æ	╫	215	D7	327
Ä	╪	216	D8	330
ì		217	D9	331
Ö	┌	218	DA	332
Ü	█	219	DB	333
É		220	DC	334
ï	▌	221	DD	335
ß	▐	222	DE	336

Roman 8	PC - 8	Decimal	Hexadecimal	Octal
Ô	■	223	DF	337
Á	α	224	E0	340
Ã	β	225	E1	341
ã	Γ	226	E2	342
Đ	π	227	E3	343
ð	Σ	228	E4	344
Í	σ	229	E5	345
Ì	μ	230	E6	346
Ó	τ	231	E7	347
Ò	Φ	232	E8	350
Õ	Θ	233	E9	351
õ	Ω	234	EA	352
Š	δ	235	EB	353
š	∞	236	EC	354
Ú	φ	237	ED	355
Ÿ	ε	238	EE	356
ÿ	∩	239	EF	357
Þ	≡	240	F0	360
þ	±	241	F1	361
·	≥	242	F2	362
μ	≤	243	F3	363
¶	∫	244	F4	364
¾		245	F5	365
—	÷	246	F6	366
¼	≈	247	F7	367
½	°	248	F8	370
ª	•	249	F9	371
º	·	250	FA	372
«	√	251	FB	373
■	η	252	FC	374
»	²	253	FD	375
±	▪	254	FE	376
		255	FF	377

PRODUCT CATALOG $\mathbf{A2}$

In this appendix, we'll describe each of the products discussed in *LaserJet Companion* and list the addresses and telephone numbers of their manufacturers. Also, whenever possible, we have included each product's suggested retail price.

In addition to the products discussed in *LaserJet Companion*, this appendix describes a few products we did not cover. This information is provided as a service to those who may be interested in these products.

PRINTERS

LaserJet Companion was written for users of HP LaserJet printers. Therefore, this section contains a short description of each member of the LaserJet printer family, along with the suggested retail price of the printers currently marketed by Hewlett-Packard.

LaserJet

The original Hewlett-Packard LaserJet is a member of the first generation of low-cost 300 dpi laser printers. The LaserJet is built around the Cannon CX laser engine, has 128K of RAM, a single 100-page paper tray, one internal font, a serial interface, and one font cartridge slot. To learn more about the LaserJet, read Chapters 1, 2, and 3. *List price:* No longer marketed. *Contact*: Hewlett-Packard Company, Boise Division, 11311 Chinden Blvd., Boise, ID 83707; 800-538-8787 (408-738-4133 in California).

LaserJet Plus

The LaserJet Plus is the direct successor to the original LaserJet. Like the LaserJet, it is built around the Cannon CX laser engine, but it features 512K of RAM upgradable to 2MB, as opposed to the LaserJet's 128K. The LaserJet Plus also features a single 100-sheet paper tray, two internal fonts, one font cartridge slot, and both parallel and serial ports. Finally, the most significant feature of the LaserJet Plus is its ability to print soft fonts. To learn more about the LaserJet Plus, read Chapters 1, 2, and 3. *List price:* No longer marketed. *Contact*: Hewlett-Packard Company, Boise Division, 11311 Chinden Blvd., Boise, ID 83707; 800-538-8787 (408-738-4133 in California).

LaserJet 500 Plus

The LaserJet 500 Plus is essentially a LaserJet Plus equipped with two 250-page paper trays. In addition, the 500 Plus has the ability to separate print jobs by shifting the position of pages as they are printed. To learn more about the LaserJet 500 Plus, read Chapters 1, 2, and 3. *List price:* No longer marketed. *Contact*: Hewlett-Packard Company, Boise Division, 11311 Chinden Blvd., Boise, ID 83707; 800-538-8787 (408-738-4133 in California).

LaserJet Series II

The LaserJet Series II replaced the LaserJet Plus as the flagship of the LaserJet printer family. The LaserJet Series II is built around the Cannon SX laser engine and features 512K of RAM upgradable to 4.5MB. The LaserJet Series II also features a single 200-sheet paper tray, three internal fonts, two font cartridge slots, and both parallel and serial ports. Finally, via its optional I/O port, the LaserJet Series II can interface with the JetScript Accessory Kit and other hardware enhancements. To learn more about the LaserJet Series II, read Chapters 1, 2, and 3. *List price:* $2,495. *Contact:* Hewlett-Packard Company, Boise Division, 11311 Chinden Blvd., Boise, ID 83707; 800-538-8787 (408-738-4133 in California).

LaserJet 2000

The LaserJet 2000, dubbed the "Jumbo Jet," is the 747 of the LaserJet printer family. The standard LaserJet 2000 Model A features 1.5MB of RAM upgradable to 5.5MB, two 250-page paper trays, 12 internal fonts, three font cartridge slots, and both serial and parallel ports. The LaserJet 2000 Model P supports all the features found in Model A, plus a 2,000-page paper input deck, while Model D supports duplex printing in addition to all Model A and Model P features.

The most significant feature of the LaserJet 2000 is its ability to print as many as 20 pages per minute. In addition, the LaserJet 2000 can automatically rotate any font—in other words, fonts designed for Landscape mode can be used in Portrait mode, and vice versa. To learn more about the LaserJet 2000, read Chapters 1, 2, and 3. *List prices*: Model A: $19,995; Model P: $21,995; Model D: $25,695. *Contact:* Hewlett-Packard Company, Boise Division, 11311 Chinden Blvd., Boise, ID 83707; 800-538-8787 (408-738-4133 in California).

LaserJet IID

The LaserJet IID is the newest addition to the LaserJet printer family. Like the LaserJet Series II, the LaserJet IID is built around the Cannon SX laser engine and features 512K of RAM upgradable to 4.5MB. The LaserJet IID also features two 200-sheet paper trays, seven internal fonts, two font cartridge slots, and both parallel and serial ports. The most significant feature of the LaserJet IID is duplex printing.

To learn more about the LaserJet IID, read Chapters 1, 2, and 3. *List price:* Unavailable. *Contact:* Hewlett-Packard Company, Boise Division, 11311 Chinden Blvd., Boise, ID 83707; 800-538-8787 (408-738-4133 in California).

APPLICATIONS

In this section, we'll provide a brief description of the applications discussed in *LaserJet Companion* and in *LaserJet Companion TechNotes*. In addition, we will provide the name, address, and telephone number of each application's manufacturer, along with the product's current list price.

dBASE III Plus

At the time *LaserJet Companion* went to press, Ashton-Tate's dBASE III Plus was the best-selling database management system for IBM PC, PS/2, and compatible systems. Although dBASE III Plus' basic support for the LaserJet is limited, it is possible to write dBASE III Plus programs that send PCL commands directly to the LaserJet. To learn more about using a LaserJet with dBASE III Plus, read Chapter 10. *List price:* $795. *Contact:* Ashton-Tate, 20101 Hamilton Ave., Torrence, CA 90502-1319; 213-329-8000.

dBASE IV

As we mentioned in Chapter 12, at the time *LaserJet Companion* went to press, Ashton-Tate was preparing to release the successor to dBASE III Plus—dBASE IV. The Cobb Group will publish *LaserJet Companion TechNotes for dBASE IV* when the product becomes available. To learn more about dBASE IV and *LaserJet Companion TechNotes for dBASE IV*, read Chapter 12. *List price:* $895. *Contact:* Ashton-Tate, 20101 Hamilton Ave., Torrence, CA 90502-1319; 213-329-8000.

DisplayWrite 4

IBM's DisplayWrite 4 is a PC- and PS/2-based successor to the popular DisplayWriter dedicated word processing system. Although its support for the LaserJet printer family is not exceptional, DisplayWrite 4 is an extremely powerful product that can produce quality LaserJet text output. To learn more about using a LaserJet with DisplayWrite 4, read Chapter 9. *List price:* $495. *Contact:* IBM Corporation, P.O. Box 152560, Irving, TX 75015; 214-550-4200.

Lotus 1-2-3

Lotus Development Corporation's 1-2-3 leads the PC, PS/2, and compatible systems spreadsheet market. While 1-2-3's support for the LaserJet family of printers is limited, it is possible to access most LaserJet features by embedding PCL commands in a worksheet. To learn more about using a LaserJet with 1-2-3, read Chapter 6. *List price:* $495. *Contact:* Lotus Development Corporation, Business Products Division, 55 Cambridge Parkway, Cambridge, MA 02142; 617-577-8500.

Microsoft Excel

One of Microsoft Excel's most impressive features is its ability to produce outstanding reports and graphs using proportionally spaced fonts and bit-mapped graphics. For this reason, Microsoft Excel, which runs under Microsoft Windows, is a perfect match for the LaserJet. To learn more about using a LaserJet with

Microsoft Excel, read Chapter 15. Also, to learn more about adding support for a LaserJet to Microsoft Windows, read Chapter 13. *List price:* $495. *Contact:* Microsoft Corporation, P.O. Box 97017, 16011 NE 36th Way, Redmond, WA 98073-9717; 206-882-8080.

Microsoft Windows

Microsoft Windows is a graphical WYSIWYG operating environment that features unified LaserJet support. In other words, once you add LaserJet support to Windows, any application that runs under Windows can access the LaserJet's features and capabilities. To learn more about adding LaserJet support to Microsoft Windows, read Chapter 13. *List prices:* Microsoft Windows/286: $99; Microsoft Windows/386: $195. *Contact:* Microsoft Corporation, P.O. Box 97017, 16011 NE 36th Way, Redmond, WA 98073-9717; 206-882-8080.

Microsoft Windows Write

Microsoft Windows Write is a rudimentary WYSIWYG word processor that is included with every copy of Microsoft Windows. While it's not known as a particularly powerful product, it can embed graphics in a document and access any LaserJet internal, cartridge, or soft font. To learn more about using a LaserJet with Microsoft Windows Write, read Chapter 16. Also, to learn more about adding LaserJet support to Microsoft Windows, read Chapter 13. *List price:* Included with Microsoft Windows. *Contact:* Microsoft Corporation, P.O. Box 97017, 16011 NE 36th Way, Redmond, WA 98073-9717; 206-882-8080.

Microsoft Word 4.0

Microsoft Word 4.0 is an extremely powerful word processor that offers an exceptional level of support for the LaserJet. For instance, you can use any LaserJet soft font in a Word 4.0 document. To learn more about using a LaserJet with Microsoft Word 4.0, read Chapter 8. *List price:* $450. *Contact:* Microsoft Corporation, P.O. Box 97017, 16011 NE 36th Way, Redmond, WA 98073-9717; 206-882-8080.

PageMaker

Aldus Corporation's PageMaker is thought by many to be the premier desktop publishing package for PC, PS/2, and compatible systems. Since it runs under Microsoft Windows, PageMaker can provide you with an on-screen WYSIWYG representation of a document and can access any LaserJet internal, cartridge, or soft font. To learn more about using a LaserJet with Aldus PageMaker, read Chapter 14. Also, to learn more about adding support for a LaserJet to Microsoft Windows, read Chapter 13. *List price:* $795. *Contact:* Aldus Corporation, 411 First Avenue South #200, Seattle, WA 98104; 206-622-5500.

Paradox

Borland International's Paradox is a powerful database management system that offers an exceptional amount of support for the LaserJet family of printers. *LaserJet Companion TechNotes for Paradox* discusses everything you need to know to get the most out of Paradox and your LaserJet. To learn more about Paradox and *LaserJet Companion TechNotes for Paradox*, read Chapter 12. *List prices:* Paradox 2.0: $725; Paradox 386: $895; Paradox OS/2: $725; Paradox for Networks: $995. *Contact:* Borland International, Inc., 4585 Scotts Valley Drive, P.O. Box 660001, Scotts Valley, CA 95066-0001; 800-543-7543.

Quattro

Borland International's Quattro is currently the leading low-cost DOS spreadsheet. One of Quattro's most attractive features is its support for the LaserJet family of printers. While we do not discuss Quattro in this book, *LaserJet Companion TechNotes for Quattro* provides all of the information you need to get the most out of Quattro and your LaserJet. To learn more about Quattro and *LaserJet Companion TechNotes for Quattro*, read Chapter 12. *List price:* $247.50. *Contact:* Borland International, Inc., 4585 Scotts Valley Drive, P.O. Box 660001, Scotts Valley, CA 95066-0001; 800-543-7543.

Ventura Publisher

When *LaserJet Companion* went to press, XEROX Ventura Publisher was the best-selling desktop publishing package for PC, PS/2, and compatible systems. While its support for LaserJet font cartridges is a bit limited, Ventura Publisher is especially popular among users of the LaserJet family of printers. To learn more about using a LaserJet with Ventura Publisher, read Chapter 11. *List price:* $890. *Contact:* XEROX Corporation, 101 Continental Blvd., El Segundo, CA 90245; 800-822-8221.

WordPerfect 5

WordPerfect 5 is the latest release of WordPerfect's most popular word processor. Among WordPerfect 5's impressive features are its outstanding support for the LaserJet and its ability to embed graphics in a document. To learn more about using a LaserJet with WordPerfect 5, read Chapter 5. *List price:* $495. *Contact:* WordPerfect Corporation, 155 N. Technology Way, Orem, UT 84058; 801-225-5000.

WordStar Professional Release 5

WordStar Professional Release 5 is the current release of MicroPro's venerable word processor. With improved LaserJet support and a new page preview function, Release 5 lets you produce quality LaserJet output. To learn more about using a LaserJet with WordStar Professional Release 5, read Chapter 7. *List price:* $495. *Contact:* MicroPro International Corporation, 33 San Pablo Ave., San Rafael, CA 94903; 800-227-8320.

XyWrite III Plus

XyQuest's XyWrite III Plus is a powerful word processor that includes an exceptional level of support for the LaserJet family of printers. While we did not discuss XyWrite III Plus in this book, *LaserJet Companion TechNotes for XyWrite III Plus* explains how to use the LaserJet with this program. To learn more about *LaserJet Companion TechNotes for XyWrite III Plus*, read Chapter 12. *List price:* $445. *Contact:* XyQuest, Inc., 44 Manning Road, Billerica, MA 01821; 508-671-0888.

UTILITIES AND ENHANCEMENTS

In this section, we'll provide a brief description of the utility software and enhancements we discussed in Chapter 18, and we'll look at several products that *LaserJet Companion* did not cover. Finally, we'll provide the name, address, and telephone number of each product's manufacturer, along with its current list price.

BitStream Fontware Installation Kits

BitStream's Fontware Installation Kits allow you to convert BitStream Typeface outlines into a standard PCL soft font of a size you specify. Each version of the Fontware Installation Kit is customized for a specific application and can add support for any fonts it creates for that application. In addition, many versions of the Fontware Installation Kit can ensure true WYSIWYG operation by creating screen fonts that match any PCL font created by the Installation Kit. For details on BitStream Fontware Installation Kits, read Chapter 18. *List prices:* Ventura Publisher: $95; Microsoft Windows: $95. *Contact:* BitStream, Inc., Athenaeum House, 215 First St., Cambridge, MA 02142; 800-522-3668 or 617-497-7514. *Notes:* Versions of the BitStream Fontware Installation Kit for Microsoft Word 4.0, WordPerfect 5, and Aldus PageMaker are included with those products free of charge. Contact Microsoft, WordPerfect, or Aldus for more information.

Font Effects

SoftCraft's Font Effects is a utility program that allows you to make radical changes to the appearance of any soft font. You can use Font Effects to add shadows to a font, or you can use it to increase a font's height and/or width. To learn more about Font Effects, read Chapter 18. *List price:* $95. *Contact:* SoftCraft, Inc., 16 N. Carroll St. #500, Madison, WI 53703; 800-351-0500 or 608-257-3300.

FontLoad

FontLoad is a soft font download utility that is packaged with a number of Hewlett-Packard soft fonts. Also available as a separate product, FontLoad is a menu-driven product that allows you to choose the soft fonts you want to download from a list. To learn more about FontLoad, read Chapter 4. *List price:* $20. *Contact:* Hewlett-Packard Company, Boise Division, 11311 Chinden Blvd., Boise, ID 83707; 800-538-8787 (408-738-4133 in California).

JetScript Accessory Kit

The JetScript Accessory Kit is a software and hardware package that adds support for Adobe's PostScript page description language to the LaserJet Series II. Designed and manufactured by QMS, Inc., the JetScript Accessory Kit contains a circuit board that requires one standard 8-bit PC slot. This board contains a 16MHz 68000 CPU and 3MB of RAM. In addition, the JetScript Accessory Kit includes a circuit board that plugs into the LaserJet Series II's optional I/O slot and a PostScript interpreter that includes support for all the fonts found in the Apple LaserWriter Plus and LaserWriter II. Utilities that allow you to configure and communicate with the PostScript interpreter and download PostScript soft fonts are also included. For more about the JetScript Accessory Kit, read Chapter 18. *List price:* $20. *Contact:* Hewlett-Packard Company, Boise Division, 11311 Chinden Blvd., Boise, ID 83707; 800-538-8787 (408-738-4133 in California).

LaserFonts is a utility program that automates the process of adding support for soft fonts to Microsoft Word, WordPerfect, and WordStar 2000. Featuring a mouse-driven, text-based user interface, LaserFonts is a perfect choice for those who find the normal soft font installation procedure to be tedious. *List price:* $180. *Contact:* SoftCraft, Inc., 16 N. Carroll St. #500, Madison, WI 53703; 800-351-0500 or 608-257-3300.

LaserFonts

PS Jet Plus is a replacement lid for the LaserJet and LaserJet Plus that adds support for Adobe's PostScript page description language. Designed and manufactured by QMS, Inc., PS Jet Plus includes support for all the fonts found in the Apple LaserWriter Plus and LaserWriter II. *List price:* $2,995. *Contact:* The Laser Connection, Inc., P.O. Box 850296, Mobile, AL 36689; 800-523-2696.

PS Jet Plus

Publisher's Typefoundry is a complete font design system that runs under Microsoft Windows. Actually two programs in one package, it allows you to create fonts with a bit editor or an outline editor. In addition, Publisher's Typefoundry is shipped with several utilities that allow you to port fonts between PostScript, PCL, and various applications such as PC Paintbrush. *List price:* $495. *Contact:* Z-Soft, Inc., 450 Franklin Road, Suite 100, Marietta, GA 30067; 404-428-0008.

Publisher's Typefoundry

As its name suggests, the SoftCraft Font Editor allows you to edit and create PCL soft fonts. One of the SoftCraft Font Editor's most important features is the graphical user interface, which allows you to draw characters as you would draw an image with a paint program. To learn more about the SoftCraft Font Editor, read Chapter 18. *List price:* $290. *Contact:* SoftCraft, Inc., 16 N. Carroll St. #500, Madison, WI 53703; 800-351-0500 or 608-257-3300.

SoftCraft Font Editor

As we pointed out in Chapters 11 and 13, Ventura Publisher and applications that run under Microsoft Windows cannot produce an on-screen WYSIWYG representation of a document unless matching screen and LaserJet fonts are available. At the time *LaserJet Companion* went to press, WYSIfonts! was the only software package with the ability to create a screen font for Ventura Publisher and Microsoft Windows that matches any PCL soft font. For more information on WYSIfonts!, read Chapter 18. *List price:* $95. *Contact:* SoftCraft, Inc., 16 N. Carroll St. #500, Madison, WI 53703; 800-351-0500 or 608-257-3300.

WYSIfonts!

As we pointed out in Chapter 4, the quality of text produced by a LaserJet is only as good as the font you are using. Therefore, in this section, we'll list several sources for LaserJet-compatible cartridge and soft fonts.

FONTS

Hewlett-Packard produces a wide range of cartridge and soft fonts and sells a number of BitStream soft font packages. Table A2-1 lists the fonts produced

Hewlett-Packard Company

and/or sold by HP at the time *LaserJet Companion* went to press. *Contact:* Hewlett-Packard Company, Boise Division, 11311 Chinden Blvd., Boise, ID 83707; 800-538-8787 (408-738-4133 in California).

TABLE A2-1

Font Cartridges

Part number	Name	List price
92286A	Courier1	$150
92286B	Tms Proportional 1	$250
92286C	International1	$150
92286D	Prestige Elite	$150
92286E	Letter Gothic	$150
92286F	Tms Proportional 2	$250
92286G	Legal Elite	$150
92286H	Legal Courier	$150
92286J	Math Elite	$250
92286K	Math Tms	$250
92286L	Courier P&L	$250
92286M	Prestige Elite P&L	$250
92286N	Letter Gothic P&L	$250
92286P	Tms Rmn P&L	$250
92286Q	Memo 1	$250
92286R	Presentazions 1	$330
92286S1	Courier Document	$250
92286S2	TmsRmn/Helv Report	$250
92286T	Tax 1	$250
92286U	Forms Portrait	$250
92286V	Forms Landscape	$250
92286W1	Bar Code 3-of-9/OCR-A	$250
92286X	EAN/UPC/OCR-B	$250
92286Y	PC Courier 1	$250
92286Z	Microsoft 1A	$330

Soft Fonts

Part number	Name	List price: $200
33412AC	TmsRmn/Helv Base Set (ASCII)	
33412AD	TmsRmn/Helv Base Set (Roman-8)	
33412AE	TmsRmn/Helv Supplemental (ASCII)	

Part number	Name	List price: $200
33412AE	TmsRmn/Helv Supplemental (Roman-8)	
33412AG	Helv Headlines	
33412DA	Letter Gothic Base Set	
33412EA	Prestige Elite Family	
33412RA	ITC Garamond	
33412SA	Century Schoolbook	
33412TA	Zapf Humanist 601	
33412UA	Headline Typefaces Collection 1	
33412RB	ITC Garamond—Roman-8	
33412SB	Century Schoolbook—Roman-8	
33412TB	Zapf Humanist 601—Roman-8	
33412UB	Headline Typefaces Collection 1—Roman-8	

These fonts are produced and/or sold by Hewlett-Packard.

BitStream Fontware Typeface Library

The BitStream Fontware Typeface Library is a collection of fonts that are based on outlines. As we mentioned in Chapter 4 and earlier in this appendix, BitStream Fontware Typeface Library outlines can be converted into standard PCL soft fonts by a Fontware Installation Kit. Table A2-2 lists the Fontware typefaces available at the time *LaserJet Companion* went to press. *List price:* $195. *Contact:* BitStream, Inc., Athenaeum House, 215 First St., Cambridge, MA 02142; 800-522-3668 or 617-497-7514.

TABLE A2-2

Baskerville	ITC Bookman
BitStream Charter	ITC Bookman Light
BitStream Cooper	ITC Galliard
BitStream Cooper Light	ITC Garamond Book
Century Schoolbook	ITC Garamond Condensed
Courier (10 pitch)	ITC Korinna Regular
Dutch (Times Roman)	ITC Souvenir Light
Futura Book	Letter Gothic (12 pitch)
Futura Light	News Gothic
Futura Medium	Prestige (12 pitch)
Goudy Old Style	Serifa
Headlines 1	Swiss (Helvetica)
Headlines 2	Swiss Condensed (Helvetica)
Headlines 3	Swiss Light (Helvetica)
Headlines 4	Zapf Calligraphic
ITC Avant Garde Gothic	Zapf Humanist

These typefaces are available from BitStream, Inc.

SoftCraft, Inc.   SoftCraft, Inc., produces a number of quality standard PCL fonts. In addition, SoftCraft markets the entire collection of BitStream Fontware Typefaces listed earlier in this appendix. At the time *LaserJet Companion* went to press, SoftCraft offered a total of 81 font disks. Each of these disks contains one or more of the fonts listed in Table A2-3. *List price:* $15 for each font disk. *Contact:* SoftCraft, Inc., 16 N. Carroll St. #500, Madison, WI 53703; 800-351-0500 or 608-257-3300.

TABLE A2-3

Roman	Proto-Indoeuropean
Fixed Width (Courier)	Greek
Classic (Times Roman)	Hebrew
Sans Serif (Helvetica)	Hebrew Sans Serif
Tall	Nouveau
Italic Unslanted	Manual Alphabet
Olde English	Modern
Formal	Block Outline
Script	Classic Shadow
Calligrapher	Bar Code/OCR
Twist	Dots/Vertical Borders
Computer	LCD Style
Math Symbols	Elegant Script
Chess	Orbit
Copyright and Symbols	Optical
Accents and Ligatures	Keys
Cyrillic	Hershey
French Classic	Persian
French Sans Serif	Hebrew
Spanish Classic	Music
Spanish Sans Serif	Borders
International Phonetic Alphabet	Overhead Projector
German	Caribbean
Indic	

SoftCraft offers 81 font disks, each of which contains one or more of these fonts.

SWFTE International Glyphix   SWFTE International's Glyphix fonts are unique in the LaserJet marketplace for one reason. With the help of a utility program known as a Glyphix Font Manager, they can be scaled "on the fly" to any size between 6 and 60 points. In addition, each Glyphix font can be slanted, made lighter, heavier, narrower, or wider, and can be filled with solid black, vertical stripes, horizontal stripes, and percentages of gray.

When we say that a Glyphix Font Manager can scale Glyphix fonts on the fly, we mean that it can convert a Glyphix outline into an actual PCL bit-mapped soft font as the font is downloaded to the LaserJet. While Glyphix Font Managers also can create normal PCL soft font data files, the ability to create a font as it is downloaded is exciting because it can save a considerable amount of space on your hard disk.

At the time *LaserJet Companion* went to press, there were two forms of the Glyphix Font Manager. The first form is a stand-alone program that is included with each font disk. This program allows you to select the Glyphix font you want to use and then creates a PCL bit-mapped version of that font, which can be immediately downloaded or written to a disk file.

The second form of the software package that allows you to use Glyphix fonts is designed specifically for use with WordPerfect and Microsoft Word. These software packages integrate tightly with WordPerfect and Microsoft Word and will automatically create any Glyphix font that you use in a document as it is being sent to the LaserJet. This is an extremely useful feature that provides you with scaling capabilities that rival Adobe's PostScript page description language. Table A2-4 lists the Glyphix fonts that were available at the time *LaserJet Companion* went to press. *List prices:* Glyphix Font Disks: $95; Glyphix MS Word Font Manager: $79; Glyphix WordPerfect Font Manager: $79. *Contact:* SWFTE International, P.O. Box 5773, Wilmington, DE 19808; 800-237-9383 or 302-733-0956.

TABLE A2-4

Font disks	Fonts
Basics	Roman (Times Roman) Helvette (Helvetica) Rockland (Rockwell) Chancelor (Zapf Chancery)
Basics II	Roman Italic Amertype (American Typewriter) Big City (Broadway) Optimis (Optima)
Decorative	Coop (Cooper Black) Abbey (Cloister Black) Beget (Benguiat) Orna
Sans Serif	Avanti (Avante-Garde) Gillies Olivia Galaxy

Font disks	Fonts
Book	Garamont (Garamond)
	Centrum (Century Schoolbook)
	Basque (Baskerville)
	Palatine (Palatino)
Fixed	Courier
	Prestige
	Letter Gothic
	Line Draw

These Glyphix fonts are available from SWFTE International.

INDEX

X

There's more!

Here's how you can expand your printing skills with even <u>more</u> software applications...

When we began to write *LaserJet Companion*, we realized it would be impossible to include every application that can be used with the LaserJet. Therefore, we focused our discussion of applications on those our research found to be most popular among LaserJet users.

LaserJet Companion TechNotes for Paradox

To supplement the applications we've included in *LaserJet Companion*, we created *TechNotes*. Each edition is comparable in length and content to a single chapter in the book.

In addition, *TechNotes* will be written to provide current information on upgrades of the products explained in *LaserJet Companion*.

To find out if an edition of *TechNotes* is available for a particular software application, call The Cobb Group toll-free at 800-223-8720.

If you use Paradox 3, Quattro, XyWrite III Plus, or the new Microsoft Word 5.0, you can order supplementary TechNotes today by mailing the card below.

Free shipping in the U.S.

BUSINESS REPLY MAIL
FIRST CLASS MAIL   PERMIT NO. 618   LOUISVILLE, KENTUCKY

POSTAGE WILL BE PAID BY ADDRESSEE

NO POSTAGE
NECESSARY
IF MAILED IN
THE UNITED
STATES

THE COBB GROUP
PO BOX 24435
LOUISVILLE KY
40224-9958